A MANUAL OF MODERN HISTORY;

CONTAINING THE

RISE AND PROGRESS OF THE PRINCIPAL EUROPEAN NATIONS, THEIR POLITICAL HISTORY, AND THE CHANGES IN THEIR SOCIAL CONDITION;

WITH A HISTORY OF

THE COLONIES FOUNDED BY EUROPEANS

BY W. C. TAYLOR, LL.D., M.R.A.S.,
OF TRINITY COLLEGE, DUBLIN.

REVISED, WITH A CHAPTER ON THE HISTORY OF THE UNITED STATES,

BY C. S. HENRY, D.D.,
PROFESSOR OF PHILOSOPHY AND HISTORY IN THE UNIVERSITY
OF THE CITY OF NEW-YORK.

WITH QUESTIONS ADAPTED FOR SCHOOLS AND COLLEGES.

FIFTH EDITION,
CAREFULLY REVISED AND CORRECTED.

NEW-YORK:
D. APPLETON & COMPANY, 200 BROADWAY.
1851.

TABLE OF CONTENTS.

MODERN HISTORY.

CHAPTER V.—*The Revival of Literature.—The Progress of Civilization and Invention.*

CHAPTER VI.—*The Reformation, and Commencement of the States-System in Europe.*

CHAPTER VII.—*The Augustan Ages of England and France.*

CHAPTER VIII.—*Growth of the Mercantile aud Colonial System.*

CHAPTER IX.—*The Age of Revolutions.*

CHAPTER X.—*The French Empire.*

CHAPTER XI.—*History of the Peace.*

CHAPTER XII.—*History of Colonization.*

CHAPTER XV.—*History of the United States.*

THE

STUDENT'S MANUAL

OF

MODERN HISTORY.

CHAPTER I.

CONSEQUENCES OF THE FALL OF THE WESTERN EMPIRE.

Section I.—*The Gothic Kingdom of Italy.*

There is no period in the annals of the human race which presents to the historical student a greater scene of confusion than the century succeeding the overthrow of the Western Empire. The different hordes of barbarians, following no definite plan, established separate monarchies in the dismembered provinces, engaged in sanguinary wars that had no object but plunder, and were too ignorant to form anything like a political system. There is consequently a want of unity in the narrative of a time when nations ceased to have any fixed relations toward each other, and history must appear desultory and digressive until some one state, rising into command, assume such importance, that the fate of all the rest may be connected with its destinies. It is necessary, before entering on the various incidents of this calamitous time, to take a geographical survey of the places occupied by the principal nations who succeeded the Romans in the sovereignty of Europe.

The Visigoths, after their establishment in Spain, began gradually to adopt the refinement of their new subjects; that peninsula had advanced rapidly in civilization under the Roman dominion, and had escaped from much of the corruption which had degraded Italy; the conquerors, more advanced than any other of the barbarians, soon learned to appreciate the advantages of social order, and began to cultivate the higher arts of life. In Pannonia, the Ostrogoths derived great improvement from their vicinity to Italy on the one side, and the court of Constantinople on the other; they were thus gradually trained to civilization, and their early adoption of Christianity secured them the benefits of literature, which was sedulously cultivated by the clergy.

Tribes of a very different character pressed into the empire from the

German forests—the Burgundians, the Lombards, and the Franks, of whom the last were long distinguished for their hostility to all refinements, and their exclusive attention to the military virtues. Still more barbarous were the Saxons and Angles; they were not only strangers to the civilization and religion of the empire, but were kept in their rude state by the practice of piracy, for which their maritime situation afforded them great facilities; their government, divided among several petty chiefs, was favorable to personal independence, and furnished a striking contrast to the absolute despotism that had been established in the Roman empire. All the Germanic tribes were remarkable for the respect which they showed to the delicacy of the female character; they neither treated their women like slaves, as most other barbarians have done, nor did they degrade them into mere objects of sensual gratification, like the Romans and Byzantines. The German woman was the companion and counsellor of her husband; she shared his labors as an equal, not as a servant. It was from the sanctity of the domestic circle among the northern nations that races of conquerors derived the firmness and courage which ensured them victory.

The northeastern part of Europe was occupied by Sclavonic tribes, differing from the Germans in language, manners, and tactics; like the Tartars of more modern times, they placed their chief reliance on their cavalry; and they were more opposed to civilization than any of the Germanic nations. Their form of government was a kind of aristocratic republic, but in war the tribes generally united under a single leader. They were very averse to fixed residences, and when they occupied a country they rarely entered the cities, but remained in their camps or in rude circular fortifications called *rings*. The Sclavonians hated the Germans, and could rarely be induced to unite with them against their common enemy, the Romans.

After the fall of the Western Empire, the court of Constantinople sunk into obscurity, from which it did not emerge for half a century, when its supremacy was restored during the memorable reign of Justinian. The Isaurian Zeno, raised to the purple by his marriage with the princess Ariadne, was forced to fly into the mountains by a fierce revolt which his mother-in-law Verina had instigated. He was restored to the throne chiefly by the aid of Theodoric, king of the Ostrogoths, who had been carefully educated as a hostage at the court of Constantinople. The turbulence of the Goths, and the faithlessness of the Byzantines, soon destroyed the amity of the two sovereigns; a desultory, but sanguinary warfare harassed the Eastern Empire, until Zeno purchased peace by ceding to Theodoric his right over Italy, or rather stimulated the Goth to undertake the conquest of that peninsula. The march of Theodoric was the emigration of an entire people; the Goths were accompanied by their wives, their children, and their aged parents, a vast multitude of wagons conveyed their most precious effects, and their store of provisions for a toilsome march undertaken in the depth of winter. Odoacer boldly prepared to meet this formidable invasion; he took post on the river Sontius (*Isonzo*) with a powerful host; but he was unable to resist the daring energy of the Goths, and his defeat gave Theodoric possession of the Venetian province as far as the walls of Verona (A. D. 489). Italy, however, was not won without further struggles: Ravenna alone sustained a siege of more than three years; but at length Odoacer capitulated (A. D. 493), and was soon after assassinated at a solemn banquet by his rival.

Theodoric secured his conquest by distributing one third of the lands of Italy to his soldiers in military tenures. This partition was effected with very little violence to the ancient possessors; the Goths were instructed to spare the people, to reverence the laws, and to lay aside their barbarous customs of judicial combats and private revenge. The Gothic sovereignty was soon extended from Sicily to the Danube, and from Sirmium (*Sirmich*) to the Atlantic ocean; thus including the fairest portion of the Western Empire. The monarch of this new kingdom showed great wisdom and moderation in his civil government, but unfortunately his attachment to the Arian heresy led him to persecute the Catholics. The legal murder of the philosopher Boethius and the venerable Symmachus were crimes which admit of no palliation; they hastened Theodoric's death, for remorse brought him to the grave in the thirty-third year of his reign (A. D. 526).

Section II.—*Reign of Justinian.*

A Dacian peasant, named Justin, who had travelled on foot to Constantinople in the reign of the emperor Leo, enlisted in the imperial guards, and, during the succeeding reigns, so distinguished himself by his strength and valor, that he was gradually raised to the command of the household troops. On the death of the emperor Anastasius, the eunuch Amantius, anxious to secure the throne for one of his creatures, intrusted Justin with a large sum of money to bribe the guards; but he used it to purchase votes for himself, and was thus elevated to the empire (A. D. 518). Totally ignorant himself, Justin was not insensible of the value of education; he made his nephew Justinian his associate in the empire; and as this prince had been instructed in all the learning of the times, he soon obtained the whole power of the state.

After the death of Justin (A. D. 527), Justinian ruled alone; but his first exercise of authority fixed a lasting stigma on his reign. He chose for his empress, Theodora, a woman of mean birth and infamous character, whose vices had disgusted even a capital so licentious as Constantinople. Among the most singular and disgraceful follies of the Eastern Empire were the factions of the circus, which arose from the colors worn by the charioteers who competed for the prize of swiftness. Green and blue were the most remarkable for their inveterate hostility, though white and red were the most ancient: all, however, soon acquired a legal existence, and the Byzantines willingly hazarded life and fortune to support their favorite color. Justinian was a partisan of the blues; his favor toward them provoked the hostility of the opposite faction, and led to a sedition which almost laid Constantinople in ashes. The disturbances first burst forth in the circus; Justinian ordered the rioters to be secured; both factions immediately turned against the monarch, the soldiers were called out, but they were unable to contend against the citizens in the narrow streets. Assailed from the tops of the houses, the barbarian mercenaries flung firebrands in revenge, and thus kindled a dreadful conflagration, which destroyed a vast number of public and private edifices. After the city had been for several days in the hands of the rioters, Justinian contrived to revive the ancient animosity between the *greens* and *blues;* the latter faction declared for the emperor, a strong body of veterans marched to the Hippodrome, or race-course, and tranquillity was restored by the slaughter of thirty thousand of the insurgents. While the internal state of the empire was thus disturbed by faction, a costly and unprofitable war was waged against the Persians, until the emperor purchased a disgraceful and precarious truce, which both he and his rival chose to designate as an endless peace.

The usurpation of the throne of the Vandals in Africa by Gelimer, who owed his success chiefly to the support of the Arian clergy, induced Justinian to undertake a war, in which he appeared both the generous friend of an allied sovereign and the protector of the Catholic faith. Belisarius, the best general of his age, was appointed to the command of the imperial forces, and a large fleet was assembled for the transport of the army in the harbor of Constantinople (A. D. 533). After the armament had been blessed by the patriarch it set sail; and, after a prosperous voyage, Belisarius effected a landing on the coast of Africa without opposition. He advanced toward Carthage, defeating the Vandals on his march, and became master of the city with little opposition. Gelimer made one effort more to save his kingdom; it was unsuccessful, his army was irretrievably ruined, and he was closely besieged in the castle where he sought refuge. The unfortunate king, after having borne the most dreadful extremities of famine, was forced to surrender unconditionally; he was carried captive to Constantinople, where he was led in the triumphal procession that honored the return of Belisarius. The dethroned monarch showed no sorrow for his fall, but consoled himself by Solomon's reflection on the instability of human greatness, frequently repeating. "Vanity of vanities, saith the preacher, all is vanity."

The murder of Amalasontha, queen of the Goths, by her ungrateful husband Theodatus, afforded Belisarius a pretext for attacking the kingdom of Italy. He sailed from Constantinople to Sicily, and easily conquered that important island (A. D. 535). Theodatus, in great terror, hasted to avert danger, by declaring himself the vassal of Justinian; but hearing in the meantime that two Byzantine generals had been defeated in Dalmatia by the Gothic troops, he passed suddenly from extreme despair to the height of presumption, and withdrew his allegiance. Belisarius soon appeared to chastise his perfidy; he transported his army across the Sicilian strait, and effected a landing at Rhegium (*Reggio*). The greater part of southern Italy, including the important city of Naples, was speedily subdued by the imperial forces; while Theodatus, secure within the walls of Rome, made no effort to protect his subjects. At length the Goths, disgusted by the incapacity and weakness of their sovereign, removed him from the throne, and chose the valiant Vitiges for their king. But Vitiges was forced to commence his reign by abandoning Rome, of which Belisarius took possession without encountering any opposition (A. D. 537). During the ensuing winter, the Goths assembled from every quarter to save, if possible, their kingdom in Italy: a powerful army, animated by dauntless spirit, was soon collected, and Vitiges led his followers to the siege of Rome. Belisarius concentrated his forces in the Eternal city, which was defended with equal skill and bravery; but famine soon appeared within the walls, and the citizens became anxious for a capitulation. A conspiracy was formed under the sanction of the pope, Sylverius, for betraying the city to the Goths; but it was discovered by an intercepted letter. Belisarius sent Sylverius into banishment, and ordered the bishops to elect a new pontiff: before however a synod could be assembled for the purpose, the general's wife, the infamous Antonina, sold the Holy See to Vigilus for a bribe of two hundred pounds weight of gold. Reinforcements soon after arrived from the east, and the Goths were forced to raise the siege of Rome, having lost one third of their number before its walls. Belisarius pursued the retreating enemy to the marshes of Ravenna, and would probably have captured that city, but for the jealousy of the eunuch Narses, whom Justinian had intrusted with the independent command of a large division of the Byzantine army. Though the differences between the two leaders were finally adjusted, the Goths had taken advantage of the interval to collect new strength; and ten thousand Burgundians, sent to invade Italy by the command of Theodobert, king of the Franks, had stormed and plundered Milan. Soon after, Theodobert passed the Alps in person at the head of one hundred thousand men. The Franks stormed Genoa, and devastated Liguria; but their excesses brought pestilence into their camp, they perished by thousands and Theodobert was induced, by his increasing distresses, to enter into terms of accommodation with the emperor. Delivered from this pressing danger, Belisarius laid siege to Ravenna, which was forced to capitulate (A. D. 539); and thus the Gothic kingdom of Italy was destroyed.

Belisarius returned to Constantinople in triumph, leading with him the captive Vitiges; he was sent to conduct the Persian war, but was soon recalled and disgraced by the ungrateful Justinian. While the conquests of Belisarius were restoring the western provinces to the empire, barbarous hordes ravaged, almost with impunity, the northeastern frontiers. Unable or unwilling to meet the Gepidæ in the field, Justinian entered into alliance with the Longobardi or Lombards (so called from their long *barts* or lances), who had just thrown off the yoke of the Heruli, and gave them settlements in Pannonia. A war of forty years' duration, between the Lombards and Gepidæ, protected the empire from the invasions of both hordes; but it was still exposed to the incursions of the Sclavonians and Bulgarians, who annually purchased a passage through the territories of the Gepidæ, and extended their inroads even into southern Greece. Commotions in the remote east brought Europeans, about this time, acquainted with new and more formidable races of barbarians, the Avars and the Turks, whose importance may justify a short digression on their origin.

The Avars, from an unknown age, possessed the mountains and deserts that border on the lake Baïkal in northeastern Asia. Thence they advanced southward under a monarch named Túlún, and extended their empire to the eastern sea, which separates Corea from Japan. The conqueror took the title of Chakan or Chagan, a name still used on the coins of the Turkish sultan. But the prosperity of the Avars was not of long duration; they were assailed by rival tribes from the north, and at the same time harassed by civil wars; while thus distressed, they were attacked by a new horde, called Thiúkhiú by the Chinese writers, but known to the Europeans as the Turks. The Avars were overthrown by these new competitors for empire, and their power totally destroyed; but their name was taken by a new nation, the Ogors or Varchonites, who after being defeated by the Turks, migrated toward Europe by the route of the Volga. They chose the false designation, because the name of the Avars was still formidable, and they preserved it on account of the terror which they saw it produced.

The Turks first appear in history as the slaves of the original Avars; they inhabited the great Altaian mountains, and were engaged in working the mines and attending the forges of those rich mineral districts. Their skill in fabricating armor and weapons was very great, and they prided themselves upon the excellence of their manufactures so much, that, when they became lords of eastern Asia, their Khakans annually forged a piece of iron in the presence of the heads of the nation. Under the guidance of Thú-men, they asserted their independence, and made slaves of their former masters. So rapid was their progress, that during the reigns of Thú-men and his successor Dizabúl, their empire was extended from the Volga to the sea of Japan. They were thus brought to the frontiers of the Byzantine and Persian dominions, and engaged in commercial relations with both, by their occupation of the countries through which the silk-trade was carried.

The great rival of Justinian was Chosroes or Nushírván, the most celebrated Persian monarch of the Sassanid dynasty; in the early part of his reign he won the affection of his subjects, by extirpating the pernicious system of policy and religion which his predecessor Kobad, seduced by an impostor named Mazdak, had patronised. His next care was to give confidence to the laboring classes by judicious laws securing the rights of industry, and by a sedulous attention to the administration of justice. Having thus secured the tranquillity and prosperity of Persia, he directed his attention to the favorite project of the Sassanides, the re-establishment of the empire of Cyrus, and perceiving that the forces of Justinian were engaged in the west, invaded Syria, at the head of a powerful army (A. D. 540). His victorious career was checked for a brief space by Belisarius, but after the recall and disgrace of that general, he urged forward his conquests with alarming rapidity. Justinian, in his distress, repented of his ingratitude; Belisarius was restored to command, and by his judicious exertions, Nushírván was forced to return across the Euphrates, loaded, however, with the spoils of western Asia. His next enterprise was the conquest of the Caucasian districts inhabited by the Lazi, the Colchians, and other semi-barbarous tribes which the Byzantines struggled to prevent, and this led to the tedious Lazic war, in which the strength of both empires was uselessly wasted. In consequence of the Persian war, Justinian entered into a treaty with the Abyssinians, whose monarch had subdued the greater part of Arabia, in the expectation of opening, by his means, a naval communication with China and India; but the design was frustrated by the reluctance of the Ethiopian monarch to engage in a doubtful contest with the power of Persia.

The provinces of Africa and Italy, acquired by the valor of Belisarius, were nearly lost by the incapacity and tyranny of his successors. Their weakness provoked the Moors to take arms; and, though these barbarians were finally reduced, the African province was changed from a fertile and populous country into a savage and silent desert. Still more dangerous was the revolt of the Goths under the gallant Totila (A. D. 541), who in a very brief space recovered the greater part of Italy. Finding his generals successively defeated, Justinian sent Belisarius to the theatre of his former glory; but he neglected to supply the hero with sufficient forces; and Rome was captured by Totila, almost in sight of the imperial army. The city was recovered soon after, and the old general gained some advantages over Totila; but finding himself unsupported, he solicited permission to return, and departed from Italy disgraced, not so much by his failure, as by the plunder he had permitted Antonina to extort from those he was sent to defend (A. D. 548). Totila, after the departure of Belisarius, again made himself master of Rome, but the maritime cities of Italy resisted his assaults, and supported the imperial interests until the eunuch Narses was sent into the peninsula (A. D. 552).

Justinian granted to this favorite what he had denied to Belisarius, a competent supply of the munitions of war; allies were entreated to send contingents, and mercenaries were hired from the principal barbarous tribes. Thus supplied, the eunuch eagerly sought to bring the Goths to an engagement; but Totila showed equal ardor for the combat, and the hostile forces soon met in the vicinity of Rome. In the very commencement of the battle the Gothic cavalry, hurried forward by their impetuosity, advanced so far beyond their infantry, that they were surrounded and cut to pieces before they could receive assistance. Totila, hasting with a chosen troop to remedy the disorder, was struck to the earth mortally wounded, and his followers instantly fled in confusion. Rome opened its gates to the conquerors; but the imperial forces, especially the barbarian mercenaries, treated the city more cruelly than the Gothic conquerors had done, and inflicted on the citizens the mingled horror of lust, rapine, and murder. The bravest of the Goths retired, after their defeat, beyond the Po, and chose Teias for their king. War was of course renewed; but in a fierce battle, which lasted two entire days, Teias was slain, and the power of the Ostrogoths irretrievably ruined. Narses had scarcely time to recover from the fatigues of this campaign, when he was summoned to repel an invasion of the Franks and Allemans; he routed them with great slaughter; and then returning to Rome, gratified its citizens by the semblance of a triumph. Italy was thus reduced to a Byzantine province, governed by the exarchs of Ravenna; and Narses himself, the first and most powerful of the exarchs, governed the whole peninsula for fifteen years.

In the meantime Belisarius had been summoned to defend the empire from the dangers with which it was menaced, by an invasion of the Bulgarians. He gained a decisive victory over the barbarians, but was prevented from improving his advantages by the intrigues of the courtiers. The Bulgarians were induced to return beyond the Danube, by the payment of a large ransom for their captives; and Justinian claimed the gratitude of his subjects for accelerating their departure by the threat of placing armed vessels in the Danube. This was the last campaign of Belisarius; he was soon after disgraced and imprisoned, under a false charge of treason: his innocence was subsequently proved, and his freedom restored, but grief and resentment hurried him to the grave; and his treasures were seized by the rapacious emperor. Eight months afterward Justinian sunk into the tomb, scarcely regretted by his subjects. He was a pious and diligent sovereign, but he wanted energy to contend against the vices of his court and the age. His talents as a legislator and statesman were great; had he acted on his own principles, he would have surpassed Augustus, but he yielded his power to the infamous Theodora, and to unworthy ministers who abused his confidence, and oppressed the empire.

Section III.—*The Establishment of the Civil Law.*

Early in his reign, Justinian directed his attention to the state of the law in his empire, and formed the useful project of digesting into a uniform code the vast mass of laws, rules, and judicial maxims, which the various interests of the Romans and Byzantines, their progress in civilization, and the inconstancy of their rulers, had produced, during the course of thirteen hundred years. He saw that the multitude of ordinances occasioned confusion and disorder, and that the heap of inconsistent decisions and regulations, formed a labyrinth in which justice went astray, and iniquity found avenues for escape. The execution of this great plan was not worthy of the design. At the head of the commission appointed to prepare the code was Tribonian, a lawyer of great eminence, but unfortunately an interested flatterer and corrupt judge; accustomed to sell justice, he altered, perverted, or suppressed many excellent laws. He frequently persuaded the emperor to destroy, by supplementary edicts called Novels, the principles of right which had been previously established in the Code and the Digest.

Justinian commenced with the Code. In an edict, dated the 3d of February, A. D. 528, addressed to the senate of Constantinople, he declared his resolution of collecting into a single volume, not merely the laws in the three previous codes of Gregory, Hermogenianus, and Theodosius, but also the laws that had been published by imperial authority since the formation of the Theodosian code. A commission of ten eminent lawyers, with Tribonian at its head, was charged with the execution of this task. They were permitted to suppress repetitions, to remove contradictory or obsolete laws, to add what was necessary for exactness or explanation, and to unite, under one head, what was spread over a great variety of laws. The work went on so rapidly, that in little more than a year the new code, containing, in twelve books, all the imperial laws from the accession of the Emperor Adrian was ready to appear. Justinian affixed the imperial seal to the new constitution (A. D. 529), and transmitted it, with a suitable edict, to Mennas, the prætorian præfect. In this edict he congratulates himself and the empire on having found commissioners possessing so much zeal, knowledge, and probity; he gives the collection the force of law, ordaining that the new code alone should be cited in courts of justice; and he commands the præfect to have this made known through the empire.

A more extensive and difficult work remained, to collect the scattered monuments of ancient jurisprudence. Justinian confided this task also to Tribonian, and gave him the power of nominating his fellow commissioners. Tribonian chose one of the magistrates who had already aided in the formation of the Code, four professors of jurisprudence, and eleven advocates of high legal reputation. These seventeen commissioners were instructed to search out, collect, and put in order, all that was really useful in the books of the juriconsults who had been authorized to make or interpret laws by preceding sovereigns; they were permitted, as in the case of the Code, to change, add, or retrench, and to fix doubtful cases by precise definitions. The emperor recommended them in settling any point, to regard neither the number nor the reputation of the juriconsults who had given opinions on the subject, but to be guided solely by reason and equity. Their collection was to be arranged in fifty books, having all the matter arranged under their respective titles, and was to be named the Digest, on account of its orderly classification, or the Pandects, because it was to contain all the ancient jurisprudence.* But the commissioners seem to have executed their task with more zeal and speed than exactness. The emperor himself did not expect that the work could be completed in less than ten years. It was necessary to examine carefully more than two thousand volumes; to discuss, compare, and reduce into order, an innumerable number of decisions; to reform some of them, to reverse others, and to classify the whole. But Tribonian, who knew that in enterprises which engage the vanity of princes, the delay between the design and execution is borne with great impatience, hurried on the work so rapidly that it was completed in three years.

On the 16th of December, 533, Justinian invested this collection with the authority of law, by a constitution of state, addressed to the senate of Constantinople, and all his subjects. In this edict he states, that the enormous chaos of ancient decisions have been reduced to a twentieth part, without the omission of anything essential, so that the order and brevity of this body of jurisprudence, and the facility with which it could be learned, took away every excuse from negligence or ignorance. He declares, that though some errors may have crept into a work of such vast magnitude, their number is very limited; and he asserts, rather too hastily, that it contains none of those inconsistent decisions which lawyers call *antinomies*.† Should any point be found deficient and obscure, he wills that recourse should be had to the imperial authority, which alone has the power to supply or interpret the laws. To prevent the recurrence of the ancient confusion, by diversity of sentiments, he forbids all commentary, permitting only the translation of the laws into Greek, with the addition of titles and paratitles—that is to say, summaries of their contents. He forbids the use of abbreviations in transcribing them, declaring that the copy in which a

* From παν, *all*, and δεχεσθαι, *to contain*. The fifty books of the Pandects are divided into four hundred and twenty-three titles, which contain nine thousand one hundred and twenty-three laws, each marked with the name of its author.

† From αντι, *contrary to*, and νομος, *law*.

contraction was found should be held of no authority, and that the transcriber should be punished for forgery. All other laws are declared to be abrogated, and are even forbidden to be cited in the tribunals; and the judges are ordered to conform in all things to the Digest from the day of the date of the edict. The emperor enjoins the three prætorian præfects to publish the Digest in their several governments, and concludes by stating that he was anxious to have this meritorious revolution effected during his third consulate, in order that a year, which heaven had blessed by a peace with Persia, and the conquest of Africa, should witness the completion of this great edifice of the laws, as a holy and august temple, in which justice should pronounce her oracles.

While the commissioners labored at the Digest, the emperor charged Tribonian, and two eminent professors, to prepare an elementary work on jurisprudence, in four books, as an introduction to the study of law. This portion of Justinian's legislation is far the most valuable part; it was finished and published a little before the Digest, and was named the Institutes.

The whole system of ancient jurisprudence was thus simplified, reduced to its essentials, and arranged in the Institutes, the Pandects, and the Code. But, after their publication, Justinian published more than two hundred supplementary edicts; and when the great collections began to be used in the courts, several errors and imperfections were discovered as might reasonably be expected in a work of such magnitude, executed with such unnecessary speed. A new commission was appointed to revise the Code; the result of its labors was a second edition, which received the imperial sanction, November 16, 534, by an edict abrogating the former imperfect Code.

The emperor reserved to himself, in express terms, the right of adding, at a subsequent time, but separately, such constitutions as he should judge necessary. These were called Novels; they limit, extend, and in some instances repeal the Code; and it is this inconsistency that has led to the suspicion of Tribonian and the prince having occasionally been guided by interest and favor, rather than by reason and equity. These Novels are one hundred and sixty-eight in number, but only ninety-eight have the force of law, having been collected into a volume in the last year of Justinian's reign.

This code was supplanted in the east by the Basilica or Greek constitutions of later emperors. In the west, Illyria was the only province by which it was received, until the overthrow of the Gothic monarchy afforded an opportunity for its introduction into Italy. The Code, way however, superseded by the laws of the Lombards, when their hordes became master of Ravenna. After Charlemagne had overthrown the Lombard monarchy, he searched Italy in vain for a copy of Justinian's legislation; it remained concealed until the twelfth century, when a copy of the Digest was found on the capture of Amalfi by the troops of the emperor Lothaire II., and presented by him to the citizens of Pisa, who had aided the imperialists in this expedition. At a later period, a copy of the Code was discovered at Ravenna, and a collection was made of the Novels which were dispersed throughout Italy. Such were the origin and revolutions of this celebrated body of legislation, the source of the civil law throughout Europe, and the great guide to the most civilized nations in supplying the defects of their several legal systems.

SECTION IV.—*History of the Silk Trade.—Introduction of the Silkworm into Europe.*

SILK was known as an article of commerce, and extensively used in the western world long before the insect that produces this precious substance, and whose nature was unknown, was brought for the first time to Constantinople. No one before the age of Justinian had even contemplated such an enterprise. It was only by long and painful journeys through the dangerous and difficult wilds of central Asia, that a merchandise could be procured, which the progress of wealth and luxury rendered almost indispensable to the civilized nations of Europe, Asia, and Africa, that surrounded the Mediterranean. The Assyrians and Medes, in the early ages, had long a monopoly of this commerce, and hence we find that garments of wrought silk are usually called Median robes by the ancient writers. In this traffic they were succeeded by the Persians, who attached great importance to the trade, and neglecting nothing that could keep it exclusively in their hands. From them the Greek and Syrian merchants of Asia purchased the silk which they transported into the western countries. Passing through such a number of hands, it was of course scarce and dear. During Justinian's reign, the Byzantines, or, as they still called themselves, the Romans, were eager to free themselves from their dependance on the Persians for the supply of this article. They tried to lower the price by purchasing from other Asiatic nations, and by making exertions to open a direct communication with the country in which the silk is produced. Their ignorance of geography was a great impediment to their success; they had very vague notions respecting the position of the regions where this desirable commodity was procured. They contented themselves with loosely describing it as part of India, or some very remote country in eastern Asia.

A few modern writers have been misled by the inaccuracy of the Byzantine historians into the belief that the country which supplied the ancient world with silk was the Punjáb, and the districts of northern India adjacent to Persia, regions where silk has never yet been produced in sufficient abundance to form an article of commerce. On the contrary, the circumstances related respecting Serica, the silk-growing country, are manifestly applicable to no place but China, where silk is still produced more plentifully than in any other part of the world. Indeed the very name Seres appears to have been derived from this commodity; for *Se*, or, as it is pronounced in the provincial dialects, Sēr, is the Chinese name for the silkworm. We also find the Sinæ identified with the Seres by the ancient geographers, and we know that *Sín*, or *Chín*, has been always the name given to China by the nations of western Asia. In the preceding pages mention has been made of the embassy sent from the Romans to the Chinese, in the age of the Antonines; and it is only necessary to add, in proof of the commercial relations between this ancient empire and the western world, that a tolerably accurate account of the revolutions in the Persian and Parthian kingdoms may be found in Chinese histories.*

The silk was imported from China in packages, which caravans of merchants brought across the extreme breadth of Asia, in a journey of two hundred and forty-three days, to the seacoast of Syria. The Persians who supplied the Romans, usually made their purchases from the Sogdians, on the banks of the Oxus, and their traffic was liable to be interrupted by the White Huns and the Turks, who successively conquered that industrious people. But the difficulties of the road between the Sogdian capital, Maracanda (*Samarcand*), and the first Chinese city in the province of Shensí, led to frequent efforts for opening a new and less perilous route, which, however, proved unsuccessful. From the time they passed the Jaxartes, the enterprising Sogdians had to contend, not only with the dangers and difficulties of the intervening deserts, but also against the wandering hordes, who have always considered the citizen and traveller as objects of lawful rapine.

It is recorded as a proof of the vast expense of the magnificent spectacles with which Julius Cæsar sought at once to dazzle and conciliate the populace, that he decorated the actors in his varied pageants with a profusion of silk dresses, which were viewed by the Italians with equal wonder and admiration. In consequence of the difficulties of transit, the vast length of desert which the caravans had to traverse and, probably, the limited supply of silk in China itself, this article bore a very high price in Rome, and was often sold for its weight in gold Silken dresses were esteemed too expensive and delicate for men, and were appropriated wholly to ladies of eminent rank and opulence. In the beginning of the reign of Tiberius, a law was passed enacting, that "no man should disgrace himself by wearing a silk dress." This might, however, have been a religious as well as a sumptuary ordinance, for it is a singular circumstance in the history of silk, that, on account of its being the excretion of a worm, several religious bodies in the East, but more especially the Mohammedans, consider it an unclean dress. Indeed, it has been decided by the unanimous consent of all the Sonnite doctors, that a person wearing a garment made entirely of silk, can not offer up the daily prayers enjoined by the Koran.

The profligate and effeminate Heliogabalus was the first of the Roman emperors who wore a garment entirely of silk; and, in consequence of his example, the custom of wearing silk soon became general among the wealthy citizens of Rome, and even extended to the provinces. It seems probable, also, that the price of the article had diminished in consequence of its beginning to be imported by the maritime route through Alexandria, instead of by caravans through the arid deserts of Tartary and Turkestan. Chinese histories inform us, that an

* The Armenians call the Chinese *Jenk*, and China *Jenistán*. Their relations with this country ascend to the beginning of the third century of our era. About that time a Chinese colony was established in Armenia. The chief of this colony was probably one of the imperial dynasty of the Huns: driven from his country by civil wars, he at first sought refuge at the court of Ardeshir, the founder of the Sassanid dynasty in Persia, thence he passed into Persia, where he was received about A. D. 260, by Tiridates, the Armenian sovereign, who gave him the province of Jaron. This personage, whose name was Mamkon, became the founder of the family of the Memigonians, who are justly celebrated in Armenian history.

ambassador from one of the Antonines came to their remote country for the purpose of concluding a commercial treaty, and this is rendered highly probable by the fact that oriental commodities became both plentiful and cheap under and after their dynasty. Ammianus Marcellinus informs us, that in his age (A. D. 370) silk was generally worn even by the lower classes.

After the restoration of a native dynasty in Persia under the Sassanides, and the establishment of the eastern empire at Constantinople, a long series of wars ensued between the Persian sovereigns, who deemed themselves legitimate inheritors of the power of Cyrus, and the Byzantine emperors, who wished themselves to be considered successors of Alexander the Great. The command of the sea of Oman gave the Persians a decided advantage over the Egyptian merchants, who were forced to import oriental commodities by the tedious and dangerous navigation of the Red sea. Until the introduction of steam navigation, the Red sea, or *Yam Suph*,* as it is called by the Orientals, was universally dreaded by voyagers. The strait at its entrance was significantly named by the Arabs *Bab-el-Mandeb*, or, "the gate of tears;" and it was a common proverb with eastern sailors, "Yam Suph is a double-locked sea; there are six months in the year that you can not get into it, and six more that you can not get out of it." But the Persians were not satisfied with this natural superiority; having it in their power to molest or cut off the caravans, which, in order to procure a supply for the Greek empire, travelled by land to China through the northern provinces of their kingdom, they laid such onerous transit duties on foreign merchants, that the Greeks were forced to abandon this branch of commerce, and purchase their silk from the Persians and Sogdians. These, with the usual rapacity of monopolists, raised the price of silk to such an exorbitant height, that the Greek manufacturers, whose looms depended on a supply of this raw material, were thrown out of employment and nearly ruined.

The Emperor Justinian, eager, not only to obtain a full and certain supply of a commodity which was become of indispensable use, but solicitous to deliver the commerce of his subjects from the exactions of his enemies, endeavored, by means of his ally the Christian monarch of Abyssinia, to wrest some portion of the silk trade from the Persians In this attempt he failed; but when he least expected it, he, by an unforeseen event, attained his great object of procuring his subjects an abundant supply of silk, independent both of ships and caravans.

Two Persian monks having been employed as Christian missionaries by some of the churches which had been established in India, pursued their evangelical labors until they had penetrated into the remote country of the Seres, or Chinese (A. D. 551). There they observed the labors of the silkworm, the mode in which these animals were fed on the mulberry-leaf; the care bestowed upon them in the several periods of insect transformation, and the attention necessary to obtaining perfect cocoons. Without such knowledge, the mere possession of the insects would have been useless; for the time that elapses while the silk-caterpillar is undergoing its changes varies according to the temperature and the quantity of nourishment with which it is supplied: the

* That is, "the Sea of Weeds."

health also of the insect and the subsequent perfection of the silk depends upon the mode in which these changes are made, and the intervals between the successive moultings of the skin, which take place before the animal attains its full growth. The Chinese calculate tha the same number of insects which would, if they had attained the full size in twenty-three or twenty-four days, produce twenty-five ounces of silk, would produce only twenty ounces if their growth occupied twenty-eight days, and only ten ounces if forty days. In order, therefore, to accelerate their growth, they supply the insects with fresh food every half hour during the first day of their existence, and then gradually reduce the number of meals as the worms grow older. It deserves to be remarked as an unnoticed fact in natural theology, that the substance on which this valuable caterpillar feeds, is the leaf of the mulberry-tree; and Providence, as if to ensure the continuance of this useful species, has so ordained it, that no other insect will partake of the same food; thus ensuring a certain supply for the little spinster.

Having made themselves acquainted with these particulars, the monks repaired to Constantinople, and revealed the information they had acquired to the Emperor Justinian. Encouraged by the liberal promises of that monarch, they undertook to bring to his capital a sufficient number of those wonderful insects to whose labors man is so much indebted. They proceeded to China, and finally accomplished the object of their mission by obtaining a competent supply of the eggs of the silkworm, which they concealed in a hollow cane. Having returned safe to Constantinople, the eggs were, under their direction, hatched by the artificial heat of a dunghill, and the insects were fed on the leaves of the wild mulberry-tree. Such care was bestowed upon them, that they soon multiplied, and worked in the same manner as in those climates where they first became the objects of human attention and care.

Justinian at first attempted to monopolize this source of profit, but the rapid increase of the worms opened the trade. A singular circumstance enables us to appreciate the speedy success of the Greeks in the manufacture of silk. Before the sixth century closed, the Turks, descending from the Altaian mountains, conquered Sogdiana. The conquered people had found the demand for silk rapidly diminishing, which they attributed to the commercial jealousy of the Persians. They complained of their losses to their new master, the Turkish khakan, who sent ambassadors to form a commercial treaty with the Persian monarch, the celebrated Nushirván. It was obviously unwise policy to strengthen the power of the new state which had been formed beyond the Oxus; and Nushirván was, besides, eager to open a direct communication with China, through the Persian gulf. To show his contempt for the offers of the Sogdians, he purchased up all their goods, and committed them to the flames. The khakan next sent ambassadors to Justinian II., who, after a toilsome journey, reached Constantinople (A. D. 571), just twenty years after the introduction of the silkworm; when, to their great astonishment, they found the Byzantines in the possession of silk of their own growth, and so skilled in its use, that their manufactures already rivalled those of China. From this time the Sogdian carrying trade declined; it was totally annihilated about the middle of the ninth century, when a fanatic insurgent, in China, murdered the foreign merchants, and cut down the mulberry-trees, to destroy the silk that enticed strangers to the celestial empire.

For nearly six hundred years, the Greeks were the only Europeans who possessed the silkworm: at length, Roger I., king of Sicily, engaged in war with the Byzantine empire, having captured some persons skilled in the production and manufacture of silk, established factories at Palermo, which rose rapidly into celebrity. Thence the trade spread into Italy, Spain, and France; but in most of these countries the manufacture was long deemed of greater importance than the production of the raw material. France owes her present superiority in the trade tc the patriotic exertions of Henry IV., who made extensive nurseries of mulberry plants, and distributed them gratuitously to all desirous of establishing plantations. James I. endeavored to introduce the production of raw silk, as a trade, into England; since his time the experiment has been frequently repeated, but it never has been attended with complete success. Similar trials have also been made in Ireland, but the result has not yet answered the expectations of the patriotic projectors.

Section V.—*The Monarchy of the Franks under the Merovingian Dynasty.*

The history of the Franks properly begins with the establishment of a large body of that nation in Belgic Gaul, under a chief named Merewig,* from whom the dynasty received the name Merovingian.† He was succeeded by his son Hilderik,‡ a brave warrior, but the slave of his passions. An insult that he offered to the wife of one of his officers occasioned a revolt; Hilderik was dethroned, and a Count Egidius, or Giles, proclaimed king. After an exile of eight years, Hilderik was restored, and the remainder of his reign appears to have passed in tranquillity. Hlodowig|| was the next sovereign: his harsh German name was softened by the Latins into Clodovecus, or Clovis, the origin of the modern Ludovicus, or Louis. At his accession (A. D. 481), Clovis had scarcely reached his twentieth year; the ardor of youth combined with the circumstances of his position to urge him to foreign conquests; for the fertility of the Belgic soil, the purity of its waters, and its atmosphere, continually attracted fresh hordes to the lower Rhine, who sought admission into the Belgic colony Clovis found it necessary to enlarge his frontiers, and invaded the Roman province. Near Soissons he encountered Syagrius, the son of his father's rival, Egidius, and gained a decisive victory. Syagrius sought refuge with the Visigoths, but that nation had lost much of its martial spirit; Alaric II., unworthy of the name he bore, sent the unfortunate general bound to Clovis, by whom he was beheaded.

The conqueror was now the most powerful monarch of his age, and the neighboring princes eagerly sought his alliance: he chose for his queen, Hlodohilde,§ or Clotilda, whose uncle was king of the Burgundians. Clotilda was a Christian; she labored earnestly to convert her husband, and especially urged him when his crown and life were en-

* Mere-wig, *eminent warrior.*

† The other Franks were named Ripe-Warians; that is, inhabitants of the banks of the Rhine.

‡ Hilde-rik, *bold in combat.*

|| Hlodo-wig, *famous warrior.*

§ Hlodo-hilde, *brilliant and noble.*

dangered by an invasion of the Germanic confederation of tribes, called the Allemans. Clovis, persuaded that he owed the great victory of Tolbiac to the prayers of Clotilda, became a convert, and received the sacrament of baptism from the bishop of Rheims (A. D. 496). He gave the prelate, as a fee, all the land he could ride round while he himself slept after dinner, a gift very characteristic of a conqueror, who felt that he had only to wake and acquire new dominions. Soon afterward he undertook new conquests. Advancing in the direction of Genabum (*Orleans*), he crossed the Loire, spreading everywhere the terror of his name. The Bretons, long subject to the Romans, consented without reluctance to a change of masters. Clovis, having traversed their country, entered Aquitaine, pillaged the houses, laid waste the fields, plundered the temples, and returned to Paris, ' leaving," as the cotemporary historian says, " nothing to the wretched inhabitants but the soil, which the Franks could not take away."

The kingdom established by Clovis extended from the Rhine to the Pyrenees, from the Alps to the ocean, but its security was very uncertain. Wherever the conqueror appeared, he met nothing but submission from the various races settled in Gaul; as soon, however, as he passed onward, his nominal subjects closed upon his rear, retaining no more trace of his march than the furrowed wave does of a vessel's keel. Neither was the Frankish monarch absolute over his own soldiers; his army was composed of freemen, who disdained to submit to despotic rule. They gave to their monarch his share of the booty, and nothing more.* When they disapproved of the expedition for which they assembled, they abandoned it without scruple; or if the monarch refused to undertake a war which they deemed advisable, they forced him to comply with their wishes, not merely by menaces, but by actual force.†

On the death of Clovis (A. D. 511), his dominions were divided between his four sons, Hildebert‡ (Childebert), Hlodomer‖ (Chlodomer), Hlodher§ (Clotaire), and Theodoric,¶ who respectively occupied the capitals of Paris, Orleans, Soissons, and Metz. This distribution gave rise to a new geographical division; all the districts between the Rhine, the Meuse, and the Moselle, received the name of Oster-rike,** since corrupted into Austrasia and the country between the Meuse, the Loire, and the ocean, was named Ni-oster-rike,†† or, as it was latinized,

* Gregory of Tours furnishes us with a curious anecdote on this subject. "About this time the army of Clovis pillaged a great number of churches and houses. His soldiers had taken away, from one of the cathedrals, a vase of surprising size and beauty. The bishop of the diocese sent a messenger to reclaim it. To this man, the king said, 'Follow me to Soissons, where the plunder will be shared, and should chance give me the vase, I will do what your prelate requires.' When they reached Soissons, they went to the place where the plunder was piled, and the king said, 'I entreat you, my brave warriors, to give me this vase in addition to my share.' Upon this, a presumptuous soldier exclaimed, 'You shall have nothing but the portion assigned you by lot.'"

† The historian quoted in the preceding note says, "After this, Clotaire and Childebert (sons of Clovis) formed the design of marching against the Burgundians. Their brother, Theodoric, was unwilling to engage in the expedition, but the Franks who followed him, said unanimously, 'If you will not join your brothers, we will quit you, and choose another leader.'"

‡ Hilde-berth, *brilliant warrior*.

‖ Hlodo-mer, *celebrated chief*.

§ Hlod-her, *celebrated and excellent*.

¶ Theod-e-rik, *brave among the people*.

** That is, *Eastern kingdom*.

†† That is, *Northeastern kingdom*.

Neustria. All that was not comprised in this division, belonged not to the Merovingian Franks, but retained its ancient name of Gaul.

Chlodomer and Theodoric engaged in war Gundumer,* king of the Burgundians. In a great battle fought near Vienne (A. D. 522), Chlodomer was slain,† but Theodoric gained a decisive victory, and added the Burgundian kingdom to his own dominions. Clotilda took the guardianship of her infant grandchildren, but the favor she showed to the three sons of Chlodomer provoked the resentment of Childebert, king of Paris. He secretly proposed to his brother Clotaire, that they should secure the persons of the young princes, shave their heads,‡ and divide their dominions. Clotaire readily joined in the project, and put the two eldest of his nephews to death; the third, saved by faithful servants, cut off his hair with his own hands, and entering into a monastery, spent a life of celibacy.‖ Ten years after this event, Theodoric

* Gundu-mer, *pacific and great.*

† "The brothers joined their forces at Veserancia, a place situated in the territory of the city of Vienna, and gave battle to Gundumer. The Burgundian having taken to flight with his army, Chlodomer pursued him, and when he was at a distance from his friends, the Burgundians, imitating the signals of the Franks, exclaimed, 'Come this way, we are thine.' He believed them, and spurred his horse into the midst of the enemy. They surrounded him, cut off his head, and fixing it on a pike, displayed it to their pursuers."—*Gregory of Tours.*

‡ To shave the head was the form of dethroning a sovereign at this period. Among the early Franks, the crown of hair was as much a symbol of royalty as the crown of gold.

‖ The account given of this transactiou by Gregory of Tours is too interesting to be omitted. "Clotaire readily adopted his brother's project, and came to Paris. Childebert had already spread a report that he and his brother had agreed to invest their nephews with royalty, and they sent a messenger to Clotilda, then residing in the same city, who said, 'Send your grandchildren, that they may be raised to the throne.' She, joyous, and knowing nothing of the plot, after having made the children eat and drink, sent them to their uncles, saying, 'Go, children, I will believe that my son is not lost, when I see you on the throne.' When the ehildren came to their uncles, they were taken and separated from their servants and governors. Then they shut them up apart, the children in one place, and the attendants in another. When this was done, Childebert and Clotaire sent Arcadius (one of their officers), to the queen, with a scissors and drawn sword. When he came into her presence, showing her these, he said, 'Thy sons, our lords, desire to know thy pleasure, gracious queen, respecting the manner in which they should treat the children. Order either their hair or their throats to be cut.' Astounded by these words, and enraged at beholding the scissors and naked sword, the queen gave vent to her wrath, and, scarcely knowing what she said, so troubled was her mind, imprudently replied, 'If they are not to reign like their father, I would rather see them dead than shaven.' Then Arcadius returned promptly to those who sent him, and said, 'You may persevere; the queen approves what you have begun, and her will is, that you complete your project.' Immediately, Clotaire, taking the eldest of the children by the arm, threw him on the ground, and stabbing him under the shoulder, put him cruelly to death. His brother, terrified at the scene, threw himself at the feet of Childebert, and kissing his knees, exclaimed, 'Help me, my good father, let me not be murdered like my poor brother.' Then, Childebert, melting into tears, said to Clotaire, 'Oh! I entreat you, my very dear brother, have the kindness to spare this child's life; if you consent to spare him, I will give you whatever you may demand.' But Clotaire, overwhelming him with reproaches, said, 'Thrust the child away, or you shall die in his stead, for you were the first to urge me to this deed, though you now shrink from its completion.' Then Childebert, alarmed, pushed the child over to Clotaire, who struck his dagger into tne boy's side, and slew him on the body of his brother. Afterward they murdered the servants and tutors. When they were dead, Clotaire mounted his horse, without showing any compunction for the murder of his died, and was succeeded by his son, Theodobert,* who took the title of king of Austrasia. His uncles attempted to deprive Theodobert of his dominions, but being daunted by the mere display of his power, they turned their arms against Spain, laid waste Arragon, Biscay, and Catalonia, stormed Pampeluna, besieged Saragossa, and were only induced to retire by a present of the tunic of St. Vincent, a relic which, in that superstitious age, was deemed an invaluable treasure.

The fame of Theodobert extended to Constantinople; Justinian endeavored to win his friendship, by the cession of the nominal claims which the empire retained over Provence, but the Austrasian monarch entered into an alliance with Totila, the emperor's enemy, crossed the Alps, and quickly subdued the greater part of northern Italy. After his return, the army he left behind met with some reverses, and the inflated vanity of Justinian led him to issue a medal, on which he styled himself Conqueror of the Franks. Theodobert was so enraged at this arrogance, that he prepared to lead an army through Hungary into Thrace, and assail Justinian in his capital, but this daring enterprise was frustrated by his sudden death; he was killed by the fall of a tree (A. D. 548), while hunting the wild buffalo, a dangerous sport, to which he was passionately addicted.

Theodobald† succeeded to the Austrasian throne, but died after an inglorious reign of seven years. Childebert soon followed him to the tomb, and thus Clotaire acquired the sole, but not the undisturbed possession of Neustria and Austrasia. His own son, Chramnè,‡ headed a revolt of the turbulent Bretons, but he was defeated and barbarously put to death, with his entire family,‖ by command of his cruel father. The chroniclers add, that Clotaire died the next year (A. D. 561), at Compeigne, on the anniversary of his son's death, and at the precise hour of the horrid butchery.

Clotaire left four sons—Charibert,§ Gontram,¶ Chilperic,** and Sigebert,†† who shared his dominions. The turbulent period that followed, is principally remarkable for the troubles occasioned by the crimes of two infamous women, Brunilda and Fredegonda, the wives of Sigebert and Chilperic. Fredegonda had won her way to the throne by murdering Galswintha, the sister of her rival; and the jealousy between

nephews, and retired with Childebert to the suburbs. The queen Clotilda, having placed the bodies on a bier, conducted them, with litanies, sacred songs, and profound grief, to the church of St. Peter's, where they were buried together. One was ten years old, and the other six. The third son, named Clodoald, was saved by the interference of some brave men, called *barons*. Renouncing his earthly kingdom, he became a clerk, and, persisting in good works, finally received priest's orders. The two kings shared among them the inheritance of Clodomer."

* Theode-bert, *very brilliant among the people.*

† Theode-bald, *vigorous above all.*

‡ Hram, *warlike.*

‖ "The two armies having come to an engagement, the count of the Bretons ran away, and was slain in flight; after which Hram (Chramnè) began to fly toward the ships he had prepared on the sea, but, while he was endeavoring to save his wife and children, he was overtaken by his father's army, made prisoner, and bound. When the news was brought to Clotaire, he ordered that the prince, together with his wife and daughters, should be burned. They shut them up in a poor hut, where Hram, extended on a bench, was strangled; they then set fire to the house, and it was consumed with all its inmates."—*Gregory of Tours.*

§ Hari-bert, *glorious in the army.*

¶ Gont-ram, *generous man.*

** Hilpe-rik, *brave in combat.*

†† Sighe-bert, *glorious conqueror.*

two ambitious and unprincipled women was aggravated, on one side, by the desire of revenge, and, on the other, by the difficulty of maintaining her dignity, when she was changed from a mistress into a wife. During the long period over which their resentments spread, it is difficult to distinguish anything but murders and assassinations, in the gloomy annals of the time. Fredegonda procured the death of Sigebert, and afterward of Chilperic and his two sons, being chiefly enraged against Merovèe,* who had married Brunilda.

Childebert inherited the kingdom of his father, Sigebert, and that of his uncle, Gontram; aided by his mother, Brunilda, he maintained a long and sanguinary struggle against Fredegonda, and her young son, Clotaire: but he died early, leaving two children to divide his distracted dominions. Both of these were destroyed by Brunilda, whose hatred they had provoked by remonstrating against her crimes, and after a dreary scene of confusion, France was again united into a single monarchy, under Clotaire II., son of Chilperic and Fredegonda (A. D. 613). His first care was to punish Brunilda, the ancient enemy of his mother and his house: she was exhibited for three days, mounted on a camel, to the derision of the army, subjected to the most cruel tortures, and finally fastened to the tail of a wild horse, which tore her wretched carcass to pieces, in the presence of the soldiers.

Clotaire published a code of laws, which enjoys some reputation; but his administration was deficient in vigor, and during his reign several encroachments were made on the royal power, by the ambitious nobles. His son, Dagobert I.,† succeeded (A. D. 628), and had the mortification to see his authority weakened by the growing greatness of the mayors of the palace: he died, after a feeble and dissolute reign (A. D. 638), but was strangely enough canonized as a saint.‡

The successors of Dagobert were mere phantoms of royalty; the entire sovereignty was possessed by the mayors of the palace, who finally acquired absolute possession of half the monarchy, as dukes of Austrasia. Pepin D'Heristal, the greatest of these nominal ministers, and real monarchs, governed France in the name of several successive kings. After his death (A. D. 714), his power descended to his grandson, Theodobald, a child only eight years of age, who was thus singularly appointed guardian to a king that was not yet sixteen. Karl,|| the

* Mere-wig, *eminent warrior.* † Dago-bert, *brilliant as the day*

‡ The cause of his canonization is singularly illustrative of the superstitions of the age. Audoald, bishop of Poictiers, while on an embassy in Sicily, was miraculously, as he declared, informed of the king's death by a holy hermit named John. This pious anchoret said, "While I was asleep last night, an old man with a long beard bade me get up, and pray for the soul of King Dagobert, who was on the point of death. I arose, and looking through the window of my hermitage, I saw, in the middle of the sea, a host of devils carrying the king's soul to hell. The unfortunate soul, grievously tormented, invoked the aid of St. Martin, St. Maurice, and St. Denis. At his cries, the spirits of these holy martyrs descended from heaven, in the midst of thunders and lightnings, delivered the king's soul, and bore it up with them through the air, singing the canticle of David, *O Lord, how happy is the man that thou hast chosen.*" Audoald recited this relation to the king's chancellor, on his return, by whom it was entered in the archives of the kingdom, and Dagobert enrolled among the number of saints.—*Gaguin.*

|| Karl, *robust.*

natural son of Pepin, better known in history by the name of Charles Martel, set aside this absurd arrangement, and succeeded to more than his father's power. His numerous victories over the Saxons, Burgundians, Frisians, &c., have rendered his name illustrious: but he is more justly celebrated for his triumph over the Saracenic invaders of France (A. D. 732), between Tours and Poictiers, by which he delivered Christendom from the imminent danger of being subjected to the Mohammedan yoke. His son, Pepin, finally compelled Chilperic III. to abdicate (A. D. 752), and the crown of France was thus transferred to the Carlovingian dynasty, from the descendants of Clovis.

SECTION VI.—*The Lombard Monarchy.*

THE Lombards were encouraged to settle on the frontiers of the empire by Justinian, who deemed that they would prove a check on the insolence of the Gepidæ. While these barbarous tribes were engaged in war, Thrace enjoyed comparative tranquillity; but when Alboin became head of the Lombard tribes, he entered into alliance with the Avars for the extirpation of the Gepidæ, purchasing their aid by a tithe of his cattle, and a promise of all the conquered lands. The emperor, Justin II., unwisely abandoned the Gepidæ to their fate; Cunimund, their monarch, hasted to encounter Alboin before he could join the Avars, but he fell in the field which proved fatal to the existence of his nation, and his scull was formed into a drinking vessel by his barbarous enemy. Rosamond, the daughter of the slaughtered king, became the prize and spouse of the victor; the bravest of the surviving Gepidæ were incorporated in the army of the Lombards. Though the Avars had contributed but slightly to the success of the war, they received a large share of the spoils; the greater part of ancient Dacia was resigned to them, and in this country their chagans ruled for more than two hundred years. Alboin's ambition was fixed on a higher object; fifteen years before, a body of Lombards had served under Narses in the conquest of Italy, and they still preserved a vivid remembrance of the wealth and fertility of the peninsula. Alboin encouraged them to hope that this fair land might yet own their sway, and to stimulate their ardor, produced some of its finest fruits at a royal feast. When his designs became known, adventurers flocked to his standard from the neighboring Slavonic and German tribes. Having made every preparation for the expedition, the Lombards resigned their lands to the Avars, on the simple promise of receiving them back, if they failed in the conquest of Italy.

As if the court of Constantinople had resolved to aid the projects of the invaders, the brave Narses was contumeliously removed from his post by the Empress Sophia; and Longinus, a person wholly unacquainted with Italy, appointed exarch in his stead. Alboin met no army to oppose him the field; few even of the cities ventured to resist his progress; Ticinum, or, as it began now to be called, Pavia, almost alone closed its gates against the conqueror, and detained him three years before its walls. It was at length forced to yield by the pressure of hunger; Alboin threatened a general massacre, but his horse happening to stumble as he entered the gates, he believed that Heaven had sent this omen to warn him against cruelty, and he assured the trembling multitude of pardon and safety. Before he could regulate the affairs of the kingdom he had so easily won, Alboin fell a victim to the revenge of his wife. One evening, heated with wine, he sent her the skull of her father Cunimund, fashioned, as has been stated, into a goblet, filled to the brim, with an insulting message, that she should rejoice with her sire. Rosamond, stifling her resentment, simply replied, "Let the will of the king be obeyed;" but she secretly resolved on vengeance and, by infamous means, procured two officers of the household to murder her husband (A. D. 573). She was compelled by the indignation of the people to fly with her paramour to the court of Ravenna, where she was poisoned by a potion which she had prepared for the partner of her guilt.

Clepho, one of the noblest of the Lombard chiefs, was chosen king after the murder of Alboin, by the great council of the nation; but at the end of eighteen months, he was stabbed by a domestic. His cruelty gave the Lombards such a distate for royalty, that after his death, they changed their form of government, and for ten years were ruled by a federation of thirty-six dukes, each of whom was chief of some important city. During this period, they made several efforts to acquire possession of some part of Gaul, but were invariably beaten by the Franks; in Italy, on the contrary, they were generally successful, adding considerably to their territories at the expense of the exarchate of Ravenna, and the other provinces dependant on the Greek empire.

A confederacy between the imperial exarch and Childebert, king of the Franks, so alarmed the Lombards that they chose Autharis, son of Clepho, for their sovereign. He established a perfectly feudal monarchy, assigning their dutchies to the dukes in perpetuity, on the condition of their giving one moiety of their revenue to support the royal dignity; they could not be deprived of their possessions except for high-treason but they held power only at the sovereign's will. A similar form of government seems to have prevailed among the Franks almost from the foundation of their monarchy; but feudal law first received a complete form among the Lombards, and the rules respecting the succession, acquisition, and investiture of fiefs among other nations, were generally derived from their code. The new monarch gained several victories over the Franks, who had been bribed to invade Italy by the Emperor Maurice, and punished the hostility of the Byzantine by subduing a great part of ancient Samnium, which he formed into the dutchy of Benevento. Autharis died without issue (A. D. 590), after a brief but glorious reign, and the crown was transferred to Agilulf, duke of Turin.

Hitherto the Lombards had been either Arians or pagans; but Agilulf, instigated by his queen, established the Catholic faith throughout his dominions, and chastised several dukes who made this change a pretext for rebellion. His son and successor, Adaluald, completed the triumph of the orthodox faith, a circumstance which tended greatly to reconcile the Italians to the supremacy of the Lombards. The Arian party was, however, sufficiently powerful to raise another to the throne; both the rivals, however, died without issue, and the general assembly chose Rotharis for their sovereign (A. D. 636). This monarch, though tainted with the Arian heresy, won the affection of all his subjects by the wise laws he enacted; he also wrested some important places from the exarch of Ravenna, and reduced the imperial interests in Italy so low, that it might be said to exist only by the sufferance of the Lombards. On his death (A. D. 652), a scene of weakness and revolution followed, which was only terminated by the accession of Grimvald, duke of Benevento (A. D. 662).

Grimvald was soon involved in war with the Franks, who invaded Italy, but were completely defeated. Scarcely had he repelled this invasion when the Byzantine emperor, Constans, appeared in Italy at the head of a powerful army, and laid siege to Benevento. But the imperialists, meeting a fierce resistance from the garrison, were soon forced to retreat, and being overtaken on their march, were routed with great slaughter. Constans fled to Sicily with the shattered remnant of his forces, and was murdered in a bath by some of his own servants. Grimvald did not long survive his triumph; he died universally lamented (A. D. 672), and his death was followed by a series of obscure and uninteresting revolutions, which, however, deluged Italy with blood.

The accession of Luitprand (A. D. 711), once more restored the prosperity of the Lombards; he enacted several wise laws, rectified the evils which during the recent disturbances had crept into the administration of justice, and won the favor of the nobles who had opposed his elevation by a judicious display of courage and prudence. Unfortunately, he was prompted by ambition to attempt the complete conquest of Italy; taking advantage of the troubles occasioned by the edicts of the emperor Leo for the destruction of images. The exarchate was invaded, and Ravenna taken; but Luitprand's success provoked the jealousy of the pope, who, though pleased with the punishment of the Iconoclasts,* was by no means gratified with the accession of power of the Lombards. At the pontiff's instigation, the Venetians aided the exarch to recover Ravenna; but the emperor Leo, instead of showing any gratitude to pope Gregory II. for his interference, sent emissaries to arrest him, and he was only saved from prison by the prompt interference of Luitprand. The Italians, provoked at Leo's fierce zeal against images, began to revolt, and several cities voluntarily submitted to the Lombard monarch, who pretended to an extravagant zeal for the Catholic faith. The pope, however, dreaded Luitprand, and sought a protection in Charles Martel against the emperor of Byzantium, who was equally hostile to the Lombards and the pontiff. Italy was now distracted by religious disputes and political jealousies, while the death of Luitprand, at this critical period (A. D. 743), afflicted the Lombards with a new series of revolutionary wars.

After some minor changes, Astulphus was chosen king (A. D. 751); during his reign, the kingdom of the Lombards touched the summit of its greatness; he subdued the exarchate of Ravenna, and changed it into a new dukedom, and then led his forces against Rome, which, nominally subject to the emperor, was really governed by the pope. Alarmed at the danger that threatened him, Pope Stephen first applied for aid to the emperor, but finding that the Byzantine court cared little

* Image-breakers.

for Italy, he appealed to Pepin, the first monarch of the Carlovingian dynasty in France. Pepin immediately crossed the Alps with a powerful army, besieged Astulphus in Pavia, and forced him to purchase peace by the cession not only of the places he had seized in the Roman dukedom, but also of the exarchate and the marches of Ancona, to the Holy See. The Franks had to return a second time to compel the fulfilment of these engagements; Astulphus once more submitted, but secretly resolved to renew the war on a favorable opportunity; before his preparations were completed, however, he was killed by a fall from his horse, and the Lombard kingdom distracted by a disputed succession.

By the aid of the pope, Desiderius prevailed in the contest; but subsequently being exposed to the jealousy of the pontifical power, he tried to secure himself by giving his daughters in marriage to Charles and Carloman, the two sons of Pepin. This alliance was of no long duration; Charles divorced his wife under pretence of her barrenness; and Desiderius, in revenge, endeavored to persuade the pope to anoint Carloman's children monarchs of the Franks. Adrian I., who then filled the pontifical chair, steadily refused; Desiderius invaded his dominions, and the pope unable to make effective resistance, placed himself under the protection of Charles, or, as he is more generally called, Charlemagne. The king of the Franks crossed the Alps, and, after a brief war, put an end to the kingdom of the Lombards by the capture of Pavia (A. D. 774). Desiderius and his family were sent into France, where they died in obscurity; Charlemagne, as conqueror, received the iron crown of Lombardy.

Section VII.—*The Anglo-Saxons.*

When Britain was deserted by the Romans, the country remained exposed to the savage incursions of the Picts and Scots; the inhabitants, unable to protect themselves, and refused aid by the emperors, who were oppressed by other barbarians, deserted their habitations, abandoned their fields, and sought shelter in the hills and woods, where they suffered equally from famine and the enemy. When the retreat of the barbarians afforded them a temporary respite, they wasted their energies in theological controversies arising out of the Pelagian heresy; and when the invasions were renewed, domestic rancor prevented their combining for their common defence. Vortigern, prince of Dumnonium, advised his countrymen to seek foreign aid; and they, forgetting prudence in the extremity of their fears, invited the Saxons to their aid from Germany.

The Saxons and Angles, from small beginnings, had gradually extended their sway from the mouth of the Rhine to the coast of Jutland; their piratical vessels scoured the seas of western Europe; and the maritime cities of Gaul, Spain, and Britain, were frequently plundered by their corsairs, or forced to purchase safety by the payment of a large tribute. Among the chiefs of their warlike tribes, none enjoyed greater authority than the two brothers Hengist and Horsa, who claimed to be descended from Woden, the tutelary god of the nation. To these leaders the application of Vortigern was made; they readily accepted his invitation, and, accompanied by about sixteen hundred of their countrymen, landed in the isle of Thanet. The Picts and Scots were subdued with so much facility, that the adventurers began to reflect how easily they might conquer a nation unable to resist such feeble invaders; instead of returning home, they invited over fresh hordes of their countrymen, and received from Germany a reinforcement of five thousand men. A long and cruel series of wars ensued, in which the Saxons and another barbarous tribe, the Angles, continually supported by crowds of volunteers from Germany, triumphed over the Britons in almost every encounter, and finally drove the miserable remnant of the nation to seek refuge in the mountains of Wales and Cornwall. The struggle lasted nearly one hundred and fifty years, and ended in the division of southern Britain into seven Saxon kingdoms, commonly called the Heptarchy.

The Christian religion was first established in the kingdom of Kent, the earliest and long the most powerful of the Saxon monarchies. Ethelbert, its sovereign, though a pagan, had married a Christian princess, Bertha, the daughter of Caribert, one of the successors of Clovis, and had promised to allow her the free exercise of her religion. Bertha, by the exercise of her conduct, acquired considerable influence over the mind both of her husband and his courtiers; her popularity was probably one of the principal motives that induced Pope Gregory the Great to send missionaries into England.* Augustine, the chief of the mission, was honorably received at the court of Ethelbert (A. D. 597), and began to preach the gospel to the people of Kent. The rigid austerity of his manners, and the severe penances to which he subjected himself, wrought powerfully upon the minds of a barbarous people, and induced them readily to believe the pretended miracles he wrought for their conversion. Ethelbert and the great majority of his subjects were soon received into the church, and Augustine was consecrated the first archbishop of Canterbury.

The petty wars between the princes of the Heptarchy are totally devoid of interest, and the history of the separate kingdoms is little more than a list of obscure names. An exception may be made in favor of Offa, king of Mercia, who zealously labored to extend the power of the Romish see in England, and founded the magnificent monastery of St. Albans. So considerable were his power and fame, that the emperor Charlemagne sought his friendship and alliance; Offa, at his desire, sent the celebrated Alcuin to the court of Charlemagne, and this learned Saxon became the emperor's preceptor in the sciences. To Alcuin, France was indebted for all the polite learning it boasted

* It is said that this prelate, while yet in a private station, beheld some Saxon youths exposed for sale in the slave-market at Rome. Struck with their beauty, he inquired to what country they belonged, and being told that they were Angli, exclaimed "They would not be *Angli*, but *Angeli* (angels), if they were Christians." Continuing his questions, he asked the name of their province; he was told *Deiri* (a district of Northumberland). "*Deiri!*" he exclaimed, "*De ira* (from the wrath of God), they are summoned to his mercy." He further asked the name of their king, and hearing that it was *Ælla*, or *Alla*, he joyously cried out, "*Allelujah!* we must endeavor that the praises of God be sung in that country." Moved by these punning allusions, he designed to visit Britain himself as a missionary, but being detained by the Roman people, he embraced the earliest opportunity of intrusting the task to qualified legates.

of in that and the following ages; the universities of Paris, Tours, Fulden, Soissons, and many others, owe to him their origin and increase; those of which he was not the superior and founder, being at least enlightened by his doctrine and example, and enriched by the benefits he procured them from Charlemagne.

The kingdom of Mercia had nearly obtained the sovereignty of the heptarchy when Egbert ascended the throne of Wessex (A. D. 799), as the kingdom of the West Saxons was called. He broke down the Mercian power, aided not a little by the hatred with which the tyrannical conduct of the Mercians had inspired the subject nations. His policy was as conspicuous as his valor, and both enabled him to unite the realm of England into an orderly monarchy, possessing tranquillity within itself, and secure from foreign invasion. This great event occurred (A. D. 827) nearly four hundred years after the first arrival of he Anglo-Saxons in Britain.

CHAPTER II.

THE RISE AND ESTABLISHMENT OF THE SARACENIC POWER.

SECTION I.—*Political and Social Condition of the East at the coming of Mohammed.*

THE reign of Justin II., the nephew and successor of Justinian, at Constantinople, was remarkable only for disgrace abroad and misery at home. At his death (A. D. 578), he bequeathed the empire to Tiberius, whose virtues amply justified his choice; but the reign of Tiberius lasted only four years; he was succeeded by Maurice, who inherited many of his predecessor's virtues as well as his crown. Soon after his accession, the attention of the emperor was directed to the unsettled state of Persia, which had been distracted by sanguinary civil wars since the death of the great Nushirván. Hormúz, the son and successor of that monarch, was deposed and slain; Bahram, a brave general but a feeble statesman, usurped the throne, and Khosrú or Chosroes, the legitimate heir, sought shelter in the Byzantine empire. Maurice levied a powerful army to restore the royal exile, and intrusted its command to Narses, a valiant general, who was himself of Persian descent. The expedition was crowned with success; Bahram, driven beyond the Oxus, died by poison, and Khosrú, grateful for his recovered throne, entered into close alliance with the emperor.

Freed from all danger on the side of Persia, Maurice resolved to turn his arms against the Avars; but the incapacity of his generals, and his own avarice, provoked the resentment of the soldiers; they mutinied, and marched to Constantinople under the command of one of their centurions, named Phocas. Had the metropolis continued faithful, this sedition might have been easily quelled; but the licentious populace, disgusted by the parsimony of their sovereign, assaulted him as he walked in a religious procession, and compelled him to seek safety in his palace. The unfortunate emperor was compelled to abdicate; Phocas was tumultuously invested with the purple, and welcomed into Constantinople by the acclamations of a thoughtless people. The tyrant commenced his reign by dragging Maurice from the sanctuary where he had sought refuge, murdering his five sons successively before his eyes, and then putting the deposed monarch to death by torture (A. D. 602). One of the royal nurses attempted to save the prince intrusted to her charge, by presenting her own child to the executioners in his stead; but Maurice refused to sanction the deceit, and as each blow of the axe fell on the necks of his children, he exclaimed, with pious resignation, "Righteous art thou, O Lord, and just are thy judgments!"

The usurpation of Phocas was basely sanctioned by Pope Gregory who received in return for his adulation the title of Universal Bishop. But the pontiff's flatteries could not save the tyrant from the resentment of his subjects, who soon discovered their error in preferring such a miscreant to the virtuous Maurice. Heraclius, exarch of Africa, invited by the unanimous voice of the empire, sailed to Constantinople: scarcely had his fleet appeared in the Hellespont, when the citizens and imperial guards entered the palace, bound Phocas in chains, and sent him a helpless captive to his rival (A. D. 610). Heraclius reproached him with his manifold vices, to which the deposed tyrant simply replied, "Wilt thou govern better?" These were the last words of Phocas: after suffering much variety of insult and torture, he was beheaded, and his mangled body thrown into the sea.

But the death of Phocas did not deliver the empire from the calamities his crimes had produced; Khosrú Parvíz had no sooner learned the sad fate of his benefactor Maurice, than he assembled the entire strength of Persia to avenge his murder. The unwise system of persecution which had been gradually established both by the Byzantine prelates and emperors, supplied the invader with allies in every province: the Jews, the Nestorians, and the Jacobites, believed, with reason, that they would find the worshippers of fire more tolerant than the orthodox Christians; and scarcely had the Persians crossed the Euphrates, when insurrections were raised in their favor throughout Syria. Khosrú, victorious in two decisive battles, was encouraged to undertake the hereditary enterprise of the Sassanid dynasty—the restoration of the Persian empire, as it existed in the age of Cyrus the Great. Heraclius had scarcely ascended the throne, when he received intelligence of the fall of Antioch; and this was soon followed by the account of the storming of Jerusalem, where the Jews, encouraged by the Persians, wreaked dreadful vengeance on the heads of their Christian persecutors (A. D. 614). The fugitives from Palestine sought refuge in Egypt, where they were hospitably entertained by the archbishop of Alexandria. But Egypt itself, where the din of arms had not been heard since the reign of Dioclesian, was invaded, conquered, and for a time annexed to the Persian empire (A. D. 616). Asia Minor was subdued with equal facility; in a single campaign, the armies of the Persians advanced from the banks of the Euphrates to the shores of the Thracian Bosphorus, and during ten years their hostile camp was in sight of the towers of Constantinople.

While Khosrú was indulging in the pride that such brilliant conquests inspired, and dazzling his subjects by the display of his magnificent plunder, he received an epistle from the almost unknown city of Mecca, written by an obscure individual, who yet claimed the king's obedience, and demanded to be recognised as the prophet of God. The grandson of Nushirván was indignant at such a claim; he tore the letter to pieces, and flung the fragments to the winds. When this was reported to the writer, Mohammed, then beginning for the first time to taste the sweets of gratified ambition, and to find his prospects enlarging as he ascended the height of power, he exclaimed, "It is thus that God will rend the kingdom of Khosrú!" a prophecy which, like many others, not a little accelerated its own accomplishment.

While the Asiatic provinces were thus a prey to the Persians, Constantinople itself was so hardly pressed by the Avars, that Heraclius was on the point of abandoning the capital, and seeking refuge with his treasures in Carthage. He was with difficulty dissuaded from this dishonorable measure by the entreaties of the patriarch; but his prospects appeared to become darker every hour; the Avars, by a treacherous attack, had nearly seized the capital, and the ambassadors sent to supplicate pardon and peace from Khosrú, were dismissed with contumely and scorn; the Persian despot declaring that he would not grant peace until either Heraclius was brought bound in chains to his footstool, or had abjured Christianity and embraced the Magian religion.

For about twelve years Heraclius had patiently witnessed the calamities of the empire without making any effort to protect his subjects; but this last insult roused his slumbering energies, and he entered on a career as glorious as his former inactivity had been disgraceful. He did not venture with his raw levies to attack the Persian camp at Chalcedon; but he passed over to the coast of Cilicia, and fortified himself on the ground where Alexander had fought the battle of Issus, not far from the modern town of Scanderoon, whose excellent harbor offered a good station for the imperial fleet. A splendid victory over the Persian cavalry enabled him to establish his winter-quarters in Cappadocia, on he banks of the Halys (*Kizil Irmak*), and to mature his plans for one of the boldest enterprises recorded in history—the invasion of Persia through its northern provinces (A. D. 623). Early in the ensuing spring, Heraclius, with a chosen band of five thousand men, sailed from Constantinople to Trebizond, assembled his forces from the southern regions, and, joined by the Christians of Armenia, entered the province of Atropatene (*Azerbiján*). Tauris (*Tabríz*), the ancient and modern capital of the country, was taken by storm, almost in sight of Khosrú's army, while the Persian monarch had neither the courage to hazard a battle, nor the justice to conclude an equitable peace. Several equally glorious campaigns followed; the greater part of Persia was overrun by the victorious Byzantines; they defeated the Asiatics wherever they encountered them, and marched in one direction as far as the Caspian, in the other to Ispahan, destroying in their progress all Khosrú's splendid palaces, plundering his hoarded treasures, and dispersing in every direction the countless slaves of his pleasure. Khosrú made no effort to stop the mighty work of ruin, and yet he rejected the terms of peace offered him by the humanity of the conqueror. His subjects soon lost all regard for a monarch whom they deemed the sole cause of the desolation of his country: a conspiracy was formed against him; he was deposed by his eldest son Shiroueh, cast into a dungeon, and put to death by an unnatural prince, who pretended that he was compelled to the parricide by the clamors and importunities of the people and nobles of the empire.

After six glorious campaigns, Heraclius returned to Constantinople, bringing with him the wood of the "True Cross," which Khosrú had taken at Jerusalem—a precious relic, which was deemed a more splendid trophy of his victories than all his spoils and conquests. The kingdom of Persia, exhausted by the late sanguinary contest, was left to perish under the accumulated evils of a dreadful famine, the disputes of proud and luxurious nobles, a succession of weak sovereigns, or rather pageants of power, and the attack of a new and terrible enemy. The flame which Mohammed had kindled in Arabia already began to spread, and to threaten an equal fate to the degraded and decaying monarchies of Byzantium and Persia.

Victory itself was fatal to Heraclius; the best and bravest of his soldiers had perished in the sanguinary war, his treasury was empty, taxes were levied with difficulty in the desolated provinces, and the emperor himself, as if exhausted by his great efforts, sunk into hopeless lethargy. While Heraclius was enjoying the empty honors of a triumph, the Saracens appeared on the confines of Syria: thenceforth the empire sunk rapidly before their fanatic valor; and in the last eight years of his reign, the emperor lost to them all that he had rescued from the the Persians.

SECTION II.—*State of Arabia at the coming of Mohammed.*

THE peninsula of Arabia is in shape a large and irregular triangle, between Persia, Syria, Egypt, and Ethiopia; its extreme length is about fifteen hundred miles, and its mean breadth about seven hundred. Though it contains several lofty ranges of mountains, the greater part of the country consists of level, sandy, and arid plains, which can support but few inhabitants. Water is difficult to be obtained; there is scarcely any wood to shelter from the direct and intense rays of a tropical sun; the winds, instead of being refreshing breezes, frequently come loaded with pestilential vapors, or raise eddying billows of sand that have overwhelmed, not only caravans, but entire armies. The high lands that border on the Indian ocean are distinguished by a superior abundance of wood and water, and hence this part of the peninsula has been called Happy Arabia: but the groves, even of this favored district, are thinly scattered; the streams, though pure, are small, and the country could only be deemed delightful by persons whose eyes were unaccustomed to vegetation, and who had often felt the want of a cooling shade or a refreshing drink. The northern part of Arabia is occupied by ranges of naked, rocky mountains, from which it received the name of Arabia Petræa, or the Stony; but notwithstanding its rugged and desert aspect, it was in ancient times the centre of a flourishing trade, being the great high road of trade between Egypt and southeastern Asia.

The Arabs are an original and unmixed race; they boast that their country has never been subdued, but the greater part of it has little that could tempt the cupidity of a conqueror. In the reign of Trajan, the Romans made Arabia Petræa a province; Yemen, or Arabia Felix, has been frequently subject to Persia, and about the time of Mohammed's appearance, the southern part of the peninsula was ruled by the Najáshi of Ethiopia. The Arab is not very robust, but he is active and well made, able to endure great fatigue, and, both from habit and education, reckless of danger. In his mental constitution, he displays quickness rather than intelligence his imagination is warm, but his judgment is not vigorous. In all his pleasures, dangers, and fatigues, he makes the horse and camel of his deserts associates rather than servants, and these animals appear to have obtained an actual superiority in Arabia. from being elevated into the companions of their masters. The horse of Arabia is equally remarkable for speed, temper, and power of endurance; and it is remarkable that the best breeds of this animal in Europe, Asia, and Africa, have been derived from an Arabian stock. The camel and dromedary of the desert are regarded by the Arab as scarcely inferior to his horse. This patient and powerful animal supplies him with milk for his sustenance, transports his property and family from one quarter of the desert to another, and when occasion requires, enables him to pursue or fly from his enemy with almost incredible speed.

The ancient religion of the Arabs was the Sabean form of idolatry which consisted in the worship of the sun, moon, and planets; but long before the coming of Mohammed, they were distracted by a great variety of creeds; some adhered to the faith of their ancestors, others embraced Judaism, and several tribes became Christians. Unfortunately Christianity, when introduced into the peninsula, had been deeply sullied by man's devices; the different Christian tribes were imbued with a fierce sectarian spirit, and hated each other more bitterly than Jews or pagans. The vivid imaginations of the Arabs led them to investigate questions beyond the powers of man's understanding; and the consequence was so abundant a supply of new doctrines, that one of the early fathers described Arabia as the land most fruitful in heresies.

The principal Arabian cities of ancient times were in Yemen; but their fame was destined to be eclipsed by the glories of Mecca and Medina, both in the Hejaz, the two great sanctuaries of the national religion. Mecca was a place of considerable trade from the earliest stages, being situated at the intersection of two important routes, that between Syria and Arabia Felix, and that between Abyssinia or upper Egypt and southeastern Asia. Commerce flourished under the sanctuary of religion. The temple of Mecca was regarded as the national metropolis of the Arabic faith, before Judaism and Christianity appeared in the peninsula; its custody raised the Koreishites to a rank above the other tribes, and the failure of the attempt made to storm it by the Ethiopians in the very year that Mohammed was born, may be considered the great check that impeded, or rather prevented, the further extension of Christianity in the country. Mecca is built in a winding valley at the foot of three barren mountains; the soil is a rock, and the waters brackish. The pastures are remote from the city, and good fruits can not be procured at a nearer place than the gardens of Tayef, which are about seventy miles distant.

The Arabs believe that Mecca was founded by Adam, and the temple erected by Abraham. Its early prosperity they ascribe to Ishmael, who fixed his residence there, because, as their traditions assert, the brackish well Zemzem was that to which Hagar was directed by the angel. It must have been a very ancient city, if, as commentators suppose, it was the Mesha which Moses mentions as inhabited by the posterity of Joktan.*

* Genesis x. and xxxi.

Medina, called Yatreb before the appearance of Mohammed, enjoys more natural advantages than Mecca; but it is not so conveniently situated for traffic. Its citizens appear to have been always jealous of the supremacy claimed by the Meccans, and this probably induced them to espouse the cause of Mohammed when he was banished by their rivals.

Literature was zealously cultivated by the ancient Arabs; they were enthusiastically attached to eloquence and poetry, for both of which, their rich harmonious language affords peculiar facilities. A meeting of the tribes was held annually, at which the poets recited their compositions, and those which were judged the best, were preserved in the public treasury. The most celebrated of these were seven poems called Moallakat, which were written on Egyptian silk in letters of gold, and suspended in the Kaaba, or temple of Mecca. Science was not similarly valued; their history was merely genealogical tables: their astronomy such a rude knowledge of the stars as served to mark the variation of the seasons; and the mechanical arts were almost wholly neglected. They used to say that God had given them four peculiarities: turbans instead of diadems; tents instead of houses; swords instead of fortresses; and poems instead of written laws.

SECTION III.—*The Preaching of Mohammed.*

MOHAMMED, the great legislator of the Arabians, and the founder of a religion which has long prevailed over the fairest portions of the globe, was born at Mecca. His father, Abdallah, was an idolater; but his mother, Emina, was a Jewess, who had been converted to Christianity, and from her early instructions he probably derived the religious impressions for which he was distinguished even in boyhood. Both his parents died while he was yet a child, but their place was supplied by his uncles, Abd-al-Motalleb, and Abu-Taleb, the latter of whom became a tender parent to the orphan. At the age of thirteen he accompanied Abu-Taleb on a mercantile journey into Syria, and soon after made his first campaign against some neighboring tribes of predatory Arabs.

From this time Mohammed appears to have engaged actively in trade. He displayed so much talent, that a rich widow, named Kadijah, appointed him her chief pastor; and after some years, was so pleased with his zeal and industry, that she gave him her hand in marriage, and made him master of her splendid fortune. After his marriage, Mohammed ranked among the first citizens of Mecca, and it must be added that he was not corrupted by good fortune. The earliest use he made of prosperity was to relieve his kind guardian and uncle Abu-Taleb, who had fallen into distress; he placed Abu-Taleb above want, and undertook the education of a portion of his family.

Little is known of Mohammed's history during the next fifteen years, but there is every reason to believe that this interval was spent in maturing his plans for the great revolution he contemplated. Every year he retired for a month to a cave in Mount Hira, near Mecca, where he spent his time in meditation and prayer. His travels as a merchant had made him acquainted with the principal forms of religion that then prevailed in the east. In Syria he met Christians of various sects Jews, Magians, and Sabæans; Arabia presented to him countless varieties of idolatry; exiles from the Persian and Byzantine empires informed him of the dangerous doctrines preached by the Mani and Mazdak. A singular dream led him to believe that he was chosen by the Deity to reconcile all these jarring creeds, and to unite mankind in the worship of the one true God. In the solitude of his cave he dreamed that the angel Gabriel appeared to him, and hailed him as a prophet. On his return he announced his mission to Kadijah, who at once recognised his claims. Her example was followed by Ali, the son of Abu-Taleb, by Abu-Beker, Othman, and a few friends accustomed to regard the recluse of Hira with reverence.

These converts were called Mussulmans, that is, persons resigned to the divine will; their faith was confirmed by revelations which Mohammed pretended to receive from Gabriel, and which, as he did not then know how to read and write, or at least but imperfectly, he communicated orally to his disciples. These revelations were preserved by them in a volume, which they called the Koran, or book that ought to be read. The progress of the new religion was slow; many of Mohammed's friends rejected his prophetic claims with something like horror, and three years elapsed before he ventured to announce his mission publicly. Having invited his friends and relatives to a splendid banquet, he declared to them that God had chosen him to preach the doctrine of the divine unity; Ali, with the generous enthusiasm of youth, warmly offered to support the prophet's claims, but many of the other guests doubted or laughed them to scorn.

Undismayed by the imperfect result of his first essay, Mohammed began to preach to the people of Mecca in the market-place. Converts were made slowly; and the guardians of the city opposed doctrines that threatened to subvert the influence they derived from the worship of the Kaaba. Several of the Mussulmans, most remarkable for their zeal, were forced by persecution to abandon their homes, and seek refuge in Abyssinia; but the spirit of Mohammed quailed not; he refused to quit Mecca, and when asked to suspend his preaching for a season, he replied, "Were my enemies to place the sun on my right hand, and the moon on my left, they would not reduce me to silence."

At one of the great annual fairs held in Mecca, Mohammed preached his mission to the merchants assembled from all parts of Arabia. Among his auditors were some citizens of Yatreb, or, as it was afterward called, Medina, whom peculiar circumstances rendered attentive to his claims. The Yatrebites had just conquered a Jewish tribe; they heard their captives boast of their speedy liberation on the coming of the Messiah, and supposing that the new prophet might be the expected deliverer, they resolved to conciliate his favor. Mohammed profited by their delusion; and this appears to have been his first direct step in imposture, though in the tangled web of human motives, it is hard to say where enthusiasm ends and fraud begins.

Inspired by his success with the Yatrebites, and some other tribes in the interior of Arabia, Mohammed, who had hitherto preached patience and submission under persecution, directed his disciples to defend themselves when attacked, declaring that all who died in defence of his person or his creed, would assuredly inherit Paradise. At the same time he averred that he had been taken up into heaven by Gabriel, and admitted to a personal interview with the Omnipotent. The Meccan chiefs, enraged at his hardihood, took measures for his destruction, and he could only save his life by a speedy retreat to Yatreb. This event, called Hejira (the flight), occurred about the fifty-third year of the prophet's age (A. D. 622), and is the era used by all Mahommedan nations.

Mohammed was received in triumph at Yatreb; he changed its name to Medinet al nábi (*the city of the prophet*), or Medina (*the city*), which it still retains. Converts flocked to Medina, and were formed into warlike bands, which infested all the roads to Mecca, and took severe vengeance for the insult offered to their master. The plunder was shared equally among the soldiers; enthusiasm generally insured success; and warriors from all parts of the peninsula were attracted by the hopes of wealth and glory. In one of the frequent encounters between the Meccans and Mussulmans, near the well Bedr, Mohammed was on the point of being defeated, when he stooped down, took up a handful of dust and flung it toward the enemy, exclaiming: "May their faces be confounded!" this simple action revived the courage of his followers; they gained a decisive victory, which he failed not to ascribe to a miraculous interposition.

After this success Mohammed made a great change in the character of his religion; hitherto he had preached patience and toleration; he now began to inculcate the doctrine of propagating the true faith by the sword, and of executing divine vengeance on idolaters and unbelievers "In the shade of the crossing cimeters," he declared, "Paradise is prefigured," and this sublime orientalism was long the favorite war-cry of his followers. The Jews became special objects of his hatred; he seems to have hoped that they would acknowledge him as their Messiah, but they were too well acquainted with their sacred Scriptures to believe that the liberator of Israel should be descended from the bondwoman. A severe defeat at Ohod increased rather than abated the pride and fanaticism of Mohammed; he ascribed it to the fault of his companions in having granted quarter to their enemies on a former occasion, and thenceforward the war assumed a most murderous and sanguinary character. The Meccans suffered much more severely than their adversaries; depending for their prosperity, and almost for their existence, on commerce, they saw their trade almost annihilated, their caravans plundered, and their flocks swept away. They made one great effort to remove their enemy, and besieged Mohammed in Medina, but were soon forced to retire with great loss. "Hitherto they have sought us," exclaimed the prophet, "it is now our turn to go in search of them."

After this defeat, the Meccans seem to have lost all courage; Mohammed rapidly became the most powerful prince in Arabia, his followers received his words as the inspired oracles of God, nor were they undeceived by the gross licentiousness in which the pretended prophet indulged. At length, he marched against Mecca, but found the defiles which lead to the city too strongly garrisoned to allow of an attack with any prospect of success. Under these circumstances, he concluded a truce, much against the will of his followers, by which a peaceful admission into the city was secured to him in the ensuing year. Feeling that his power was now established, Mohammed sent ambassadors, inviting the most powerful kings of the earth, especially the emperors of Persia and Constantinople, to become his disciples. Khosrú Parvíz, who then ruled in Irán, was indignant at receiving a letter, in which "a poor lizard-eater," as the Arab was then called by his haughty neighbors, dared to place his name before that of "the king of kings." He tore the paper to pieces, and dismissed the ambassador with insult; when this was told to Mohammed, he exclaimed, "Thus God hath torn his kingdom." The Byzantine emperor, Heraclius, treated the message with respect, though he declined acceding to the invitation. During the year that preceded the pilgrimage to Mecca, Mohammed subdued several of the surrounding tribes that had hitherto spurned his power; but the seeds of mortal disease were sown in his constitution by a dose of poison, which a Jewess administered as a test of his prophetic pretensions.

At length the day arrived which was to consummate the triumph of Islamism; Mohammed made his public entry into Mecca with unparalleled magnificence; he did homage to the national faith by worshipping in the Kaaba; and such was the effect produced by his presence, that many of his former enemies, and among others, the chief guardian of the idolatrous sanctuary, proclaimed themselves his disciples. Soon after this success he began his first foreign war. The ambassador he sent to the Byzantine governor of Bosrah, having been murdered at Muta, a little town south of the Dead sea, an army was sent under the command of Zeid, the freedman of the prophet, to avenge the insult. The Mussulman general, and the two officers that succeeded, were slain; but the command devolving upon Khaled, the son of Walid, he obtained a decisive victory, and returned to Medina laden with booty. This success induced Mohammed to break his truce with the Meccans; disregarding their remonstrances and offers of submission, he marched against the city; an entrance was forced by the fiery Khaled, and the prophet with difficulty prevented his followers from involving his fellow-citizens in one promiscuous massacre. The Kaaba became the property of the conqueror; all traces of idolatry were removed from this national sanctuary; the only emblem of former superstition permitted to remain, was the celebrated Black Stone, an aërolite which the Arabs had venerated from an unknown age, the reverence for which was too deeply graven in their hearts to be easily eradicated. This success led to the subjugation of most of the northern Arabian tribes; ambassadors flocked to congratulate the prophet from every side; the lieutenant Khosrú, at the western side of the Euphrates, became a Mussulman; the governor of the provinces that the Najáshí of Abyssinia held in Arabia, followed the example; and Mohammed might be regarded as the undisputed sovereign of the peninsula. His two great objects seemed thus to be effected; Arabia was liberated from the yoke of foreign powers, and the Arabs began to regard themselves as one nation. A second expedition against the southern provinces of the Byzantine, or, as it was still called, the Roman empire, was crowned with success; and so rapid had been the progress of Islamism, that when the prophet performed his last pilgrimage to Mecca, his followers amounted to nearly one hundred thousand warriors, independent of women, slaves, and other attendants.

On his return to Medina, the poison which Mohammed had taken from a Jewess, who is said to have taken this means of testing his claim to the title of Messiah, began to show its effects. He was seized with mortal disease; and, at his own request, was removed to the house of his favorite wife Ayesha, on whose prudence he depended for concealing any incautious avowal he might make under the pressure of sickness. On the 8th of June, 632, he died, declaring with his last breath that he was about "to take his place with his fellow-citizen on high," meaning the angel Gabriel. He made no will, he appointed no successor, owing to the contrivance of Ayesha, who feared that Ali, the cousin and son-in-law of the prophet, would be nominated the heir of his power; and that she would thus be inferior to her beautiful step-daughter, Fatima, the wife of Ali.

Section IV.—*Early Progress of the Saracens.*

The fabric of Islamism was shaken to its very foundation after Mohammed's death, by the disputes that arose respecting the choice of a successor. Ali had the best hereditary claims, but his literary tastes, and ascetic manners, rendered him unpopular with the fierce soldiery; and he had a powerful enemy in Ayesha, whom he had once charged with infidelity. After three days of fierce dispute, the controversy was decided by Omar's proffering the oath of fidelity to Abú Bekr, the father of Ayesha, and one of Mohammed's most faithful followers.

Abú Bekr assumed the title of Khaliph, or vicar, which thenceforth became the designation of the Saracenic emperors. Having superintended the sepulture of his illustrious predecessor at Medina, the khaliph sent an army against Mosseilama, an impostor, who, following the example of Mohammed, attempted to found a new religion. Mosseilama and his followers were exterminated by the gallant Khaled, surnamed from his fiery valor "the sword of God," and Islamism was thenceforward established in Arabia.

Perceiving that it was necessary to find employment for the energetic spirits by which he was surrounded, Abú Bekr prepared to invade the Byzantine and Persian empires, both of which had fallen into a state of deplorable weakness. Osâma, the son of Zeid, ravaged Syria, while the province of Irák, the ancient Babylonia, was subdued by Khaled. The conquest of Syria was a more important enterprise; circulars announcing the undertaking, were sent to the principal Arabian tribes; and the army which assembled on the occasion was the most numerous that had yet been raised by the Saracens. The emperor Heraclius, alarmed at the approach of such formidable forces, sent a large detachment to meet the enemy on the frontiers, which was defeated with great slaughter. But the imperialists were more successful at Gaza, where they gained a victory over a Moslem division, commanded by Abu Obeidah. The Khaliph invested Amrú with the supreme command of the expedition, but intrusted Obeidah's division to Khaled.

The latter made himself master of the city of Bosra, and after gaining several other advantages over the Romans, laid siege to Damascus.

Jerusalem was regarded with as much veneration by the Mussulmans as by the Jews or Christians, and Abú Bekr felt that the capture of so holy a city would give immense strength to the cause of Islám. In his celebrated directions to his generals he displays great knowledge of the country as well as much political wisdom But these directions are still more remarkable for their almost verbal coincidence with a passage in the Book of Revelations (chap. ix. verse 4), which most commentators have regarded as a prophetic description of the Saracens. A reference to the passage will enable the reader to see the striking similarity between the language of the apostle and of the khaliph. When the army was assembled, Abú Bekr addressed the chief commander in the following terms: "Take care, Yezid-Abn-Abu Sofian, to treat your men with tenderness and lenity. Consult with your officers on all pressing occasions, and encourage them to face the enemy with bravery and resolution. If you conquer, spare the aged, the infirm, the women, and the children. Cut down no palm-trees, destroy not the fields of corn. Spare all fruit-trees, slay no cattle but such as are absolutely necessary for food. Always preserve your engagements inviolate; spare the religious persons who dwell in monasteries, and injure not the places in which they worship God. As for those members of the synagogue of Satan, who shave their crowns, cleave their sculls, unless they embrace Islamism, or pay tribute."

But Jerusalem was not the only city to which sanctity was ascribed in the Mussulman traditions; it was reported that Mohammed, after viewing the lovely and fertile plains in which Damascus stands, from one of the neighboring heights, proclaimed it to be the earthly paradise designed to be the inheritance of true believers. The fiery Khaled recited this tradition to his enthusiastic followers as he led them before the walls, and thus excited their ardor for the siege to a fury that bordered on insanity.

Heraclius sent an army of 100,000 men to relieve the capital of Syria, but the imperialists were thrice routed; and in the last of these battles more than half their number fell in the field. This calamity led to the fall of Damascus, one side of which was stormed by Khaled, just as the other capitulated to Abu Obeidah. A warm dispute arose between the generals as to the claims of the citizens to the benefit of the capitulation; but mercy finally prevailed, and the lives of the Damascenes were spared. Abú Bekr died on the very day that Damascus was taken (A. D. 634); his memory was justly venerated, not only because he pointed the Saracens the way to conquest beyond Arabia, but because he gave their religion its permanent form, by collecting the scattered passages of the Koran, and arranging them in the order which they hold to the present day.

His character was remarkable for generosity and moderation; he did not reserve for himself any portion of the vast wealth acquired by his victorious armies, but distributed his share to his soldiers and to the poor. He was always easy of access; no petitioner for mercy or claimant of justice went unheard from his presence; both by precept and example he labored to maintain the republican simplicity so remarkable in the early history of the Saracens; and though the partisans of Ali regard him as a usurper, they still reverence his memory on account of his moderation and his virtue.

Omar was chosen second khaliph by the unanimous consent of the army. Soon after his accession he received the intelligence of the capture of Damascus; but instead of evincing his gratitude, he yielded to the suggestions of petty jealousy, and transferred the command of the army from Khaled to Abu Obeidah. The conquest of Syria was followed by the subjugation of Persia. Yezdijird, the last monarch of the Sassanid dynasty, sent a large army to recover Irák, under the command of Ferokshad, a general of high reputation. Saad-ebn-Wakass, the leader of the Saracens, relying upon the impetuous courage of his soldiers, eagerly sought a general action; and Ferokshad, after many vain efforts to protract the war, was forced to a decisive engagement in the plains of Kadseah, or Kadesia. The battle lasted several days, and ended in the almost total annihilation of the Persian army, while the loss of the Arabs did not exceed three thousand men. The celebrated standard of Persia, originally the apron of the patriotic blacksmith Gávah, but which had been enlarged, by successive monarchs, to the length of twenty-two feet and the breadth of fifteen, enriched with jewels of the highest value, fell into the hands of the conquerors and was broken up for distribution. Nor was this the only rich booty obtained by the "sons of the desert," who were yet ignorant of its value. "I will give any quantity of this yellow metal for a little white," was an exclamation made, after the battle was over, by an Arabian soldier, who desired to exchange gold, which he had never before seen, for silver, which he had learned to appreciate (A. D. 638).

Yezdijird assembled a new army in the northern and eastern provinces, while the khaliph reinforced the invaders with fresh bodies of enthusiasts. The battle which decided the fate of Persia was fought at Navahend (A. D. 641). Noman, the leader of the Saracens, attacked the Persians in their intrenchments; nothing could resist the fury of the onslaught; the Persian lines were completely broken; it was a carnage rather than a battle. For ten years Yezdijird, "a hunted wanderer on the wild," protracted a faint but unyielding resistance; he was at length slain by a miller with whom he had sought refuge (A. D. 651). Thus ended the dynasty of Sassan, which ruled Persia for four hundred and fifty years, and the memory of which is still cherished by a nation, whose ancient glory is associated with the fame of Ardeshír, Shah-púr, and Nushirván.

Nor were the Saracens less successful in Syria; Abu Obeidah's caution tempered the fiery zeal of Khaled, and rendered victory more secure, though less rapid. City after city yielded to the Moslems, and the army which Heraclius sent to the defence of his unfortunate subjects was irretrievably ruined in the battle of Yermûk. Inspired by this victory, Abu Obeidah laid seige to Jerusalem, and in four months reduced the garrison to such distress, that a surrender was unavoidable. The Khaliph Omar came in person to receive the submission of the holy city. His equipage was a singular characteristic of the simplicity that still prevailed among the Saracens. He rode upon a red camel, with a sack of corn and water-bag slung from the saddle, to supply his wants during the journey. A wooden platter was the only utensil he brought with him; his dress was of camel's hair, coarse and torn; a single slave constituted his attendance and escort. In this guise he reached the Moslem camp, where he recited the public prayers, and preached a sermon to his troops. He then signed the capitulation, securing to the Christians of Jerusalem protection in person, property, and religious worship, on the payment of a moderate tribute, and entered the city in triumph (A. D. 637). In his triumphal entry the khaliph marched at the head of his troops, in familiar conversation with Sophronius, the Christian patriarch of Jerusalem, whom he hoped to protect from the fanaticism of his followers by this exhibition of confidence. Nor was this the only proof of good faith displayed by Omar; he refused to pray in any of the Christian churches, lest the Mussulmans should take advantage of his example and convert it into a mosque. He chose the ground on which the temple of Solomon anciently stood for the foundation of the mosque which bears his name; and as it was covered with filth of every kind, he set the example of clearing the spot, to his soldiers, by removing some of the rubbish in his robe.

Aleppo, the ancient Berœa, was the next city besieged by the Saracens; it was valiantly defended for four months, but was finally taken by assault, and its governor, Gukinna, with several of his principal officers, embraced the Mohammedan faith. Antioch and Cæsarea were taken with less difficulty; the emperor Heraclius fled from the province, and his son, after a few unsuccessful efforts, followed him to Constantinople. In six years from their first appearance in Syria, the Saracens completed the conquest of that province, and of Palestine, and secured their acquisitions by occupying the mountain-fortresses on the borders of Cilicia. Egypt was next attacked by Amrú, and subdued without much difficulty. Alexandria alone made a vigorous defence; but it was finally taken by storm, and its valuable library consigned to the flames, through the fanaticism of Omar, who was ignorant of literature and science. In the midst of these triumphs the Khaliph Omar was assassinated by a slave (A. D. 643). During his reign of ten years and a half, the Saracens could boast that they had subdued Syria, Chaldæa, Persia, and Egypt; taken thirty-six thousand cities, towns, and castles; destroyed four thousand Christian churches, fire and idol temples, and built fourteen hundred mosques.

Omar's memory is held in the highest veneration by the Soonnees, and is eqally execrated by the Sheeahs. His severity and simplicity, which bordered on barbarism, are strikingly contrasted with the luxury and magnificence of his successors. He had no state or pomp, he lived in a mean house; his mornings were spent in preaching or praying at the mosque, and during the rest of the day he was to be found in the public market-place, where, clothed in a tattered robe, he administered justice to all comers, directed the affairs of his increasing empire, and received ambassadors from the most powerful princes of the east. To him the Arabs are indebted for the era of the Hejira; before his reign they counted their years from such epochs as wars, famines, plagues, remarkable tempests, or harvests of unusual plenty. He was the first to establish a police in Medina and the other great cities of the empire. Before his reign, the Arabs, accustomed to lawless independence, would admit of no restraint, and the immense conquests of the Saracens had caused such a concourse of strangers in the seats of government, that cities became nearly as insecure places of residence as the open country. Omar also established a regular system of pay for soldiers in the field, and he also instituted pensions for the wounded and disabled soldiers; indeed the old companions of Mohammed, those who had borne the dangers and difficulties that beset the prophet in the earlier part of his career, having been rendered incapable of acquiring fresh plunder by wounds and age, would have perished miserably but for the provision which Omar made for their support in their declining years.

Omar, by his will, appointed six commissioners to elect a new khaliph, and their choice fell on Othman-ebn-Affán, whose pliancy of disposition appears to have been his chief recommendation. The change of their sovereign did not abate the rage for conquest among the Saracens. They ceased to limit their exertions to land; a fleet fitted out by Moawiyáh, the governor of Syria, subdued the island of Cyprus (A. D. 647), while the Syrian and Egyptian armies penetrated into Armenia and Nubia. The island of Rhodes was a still more important acquisition: it yielded to Moawiyáh almost without a struggle; its celebrated Colossus was broken to pieces and sold to a Jew, who loaded nine hundred camels with the metal that it contained. Othman's weakness soon rendered him odious to his warlike subjects. The Egyptian army revolted, and marched to besiege him in Medina; their discontents were appeased for a time by the exertions of Ali, but the insurgents having reason to suspect that the khaliph meditated vengeance, retraced their steps, and murdered him in his palace (A. D. 656). The Koran, stained with the blood of Othman, is said to be still preserved at Damascus.

Immediately after the murder of Othman, Ali, the cousin and son-in-law of the prophet, was proclaimed khaliph. His accession was the signal for disorders, which threatened the speedy ruin of the Saracenic empire. His old enemy Ayesha, the widow of Mohammed, excited a revolt in Arabia, affecting to avenge the murder of Othman, though she had more than consented to his death; Moawiyáh headed a revolt in Syria; and the turbulent army of Egypt set their sovereign's authority at defiance. The first combat was against the partisans of Ayesha, who were routed with great slaughter, and she herself made prisoner. Ali not only spared the life of this turbulent woman, but assigned her a large pension.

Moawiyáh was a far more dangerous enemy. By his affected zeal for religion, he had won the friendship of many of the companions of the prophet, while his descent from the ancient chiefs of Mecca procured the support of many who had yielded reluctantly to the sway of Mohammed. The rival armies met in the plains of Saffein, on the western bank of the Euphrates, and more than ninety days were spent in undecisive skirmishes. At length Moawiyáh, finding his forces rapidly diminishing, adopted the following singular expedient, on the recommendation of Amrú; he ordered a copy of the Koran to be fixed on the top of a pike, and directed a herald to proclaim, in the presence of both armies, that he was willing to decide all differences by this sacred code. Ali's soldiers forced him to consent to a truce; two commissioners were chosen to regulate the articles of peace; and Amrú, who appeared on the part of Moawiyáh, contrived to have his friend proclaimed khaliph. The war was renewed, but no decisive battle was fought. At length some enthusiasts met accidentally at Mecca and began to discuss the calamities that threatened the ruin of Islamism. One of them remarked that no one of the claimants of the throne deserved to reign, since they had jointly and severally inflicted great sufferings on the faithful, and brought religion into jeopardy. Three of them then agreed to devote themselves for the public good, and on the same day to assassinate Amrú, Moawiyáh, and Ali. The two former escaped; Ali became a victim (A. D. 661), and Moawiyáh, without much resistance, became chief of the Saracenic empire, and founded the Ommiade dynasty of khaliphs.

There is a tradition that Mohammed, a little before his last illness, declared, "The khaliphate will not last more than thirty years after my death;" if this prediction was not devised after the event, it was singularly fulfilled by the murder of his nephew and son-in-law. Ali's memory is justly venerated by the Mussulmans; he was inferior in statesmanship to his predecessors, but he was certainly the most amiable of the khaliphs. His mildness, placidity, and yielding disposition, which rendered him so beloved in private life, were however fatal to him in an age of distraction and civil warfare. His family continued to be revered long after his death; but their popularity excited the jealousy of succeeding khaliphs, and most of them perished by open violence or secret assassination. The martyrdom of Hassan and Hossein, the sons of Ali, is yearly celebrated by the Sheeahs of India and Persia with great solemnity; and on these occasions the affecting incidents of these events are so vividly represented, that travellers would suppose the bursts of grief they witness, to be caused by some recent and overwhelming calamity.

During these commotions the career of Saracenic conquest had been suspended; but under the Ommiade dynasty the military spirit of the Arabs was restored to its former strength. Egypt furnished an excellent key to southern Europe and western Africa. Thrice the Saracens were compelled to abandon their enterprise against the countries west of Egypt; but at length their perseverance was crowned with success, and the creed of Mohammed was extended through northern Africa to the shores of the Atlantic.

Count Julian, a Gothic noble, irritated by the treatment he had received from his sovereign, Roderic, invited the Saracens into Spain (A. D. 710). A numerous army of adventurers crossed the straits, and, aided by the resentment of the persecuted Jews, subdued the entire peninsula, with the exception of a small district in the Asturian mountains. Not content with this success, the Saracens crossed the Pyrenees, and advanced through France to the Loire: they even meditated a plan of conquest, which would have subjected all Christendom to their yoke; they proposed to conquer France, Italy, and Germany, and then descending the Danube to exterminate the Greek empire, whose capital they had already twice assailed. The valor of Charles Martel, who completely defeated the Saracens in a memorable battle, that lasted seven days (A. D. 732), rescued Europe from the Mohammedan yoke. His grandson, Charlemagne, drove the Saracens back to the Ebro; and though they subsequently recovered their Spanish provinces, they were forced to respect the Pyrenees as the bulwark of Christendom.

The revolution which transferred the khaliphate from the descendants of Moawiyáh to the posterity of Abbas, the uncle of Mohammed, led to the dismemberment of the empire. Mohammed, the grandson of Abbas, had long been engaged in forming a party to support the rights of his house, and from his obscure residence in Syria, sent emissaries into the remotest parts of the empire, to secure partisans for an approaching struggle. On the death of Mohammed, his son, Ibrahim, succeeded to his influence and his claims; he sent Abu Moslem as the representative of his party into Khorassan, and there that intrepid warrior for the first time raised the black standard of the house of Abbas. From this time the parties that rent the Saracenic empire were distinguished by the colors chosen as their cognizance; black was the ominous badge of the Abbassides, white of the Ommiades, and green of the Fatimites, who claimed to be descended from Mohammed, through Fatima, the daughter of the prophet and the wife of Ali. Abúl Abbas, surnamed Al Saffah, or the Sanguinary, overthrew the last of the Ommiade line near the river Jab, and not only put him to death, but massacred all the princes of his family whom he could seize, broke open the sepulchres of all the khaliphs from Moawiyáh downward, burned their mouldering contents, and scattered the ashes to the winds.

Ninety members of the Ommiade family were living at Damascus after their submission, under what they believed the safe protection of Abdallah-Ebn-Ali, the uncle of the khaliph. One day, when they were all assembled at a feast to which they had been invited by the governor, a poet, according to a preconcerted arrangement, presented himself before Abdallah and recited some verses enumerating the crimes of the house of Moawiyáh, calling for vengeance on their devoted heads, and pointing out the dangers to which their existence exposed the house of Abbas. "God has cast them down," he exclaimed; "why dost not thou trample upon them?"

This abominable exhortation fell upon willing ears; Abdallah gave the signal to the executioners whom he had already prepared, and ordered the ninety guests to be beaten to death with clubs in his presence. When the last had fainted under the hands of the executioner, he ordered the bodies of the dead and dying to be piled together, and carpets to be thrown over the ghastly heap. He then, with the rest of his guests, ascended this horrible platform, and there they revelled in a gorgeous banquet, careless of the groans and agony below!

Abd-er-rahman, the youngest son of the late khaliph, alone escaped from this indiscriminate massacre. After a series of almost incredible adventures, he reached Spain, where the Saracens, fondly attached to the memory of Moawiyáh, chose him for their sovereign, and he thus became the founder of the second dynasty of the Ommiade khaliphs.

This example of separation was followed by the Edrissites of Mauritania, and the Fatimites and Aglabites of eastern Africa. Bagdad, founded by Almansúr, became the capital of the Abbasside dynasty. The khaliphs of this line were generous patrons of science, literature, and the arts, especially Harún-al-Rashid, the hero of the Arabian Nights, and his son Al Mamún. The love of learning spread from Bagdad into the other Saracenic countries; the Ommiade khaliphs founded several universities in Spain, the Fatimites established schools in Egypt, and the Mahommedan nations were distinguished for their attainments in physical science, while Europe remained sunk in barbarism. The Saracenic empire gradually passed from splendor into weakness; the Turkish mercenaries employed by the later khaliphs became the masters of their sovereign; and the dignity, after being long an empty title, was finally abolished (A. D. 1258).

CHAPTER III.

RESTORATION OF THE WESTERN EMPIRE.

SECTION I.—*The Life of Charlemagne.*

WHEN the last of the feeble descendants of Clovis was dethroned by Pepin, France, by being brought into close connexion with the See of Rome, became the most prominent state in Europe, and the foundation was laid for the system of policy which has since prevailed in Europe, by the union of the highest ecclesiastical authority with the most extensive civil power. Many circumstances had previously conspired to give the popes, as the bishops of Rome were called from an unknown period, great and commanding authority over the Christian nations of the West. Among the most influential, was the extravagant claim to the ancient sway of the Cæsars, gravely urged by the Byzantine emperors, when they had neither means nor ability to support their pretensions. Wearied by the pride and cruelty of the Greeks, the Italians supported the papal power as a counterpoise to the imperial, and were eager to have the bishop of Rome recognised as head of the Christian church, to prevent the title from being usurped by the patriarch of Constantinople. The recognition of Pepin's elevation to the throne of France was something more than a mere form: it was a ratification of his claims by the only authority that was respected by the nations of western Europe. In return, Pepin gave military aid to the popes, in their wars with the Lombards, and openly proclaimed himself the champion of the church. The French king intrusted the command of the armies he employed in Italy to his youthful son, Karl, better known by his French name, Charlemagne. The prince, thus early brought into public life, displayed more than ordinary abilities, both as a general and a statesman; he acted a distinguished part in the subjugation of Aquitaine, and deservedly obtained the fame of adding that fine province to the dominions of the Franks.

Pepin did not long survive this acquisition; pursuing the pernicious policy which had already proved so destructive to the preceding dynasty, he divided his dominions between his sons Charles and Carloman Their mutual jealousies would have exploded in civil war, but for the judicious interference of their mother Bertha. At length Carloman died suddenly; his wife and children fled to the Lombards, his subjects, with one accord, resolved to have Charlemagne for their sovereign, and thus the French monarchy was again reunited under a single head. The protection granted to the family of Carloman was not the only ground of hostility between Charlemagne and the Lombard king Desiderius; Charlemagne had married, and afterward repudiated, that monarch's daughter; Desiderius menaced war, but had not the means of executing his threats; Charlemagne was prevented from crossing the Alps, by the appearance of a more formidable enemy on his eastern frontiers.

The Saxons, and other Germanic tribes, were still sunk in idolatry: they frequently devastated the frontier provinces of the Christian Franks, and showed particular animosity to the churches and ministers of religion. A missionary, St. Libuinus, had vainly endeavored to convert the Saxons by denouncing the vengeance of Heaven against their idolatry; irritated by his reproaches, they expelled him from their country burned the church erected at Daventer, and slew the Christians. The general convocation of the Franks, called from the time of meeting the Champ de Maï, was at the time assembled at Worms under the presidency of Charles; its members regarded the massacre at Daventer as a just provocation, and war was declared against the Saxons. As the assembly of the Champ de Maï was at once a convention of the estates and a review of the military power of the Franks, an army was in immediate readiness: Charlemagne crossed the Rhine, captured their principal fortresses, destroyed their national idol, and compelled them to give hostages for their future good conduct. He had scarcely returned home, when he was summoned into Italy, to rescue the pope from the wrath of Desiderius, who, enraged at the pontiff's refusal to recognise the claims of the sons of Carloman, had actually laid siege to Rome. Like Hannibal in ancient, and Napoleon in modern times, Charlemagne forced a passage over the Alps, and was actually descending from the mountains before the Lombards knew of his having commenced his march. Desiderius, after vainly attempting to check the Franks in the defiles, abandoned the field, and shut himself up in Pavia. The city was taken after a year's siege: during the interval, Charlemagne visited Rome, and was received with great enthusiasm by the pope and the citizens. Soon after his return to his camp Pavia surrendered, Desiderius and his queen were confined in separate monasteries, and the iron crown, usually worn by the kings of Lombardy, was placed upon the head of the French monarch.

The Saxons and Lombards made several vigorous efforts to shake off the yoke, but their insurrections were easily suppressed; while, however, alarming discontents prevailed in both nations, Charlemagne was involved in a new and perilous war. A Saracenic prince sought refuge in the French court, and persuaded the monarch to lead an army over the Pyrenees. The frontier provinces were easily subdued, owing to the disputes that divided the Mohammedans in Spain. Charlemagne gained a decisive victory over the Saracens at Saragossa, but before he could complete his conquest, he was recalled home by a new and more dangerous revolt of the Saxons. The rear-guard of the French, commanded by the gallant Roland, was treacherously assailed on its return, by the Gascons, in the defiles of Roncésvalles, and almost wholly destroyed. The celebrated valley of Roncesvalles is the line of communication between France and Navarre; the road through it is rugged and tortuous, with narrow gorges between steep mountains. While the Franks were toiling through these defiles, the Gascons and Navarrese formed ambuscades on the summits of the mountains, concealed by the thick forests with which they abound. After the greater part of the army had passed, the mountaineers suddenly rushed down the steeps, fell upon the rear-guard, and the divisions intrusted with the charge of the baggage. The Franks were surprised but not disheartened; they made a desperate resistance, and vainly tried to cut their way to the main body; but the assailants had the advantage of a light equipment and a favorable position; the whole of the rear-guard was cut off, and the baggage plundered before Charlemagne knew that they were endangered; and the mountaineers disappeared so rapidly with their booty that all pursuit was unavailing. Such was the battle of Roncesvalles, which has been strangely exaggerated and misrepresented by writers of romance.

But though the legendary account of Roncesvalles contains a very small portion of truth, it is not devoid of historical importance, because there never was a history which possessed wider influence than this romantic tale. It was by singing the song of Roland that the Normans were encouraged at the battle of Hastings, and the French inspired to their most glorious deeds. We must therefore give an abstract of the ancient tradition.

According to the legend, Charlemagne, in a war which lasted more than seven years, had nearly completed the conquest of Spain. The Moorish monarch, whom the romancers are pleased to designate Marsiles, in dread of total ruin held a council of his principal emirs and nobles, who unanimously recommended him to conciliate Charles by immediate submission. A Saracen ambassador, with the usual inconsistency of romance, is said to have been pitched close to the Spanish marches, and he addressed the monarch in the following words: "God protect you! Behold here are presents which my master sends; and he engages if you withdraw from Spain to come and do you homage at Aix-la-Chapelle."

Charlemagne summoned his twelve paladins to council, to deliberate on this offer. Roland strenuously opposed entering into any terms with an infidel, and declared that it was their duty to rescue Spain from the dominion of the crescent, and place it under the banner of the cross. Two of the paladins, however, Ganelon and the duke Naimes, maintained that it was contrary to the rules of chivalry to refuse grace to a conquered enemy. Charlemagne, who in the romances is represented as a perfect model of knightly courtesy, yielded to the arguments of the friends of peace, and inquired which of his peers would undertake to return with the ambassador, and bear back a suitable reply to the king Marsiles. Ganelon proffered his services, but Roland contemptuously declared him unfit for such a duty, and offered himself in his stead.

A warm debate arose in the council; Ganelon, irritated by the scorn with which Roland treated his pretensions, and indignant at some imputations on his fidelity and courage, said angrily to his rival, "Take care that some mischief does not overtake you." Roland, among whose virtuous qualities moderation can not be enumerated, replied, "Go to, you speak like a fool! We want men of sense to carry our messages; if the emperor pleases, I will go in your place." In great irritation Ganelon replied, "Charles is commander here; I submit myself to his will." At these words Roland burst into an immoderate fit of laughter but this act of discourtesy so offended the rest of the paladins, that with one voice they recommended Ganelon as the most suitable ambassador to be sent to Marsiles.

The Saracenic ambassador had received private information of the angry discussion which had taken place in the imperial council. As he returned to his court, he took every opportunity of reminding Ganelon of the insult he had received, and though he did not immediately succeed, he certainly weakened the paladin's loyalty, and led him secretly to deliberate on the possibility of obtaining revenge by means of treason. At his first interview with Marsiles, he maintained the pride and dignity of a French chevalier. "Charles is now old," said the Moorish monarch, "he must be close upon a hundred years of age; does he not think of taking some repose?" Ganelon firmly replied, "No! no! Charles is ever powerful; so long as he has round him the twelve peers of France, but particularly Oliver and Roland, Charles need not fear a living man." Subsequent conversations, however, enabled the Moorish monarch to work upon Ganelon's cupidity, and his jealousy of Roland, so effectually, that he agreed to supply him with such information as would enable him to cut off the rear of the Christian army, when it returned to Roncesvalles, according to the terms of the treaty.

Ganelon returned to the Christian camp, and informed the emperor that Marsiles had consented to become his vassal, and pay him tribute. Charles immediately gave orders that the army should return to France; he took the command of the van in person; the rear-guard intrusted with the care of the baggage and plunder, followed at a little distance through the passes of Roncesvalles.

In the meantime Marsiles had collected an immense army, consisting not merely of his own subjects, but of numerous auxiliaries from Barbary, Morocco, and the wild tribes in the interior of Africa. According to the instructions of Ganelon, he sent large detachments of his men to occupy the woods and mountains which overhung "the gloomy Roncesvalles' strait."

When the Christians were involved in the pass, they were suddenly attacked, at the same moment, in front, flank, and rear. Oliver clambered up a tree in order to discover the number of the enemy. Perceiving that their hosts were vastly superior to the French, he called out to Roland, "Brother in arms! the pagans are very numerous, and we Christians are few; if you sounded your horn the emperor Charles would bring us succor." Roland replied, "God forbid that my lineage should be dishonored by such a deed! I will strike with my good sword Durandel; and the pagans falling beneath my blows, will discover that they have been led hither by their evil fate." "Sound your horn, companion in arms!" reiterated Oliver; "the enemies hem us in on every side." "No!" repeated Roland, our Franks are gallant warriors; they will strike heavy blows, and cut through the host of the foul paynim." He then prepared his troops for action. Archbishop Turpin, perceiving that the fight would be desperate and bloody, commanded all the soldiers to kneel, and join in a general confession of faith, after which he bestowed upon them absolution, and his episcopal benediction.

The Christians made a gallant defence; but numbers finally trium, ued over valor. "Down went many a noble crest; cloven was many a plumed helmet. The lances were shivered in the grasp of Christendom's knights, and the swords dropped from their wearied arms." Turpin, Oliver, and Roland, still survived, and faintly maintained the fight. At length, Roland turning to Oliver, exclaimed, "I will sound my horn, Charles will hear us, and we may yet hope again to see our beloved France." "Oh! shame and disgrace," answered Oliver, "why did you not sound when first I asked you? The best warriors of France have been sacrificed to your temerity: we must die with them!" Turpin, however, insisted that the horn should be blown as a signal to the emperor; and Roland blew such a blast, that the blood spurted from his mouth, and his wounds, opened afresh, poured forth torrents. Charles, though thirty leagues distant, heard the sound, and said, "Our men are engaged at disadvantage; we must haste to their assistance." "I do not believe it," replied the traitor Ganelon, and dissuaded the emperor. Roland once more, with his dying breath, rung a wailing blast from the horn. Charles knew the character of the sound. "Evil has come upon us," he exclaimed; "those are the dying notes of my nephew Roland!" He hastily returned to Roncesvalles; but Roland, and all his companions, lay dead upon the plain, and the emperor could only honor their corpses with Christian burial.

Such are the salient points in the old romance, on which the song of Roland is founded. So late as the close of the fifteenth century the narrative was received as an historical fact; and when John, king of France, a little before the fatal battle of Poictiers, reproached his nobles that there were no Rolands to be found in his army, an aged knight replied, "Sire, Rolands would not be wanting, if we could find a Charlemagne."

The devastations of the Saxons, which recalled Charlemagne from Spain, exceeded anything which Europe had witnessed since the days of Attila. Witikind, prince of Westphalia, was the leader of this dangerous revolt; he had united his countrymen into one great national confederacy, and long maintained a desperate struggle against the whole strength of the French monarchy. He was at length irretrievably routed, and submitting to the conqueror, became a Christian. Several minor revolts in his extensive dominions troubled the reign of Charlemagne, but he quelled them all, and secured the tranquillity of Germany, both by subduing the Saxons, and destroying the last remnant of the barbarous Avars who had settled in Hungary. The brief intervals of tranquillity were spent by this wise monarch in extending the blessings of civilization to his subjects, by establishing schools, and patronising science and literature. In these labors he was assisted by Alcuin, an English monk, the most accomplished scholar of his age. Such was the fame of the French monarchy at this time, that embassies came to the court from the most distant contemporary sovereigns. The most remarkable was that sent from the renowned Harún-er-Rashíd, khaliph of Bagdad; among the presents they brought were some beautiful pieces of clock-work, which were regarded as something almost miraculous in western Europe, where the mechanical arts were still in their infancy.

But in the midst of these glories Charlemagne was alarmed by the appearance of a new enemy on the coasts of France, whose incursions, though repelled, filled the monarch's prescient mind with sad bodings of future danger. These were the Northmen, or Normans, pirates, from the distant shores of Scandinavia, whose thirst of plunder was stimulated by the desire of revenging the wrongs that their idolatrous brethren, the Saxons, had endured. At their first landing in France, they had scarcely time to commit any ravages, for they fled on the news of the dreaded king's approach. Charlemagne saw their departing ships without exultation; he burst into tears,* and predicted that these "sea-kings" would soon prove a dreadful scourge to southern Europe.

Probably about the same time that Charles was excited by the appearance of these pirates, whose ferocity and courage he had learned to dread during his expeditions into the north of Germany, three ships of a similar character to those described, entered one of the harbors on the southeastern coast of Britain, about a century and a half after the Anglo-Saxons had established their dominion over the southern part of the island, and given it the name of Angle-Land, or England.

Here the sight of the strange ships produced the same doubts as in France. The Saxon graf, or magistrate of the district, proceeded to the shore to inquire who these strangers were, and what they wanted. The foreigners, who had just disembarked, attacked him and his escort without provocation, slew them on the spot, pillaged the neighboring houses, and then returned to their vessels. Some time elapsed before it was discovered that these pirates were the Danes, or Normans, names with which the ears of Anglo-Saxons were destined soon to form a terrible familiarity.

Soon after the retreat of the Normans, Charlemagne was induced to visit Italy, both to quell the rebellion of the duke of Beneventum, and to rescue Pope Leo from his insurgent subjects. He succeeded in both enterprises, and the grateful pontiff solemnly crowned his benefactor EMPEROR OF THE WEST. A project was soon after formed for re-establishing the ancient Roman empire, by uniting Charlemagne to the Byzantine empress, Irene, but this was prevented by the factions of Constantinople; the degraded Greeks dreaded nothing so much as the vigorous administration of such a sovereign as the restorer of the Western Empire.

Charlemagne intended to divide his dominions equally between his three sons; but two of them died while the arrangements were in progress, and Louis, the weakest in mind and body, became sole heir to the empire. His claims were solemnly recognised in a national assembly of the Frank nobility, at Aix-la-Chapelle; soon after which, the emperor died, in the seventy-second year of his age, universally lamented throughout his extensive dominions.

* The monk of St. Gall tells us, that when Charlemagne was asked the cause of these tears, he replied, "My faithful friends, do you inquire why I weep thus bitterly? Assuredly it is not that I dread any annoyance to myself from the piracy of those wretches; but I am deeply affected to find that they have dared to visit these coasts even in my lifetime; and violent grief overwhelms me, when I look forward to the evils they will inflict on my subjects."

Section II.—*Decline and Fall of the Carlovingian Dynasty.*

The Western Empire, established by Charlemagne, extended from the Ebro in the west to the Elbe and Raab in the east, and from the dutchy of Beneventum and the Adriatic sea to the river Eyder, which separated the Germanic tribes from the Scandinavian hordes, or, as they began about this time to be called, the Danes and Normans. It consequently included all ancient Gaul, a great portion of Spain and Italy, several islands in the Mediterranean, especially Corsica, Sardinia, and the Baleares, western and northern Germany, with a considerable part of Pannonia, or Hungary. No other European power could compete with that of the Franks; the monarchies of Norway, Denmark, Sweden, Poland, and Russia, were not yet founded; England was still divided by the Heptarchy; the Saracenic empire in Spain was distracted by civil commotions, and the Christian kingdom of the Asturias was barely struggling into existence; finally, the Byzantine empire was sunk into hopeless lethargy, and owed its continued existence only to the decay of the spirit of enterprise among the Arabs, after the seat of the Khaliphate was removed to Bagdad. But the continuation of an empire including so many nations essentially different in interests, habits, and feelings, required a superior genius in the sovereign. Louis the Debonnaire, the son and successor of Charlemagne, was deficient in every quality that a ruler should possess; foolish, weak, and superstitious, he could not make himself beloved, and he failed to inspire fear. Yielding to the suggestions of his queen, Hermengarde, Louis sanctioned the murder of his nephew Bernard, and forced the three natural sons of Charlemagne to assume the clerical tonsure, by which they were for ever prevented from taking a share in temporal affairs. These crimes had scarcely been committed when Louis became the victim of remorse. Unable to stifle the reproaches of conscience, he appeared before the general assembly of his subjects, and publicly confessed that he had been deeply criminal in consenting to the murder of Bernard, and in forcing his brothers to enter religious orders; he humbly besought pardon from all present, solicited the aid of their prayers, and undertook a solemn penance. This strange scene rendered Louis contemptible in the eyes of his subjects; some doubted his sincerity, others questioned his motives, but all believed this public confession a needless sacrifice of the royal dignity.

Louis chose for his second wife, Judith, the daughter of a Bavarian count. His three sons were indignant at a marriage which threatened to produce new sharers in their inheritance, but nearly four years elapsed without any appearance of such an event. At length the empress gave birth to a child, afterward known as Charles the Bald, who was popularly said to be the son of her unworthy favorite, Bernard, count of Barcelona. The three former sons of Louis not only refused to acknowledge their new brother, but took up arms to force their father to dismiss his ministers and divorce his wife. After a desultory war Louis prevailed over his rebellious children, but the fatigues of campaigning broke down his feeble constitution, and put an end to his inglorious life. The seeds of discord were thickly sown during his life, they were forced into maturity after his death by his unwise distribution of his dominions between his three sons.

Scarcely had Louis been laid in the grave, when his sons Louis the Germanic and Charles the Bald took up arms against their elder brother Lothaire, and engaged him in a general battle at Fontenay, which proved fatal to the flower of the ancient Frank nobility (A. D. 841). After a desultory war, the brothers finally agreed on a partition of the empire, by which Lothaire obtained Italy, and the eastern provinces of France; Louis received his father's Germanic dominions; and to Charles were assigned the provinces of France west of the Saône and the Rhone, together with the Spanish marches (A. D. 843). Thus Charles the Bald may be considered as the founder of the French monarchy properly so called, for hitherto the sovereigns of the Franks were Germans in language, customs, country, and blood. It is unnecessary to detail the petty revolutions in the family of Charlemagne; it is sufficient to say, that the empire was momentarily reunited under Charles the Fat, younger son of Louis the Germanic (A. D. 884), but he being deposed by his subjects, its dissolution became inevitable; from its fragments were formed the kingdoms of Italy, France, and Germany, with the states of Lorraine, Burgundy, and Navarre.

These new states owed their origin less to the disputes that convulsed the Carlovingian family than to the exorbitant power of the nobles, which had been increasing rapidly from the death of Charlemagne. The titles of duke and count were not in that age merely honorary; they conferred nearly despotic sway over the provinces. The great feudatories of the crown were invested, not merely with the administration of justice and regulation of police in their respective districts, but had also the command of the army and the direction of the revenue. It is easy to see that the union of such different and important departments of government in a single person must necessarily have been dangerous to royal authority, and constantly tempted ambitious nobles to proclaim their independence. Charlemagne saw this evil, and endeavored to abate the danger by dividing the great dutchies into several counties; but in the civil wars among his posterity, rival competitors, to secure the support of powerful feudatories, offered the restored dutchies as tempting bribes, and further weakened themselves by alienating the royal domains to secure the favor of the church Taking advantage of this impolicy, the dukes and counts contrived to make their dignities hereditary; and this dangerous innovation was not only sanctioned by Charles the Bald, but extended to all fiefs (A. D. 877), in a parliament held at Chiersi, toward the close of his reign. The principle of inheritance, thus introduced, may be regarded as the foundation of the feudal system, and the source of the calamitous wars between rival nobles which convulsed all central and southwestern Europe.

The Normans, like the Saxons and Franks, were a branch of the great Teutonic race; but the conversion of the latter to Christianity was viewed by their brethren of the north as an act of treason against the national religion of Germany, and their indignation was still farther exasperated, by the tales of wrong and suffering related by the crowds of idolatrous Saxons, who fled to the isles of the Baltic from the merciless persecutions of Charlemagne. The maritime Teutones from the earliest ages were distinguished by their hardihood, their ardent passion for adventure, and their contempt of death. They navigated the dangerous seas of the north with more courage and freedom, than the Greeks and Romans exhibited in the Mediterranean; they did not despair when they lost sight of land; they did not come to anchor when clouds obscured the stars. On board every vessel there was a cast of hawks or ravens, and when the adventurers were uncertain in what direction the land lay, they let loose one of the birds, knowing that he would make with instinctive sagacity for the nearest coast, and by his flight they steered their course. Toward the close of the eighth century the Normans became formidable as pirates to western Europe: they particularly infested the coast of Britain, Ireland, and France. Their leaders assumed the proud title of sea-kings, though the limits of each royalty did not extend beyond the deck of a single vessel, and all superiority was at an end when the expedition was over. A sea-king had only to announce his intention of undertaking some buccaneering enterprise, and he was sure to find crowds of adventurous youth ready to volunteer their services as his associates. Whither the adventurous sea-king would steer, provided that there appeared a reasonable chance of plunder, was a matter of perfect indifference to him and his associates. They effected a landing when least expected; no mercy was shown to age or sex, the fate of those who submitted or resisted was alike, but the special objects of their vengeance were the clergy and the churches, because they regarded themselves as the avengers of the insults offered to Odin, and of the persecutions with which Christian sovereigns afflicted their worshippers in their dominions. Sir Walter Scott has drawn the character of an ancient sea-king with so much poetic force and historic truth, that the extract will supersede the necessity of further description.

"Count Witikind came of a regal strain,
And roved with his Norsemen the land and the main;
Wo to the realms which he coasted! for there
Was shedding of blood and rending of hair,
Rape of maiden and slaughter of priest,
Gathering of ravens and wolves to the feast!
When he hoisted his standard black,
Before him was battle, behind him wrack:
And he burned the churches, that heathen Dane,
To light his band to their barks again.

On Erin's shores was his outrage known,
The winds of France had his banners blown;
Little was there to plunder, yet still
His pirates had forayed on Scottish hill;
But upon merry England's coast,
More frequent he sailed, for he won the most.
So far and wide his ravage they knew,
If a sail but gleamed white 'gainst the welkin blue
Trumpet and bugles to arms did call,
Burghers hastened to man the wall;
Peasants fled inland his fury to scape,
Beacons were lighted on headland and cape;
Bells were tolled out, and aye as they rung
Fearful and faintly the gray brothers sung,
'Save us, St. Mary, from flood and from fire,
From famine and pest, and Count Witikind's ire.'"

Thierry has collected the principal characteristics of a sea-king from the Icelandic sagas. "He could govern a vessel as the good rider manages his horse, running over the oars while they were in motion. He would throw three javelins to the mast-head and catch them alternately in his hand without once missing. Equal under such a chief, supporting lightly their voluntary submission, and the weight of their coat-of-mail, which they promised themselves would soon be exchanged for an equal weight of gold, the pirates held their course gayly, as their old songs express it, along the track of the swans. Often were their fragile barks wrecked and dispersed by the north sea-storm, often did the rallying sign remain unanswered, but this neither increased the cares nor diminished the confidence of the survivors, who laughed at the wind and waves from which they had escaped unhurt. Their song in the midst of the tempest was :—

"The force of the storm helps the arms of our rowers,
The hurricane is carrying us the way which we should go."

Nearly all the information which we possess respecting these formidable pirates is derived from the *sagas*, or songs of the Skalds ; these singular compositions are unlike any other form of literature, they are records of adventure in verse or measured prose, in which no notice is taken of historical events, and no regard paid to chronology.

The Skalds, or bards, were more honored by the Scandinavians than their priests ; indeed it is doubtful whether they had any regular sacerdotal caste, or order. Some of their heroes prided themselves on defying the gods themselves ; thus Gauthakor, when asked his religion, by Olaf the saint, who was anxious to introduce Christianity among his countrymen, replied : "My brothers in arms and I are neither Christians nor pagans. We have no faith but in our arms, and our strength to vanquish our enemies, and those we have ever found sufficient." So far was the character of a pirate or Vikingar from being disgraceful, that it was eagerly sought by men of the highest rank, and was only accorded to those who had given distinguished proofs both of their bravery in battle and their skill in navigation. An ancient law enacted, that a man in order to acquire glory for bravery, should attack a single enemy, defend himself against two, and not yield to three, but that he might without disgrace fly from four.

Every king, whether of sea or land, had a chosen band of champions, called Kempe ; warriors pledged to the personal service of their chief, and whose only hope of advancement arose from the performance of some exploit, which common fame, and the songs of the Skalds, might spread over the north.

Each sea-king laid down the rules for the government of his own champions, and fame was assigned to him whose regulations were the most strict and rigorous. Thus we are told, that Half, and Hiorolf, the sons of a Norwegian king, both devoted themselves to maritime adventure, or, in plain terms, to piracy.

Hiorolf collected a great number for ships, which he manned with volunteers of every kind both of serfs and freemen ; he was defeated in all his expeditions. On the other hand his brother Half had only one ship, but his crew were all picked men. They were at first but twenty-three in number, all descended from kings; the troop was subsequently increased to sixty.

To obtain admission into the company, it was necessary that the champion should lift up a large stone which lay in the front of Half's residence, and which could not be moved by the force of twelve ordinary men. These champions were forbidden to take women and children, to seek a refuge during a tempest, or to dress their wounds before the battle was ended. Eighteen years Half's band carried terror to all the shores of western Europe. Finally, when the sea-king was returning to enjoy the wealth he had acquired, his vessel, overladen with plunder, appeared on the point of sinking within sight of the Norwegian shore. The brave crew immediately drew lots to determine who should throw themselves into the sea, for the purpose of saving their chief and the cargo; those on whom the lot fell, instantly jumped overboard and swam to shore, while the vessel relieved of the weight reached the harbor in safety.

Sometimes these warriors, like the Malays in Java, were seized with a kind of phrensy, either arising from an excited imagination, or from the use of stimulating liquors. In this state they were called "*berserker*," a word of frequent occurrence in the sagas. While under the influence of this madness, the champions committed the wildest extravagances; they danced about, foamed at the mouth, struck indiscriminately at friends and foes, destroyed their own property, and like the mad Orlando waged war against inanimate nature, tearing up rocks and trees. Sivald, king of Sweden, had five sons, all of whom became *berserker;* when the fit was on them they used to swallow burning coals and throw themselves into the fire. They and their father were slain by Halfdan, whom Sivald had previously dethroned, the nation having become impatient of the extravagances of the frantic princes. Halfdan had a contest with another berserker, named Hartben, who came to attack him accompanied by twelve champions. Hartben was a formidable pirate, but when the fit was on him it was as much as his twelve companions could do to prevent him devastating everything around him. Halfdan challenged the pirate and his entire crew. Such an insult so inflamed Hartben, that he was immediately seized with a fit of phrensy during which he killed six of his companions; he rushed against the king with the remaining six, but the pirates were slain, by the irresistible blows of the mace of Halfdan.

The sons of Arngrim, king of Helegoland, the most celebrated pirates of their age, are described as suffering severely from the *berserk* madness; when under its influence they slaughtered their crews and destroyed their shipping: sometimes they landed on desert places and vented their fury on the stocks and stones. After the fit was over they lay quite senseless from sheer exhaustion.

A sea-king rarely condescended to the blandishments of courtship. If he heard of any noble or royal damsel celebrated for beauty, he at once demanded her from her father, and if refused, equipped a vessel to take her away by force. He generally brought away, if successful, her dowry at the same time, and thus could boast of a double victory.

A Swedish pirate named Gunnar, having heard the Skalds celebrate the charms of Moalda, a Norwegian princess, sent to her father Regnald a peremptory demand for the fair lady's hand. Regnald rejected such a suitor with scorn, but aware of the consequences of a refusal, he made instant preparations for defence. Before marching against the pirates, he had a cavern hollowed out in the mountains, within which he concealed the princess and his choicest treasures, leaving her a proper supply of provisions. Scarcely were his arrangements completed than the fierce Gunnar appeared off the coast; Regnald met the pirates on the shore, a desperate battle ensued, and the king was slain. After his victory Gunnar sought out the place where Moalda was concealed, and carried away the princess with her treasures to Sweden. A second and a third conquest of this kind often followed the first, for polygamy was sufficiently common among these adventurers. The ladies themselves could not view with indifference heroes who risked their lives to obtain their hands, and whose exploits, immortalized by the Skalds, were sung in all the islands and in all families.

France suffered most severely from their hostilities ; their light barks ascended the Seine, the Loire, the Garonne, and the Rhone, carrying fire and sword into the very centre of the kingdom. Most of the principal cities were laid waste ; Paris itself was thrice taken and pillaged ; and the French, at length losing all courage, refused to meet the northern warriors in the field, but purchased their retreat with large bribes. This remedy was necessarily as inefficacious as it was disgraceful, for it stimulated the barbarians to fresh incursions in the assured hope of gain. Nor were the Normans regardless of permanent conquests ; Ruric, a leader of their adventurous bands, founded the Russian monarchy toward the close of the ninth century; Iceland was colonized, and the greater part of Ireland subdued, at a still earlier period; and the northern and western islands of Scotland were successively occupied as convenient stations for their piratical navies. Finally, they obtained fixed establishments in France; the province of Neustria, now called Normandy, was ceded to Rolf or Rollo, the chief of a large horde of these northern pirates, by Charles the Simple (A. D. 912) ; the province gained great advantages by the exchange, for Rollo becoming a Christian, was baptized by the name of Robert, and applied himself with equeal diligence and success to improve the condition of his new subjects.

Charles also ceded to Rollo all the pretensions of the crown to that part of Brittany which no longer recognised the sovereignty of the kings of France, and Rollo came to the borders of his new province to perform liege homage and confirm the articles of peace. The Norman swore allegiance to Charles, who in return presented his daughter to the adventurer, and gave him the investiture of Neustria. The French prelates, who assumed the regulation of the ceremonials employed on all solemn occasions, had introduced the degrading prostrations of the Orientals into the forms of European homage; they now informed Rollo that after receiving a gift of so much value, he should on his bended knees kiss the feet of the king. " Never," replied the haughty barbarian, " will I bend my knees before another mortal—never will I kiss the foot of man." As the prelates, however, were urgent, he ordered one of his soldiers to perform the ceremony in his stead. The soldier advancing, rudely seized the foot of Charles, and by a sudden jerk threw the monarch on the ground. The Normans who witnessed the transaction, applauded their comrade's insolence, while the French nobles deemed it prudent to conceal their indignation. The ceremony was continued as if nothing had happened; the several Norman lords took the usual oaths of allegiance, after which the king returned to Laon. He had chosen this city for his capital, because Paris was included in the fief of one of the great vassals of the crown.

The establishment of the Normans in Neustria put an end to the system of piracy and plunder which for more than a century had devastated western Europe; the repetition of pillage had so wasted Germany, Gaul, and Britain, that the plunder to be acquired no longer repaid the hazards of an expedition, and as war was no longer profitable, Rollo resolved to cultivate the arts of peace. To prevent the future incursions of his countrymen, he fortified the mouths of the rivers, restored the walls of the cities, and kept his subjects in constant military training. Under Rollo the feudal system, which had been slowly forming, received its full development; immediately after his baptism, he divided the lands of Neustria among his principal followers, to each of whom he gave the title of count, and these counts subdivided the land among their soldiers. The Normans displayed the same ardor in cultivating their new estates which they had formerly shown in devastating them; the peasants resumed the cultivation of their fields; the priests restored their ruined churches; the citizens resumed their trading occupations; strangers were invited from every country to cultivate the waste lands: and the most rigorous laws were enacted for the protection of person and property. Robberies were so efficiently checked, that Rollo, as a bravado, hung up a golden bracelet in a forest near the Seine, which remained untouched for three years.

While the Normans devastated the coasts, central Europe was devastated by the Hungarians, or, as they called themselves, the Magyars, who extended their ravages into Greece and Italy. Germany suffered most from their hostilities, and was the longest exposed to their fury. These incursions, to which must be added occasional enterprises of the Sclavonians and Saracens, destroyed the political institutions that Charlemagne had formed, and threw Christendom back into the barbarism from which it had just begun to emerge. England, under the government of Alfred, for a brief space preserved the elements of civilization; he expelled the Normans from the island (A. D. 887), restored the ancient seminaries of learning, and founded new schools. But his glorious reign was followed by fresh calamities; the Danish-Normans reappeared in England, and spread trouble and desolation throughout the country.

From the reign of Charles the Bald, the royal authority rapidly declined in France, while the power of the feudal lords constantly increased. The dukes and counts, usurping regal rights, raised, on the slightest, or without any provocation, the standard of revolt: the kings, to gain some, and secure the allegiance of others, abandoned to them successively the most valuable royal domains and privileges, until the Carlovingian monarchs, so far from being able to counterbalance the power of the nobility, were unable to support the expenses of their own courts. A change of dynasty was thus rendered inevitable, and the throne was certain to fall to the lot of the most powerful or most daring of the nominal vassals. This event, which had been long foreseen, took place on the death of Louis the Sluggard, the last of the Carlovingian dynasty, who died without issue at the early age of twenty (A. D. 987). Hugh Capet possessed already the centre of the kingdom; he was count of Paris, duke of France and Neustria, while his brother Henry held the dutchy of Burgundy. It was not difficult for so powerful a noble to form a party, by whose favor he was invested with the title, after having long enjoyed the power of royalty (A. D. 987). Charles of Lorraine, the late king's uncle, took up arms in defence of his hereditary rights; but he was betrayed to his rival by the bishop of Laon, and ended his days in prison. Hugh became the founder of the Capetian dynasty in France, a branch of which still retains possession of that crown. But for many years after the accession of Hugh Capet, France was an aristocratic republic rather than a monarchy, for the royal authority was merely nominal. The domains of the count of Paris were indeed annexed to the crown, and thus the Capetians had greater territorial possessions, and consequently greater influence, than the Carlovingians. But the peers of France, as the great feudatories were called, still preserved their independence: and their tacit assent to Hugh's usurpation was anything rather than a recognition of his authority. In the south of France, Languedoc, no notice was taken of Hugh's elevation; and the inhabitants for many years dated their public acts by the nominal reigns of the children of Charles of Lorraine.

Section III.—*The Foundation of the Germanic Empire.*

From the first foundation of the Germanic empire by the treaty of Verdun, the royal authority was extremely limited, and Louis, its monarch, was obliged to swear in a national assembly, held at Marone (A. D. 851), that "he would maintain the states in all their rights and privileges." His youngest son, Charles the Fat, was deposed by his subjects; and Arnold, the natural son of Prince Carloman, was elected to the vacant throne. The custom of electing emperors was thus established in Germany, and it continued almost to our own times. Arnold was succeeded by his son Louis; the states chose Conrad, duke of Franconia, as his successor, to the exclusion of Charles the Simple, king of France, the legitimate heir male of the Carlovingians. On the death of Conrad, the states elected Henry, surnamed the Fowler, as his successor (A. D. 919), the first of the Saxon dynasty of kings and emperors.

Henry I., by his civil and military institutions, raised Germany to the highest rank among the states of Europe. Profiting by the intestine commotions of France, he conquered the province of Lorraine which he divided into two dutchies, that of Upper Lorraine, or the Moselle, and that of Lower Lorraine, or Brabant. The former retained the name of Lorraine; it was long governed by the family of Gerard, duke of Alsace, whose descendants obtained the Germanic empire in the eighteenth century. Brabant was assigned to Godfrey, count of Louvain, whose descendants retained it, with the title of duke, until, on the failure of male heirs, it passed by marriage into the hands of the dukes of Burgundy, who thus found means to render themselves masters of a great portion of the Netherlands. Henry successfully repelled the invasions of the Sclavonians and Hungarians; by the defeat of the latter he freed the Germans from the disgraceful tribute with which they had been compelled to purchase the forbearance of these barbarians, and the memory of his victory was annually commemorated by a grateful people for several succeeding centuries.

The great merits of Henry secured the election of his son Otho to the Germanic throne. His reign was disturbed by frequent revolts of the powerful feudatories; their faction and insubordination effectually prevented him from giving his subjects a code of laws, the great object of his ambition; he was forced to yield to the turbulent spirit of the times, and leave some more fortunate sovereign to gather the laurels of a legislator. One incident will serve to mark the character of the age better than any labored dissertation. During one of the national assemblies or diets, it was debated "whether children could inherit the property of their fathers during the lifetime of their grandfathers." After a long discussion, in which the point became more obscure than ever, it was gravely resolved to leave the matter to the decision of a duel. An equal number of combatants, chosen on both sides, entered the lists; the champions of the children prevailed, and thenceforward the law of inheritance was considered to be fixed.

Italy had been raised into a kingdom after the partition of the Carlovingian dynasty, and several of its princes had taken the imperial title; but the government of these feeble rulers exposed the peninsula to dreadful calamities; it was harassed by the private wars of the nobles, and devastated by invasions of the Hungarians and Saracens. Adelaide, the widow of Lothaire, king of Italy, menaced with the loss of her dominions by Berenger, or Berengarius the Younger, supplicated the aid of Otho, and her request was strenuously supported by Pope John XII. (A. D. 951). Otho passed into Italy, conquered several of the strongest cities, and gave his hand in marriage to the queen whom he had come to protect. Berenger was permitted to retain the crown of Italy on condition of doing homage to Otho; but the tyranny and faithlessness of this prince excited such commotions, that the German sovereign was once more summoned to cross the Alps by the united entreaties of the Italian princes and prelates. Otho entered Italy at the head of an army which his rival could not resist; he marched directly to Rome, where he was received with the greatest enthusiasm (A. D 962). The pope revived in his favor the imperial title, which had been thirty-eight years in abeyance, proclaimed him Augustus, crowned him emperor of the Romans, and acknowledged him Supreme Head of the Church. But the pontiff's gratitude was not of long duration; enraged by the emperor's remonstrances against his vicious courses, he took advantage of Otho's absence in pursuit of Berenger to enter into alliance with Adelbert, the son of his ancient enemy, to form a secret league for the expulsion of the Germans from Italy.

Otho heard the intelligence of John's treachery with great indignation; he returned to Rome, held a council, in which the pope was accused of the most scandalous immoralities, and on his refusal to appear, he was condemned as contumacious, deposed, and a new pontiff, Leo VIII., elected in his stead. All Italy, as far as the ancient kingdom of the Lombards extended, thus fell under the sway of the Germans ; there were only some maritime places in Lower Italy which, with Apulia and Calabria, still remained subject to the Greeks. Otho transmitted this kingdom, with the imperial dignity, to his successors on the German throne ; but from his reign to that of Maximilian I., no prince took the title of emperor until he had been consecrated by the pope. Maximilian designated himself "Emperor Elect" (A. D. 1508), and his example was followed by his successors down to our times.

Otho I. died after a prosperous reign (A. D. 975), and was succeeded by his son Otho II. His reign was occupied in sanguinary wars, which harassed Germany and Italy. Otho having married the Greek princess Theophania, claimed the provinces of Apulia and Calabria as her dowry. After a tedious struggle, the emperor was mortally wounded by a poisoned javelin in a battle with the Greeks (A. D. 983). His death is said to have been accelerated by indignation at the joy which Theophania showed for the victory of her countrymen, though it was obtained over her own husband.

Otho III., when elected successor to his father, was only twelve years of age ; ambitious rivals prepared to dispute his title, but the affection of the Germans for his family enabled him to triumph over all opposition. His authority was more fiercely questioned in Italy, where Crescentius, an ambitious noble, became such a favorite with the Roman populace, that he deposed Pope Gregory, and gave the pontifical dignity to John XVI. Otho hastened to Italy, captured Rome, and put both Crescentius and John to death. These severities did not quell the turbulence of the Italians ; fresh insurrections soon compelled the emperor to return to the peninsula, where he was poisoned by the widow of Crescentius, whom he had seduced under a promise of marriage (A. D. 1002). He died without issue.

After some competition, the electors chose Henry, duke of Bavaria, descended from the Othos in the female line, emperor of the West. His reign was disturbed by repeated insurrections, both in Germany and Italy ; he succeeded in quelling them, but was so wearied by these repeated troubles, that he seriously designed to abdicate and retire into a monastery. The clergy took advantage of his piety and liberality to extort from him several rich donations, which proved, in an after age, the cause of much evil. His death (A. D. 1024) put an end to the Saxon dynasty.

Conrad II., duke of Franconia, being chosen by the electors, united the kingdom of Burgundy, or, as it was called, Arles, to the empire. But this was an acquisition of little real value ; the great vassals of the kingdom, the counts and bishops, preserved the authority they had usurped in their respective districts, leaving the emperors a merely nominal sovereignty. It is even probable that the high authority possessed by the Burgundian lords, induced the German nobles to arrogate to themselves the same prerogatives. The power of the clergy was increasing even more rapidly than that of the nobles, for they extorted fresh privileges and grants from every successive sovereign ; Conrad, who was naturally of a generous disposition,* impoverished the state by imitating the unwise liberality of his predecessors. Italy, during this reign and that of Conrad's son and successor, Henry III., continued to be distracted by rival factions; but Henry was an energetic supporter of the imperial authority; he deposed three rival popes, who claimed succession to St. Peter at the same time, and gave the pontifical chair to a German prelate, Clement II. He even exacted an oath from the Romans, that they would never elect a pope without having previously received the imperial sanction. The imperial power, wielded by an energetic monarch like Henry, was still formidable, but its resources were exhausted; and when a feebler sovereign attempted to exercise the sway over the church which his father had held, he found the papacy stronger than the empire.

The great struggle between the papal and imperial power began in the reign of Henry IV., whose long minority, for he succeeded his father when only five years old, necessarily weakened the influence of the sovereign. On the other hand, the circumstances of Europe, at this crisis, were peculiarly favorable to the policy of the popes. The Saxon line, restored in England by Edward the Confessor, had lost its nationality: Edward conferred the chief ecclesiastical dignities of his kingdom on foreigners, or persons remarkable for their foreign attachments; and thus those who wielded the power of the church in the island, were more like missionaries, laboring for the benefit of a distant see, than clergymen, attentive only to their flocks. In Spain, the new provinces wrested from the Moors, when the unity of their empire was destroyed by the subversion of the Ommiade khaliphs, became closely attached to the Roman see. The spread of Christianity in Norway, Poland, Russia, and the other northern states, gave additional vigor to the papal power; for the Northerns, with all the zeal of new converts, became eager to prove their sincerity by some enterprise in support of the pontiff, whom they regarded as the great director of their faith.

But the most potent allies obtained by the church were the Normans of England and Italy. William, the natural son of Robert, duke of Normandy, had been nominated heir of the English throne by Edward he Confessor, who had no right to make any such appointment. Harold, the son of Godwin, earl of Kent, was the favorite of the English people, and it was generally known that he would be elected to the throne on the death of the confessor. Unfortunately Harold's brother was detained as a hostage in Normandy, and in spite of the warnings of King Edward, he crossed the sea in order to obtain his deliverance. The vessel in which the Saxon chief crossed the channel was wrecked near the mouth of the Somme, and, according to the barbarous custom of the age, the court of Ponthieu seized upon the shipwrecked strangers, and threw them into prison, for the purpose of obtaining large ransom. Harold and his companions appealed to Duke William, who procured their liberation, and invited them to his court. A grand council of the Norman prelates and nobles was then convoked, in whose presence

* Many remarkable anecdotes are related of Conrad's generosity; one deserves to be recorded. A gentleman having lost his leg in the imperial service, Conrad ordered that his boot should be filled with gold coins, to defray the expenses of his cure.

William required Harold to swear that he would support with all his might William's succession to the crown of England, so soon as a vacancy should be created by the death of Edward. Harold's life was in the duke's power, and he consented to take the oath, secretly resolving to violate its obligations. But an artifice was employed, which, in that superstitious age, was supposed to give the oath such sanctity as to render its violation an inexpiable crime. By the duke's orders, a chest was secretly conveyed into the place of meeting, filled with the bones and relics of the saints most honored in the surrounding country, and covered with a cloth of gold. A missal was laid upon the cloth, and at William's summons Harold came forward and took the required oath, the whole assembly joining in the imprecation, "So help you God, at his holy doom." When the ceremony was concluded, the cloth of gold was removed, and Harold shuddered with superstitious horror when he found that his oath had been taken on the relics of saints and martyrs.

On Edward's death, Harold, notwithstanding his oath, allowed himself to be elected king by the English nobles and people; but the papal clergy refused to recognise his title, the pope issued a bull excommunicating Harold and his adherents, which he sent to Duke William, accompanied by a consecrated banner, and a ring, said to have contained one of St. Peter's hairs, set under a valuable diamond. Thus supported by the superstitious feelings of the period, William found no difficulty in levying a numerous army, with which he passed over into England. The fate of the kingdom was decided by the battle of Hastings, in which Harold and his bravest soldiers fell. William found little difficulty in completing the conquest of England, into which he introduced the inheritance of fiefs, and the severities of the feudal law. He deprived the native English nobles of their estates, which he shared among his own needy and rapacious followers, and he treated his new subjects with more than the cruelty that barbarous conquerors usually display toward the vanquished.

About the same time, some Norman adventurers laid the foundation of the kingdom of the Two Sicilies, in southern Europe. The provinces that compose it were shared among the Lombard feudatories of the empire, the Greeks, and the Saracens, who harassed each other with mutual wars. About a hundred Normans landing on the coast (A. D. 1016), offered their services to the Lombard princes, and displayed so much valor, that they obtained from the duke of Naples a grant of territory, where they built the city of Aversa. Encouraged by their success, Tancred, with another body of Norman adventurers, undertook the conquest of Apulia, which was completed by his son, Robert Guiscard. This warrior subdued Calabria also, and took the title of duke of both provinces. To secure his possessions, he entered into alliance with the pope, securing to the pontiff homage, and an annual tribute, on condition of receiving investiture. Nicholas II., who then filled the chair of St. Peter, willingly ratified a treaty by which the papacy gained important advantages, at the price of an empty title; he stimulated Guiscard to undertake the conquest of Sicily also, an enterprise in which that adventurer completely succeeded. Thus, at the moment that the papacy was about to struggle for power with the empire, the former had been strengthened by the accession of powerful allies and vassals, while the latter had given away the greater part of its strength by the alienation of its domains, to gratify the church, or to win the favor of feudatories whose influence was already formidable.

SECTION IV.—*State of the East from the Establishment to the Overthrow of the Khaliphate.*

THE history of the Byzantine empire, in the ninth, tenth, and eleventh centuries, is little better than a tissue of usurpation, fanaticism, and perfidy. "Externally surrounded by foes, superior in numbers, in discipline, and in valor, it seemed as if its safety was guarantied by cowardice, and its security confirmed by defeat. Internally were at work all the causes that usually effect the destruction of states: dishonor and profligacy triumphant in the palace; ferocious bigotry, based at once on enthusiasm and hypocrisy, ruling the church; civil dissensions, equally senseless and bloody, distracting the state; complete demoralization pervading every rank, from the court to the cottage; so that its existence seemed owing to the antagonising effect of the causes that singly produce the ruin of empires." In the tenth century these causes seemed to have reached their consummation; emperor after emperor perished by poison, or the dagger of the assassin; parricide and fratricide were crimes of such ordinary occurrence, that they ceased to excite feelings of horror or disgust. Theological disputes, about questions that pass the limits of human knowledge, and a jealous rivalry between the patriarch of Constantinople and the pope of Rome, produced a division between the eastern and western churches, which the disputes respecting the Bulgarians aggravated into a formal schism. These barbarians were converted to Christianity by Greek and Latin missionaries; the patriarch and the pope contended for the patronage of the new ecclesiastical establishments; the Greeks prevailed in the contest, and forthwith banished their Latin adversaries, while the court of Rome took revenge by describing the Greeks as worse than the worst of the heathen. A brief display of vigor by Nicephorus, Phocus, and John Zimisces, arrested the progress of the Saracens, who were forming permanent establishments within sight of Constantinople. But Zimisces was poisoned at the very moment when his piety, courage, and moderation, had averted impending ruin, and promised to restore some portion of the empire's former strength and former glory. His feeble successors swayed the sceptre with unsteady hands, at a time when the empire was attacked by the fiercest enemies it had yet encountered, the Normans in Sicily, and the Seljukian Turks in Asia Minor.

The names Turk and Tartar are loosely given to the inhabitants of those regions which ancient authors included under the designation of Scythia. Their uncivilized tribes possessed the countries north of the Caucasus and east of the Caspian, from the river Oxus to the wall of China: hordes issuing from these wide plains had frequently devastated the empire of Persia, and more than once placed a new race of sovereigns on the throne. It was not, however, until the eighth century that they were themselves invaded in turn; the Saracens, in the first burst of their enthusiasm, passed the Oxus, subdued Kharasm and Transoxiana, and imposed the religion and law of Mohammed on a race of warriors more fiery and zealous than themselves. Soon after the establishment of the khaliphate at Bagdad, the Saracenic empire began to be dismembered, as we have already stated, and the khaliphs, alarmed by the revolt of their armies, and surrounded only by subjects devoted to the arts of peace, began to intrust the guard of their persons and their capital to foreign mercenaries. Al Moutassem was the first who levied a Turkish army to protect his states (A. D. 833); and even during his reign, much inconvenience was felt from the pride and insolence of soldiers unconnected with the soil they were employed to defend. The evil went on daily increasing, until the emirs, or Turkish commanders, usurped all the real authority of the state, leaving to the khaliphs the outward show and gewgaws of sovereignty, with empty titles, whose pomp was increased as the authority they pretended to represent was diminished. The revolution was completed in the reign of Al Khadi (A. D. 936); hoping to arrest the progress of the revolution, he created a new minister, called the Emir-al-Omra,* to whom far greater powers were given than had been intrusted to the ancient viziers. This, as might have been expected, aggravated the evil it was designed to prevent. The family of the Bowides, so called from their ancestor Buyáh, usurped this high office and the sovereignty of Bagdad; the khaliph was deprived of all temporal authority, and was regarded simply as the chief Imán, or pontiff of the Mohammedan faith.

Such was the state of the khaliphate, when a new horde from the interior of Turkestán appeared to change the entire face of Asia. This horde, deriving its name from Seljúk, one of its most renowned chiefs, was invited to cross the Oxus by the Ghaznevid† sultans,‡ who had already established a powerful kingdom in the east of Persia, and subdued the north of Hindostan. The Seljukians finding the pasturages of Khorassan far superior to those of their native country, invited new colonies to the fertile land; they soon became so powerful that Togrul Beg proclaimed himself a sultan, and seized several of the best provinces belonging to the khaliphate. Finally, having taken Bagdad, he became master of the khaliph's person (A. D. 1055) and succeeded to the power which had formerly been possessed by the Bowides. Togrul transmitted his authority to his nephew and heir, the formidable Alp Arslan.§ This prince renewed the war against the Greek empire, obtained a signal victory over its forces in Armenia, and took the emperor,

* "Lord of the lords," or "Commander of the commanders."

† The Ghaznevid dynasty was founded by Sebektagén, who is said to have been originally a slave (A. D. 977). But his fame is eclipsed by that of his son Mahmúd, whose conquests in northern India rival those of a hero of romance. His desire of conquest was rendered more terrible to those he attacked by his cruel bigotry, for in every country that he subdued, the horrors of war were increased by those of religious persecution. At his death, the empire of Ghizni included a great part of Persia, Afghanistan, and northern India, to the provinces of Bengal and the Deccan. But the rise of this great dynasty was not more rapid than its downfall, which we may date from the death of that monarch, to whom it owes all its lustre in the page of history (A. D. 1028). Little more than a century after Mohammed's death, the last of the Ghaznevids was deposed by Mohammed Gourí, the founder of a new dynasty, equally transitory as that which it displaced.

‡ The title of sultan, which in the Chaldaic and Arabic languages signifies a sovereign, was first assumed by the Ghaznevid princes.

§ His name signifies the Conquering Lion.

Romanus Diogenes, prisoner (A. D. 1070). The distractions produced by this event in the Byzantine dominions, enabled the Turks not only to expel the Greeks from Syria, but also to seize some of the finest provinces in Asia Minor.

Under Malek Shah, the son and successor of Alp Arslan, the Seljukian monarchy touched the summit of its greatness. This wise prince extended his dominions from the Mediterranean to the wall of China. Guided by the wise counsels of the vizier, Nezam-al-Mulk, the sultan ruled this mighty empire with great justice and moderation, Asia enjoyed tranquillity, to which it had been long unaccustomed, and learning and civilization began to revive.

In the midst of this prosperity, a circumstance occurred, which, though little noticed at the time, became the source of unparalleled misfortunes to the east. This was the seizure of the mountain-castle of Alamút, and the foundation of the order of the Assassins, by Hassan Sabah. This formidable enthusiast had become a convert to the Ismaëlian doctrines, in which the creed of Islam was mingled with the darker and more gloomy superstitions of Asiatic paganism. His followers, persuaded that obedience to the commands of their chief would ensure their eternal felicity, never hesitated to encounter any danger in order to remove his enemies. Emissaries from the formidable Sheikh al Jebal* went in disguise to palaces and private houses, watching the favorable opportunity of striking the blow, to those who had provoked the hostility of their grand master. So dreadful was this scourge that oriental historians, during a long period of their annals, terminate their account of each year with a list of the men of note who had fallen victims during its course to the daggers of the assassins. After the death of Malek Shah (A. D. 1092), disputes arose between his sons, which led to sanguinary civil wars, and the dismemberment of the empire. Three powerful sultanies were formed from its fragments, namely, Iran, Kerman, and Rúm, or Iconium. That of Iran was the most powerful, for it possessed the rich provinces of Upper Asia, but its greatness soon declined. The emirs, or governors of cities and provinces, threw off their allegiance, and under the modest title of Atta-begs,† exercised sovereign authority. The Seljukians of Rúm, known to the crusaders as the Sultans of Nice, or Iconium,‡ were first raised into notice by Soleiman. Their history is important only from its connexion with that of the crusades. These divisions were the cause of the success which attended the early wars of the Christians in Palestine, and of the qualified independence of the late khaliphs, who shook off the Seljúkian yoke, and established themselves in the sovereignty of Irak Arabi, or the province of Bagdad.

* "Lord of the Mountain;" from the equivocal sense of the Arabic word *Sheikh*, the name is commonly translated "Old Man of the Mountain."

† *Atta-beg* is a Turkish word, and signifies "father or guardian of the prince."

‡ Cogni, or Iconium, is a city of Lycaonia, which these sultans made their capital, after Nice had been taken by the crusaders.

CHAPTER IV.

GROWTH OF THE PAPAL POWER.

Section I.—*The Origin of the Papacy.*

There is nothing more remarkable in the clerical organization of Christianity at its first institution, than its adaptation to all times and al circumstances. Without entering into any controverted question, we may generally state, that in the infant church provision was made for self-government on the one hand, and general superintendence on the other; and that, before the gospel was preached beyond the bounds of Judæa, the two great principles of the independence of national churches, and the authority of a council to ensure the unity of the faith, were fully recognised. Infidels have endeavored to trace the form of church government to Constantine, though the slightest glance at the history of the preceding age suffices to prove that the ecclesiastical constitution was, long before that emperor's accession, perfected in all its parts. The management belonged to the local priesthood, the government to the bishops, the superintendence of all to the council. This is the general outline of the apostolic model, and we may see in it one mark, at least, of a more than human origin, its capability of unlimited expansion.

The best institutions are open to abuse, and the Christian clergy were exposed to two different lines of temptation, both, however, tending to the same point, acquisition of power. The emperors of Constantinople endeavored to make the clergy their instruments in establishing a perfect despotism, while the people looked upon their spiritual guides as their natural protectors against the oppressions of their temporal rulers. Under these circumstances, episcopacy formed a new power in the empire, a power continually extending, because it was soon obvious that a common faith was the only bond which would hold together nations differing in language, institutions, and blood. But this political use of Christianity naturally suggested a gross and dangerous perversion of its first principles; when unity of faith appeared to be of such great value, it was natural that toleration should be refused to any great difference of opinion, and consequently, persecuting edicts were issued against paganism and heresy. This false step led to a still more dangerous confusion between spiritual and temporal power; when ecclesiastical censures produced civil consequences, the priest was identified with the magistrate, and every hour it became more difficult to separate their functions. In the decline of the empire also, the temporal power was deservedly hated and despised; a profligate court, a venal magistracy, and a cowardly soldiery, constituted the ordinary materials of the imperial government; and, compared with these, the sacerdotal body, in the worst stage of its degradation, had powerful claims to respect, if not to esteem.

It is of importance to remember that the corruption of the episcopal power was produced by the general corruption of the empire, and consequently, instead of furnishing an argument against episcopacy as an institution, it may rather be urged as a proof of its excellence. The church had fallen, indeed, from its original purity, but the state was a mass of unmixed evils; ecclesiastical power was frequently abused, but the temporal authorities scarcely went right by accident; whatever principles of justice and rectitude remained in the world, owed their conservation to the Christian clergy; and to the examples of ecclesiastical traffic there might easily be opposed a longer and more honorable list of instances, in which bishops supported the dignity of their order, by protecting the interests of morality against the craft of courtiers and the vices of sovereigns.

While the discipline of the church was injured by the clergy having temporal power forced upon them—in the first instance at least—without their solicitation, the doctrines of Christianity were corrupted by a practice arising from the best feelings of our nature. The saints and martyrs who had faced danger, torture, and death, to promulgate Christianity, were remembered with just gratitude, when that religion became triumphant. Their bones were removed from unhonored graves to tombs more worthy of their virtues, and a generation enjoying the advantages that their toils and their blood had purchased, testified its thankfulness by rich offerings at their shrines. Thus the avaricious and the designing were tempted to multiply the number of relics, and to exaggerate their importance, until the feeling of thankful reverence was gradually changed into one of religious adoration. These steps in the progress of error were easy, they were likewise profitable; crafty men propagated stories of miracles wrought at the tombs of the martyrs, prayers were soon addressed to persons supposed to be possessed of such supernatural powers, the invocation of saints and the worship of relics naturally led to the introduction of images and pictures, and to the revival of many pagan ceremonies, which had, perhaps, never fallen into complete oblivion.

But an ecclesiastical establishment must not bear the entire blame of the introduction of image-worship into the Christian church. The desire of possessing representations of those whom we venerate is natural to the human mind; and in an age of ignorance, the symbols of a creed were found useful aids in teaching the multitude the historical facts of Christianity. It must, however, be observed, that the ignorance and credulity of the laity had a far greater share in leading to a corrupt use of images, than the craft of the clergy: the perversion was in many, perhaps in most instances, forced upon the priesthood by the flock, and it was still further supported by the monastic bodies, which have in every age been the most prominent among the originators and supporters of every superstition.

The monastics were the first who introduced what is called the voluntary principle, into the Christian church; they were also the first to allow self-ordained instructers to interfere with the duties of the proper pastors. Fanaticism and superstition were the necessary results of these disturbing forces, and by none was the progress of evil more seriously lamented than by the parochial clergy and the regular bishops.

The charge of idolatry was justly urged against the Christian church in the beginning of the eighth century, both by the Jews and the Mohammedans. The latter were far the more formidable, for to the arguments of truth they added the weight of victory. There was scarcely an eastern city which was not fortified by the possession of some miraculous image, supposed to be the palladium of its safety; but in spite of this protection they had fallen, one after the other, into the hands of the Mussulmans. Ashamed of the reproaches they encountered, and convinced practically of the insufficiency of these objects of their devotion, many of the eastern bishops began to oppose the worship of images, but their exertions were rendered unavailing, by the influence and obstinacy of the monks, until Leo the Isaurian ascended the throne of Constantinople.

A fierce struggle ensued: the Iconoclasts, as the opposers of images were called, made a vigorous effort to restore the purity of the Christian worship, and at the synod of Constantinople (A. D. 754) three hundred and thirty-eight bishops pronounced and subscribed a unanimous decree, that "all visible symbols of Christ, except in the eucharist, were either blasphemous or heretical; that image-worship was a corruption of Christianity, and a revival of paganism; that all such monuments of idolatry should be broken or erased; and that those who should refuse to give up the objects of their private superstition, should be deemed guilty of disobedience to the authority of the church and of the emperor."

The enemies of the Iconoclasts have spared no terms of reproach in denouncing the proceedings of this synod, but an impartial view of the authentic relics of its proceedings, which have been preserved, proves that its members displayed more of reason and piety than could have been expected in their age. They seem, indeed, to have felt that they were fighting the battle of episcopacy against monachism, and that the safety of their order was compromised by the assumptions of volunteer instructers; but they made no direct attack upon monastic institutions, and only assailed the abuses which they encouraged.

Six successive emperors supported the cause of reason and religion against idolatry in the eastern church, but the worshippers of images finally triumphed. Still, down to a very late period, there were prelates in the East who resisted the corruption, and the Armenians especially refused to admit images into their churches even in the twelfth century. But the contest was decided much sooner in western Europe, by the promptitude with which Pope Gregory II. appealed to arms against his sovereign and the Iconoclasts. The ambitious pontiff found sufficient support in the national enmity between the Greeks and Latins; he had the art to persuade the Italians that there was some connexion between the new superstition and their hereditary glory; and that, while they supported the worship of images, they were imposing a necessary restraint on Byzantine tyranny. The Lombards embraced the religious pretext to expel the Greeks from Italy; but the pope, finding that the conquerors were anxious to impose a yoke upon him more grievous than that which had just been shaken off, invoked the assistance of the Franks. Supported by the arms of Pepin and Charlemagne, the popes maintained the independence of the Roman territories, and were thus raised to the rank of temporal princes. Grateful for the aid they received, the pontiffs, as has been already mentioned, decided that it was lawful for the Franks to depose an imbecile sovereign, and substitute in his place one who had proved an able protector of the state, and a generous benefactor to the church; and in consequence of this sentence, Pepin was solemnly crowned at Paris.

The proper history of the papacy begins at this union of temporal and spiritual jurisdiction. Three transactions combined to give it form: the revolt against Leo, the establishment of the Roman principality, and the coronation of Pepin. In the first of these, the popes were hurried forward by circumstances to lengths which they had not anticipated; neither the second nor third Gregory wished to destroy completely the power of the Byzantine emperor, and they continued to acknowledge the successors of Constantine as their rulers, until the Lombards subverted the exarchate of Ravenna. But in spite of their moderation, real or affected, they had established to some extent the dangerous precedent, that the heresy of a sovereign justifies a withdrawal of allegiance in his subjects, though they themselves never asserted such a principle, and indeed seem never to have contemplated it.

The independence of the Roman principality, and the establishment of the pope as a temporal sovereign, necessarily resulted from the dread which the Latins, but especially the Romans, had of the Lombards. It was impossible to revert to the sovereigns of Constantinople; independent of the unpopularity produced by their Iconoclast propensities, they wanted the power of retaining the Italian provinces, even if the government had been offered them; there was no choice between the assertion of independence and submission to the Lombards; there were no materials for constructing a national government outside the precincts of the church, and the popes consequently became princes by the pressure of a necessity which was confessed by the unanimous consent of their subjects.

In sanctioning the usurpation of Pepin, Pope Zachary pronounced his opinion more as a statesman than a prelate. There was an obvious expediency for dethroning the weak Chilperic, and giving the title of king to him who really exercised the functions of royalty. There was nothing authoritative in the sentence—it did not command the Franks to dethrone one king and elect another—it merely declared that considerations of public safety justified a people in changing its rulers: it did nothing new, but it ratified what had been done already. But the new dynasty eagerly sought in the proceeding for a confirmation of their defective title; it was Pepin and his friends, rather than the pontiff, who perverted the opinion of a casuist into the sentence of a judge and the oracle of a prophet.

Thus popery, like most human institutions, was founded on opinions in which truth and falsehood were strangely mixed; and it is fortunately easy to separate the parts. In rejecting the Byzantine yoke, the popes asserted a right to resist, but not to depose, sovereigns; in becoming temporal princes, they declared that there could be a union between civil and ecclesiastical jurisdictions, but not that they were necessarily connected, and still less that they were inherited of right by the successors of St. Peter: finally, in the most equivocal case, the sanction of Pepin's election, the pope put forward the expediency of having an intelligent umpire to decide in cases of a dispute, not that he was necessarily that umpire; and still less that he had authority to act as supreme judge in a court of appeal. It is sufficiently obvious, however, that the truths are easily capable of being perverted into the falsehoods, and that there were strong temptations to the change. Ere a generation had passed away, the truths sank into oblivion, and the falsehoods were everywhere proclaimed as the true foundations of the papal system.

Section II.—*The early Development of the Political System of the Papacy.*

The Iconoclast controversy, and the mutual obligations of the popes and the Carlovingian family, form the important links between ancient and modern history, as well as between civil and ecclesiastical affairs. Pepin recognised the pope's arbitration as an authoritative act, though, as we have seen, it was merely an opinion founded on expediency, and furthermore might have been justified on constitutional grounds, for the monarchy of the Franks was originally elective, and the principle of hereditary right was an innovation gradually introduced by the successors of Clovis. But Pepin naturally felt that he would weaken the title of his sons to the succession, if he rested his claims on popular election; and he was therefore anxious to invest his dynasty with the mysterious sanction of religion. It is doubtful whether the Roman pontiffs foresaw the importance of the measures they adopted, but prudence and prophecy united could scarcely have suggested better means for extending the papal power. They revived the Jewish ceremonial of anointing kings; and Pepin, as well as his successors, regarded this ceremony as an assertion of a divine right to the crown; while the popes represented it, not as a simple recognition, but almost an appointment of the sovereign. Both the kings and the pontiffs shared in a profitable fraud, which gave security to the one, and power to the other; the Frank nobles murmured, without being able to discover the exact nature of the principles which destroyed for the future their ancient rights of election, though these principles were very intelligibly expressed by a new effort of Pope Stephen to gratify the new dynasty. Pressed by his enemies in Italy, Stephen III. sought Pepin's court to obtain aid, and gratified the monarch by solemnly crowning both his sons. In Pepin's case, the coronation had followed the election; and thus the popular rights were abolished almost at the moment that they were most strongly asserted. Royalty and popery gained, but not in equal proportions: for though the principles of divine right and inheritance by descent were established for kings, the higher power of pronouncing on these rights was reserved for the pontiffs.

The Carlovingians, grateful for the security thus given to their title, enlarged the papal dominions by territories wrested from the Lombard kingdom—the Greek exarchate. To secure these acquisitions, the pontiffs had recourse to a more daring fraud than any they had yet perpetrated: a forged deed was produced, purporting to be a donation from the first Christian emperor, Constantine, to the successors of St. Peter, of the sovereignty over Rome, Italy, and the western provinces. Thus the gift of the French monarch was made to appear the restitution of ancient possessions, and the temporal power of the popes, while yet in its infancy, was invested with the sanction of remote antiquity. It is useless to expose the falsehood of this audacious forgery, which is now condemned by even the most bigoted writers of the Romish church; but in its day it was universally received as valid, and was long regarded as the legal instrument by which the papal power was established.

Adrian I. was the pontiff who first combined the elements of the papacy into a system. He was startled at the very outset by a difficulty which seemed to threaten the foundation of his power. The Greek emperess, Irene, who administered the government during the reign of her son, Constantine the Porphyrogennete, re-established the worship of images, and persecuted the Iconoclasts. Adrian, however, was naturally reluctant to return under the Byzantine yoke, and were he even so inclined, he would probably have been prevented by the Romans; the popes had tasted the pleasures of sovereignty, and the people of freedom; neither, therefore, would sacrifice such advantages to the Greeks. A closer union was made with the Franks, though Charles and his bishops had stigmatized the worship of images, and declared they should be regarded only as objects of reverence. But the pope foresaw that the use of images would soon lead to their adoration, and he courted Charlemagne as a friend and protector.

Leo III., who succeeded Adrian, sent to Charlemagne the standard of Rome, requesting him to send delegates to receive the allegiance of the Romans. From the latter circumstance, it has been rather hastily inferred that the popes acknowledged the sovereignty of Charles; but, in truth, the relations between the pontiffs and the Frank monarchs were purposely left indefinite; any attempt to state them would have shown that the claims of both were irreconcilable, but their mutual interests required that they should combine, and each avoided explanations that might provoke a contest.

Leo soon experienced the benefits of his moderation; driven from Rome by the relatives of the late pope, he sought refuge among the Franks; and Charlemagne not only sent him back with a powerful escort to his capital, but went thither in person to do him justice. Leo was permitted to purge himself by oath of the crimes laid to his charge, and, in gratitude for his acquittal, he solemnly crowned Charles, Emperor of the West. The ceremony was performed on the festival of Christmas, in the last year of the eighth century; and the pontiff who had so recently stood before his sovereign as a criminal making his defence, now appeared as his superior, conferring on him the highest earthly title by the authority of Heaven.

There was obvious danger to papal ambition in the establishment of an empire; the successors of the Cæsars must of necessity have been formidable rivals to the successors of St. Peter; but there were many important advantages to be gained, which did not escape the notice of the crafty pontiffs. The secure enjoyment of their temporal dominions, as the most honorable species of fief or benefice, was obviously an immediate result, but there was a remote one of much greater importance, the change of the precedence, universally conceded to the Romish see, into an acknowledgment of its supremacy.

It is not easy to discover at what time the papacy directly fixed its attention upon destroying the independence of national churches, but assuredly the period was not very remote from that which we have been considering. The contests between the bishops of Rome and Constantinople, like those of more modern times between the archbishops of York and Canterbury, were struggles for dignity rather than power. The primacy which Boniface III. assumed, by taking the title of universal bishop, was nothing more than presidency: this was a good foundation for a future claim to supremacy, but there is no proof that any such claim was contemplated by Boniface, and every probability is against the supposition.

But when the independence of nations was compromised by the establishment of an empire, it was very natural that the independence of national churches should also be endangered. In the age of Charlemagne, law, order, and intelligence, had no sure support but religion: the popular opinion identified with ecclesiastical influence all that society enjoyed or hoped for; it was the bond that held the discordant parts of the empire together, and the emperor joined with the pope in giving it strength and unity.

The death of Charlemagne relieved the pontiffs from the pressure of imperial power; his successor, Louis the Debonnaire, had not strength of mind sufficient to support the weight of empire, while the popes stood ready to grasp the reins of power as they slipped from his hands; they began to exercise their pontifical functions immediately after their election, without waiting for the confirmation of their power, and Louis, embarrassed by nearer dangers, was unable to punish the usurpation. Louis divided his empire among his sons; a fatal error, for in their contests for supremacy the sovereign authority was sacrificed to the feudal lords, and to the spiritual power.

It must, however, be confessed, that the usurpations of the church, during the sanguinary wars between the successors of Charlemagne, were almost rendered necessary by the circumstances of the time. The competitors for empire were weak and cruel, the profligacy of the feudal lords was only equalled by their ignorance, and the church alone preserved the semblance of justice. The clergy of all ranks profited by the popular opinion in their favor; usurpation followed usurpation without provoking opposition: Charles the Bald acknowledged the right of the bishops to depose him, and the bishops of his council bound themselves by a canon to remain united, "for the correction of kings, the nobility, and the people." This gross assumption was applauded by the laity, at once ignorant, wicked, and devout: it was felt by all parties that supreme power should exist somewhere; kings, nobles, and commons, equally felt the want, and, in a greater or less degree, the consciousness that it could not safely be intrusted to themselves. Nicholas I., more bold than any of his predecessors, constituted himself the judge of bishops and kings: he deposed the archbishop of Ravenna for asserting his independence, and would not permit him to be restored until he acknowledged himself a vassal of the holy see: he even cited the king of Lorraine to appear before his tribunal (A. D. 860). Lothaire, king of Lorraine, had divorced his first wife, Theutberga, on a charge of adultery, and, by the advice of his council, chosen a beautiful young lady, called Valdrade, for his second queen. The pope annulled the second marriage, and compelled Lothaire to take back his first wife; he persevered in enforcing his edict, even after Theutberga herself had submitted to the pretensions of her rival.

Adrian II. was chosen successor to Nicholas; the imperial ambassadors were excluded from the election, and their remonstrances treated with neglect. He interfered on the side of justice, to secure the inheritance of Lorraine for the emperor Louis II., but the pontiff was foiled by the firmness of Charles the Bald, and his claims to decide between the competitors refuted by Hincmar, archbishop of Rheims. Adrian resolved to conciliate the prince whom he could not subdue, and won Charles to submission by promising him the succession to the empire. This project was executed by Adrian's successor, John VIII.; finding that the king of France was determined to have the title of emperor on any terms, he made him stipulate to acknowledge the independence of Rome and its territory, and to confess that he only held the empire by the gift of the pope.

In an assembly held at Pavia (A. D. 878), Charles was recognised by the Italian prelates and nobles in the following memorable words: "Since the Divine favor, through the merits of the holy apostles and of their vicar Pope John, has raised you to the empire, according to the judgment of the Holy Ghost, we elect you unanimously for our protector and lord." The pontiff by no means suffered Charles to forget that the empire was his gift: when the Saracens invaded Italy, he wrote to Charles, reproaching him for his delay in affording succor, and desiring him, "to remember the hand that had given him the empire, lest, if driven to despair, we should change our opinion."

But while the popes were thus triumphant over the emperors, they were severely harassed by the turbulent feudal lords, who had taken advantage of the weakness of their sovereign, to establish a virtual independence. They interfered in the pontifical elections, and generally controlled them; they insulted, imprisoned, and murdered the pontiffs; while the claims of the apostolic see to complete supremacy were tacitly acknowledged throughout Europe, it was itself held in disgraceful servitude by petty tyrants. Two infamous prostitutes, by their influence with the profligate nobles, procured the throne of St. Peter for their paramours, and their illegitimate children; and the disorders of the church finally attained such a height that the imperial power was once more raised above the papal, and Pope John XII. deposed by the emperor Otho.

The vices of this dark period are not justly attributable to popery; they were the result of feudalism, and so far as the papal system was able to exert any influence, it was employed in counteracting these evils. The great error of the pontiffs was, that they did not arrange a judicious plan for elections; they left their power thus exposed to the disturbances of a disputed succession which had already proved fatal to the imperial power: had the arrangements been such as to prevent any lay interference, ecclesiastical influence would have gone on increasing without interruption. But the vice and violence of the Roman nobles rendered popery, as a system, for a time inoperative, and prevented a Nicholas from anticipating a Hildebrand

SECTION III.—*The Struggle for Supremacy between the Popes and Emperors.*

OTHO, deservedly called the Great, was the third emperor of Germany, elected by the suffrage of the German princes. His high character pointed him out to Pope John XII. as a proper protector for the church and the republic, against the fierce nobles of Lombardy, but especially against Berengarius, who claimed the kingdom of Italy. Otho crossed the Alps, tranquillized Italy, and was rewarded with the iron crown of Lombardy, and the revived title of Emperor of the West. But both the pope and the Romans were jealous of their benefactor, and even during the ceremony of his coronation, Otho had to take precautions against the daggers of assassins. John soon found that the German emperor was not content with an empty title; enraged at the progress of the imperial authority, he entered into a secret compact with Adelbert, the son of his ancient enemy, to expel foreigners from Italy, and, at the same time, he invited the Hungarians to invade Germany.

Otho promptly returned to Italy, and having entered Rome, he compelled the nobles and people to renew their oath of allegiance. He then summoned a council for the trial of Pope John, whose immoralities were flagrant and notorious. The charges against the pontiff contained a dreadful catalogue of crimes, but we can not vouch for the integrity of the witnesses, or the impartiality of the court. There is, however, no doubt that John was a licentious profligate, whose vices not only disgraced his station, but were shocking to humanity. The pope refusing to appear before the tribunal, was condemned as contumacious, after having been twice summoned in vain. Leo VIII. was elected to the papacy, in the room of John, and he not only took an oath of obedience and fidelity to the emperor, but issued a bull, ordaining that Otho and his successors should have a right of appointing the popes, and investing bishops and archbishops; and that none should dare to consecrate a bishop without the permission of the emperor.

This fatal blow to the papacy was unpopular with the bishops; they complained that Leo had subverted, at one blow, the structure which his predecessors had toiled to raise during two centuries. When John, after the emperor's departure, returned to Rome, he easily procured the deposition of Leo, and the acknowledgment of his own claims. The restored pope began to exercise great cruelties against his opponents; but in the midst of his career, he was assassinated by a young nobleman, whom he had rivalled in the affections of his mistress. Such horror had this pontiff's crimes inspired, that many of the Romans believed that Satan in proper person had struck the fatal blow which sent him to his dread account, "with all his imperfections on his head."

The adherents of John still refused to acknowledge Leo, and without consulting the emperor, they chose Benedict to succeed the murdered pontiff. But the return of Otho threw them into confusion: Benedict hastily tendered his submission to Leo, by whom he was banished; and the Roman nobility and clergy promised the emperor that they would never confer the papal dignity on any but a native of Germany. On the death of Leo, the electors, obedient to their promise, chose John XIII. by the emperor's permission. The pope was too grateful to his sovereign, to resist the encroachments of the imperial power on the city and the church: the turbulent Romans revolted and threw John into prison, but Otho soon came to suppress these disturbances. He restored John, and severely punished the authors of the revolt. Thus the political system of popery seemed utterly ruined, the pontiff ruled the Roman states as a lieutenant instead of a prince, and, far from being regarded as the supreme umpire of monarchs, he was reduced to the condition of a subject.

We have seen that the papacy owed its first success to the national hatred between the Latins and the Byzantines; strength for a new struggle to retrieve its fortunes was derived from the animosity with which the Germans were regarded by the Italians. The death of Otho (A. D. 973), was the signal for new convulsions in Italy; the feudal lords aimed at independence, the cities tried to establish freedom; Pope John tried to uphold the imperial cause, but he was arrested by Cincius, the head of the popular party, and strangled in prison.

Cincius and his faction chose Boniface VII. for their spiritual head; the aristocratic party, headed by the counts of Tuscany, elected Benedict VII.; the former was soon driven from the capital; he sought shelter at Constantinople, where he strenuously urged the Greek emperors to invade Italy. These princes took his advice, and, uniting themselves with the Saracens, subdued Apulia and Calabria. Otho II. vanquished these enemies; but when he returned to Germany, Boniface came back to Italy, made himself master of Rome, and threw his rival into prison, where he was starved to death. Four months afterward the murderer died suddenly, and was succeeded by John XV.

So low had the papacy now sunk, that the whole of John's reign was occupied by a struggle for the government of the city of Rome. Crescentius, an ambitious noble, eager to establish his own despotism under the name of freedom, persuaded the citizens to reject the authority both of the pope and the emperor. Otho II. crushed the revolt, and so firmly established the imperial authority, that he was enabled to nominate one of his creatures successor to John; and the cardinals received as their head Bruno, a Saxon stranger, who took the title of Gregory V.*

Crescentius had little trouble in exciting a new insurrection; but the Italians were too feeble to contend with the entire strength of the empire; they were defeated with ruinous loss; their leader was captured and beheaded. On the death of Gregory, Otho nominated Gerbert to the papal dignity, and he was installed under the title of Sylvester II. Although he did not foresee the consequences, Sylvester may be re

* Every pope changes his name on his accession, in imitation of St. Peter, whom our Lord called Cephas, or Peter, instead of Simon.

garded as the first who made any progress in restoring the power of popery. His personal virtues removed the scandal which had long weakened the influence of his see, his patronage of learning restored to the church its superiority in intelligence, and, through his intimacy with the emperor, he obtained a renewal of the temporal grants which Charlemagne and Pepin had made to his predecessors. The popes now began to support the imperial cause against the turbulent nobles of Italy; in return they were aided by the emperors in their struggles with the Roman princes and citizens; but by this alliance the pontiffs were the principal gainers, for the emperor's attention was distracted by various objects while the popes were always on the spot to secure the fruit of every victory. So rapidly had their power been retrieved, that when Benedict VIII. crowned the emperor Henry, to whom he owed the preservation of his dignity, he demanded of his benefactor, before he entered the church: "Will you observe your fidelity to me and my successors in everything?" and the emperor had the weakness to answer in the affirmative.

But the factions of the Roman nobles and citizens prevented the papal power from being consolidated; three rival popes, each remarkable for his scandalous life, shared the revenues of the church between them (A. D. 1045); they were finally persuaded to resign by John Gratian, a priest of piety and learning, and he was elected to the vacant throne by the title of Gregory VI. The emperor Henry procured the deposition of Gregory, and the election of Clement II.

The most remarkable of the deposed popes was Benedict IX.; he was the son of a Tusculan count, and was raised to the chair of St. Peter at the early age of ten years. His vices induced the Romans to raise rivals against him; but, supported by the aristocratic faction, he would probably have held his place, had he not been bribed to resign in favor of Gregory. The agent in this transaction was Hildebrand, the son of humble parents, who had raised himself by the force of his abilities and his reputation for piety to high rank in the church, and commanding influence in the state. Gregory was undoubtedly a better ruler than his immediate predecessors; he expelled the robbers and freebooters who infested the roads around Rome; he opened a secure passage for the pilgrims who wished to visit the shrine of St. Peter, and he vigorously exerted himself to reform the administration of justice. It was imprudent in the emperor Henry to depose such a man at the instigation of the enemies of order; Clement II. felt great aversion to the proceeding, and very reluctantly consented to his own elevation.

Gregory and Hildebrand, to the great regret of the Italian people, and especially the citizens of Rome, were driven into exile; they retired to the celebrated monastery of Clugni, where Gregory died of vexation, leaving Hildebrand the heir of his wealth and his resentment. Clement was poisoned by an emissary of Benedict nine months after his consecration; and his successor, Damasus II., shared the same fate. When the news reached Hildebrand, he immediately departed from the imperial court, hoping to have some influence in the nomination of the next pope, but on the road he learned that the Diet of Worms, directed by the emperor, had elected Bruno, bishop of Toul, under the title of Leo IX.

We have now reached an important crisis in the struggle between the papal and the imperial power; the latter had touched the highest point of its greatness, and was destined to fall by the dauntless energies of one man, Hildebrand, the humble monk of Soano by birth, the controller of the destiny of nations by talent and position.

Section IV.—*Revival of the Papal Power.*

from A. D. 1048 to A. D. 1070.

We have seen that papal usurpation began by an attack on the power of the Greek empire, and prevailed over the Byzantine court, because it was supported by the public opinion of western Europe. To secure its acquisitions, the papacy entered into alliance with the Carlovingian dynasty on terms favorable to both; but in the struggle that followed the partition of Charlemagne's empire, it was shorn of its strength, for the growth of its greatness was too rapid to be permanent. When the nobles of Italy had attained the rank of petty princes, the territorial possessions of the church, naturally excited their cupidity, and when the German emperors had extended their sway beyond the Alps, they felt that a controlling influence in the papal elections was necessary to the permanence of their power. Had both combined, the papacy would have been annihilated, the pope would have been a mere vassal of the emperor, and his temporal dominions would have been rent in sunder by rival princes. But even when the papacy was enslaved, either to aristocratic factions, or to despotic autocrats, it was secretly collecting materials for its liberation and future triumph. It was generating an opinion which gave the papacy, as an institution, greater strength and surer permanence than it possessed in the days of its former prosperity.

It was under the pressure of the feudal system that the organization of popery was completed and defined; opposed both to princes and emperors, it was thrown for support entirely on the people. By its numerous gradations of rank, the church of the middle ages linked itself with every class of the community: its bishops were the companions of princes; its priests claimed reverence in the baronial hall; its preaching friars and monks brought consolation to the cottage of the suffering peasant. Great as were the vices of individuals, the organization of the clerical body continued to be respectable, and this was an immense advantage when every other portion of civilized society was a mass of confusion. When the distinction of caste was rigidly established in all the political forms of social life, the church scarcely knew any aristocracy but that of talent; once received into holy orders, the serf lost all traces of his bondage; he was not merely raised to an equality with the former lord, but he could aspire to dignities which threw those of temporal princes into the shade. The clerical was thus identified with the popular cause, and the bulk of the laity not only received the claims of the priesthood, but gave them additional extension.

Hildebrand was the first who perceived the tendency and the strength of this current, and he probably was sincere in his belief that the church supplied the only means by which the regeneration of Europe could be effected. Feudalism, the worst of foes to social order, stood opposed to the sovereignty of the monarch and the liberty of the subject; the emperors were too weak, the people too ignorant, to struggle against it; and the wise arrangements of Providence, by which good has been so frequently wrought out of evil, made the revival of popery the instrument by which Europe was rescued from barbarism. Hildebrand's personal character is really a matter of no importance; his measures in the present age would justly subject him to the charge of extravagant ambition and blundering tyranny; but in the eleventh century, every one of these measures was necessary to counteract some evil principle, and milder or more justifiable means would not have been adequate to the occasion. We must not pass sentence on an institution without examining the opinion on which it is founded; and before we judge of the opinion, we must estimate the circumstances by which it was engendered. The disorganized state of Europe produced a strong opinion that some power for appeal and protection should be constituted; a power with intelligence to guide its decisions, and sanctity to enforce respect for them: the revived papacy seemed an institution suited to these conditions, and under the circumstances it was capable of being rendered the great instrument for reforming civil society.

Hildebrand's own writings prove that his design was to render the papacy such an institution as we have described; it was indeed a beautiful theory to base power upon intelligence, and concentrate both in the church. But Hildebrand did not make a discovery which too often has eluded reformers and legislators, that his plan was suited only to peculiar circumstances, that it was only applicable to a period when state power was corrupt and popular intelligence restricted, and that to give it permanence was to extend its duration beyond the period of its utility, and consequently prepare the way for its becoming just as mischievous as the evils it had been devised to counteract.

This general view of the state of society will enable us to form a better judgment of the struggle in which Hildebrand engaged than could be done if we confined ourselves to a simple narrative; we shall now proceed to relate the course adopted by the enterprising monk to exalt the spiritual power.

Leo IX., on whom the emperor, as we have said, conferred the papacy, was a prelate of virtuous principles and strict integrity, but he was a man infirm of purpose, and weak in understanding. Hildebrand was well aware of the advantages that might be derived from the pope's character, and in his first interview he gained such an ascendency over Leo's mind, that henceforth the pope was a passive instrument in the hands of his adviser. The pontiff naturally dreaded that the circumstance of his having been nominated by the emperor, and elected by a German diet, would render him unpopular in Italy; but Hildebrand smoothed the way, and by his personal influence secured Leo a favorable reception at Rome. This service was rewarded by an accumulation of dignities; Hildebrand soon united in his person the titles and offices of cardinal, sub-deacon, abbot of St. Paul, and keeper of the altar and treasury of St. Peter. The clergy and people of Rome applauded these proceedings, because the favorite had induced Leo to gratify the national vanity, by submitting to the form of a new election immediately after his arrival in the city.

Leo made unremitting exertions to reform the clergy and the monastic orders ; but, in the fifth year of his reign he marched against the Normans, who were ravaging the south of Italy, and was unfortunately taken prisoner. Though the conquerors showed every respect to their captive, the misfortune weighed heavily on his proud spirit; and his grief was aggravated by the reproaches of some of his clergy, who condemned him for desecrating his holy office by appearing in arms. He died of a broken heart soon after his liberation, and the deposed Benedict IX. seized the opportunity of reascending the papal throne.

Hildebrand was opposed to the imperial influence, but he hated more intensely the nearer and more dangerous power of the Italian nobles, and therefore he became an active and energetic opponent of their creature, Benedict. The monastic orders supported one whom they justly regarded as the pride and ornament of their body, and by their means Hildebrand gained such a commanding influence over the Roman people, that he could truly represent himself to the emperor as their delegate in choosing a new pope. Henry nominated a German bishop to the dignity, who took the name of Victor II., and the cardinal-monk hoped to exercise the same authority in the new reign that he had possessed under Leo IX. The pope, however, soon became weary of having "a viceroy over him;" he sent his ambitious minister into France with the title of legate, under the honorable pretext of correcting the abuses that had crept into the Gallican church. Hildebrand performed his task with more rigor than it would have been prudent for a less popular minister to display; he excommunicated several immoral priests and bishops, and even sentenced some monks to death for a breach of their monastic vows. After a year's absence he returned to Rome more powerful than ever, and Victor was content to receive him as his chief adviser and director.

In the meantime the emperor Henry died, and was succeeded by his son of the same name, who was yet an infant. Hildebrand was too sagacious not to discover the advantage with which the papal power would struggle against the imperial during a minority, and he secretly prepared for the contest. The death of Victor, speedily followed by that of his successor, Stephen IX., delayed, but did not alter, the cardinal-monk's intentions, for circumstances compelled him to appear as an advocate of the imperial authority.

On the death of Stephen, the aristocratic faction, presuming on the minority of the emperor, rushed at night, with a body of armed men, into the Vatican church, where they declared John, bishop of Velitri, one of heir body, pope, with the title of Benedict X. Hildebrand received this intelligence as he returned from Germany; it was brought to him by the terrified cardinals and bishops who had fled from Rome; he assembled the fugitives at Sienna, and prevailed upon them to elect the bishop of Florence, who took the name Nicholas II. The emperor's sanction was easily procured for the latter election, and the imperial court was persuaded that it was supporting its own interests when it placed Nicholas upon the papal throne.

Circumstances soon occurred to prove that the Germans had been deluded; Nicholas assembled a council at Rome, in which it was decreed that the cardinals alone should in future have a voice in the election of the pope; but to avoid any open breach with the emperor, a clause was added, reserving to him all due honor and respect. A less equivocal proceeding soon followed; the Normans, who had settled in the south of Italy, had become more amenable to the church than they had been in the days of Leo. The lust of conquest was abated, and they were now anxious to obtain some security for their possessions; they therefore tendered their alliance and feudal allegiance to the pope, on condition of his confirming their titles. By the advice of Hildebrand, Nicholas gave to Richard Guiscard the principality of Capua, and granted Robert Guiscard the title of duke, with the investiture of all the lands he had conquered, or should conquer, in Sicily, Apulia, and Calabria.

The pope readily granted that to which he had no right, a proceeding that might have cost him dear, if the old emperor had survived: the Normans, in return, lent their aid to punish the enemies of Nicholas in the Roman territory. The lands of the turbulent aristocracy were ravaged with unsparing cruelty, and it is to the desolation thus produced, that the depopulation of the country round Rome, even at the present day, must be attributed.

While Hildebrand was maturing his plans for re-establishing the papacy, many circumstances occurred, which proved the expediency of establishing a central controlling power in the church. The ecclesiastics of Milan had been, for nearly two hundred years, independent of the holy see, and their church had become the scandal of Italy. Benefices were openly sold, immoralities flagrantly practised, until at length a respectable portion of the laity requested the interference of the pope. Peter Damian was sent as a legate to Milan, but the populace, incited by the priests, raised a formidable insurrection, and threatened to murder him for menacing their independence. Peter, undismayed, ascended a pulpit in one of their principal churches, and made such an effective discourse, that the rioters not only submitted, but encouraged him to pursue his task of investigation. The inquiry proved, that nearly every priest in Milan had purchased his preferment, and lived with a concubine. The archbishop, after an obstinate resistance, was brought to confess, that he had transgressed the canons; but he was pardoned by the legate, on condition of swearing, with his clergy, to observe the ecclesiastical rules for the future. Scarcely, however, had the legate departed, when the clergy assailed the archbishop for betraying the rights of their church, and compelled him to retract the conditions to which he had so recently sworn. The troubles in Milan burst out afresh, and the profligacy of the clergy seemed to have been increased by the temporary interruption.

Ere Nicholas could make any effort to terminate these disorders, he was seized by a mortal disease; his death made a great change in the political aspect of Italy, for the church party, encouraged by Hildebrand, set both the emperor and the aristocracy at defiance. The cardinals and bishops, without waiting for the imperial sanction, conferred the papacy on Anselmo, bishop of Lucca, who took the title of Alexander II.; on the other hand, the counts of Tuscany, hoping to recover the lands that had been wrested from them by the Normans, declared that they would support the emperor's right of nomination. The Roman nobles had hitherto owed their partial success to their having sup ported a national prelate; they soon found that their strength was gone, when they gave their aid to a foreign competitor. Supported by a German and Lombard army, Cadislaus, who had been chosen by the emperor, appeared before the gates of Rome, but the citizens refused him admission. At first the imperialists gained some advantages, but the arrival of Duke Godfrey, with an auxiliary force of Normans, changed the fortunes of the war, and Cadislaus was compelled to make a hasty retreat. He sought refuge in the castle of St. Angelo, where he was closely besieged. Soon afterward, the young emperor, having been removed by a stratagem from the protection of his mother, was placed under the control of the archbishops of Bremen and Cologne; at their instigation he recognised Alexander as the legitimate pope, and Cadislaus, finding himself abandoned by his principal protector, fled in disguise from the castle of St. Angelo to his native diocese, where he died in obscurity.

During the brief reign of Alexander, Hildebrand was the real governor of the church. As soon as the war with Cadislaus was ended, he directed his attention to the affairs of Milan, excommunicating the perjured archbishop, and ordering that all the priests who were married, or who lived in concubinage, should be ejected from their cures. Supported by the populace and a large body of the nobles, the papal legate not only enforced this decree, but obtained from the clergy and people a solemn oath, that, for the future, they would hold no election of a bishop valid, unless it was confirmed by the pope.

The excommunicated archbishop resigned his see, and sent the insignia of his office, the pastoral rod and ring, to the emperor. Godfrey, a deacon of Milan, was appointed to supply the vacancy by the imperial council; but the citizens of Milan refused to receive him, and chose for their archbishop, Atto, a nominee of the pope. A fierce war raged between the rival prelates, and Alexander, indignant at the support that Godfrey received from the emperor, summoned that prince to appear before his tribunal, on a charge of simony, and granting investitures without the approbation of the see of Rome.

Neither the ambition nor the cares of Pope Alexander, or rather his instigator Hildebrand, were confined to the Italian peninsula. By means of the popularity which the pretensions of the mendicant friars had given their order throughout Europe, he established an interest for himself in every part of Christendom. Faithful agents kept a strict watch over the proceedings of the emperor Henry, legates were sent to Denmark and Norway, the allegiance of the king of Bohemia was secured by permission to wear the mitre, and the virtual independence of the Anglo-Saxon church was destroyed by the Norman conquest, to the success of which the interference of the pope and of Hildebrand materially contributed.

The pretexts of the pontiffs are characteristics of the superstitions of the age. Harold, the last Saxon monarch of England, had, during an accidental visit to Normandy, been forced to swear that he would favor the succession of William, whose claims were founded on a real or pretended promise of Edward the Confessor. This compulsory oath, it seems, would not have been considered binding, had not Harold unwittingly sworn it on a chest of relics, collected from all the surrounding churches. When, therefore, on the death of Edward, he accepted he crown, proffered to him by the free voice of the Anglo-Saxons, he was regarded, not as a patriot resolved to maintain his country's independence, but as a perjured wretch who had trampled on the most solemn obligations. Hildebrand eagerly seized this opportunity of establishing the papal supremacy over a national church, whose claims to independence had long given offence at Rome. At his instigation, the claims of the Norman duke to the English crown were solemnly recognised by the papal council: a bull containing this decision was sent to William, together with a consecrated standard, and a ring, said to contain a hair from the head of St. Peter, enclosed in a diamond of considerable value. But we learn from a letter, subsequently addressed by Hildebrand to the conqueror, that there were some in the conclave who opposed this iniquitous interference with the rights of nations, and severely reproached the cardinal-monk for advocating the cause of a tyrannical usurper.

But Hildebrand did not extend to the Normans in Italy the same favor that he showed to their brethren in England. Aided by the forces of the countess Matilda, a devoted adherent of the church, and heiress to a considerable territory, he forced them to resign the districts they had wrested from the holy see. Anxious to retain this sovereignty, Hildebrand violently opposed a marriage between the countess and Godfrey Gobbo, a son whom her step-father had by a former wife, before his marriage with her mother. Such a union, indeed, was warranted by the strict letter of the canonical degrees, but still it was, in some degree, revolting to the feelings. Gobbo was excommunicated, but Hildebrand secretly hinted that he might be reconciled to the church, on making proper submissions.

But all these political struggles were cast into the shade, by the daring citation of the emperor Henry: every one regarded it as a declaration of war between the spiritual and temporal authorities, and it must have been obvious to all, that the death of Alexander II. only delayed the contest. More had been done during the reign of this pope to extend the authority of the papacy, than in any former pontificate, but this must not be attributed either to the faults or to the merits of Alexander, who was a mere instrument in the hands of his ambitious minister. The monks, to raise Hildebrand's fame, published tales of the numerous miracles he wrought, which were greedily received by the superstitious populace, and tended greatly to extend his influence. we have taken no notice of these legends; a greater miracle than any they record, is, that rational beings should be found sufficiently credulous to believe and repeat such monstrous absurdities.

Section V.—*Pontificate of Gregory VII.*

FROM A. D. 1073 TO A. D. 1086.

There were few statesmen in any part of Christendom, who did not dread the accession of Hildebrand to the papacy, but there were none prepared to provoke his resentment by interfering to prevent his election. The irregular and precipitate manner in which he was chosen, seems to prove that some opposition was dreaded by his partisans; and

Hildebrand himself found it necessary to disarm hostility, by an affectation of submission to the emperor. He wrote to Henry, that he had been chosen against his will, that he had no wish for the office, and that he would not be consecrated without the imperial sanction. Deceived by this hypocrisy, Henry ratified the irregular election, and Hildebrand was enthroned with the title of Gregory VII.

No sooner was he secured on the throne, than he began to put in execution his favorite plan for securing the independence of the church, by preventing lay interference in the collation of benefices. Before he had been a month elected, he sent a legate into Spain, to reform the ecclesiastical abuses of that kingdom; but principally to claim for the apostolic see all the conquests that had recently been made from the Moors, under the pretence that the Spanish peninsula, before the Saracenic invasion, had been tributary to the successors of St. Peter. Henry was so much daunted by this and similar displays of vigor, that he sent a submissive letter to the pontiff, acknowledging his former errors in his dispute with Alexander, which he attributed to his youth and the influence of evil counsellors, desiring him to arrange the troubles in the church of Milan at his discretion, and promising to assist him in everything with the imperial authority.

The two great objects of the pope were, to enforce the celibacy of the clergy, and the papal right to the investiture of bishops. The former of these projects was a matter of discipline, defended on plausible grounds of expediency. Its advocates pleaded that a clergyman unencumbered with the cares of a family could devote his whole attention to the flock intrusted to his charge; and that a bishop without children would be free to exercise his patronage without being warped by domestic affection. On the other hand, men were thus forced to sacrifice the noblest and best of human feelings; they were denaturalized, cut off from the influences of social life: the church became the country and the home of every person who embraced the ecclesiastical profession. After ordination, the priest and the bishop were no longer Germans, Spaniards, or Englishmen; they were Romans—ministers and peers of a mighty empire, that claimed the dominion of the whole globe. Like the envoy or minister of any foreign government, a member of the Romish hierarchy observes the laws of the state in which his master may have placed him, and respects for a time the authority of the local magistrate: but his order is his country, the pontiff is his natural sovereign, and their welfare and their honor are the appropriate objects of his public care. The constant sight of such a sacrifice of the natural feelings of mankind, was obviously calculated to win the respect of the laity, and gain credence for the superior sanctity that was supposed to invest the character of a priest.

The pope's determination to destroy the practice of lay investitures, was defended on more plausible grounds. The administration of ecclesiastical patronage by the emperor and other temporal princes, was liable to great abuses, and had actually led to many: they supplied vacancies with the ignorant, the depraved, and the violent; they sought for the qualifications of a soldier or a politician, when they had to elect a bishop. In a dark age, when monarchs and nobles were rarely able to write their own names; when the knowledge of the alphabet, even in aristocratic families, was so rare as to be deemed a spell against witchcraft; and when the fierce qualities of a warrior were valued more highly than the Christian virtues, it seemed almost necessary to render appointments in the church independent of the state. But to this obvious expediency, Gregory VII. added a blasphemous claim of right, as Christ's vicar on earth, and inheritor of his visible throne. While, however, we condemn such impious assumptions, we should not refuse to Hildebrand the credit of higher and purer motives than those of personal aggrandizement, mingling in his schemes for extending his own power and that of his successors. It is undeniable that the corporate authority he procured for the church became, in many European countries, a source of much benefit during the middle ages, overawing the violent, protecting the forlorn, mitigating the prevailing ferocity of manners, and supplying in various ways the defects of civil institutions.

Gregory having assembled a general council at Rome, ordained, by consent of the bishops present, that if any one should accept investiture from a layman, both the giver and the receiver should be excommunicated; that the prelates and nobles who advised the emperor to claim the collation of benefices should be excommunicated; and that all married priests should dismiss their wives, or be deposed. These decrees were communicated to the sovereigns of Europe by Gregory himself, in letters that must ever remain a monument of his consummate abilities. His monstrous claims for the universal supremacy of the church and of the Romish see, are proposed in a tone of humility and candor, well calculated to win the unthinking and unwary; his dictations assume the form of affectionate suggestions, and his remonstrances resemble those of a tender and affectionate father.

But the pope did not confine his exertions to mere words; he obliged the Normans to quit their conquests in Campania, proposed a crusade against the Saracens, who were menacing Constantinople, and offered a province in Italy to Sweno, king of Denmark, under the pretence that the inhabitants were heretics. The emperor Henry was not deceived by Gregory's professions; he hated the pontiff in his heart, and had good reason to believe that the enmity was reciprocal. It was therefore with mingled jealousy and indignation that he saw a new power established which more than rivalled his own, and he entered into a secret alliance with the Normans against their common enemy. In the meantime, a conspiracy was formed against the pope in Rome itself by some of the aristocracy, whose privileges he had invaded. Cincius, the prefect of the city, arrested the pontiff while he was celebrating mass on Christmas day, and threw him into prison; but the populace soon rescued their favorite, Cincius would have been torn to pieces but for Gregory's interference, and all who had shared in this act of violence were banished from the city. Soon afterward, Gregory cited the emperor to appear before the council at Rome, to answer to the charge of protecting excommunicated bishops, and granting investitures without the sanction of the holy see. Henry, enraged by the insult, and relieved from his anxieties in Germany by a recent victory over the Saxons, resolved to temporize no longer. He assembled a synod at Worms, of the princes and prelates devoted to his cause, and procured sentence of deposition against Gregory, on a charge of simony, murder, and atheism.

Gregory was far from being disheartened by the emperor's violence; he assembled a council at Rome, solemnly excommunicated Henry, absolved his subjects in Germany and Italy from their oath of allegiance, deposed several prelates in Germany, France, and Lombardy, and published a series of papal constitutions, in which the claims of the Roman pontiffs to supremacy over all the sovereigns of the earth were asserted in the plainest terms.

The most important of these resolutions, which form the basis of the political system of popery, were—

That the Roman pontiff alone can be called universal.

That he alone has a right to depose bishops.

That his legates have a right to preside over all bishops assembled in a general council.

That the pope can depose absent prelates.

That he alone has a right to use imperial ornaments.

That princes are bound to kiss his feet, and his only.

That he has a right to depose emperors.

That no synod or council summoned without his commission can be called general.

That no book can be called canonical without his authority.

That his sentence can be annulled by none, but that he may annul the decrees of all.

That the Roman church has been, is, and will continue, infallible.

That whoever dissents from the Romish church ceases to be a catholic Christian.

And, that subjects may be absolved from their allegiance to wicked princes.

Some cautious prelates advised Gregory not to be too hasty in excommunicating his sovereign; to their remonstrances he made the following memorable reply: "When Christ trusted his flock to St. Peter, saying, 'Feed my sheep,' did he except kings? Or when he gave him the power to bind and loose, did he withdraw any one from his visitation? He, therefore, who says that he can not be bound by the bonds of the church, must confess that he can not be absolved by it; and he who denies that doctrine, separates himself from Christ and his church."

Both parties now prepared for war, but all the advantages were on the side of Gregory At the very commencement of the struggle, Gobbo, the most vigorous supporter of the emperor, died, and his widow, the countess Matilda, placed all her resources at the disposal of the pontiff. So completely, indeed, did this princess devote herself to support the interests of Gregory, that their mutual attachment was suspected of having transgressed the limits of innocence. The duke of Dalmatia, gratified by the title of king, and the Norman monarch of Sicily, proffered aid to the pontiff; even the Mohammedan emperor of Morocco courted his favor, and presented him with the liberty of the Christian slaves in his dominions.

Henry, on the contrary, knew not where to look for support; in every quarter of his dominions monks and friars preached against their sovereign, and the prelates by whom he had been supported · the Saxon nobles eagerly embraced a religious pretext to renew their insurrection; the dukes of Suabia and Carinthia demanded a change of dynasty; even the prelates who had been most zealous in urging Henry forward, terrified by threats of excommunication, abandoned his cause. A diet was assembled at Tribur, attended by two papal legates, in which it was resolved that Henry should be deposed, unless within a limited period he presented himself before the pope and obtained absolution.

The prelates and nobles of Lombardy alone maintained their courage, and boldly retorted the excommunications of Gregory. Animated by the hope of obtaining their efficient aid, Henry resolved to cross the Alps instead of waiting for Gregory's arrival in Germany. The hardships which the unfortunate monarch underwent during this journey, in the depth of a severe winter—the dangers to which he was exposed from the active malice of his enemies—the sight of the sufferings of his queen and child, who could only travel by being enclosed in the hides of oxen, and thus dragged through the Alpine passes—would have broken a sterner spirit than Henry's. He entered Lombardy completely disheartened, and, though joined by considerable forces, he thought only of conciliating his powerful enemy by submission. Having obtained a conference with the countess Matilda, Henry prevailed upon her to intercede for him with the pope; and her intercession, supported by the principal nobles of Italy, induced Gregory to grant an interview to his sovereign.

On the 21st of January, 1077, Henry proceeded to Canosa, where the pope resided, and was forced to submit to the greatest indignities that were ever heaped upon imperial majesty. At the first barrier, he was compelled to dismiss his attendants; when he reached the second, he was obliged to lay aside his imperial robes, and assume the habit of a penitent. For three entire days he was forced to stand barefooted and fasting, from morning till night, in the outer court of the castle, during one of the severest winters that had ever been known in northern Italy, imploring pardon of his transgressions from God and the pope. He was at length admitted into the presence of the haughty pontiff, and, after all his submissions, obtained, not the removal, but the suspension of the excommunication.

Such harsh treatment sank deep into Henry's mind; and his hostility to Gregory was exasperated by the pontiff accepting a grant of the countess Matilda's possessions for the use of the church, which would legally revert to the empire after her decease. The reproaches of the Lombards also induced him to repent of his degradation, and he renewed the war by a dishonorable and ineffectual attempt to arrest Gregory and Matilda. In the meantime the discontented nobles of Germany had assembled a diet at Fercheim, deposed their sovereign, and elected Rodolph, duke of Suabia, to the empire. This proceeding greatly embarrassed the pope; he dared not declare against Henry, who was powerful in Italy, and if he abandoned Rodolph, he would ruin his own party in Germany. He resolved to preserve a neutrality in the contest, and in the meantime he directed his attention to the internal state of the church, which had for some time been distracted by the controversy respecting the eucharist.

It is not easy to determine by whom the doctrine of transubstantiation was first broached: Selden very justly says, "This opinion is only rhetoric turned into logic," and it is easy to see how the spiritual presence of our Savior in the holy communion might, in a dark and ignorant age, be represented as an actual change of the consecrated elements into his material substance. We are not concerned with the theological errors of this doctrine; our subject only requires us to notice the political purposes to which it was applied. No article of faith was better calculated to exalt the power of the priesthood; it represented them as daily working a miracle equally stupendous and mysterious; true, its nature was incomprehensible, but this circumstance, instead of exciting a suspicion of its absurdity, only increased the reverence with which it was regarded. We must not then be surprised at the zeal that the Romish priesthood has ever manifested in defending an opinion which has so materially strengthened its influence. The confessor to the queen of Spain is said to have rebuked the opposition of a nobleman, by saying, "You should respect the man who every day has your God in his hands and your queen at his feet." In this brief sentence, the purpose of the doctrine is distinctly stated; it conferred political power, and was therefore to be defended at all hazards. But common sense frequently revolted at a doctrine contracted by sight, feeling, and taste; in the eleventh century it was ably exposed by Berengarius, a priest of Tours, who assailed it at once with ridicule and with argument. But in his eightieth year, Berengarius was prevailed upon by Gregory to renounce his former opinions, and transubstantiation was generally received as an article of faith.

A victory obtained by Rodolph induced Gregory to depart from his cautious policy; he excommunicated Henry, and sent a crown of gold to his rival. The indignant emperor summoned a council in the mountains of the Tyrol, pronounced Gregory's deposition, and proclaimed Gilbert, archbishop of Ravenna, pope, by the name of Clement III. Gregory immediately made peace with the Normans, and, supported by them and the Countess Matilda, he bade his enemies defiance. But in the meantime, Rodolph was defeated and slain, the discontented Germans were forced to submit to the imperial authority and Henry, at the head of a victorious army, crossed the Alps. The Norman dukes, engaged in war with the Greek emperors, neglected their ally, and the forces of the countess Matilda were unable to cope with the imperialists. Twice was Henry driven from before the walls of Rome; but the third time he gained an entrance, by a lavish distribution of bribes, and procured the solemn installation of Clement. The emperor's departure left his partisans exposed to the vengeance of Gregory; the pontiff returned at the head of a Norman army, and gave the city to be pillaged by his barbarous auxiliaries. Having reduced Rome almost to a mass of ruins, Gregory retired to Salerno, where he was seized with a mortal disease. He died unconquered, repeating with his latest breath the excommunications which he had hurled against Henry, the antipope, and their adherents. He viewed his own conduct in the struggle with complacency, and frequently boasted of the goodness of his cause. "I have loved righteousness and hated iniquity," he exclaimed, "and it is therefore I die an exile."

Gregory may be regarded as the great founder of the political system of popery; and therefore, while he is extolled by some historians as a saint, others have described him as a disgrace to humanity. But the character of this remarkable man was formed by his age, and developed by the circumstances that surrounded him. He was the representative both of popery and democracy, principles apparently inconsistent, but which in ancient and modern times have frequently been found in close alliance. With the sanctity of the church he shielded the people; with the strength of the people he gave stability to the church. In the course of his long career as the secret and as the acknowledged ruler of the papacy, he displayed unquestionable abilities of the highest order; his pretensions to ascetic piety gained him the enthusiastic admiration of the multitude; the soldiers regarded him as a brave warrior and successful general; the higher ranks of the clergy yielded in the council to his fervid eloquence and political skill. His very faults became elements of his success: he was severe, vindictive, and inexorable: he knew not what it was to forgive; none of his enemies could elude the patient search and the incessant vigilance with which he pursued those against whom he treasured wrath. It was his custom to witness the execution of those whose death he decreed; and it was awful to contemplate the serenity of his countenance and the placidity of his manners while he presided over tortures and massacres. It can not, therefore, be a matter of wonder that the power of such a man should have swept over Christendom like a torrent, and hurried everything into the vortex of his new and gigantic institutions.

Section VI.—*The War of Investitures.*

FROM A. D. 1086 TO A. D. 1152.

Henry gained only a brief respite by the death of his formidable and inveterate antagonist. Victor III. was elected by the cardinals, and during his brief reign he gained several advantages over the imperial party. He was succeeded by Urban II., the friend and pupil of Gregory, who commenced his pontificate by sending an encyclical letter to the Christian churches, declaring his resolution to adhere to the political system of his deceased master. Supported by the Normans, Urban entered Rome, and assembled a council of one hundred and fifteen bishops, in which the emperor, the antipope, and their adherents, were solemnly excommunicated. At the same time he negotiated a marriage between Guelph, son of the duke of Bavaria, a distinguished supporter of the papal cause in Germany, and the countess Matilda. From this union, the present dukes of Brunswick and Lunenburgh, and the reigning family of England, trace their descent. Henry marched into Italy, and though vigorously opposed by Guelph, gained several important advantages; but the papal intrigues raised enemies against him in the bosom of his family; his eldest son Conrad rebelled, and was crowned king of Italy by Urban. This revolt compelled Henry to abandon his recent acquisitions, and retire toward the Alps.

A council was summoned to meet at Placentia, and so large a number of bishops assembled, that no church could contain them, and they were forced to deliberate in the open air. Most of Gregory's decrees were re-enacted; but, in addition to the affair of investitures, the attention of the council was directed to the rapid progress of the Mohammedans in the east, and the dangers that threatened the empire of Constantinople (A. D. 1095). The tales of the persecutions to which the Christian pilgrims were exposed by the ferocious Turks, who had become masters of the Holy Land, had excited general indignation throughout Europe. Peter the Hermit, a wild fanatic, preached everywhere the necessity of rescuing the faithful from the infidel Saracens, as he ignorantly called the Turks, and such a flame was kindled by his exertions, that a decree was issued by the council of Clermont, authorizing the first crusade; and at the same time the king of France, in whose dominions the council met, was excommunicated, and could only obtain absolution by humiliating submissions.

The general insanity diffused through Europe by the preaching of the first crusade, the multitudes that abandoned their homes to follow Walter the Pennyless or Godescald the Fanatic, the massacres of the Jews, the sufferings and exploits of the disciplined adventurers that marched under the banners of Godfrey, will form the subject of the next section; it is enough here to say that the general fanaticism proved of essential service to the papal cause, and that the partisans of Henry suffered severely from the fury of the crusaders in their passage through Italy.

Paschal II. was the successor of Urban, and, like him, steadfastly pursued the policy of Gregory; he easily triumphed over the antipope, who died of a broken heart, and he urged a second general crusade, which the reverses of the Christians in the Holy Land rendered necessary. To consolidate the papal structure, he assembled a council at Rome, and procured the enactment of a new oath, to be taken by all ranks of the clergy. By this oath they abjured all heresy, they promised implicit obedience to the pope and his successors, to affirm what the holy and universal church confirms, and to condemn what she condemns (A. D. 1104). Soon after, the old emperor, Henry, was treacherously arrested by his own son Henry V., and deprived of his imperial dignity: he subsequently escaped, but before hostilities made any progress, he died of a broken heart. The bishop of Liege honorably interred the body of his unfortunate sovereign, but papal enmity pursued Henry beyond the grave; the benevolent prelate was excommunicated, and could only obtain absolution by disinterring the corpse.

Though Henry V. owed his throne to papal influence, he would not yield the imperial right to granting investitures, and his example was followed by the kings of England and France. The form in which monarchs gave investiture by bestowing a pastoral ring and staff, was regarded by the popes as an interference with their spiritual jurisdiction, and when the form was altered, they gave no further trouble to the English and French monarchs, but, in their disputes with the emperors, they not only forbade ecclesiastics to receive investiture from laymen, but even to take an oath of allegiance to them.

The fifth Henry proved a more formidable enemy to the papacy than his father; he led an army into Italy, made Paschal prisoner, compelled him to perform the ceremony of his coronation, and to issue a bull securing the right of investiture to the emperor and his successors. But the remonstrances of the cardinals induced the pope to annul the treaty, and he permitted Henry to be excommunicated by several provincial councils. The pontiff, however, did not ratify the sentence until the death of the countess Matilda, and the disputes about her inheritance created fresh animosities between the empire and the holy see.

The death of Paschal prevented an immediate war. His successors Gelasius II. and Calixtus II., however, supported his policy, and, after a long struggle, the emperor was forced to resign his claim to episcopal investitures, but he was permitted to retain the investiture of the temporal rights belonging to the sees.

During the pontificate of Honorius II., the successor of Calixtus, the church of Ireland, for the first time, was brought under the supremacy of the pope by the exertions of St. Malachi, a monk of great influence and reputation. The greater part of the reign of Honorius was spent in a contest with the Normans in southern Italy, whom he forced to continue in their allegiance.

Innocent II. and Anacletus, elected by rival factions, were both enthroned the same day, and the papacy was consequently rent by a schism. Anacletus was the grandson of a converted Jew; he possessed great wealth, was a favorite with the Roman populace, and had an undoubted majority of the cardinals in his favor, yet he is stigmatized as an antipope. This was principally owing to the exertions of the celebrated St. Bernard, who warmly espoused the cause of Innocent, and procured him the support of the king of France and the German emperor. On the death of Anacletus, his party elected another antipope, but he soon made his submission to Innocent, and the schism was appeased.

A general council was soon afterward assembled at Rome (A. D. 1139), at which no less than a thousand bishops were present; several ordinances were made for completing the ecclesiastical organization of the church. The opinions of Arnold of Brescia were condemned at this council; they were derived from the celebrated Abelard, whose controversy with St. Bernard began to excite universal attention.

Abelard was generally regarded as the most accomplished scholar and the best logician in Europe; crowds of disciples flocked to hear his lectures, and though he did not break through the trammels of scholastic philosophy, he gave an impulse to the spirit of inquiry which, in a future age, produced beneficial effects. St. Bernard, whose opinions were invested by the bishops with a kind of apostolic authority, accused Abelard of teaching heretical opinions respecting the doctrine of the trinity. Abelard denied the imputation, and the dispute turned on metaphysical subtleties, to which neither party affixed a definite meaning. Abelard's opinions were condemned by a council at Sens, but he was permitted to retire into the monastery of Clugny, where he died in peace.

This obscure controversy was the first symptom of the struggle between scholastic divinity and philosophy. Abelard was subdued, but he bequeathed his cause to a succession of faithful disciples, who gradually emancipated knowledge from the confinement of the cloister, and liberated the human mind from the thraldom of popery. Abelard's opinions were purely theological; his disciple, Arnold of Brescia, abandoning his master's mysticism, directed his attention to the reform of the church and of the government. He declared that the political power and wealth of the clergy were inconsistent with the sanctity of their profession, and he began to preach these doctrines in Italy and Germany; so great was his influence, that he was invited to Rome, in order to revive the republic. Innocent II., Celestine II., Lucius II., and Eugenius III., had to struggle with "the politicians," as the followers of Arnold were called, for the maintenance of their domestic power; and during this period the aggressions of popery on the rights of kings and nations were suspended. Rome set the example of resistance to the pontiffs; Italy, for a brief space, furnished the boldest opponents to the papal usurpations; but when Europe began to profit by the example, the Italians discovered that the overthrow of the papacy would diminish the profits which they derived from the payments made by superstition and ignorance to the Roman exchequer; and they lent their aid to the support of the lucrative delusion they had been the first to expose, and even yielded their liberties to the pontiffs, on condition of sharing in their unhallowed gains.

The claims of the popes to spiritual and temporal power, the means they employed to effect their object, their struggle against royal power on the one side, and national independence on the other, form the most important part of European history during several centuries. A calm and careful examination of the origin and growth of the papal system is therefore necessary to a right understanding of the social condition of Europe in the ages preceding the Reformation. To render this portion of history satisfactory to the student, it is necessary to trace back the early history of Christianity, and point out some of the corruptions by which its purity was early disfigured.

Section VII.—*The Crusades.*

The wars undertaken by the crusaders for the conquest of Palestine, at the instigation of the popes, form an essential part of the history of the great struggle between the spiritual and temporal powers. To understand aright the influence they exercised, it will be necessary to cast a retrospective glance at their origin, and at the state of society in the eastern and western world, when first this great movement began.

Pilgrimages to Jerusalem, and the localities that had been hallowed by our blessed Savior's presence, were common in the earliest ages of the church. They began to multiply very rapidly at the beginning of the eleventh century, in consequence of an opinion very generally diffused, that the end of the world was at hand; many persons sold their estates, and migrated to the Holy Land, to wait there the coming of the Lord. While the Saracens remained masters of Palestine, they encouraged and protected visiters whose arrival brought them considerable profit, but when the Seljúkian Turks wrested the country from the khaliphs of Egypt, the pilgrims were subjected to every extortion and outrage that fanaticism and ignorance could dictate. Their sad recital of the calamities they were forced to endure excited universal indignation, and Gregory VII. was the first to propose a general arming throughout Christendom, for the purpose of driving the Turks beyond the Euphrates. The time was not propitious for such an undertaking; the wars of the empire engaged the attention and employed the arms of the chief military leaders. But when the Normans had completed the conquest of England and the two Sicilies, when the imperial power had sunk before the popes in Italy and the feudal princes in Germany, vast hordes of military adventurers who remained without employment, ready to embrace any cause that promised to gratify their love of glory and plunder. At this moment an enthusiastic monk, usually called Peter the Hermit, indignant at the oppression of the Christians, which he had witnessed in Palestine, began to preach the duty of expelling the infidels from the patrimony of Christ, and by his energetic labors, widely diffused his own fanaticism.

Peter's zeal was vigorously seconded by Pope Urban II.; the pontiff went personally to France, and held a council at Clermont (A. D. 1095), where the war was sanctioned with great enthusiasm, and multitudes assumed the badge of the cross, as the symbol of their enlistment. The first hordes of crusaders were ignorant fanatics, guided by men of no note or experience. They marched without order or discipline, pillaging, burning, and plundering the countries that they traversed. So great was the delusion that whole families joined in these wild expeditions; farmers were seen driving carts containing their wives and children in the line of march, while boys bearing mimic implements of war, sported round, mistaking every stranger for a Turk, and every new town for Jerusalem. Most of these wretches perished by fatigue, famine, disease, or the swords of the people they had outraged, but not before their excesses had indelibly stigmatized the cause in which they were engaged. The Jews along the Rhine suffered most severely from these fanatics, who were persuaded that the sacrifice of this unfortunate race would be the best propitiation for the success of their expedition. Myriads of the hapless Jews were massacred with every torture and indignity that malice could suggest; whole families committed suicide by mutual agreement; a few submitted to be baptized, and purchased safety by apostacy. The archbishop of Mayence exerted all the means in his power to protect the wretched victims, but had the mortification to witness the murder of those who sought refuge in his own palace.

At length a regular army was organized, under the command of Godfrey of Bouillon, duke of Lower Lorraine, one of the most celebrated generals of the age. No sovereign joined his standard, but the leading nobility of Christendom were enrolled among his followers, among whom may be mentioned, Robert, duke of Normandy, eldest son of William the Conqueror, Hugh, brother of the king of France, Bohemond, prince of Tarentum, and Raymond, count of Toulouse. When the divisions of this formidable army arrived near Constantinople, Alexis, who then ruled the Byzantine empire, was naturally terrified by the appearance of hosts too powerful to be received as auxiliaries, and too formidable to be rejected as enemies. The crafty Greek had recourse to treachery and dissimulation; after a disgusting train of fraudulent negotiations, the Latin warriors passed into Asia, leaving behind them worse enemies in the Christians of the Byzantine empire, whom it was part of their object to protect, than the Turks they had come to assail. Their early career in Asia was glorious, but purchased at an enormous expenditure of life. Nicea, the capital of the sultany of Rúm, was taken; a great victory over the sultan Soleiman opened a passage into Syria; Antioch was captured after a seige of unparalleled difficulty, and finally, Jerusalem, which had been recently wrested from the Turks by the Egyptians, fell before the arms of the crusaders, and became the capital of a new kingdom (A. D. 1099).

Jerusalem was obstinately defended by the Mussulmans; they hurled beams and stones on the heads of those who tried to scale the walls, and flung burning oil and sulphur on the moveable towers and bridges employed by the assailants. The crusaders displayed equal energy, but on the second day of assault, just as they were sinking under the united effects of weariness and a burning sun, Godfrey declared that he saw a celestial messenger on the Mount of Olives, cheering the Christians to the combat. The enthusiasm awakened by such a declaration bore down every obstacle; the crusaders made good their lodgement on the wall, and the Mohammedans fled into the city. Amid the most rapturous shouts of triumph the banner of the cross was planted on the towers of Jerusalem, and as it unfurled itself in the wind, many of the bravest warriors wept for joy. But the triumph was sullied by an indiscriminate and unsparing massacre; a helpless crowd sought shelter in the mosque of Omar, but the gates were speedily forced and the fugitives butchered; the knights boasted that they rode in Saracen blood up to the knees of their horses. The massacre lasted all day, but when the shades of evening began to close around, the crusaders suddenly recollected that they were in the midst of those places which had been hallowed by the presence and sufferings of their Savior. As if by some common and supernatural impulse, the savage warriors were suddenly changed into devout pilgrims; each hasted to remove from his person the stains of slaughter; they laid aside their weapons, and in the guise of penitents, with bare heads and feet, streaming eyes and folded hands, they ascended the hill of Calvary and entered the church of the Holy Sepulchre. The services of religion were performed by the clergy of Jerusalem, who hailed their deliverers with enthusiastic gratitude.

Godfrey of Bouillon was chosen sovereign of Palestine; he refused the title of king, declaring that Christ was the true monarch of the Holy Land, and declined to wear a crown of gold, where his Savior had borne a crown of thorns. Baldwin, his brother and successor, was less scrupulous; he assumed the royal ensigns and title, and transmitted the throne to his cousin, Baldwin du Bourg, whose posterity continued to reign in Palestine until the kingdom was overthrown by Saladin (A. D. 1187). Several minor states were established by the crusaders, of which the most remarkable were the county of Edessa, the principality of Antioch, the county of Tripoli, and, at a later period, the kingdom of Cyprus. None of these states had long duration; the Christians of the east, continually assailed by powerful enemies, could not be persuaded to unite cordially for mutual defence; victories were scarcely less calamitous to them than defeats, on account of the difficulty of obtaining reinforcements from Europe; and though the crusading enthusiasm endured for two centuries, its heat gradually abated, and nothing would have kept it alive but the privileges and grants made by the popes, and the principal European potentates, to those who joined in such expeditions. Six principal crusades followed the first great movement; they were all either unsuccessful or productive of advantages as fleeting as they were trivial.

Forty-eight years after Jerusalem had been taken by the Christians, the emperor, Conrad III., and Louis VII., king of France, undertook a second crusade to support the sinking fortunes of their brethren in Palestine (A. D. 1117). The Atta-beg Zenghi, who had, by his superior prowess, obtained the chief command over the Turkish tribes in Irak, attacked the Christian territories beyond the Euphrates, and made himself master of Edessa, justly regarded as the bulwark of the kingdom of Jerusalem. Conrad proceeded to Constantinople, without waiting for his ally. He had to encounter the treacherous hostility of the Byzantine emperor, which proved fatal to an army containing the flower of German chivalry, including a troop of noble ladies who served in the attitude and armor of men. Manuel, who then held the throne of Constantinople, gave the sultan secret intelligence of the German line of march, and furnished Conrad with treacherous guides. After a glorious but unsuccessful battle on the banks of the Mæander, Conrad was forced to retreat; he met the French advancing from the Bosphorus, and the contrast of his own condition with the pomp of Louis, led him to desert the cause. The French, undismayed and unwarned, pursued their march with inconsiderate speed; their rear-guard was surprised by the Turkish troops, while the van was at a considerable distance, and the greater part put to the sword. Louis brought the shattered remnant of his forces by sea to Antioch; the Christians of Palestine joined him in an unsuccessful siege of Damascus, after which the monarch returned to Europe, dishonored by a faithless wife, and deserted by ungrateful allies. This disgraceful termination of an expedition from which so much had been expected, diffused feelings of melancholy and surprise throughout Europe. St. Bernard, abbot of Clairvaux, through whose influence the crusade was undertaken, had to encounter the storm of public indignation; he was stigmatized as a lying prophet, who, by pretended inspiration and false miracles, had lured myriads to a miserable doom. But Bernard was not daunted by these reproaches; he replied to those accusations by pointing out the true causes of the failure, the follies and vices of the crusaders themselves; he asserted that a new expedition, undertaken in a spirit of piety, would be crowned with success; and he urged the states of Christendom to combine in one great effort for securing the kingdom of Jerusalem. His efforts to revive the crusading spirit were, however, unavailing, and death surprised him in the midst of his exertions.

Noureddín,* the son of Zenghi, destroyed the dynasty of the Fatimite khaliphs in Egypt. His favorite, Saladin,† usurped the government of Egypt, and, though a Kurd by descent, became the favorite hero both of the Turks and Arabs. On the death of his ancient master, Saladin invaded the Christian territories, and, after a brief siege, made himself master of Jerusalem (A. D. 1187). The loss of the holy city filled all Europe with sorrow; the emperor, Frederic I., the lion-hearted

* Núr-ed-dín signifies "the light of religion."
† Salah-ed-dín signifies "the safety of religion."

Richard of England, Philip Augustus of France, and several minor princes, assumed the cross, while the maritime states of Italy, by sending immediate reinforcements to the garrisons on the coasts of the Mediterranean, arrested the progress of Saladin. Frederic advanced through the Byzantine territories, harassed at every step by Greek fraud and treachery. Having wintered at Adrianople, he crossed the Hellespont, defeated the Turks in several engagements, and stormed the city of Iconium. But in the midst of his glorious career he was drowned in the river Cydnus (A. D. 1190). The army persevered, and joined the eastern Christians in the famous siege of Acre.

While Acre was closely pressed by the Christians, the besiegers were, in their turn, so strictly blockaded by Saladin, that they suffered more than the garrison. The kings of England and France, however, followed by the flower of their dominions, appeared together as companions in arms, and reached Palestine by sea. The siege of Acre was so vigorously prosecuted after the arrival of the English that the town was soon forced to surrender, and the Christians began to indulge the hope of recovering Jerusalem. Their expectations were frustrated by the jealousy which arose between the French and the English; Philip, unable to brook the superiority which Richard acquired by his military prowess, and perhaps, in some degree, by his wealth, returned home, leaving a part of his army under the command of the duke of Burgundy, for the defence of the Holy Land. But the animosity between the French and English parties was increased rather than abated by the departure of Philip; the envy of his companions rendered the valorous exertions of Richard unavailing; he entered into a treaty with Saladin, obtaining for the Christians free access to Jerusalem and the Holy Sepulchre, and then hasted home to defend his dominions from the attacks of his ancient rival (A. D. 1192). On his return, the English monarch was seized and imprisoned by the duke of Austria, whom he had grievously insulted in Palestine; he was subsequently resigned to the custody of the emperor of Germany, from whom he had to purchase his liberation by the payment of a large ransom. The illustrious Saladin did not long survive the departure of the royal crusader; he died at Damascus, and the disputes that arose respecting his inheritance, prevented the Mohammedans from completing the destruction of the Latin kingdom of Palestine.

The fourth crusade was undertaken at the instigation of Innocent III. (A. D. 1202), aided by a fanatic preacher, Foulke of Neuilly. The fervor of enthusiasm was now abated; no great sovereign joined in the enterprise, but several of the most potent feudatories offered their services, and Boniface, marquis of Montferrat, was chosen commander-in-chief. The crusaders obtained transports from the Venetians, by conquering Zara, in Dalmatia, for the republic of Venice, in spite of the threats and remonstrances of the pope, who was justly indignant at seeing their first efforts directed against a Christian city. But this departure from their original design was followed by a still more remarkable deviation; instead of proceeding to Palestine, they sailed against Constantinople, to dethrone the usurper, Alexius Angelus. The crusaders succeeded in restoring the lawful emperor, Isaac, to his empire; but the reward they claimed for their services was extravagant, and

Isaac's efforts to comply with the stipulations provoked such resentment, that he was deposed by his subjects, and put to death, together with his son. The crusaders instantly proclaimed war against the usurper, Mourzoufle, laid siege to Constantinople, took the city by storm, pillaged it with remorseless cruelty, and founded a new Latin empire on the ruins of the Byzantine (A. D. 1204). Baldwin, count of Flanders, was chosen sovereign of the new state, which, under five Latin emperors, lasted little more than half a century. Constantinople was recovered by the Greeks (A. D. 1261), and the hopes of uniting the eastern and western churches, which the possession of the Byzantine capital had inspired, were blighted for ever.

The fifth crusade was conducted by the king of Hungary. Two hundred thousand Franks landed at the eastern mouth of the Nile, persuaded that the conquest of Egypt was a necessary preliminary to the recovery and safe possession of Palestine (A. D. 1218). After having obtained some important successes, their cause was ruined by the arrogance and presumption of the papal legate, who assumed the direction of the army. They purchased some trivial concessions, by evacuating all their conquests; and the pope, who at first proposed to come in person to their assistance, was too busily engaged in checking the progress of heresy, to venture on an expedition to Palestine.

Frederic II., emperor of Germany, led a formidable army to Palestine, after having been excommunicated by Pope Gregory IX. for delaying his expedition, a sentence which was renewed because he ventured to sail without waiting for the papal orders (A. D. 1228). This war exhibited the strange anomaly of a champion of the cross exposed to the bitterest hostility of the church. Frederic was everywhere victorious, but the papal legates and the priests harassed him by constant opposition; a crusade was preached against him in Italy, and efforts were made to weaken his authority in his own hereditary dominions. On receiving this intelligence, Frederic concluded an equitable treaty with the sultan Melek Kamel, crowned himself at Jerusalem, for no ecclesiastic would perform the ceremony, and returned to Europe, after having effected more for the Christians of Palestine than any of their former protectors. Gregory again hurled anathemas against a prince who had made a treaty with the infidels; but Frederic's vigorous exertions soon changed the aspect of affairs; he reduced those who had rebelled during his absence, dispersed the papal and Lombard troops, and won absolution by his victories.

Tranquillity, which endured fifteen years, raised the Latins of Palestine to a prosperous condition; but a new and more formidable enemy, issuing from the deserts of Tartary, subverted the kingdom which had been founded at such an expense of blood and treasure. The Khorasmian Turks, driven from their native deserts by the Mongols, threw themselves upon Palestine, stormed Jerusalem, subverted the Latin principalities, and the small Turkish states in Syria. Jerusalem, and the greater part of Palestine, was subsequently annexed to the sultany of Egypt.

Louis IX., of France, commonly called St. Louis, led the ninth crusade. Egypt was the scene of his operations; after obtaining some important triumphs, he was defeated, made prisoner, and forced to purchase his freedom by the payment of a large ransom (A. D. 1250). The pope's inveterate hostility to Frederic was one of the chief causes that led to the ruin of this crusade. At the moment that Louis sailed, Innocent was preaching a crusade against the emperor in Europe, and the Dominicans were stimulating their hearers to rebellion and assassination. The lamentable loss of the French army, the captivity of the "most Christian king," and the utter ruin of the Latin kingdom in Palestine, failed to shake the obstinacy of the pontiff. It seemed even that the death of Frederic redoubled his fury, as if his prey had escaped from his hands. "Let the heavens rejoice, and let the earth be glad," was his address to the clergy of Sicily, "for the lightning and the tempest, wherewith God Almighty has so long menaced your heads, have been changed, by the death of this man, into refreshing zephyrs and fertilizing dews."

Untaught by calamity, he prepared for a second crusade; on his voyage to the place of rendezvous, he was induced to steer to Tunis, in the wild hope of baptizing its king (A. D. 1270). Instead of a proselyte, Louis found a tedious siege, and a mortal disease. On his death, the remnant of his army was led back to Europe without making any further effort. The fate of Palestine was for a time delayed by the valor of Edward I., of England, who extorted a three years' truce from the Mohammedans. At length, some excesses of the Latins provoked the resentment of the Mameluke sultan, Khalil; he resolved to expel them completely from Palestine, and laid siege to their last stronghold, Acre (A. D. 1291). The city was taken after a tedious siege, and after its fall the title of King of Jerusalem, still preserved by the Christian princes, became an empty name.

Section VIII.—*The Crusade against the Albigenses.*

It has been already mentioned that the growth of heresy was beginning to alarm the advocates of papal supremacy in the reign of Alexander III., and that a general council had pronounced a solemn decree against the Albigenses. But the feudal lords of France and Italy were slow in adopting an edict which would have deprived them of their best vassals, and the new opinions, or rather the original doctrines of Christianity, were secretly preached throughout the greater part of Europe. It may be conceded to the defenders of the papal system that there were some among the preachers of a reformation who had given too great a scope to their imaginations, and revived many of the dangerous errors of the Manichæans and Paulicians. There seems no just cause for doubting that a few enthusiasts ascribed the Old Testament to the principle of Evil; because, as they asserted, "God is there described as a homicide, destroying the world by water Sodom and Gomorrah by fire, and the Egyptians by the overflow of the Red sea." But these were the sentiments of a very small minority; the bulk of the Albigensian reformers protested simply against the doctrine of transubstantiation, the sacraments of confirmation, confession, and marriage, the invocation of saints, the worship of images, and the temporal power of the prelates. Their moral character was confessed by their enemies, but while they acknowledged its external purity, they invented the blackest calumnies respecting their secret practices, without ever bringing forward a shadow of proof, and consequently without incurring the hazard of refutation. The progress of reform was silent; for the efforts of the *paterins*, or Albigensian teachers, were directed rather to forming a moral and pure society within the church, than to the establishment of a new sect. They seemed anxious to hold the same relation to the Romish establishment that John Wesley designed the Methodists to keep toward the church of England. Their labors generated an independence of spirit and freedom of judgment which would probably have led to an open revolt, had not Innocent III. discerned the danger to which the papal system was exposed, and resolved to crush freedom of thought before its exercise would subvert his despotism.

Innocent's first step was to enlist cupidity and self-interest on his side; he abandoned to the barons the confiscated properties of heretics, and ordered that the enemies of the church should be for ever banished from the lands of which they were deprived. He then sent commissioners into the south of France, to examine and punish those suspected of entertaining heretical opinions, and thus laid the first foundation of the Inquisition. The arrogance and violence of these papal emissaries disgusted every class of society; finding that their persecutions were unpopular, they resolved to support their power by force of arms, and they were not long in discovering the materials of an army.

Raymond VI., count of Toulouse, was engaged in war with some of the neighboring barons, and Peter de Castelnau, the papal legate, offered to act as mediator. He went to the barons, and obtained from them a promise that, if Raymond would consent to their demands, they would employ all the forces they had assembled to extirpate heresy. Castelnau drew up a treaty on these conditions, and offered it to Raymond for his signature. The count was naturally reluctant to purchase the slaughter of his best subjects, by the sacrifice of his dominions, and the admission of a hostile army into his states. He peremptorily refused his consent, upon which Castelnau excommunicated Raymond, placed his dominions under an interdict, and wrote to the pope for a confirmation of the sentence.

Innocent III. confirmed the legate's sentence, and began to preach a crusade; but his violence transcended all bounds, when he learned that Castelnau had been slain by a gentleman of Toulouse whom he had personally insulted (A. D. 1208). Though Raymond appears to have had no share in this murder, it was against him that the papal vengeance was principally directed: he was excommunicated, his subjects absolved from their oath of allegiance, and the French king was invited to despoil him of his estates.

Philip Augustus was too busily engaged in wars with the king of England and the emperor of Germany to turn his attention to the extirpation of heresy; but he permitted a crusade against the Albigenses to be preached throughout his dominions, and the monks of Citeaux became the chief missionaries of this unholy war; they promised the pardon of all sins committed from the day of birth to death, to those who fell in the war, unlimited indulgence, the protection of the church and a large share of spoil to all who survived. While the monks were enlisting ferocious bands of wretches, who believed that they might expiate their former crimes by the perpetration of fresh atrocities, Innocent was preparing a new mission to Languedoc, whose savage brutalities exceeded even those of the crusaders. A new monastic order was instituted, at the head of which was placed a Spaniard named St. Dominic, whose special object was to extirpate heresy, by preaching against the doctrines of those who dissented from the church, and punishing with death those who could not be convinced by argument. This institution, too well known by the dreaded name of the Inquisition, appears to have been originally planned by the bishop of Toulouse, who introduced it into his diocese about seven years before it was formally sanctioned by Pope Innocent at the council of Lateran.

Raymond VI., and his nephew Raymond Roger, viscount of Albí, alarmed at the approaching danger, presented themselves before the papal legate, Arnold, abbot of Citeaux, to avert the coming storm by explanations and submissions. They protested that they had never sanctioned heresy, and that they had no share in the murder of Castelnau. The severity with which they were treated by the legate, convinced the young viscount that nothing was to be hoped from negotiation, and he returned to his states, resolved to defend himself to the last extremity: the count of Toulouse showed less fortitude; he promised to submit to any conditions which the pope would impose.

Raymond's ambassadors were received by the pope with apparent indulgence; but the terms on which absolution were offered to the count could scarcely have been more severe. He was required to make common cause with the crusaders, to aid them in the extirpation of heretics—that is, his own subjects—and to give up seven of his best castles as a pledge of his intentions. Innocent declared that, if Raymond performed these conditions, he would not only be absolved, but taken into special favor; yet, at the very same moment, the pope was inflexibly resolved on the count's destruction.

In the spring of the year 1209, all the fanatics who had taken arms at the preaching of the monks of Citeaux, began to assemble on the borders of Languedoc; the land was spread in beauty before them—ere long it was to be a howling wilderness. Raymond VI. sank into abject cowardice; he yielded up his castles, he promised implicit submission to the legate, he even allowed himself to be publicly beaten with rods before the altar, as a penance for his errors. As a reward for his humiliation, he was permitted to serve in the ranks of the crusaders, and to act as their guide in the war against his nephew.

Raymond Roger showed a bolder spirit; finding the papal legate implacable, he summoned his barons together, and having stated all his exertions to preserve peace, made a stirring appeal to their generosity and their patriotism. All resolved on an obstinate defence; even those who adhered to the church of Rome justly dreaded the excesses of a fanatical horde eager to shed blood, and gratify a ruffian thirst for plunder. The crusaders advanced: some castles and fortified towns were abandoned to them; others not subject to the imputation of heresy were allowed to ransom themselves; Villemur was burned, and Chasseneuil, after a vigorous defence, capitulated. The garrison was permitted to retire, but all the inhabitants suspected of heresy, male and female, were committed to the flames amid the ferocious shouts of the conquerors, and their property abandoned to the soldiery.

Beziers was the next object of attack; the citizens resolved to make a vigorous resistance, but they were routed in a sally by the advanced guard of the crusaders, and so vigorously pursued, that the conquerors and conquered entered the gates together. The leaders, before taking advantage of their unexpected success, asked the abbot of Citeaux how they should distinguish Catholics from heretics; the legate's memorable answer was, "Kill all: God will distinguish those who belong to himself." His words were too well obeyed; every inhabitant of Beziers was ruthlessly massacred, and when the town was thus one immense slaughter-house, it was fired, that its ruins and ashes might become the monument of papal vengeance.

Carcasonne was now the last stronghold of Raymond Roger, and t was gallantly defended by the young viscount. Simon de Montfort, the leader of the crusaders, found himself foiled by a mere youth, and was detained for eight days before he could master the suburbs and invest the town.

Peter II., king of Aragon, whom the viscount of Albi and Beziers recognised as his suzerain, took advantage of this delay to interfere in behalf of the young lord, who was his nephew as well as his vassal. The egate, unwilling to offend so powerful a sovereign, accepted his mediation, but when asked what terms would be granted to the besieged, he required that two thirds of Carcasonne should be given up to plunder. Raymond Roger spurned such conditions; Peter applauded his courage, and personally addressed the garrison. "You know the fate that waits you; make a bold defence, for that is the best means of finally obtaining favorable terms." The prudence of this advice was proved by the legate's consenting to a capitulation; but when the viscount, trusting to the faith of the treaty, presented himself in the camp of the crusaders, he was treacherously arrested, and thrown with his attendants into prison. Warned by the fate of their leader, the citizens of Carcasonne evacuated the town during the night, but some of the fugitives were overtaken by the cavalry of the crusaders; the legate selected a supply of victims from his prisoners; four hundred of them were burned alive, and about fifty were hanged.

It seemed that the object of the crusade was obtained; the count of Toulouse had submitted to every condition, however humiliating; the viscount of Narbonne abandoned every notion of resistance; and the gallant lord of Beziers was a prisoner. The crusaders too began to grow weary of the war; the French lords were ashamed of the cruelties they had sanctioned, and the faith they had violated; the knights and common soldiers, having completed the term of their service, were anxious to revisit their homes. But the legate, Arnold, was still unsatisfied; he summoned a council of the crusaders, and tried to induce them to remain, in order that they might protect their conquests of Beziers and Carcasonne, the investiture of which he conferred on Simon de Montfort, earl of Leicester. But the greater part of the French nobles refused to remain longer, and Montfort had to defend his new acquisitions with the vassals from his own estates. The gallant

Raymond Roger was detained a close prisoner in his own baronial hall at Carcasonne, where he soon died, the victim of a dysentery, produced by grief, or, as was generally suspected, by poison.

The armies of the crusaders withdrew; they left a desert, and called it peace; but the sufferings of the Albigenses were not exhausted; the monks of the Inquisition, attended by trains of executioners, went at their will through the land, torturing and butchering all who were suspected of heresy. Nor were the monks of Citeaux idle; they had found honor and profit in preaching a crusade, and they were not disposed to relinquish the lucrative employment. Thus a new crusade was preached when there was no enemy to combat, and new hordes of fanatics were poured into Languedoc. They forced their chiefs to renew the war, that the exertions of those who profited by preaching extermination should not be lost, and that the bigotry of those who hoped to purchase their salvation by murder should not remain ungratified.

Strengthened by these reinforcements, Simon de Montfort threw off the mask of moderation, and declared war against the unfortunate count of Toulouse. Raymond was once more excommunicated, and his dominions placed under an interdict. But the earl of Leicester soon found that he had been premature in his hostilities; the king of Aragon refused to receive his homage for the viscounties of Beziers and Carcasonne, declaring that he would support the claims of the legitimate heir, Raymond Trencanel, the only son of the unfortunate Raymond Roger, a child about two years old, who was safe under the guardianship of the Count de Foix. A dangerous insurrection was raised in the states so recently assigned to Montfort; and out of the two hundred towns and castles that had been granted to him, eight alone remained in his possession.

The count of Toulouse was too much afraid of ecclesiastical vengeance to defend himself by arms; he sought the protection of the king of France, and he went in person to Rome to implore absolution. Innocent promised him pardon on condition of his clearing himself from the charge of heresy and of participation in the murder of Castelnau; but when he presented himself before the council, he found that his judges had been gained over by his inexorable enemy, the abbot of Citeaux, and instead of being permitted to enter on his defence, he was overwhelmed by a series of new and unexpected charges. His remonstrances were neglected, his tears afforded theme for mockery and insult, and the sentence of excommunication was formally ratified.

In the meantime the crusaders, under Simon de Montfort, pursued their career of extermination; those whom the sword spared fell by the hands of the executioner; and the ministers of a God of peace were found more cruel and vindictive than a licentious soldiery. Even the king of Aragon became alarmed, and sought to secure the friendship of the papal favorite, by affiancing his infant son to a daughter of De Montfort. The monarch probably expected that by this concession, he would obtain more favorable terms for Raymond, and he accompanied the count to Arles, where a provincial council was assembled. The terms of peace fixed by the legate were so extravagant, not to say absurd, that even Raymond rejected them, and secretly withdrew from the city in company with the king of Aragon. Once more the count was excommunicated, pronounced an enemy of the church and an apostate from the faith, and declared to have forfeited his title and estates.

The war was now resumed with fresh vigor; after a long siege, De Montfort took the strong castle of Lavaur by assault, hanged its brave governor, the lord of Montreal, and massacred the entire garrison. "The lady of the castle," says the Romish historian, "who was an execrable heretic, was by the earl's orders thrown into a well, and stones heaped over her: afterward, the pilgrims collected the numberless heretics that were in the fortress, and burned them alive with great joy."

The same cruelties were perpetrated at every other place through which the crusaders passed; and the friends of the victims took revenge, by intercepting convoys, and murdering stragglers. It was not until he had received a large reinforcement of pilgrims from Germany, that the earl of Leicester ventured to lay siege to Toulouse. Raymond, in this extremity, displayed a vigor and courage, which, if he had manifested in the earlier part of the war, would probably have saved his country from ruin. He made so vigorous a defence, that the crusaders were forced to raise the siege, and retire with some precipitation.

The friendship between the monks of Citeaux and the crusaders soon began to be interrupted by the ambition of the former. Under pretence of reforming the ecclesiastical condition of Languedoc, they expelled the principal prelates, and seized for themselves the richest sees and benefices. The legate, Arnold, took for his share the archbishop of Narbonne, after which he abandoned Montfort, and went to lead a new crusade against the Moors in Spain. Innocent III. himself paused for a moment in his career of vengeance, and, at the instance of the king of Aragon, promised Raymond the benefit of a fair trial. But it is easier to rouse than to allay the spirit of fanaticism; disobeyed by his legates, and reproached by the crusaders, the pope was compelled to retrace his steps, and abandon Raymond to the fury of his enemies.

The king of Arragon came to the aid of his unfortunate relative, and encountered the formidable army of the crusaders at Muret; but he was slain in the beginning of the battle; the Spanish chivalry, disheartened by his fall, took to flight; and the infantry of Toulouse, thus forsaken, could offer no effective resistance. Trampled down by the pilgrim-knights, the citizens of Toulouse who followed their sovereign to the field, were either cut to pieces, or drowned in the waters of the Garonne.

Philip Augustus had triumphed over his enemies, the king of England and the emperor of Germany, just when the victory of Muret seems to have confirmed the power of De Montfort. But the ambitious adventurer derived little profit from his success, for the court of Rome began to dread the power of its creature (A. D. 1215). His influence with the papal legates and the prelates who had directed the crusade was, however, still very great, and he procured from the council of Montpellier the investiture of Toulouse and all the conquests made by "the Christian pilgrims." Philip Augustus was by no means disposed to acquiesce in this arrangement; he sent his son Louis with a numerous army into the south of France, under pretence of joining in the crusade, but really to watch the proceedings of De Montfort. Louis subsequently returned to accept the proffered crown of England, and the quarrel in which this proceeding involved him with the pope diverted his attention from Languedoc.

Arnold of Citeaux, having returned from his Spanish crusade, took possession of his archbishopric of Narbonne, where he began to exercise the rights of a sovereign prince. Simon de Montfort, who had taken the title of duke of Narbonne in addition to that of count of Toulouse, denied that his old companion in arms had a right to temporal jurisdiction; he entered the city by force, and erected his ducal standard. Arnold fulminated an excommunication against De Montfort, and placed the city under an interdict while he remained in it; he found, however, to his great surprise and vexation, that these weapons were contemned by the formidable champion of the church. But a more vigorous enemy appeared in the person of Raymond VII., son of the count of Toulouse, who, in conjunction with his father, made a vigorous effort to recover the ancient inheritance of his race. Simon de Montfort, contrary to his own better judgment, was induced by Foulke, bishop of Toulouse, to treat the citizens with treacherous cruelty for showing some symptoms of affection to their ancient lord; the consequence was, that they took advantage of his absence to invite Raymond to resume his power; and on the 13th of September, 1217, the count was publicly received into his ancient capital amid universal acclamations.

Simon, by the aid of the papal legate and the clergy, was able to collect a large army, but the bravest of the crusaders had either fallen in the preceding wars, or returned disgusted to their homes. Every one now knew that heresy was extinguished in Languedoc, and that the war was maintained only to gratify private revenge and individual ambition. De Montfort laid siege to Toulouse, but he was slain in a sally of the inhabitants, and his son Almeric, after a vain effort to revenge his death, retired to Carcasonne.

The Albigensian war was not ended by the death of its great leader. Almeric de Montfort sold his claims over Languedoc to Louis VIII., king of France; and though this prince died in the attempt to gain possession of Toulouse, the war was so vigorously supported by the queen-regent, Blanche, that Raymond VII, submitted to his enemies, and his dominions were united to the crown of France (A. D. 1229). The Inquisition was immediately established in these unhappy countries, which have never since recovered completely from the calamities inflicted upon them by the ministers of papal vengeance.

SECTION IX.—*Consequences of the Crusades.*

THOUGH the popes did not succeed in establishing their supremacy over the eastern churches, yet they derived very important advantages from the wars of the crusaders. Not the least of these was the general recognition of their right to interfere in the internal management of states; they compelled emperors and kings to assume the cross; they levied taxes at their discretion on the clergy throughout Christendom for the support of these wars; they took under their immediate protection the persons and properties of those who enlisted, and granted privileges to the adventurous warriors, which it would have been deemed impiety to contravene. Those who joined in these wars, frequently bequeathed their estates to the church, in the not improbable case of their death without heirs; those whom cowardice or policy detained at home, atoned for their absence by founding ecclesiastical endowments.

While the papal power increased, that of monarchs declined; in Germany, the Hohenstauffen gradually lost all influence; in England, the barons extorted a charter from John, and the Hungarians chiefs placed similar restrictions on their sovereign. Peculiar circumstances led to a contrary result in France; many of the great feudatories having fallen in a distant land, the monarchs were enabled to extend their prerogatives, while their domains were increased by seizing the properties of those who died without feudal heirs, or of those who were suspected of heretical opinions. The Christian kings of Spain and northern Europe derived also some profit from the fanaticism of the age, being aided by troops of warlike adventurers, in extending their dominions at the expense of their Mohammedan and pagan neighbors.

Chivalry, though older than the crusades, derived its chief influence and strength from these wars. The use of surnames, coats of arms, and distinctive banners, became necessary in armies composed of men differing in language, habits, and feelings, collected at hazard from every Christian kingdom. Tournaments were the natural result of pride and courage, in warriors naturally jealous of each other's fame, while the institution of the military orders invested knighthood with a mysterious religious sanction. The first of these was the order of the Hospitallers, or Knights of St. John of Jerusalem, known subsequently as the Knights of Malta. They were formed into a confraternity by Pope Pascal (A. D. 1114), but their order was greatly enlarged by Pope Calixtus. They bore an octagonal white cross on their black robes, and were bound to wage war on infidels, and attend to sick pilgrims. After the loss of the Holy Land, they removed successively to Cyprus, Rhodes, and Malta. Their order held Malta until A. D. 1798, when they were deprived of their last possession by Napoleon.

The Knights Templars, distinguished by the red cross, were instituted soon after the Hospitallers. Their original duty was to keep the roads free for the pilgrims that visited the Holy Sepulchre, but as their numbers increased, they became the great bulwark of the Christian kingdom of Palestine, and the possessors of rich endowments in every part of western Europe.* At length their wealth excited the cupidity of monarchs; they were overwhelmed by a mass of forged accusations; many of the noblest knights were put to death by torture, and the order wholly abolished at the council of Vienne (A. D. 1312).

The Teutonic order was originally a confraternity of German knights, formed during the seige of Acre, for the relief of the sick and wounded It was formally instituted by Pope Celestin III. (A. D. 1192), and a

* The Temple in London belonged to the Red-cross knights; the Hospitallers possessed a splendid preceptory in Clerkenwell, part of which is still standing.

code of regulations prescribed for its direction. Their ensign was a black cross, on a white robe. They subdued the kingdom of Prussia (A. D. 1230), of which they held possession until the progress of the Reformation gave that country to a protestant prince (A. D. 1525). The last great order was that of St. Lazarus, instituted originally for superintending the treatment of leprosy, a loathsome disease which the crusaders introduced into Europe. It soon became military, like the preceding, but never rose to similar eminence.

The Italian maritime states supplied the crusaders with transports, and conveyed to them provision and the munitions of war. This traffic led to a rapid increase in the commerce and navigation of the Mediterranean; a taste for spices and other articles of oriental luxury was gradually diffused throughout Europe, and trading depôts were formed by Venice, Genoa, and other Italian powers, on the shores of the Levant, and the coasts of the Greek empire. Several French towns imitated this example, and in the remote north an association was formed for the protection and extension of commerce between the cities of Lubeck and Hamburgh (A. D. 1241), which laid the foundation of the Hanseatic league. The progress of industry, the encouragement which sovereigns found it their interest to grant to trade, and their anxiety to check the arrogance and rapacity of their feudal vassals, led to a great change in most European countries, the establishment of municipal institutions.

The royal authority gained considerably by the extension of municipal freedom. The cities and towns saw that the sovereign was the person most interested in protecting their growing freedom, and they therefore gladly gave him their support in his struggles with the aristocracy and the clergy. The emancipation of the serfs was a consequence of municipal freedom. The free cities granted protection to all who sought shelter within their walls, and the nobles saw that they must either ameliorate the condition of their vassals, or witness the depopulation of their estates. Liberty thus gradually recovered its right civilization consequently began to extend its blessings over society.

The imperial house of Hohenstauffen fell from its pride of place on the death of the emperor Frederic II., the great opponent of the papacy (A. D. 1250). His son Conrad fell a victim to disease, after a brief but troubled reign; and the anarchy which succeeded in Germany, is justly named the calamitous period of the great interregnum. William of Holland, and an English prince, Richard, earl of Cornwall, were successively elected emperors, and enjoyed little more than the title. At length, Rodolph, count of Hapsburgh, was chosen (A. D. 1273) and showed himself worthy of the crown by his energy in suppressing the predatory wars that were waged by his vassals. In the meantime, the popes, in defiance of the rights of the Hohenstauffen, had bestowed the kingdom of Naples on Charles, duke of Anjou brother to the king of France.

The cruelties of Charles led the Italians to invite young Conradin to assert the hereditary claims of his family. At the age of sixteen this brave prince entered Italy, where he was enthusiastically received. But the Italians were not able to compete with the French in the field, when Conradin encountered Charles, his followers broke at the first onset, and he remained a prisoner. The duke of Anjou subjected the young prince to the mockery of a trial, and commanded him to be executed.

Thus fell the last prince of the house of Suabia, which had long been the most formidable obstacle to papal usurpation. The triumph of the papacy appeared complete : Italy was severed from the German empire ; but the peninsula recovered its independence only to be torn in sunder by factions ; the church did not succeed to the empire, and the pontiffs found that the spirit of freedom, which they had themselves nurtured, was a more formidable foe than the sovereigns of Germany.

Section X.—*Formation and Constitutional History of the Spanish Monarchy.*

For several hundred years after the great Saracen invasion in the beginning of the eighth century, Spain was broken up into a number of small but independent states, divided in their interests, and often in deadly hostility with one another. By the middle of the fifteenth century, the number of states into which the country had been divided was reduced to four; Castile, Aragon, Navarre, and the Moorish kingdom of Granada. The last, comprised within nearly the same limits as the modern province of that name, was all that remained to the Moslems of their once vast possessions in the peninsula. Its concentrated population gave it a degree of strength altogether disproportioned to the extent of its territory ; and the profuse magnificence of its court, which rivalled that of the ancient khaliphs, was supported by the labors of a sober industrious people, under whom agriculture and several of the mechanic arts had reached a degree of perfection probably unequalled in any other part of Europe during the middle ages.

The little kingdom of Navarre, embosomed within the Pyrenees, had often attracted the avarice of neighboring and more powerful states. But since their selfish schemes operated as a mutual check upon each other, Navarre still continued to maintain her independence when all the smaller states had been absorbed in the gradually increasing dominion of Castile and Aragon. This latter kingdom comprehended the province of that name, together with Catalonia and Valencia. Under its auspicious climate and free political institutions, its inhabitants displayed an uncommon share of intellectual and moral energy. Its long line of coast opened the way to an extensive and flourishing commerce ; and its enterprising navy indemnified the nation for the scantiness of its territory at home by the important foreign conquests of Sardinia, Sicily, Naples, and the Balearic Isles.

The remaining provinces of the peninsula fell to the crown of Castile, which, thus extending its sway over an unbroken line of country from the bay of Biscay to the Mediterranean, seemed, by the magnitude of its territory, to be entitled to some supremacy over the other states of the peninsula ; especially as it was there that the old Gothic monarchy may be said first to have revived after the great Saracen invasion This claim, indeed, appears to have been recognised at an early period of her history.

The Saracens, reposing under the sunny skies of Andalusia, so congenial with their own, seemed willing to relinquish the sterile regions of the north to an enemy whom they despised. But when the Spaniards, quitting the shelter of their mountains, descended into the open plains of Leon and Castile, they found themselves exposed to the predatory incursions of the Arab cavalry. It was not until they had reached some natural boundary, as the river Douro, that they were enabled, by constructing a line of fortifications behind this natural fence, to secure their conquests. Their own dissensions were another cause of their tardy progress. More Christian blood was wasted in these national feuds than in all their encounters with the infidel. The soldiers of Fernan Gonçales, a chieftain of the tenth century, complained that their master made them lead the lives of very devils, keeping them in the harness day and night, in wars not against the Saracens, but one another.

These circumstances so far checked the energies of the Christians, that a century and a half elapsed after the invasion before they had penetrated to the Douro (A. D. 850), and nearly thrice that period before they had advanced the line of conquest to the Tagus (A. D. 1147), notwithstanding this portion of the country had been comparatively deserted by the Mohammedans. But it was easy to foresee that a people living as they did under circumstances favorable to the development of both physical and moral energy, must ultimately prevail over a nation oppressed by despotism, and the effeminate indulgence to which it was naturally disposed by a sensual religion and a voluptuous climate. In truth, the early Spaniard was urged by every motive which can give energy to human purpose. His cause became the cause of Heaven The church published her bulls of crusade, offering liberal indulgences to those who served, and paradise to those who fell in the battle against the infidel. Indeed, volunteers from the remotest parts of Christian Europe eagerly thronged to serve under his banner, and the cause of religion was debated with the same ardor in Spain as on the plains of Palestine.

To the extraordinary position in which the nation was placed may be referred the liberal forms of its political institutions, as well as a more early development of them than took place in other countries of Europe. From the exposure of the Castilian towns to the predatory incursions of the Arabs, it became necessary, not only that they should be strongly fortified, but that every citizen should be trained to bear arms in their defence. An immense increase of consequence was given to the burgesses, who thus constituted the most effective part of the national militia. To this circumstance, as well as to the policy of inviting the settlement of frontier places by the grant of extraordinary privileges to the inhabitants, is to be imputed the early date, as well the liberal character of the charters of community in Castile and Leon. These, although varying a good deal in their details, generally conceded to the citizens the right of electing their own magistrates for the regulation of municipal affairs. In order to secure the barriers of justice more effectually against the violence of power, so often superior to law in an imperfect state of society, it was provided in many of the charters that no nobles should be permitted to acquire real property within the limits of the municipality; that no fortress or palace should be erected by them there; that such as might reside within the territory of a chartered city or borough should be subject to its jurisdiction, and that any violence offered by the feudal lords to its inhabitants might be resisted with impunity. Thus, while the inhabitants of the great towns in other parts of Europe were languishing in feudal servitude, the Castilian corporation, living under the protection of their own laws and magistrates in time of peace, and commanded by their own officers in time of war, were in full enjoyment of all the essential rights and privileges of freemen.

The earliest instance on record of popular representation in Castile, occurred at Burgos in 1169; nearly a century antecedent to the first convocation of the English house of commons, in the celebrated Leicester parliament. Each city had but one vote whatever might be the number of its representatives. The nomination of the deputies was originally vested in the householders at large, but was afterward confined to the municipalities; a most mischievous alteration which subjected their election eventually to the corrupt influence of the crown. They assembled in the same chamber with the higher orders of the nobility and clergy; but on questions of importance retired to deliberate by themselves. After the transaction of other business, their own petitions were presented to the sovereign; and his assent gave them the validity of laws. The Castilian commons, by neglecting to make their money grants dependant on corresponding concessions from the crown, relinquished that powerful check on its operations so beneficially exerted in the British parliament, but in vain contended for even there until a period much later than that now under consideration. Whatever may have been the right of the nobility and clergy to attend the Cortes, their sanction was not deemed essential to the validity of legislative acts; for their presence was not even required in many assemblies of the nation which occurred in the fourteenth and fifteenth centuries. The extraordinary power thus committed to the commons was, on the whole, unfavorable to their liberties. It deprived them of the sympathy and co-operation of the great orders of the state, whose authority alone could have enabled them to withstand the enactments of arbitrary power, and who in fact did eventually desert them in their utmost need.

But notwithstanding these defects, the popular branch of the Castilian Cortes, very soon after its admission into that body, assumed functions and exercised a degree of power superior to that enjoyed by the commons in other European legislatures. It was soon recognised as a principle of the constitution, that no tax should be imposed without the consent of the representatives of the people. The commons showed a wise solicitude in regard to the mode of collecting the public revenue. They watched carefully over its appropriation to its destined uses. A vigilant eye was kept on the conduct of public officers, as well as on the right administration of justice, and commissions were appointed by the Cortes to inquire into any suspected abuses of judicial authority. They entered into negotiations for alliances with foreign powers, and by determining the amount of supplies for the maintenance of troops in time of war, preserved a salutary check over military operations. The nomination of regencies was subject to their approbation, and they defined the nature of the authority to be intrusted to them. Their consent was esteemed indispensable to the validity of a title to the crown; and this prerogative, or at least the shadow of it, long continued to survive the wreck of their ancient liberties. Finally they more than once set aside the testamentary provisions of the sovereign in regard to the succession.

It would be improper to pass by without notice an anomalous institution peculiar to Castile, which sought to secure the public tranquillity by means which were themselves scarcely compatible with civil subordination. This was the celebrated *Hermandad*, or "Holy Brotherhood," which was designed as a substitute for a regularly-organized police. It consisted of a confederation of the principal cities, bound together by solemn league and covenant for the defence of their liberty in seasons of civil anarchy. Its affairs were conducted by deputies, who assembled at stated intervals for the purpose, transacting their business under a common seal, enacting laws which they were careful to transmit to the nobles and the sovereign, and enforcing their measures by an armed body of dependants. This wild kind of justice, so characteristic of an unsettled state of society, repeatedly received the legislative sanction; and however formidable such a popular engine may have appeared to the eye of a monarch, he was often led to countenance it by a sense of his own impotence, as well as of the overweening power of the nobles, against whom it was principally directed. Hence these associations, though the epithet may seem somewhat overstrained, have received the appellation of "Cortes Extraordinary."

With these immunities the cities of Castile attained a degree of opulence and splendor unrivalled, unless in Italy, during the middle ages. At a very early period indeed their contact with the Arabs had familiarized them with a better system of agriculture and a dexterity in the mechanic arts unknown in other parts of Christendom. Augmentation of wealth brought with it the usual appetite for expensive pleasures but the surplus of riches was frequently expended in useful public works.

The nobles, though possessed of immense estates and great political privileges, did not consume their fortunes or their energies in a life of effeminate luxury. From their earliest boyhood they were accustomed to serve in the ranks against the infidel, and their whole subsequent lives were occupied either with war, or those martial exercises which reflect the image of it. Looking back with pride to the ancient Gothic descent, and to those times when they had stood forward as the peers, the electors of their sovereign, they would ill brook the slightest indignity at his hand. Accordingly we find them perpetually convulsing the kingdom with their schemes of selfish aggrandizement. The petitions of the commons are filled with remonstrances on their various oppressions, and the evils resulting from their long desolating feuds.

The over-weening self-confidence of the nobles, however, proved their ruin. They disdained a co-operation with the lower orders in defence of their privileges, when both were assailed by the Austrian dynasty, and relied too unhesitatingly on their power as a body, to feel jealous of their exclusion from the national legislature, where alone they could make an effectual stand against the usurpations of the crown.

The long minorities with which Castile was afflicted, perhaps more than any country in Europe, frequently threw the government into the hands of the principal nobility, who perverted to their own emolument the high powers intrusted to them. They usurped the possessions of the crown, and invaded some of its most valuable privileges; so that the sovereign's subsequent life was frequently spent in fruitless attempts to recover the losses of his minority. He sometimes, indeed, in the impotence of other resources, resorted to such unhappy expedients as treachery and assassination.

Section XI.—*Survey of the Constitution of Aragon.*

Aragon was first raised to political importance by its union with Catalonia, including the rich country of Barcelona, and the subsequent conquest of the kingdom of Valencia. The ancient country of Barcelona had reached a higher degree of civilization than Aragon, and was distinguished by institutions even more liberal than those we have described in the preceding section as belonging to Castile. It was in the maritime cities, scattered along the coasts of the Mediterranean, that the seeds of liberty, both in ancient and modern times, were implanted and brought to maturity. During the middle ages, when the people of Europe generally maintained a toilsome and unfrequent intercourse with each other, those situated on the margin of this great inland sea found an easy mode of communication across the great highway of its waters. Among these maritime republics, those of Catalonia were eminently conspicuous. By the incorporation of this country, therefore, with the kingdom of Aragon, the strength of the latter was greatly augmented. The Aragonese princes, well aware of this, liberally fostered the institutions to which the country owed its prosperity, and skilfully availed themselves of its resources for the aggrandizement of their dominions. The Catalan navy disputed the empire of the Mediterranean with the fleets of Pisa, and still more with those of Genoa. With its aid the Aragonese monarchs achieved successfully the conquest of Sicily, Sardinia, and the Balearic isles, which they annexed to their empire. It penetrated into the farthest regions of the Levant, and a Catalan armament conquered Athens, giving to their sovereign the classical title of duke of that city.

But though the dominions of the kings of Aragon were thus extended abroad, there were no sovereigns in Europe whose authority was so limited at home. The national historians refer the origin of their government to a written constitution of about the middle of the ninth century, fragments of which are still preserved in certain ancient documents and chronicles. On the occurrence of a vacancy in the throne at this epoch, a monarch was elected by the twelve principal nobles, who prescribed a code of laws, to the observance of which he was compelled to swear before assuming the sceptre. The import of these laws was to circumscribe within very narrow limits the authority of the sovereignty, distributing the principal functions to a *justicia* or justice; and these peers were authorized, if the compact should be violated by the monarch, to withdraw their allegiance, and in the bold language of the ordinance "to substitute any other ruler in his stead, even a pagan if they listed." The great barons of Aragon were few in number, they claimed descent from the twelve electoral peers we have described, and they very reluctantly admitted to equality those whom the favor of the sovereign raised to the peerage. No baron could be divested of his fief unless by public sentence of the justice and the cortes. The nobles filled of right the highest offices in the state ; they appointed judges in their domains for the cognizance of certain civil causes, and they exercised an unlimited criminal jurisdiction over certain classes of their vassals. They were excused from taxation, except in specified cases ; were exempted from all corporal and capital punishments ; nor could they be imprisoned, though their estates might be sequestrated, for debt. But the laws conceded to them privileges of a still more dangerous character. They were entitled to defy and publicly renounce their allegiance to their sovereign, with the whimsical privilege in addition, of commending their families and estates to his protection, which he was obliged to protect until they were again reconciled. The mischievous right of private war was repeatedly recognised by statute. It was claimed and exercised in its full extent, and occasionally with circumstances of peculiar atrocity.

The commons of Aragon enjoyed higher consideration, and still larger civil privileges, than those of Castile. For this they were perhaps somewhat indebted to the example of their Catalan neighbors, the influence of whose democratic institutions naturally extended to other parts of the Aragonese monarchy. The charters of certain cities accorded to their inhabitants privileges of nobility, particularly those of immunity from taxation ; while the magistrates of others were permitted to take their seats in the order of the lesser nobles. By a statute passed in 1307, it was ordained that the cortes should assemble triennially. The great officers of the crown, whatever might be their personal rank, were jealously excluded from their deliberations. It was in the power of any member to defeat the passage of a bill, by opposing to it his *veto* or dissent formally registered to that effect. He might even interpose his negative on the proceedings of the house, and thus put a stop to the prosecution of all further business during the session. During the interval of the sessions of the legislature, a committee of two from each department was appointed to preside over public affairs, particularly in regard to the revenue and the security of justice ; with authority to convoke a cortes extraordinary, whenever the exigency might demand it.

The cortes exercised the highest functions, whether of a deliberative, legislative, or judicial nature. It had a right to be consulted on all matters of importance ; especially on those of peace or war. No law was valid, no tax could be imposed without its consent ; and it carefully provided for the application of the revenue to its destined uses. It determined the succession to the crown ; removed obnoxious ministers ; reformed the household and domestic expenditure of the monarch ; and exercised the power in the most unreserved manner of withholding supplies, as well as of resisting what it regarded as an encroachment on the liberties of the nation.

The governments of Valencia and Catalonia were administered independent of each other long after they had been consolidated into one monarchy, but they bore a very near resemblance to the constitution of Aragon. The city of Barcelona, which originally gave its name to the county of which it was the capital, was distinguished from a very early period by ample municipal privileges. Under the Aragonese monarchs, Barcelona had so well profited by the liberal administrations of its rulers as to have reached a degree of prosperity rivalling that of any of the Italian republics. The wealth which flowed in upon Barcelona, and the result of the activity and enterprise which the merchants of the place exhibited, was evinced by the numerous public works in which it set an example to all Europe. Strangers who visited Spain in the fourteenth and fifteenth centuries, expatiate on the magnificence of this city, its commodious private edifices, the cleanliness of its streets and public squares, and on the amenity of its gardens and cultivated environs.

But the peculiar glory of Barcelona was the freedom of its municipal institutions. The government consisted of a senate or council of one hundred, and a body of *corregidores* or counsellors, varying at times from four to six in number; the former intrusted with the legislative, the latter with the executive functions of administration. A large proportion of these bodies was selected from the merchants, tradesmen, and mechanics of the city. They were invested, not merely with municipal authority, but with many of the rights of sovereignty. They entered into commercial treaties with foreign powers; superintended the defence of the city in time of war; provided for the security of trade; granted letters of reprisal against any nation who might violate it; and raised and appropriated public money for the construction of useful works, or the encouragement of such commercial adventures as were too hazardous or expensive for individual enterprise.

Under the influence of these democratic institutions, the burghers of Barcelona, and, indeed, of Catalonia in general, which enjoyed more or less of a similar freedom, assumed a haughty independence of character, beyond what existed among the same class in other parts of Spain; and this, combined with the martial daring fostered by a life of maritime adventure and warfare, made them impatient, not merely of oppression, but of contradiction on the part of their sovereigns, who have experienced more frequent and more sturdy resistance from this part of their dominions than from any other. Navogiers, the Venetian ambassador to Spain early in the sixteenth century, although a republican himself, was so struck with what he deemed the insubordination of the Barcelonians, that he asserts, "The inhabitants have so many privileges that the king scarcely retains any authority over them; their liberty," he adds, "should rather go by the name of licentiousness."

Such, in the earlier stages of Spanish history, were the free constitutions of Castile and Aragon; but when these two kingdoms were united into one great monarchy, it became the settled policy of the sovereigns to destroy all the institutions by which the liberties of the people were secured. As the power of the Mohammedans grew weaker, the kings of Castile had less reason to grant municipal privileges on condition of defending the frontiers; and their nobles, continually engaged in mutual dissensions, were unable to check the inroads of the crown on their aristocratic privileges. The nobles of Aragon, indeed, were always ready to combine in a common cause, and it was aptly said by one of the monarchs, in reference to these two aristocracies, that "it was equally difficult to divide the nobles of Aragon, and to unite those of Castile." But union availed little to the Aragonese nobles, when the seat of government was placed beyond the sphere of their influence, and when Castilian armies were ready to crush the first appearance of insurrection. It is also to be remarked, though rather in anticipation of what we shall have to discuss hereafter, that the conquest of America not merely gave the kings of Spain vast supplies of gold, without their being compelled to have recourse to their parliaments or cortes, but it also enabled them to create many lucrative monopolies, for which the Spanish nobles bartered the privileges of their order and the rights of the people. There is a closer connexion between freedom of trade and freedom of institutions than is generally imagined: every protected interest exists at the expense of all the other classes of the community, and being itself based on injustice, must connive at injustice in others. Prospective loss, however great, is constantly hazarded by the ignorant and unthinking for immediate gain, however small, and it was this selfish folly which mainly enabled the Austrian line of Spanish monarchs to overthrow the ancient constitution of their country, and to render Spain a memorable and sad example of the great truth, that a land of monopoly soon becomes a land of slavery, and eventually a land of misery.

Section XII.—*State of Western Europe at the commencement of the Fourteenth Century.*

Rodolph of Hapsburgh had no sooner obtained possession of the empire, than he resolved to strengthen the sovereign authority, by annexing some of the great fiefs to the crown. The usurpation of the dutchy of Austria by Ottokar, king of Bohemia, afforded him a pretext for interfering in the disposal of that province; he defeated Ottokar, and deprived him not only of Austria, but also of Styria, Carinthia, and Carniola, which were formed into a new principality, and the investiture given to Albert, the emperor's son (A. D. 1282), who founded the imperial house of Austria.

But while the emperor's authority was extended in Germany, it was almost unknown in Italy, where the republican cities generally withdrew even nominal allegiance from their former masters. Of these commercial states Venice was the most important. This city had been originally founded by some refugees who sought shelter in the islands and lagoons of the Adriatic, from the ferocity of the Huns (A. D. 452); but it first rose into importance under the doge Pierre Urseolo II. (A. D. 992), who obtained freedom of commerce for his fellow-citizens from the Byzantine emperor and the sultan of Egypt, and subjected the maritime cities of Istria and Dalmatia. In the wars between the empire and the papacy, they had generally supported the latter; Pope Alexander III., as a reward for their services, conferred on them the sovereignty of the Adriatic, and hence arose the singular ceremony of celebrating annually a mystic marriage between that sea and the Venetian doge. The crusades tended greatly to extend the power of the republic, especially the fourth, in which, as we have already stated, the Greek empire was dismembered. On this occasion, the Venetians received from their allies several maritime cities in Dalmatia, Albania, Epirus, and Greece, the islands of Crete, Corfu, Cephalonia, and several others in the Ionian cluster.

But the increasing wealth of Venice led to a fatal change in its political constitution. The government was originally democratic, the power of the doge being limited by a council, who were freely chosen by the citizens. Several tumults at these elections furnished the doge, Peter Grandenigo, with an excuse for proposing a law abrogating annual elections, and rendering the dignity of councillor hereditary in the families of those who were at the period members of the legislative assembly (A. D. 1298). This establishment of a close aristocracy led to several revolts, of which that headed by Tiepolo was the most remarkable (A. D. 1310). After a fierce battle within the city, the insurgents were routed; ten inquisitors were chosen to investigate the conspiracy, and this commission was soon rendered permanent under the name of the Council of Ten, the most formidable tribunal ever founded to support aristocratic tyranny.

Genoa, like Venice, owed its prosperity to its extensive commerce, which flourished in spite of the several political convulsions that agitated the republic. The Genoese embraced the cause of the Greek emperors, and helped them to regain Constantinople. Their services were rewarded by the cession of Caffa, Azov, and other ports on the Black sea, through which they opened a lucrative trade with China and India. They obtained also Smyrna, and Pera, a suburb of Constantinople, together with several important islands in the Archipelago. Nor were they less successful in extending their power in Italy and the western Mediterranean, though they had to contend against powerful rivals in the citizens of Pisa. The mutual jealousies of these republics, and the anxiety of both to possess the islands of Corsica and Sardinia, led to a long and sanguinary war. It ended (A. D. 1290) in the complete overthrow of the Pisans, whose commerce was annihilated by the loss of the island of Elba, and the destruction of the ports of Pisa and Leghorn.

Charles of Anjou did not long enjoy the kingdom of the Two Sicilies. His subjects justly hated him for the murder of Conradin, and the insolence of the French soldiery confirmed their aversion. An atrocious insult offered to a Sicilian lady, provoked the celebrated insurrection, commonly called the Sicilian Vespers* (A. D. 1282), in which all the French residents in Sicily were massacred, with the exception of William Parcellet, whose virtues honorably distinguished him from his countrymen. The islanders placed themselves under the protection of the king of Aragon, and Charles, though aided by the pope, was unable to regain his authority over them.

Pope Martin, who was warmly attached to Charles of Anjou, excommunicated the king of Aragon, and placed his kingdom under an interdict; and, finding these measures ineffectual, he preached a crusade against him, and gave the investiture of his states to the count of Va-

* The evening prayers in the catholic church are called Vespers, and the revolt commenced as the congregation were assembling at Palermo for the evening service, during the festival of Easter. Some historians describe this massacre as the result of a deep and long-planned conspiracy; but it is much more likely to have been simply a sudden outbreak of popular indignation.

lois, second son of the king of France. He proclaimed Charles of Anjou champion of the holy church, and declared that this sanguinary tyrant was a prince chosen by God himself. The pope, who thus bestowed crowns, and exonerated subjects from their allegiance, was unable to maintain himself in his own capital; and while he hoped to humble kings, could not enforce the obedience of the Roman citizens. But this is not the only instance of a similar anomaly in the history of the papacy. Peter of Aragon, feigning obedience, exchanged his title of king for that of a simple knight, retaining, however, all the power of royalty; but dreading the succors that the king of France sent to his uncle more than the papal menaces, he sought out means of gaining time to organize the defence of Sicily. Knowing the vain-glorious disposition of his rival, Peter proposed that Charles and he, with a hundred knights at each side, should decide their respective titles in a combat, near Bordeaux. The duke of Anjou, elated by the hopes of a duel with a prince who added to his modest title, "Knight of Aragon," the sounding designations, "Lord of the Seas, and Father of Three Kings," accepted the terms; and, while he prepared for the expected field, neglected his preparations for war. Martin fulminated against the duel, single combats being forbidden by the church; but Peter had never intended to expose himself to the chance, and on the appointed day Charles discovered, from the non-appearance of his adversary, that he had been baffled by superior policy, perhaps we should rather say, perfidy.

Martin more than shared the indignation of his favorite; he renewed the preaching of the crusade against Peter, granting to all who fought in the papal cause the same indulgences assigned to those who joined in the expeditions for the recovery of Palestine; and he sent ambassadors urging the French king to hasten the invasion of Aragon. It is not easy to conceive how monarchs could be blind to the consequences of accepting these proffered crowns; they thus recognised the principle of the pope's right to depose sovereigns, and sanctioned a power which might at any time be employed against themselves or their successors. But the lessons of prudence are slow in penetrating hearts fascinated by ambition or fanaticism.

The anathemas of Martin did not deprive Peter of his crown; they scarcely even checked the current of his fortunes. All his subjects, clergy, nobles, and commons, ostentatiously displayed their attachment to their sovereign, and laughed the papal decrees to scorn. The Aragonese admiral defeated the fleet of the duke of Anjou within sight of Naples, and made his son, Charles the Lame, a prisoner (A. D. 1284). This scion of a detested race would not have escaped the fury of the Messenians, who wished to sacrifice him in revenge for the murder of Conradin, only for the generous interference of Queen Constance, Manfred's daughter, who rescued him from the fury of the populace, and sent him for security to Catalonia. Charles of Anjou did not long survive this calamity; the remembrance of his former triumphs and prosperity, his pride, his contempt for his enemies, and shame for having been baffled by policy, aggravated the mortification of a defeat which he no longer had power to retrieve.

Spain continued divided into several small kingdoms, Christian and

Mohammedan. To the former belonged Navarre, Aragon, and Castile, of which the last two were gradually extending themselves at the expense of their Mohammedan neighbors. The Castilian monarch, Alphonso I., captured Madrid and Toledo (A. D. 1085); he would probably have expelled the Moors from Spain, had not a new burst of fanaticism in Africa supplied the Mohammedans with hordes of enthusiastic defenders in the moment of danger. The Moors not only recovered their strength, but became so formidable, that Pope Innocent III. published a crusade against them. A numerous Christian army assembled on the confines of Castile and Andalusia; they encountered their enemies near the city of Uleda, and inflicted on them a defeat, from which the Spanish Mohammedans never recovered (A. D. 1212). Ferdinand III., king of Castile and Leon, profiting by the weakness of the Moors, subdued the little kingdom of Cordova, Murcia, and Seville (A. D. 1256), so that the Mohammedans were reduced to the single kingdom of Granada.

The crusade in Spain led to the foundation of a new kingdom in Europe. Henry of Burgundy, a member of the royal family of France, was so eminently distinguished by his valor in the Mohammedan wars, that Alphonso VI., king of Castile, gave him his daughter in marriage, with the investiture of the country of Portugal as her dowry. Henry enlarged his territory at the expense of the Mohammedans, but his fame was eclipsed by that of his son Alphonso, whom his soldiers proclaimed king on the glorious field of battle in which the power of the Mohammedans was destroyed (A. D. 1139). To secure his new royalty, Alphonso placed himself and his kingdom under the protection of the holy see, and declared himself a liege subject of the pope. His successors found the Roman pontiffs by no means slow in availing themselves of the power thus ceded to them; several violent struggles were made by the kings to free themselves from the yoke, but the power of the popes prevailed, and a treaty was concluded, by which the Portuguese clergy were secured in extensive possessions, almost royal privileges, and a complete exemption from secular jurisdiction (A. D. 1289).

As the governments of France and England began to assume a stable form, rivalry arose between the two nations, which led to a long series of sanguinary wars. From the time of Capet's usurpation, the policy of the French kings had been to lessen the power of the great feudatories; and it was a perilous error in Philip I. to sanction the duke of Normandy's conquest of England, for he thus permitted a vassal, already dangerous, to become his rival sovereign. The danger was greatly increased when Louis VII. divorced his faithless wife Eleanor, the heiress to the provinces of Guienne, Poitou, and Gascony. She married Henry II., king of England, and thus enabled him to add her inheritance to that of the Plantagenets in France, which included the dutchies of Normandy and the counties of Anjou and Maine (A. D. 1252). The vassal was now more powerful than his sovereign; the throne of France indeed would scarcely have been secure, had not the family disputes of the Plantagenets, secretly fomented by the wicked Eleanor, caused Henry's sons to revolt against their indulgent father, and brought that able sovereign with sorrow to his grave. Philip Augustus was the founder of the greatness of the French monarchy. The Plantagenets of England sank rapidly before his superior talents. Richard I. was nothing more than a brave warrior, and unable to compete with the policy of his rival; his successor, John, was neither a soldier nor a statesman; he provoked the resentment of all his subjects, and while assailed in England by the discontented barons, and menaced abroad by the pope, he was deprived of most of his continental dominions by the watchful king of France. Philip's neighbors, and many of his vassals, were alarmed at the vast increase of his power after his conquest of the Norman provinces; they formed a league against him, but at the battle of Bouvines (A. D. 1214), he triumphed over the united forces of the Germans, the English, and the Flemings, and by this victory secured the possession of his acquisitions.

After the death of Nicholas (A. D. 1292), the papacy, as if exhausted by its own excesses, seemed to have fallen into a lethargy. The holy see remained vacant for two years and three months; an interval which the heads of the church might have improved to accommodate the ecclesiastical system to the improved state of intelligence, and the consequent changes in the wants and wishes of Europe But, in an evil hour, they had adopted the doctrine of infallibility, and believed themselves bound to keep their system stationary while everything around was in progress. In a former age the papacy had taken the lead in the advancement of intelligence; the clergy and the friars were the missionaries of knowledge; but the church had now fallen into the rear; kings, not pontiffs, were the patrons of learning; in the new contest between the spiritual and temporal powers, we shall find the latter conquering, because on their side were ranged all who took a share in the advancement of civilization. Intelligence, emancipated from the cloister, found a temporary abode in the palace, and finally spread even to the cottage; the popes became its enemies from the moment it quitted their protection, but they were necessarily vanquished in the struggle; one age beheld monarchs despise the deposing power, the next witnessed the pope's authority a mockery, and his very name a reproach in one half of Europe.

The vacancy in the papacy became the signal for civil wars in Rome, and throughout Italy; superstition attributed these calamities to the cardinals, who left the church without a head: an insane hermit stimulated the populace to menace them with death unless they proceeded to an election, and they chose a feeble, ignorant, old fanatic, who took the name of Celestine IV. Though destitute of any other qualification, Celestine had at least the pride of a pontiff—the bridle of the ass, on which, with blasphemous imitation, he made his public entry into Aquilla, was held by two kings, Charles II., the perjured sovereign of Naples, and his son Charles Martel, nominal king of Hungary. But the cardinals soon became weary of an idiot monk forced upon them by an insane hermit; Benedict Cajetan worked upon the weak mind of Celestine to resign a dignity which he was unable to maintain, and, having previously gained the suffrages of the college, ascended the throne under the name of Boniface VIII.* In its altered circumstances, the

* Almost the only thing memorable in the pontificate of Celestine, is the fabled miracle of the chapel of Loretto, which was said to have been transported by angels from Nazareth to the place where it now stands, that it should not be

papacy thus found a ruler who had fortitude and courage sufficient to maintain its pretensions against the kings who had now begun to discover their rights; but the defeat of the pontiff added one to the many examples that history affords of the failure of antiquated pretensions when opposed to common sense and common honesty.

Section XIII.—*Pontificate of Boniface VIII.*

Most historians assert that Boniface had recourse to very treacherous artifices, in order to obtain the resignation of Celestine: however this may be, the abdicated pontiff was immediately shut up in a prison, lest his scruples, or his remorse, should trouble his successor. Boniface, to the ambition and despotic character of Gregory VII, added a more crafty manner, and more dissimulation, than had been recently seen in the chair of St. Peter. He aspired to universal sovereignty over ecclesiastics, princes, and nations; and he diligently sought out means for rendering them submissive to his laws. Aware that it would be impossible to revive the crusading passion in Europe, he resolved to make the recovery of Palestine a pretext for interfering in the quarrels of sovereigns. He wrote to Philip the Fair, king of France, to Edward I. of England, and to Adolphus, emperor of Germany, commanding them, under pain of excommunication, to accommodate their differences; and he mediated a peace between the sovereigns of France and Aragon.

James, king of Aragon, anxious to conciliate the pope, resigned his pretensions to Sicily; but the islanders, detesting the house of Anjou, and despising the commands of a sovereign who had so weakly abandoned his rights, crowned Frederic, the brother of James, at Palermo, and expelled the papal legates. Excommunications were fulminated against the Sicilians, and the sovereign of their choice; even the feeble James was induced to arm against his brother, and aid in his expulsion from the island; and this violation of natural ties was rewarded by the cession of Sardinia and Corsica, over which the pope had not a shadow of right. But the ambition of Boniface was not limited to bestowing islands and Italian principalities; he resolved to establish his authority over the most powerful sovereigns of Europe.

Philip the Fair was one of the most able monarchs in Christendom, resolute in establishing his influence over the great vassals of the crown, he strengthened himself by the support of his people, and resolved that the nobles and the clergy should, henceforth, form classes of his subjects. Feudal anarchy disappeared, and equal jurisdiction was extended over all ranks; the lower classes were delivered from the most galling burdens of vassalage, and the despotism of the sovereign became a blessing to the nation. In the midst of his career he received an embassy from the pope, commanding him to spare a conquered vassal, to abstain from taxing the clergy, and to submit his disputes with the count of Flanders to the arbitration of the holy see. Philip spurned these demands, upon which the pope issued the celebrated bull, called, from the words with which it commences, *Clericis*

polluted by the Saracens. This absurd story was long credited by the Romanists, but it is now derided even in Italy.

laicos, excommunicating the kings who should levy ecclesiastical subsidies, and the priests who should pay them; and withdrawing the clergy from the jurisdiction of lay tribunals.

This attempt to establish a theocracy, independent of monarchy excited general indignation. In England, Edward ordered his judges to admit no causes in which ecclesiastics were the complainants, but to try every suit brought against them, averring that those who refused to contribute to the support of the state, had no claim to the protection of the law. This expedient succeeded, and the English ecclesiastics hastened to pay their subsidies, without further compulsion. Philip the Fair exhibited even more vigor; he issued an edict prohibiting the export of gold, silver, jewels, provisions, or munitions of war, without a license; and he forbade foreign merchants to establish themselves in his dominions. Boniface, aware that these measures would destroy the revenue which the court of Rome derived from France, remonstrated in urgent terms, explained away the most offensive parts of his former bull, and offered several advantages to the king if he would modify his edicts. Philip allowed himself to be persuaded; the bull *Clericis laicos* was rendered less stringent: Louis IX. was canonized, and Philip could boast of having a saint for an ancestor; finally, the pope promised that he would support Charles of Valois, as a candidate for the empire. Dazzled by these boons, the French monarch accepted the arbitration of the pope, in his disputes with the king of England and the count of Flanders. But Boniface, to his astonishment, decided that Guienne should be restored to England, that all his former possessions should be given back to the count of Flanders, and that Philip himself should undertake a new crusade. When this unjust sentence was read in the presence of the French court, by the bishop of Durham, Edward's ambassador, the king listened to it with a smile of contempt; but the count of Artois enraged at such insolence, snatched the bull, tore it in pieces, and flung the fragments into the fire. This was the only answer returned: Philip, heedless of the pope's anger, renewed the war.

Boniface VIII. little dreamed that Philip's resistance would be so energetic, or of such dangerous example; but he prepared for the coming struggle, by securing his authority in Italy, and especially in Rome, where the papal power had been long controlled by the factious nobles. Immediately after his elevation to the pontificate, he had caused himself to be elected senator, but the Ghibellines rendered the dignity of such a magistrate very precarious; it was necessary to destroy them, and in this instance personal vengeance was united to the projects of ambition. The leaders of the Ghibelline faction at Rome were the illustrious family of the Colonna: two cardinals of that name had strenuously resisted the abdication of Celestine, and had long been marked out as victims. Under the pretext of their alliance with the kings of Sicily and Aragon, they were summoned to appear before the papal tribunal; but, justly dreading that their doom was predetermined, they fled to their castles, protesting against the sentence of him whom they denied to be a legitimate pope. Boniface hurled the most terrible anathemas against them, declaring them infamous, excommunicate, and incapable of any public charge, to the fourth generation: he devoted them to the fires of the Inquisition, and preached a crusade for their destruction. Intimidated for a moment, the Colonnas submitted, and surrendered their town of Palestrina as a pledge of their fidelity. No sooner was Boniface master of this stronghold, than, regardless of his oaths, he levelled the fortress to the ground, forbade it to be rebuilt, renewed his persecutions against the Colonnas, and compelled them to fly from Italy. They sought shelter at the court of France, where they were hospitably received by Philip, who thus gave a signal proof of his independence and his generosity.

Boniface was alarmed, but not dismayed; he resolved to lull the king's vigilance by stimulating his ambition: for this purpose he proposed to dethrone Albert, emperor of Germany, and give the crown to Charles of Valois, whom he had already created imperial vicar, and captain-general of the holy church. Philip turned a deaf ear to this tempting proposal; he even entered into alliance with Albert, and cemented the union by giving his sister in marriage to the emperor's son, Rodolph, duke of Austria. Boniface was enraged at this disappointment, but his attention was diverted by the institution of a jubilee, to mark the commencement of a new century (A. D. 1300). He published a bull, promising full pardon and remission of all sins to those who, being confessed and penitent, should visit the tombs of the apostles at Rome, during fifteen days. Multitudes of pilgrims, anxious to obtain the benefits of the crusades, without the perils of war, flocked to the city, and, by their liberal expenditure, greatly enriched the Romans. This profitable contrivance was renewed by the successors of Boniface, at intervals of fifty years, and proved to be an efficacious means of recruiting the papal treasury.

Scarcely had the jubilee terminated, when the disputes between the pope and the king of France were revived, in consequence of the rival claims for supremacy, between the archbishop and the viscount of Narbonne. The king supported his vassal; the prelate appealed to the pope, and Boniface promptly responded to the call. A legate was sent to Philip, and the choice of an ambassador was almost a declaration of war. The pope's messenger was the bishop of Pamiers, a rebellious subject, whose treasons were notorious, and whose insolence to his sovereign excited general indignation. The seditious prelate was driven from the court; but the king, instead of bringing him to trial, complained to his metropolitan, the archbishop of Narbonne, and demanded justice. Boniface addressed an insolent bull to the king, summoned the French bishops to meet at Rome, to consult respecting the doom that should be pronounced on their sovereign, and invited Philip himself to be present at this unprecedented conclave. But the king, supported by the legists or professors of the law, a body rising rapidly into importance, defied the papal power, and appealed to the good sense of his people. Boniface had sent a bull, known in history by the name *Ausculta fili*,* to France, in which all the delinquencies of Philip, not only toward the church, but every class of his subjects, were portrayed with apparent moderation, but with great vigor and eloquence. Peter Flotte, the royal chancellor, presented an abridgment of this document to the great council of the nation, craftily culling out those passages in

* "Listen, son," the words with which it commenced.

which the papal pretensions were most offensively put forward. This document, called "the little bull," was as follows:—

"Boniface, bishop, servant of the servants of God, to Philip, king of the Franks. Fear God and keep his commandments. We desire you to know that you are subject to us in temporal as well as in spiritual affairs; that the appointment to benefices and prebends belongs not to you; that if you have kept benefices vacant, the profits must be reserved for the legal successors; and if you have bestowed any benefice, we declare the appointment invalid, and revoke it if executed. Those who oppose this judgment shall be deemed heretics."

Philip ordered this declaration to be publicly burned, and he published a memorable reply, which, however, was probably never sent to Rome. It is a very remarkable proof of the decline of the papal power that such a manifesto should be issued, and presented to the states-general of France, as their monarch's answer to the supreme pontiff. The letter of the king is thus given by historians:—

"Philip, by the grace of God, king of the French, to Boniface, claiming to be pope, little or no greeting. May it please your sublime stupidity to learn, that we are subject to no person in temporal affairs; that the bestowing of fiefs and benefices belongs to us by right of our crown; that the disposal of the revenues of vacant sees, is part of our prerogative; that our decrees, in this respect, are valid, both for the past and for the future; and that we will support, with all our might, those on whom we have bestowed, or shall bestow, benefices. Those who oppose this judgment shall be deemed fools or idiots."

The manifestos sent to Rome by the three orders of the states-general, the nobles, the clergy, and the commons, are of greater importance to the historian than "the little bull" or the royal reply. That of the French barons was addressed to the college of cardinals; it openly accused the pope of having periled the unity of the church by his extravagant ambition, and it denied, in the strongest terms, his right to appellate jurisdiction over the kingdom of France. The clergy addressed Boniface himself in a measured and respectful tone, but they declared that they had taken a new oath to their sovereign, that they would firmly maintain the independence of his crown. The declaration of the commons has not been preserved, but like that of the nobles, it appears to have been addressed to the college of cardinals. The court of Rome was alarmed, letters of explanation were sent to the different orders, but the pope declared he would not write to the king, whom he considered subject to the sentence of excommunication.

While Boniface VIII. was thus engaged with France and its ruler, he did not lose sight of his pretensions over other kingdoms. Edward of England, having overcome the feudal turbulence of his vassals, was about to undertake the conquest of Scotland, when the holy see forbade the enterprise. Edward in reply traced his right to Scotland, up to the age of the prophet Samuel, and a synod of the English clergy declared, that the claims of their sovereign were better founded than those of the pontiff. A legate, by command of Boniface, labored to pacify Hungary, which was divided between the grandson of Charles the Lame, king of Naples, and Andrew the Venetian. On the death of the latter prince, the Hungarian barons, fearing the loss of their liberties under a king imposed upon them by the church, elected for their sovereign the son of the king of Bavaria, and he was solemnly crowned by the archbishop of Colreza. The pope wrote fierce denunciations against the election, and even commanded the king of Bavaria to dethrone his own son. But though Hungary refused submission, the obedience of Spain consoled the pontiff; he declared the marriage of Sancho the Brave valid, after his death, and in consequence of this decision, Ferdinand IV., the eldest son of that monarch, was permitted to retain the kingdom of Castile.

Though Philip had ordered that the goods of all the clergy who quitted the kingdom should be confiscated, many of the prelates braving the penalty, proceeded to the court of Rome. Conscious that this disobedience portended a struggle between the spiritual and temporal power, the French king took the unexpected precaution of denouncing the horrors of the inquisition, and thus representing royalty as the shield of the people against the tyranny of the priesthood. Boniface, encouraged by the presence of the French bishops, yielded to the impetuosity of his passions, and issued the famous bull *Unam sanctam*, in which the claims of the papacy to universal dominion are stated with more strength and precision than the court of Rome had yet ventured to use. After this document had been sanctioned by the council, a legate was sent to France, whose instructions contained the demand that the king should not oppose the prelates who wished to travel, the disposal of benefices by the holy see, or the entrance of legates into his kingdom; that he should not confiscate the properties of ecclesiastics, nor bring them to trial, before civil courts; that the king should appear in person at Rome, and answer to the charge of having burned a bull sealed with the effigies of the holy apostles; and finally, that he should recompense the losses occasioned by the depreciation of the currency, and abandon the city of Lyons to its archbishop, as an ecclesiastical fief. Philip the Fair, undaunted by the threat of excommunication, peremptorily rejected all these demands, and in his turn caused Boniface to be accused by William de Nogaret, the royal advocate, of usurpation, heresy, and simony. The advocate required that a general council should be summoned to investigate these charges, and that the pope should be detained in prison until his guilt or innocence should be decided.

Boniface was now seriously alarmed; when he ascended the throne, Celestine had declared "This cardinal, who stole like a fox into the chair of St. Peter, will have the reign of a lion, and the end of a dog;" his violence in the struggle with the king of France, tended to realize both predictions. But it was necessary to obtain allies, and Frederic, king of Sicily, was won over to declare himself a vassal of the holy see, by obtaining the recognition of his royal title, and absolution from the many anathemas hurled against him. The emperor Albert was similarly prevailed upon to recognise the extravagant pretensions of the papacy, on obtaining a bull confirming his election; he even issued letters patent confessing that the imperial power was a boon conferred at the pleasure of the holy see. Thus strengthened, Boniface laid aside all appearance of moderation, and solemnly excommunicated the contumacious king of France.

Philip on the other hand assembled the states of his realm at the Louvre, and presented to them a new act of accusation against Boniface, in which he was charged with the most detestable and unnatural crimes. It was voted that an appeal should be made to a new pope and a general council, and so general was the disapprobation of the pontiff's ambitious schemes, that the greater part of the French ecclesiastical dignitaries, including nine cardinals, sent in their adhesion to the appeal.

Boniface met the storm with firmness; he replied to the charges urged against him with more temper than could have been anticipated, but he secretly prepared a bull of excommunication, depriving Philip of his throne, and anathematizing his posterity to the fourth generation.

This final burst of hostility was delayed until the 8th of September (A. D. 1303), when the Romish church celebrates the nativity of the blessed Virgin, and Boniface awaited the day in the city of Anagni.

On the eve of the Virgin's nativity the pope had retired to rest, having arranged his plans of vengeance for the following day; he was suddenly roused by cries of "Long live Philip! Death to Boniface!" Nogaret, at the command of the king of France, had entered Anagni with three hundred cavaliers, and being joined by some of the townsmen, was forcing his way into the palace. Sciarra Colonna and Nogaret rushed together into the chamber of Boniface; they found the old man clothed in his pontifical robes, seated on his throne, waiting their approach with unshaken dignity. They made him their prisoner, and prepared for his removal to France until a general council. But Nogaret having unwisely delayed three days at Anagni, the citizens and the neighboring peasants united to liberate the pontiff; Colonna and his French allies were forced to abandon their prey, and could only save their lives by a rapid flight. Boniface hastened to Rome; but fatigue, anxiety, and vexation, brought on a violent fever, which soon put an end to his troubled life.

The reign of Boniface was fatal to the papal power; he exaggerated its pretensions at the moment when the world had begun to discover the weakness of its claims; in the attempt to extend his influence further than any of his predecessors, he exhausted the sources of his strength, and none of his successors, however ardent, ventured to revive pretensions which had excited so many wars, shed so much blood, and dethroned so many kings. The priesthood and the empire, fatigued by so long and disastrous a struggle, desired tranquillity, but tranquillity was for the court of Rome a political death. The illusion of its own omnipotence vanished with the agitations by which it had been produced, and new principles of action began to be recognised in its policy.

The death of Boniface marks an important era in the history of popery; from this time we shall see it concentrating its strength, and husbanding its resources; fighting only on the defensive, it no longer provokes the hostility of kings, or seeks cause of quarrel with the emperors. The bulls that terrified Christendom must repose as literary curiosities in the archives of St. Angelo, and though the claims to universal supremacy will not be renounced, there will be no effort made to enforce them. A few pontiffs will be found now and then reviving the claims of Gregory, of Innocent, and of Boniface; but their attempts will be found desultory and of brief duration, like the last flashes, fierce but few, that break out from the ashes of a conflagration.

Benedict XI., the successor of Boniface, hasted to exhibit proofs of the moderation which results from defeat. Without waiting for any solicitation, he absolved Philip the Fair from the anathemas fulminated against him by Boniface; recalled the Colonnas from exile, and encouraged the Roman people to restore the ancient inheritance of that illustrious family; finally, he exerted himself to reconcile the Guelphs and Ghibellines in Tuscany, but unfortunately without effect. His early death prepared the way for a new crisis, in which the political system of the papacy was destined to suffer greater shocks than any to which it had been yet exposed, and to give fresh proofs that it could not be improved, even by the stern lessons of adversity.

Section XIV.—*State of England and the Northern Kingdoms at the Commencement of the Fourteenth Century.*

William the Conqueror reduced the Saxon population of England to the most degrading state of vassalage, but he could not destroy the love and memory of their ancient laws and liberties retained by the nation His sons, William Rufus, and Henry I., were successively enabled to seize the throne in prejudice of the rights of their elder brother Robert, by promising to restore the ancient laws of the kingdom. Henry, to conciliate the English more effectually, married a princess of Saxon descent; on his death he bequeathed the crown to the surviving child by this marriage, Matilda, the wife of Geoffry Plantagenet, earl of Anjou. This arrangement was defeated by the usurpation of Stephen. England was convulsed by a civil war, which was terminated by Stephen's adopting Henry, Matilda's son, as his successor.

Henry II., the first of the Plantagenet dynasty, on ascending the throne, united to England the dutchy of Normandy, the county of Anjou, and the fairest provinces of northwestern France (A. D. 1154). To these he added the more important acquisition of Ireland, partly by a papal donation, and partly by right of conquest.

Ireland was at this period divided into five petty sovereignties, whose monarchs harassed each other by mutual wars, and could rarely be induced to combine for their common interest. The island had been frequently devastated, and once completely subdued, by the Danes; several septs of these foreigners retained possession of the chief commercial cities, and even the king of Man was formidable to a country distracted by intestine wars. When their Norman brethren conquered England, the Danes in Ireland entered into a close correspondence with William and his successors, a circumstance which probably first suggested to Henry the notion of conquering the island. He applied to the pope for a sanction of his enterprise. Adrian, the only Englishman that ever filled the papal throne, was at that time the reigning pontiff; his desire to gratify his native sovereign was stimulated by his anxiety to extend the papal authority. The Irish church had been long independent of Rome; and the connexion between its prelates and the papacy was as yet insecure; it was therefore on the condition of subjecting Ireland to the jurisdiction of the Romish church that a bull was issued, granting Henry permission to invade the country. The bitter feuds in the Plantagenet family, and the state of his continental dominions, long prevented the English monarch from availing himself of this permission. At length Dermod, king of Leinster, driven from his dominions by a rival sovereign, sought English aid, and was permitted to engage the services of Strongbow, and some other military adventurers, on condition of doing homage for his kingdom to Henry. The rapid successes of Strongbow awakened Henry's jealousy; he went to Ireland in person, and received the submission of its principal sovereigns (A. D. 1172). He returned without completing the conquest of the country, a circumstance productive of much misery and bloodshed through several successive centuries.

The reign of Richard I. was a period of little importance in English history; but that of his brother and successor, the profligate John, led to the most important results. The barons, provoked by his tyranny and his vices, took up arms, and compelled him to sign the Great Charter, which laid the first permanent foundation of British freedom; the pope forced him to resign his crown, and to receive it back again, only on condition of vassalage to the holy see, while Philip Augustus took advantage of these circumstances to deprive the English monarchs of most of their continental possessions. John's death saved England from becoming a province of France: absolved by Pope Innocent III. from his oath, he ventured to abrogate the Great Charter, upon which the English barons proffered the crown to Louis, the eldest son of Philip Augustus, who invaded England with the fairest prospects of success. John was completely defeated (A. D. 1216); he fled toward Scotland, but died upon the road. The English, already disgusted, with their French allies, embraced this opportunity of rallying round Prince Henry, and Louis was glad to conclude a treaty for abandoning the island.

Henry III. was a monarch wholly void of energy; it was his misfortune to fill the throne at one of the most turbulent periods of English history, without talents to command respect, or resolution to enforce obedience. During his long reign, England was engaged in few foreign wars, but these were generally unfortunate. On the other hand, the country was agitated by internal commotions during the greater part of the fifty years that he swayed the sceptre. The discontent of the prelates and barons at the favor that the king showed to foreigners induced them to form an association, by which the king was virtually deposed, and the supreme authority vested in a committee of peers, with the earl of Leicester at its head. Leicester introduced an important change into the constitution, by summoning representatives of counties, cities, and boroughs, to unite with the barons in the great council of the nation (A. D. 1265). This innovation laid the basis for the house of commons, which henceforth had an increasing share in English legislation. The tyranny of the barons being found less endurable than that of the king, Henry was restored to his former power; and his authority seemed fixed so permanently, that Prince Edward led an armament to the Holy Land, in aid of the last crusade of St. Louis. Henry died during his son's absence (A. D. 1272); but though two years elapsed before Edward's return home, the tranquillity of the country continued undisturbed.

The chief object of Edward's ambition was to unite the whole of Great Britain under one sovereignty. Under the pretext of the Welsh prince, Llewelyn, having refused homage, he invaded the country, and completely subdued it, but not without encountering a desperate resistance. The English monarch stayed more than a year in Wales to complete its pacification, and during that time his queen, Eleanor, gave birth to a son in the castle of Carnarvon (A. D. 1284). The Welsh claimed the child as their countryman, and he was declared Prince of Wales, a title which has ever since been borne by the eldest sons of the English kings.

The failure of the direct heirs to the crown of Scotland gave Edward a pretence for interfering in the affairs of that kingdom. Three competitors, Baliol, Bruce, and Hastings, laid claim to the crown; to avert the horrors of civil war, they agreed to leave the decision to Edward; and he pronounced in favor of the first, on condition of Baliol's becoming a vassal to the king of England. Baliol soon grew weary of the authority exercised over him by Edward, and made an effort to recover his independence; but being defeated and taken prisoner, he abdicated the throne (A. D. 1296), and was confined in the Tower of London. The Scottish nation, though vanquished, was not subdued; several insurrections were raised against the English yoke; but after the defeat and capture of the Scottish hero, Sir William Wallace, all hope of independence seemed to have vanished. At length, Robert Bruce raised the standard of revolt, and was crowned king at Scone (A. D. 1306). Edward once more sent an army into Scotland, and soon followed in person to subdue that obstinate nation. His death on the border (A. D. 1307) freed Bruce from his most dangerous foe; and in the following reign the independence of Scotland was established by the decisive battle of Bannockburn (A. D. 1314).

The northren kingdoms of Europe, in the thirteenth and fourteenth centuries, offer little to our notice but scenes of horror and carnage. The natural ferocity and warlike spirit of the Northmen, the want of fixed rules of succession, and the difficulty of finding employment for turbulent spirits in piratical expeditions when the increase of civilization had given consistency to the governments of the south, and enabled them to provide for the protection of their subjects, multiplied factions, and produced innumerable civil wars. Crusades, however, were undertaken against the Sclavonian and other pagan nations, by which the kings of Denmark and Sweden added considerably to their dominions, and gave them a high rank among the states of Europe. Prussia and Livonia were subdued by the knights of the Teutonic order; and Hungary, after having been almost ruined by the Mongolian hordes, began gradually to recover its importance after the retreat of these barbarians (A. D. 1244).

SECTION XV.—*Revolutions in the East in consequence of the Mongolian Invasion.*

THERE is no phenomenon more remarkable in history than the rise, progress, and extent of the Mongolian empire. Jenghiz Khan, in a single reign, issuing from a petty principality in the wilds of Tartary, acquired an empire stretching about six thousand miles from east to west, and at least half that space from north to south, including within its limits the most powerful and wealthy kingdoms of Asia.

The Mongols were first raised into eminence by Jenghiz Khan; his original name was Temujín, and he was the chief of a small horde which his father's valor had elevated above the surrounding tribes. At an early age he was invited to the court of Vang Khan, the nominal head of the tribes of the Tartarian deserts, and received the hand of that potentate's daughter in marriage. Mutual jealousy soon led to a war between Temujín and his father-in-law; the latter was slain in battle, and Temujín succeeded to his authority. On the day of his installation, a pretended prophet named Kokza, addressing the new sovereign, declared that he was inspired by God to name him Jenghiz Khan, that is, supreme monarch, and to promise him the empire of the universe.

Inspired by this prophecy, which, however, he is suspected of having suggested, Jenghiz zealously labored to establish military discipline among the vast hordes that flocked to his standard; and when he had organized an army, he invaded those provinces of northern China called Khatai by the oriental writers, and Cathay by our old English authors. In five years this extensive country was subdued, and Jenghiz directed his arms westward, provoked by an outrage of the sultan of Kharasm. This kingdom of Kharasm was among the most flourishing in central Asia; the literary eminence of Bokhara, and the commercial prosperity of Samarcand, were celebrated throughout the East. The sultans Mohammed and his son and successor, Jalaloddín, were monarchs of dauntless bravery, but nothing could withstand the fury of the Mongols, and not only Kharasm, but the greater part of northern and eastern Persia, full under the sway of Jenghiz. Astrachan was taken by a Mongolian detachment, and some of the hordes pushed their incursions as far as the confines of Russia. Jenghiz died in his seventy-sixth year (A. D. 1227), continuing his career of conquest almost to the last hour of his life. Few conquerors have displayed greater military abilities, none more savage ferocity. He delighted in slaughter and devastation; his maxim was to slaughter without mercy, all that offered him the least resistance.

The successors of the Mongolian conqueror followed the course he had traced. They completed the subjugation of China, they overthrew the khaliphate of Bagdad (A. D. 1258), and rendered the sultans of Iconium tributary. Oktaï Khan, the immediate successor of Jenghiz, sent two armies from the centre of China, one against the peninsula of Corea, the other to subdue the countries north and east of the Caspian. This latter army, under the guidance of Batú Khan, penetrated and subdued the Russian empire (A. D. 1237); thence the Mongols spread into Hungary, Poland, and Silesia, and even reached the coasts of the Adriatic sea. The dutchy of Wladimir was the only native Russian dynasty that preserved its existence; it owed its good fortune to Alexander Newski, whose prudent measures conciliated the favor of the conquerors, and secured him a tranquil reign. After the death of Kublaï Khan, the grandson of Jenghiz, the Mongolian empire was partitioned by the provincial governors, and gradually sank into decay.

The overthrow of the Seljúkian sultans and the Fatimite khaliphs, by Noureddin and Saladin, has been already mentioned. The dynasty of the Ayúbites was founded by Saladin's descendants in Syria and Egypt, and this, after having been divided into several states, was overthrown by the Mamelukes in the thirteenth century.

The Mamelukes were Turkish captives, whom the ferocious Mongols sold into slavery; great numbers of them were imported into Egypt in the reign of Sultan Saleh, of the Ayúbite dynasty. This prince purchased multitudes of the younger captives, whom he formed into an army and kept in a camp on the seacoast, where they received instruction in military discipline.* From this they were removed to receive the charge of the royal person, and the superintendence of the officers of state. In a short time, these slaves became so numerous and so powerful that they were enabled to usurp the throne, having murdered Túran Shah, the son and successor of Saleh, who had vainly endeavored to break the yoke which the Mamelukes had imposed upon their sultan (A. D. 1250). This revolution took place in the presence of St. Louis, who had been taken prisoner at the battle of Mansurah, and had just concluded a truce for ten years with Túran Shah. The Mameluke insurgent, named at first regent or atta-beg, was finally proclaimed sultan of Egypt.

The dominion of the Mamelukes over Egypt lasted for more than two centuries and a half. Their body, constantly recruited by Turkish and Circassian slaves, disposed of the throne at its pleasure; the boldest of their chiefs, provided he could prove his descent from Turkestan, was chosen sultan. Notwithstanding the frequent wars and revolutions necessarily resulting from the licentiousness of military election, the Mamelukes made a successful resistance to the Mongols, and after the death of Jenghiz Khan's immediate heirs, conquered the kingdoms of Aleppo and Damascus, which the Mongolian khans had taken from the Ayúbites (A. D. 1260). The surviving princes of the Ayúbite dynasty in Syria and Arabia tendered their submission to the Mamelukes, who were thus masters of all the ancient Saracenic possessions in the Levantine countries, with the exception of the few forts and cities which were still retained by the Franks and western Christians. The Mamelukes soon resolved to seize these last memorials of the crusades. They invaded the principalities of Antioch and Tripoli, which were subdued without much difficulty. A fierce resistance was made by the garrison of Acre, but the town was taken by assault and its gallant defenders put to the sword. Tyre soon after surrendered by capitulation (A. D. 1291), and thus the Christians were finally expelled from Syria and Palestine.

* Hence they were called the Baharite or Maritime Mamelukes, to distinguish them from the Borjite or Garrison Mamelukes, another body of this militia, formed by the Baharite sultan, Kelaún, to counterbalance the authority usurped by the Turkish emirs. The Borjites derived their name from the forts which they garrisoned; they soon increased in power, and made the Baharite dynasty undergo the fate it inflicted on the Ayúbite sultans. They rose against their masters (A. D. 1382), gained possession of the supreme authority, and placed one of their chiefs on the throne of Egypt. The Borjites in their turn were overthrown by the Ottomans (A. D. 1517).

CHAPTER V.

THE REVIVAL OF LITERATURE; THE PROGRESS OF CIVILIZATION AND INVENTION.

Section I.—*Decline of the Papal Power.—The Great Schism of the West.*

Clement V., elevated to the papacy by the influence of the French king, Philip the Fair, to gratify his patron, abstained from going to Rome, had the ceremony of his coronation performed at Lyons, and fixed his residence at Avignon (A. D. 1309).

Philip further insisted that the memory of Boniface should be stigmatized, and his bones disinterred and ignominiously burned. Clement was afraid to refuse; but, at the same time, he dreaded the scandal of such a proceeding, and the danger of such a precedent; he therefore resolved to temporize, and persuaded Philip to adjourn the matter until a general council should be assembled. But some sacrifice was necessary to appease the royal thirst for vengeance, and the illustrious order of the Templars was sacrificed by the head of that church it had been instituted to defend. On the 13th of October, 1307, all the knights of that order were simultaneously arrested; they were accused of the most horrible and improbable crimes; evidence was sought by every means that revenge and cupidity could suggest; the torture of the rack was used with unparalleled violence to extort confession; and sentence of condemnation was finally pronounced on these unfortunate men, whose only crime was the wealth of their order, and their adherence to the papal cause in the reign of Boniface.

The assassination of the emperor Albert inspired Philip with the hope of procuring the crown of Charlemagne for his brother, and he hastened to Avignon to claim the promised aid of the pope. But though Clement had abandoned Italy to tyrants and factions, he had not resigned the hope of re-establishing the papal power over the peninsula, and he shuddered at the prospect of a French emperor reconciling the Guelphs and Ghibellines, crushing opposition by the aid of his royal brother, and fixing the imperial authority on a permanent basis; he therefore secretly instigated the German princes to hasten the election, and Henry VII. of Luxemburg was chosen at his suggestion. Though Henry possessed little hereditary influence, his character and talents secured him obedience in Germany; he had thus leisure to attend to the affairs of Italy, which no emperor had visited during the preceding half century. He crossed the Alps with a band of faithful followers; the cities and their tyrants, as if impressed by magic with unusual respect for the imperial majesty, tendered him their allegiance, and the peninsula, for a brief space, submitted to orderly government. But the rivalry of the chief cities, the ambition of powerful barons, and the intrigues of Clement, soon excited fresh commotions, which Henry had not the means of controlling.

The council of Vienne had been summoned for the posthumous trial of Boniface VIII., and an examination of the charges brought against the Templars (A. D. 1309). Twenty-three witnesses gave evidence against the deceased pontiff, and fully established the charges of profligacy and infidelity; but Clement's own immoralities were too flagrant for him to venture on establishing such a principle as the forfeiture of the papacy for criminal indulgences, and the confession that Christianity had been described by a pope as a lucrative fable, was justly regarded as dangerous, not only to the papacy, but to religion itself. Philip was persuaded to abandon the prosecution, and a bull was issued acquitting Boniface, but, at the same time, justifying the motives of his accusers. The order of the Templars was formally abolished, and their estates transferred to the Hospitallers, or Knights of St. John of Jerusalem; but the Hospitallers were forced to pay such large sums to Philip and the princes who had usurped the Temple lands, that they were impoverished rather than enriched by the grant. The council passed several decrees against heretics, and made some feeble efforts to reform the lives of the clergy; finally, it ordained a new crusade, which had no result but the filling of the papal coffers with gifts from the devout, bribes from the politic, and the purchase-money of indulgences from the cowardly.

When the emperor Henry VII. was crowned at Rome, he established a tribunal to support his authority over the cities and princes of Italy; sentence of forfeiture was pronounced against Robert, king of Naples, on a charge of treason, and this prince, to the great indignation of the French monarch, was placed under the ban of the empire. The pope interfered to protect the cousin of his patron, Philip; the wars between the papacy and the empire were about to be renewed, when Henry died suddenly at Bonconventio, in the state of Sienna. It was generally believed that the emperor was poisoned by his confessor, a Dominican monk, who administered the fatal dose in the eucharist. Clement fulminated two bulls against Henry's memory, accusing him of perjury and usurpation; he also annulled the sentence against Robert of Naples, and nominated that prince imperial vicar of Italy.

The death of Henry exposed Germany to the wars of a disputed succession; that of Clement, which soon followed, produced alarming dissensions in the church. Philip did not long survive the pontiff, and his successor, Louis X., was too deeply sunk in dissipation to regard the concerns of the papacy. Twenty-seven months elapsed in contests between the French and Italian cardinals, each anxious to have a pontiff of their own nation. When first they met in conclave, at Carpentras, the town was fired in a battle between their servants, and the cardinals, escaping from their burning palace through the windows, dispersed without coming to any decision. At length, Philip the Long, count of Poictiers, assembled the cardinals at Lyons, having voluntarily sworn that he would secure their perfect freedom. During their deliberations, the death of Louis X. gave Philip the regency, and soon after the crown of France; the first use he made of his power was to shut up the cardinals in close conclave, and compel them to expedite the election. Thus coerced, they engaged to choose the pontiff who should be nominated by the Cardinal de Porto; this prelate, to the great surprise of all parties, named himself, and was soon after solemnly installed at Avignon, under the title of John XXII.

Europe was at this period in a miserable state of distraction. Italy was convulsed by the civil wars between the Guelphs and Ghibellines, whose animosities were secretly instigated by the intrigues of the king of Naples; Spain and Portugal were harassed by the struggles between the Christians and the Moors; England and France were at war with each other, while both were distracted by internal commotions; two emperors unfurled their hostile banners in Germany; and, finally, the Ottoman Turks were steadily advancing toward Constantinople. In these difficult times, John displayed great policy; he refused to recognise either of the rivals to the empire, and took advantage of their dissensions to revive the papal claims to the supremacy of Italy. But the battle of Muhldorf having established Louis of Bavaria on the imperial throne, John, who had previously been disposed to favor the duke of Austria, vainly attempted to gain over the successful sovereign. Louis sent efficient aid to the Ghibellines, and the papal party in Italy seemed on the point of being destroyed. John, forced to seek for allies, resolved to offer the imperial crown to Charles the Fair, who had just succeeded his brother Philip on the throne of France. The Germans, ever jealous of the French, were filled with indignation when they heard that the pope was endeavoring to remove their popular emperor; Louis summoned a diet, in which he publicly refuted the charges brought against him by the court of Avignon; several learned men published treatises to prove the subordination of the ecclesiastical to the imperial authority; the chapter of Freysingen expelled the bishop for his attachment to the pope; and the citizens of Strasburg threw a priest into the Rhine, for daring to affix a copy of John's condemnation of Louis to the gates of the cathedral. Even the religious orders were divided; for, while the Dominicans adhered to the pope, the Franciscans zealously supported the cause of the emperor.

Irritated rather than discouraged by anathemas, Louis led an army into Italy, traversed the Appenines, received the iron crown of Lombardy at Milan, and, advancing to Rome, found a schismatic bishop willing to perform the ceremony of his coronation. It was in vain that John declared these proceedings void, and issued new bulls of excommunication; the emperor conciliated the Guelphs by his real or pretended zeal for orthodoxy, and, confident in his strength, ventured to pronounce sentence of deposition and death against John, and to procure the election of Nicholas V. by the Roman clergy and people. The Franciscans declared in favor of the antipope, who was one of their body; and if Louis had shown prudence and forbearance equal to his vigor, the cause of Pope John would have been irretrievably ruined. But the avarice of the emperor alienated the affections, not only of the Romans, but of many Italian princes, who had hitherto been attached to the Ghibelline party; he was deserted by his chief supporters, and he embraced the pretext afforded him by the death of the duke of Aus tria, to return to Bavaria. Nicholas, abandoned by his allies, was forced to surrender to the pope, and only obtained his life by submitting to appear before John, with a rope round his neck, and to ask pardon of the pope and the public, for the scandal he had occasioned (A. D. 1330). Though by this humiliation the antipope escaped immediate death, he was detained a close prisoner for the remainder of his days, "treated," says a contemporary, "like a friend, but watched like an enemy."

The emperor would doubtless have suffered severely for his share in the elevation of Nicholas, had not the church been disturbed by a religious controversy. In a discourse at Avignon, the pope maintained that the souls of the blessed would not enjoy the full fruition of celestial joys, or, as he termed it, "the beatific vision," until the day of judgment. The university of Paris, and several leaders of the mendicant orders, declared that such a doctrine was heretical; Philip of Valois, who had only recently obtained the crown of France, required that the pope should retract his assertions, and John was compelled to appease his adversaries by equivocal explanations. The dispute afforded the emperor a pretext for refusing obedience to the papal bulls, and appealing to a general council; new wars were about to commence, when John died at Avignon, leaving behind him the largest treasure that had ever been amassed by a pontiff.

It was not without cause that the Italians named the sojourn of the popes in Avignon, "the Babylonish captivity." The strength of the papacy was shaken to its very foundation, when its possessors appeared mere dependants on the kings of France, the instruments of war and of power, whose possession monarchs contested, while they spurned their authority. The successor of John owed his election to his promise, that he would not reside at Rome: he took the title of Benedict XII., and began his reign by an attempt to restore peace to the church and to the empire. Philip of Valois had other interests, and he compelled the pope to adopt his views. Edward III. was preparing to assert his claims to the crown of France, and Philip feared that he would be supported by his brother-in-law, the emperor; he therefore threatened Benedict with his vengeance, if he should enter into negotiations with Louis, and, as a proof of his earnestness, he seized the revenues of the cardinals. The king of England and the German emperor, aware that the pope was a mere instrument in the hands of their enemies, disregarded his remonstrances and derided his threats. Benedict had not courage or talents adequate to the crisis; his death delivered the papacy from the danger of sinking into contempt, under a feeble ruler, who sacrificed everything to his love of ease; the cardinals, in choosing a successor, sought a pontiff whose energy and ambition might again invest the church with political power.

Clement VI., unanimously chosen by the electors, commenced his reign by claiming the restoration of those rights of the holy see which had fallen into abeyance during the government of his feeble predecessor. The Romans sent a deputation to request that he would return to the city, and appoint the celebration of a jubilee at the middle of the century; Clement granted the latter request, but he refused to visit Rome, through dread of the turbulent spirit of its inhabitants (A. D. 1343). But Clement did not neglect the affairs of Italy, though he refused to reside in the country: Roger, king of Naples, at his death bequeathed his kingdom to his daughter Jane, or Joan, and named a council of regency: Clement insisted that the government, during the minority of the princess, belonged to the holy see; he, therefore, annulled the king's will, and sent a papal legate to preside over the administration. The emperor Louis V. sent an ambassador to the pope, soliciting absolution; Clement demanded humiliating submissions, which were indignantly refused; upon which the anathemas were renewed, and the German electors were exhorted to choose a new sovereign. As if resolved to brave all the princes that opposed the king of France, Clement nominated cardinals to the vacant benefices in England; but Edward III., supported by his clergy and people, refused to admit the intruders; nor could any threats of ecclesiastical censure shake his resolution. About the same time, Clement conferred the sovereignty of the Canary islands on Prince Louis of Spain, as Adrian had given Ireland to the English king. "In these grants," says Henry, "the pretensions of the popes seem to be less remarkable than the credulity of princes."

The pusillanimity of Louis V. is more surprising than the credulity of those who obtained papal grants to confirm questionable titles; though supported by all the princes and most of the prelates in Germany, the emperor sought to purchase pardon by submission; but the Diet would not allow the extravagant claims of the pope to be recognised, and the humiliations to which Louis submitted alienated his friends, without abating the hostility of his enemies.

But Italy was now the theatre of events calculated to divert public attention from the quarrels of the pope. Jane, queen of Naples, had married Andrew, brother to the king of Hungary, whose family had ancient claims on the Neapolitan crown. Political jealousy disturbed the harmony of the marriage; a conspiracy was formed by the courtiers against Andrew; he was murdered in his wife's bed, and she was more than suspected of having consented to the crime. Clement shared the general indignation excited by this atrocity, and, in his chimerical quality of suzerian of Naples, ordered that a strict search should be made after the murderers, against whom he denounced sentence of excommunication (A. D. 1346). Jane soon conciliated the pontiff, and purchased a sentence of acquittal, by selling her pretensions to the county of Avignon for a very moderate sum, which, it may be added, was never paid. But the king of Hungary was not so easily satisfied; he levied a powerful army to avenge the murder of his brother; and the emperor of Germany gladly embraced the opportunity of venting his resentment on the Guelphs and the partisans of the king of France, to whose intrigues he attributed the continuance of the papal excommunications.

Clement saw the danger with which he was menaced by the Hungarian league; to avert it, he negotiated with the king of Bohemia, and prevailed upon some of the German electors to nominate that monarch's son, Charles, marquis of Moravia, to the empire. The new sovereign agreed to recognise all the extravagant claims of the popes, which his predecessors had so strenuously resisted; but no real authority was added to the papacy by this degradation of the empire; even Clement was aware that his authority should be supported by artifice and nego tiation, rather than by any direct assertion of power.

While the princes of Europe were gradually emancipating themselves from the thraldom of the pontiffs, a remarkable revolution wrested Rome itself from their grasp, and revived for a moment the glories of the ancient republic. Rienzi, a young enthusiast of great learning, but humble origin, addressed a pathetic speech to his countrymen on the deplorable state of their city and the happiness of their ancient liberty. Such was the effect of his eloquence, that the citizens immediately elected him tribune of the people, and conferred upon him the supreme power (A. D. 1347). He immediately degraded the senators appointed by the pope, punished with death several malefactors of high rank, and banished the Orsini, the Colonnas, and other noble families, whose factions had filled the city with confusion. The messengers sent by the tribune to announce his elevation were everywhere received with great respect; not only the Italian cities, but even foreign princes, sought his alliance; the king of Hungary and the queen of Naples appealed to him as a mediator and judge, the emperor Louis sought his friendship, and the pope wrote him a letter approving all his proceedings. Such unexpected power intoxicated the tribune; he summoned the candidates for the empire to appear before him, he issued an edict declaring Rome the metropolis of the world, and assumed several strange titles that prove both his weakness and his vanity. This extravagance proved his ruin; Rienzi was excommunicated by the pope, the banished nobles entered Rome, the fickle populace deserted the tribune, and after wandering about for some time in various disguises, he was arrested by the papal ministers, and sent to Avignon, where he was detained a close prisoner.

In the meantime, the king of Hungary had entered Italy; Jane, whose recent marriage to the duke of Tarentum, one of the murderers of her husband, had given great offence to her subjects, abandoned the Neapolitan territories at his approach, and sought refuge at Avignon. But a dreadful pestilence, which at this time desolated southern Europe, compelled the king of Hungary to abandon the territories he had so easily acquired. About the same time, the death of the emperor Louis left Charles without a rival; and Clement resolved to take advantage of the favorable juncture to restore the papal authority in Italy. He ordered a jubilee to be celebrated at Rome; he excommunicated Visconti, archbishop of Milan, but afterward sold absolution to this prelate, who was formidable as a statesman and a soldier; finally, he persuaded the king of Hungary and the queen of Naples to submit their differences to his arbitration. But the court of Avignon was devoted to the house of Anjou; it did not venture to pronounce the queen innocent, but it declared that a weak woman could not resist the temptations of evil spirits, and decided that she should be restored to her kingdom on paying a subsidy to the king of Hungary. That generous prince refused the money, declaring that he had taken up arms to avenge the murder of his brother, not to gain a paltry bribe. Thus the pontiff still seemed the arbitrator of kings; some years before he had engaged Humbert, a prince of southern France, to bequeath his dominions to the French king, on the condition that the eldest son of that monarch should take the title of dauphin; he had been victorious, though by accident, in his contest with the emperor Louis, and at his death Clement left the papacy in full possession of all its titles to supreme power.

But while the nominal authority of the papacy was as great as ever, its real power was considerably weakened. Innocent VI., unable to escape from the yoke which the kings of France had imposed on the popes during their residence at Avignon, resolved to recover the ancient patrimony of St. Peter; Rienzi was summoned from his dungeon, and was sent back to Rome with the title of senator. But the turbulent Romans soon grew weary of their former favorite and Rienzi was murdered by the populace, at the time he was most zealously laboring to chastise the disturbers of public tranquillity, and rescue the people from the oppression of the nobles (A. D. 1354). Soon afterward the emperor Charles IV. entered Rome, and, by the permission of the pope, was solemnly crowned. This feeble prince negotiated with all parties, and betrayed all; he sold liberty to the cities, because he had neither the military force nor the political power to defend a refusal, and he submitted to receive a passport from the pope, and to abide in Rome only the limited period prescribed by the jealousy of the pontiff.

But though the popes, during their residence at Avignon, favored the discords of Italy, stimulated the mutual animosity of the Guelphs and Ghibellines, and encouraged civil war in the empire, they were desirous to terminate the sanguinary struggles for the crown of France, and made several efforts to reconcile the English Edward to the house of Valois. Edward was not to be checked in his career of victory; the glory of the French arms was destroyed at Crecy, and the king of France himself became a prisoner at Poictiers. It was through the mediation of Innocent VI. that King John recovered his liberty, and the war between England and France was terminated by the peace of Bretigny. Soon after his deliverance, John, distressed for money, was induced by a large bribe to give his daughter in marriage to Visconti, the most formidable enemy of the church, while Innocent was too occupied by nearer dangers to prevent an alliance so injurious to his interests. The numerous bands of mercenaries, who were thrown out of employment by the restoration of peace, formed themselves into independent bands, called Free Companies, and quitting the southern districts of France, already desolated by frequent campaigns, directed their march toward Provence. The anathemas hurled against them neither retarded their progress nor diminished their number; a crusade was vainly preached; no soldiers would enlist, when the only pay was indulgences; the plundering hordes approached Avignon, and the treasures of the ecclesiastics were on the point of falling into the hands of these unscrupulous spoilers. By paying a large bribe, and giving them absolution for all their sins, Innocent prevailed upon the Free Companies to turn aside from Avignon and enter into the service of the marquis of Montferrat, who was engaged in the war against the Visconti.

Urban V. succeeded Innocent, and though, like him, inclined to favor the king of France, he became convinced that the residence of the popes at Avignon was injurious to his interests. The emperor solicited Urban to visit Rome, and the Free Companies having again extorted a large bribe, for sparing Avignon, the pope hasted to leave a residence where he was exposed to insult and subservient to foreign authority. The pope was received in Italy with great joy, the emperor Charles hastened to meet him, and gave the last example of imperial degradation, by leading the horse on which the pontiff rode when he made his triumphal entry into Rome (A. D. 1368). This spectacle, instead of gratifying the Italians, filled them with rage; they treated the emperor with so much contempt, that he soon returned to Germany; and Urban finding that he could not check the republican licentiousness which had so long prevailed in Rome and the other cities of the patrimony of St. Peter, began to languish for the more tranquil retirement of Avignon. The only advantage he gained by his visit to Italy, was the empty honor of seeing the emperor of the east bow at his footstool, and offer as the reward of aid against the Turks, the union of the Greek and Latin churches. But Urban could not prevail upon the western princes to combine in defence of Constantinople; and the Greek emperor would have been unable to gain the consent of his subjects to lay aside either the peculiar ceremonies or doctrines that had severed their church from the papacy. The renewal of the war between France and England, when Charles V. succeeded the imbecile John, afforded Urban a pretext for returning to Avignon. Death seized him soon after he reached the city, and Gregory XI. was chosen his successor.

Gregory's great object was to break the power of the Visconti, who had become the virtual sovereigns of northern Italy; but he did not neglect the general interests of the church, exerting himself diligently to suppress heresy. The emperor created the pontiff his vicar, and Gregory, to support his authority, took some of the free companies into pay, and among the rest a band of Englishmen commanded by John Hawkwood. It was of importance to gain over the city of Florence; the papal legate thought that this object could best be obtained by producing a famine, and stimulating the citizens by the pressure of want to rise against their government. In pursuance of this infamous policy, means were taken to cut off the import of corn, while Hawkwood ravaged the territory of the city and destroyed the harvests. Of all the Italian people, the Florentines had been the most constant in their attachment to the cause of the holy see—their indignation was therefore excessive, and their hate implacable.

A general revolt against the papal power was soon organized through Italy by the outraged Florentines; they embroidered the word LIBERTAS on their standards in letters of gold, while their emissaries preached freedom in the cities, in the castles, and in the cottages; the summons was eagerly heard, and the states of the church soon refused to recognise the sovereignty of its head. Gregory sent new legates and menaced the confederates with excommunication; he pronounced sentence of excommunication against the Florentines, exhorting all princes to confiscate the property of those who should be found in their several dominions, and to sell their persons into slavery;—an iniquitous edict, which was partially acted upon both in France and England: new hordes of mercenaries were taken into pay, and when the citizens of Bologna applied to the legate for pardon, he replied that he would not quit their city until he had bathed his hands and feet in their blood. The Florentines were undaunted, but the dis union and mutual jealousies between the other confederates proved fatal to the national cause; the citizens of Rome were anxious to have the pontifical court restored to their city, and to obtain this desirable object, they willingly sacrificed their claims to freedom. In their state of moral degradation, indeed, they were unable to appreciate the advantages of rational liberty, and unfit to exercise its privileges.

During these commotions in Italy, Gregory, being informed of the reformed doctrines, or, as he called them, the heresies published in England by John Wickliffe, wrote to the chancellor and university of Oxford, severely reproving them for permitting such opinions to be promulgated, and ordaining that Wickliffe should be brought to trial before an ecclesiastical tribunal. Similar letters were sent to Richard II., the young king of England, who had just succeeded his grandfather Edward III., but the duke of Lancaster and several other nobles took the reformer under their protection; Wickliffe was rescued from the malice of his enemies, while his doctrines rapidly, though secretly, spread not only through Italy, but through Germany. The chief articles he was accused of teaching, were, that the wafer in the eucharist, after consecration, is not the real body of Christ, but its figure only; that the Roman church had no right to be the head of all churches; that the pope has no more authority than any other priest; that lay patrons may, and ought to, deprive a delinquent church of its temporal possessions; that the gospel was sufficient to direct any Christian; that no prelate of the church ought to have prisons for punishing delinquents. The publication of these sentiments enraged Gregory, who had, from the very commencement of his reign, shown himself a virulent persecutor, and procured the burning of several unfortunate wretches accused of heresy, both in France and Germany. Scarcely had he made his triumphal entry into Rome, when he prepared to take some effective measures for checking the progress of innovation. But domestic troubles soon engaged his attention; the Romans, who had received him on his first arrival with so much enthusiasm, soon began to brave his authority and disobey his edicts; baffled in his expectations of peace and power, he even contemplated returning to Avignon, where part of the papal court still continued. But before taking this step, he resolved to secure the tranquillity of Italy, and, if possible, avert the divisions which he foresaw would probably trouble the church after his death (A. D. 1378). A congress was opened at Serazanæ, but before its deliberations could produce any important result, Gregory was seized with mortal illness, and all hopes of peace were destroyed by the schism which arose respecting the choice of his successor.

The death of Gregory XI. was the commencement of a new era for the ancient capital of the world, from which the popes had been absent during so many years. Pride, interest, and self-love, combined to attach the Romans to the papacy; had they combined with the Florentines, it is possible that the cities of Italy might have formed a confederacy sufficiently strong to defy an absent pope, and an emperor powerless and distant; perhaps they might even have solved the problem which still continues to baffle statesmen, and form a federative union in Italy. But the Romans were incapable of such profound views; they looked to nothing beyond the advantages to be derived from the residence of the papal court; and, instead of aiming at reviving their ancient glory, they contented themselves with disputing the profits that had hitherto been enjoyed by the city of Avignon.

No sooner had the cardinals, the majority of whom belonged to the French party, shut themselves up in a conclave, than the Romans were filled with alarm lest a Transalpine prelate should be chosen, who would establish his court at Avignon. They assembled in arms round the Vatican, and by their menaces sent terror into its inmost recesses. They demanded that the new pope should be an Italian; this was the only virtue they required in the successor of St. Peter. The French cardinals, already disunited, were intimidated by these clamors; they gave their votes to a Neapolitan archbishop, who took the title of Urban VI.

The cardinals seem to have expected that Urban, who was celebrated for his modesty, his humility, and his skill in the canon law, would have acknowledged that his election was vitiated by the force that had been used, and that he would therefore have abdicated the pontificate. But Urban soon convinced them of their error; he not only showed a determination to retain his power, but openly set the discontented cardinals at defiance. In a public discourse, immediately after his coronation, he severely reprehended their pomp and luxury, threatened to punish those who had been convicted of receiving bribes, and reproached some of them by name for corresponding with the enemies of the church. Exasperated by this austerity, the discontented cardinals fled to Anagni, proclaimed the late election void, sent circulars to all Christian princes warning them not to acknowledge Urban, took a body of Bretons into their pay, and, relying on the protection of this military force, excommunicated the new pope as an apostate usurper. The duke of Brunswick, the husband of Jane, queen of Naples, alarmed at the prospect of a schism, attempted to mediate; but his efforts to effect a reconciliation were baffled by the resentment of the cardinals and the haughtiness of Urban. On all sides proposals were made to assemble a general council, but the pope, the cardinals, and the emperor, disputed the right of convocation; the fortune of war could alone determine the fate of the church.

Urban showed no desire to conciliate his opponents; he announced a speedy creation of new cardinals to overwhelm their votes, and threatened the queen of Naples for granting them protection. He showed similar severity in his conduct to the Roman aristocracy, and, on a very slight pretext, ventured to deprive the count of Fondi of his fiefs. The count at once declared himself a partisan of the cardinals; he gave them shelter in the town of Fondi, where, protected by Neapolitan troops, they proceeded to a new election. It is said by many historians that they would have chosen the king of France, Charles V., had not his being maimed in the left arm incapacitated him from performing the ceremonies of the mass; but their selection was scarcely less swayed by temporal motives when they gave their votes to Cardinal Robert of Geneva, who assumed the title of Clement VII. This prelate had served in the field, and even acquired some reputation as a warrior; but he was generally and justly hated by the Italians for having massacred all the inhabitants of Cesena during the Florentine war.

The death of the emperor Charles IV. added new troubles to the complicated policy of Europe; that despicable slave of superstition had purchased from the venal electors the nomination of his son Wenceslaus as his successor; and the young prince, from the moment of his succession, gave himself up to the practice of the meanest vices, and wallowed in disgusting debauchery. These crimes, however, did not prevent him from enjoying the favor of Urban, whose cause he warmly espoused—a merit which, in the eyes of the pontiff, compensated for the want of all the virtues.

The queen of Naples declared in favor of Clement, and invited him to her court. So great, however, was the hatred of a French pontiff, that, in spite of the turbulent disposition of Urban, the defection of the cardinals, the authority of the queen, and the jealousy of the states so recently at war with the court of Rome, all Italy declared against Clement, and the Neapolitans showed such hatred to his cause, that he was forced to escape by sea to Marseilles, whence he proceeded to establish his court at Avignon.

The king of France, Charles V., had eagerly espoused the cause of the cardinals who had elected the antipope; most of them were his subjects, and all were devoted to the interests of France; he therefore declared himself the partisan of Clement, trusting that he would obtain important political advantages by the residence of the pope at Avignon. Unfortunately the result was to involve his kingdom in a ruinous war, which long doomed France to loss and calamity.

Urban's vengeance was promptly directed against the queen of Naples, whose supposed murder of her husband, thirty years before, was still remembered to her disadvantage; he declared that she had forfeited her right to the throne, which he conferred on her cousin Charles of Durazzo; and to support this king of his vengeance, he not only sold ecclesiastical benefices, but pledged the plate belonging to the churches. Jane, driven from her kingdom, adopted the duke of Anjou as her son and successor; the French monarchs believed themselves bound to support his claims, and exhausted their resources in the effort.

All Europe was divided by the schism: Italy, Holland, Germany, Bohemia, Poland, Hungary, Flanders, and England, declared for Urban; while Clement was supported by Spain, Navarre, Scotland, Savoy, Lorraine, and France. The rival popes hurled anathemas against each other; excommunication was answered by excommunication; and both prepared piles to burn the partisans of their adversary as heretics. Charles V. set the example, by issuing an edict confiscating the property and life of those who ventured to recognise Urban in his dominions. Urban retorted, by preaching a crusade against Charles; the English eagerly seized this pretext for renewing war against France, and a powerful army entered Britanny to support its duke against his liege lord.

The death of Charles V., and the minority of his son Charles VI added to the embarrassments of France; the duke of Anjou seized the royal treasures to support his claims on Naples; the new taxes imposed upon the people provoked insurrection; the revolters were punished with remorseless cruelty, and they, on the other hand, practised horrible retaliations whenever they had an opportunity. Charles Durazzo, in the meantime, found little difficulty in taking possession of the Neapolitan territories; Jane, abandoned by her subjects, was forced to surrender to her cousin, and, by his command, was strangled in prison (A. D. 1382). Louis of Anjou immediately claimed her inheritance and, having obtained the investiture of Naples from Clement, entered Italy at the head of fifteen thousand men. No opposition was offered to the French in their passage; Louis reached the frontiers of the Abruzzi in safety, and was there joined by several Neapolitan nobles attached to the memory of Jane, and anxious to avenge her death.

Durazzo was unable to meet his enemy in the field; but he garrisoned his fortresses, encouraged the peasantry of the Abruzzi to harass the French by a guerilla warfare, and destroyed all the forage and provisions in the open country. Famine and pestilence wasted the gallant chivalry of France; the duke of Anjou fell a victim to a fever, whose severity was aggravated by his disappointment; his army dispersed, and many noble barons, who had joined his banners, were forced to beg their way home, amid the jeers and insults of the Italians. The English, commanded by the bishop of Norwich, made a feeble attack upon the schismatic French; they were defeated, and the bishop returned with shame to his diocese.

Urban disapproved of the cautious policy of Durazzo, and, proceeding to Naples, began to treat the king as his vassal; Charles temporized, until the death of the duke of Anjou delivered him from pressing danger, but then he refused all obedience to the pope, and treated him so uncivilly, that Urban removed to Nocera. Several of the cardinals, weary of the tyranny to which they were subjected, plotted the murder of the pope; but their conspiracy was discovered, and six of them were sentenced to suffer the tortures of the rack that they might be compelled to betray their accomplices. Urban personally superintended these cruelties, and suggested new modes of torture to the executioners. When confessions were thus obtained, he degraded the cardinals from their dignity, and pronounced sentence of excommunication, not only against them, but against the king and queen of Naples, the antipope Clement, his cardinals, and his adherents. Durazzo, justly enraged, marched against Nocera, and captured the town; but the pope found shelter in the citadel, from which he, several times-a-day, fulminated anathemas with bell and candle against the king of Naples and his army. Urban at length made his escape, and, embarking on board some Genoese galleys, reached Genoa in safety, where he was honorably received by the doge, who deemed the city honored by his presence. During his flight, he ordered the bishop of Aquila to be murdered, suspecting that he meditated desertion; and soon after he put to death five of the guilty cardinals, sparing the sixth, who was an Englishman, at the intercession of Richard II.—a monarch who had given the weight of England's influence to Urban's cause.

Clement VII. did not conduct himself one whit better than his rival; he insulted and imprisoned the German and Hungarian ambassadors, who were sent to propose expedients for terminating the schism, his exactions from the churches that acknowledged his authority alienated the minds of those whom their political position had ranged on his side; his intrigues and his servility were offensive to the kings that supported him. The double papacy was found a heavy tax on Christendom; each pontiff collected around him a court of dissolute and prodigal cardinals, whose lavish expenditure was supported by alienating the revenues of all the benefices within their grasp.

But the kingdom of Naples was especially destined to suffer from the schism; the rival pontiffs claimed the right of bestowing the Neapolitan crown at their discretion, and their pretensions perpetuated civil discord. Charles Durazzo quitted his kingdom to seek a new crown in Hungary, but fell a victim to assassins in the hour of success; Margaret, his queen, on receiving the news, assumed the regency, and caused her son Ladislaus to be recognised as sovereign by the states of the realm. But Urban VI., who had excommunicated Charles Durazzo, pretended that the kingdom of Naples reverted as a vacant fief to the holy see, and began forming a party against the queen. Clement on his side raised a similar claim, and sold the church plate to pay troops; he zealously supported the house of Anjou, and employed Otho of Brunswick, the widower of the unfortunate Jane, to expel the family of Durazzo.

Hitherto the division in the church had been political; a doctrinal controversy, however, was added to the schism, which, though it led to no immediate results, deserves to be briefly described. A Dominican doctor of divinity, John de Monçon, preaching on the doctrine of original sin, declared that the virgin Mary was conceived in sin. But the faculty of theology in the university of Paris, the Sorbonne, declared that his assertion was an impious outrage against the mother of Christ: the doctors added that the prophesied sacrifice of Christ had an effect before its accomplishment, on his birth and that of his mother, and to this exemption from the ordinary law of humanity, they gave the name of the Immaculate Conception.

The worship of the virgin Mary has always been the most popular portion of the Romish liturgy; the doctrine of the Sorbonne seemed to confer new honor upon her name, and it was ardently received by multitudes of ignorant enthusiasts.

Monçon, alarmed at the ferment he had unwittingly excited, fled to Avignon. The entire order of the Dominicans, enraged to find one of their brethren accused of heresy, sent seventy of their most eminent doctors to support Monçon's opinions before the papal tribunal. The Sorbonne, on the other hand, deputed its most eminent professors to prosecute Monçon, and procure the condemnation of his opinions. The pope was sorely embarrassed; the opposing parties were so powerful that he did not wish to alienate either; and he, therefore, had recourse to the expedient of dismissing Monçon secretly, and sending him to seek refuge in Aragon.

But the theologians of the Sorbonne would not rest satisfied with an imperfect victory; profiting by the popular ferment to work on the mind of their sovereign, Charles VI., they persuaded the king, who had not yet attained his twenty-first year, and whose ignorance was extreme, to undertake the decision of a question beyond the limits of human knowledge. The young and stupid king took upon himself to maintain that the virgin Mary was free from the stain of original sin; he even sent to prison all who denied the doctrine of the Immaculate Conception.

Clement VII., always in fear of being sacrificed to his rival, Urban VI., and relying for support chiefly on the court of France, did not venture to make any further resistance. He issued a bull condemning John de Monçon, and all his adherents: he permitted the king to institute a new festival in honor of the Immaculate Conception. The whole order of St. Dominic was degraded to the lowest rank of monastics, and it was ordained that no one of their body should, in future, hold the office of confessor to the king.

Urban VI. paid little regard to theological controversies; he was more anxious to re-establish his authority over southern Italy. But as he marched toward Naples, his troops mutinied for want of pay, and he was forced to return to Rome. The citizens proved to be as discontented as the soldiers; to stifle their murmurs he published a bull for the celebration of a jubilee the following year at Rome, and ordered that this solemnity should be repeated every thirty-three years, according to the number of years that Christ remained upon earth. He hoped that this festival would enrich the Romans and himself, but he died before the time for its celebration (A. D. 1389). It is supposed that his end was hastened by poison, for his most ardent supporters were weary of his tyranny.

A few days after the death of Urban, the cardinals at Rome chose a new pontiff, who took the title of Boniface IX., and commenced his reign by an interchange of anathemas and excommunications with his rival at Avignon. More prudent than his predecessor, Boniface hasted to make terms with the family of Durazzo at Naples; he recognised young Ladislaus as a legitimate king, and sent a legate to perform the ceremony of his coronation. Ladislaus, in return, took an oath of fidelity and homage, binding himself never to recognise the antipope at Avignon.

Clement VII. strengthened himself by a closer union with the king of France, whom he induced to visit Avignon, and to witness the ceremony of the coronation of Louis II. of Anjou, as king of Naples. The imbecile Charles was so gratified by his reception, that he projected a crusade against Rome, but he was soon induced to abandon his purpose, and he gave very feeble aid to his cousin of Anjou, when he prepared an armament to invade the Neapolitan territories. The doctors of the Sorbonne became eager to terminate the schism; and, encouraged by their success in the controversy of the Immaculate Conception, they presented to the king a project for restoring the peace of the church, by compelling the rival popes to resign, and submit the choice of a new pontiff to a general council (A. D. 1394). Though this counsel was not favorably received by the king, it gave great alarm to Clement, and agitation of mind is supposed to have produced the apopletic fit which occasioned his death.

The French ministers wrote to the cardinals at Avignon, urging them to embrace the opportunity of terminating the schism; but these prelates hasted to conclude a new election without opening the letter, with the contents of which they were acquainted. Peter de Luna, cardinal of

Aragon, was nominated pope ; he took the name of Benedict XIII., and the schism became wider than ever. When the news of the election reached Paris, Charles, instead of recognising the pope of Avignon, convoked the clergy of his kingdom to deliberate on the means of restoring peace to the church. After some delay, the convocation met, and came to the inconsistent resolution of recognising Benedict, and proposing that the schism should be terminated by the abdication of the two popes. Ambassadors were sent with this proposal to Avignon, but a ridiculous though insuperable difficulty prevented the success of their negotiations. The plenipotentiaries on both sides preached long sermons to each other, until the French princes who were joined in the legation, completely fatigued, and seeing no probable termination of the conference, returned home indignant and disappointed. The king of England and the emperor of Germany joined the French monarch in recommending the double application ; Boniface declared his readiness to resign, if Benedict would set the example, but the latter pontiff absolutely refused submission. An army was sent to compel him to obedience ; Avignon was taken, and Benedict besieged in his palace, but his obstinacy continued unshaken, and the party feuds which the weakness of the king encouraged in France, gave him hopes of final triumph.

The state of the western governments tended to protract the schism of the church ; the king of France fell into idiotcy ; Richard II. was deposed in England by his cousin Henry IV. ; the duke of Anjou was driven from Naples ; the Byzantine emperor and the king of Hungary were harassed by the Turks, whose increasing power threatened ruin to both ; the Spanish peninsula was distracted by the Moorish wars ; and the emperor Wenceslaus was forced to abdicate by the German electors. Boniface took advantage of these circumstances to establish the papal claim to the first-fruits of all ecclesiastical benefices, and to render himself absolute master of Rome, by fortifying the citadel and castle of St. Angelo. The Roman citizens were deprived of the last shadow of their former franchises ; the readiness with which they submitted, is, however, a sufficient proof that they were unworthy of freedom. The pope did not long survive this triumph ; the Roman cardinals elected Innocent VII. to supply his place ; but he died about twelve months after his elevation, and was succeeded by Gregory XII. (A. D. 1406). Benedict having, in the meantime, recovered his freedom, protested against the Roman elections, but offered to hold a personal conference with Gregory for reconciling all their differences. The cardinals, weary of these controversies, deserted the rivals, and having assembled a general council at Pisa, elected a third pope, who took the title of Alexander V.

There were now three heads to the Christian church : Ladislaus and some of the Italian cities supported Gregory ; the kings of Scotland and Spain adhered to Benedict ; while Alexander was recognised in the rest of Christendom. The disputes of these hostile pontiffs had greatly tended to enfranchise the human mind, and weaken the hold of superstition. Wickliffe's doctrines spread in England, and in Germany they were advocated by John Huss, who eloquently denounced the corruptions that debased the pure doctrines of Christianity. Pope

Alexander was preparing to resist the progress of the courageous reformer, when his death threw the affairs of the church into fresh confusion.

The presence of an armed force induced the cardinals to elect John XXIII., whose promotion gave great scandal, as he was more remarkable for his military than his religious qualifications (A. D. 1411). John soon compelled Ladislaus to abandon Gregory's party; he then assembled a general council at Rome, where sentence of condemnation was pronounced on the doctrines of Huss and Wickliffe. But Ladislaus soon grew weary of peace; he led an army against Rome, plundered the city, and compelled the pope to seek protection from Sigismond, emperor of Germany. John consented very reluctantly to the imperial demand, that the schism should finally be terminated by a general council; he made an ineffectual effort to have the assembly held in one of his own cities, but Sigismond insisted that it should meet in Constance. John then attempted to interpose delays, but the general voice of Christendom was against him; he jndged his situation accurately, when, pointing to Constance from the summit of the Alps, he exclaimed, "What a fine trap for catching foxes!"

The attention of all Christendom was fixed upon the deliberations of the council of Constance, whither bishops, ambassadors, and theologians, flocked from every part of Europe (A. D. 1415). John Huss, having obtained the emperor's safe conduct, appeared before the council to defend his doctrines, but Sigismond was persuaded to forfeit his pledge, and deliver the courageous reformer to his enemies, to be tried for heresy. Pope John was not treated better; a unanimous vote of the council demanded his abdication; he fled to Austria, but he was overtaken and detained in the same prison with Huss, until he ratified the sentence of his own deposition. Gregory XII. soon after abdicated the pontificate, but Benedict still continued obstinate; his means of resistance, however, were so trifling, that the council paid little attention to his refusal. John Huss, and his friend Jerome of Prague, were sentenced to be burnt at the stake as obstinate heretics, but their persecutors could not stop the progress of the truth; the Hussites in Bohemia had recourse to arms for the defence of their liberties, and, under the command of the heroic Zisca, maintained the cause of civil and religious liberty, in many glorious fields.

The emperor, the princes of Germany, and the English deputies, strenuously urged the council to examine the abuses of the church, and form some plan for its thorough reformation; but the prelates, fearing that some proposals might be made injurious to their interests, steadily resisted these efforts; declaring that the election of a pope ought to have precedence of all other business. After long disputes, the choice of the electors fell on Otho Colonna, a Roman noble, who took the title of Martin V. The new pontiff combined with the cardinals to strangle all the plans of reform, and the council, from whose deliberations so much had been expected, terminated its sittings, without having applied any effectual remedy to the evils which had produced the schism. A promise, indeed, was made, that another council would be convened, for the reform of the church, at Pavia, but no one cared to claim its performance; the conduct of those who met at Constance convinced the world that no effectual redress of grievances could be expected from such assemblies.

The projects of reform, begun at Constance, were revived at the council of Basle (A. D. 1431); but Eugenius IV., the successor of Martin, soon felt that the proposed innovations would be fatal to the papal authority, and dissolved the council. This precipitancy caused another schism, which lasted ten years; but at length the ex-duke of Savoy, who had been chosen pope by the partisans of the council, under the name of Felix V., gave in his submission; and the council, from whose labors so much had been expected, ended by doing nothing. Still the convocations of the prelates of Christendom at Constance and Basle struck a fatal blow against the despotism of the popes. Henceforth monarchs had, or seemed to have, a court of appeal—one so dreaded by the pontiffs, that the mere dread of its convocation procured from them liberal concessions. But a new and more formidable enemy to the despotism of the pontiffs than the resistance of kings or of councils, was the progress of literature and knowledge, which brought the extravagant claims of spiritual and temporal rulers to be investigated on their real merits, not according to their asserted claims.

SECTION II.—*First Revival of Literature, and Inventions in Science.*

IN the controversy between Philip the Fair and Boniface VIII., literary talent was for the first time employed against the church by John of Paris, a celebrated Dominican, who advocated the royal independence with great zeal and considerable ability. The celebrated poet Dante Alighieri, who may be regarded as the founder of Italian literature, and almost of the Italian language, followed the same course, advocating strenuously the cause of the emperor Louis of Bavaria. Their example was a model for many other writers, who laid aside the shackles of authority, and supported the independence of states. But literature itself was subject to trammels which checked the progress of improvement It was deemed a crime scarcely less than heresy, to doubt of any explanation given by the schoolmen of physical, mental, or moral phenomena. Roger Bacon, a Franciscan monk, was the first who revived experimental science; he made several important discoveries in mechanics and chymistry, but his great merit is to be found, not so much in his various inventions and projects, as in the bold appeal which he made to experiment, and the observation of nature. His lectures at Oxford, published under the title of "Opus Majus" (A. D. 1266), raised against him a host of enemies; he was prohibited from giving instructions in the university, and was subjected to confinement in his convent. His scientific discoveries were deemed a species of magic in that age o' ignorance; he was the first of the long list of victims of ecclesiastical persecution, and the leader of a long line of patriots who supported the cause of intellectual and moral liberty against the odious encroachments of spiritual despotism. The emancipation of literature accompanied that of science; the impulse which Dante had given to the cultivation of Italian poetry was long felt; he was followed by Petrarch and Boccacio, whose writings at once elevated the character and formed the language of their countrymen

Several new inventions, or perhaps importations from the remote East, accelerated the progress of men in learning and the arts. Of these we may mention more particularly the art of forming paper from linen-rags, painting in oil, the art of printing, the use of gunpowder, and of the mariner's compass.

Before the invention of linen-paper, parchment was generally used in Europe, both for copying books and preserving public records. This material was scarce and dear. When the Arabs conquered Bokhara (A. D. 704), they are said to have found a large manufactory of cotton-paper at Samarcand, which is not improbable, as the fabric was known in China before the Christian era. They brought the knowledge of the art into their western territories, but the scarcity of the materials long impeded its progress. At length, in the thirteenth century, it was discovered that linen would answer all the purposes of cotton; but when, where, or by whom, this valuable discovery was made, can not be ascertained. The first great factory of linen-paper of which we have any certain accounts, was established at Nuremberg (A. D 1390), but there is reason to believe that paper was manufactured in western Europe a century earlier.

The invention of painting in oils is usually attributed to two brothers, Van Eyck, of whom the younger, called John of Bruges, flourished toward the close of the thirteenth century. The invention, however, is of much earlier date, but the brothers deserve the merit of having brought it into practical use, and carried it to a high degree of perfection. Owing to this invention, modern paintings excel the ancients both in finish of execution and permanence.

More important than either of these was the invention of printing, which seems to have been at least partially derived from the East. Solid blocks of wood, graven with pictures and legends, were used in China from a very remote period. The great improvement of having separate types for each letter, was made by John Gutenberg, a citizen of Mayence (A. D. 1436); he used small blocks of wood, but the matrix for casting metal types was soon after devised by Peter Schoeffer, of Gemheim. Gutenberg established the first printing-press known in Europe, at Strasburg; thence he removed to Mayence, where he entered into partnership with John Fust, or Faustus, whose ingenuity greatly contributed to perfect the invention. Gutenberg did not put his name to any of the books he printed; Faustus, more ambitious of fame, placed his name and that of his partner to his celebrated Psalter, and thus received no small share of the glory that properly belonged to the first discoverer. The art of engraving on copper, was discovered about the same time as the use of moveable types, but its history is very obscure.

Scarcely less important than printing was the manufacture and use of gunpowder. The explosive power of saltpetre was probably known in the east from a very remote age. With less certainty we may conjecture that the process of compounding saltpetre with other ingredients, was brought from the remote east by the Saracens. Friar Bacon, the first European writer who describes the composition of gun powder, derived his knowledge of chymistry chiefly from the Arabian writers who were the originators of that science. The employment of gunpowder for throwing bullets and stones began in Europe abou the commencment of the fourteenth century; it was introduced by the Saracens in their Spanish wars; and the first certain account of this change in warfare, is in an Arabian history of the siege of Baza, by the king of Granada (A. D. 1312). It is generally supposed that the Genoese were the first who used powder in mines, to destroy walls and fortifications, at the siege of Seranessa (A. D. 1487). Bombs and mortars are said to have been invented by Malatesta, prince of Rimini (A. D. 1467); and about the same time guns, or rather portable cannons, began to be used by soldiers. Several circumstances prevented the immediate adoption of firearms and artillery in war: long habit made many prefer their ancient weapons; the construction of cannons was imperfect, they were made more frequently of wood, leather, or iron hoops, than solid metal, and were therefore liable to burst; the gunpowder was of imperfect manufacture, and frequently failed in the field. Above all, the mail-clad chivalry of Europe opposed a change in the art of war which greatly lowered the value of knights and cavalry.

The last great invention that requires notice, is the polarity of the magnet, and its application to the mariner's compass. It was generally believed that the inventor of this precious instrument was Flavio Gioia, a native of Amalfi, in the kingdom of Naples; and so precise were the historians, that they specified the date of the invention as either A. D. 1302, or 1303. A more careful examination of the subject showed that the magnet's polarity had been noticed by Chinese, Arabian, and even European writers, long before the commencement of the fourteenth century.

The time when the polarity of the magnet was first known to the Chinese is lost in the night of antiquity. But many centuries before the Christian era, this property of the loadstone was applied to the construction of magnetic chariots; but it was probably not until the Chinese began to direct their attention to navigation, under the Tsin dynasty, that is, between the middle of the third and the commencement of the fifth centuries of our era that it was used for the guidance of vessels at sea. We have no certain account of the introduction of the compass into Europe, but writers of the twelfth century, speaking of it, as far as we know for the first time, mention it as a thing generally known. From this sudden notoriety of the polarity of the magnet, it seems probable that its use had been practically known to sailors, before it engaged the attention of the learned. Only one century previous to this notoriety, we find that the northern navigators had no better expedient for directing their course, than watching the flight of birds. "The old northern sailors," says a Danish chronicle, "took a supply of ravens for their guides; they used to let these birds fly from their barks when in the open sea; if the birds returned to the ship, the sailors concluded that there was no land in sight, but if they flew off, the vessels were steered in the direction of their flight." The improvements in the compass were made by slow degrees, and for the most important of them the world is indebted to Englishmen.

SECTION III.—*Progress of Commerce.*

FROM the beginning of the fourteenth to the middle of the fifteenth century the commerce of Europe was engrossed by the Italian, Hanseatic, and Flemish cities. The Italians, but more especially the Florentines, Genoese, and Venetians, possessed the trade of the Levant. The jealousy of the rival republics led to sanguinary wars, which ended in rendering the Venetians supreme in the Mediterranean. The manufacture of silk, which had been introduced into Sicily from Greece, spread thence into various parts of Italy, but the largest factories were established at Venice. This city supplied the greater part of Europe with silks, spices, and Asiatic produce. Italian merchants, commonly called Lombards, carried these goods into the northern and western kingdoms. The privileges and exemptions granted them by sovereigns, enabled them to rule the traffic of Europe, and to become the chief bankers and money-dealers in its different states.*

But all the Italian free cities did not enjoy equal prosperity. The states of Lombardy that had wrested their freedom from the German emperors, soon fell into anarchy. Disgusted with the advantages by which they knew not how to profit, some voluntarily resigned their liberties to new masters, while others yielded to usurpers. Thus the marquis of Este became lord of Modena and Reggia (A. D. 1336); the house of Gonzago gained possession of Mantua, and the Visconti took the title of dukes of Milan (A. D. 1395). Florence retained its freedom and prosperity for a longer period. It was not until the reign of the emperor Charles V. (A. D. 1530), that its republican form of government was abolished, and the supreme authority usurped by the princely family of the Medicis.

The rivalry between the Genoese and the Venetians led, as we have already mentioned, to long and deadly wars. The last and most memorable of these, was that called the war of Chiozza (A. D. 1379), in which the Genoese received so severe a check, that they were no longer able to contest the supremacy of the sea with their rivals.

But these wars were not the only cause of the decline of Genoa; the streets of the city frequently streamed with the blood of rival factions; the nobles and commons fought for supremacy, which want of internal union prevented either party from maintaining; and at length, incapable of governing themselves, they sought the protection of foreign powers. With their usual inconstancy, the Genoese were ever changing masters; twice they placed themselves under the king of France, but after a short experience of French rule, took for their sovereign, first the marquis of Montferrat, and afterward the duke of Milan. From the year 1464, Genoa remained a dependancy on the dutchy of Milan, until 1528, when it recovered its former freedom.

While the power of the Genoese republic was declining, that of Venice was increasing by rapid strides. The permanence given to its government by introducing the principle of hereditary aristocracy, saved

* The street in London where these foreigners were settled, still retains the name of Lombard street, and continues to be the chief seat of banking establishments. It is not generally known that the three balls exhibited over pawnbroker's shops, are the arms of Lombardy, and have been retained as a sign, ever since the Lombards were the sole money-lenders of Europe.

the states from internal convulsions, while the judicious establishment of commercial stations, on the shores of the Adriatic and Levant, secured and fostered its trade. The greatest advantage that the Venetians obtained over their commercial rivals, arose from their treaty with the sultan of Egypt (A. D. 1343), by this alliance, the republic obtained full liberty of trade in the Syrian and Egyptian ports, with the privilege of having consular establishments at Alexandria and Damascus. These advantages soon enabled them to acquire supreme command over the trade of central and southern Asia; the spices and other commodities of India were brought to Syrian markets, and the Genoese establishments on the Black sea soon became worthless. The territorial acquisitions of the republic on the northern coasts of the Adriatic, formed a powerful state about the middle of the fifteenth century. But the power of the republic was less secure than it appeared; oppressive to its dependancies, it provoked hostile feelings, which only waited for an opportunity to blaze forth in open rebellion; insolent to all the surrounding powers, a secret jealousy and enmity were excited, which, at no distant date, exposed Venice to the resentments of a league too powerful to be resisted.

We have already mentioned the Hanseatic confederation of the commercial cities in northern and western Europe, to protect their trade from pirates and robbers. In the fourteenth century, the league became so extensive as to form an important power, that claimed and received the respect of kings and emperors. The maritime cities of Germany, from the Scheldt and the isles of Zealand, all round to the borders of Livonia, joined the confederacy, and several cities in the interior sought its protection, and admission into its alliance. The first known act of confederation was signed by the deputies of the several cities at Cologne (A. D. 1364). All the allied cities were divided into four circles, whose limits and capitals varied at different periods; the general administration of the confederacy was intrusted to a confederacy which assembled triennially at Lubeck. In the early part of the fifteenth century, no less than eighty cities sent delegates to the congress, while many others were connected with the league, though they had not the power of sending delegates. Possessing the exclusive commerce of the Baltic sea, the Hanse towns exercised the right of making war and peace, and forming alliances; they equipped powerful fleets and waged successful wars with the northern sovereigns that attempted to interfere with their monopoly, or limit the privileges extorted from the ignorance or weakness of their predecessors.

The principal marts were Bruges for the Flemish countries, London for England, Bergen for Norway, and Novogorod for Russia. In the close of the fifteenth century, Novogorod was deprived of its republican constitution, and the merchants migrated to Narva and Revel. Through the Flemings the Hanseatic commercial cities were brought into connexion with those of Italy; the merchants of both met in the fairs and markets of Bruges, where the produce of the unexplored north was exchanged for that of the unknown regions of India. The progress of trade, and the intercourse thus effected between remote nations, excited a love for maritime and inland discovery, which soon produced important changes, and aided the other causes that necessarily led to the overthrow of the confederation.

Extensive as was the commerce of the Hanseatic cities, it possessed neither permanence nor durability. Having neither produce nor manufactures of their own, the merchants had merely a carrying trade, and the produce of simple barter; consequently the progress of industry, especially in countries where the useful arts were cultivated, raised powerful rivals against them, and gave commerce a new direction. The establishment of stable government was also injurious to a confederation; the German princes gradually recovered their supremacy over the cities that had been withdrawn from their authority. This result was hastened by the internal dissensions of the confederate cities. When the northern sovereigns, enlightened on the advantages that their subjects might derive from commerce, assailed the privileges of the Hanse towns by force of arms; many of the southern cities withdrew themselves from the league; and the northern confederates, thus deserted, were unable to preserve their monopoly of the Baltic trade, which they were forced to share with the merchants of England and Holland. The confederacy thus gradually declined, until in the seventeenth century, this league, once so extensive, included only the cities of Hamburg, Lubeck, and Bremen.

In Flanders, commercial prosperity was based on manufacturing industry; the Flemings supplied the principal markets of Europe with cloth in the thirteenth and fourteenth centuries; while, through the commercial cities of Italy, they were enabled to send the produce of their looms to the ports of the Levant, and exchange them for spices, jewels, and other articles of oriental luxury. The wealth, the population, and the resources of these cities, rendered the earls of Flanders more wealthy, and scarcely less powerful than their nominal sovereigns, the kings of France. When Edward I. of England wished to recover Guienne, which had been wrested from his predecessors, he sought the alliance of Guy de Dampierre, earl of Flanders, and proposed to make the earl's daughter, Philippa, his queen; being attracted both by her personal charms and the enormous sums promised as her dowry. So great was the lady's wealth, and such the importance attached to the Flemish alliance, that Philip the Fair had recourse to the most infamous treachery in order to defeat the marriage. As he was the godfather of the young lady, he invited her and the earl to pay him a visit in Paris; but no sooner did they reach the capital than he threw them both into prison, declaring that the marriage of so wealthy an heiress could not be arranged without the consent of the superior lord, and that the earl was guilty of felony in promising the hand of his daughter to an enemy of the kingdom. Guy escaped from prison, but his daughter died a captive, under circumstances which led to a strong suspicion of poison; the earl, believing, or feigning to believe the charge, assembled his chief vassals at Grammont, and there, in the presence of the ambassadors from England, Germany, and Lorraine, he solemnly renounced his allegiance to the crown of France, and proclaimed war against Philip. Such was the commencement of the long series of Flemish wars, which early assumed the form of a desperate struggle between the mercantile and landed aristocracy.

Commerce and manufactures had brought together a large and wealthy population into the cities of Flanders; the burgesses had purchased charters of privileges from their respective lords, being well aware that municipal freedom was necessary to commercial prosperity; they began to rival their former masters in wealth and influence, and they formed an order of their own, which was as much respected in the trading communities as the landed aristocracy in the rural districts. The nobles soon began to view the rapid progress of the merchants and traders with jealousy and dislike. Not only were the lords grieved at the loss of their power to distort discretionary imposts, but they regretted the growth of that mercantile wealth which invested counting-houses and stores with a political influence not inferior to that which had hitherto attached exclusively to castles and estates. Municipal immunities were found to be at variance with feudal privileges; neither the merchants nor the nobles would make such concessions as might form the basis of a reasonable compromise, and war was thus rendered inevitable. Under the guidance of several eminent and popular leaders, particularly the two Artaveldes, the mercantile Flemings maintained a long and vigorous warfare against their earls and aristocracy, though the latter were supported by the whole power of France. At the close of the contest, the trading cities preserved their immunities; but in the course of the war, capitalists had been ruined, artisans had fled to more peaceful lands, the nobles were impoverished, and the peasants reduced to despair. Though the Flemings continued to retain a large share of their commercial and manufacturing supremacy, they had the mortification to witness the rise of a powerful rival in England, where the woollen manufacture gradually attained to a greater height than it had reached even in Flanders.

Wool was the most important article of British produce; and about the middle of the fourteenth century, we find that wool constituted about thirteen fourteenths of the entire exports of the kingdom.

Little cloth was made in England, and that only of the coarsest description, until Edward III., in the year 1331, invited weavers, dyers, and fullers, to come over from Flanders and settle in England, promising them his protection and favor on condition that they would carry on their trades here, and teach the knowledge of them to his subjects. The native wool-growers and merchants looked upon these foreign manufacturers with very jealous eyes, especially when Edward created a monopoly in their favor, by prohibiting the wearing of any cloth but of English fabric; and many petitions are preserved from the weavers of woollen stuffs, complaining of the heavy impositions laid upon them by the corporations, in which the corporation of Bristol is especially conspicuous. The manufacture, however, took root and flourished, though it received a severe check from the jealousy of parliament, which, by a very unwise law, prohibited the export of woollen goods, and permitted that of unwrought wool.

The land-owners of England were slow in discovering that their own prosperity was connected with that of the manufacturing interest. Their avowed object in legislation was to keep up the high price of the raw material, the wool grown upon their estates; and their had the honesty to say so in the preamble to a statute (14 Rich. II. c. 4) prohibiting any denizen of England from buying wool except from the owners of the sheep and for his own use. This of course closed the home market; the grower, in his anxiety to grasp the profits of the wool-merchant and retailer in addition to his own, found that he had turned off his best customers; and we learn from a contemporary historian that the growers were reduced to the greatest distress by having the accumulated stock of two or three years left on their hands.

In the reign of Henry VI., not more than a century after its introduction, the woollen manufacture had thriven so well, that it was made to contribute to the revenue, and we were enabled to compete with the nations by whom we had been taught it, on equal terms: a reciprocity law, passed at this time, ordains, that "if our woollen goods were not received in Brabant, Holland, and Zealand, then the merchandise growing or wrought within the dominions of the duke of Burgundy shall be prohibited in England under pain of forfeiture." But there was already a growing jealousy between the landed and manufacturing interests, caused by the rise in the price of labor, resulting from increase of employment; for so early as the reign of Henry IV., an act was passed that "no one should bind his son or daughter to an apprenticeship, unless he was possessed of twenty shillings." This attempt to limit the supply of labor in manufacture would have wholly destroyed the woollen trade, had not the first monarch of the house of Tudor granted an exemption from the act to the city of Norwich, and subsequently to the whole county of Norfolk.

The besetting error of legislators in this age was the belief, that gold and silver had some inherent and intrinsic value in themselves, independent of their exchangeable and marketable value. They could not understand that the very essence of all commerce is barter, and that money only serves as a third term or common measure for ascertaining the comparative value of the articles to be exchanged. Ignorant of this fact, they made several attempts to compel foreigners to pay for English goods in money. In 1429, a law was passed, that no Englishman should sell goods to foreigners except for ready money, or other goods delivered on the instant.

This was such a fatal blow to trade, that, in the very next year, the parliament was compelled to relax so far as to admit of the sale of goods on six months' credit. With equal wisdom, and for the same perplexing reason, "the prevention of the exportation of treasure out of the country," a law was passed prohibiting "foreign merchants from selling goods in England to any other foreigner." This precious piece of legislation did not, of course, prevent the exportation of the precious metals, but it prevented the import of merchandise and of bullion, a result which quite perplexed the legislature, but did not lead to the abolition of the foolish law

Henry VII., removed a still greater check to industry, by restraining the usurpations of corporations. A law was enacted, that corporations should not pass by-laws without the consent of three of the chief officers of state; they were also prohibited from exacting tolls at their gates The necessity of legislative interference was proved by the conduct of the corporations of Gloucester and Worcester, which had actually imposed transit tolls on the Severn—these, of course, were abolished. But the monarch was not superior to the prejudices of his age; he affixed prices to woollen cloths, caps, and hats, which, of course, led to a deterioration of the several articles. Yet this law was highly extolled as a master-stroke of policy by the statesmen of the day.

The parliaments in the reign of Henry VIII., were too busily engaged in enforcing the king's caprices, by inconsistent laws against heresy and treason, to pay much attention to trade and commerce. One circumstance, however, connected with the woollen trade deserves to be noticed. So greatly had our woollen manufactures increased, that the Flemings, no longer able to compete with the English as producers, entered into the carrying trade, bought the English commodities, and distributed them into other parts of Europe. In 1528, hostilities commenced between England and the Low Countries; there was an immediate stagnation of trade; the merchants having no longer their usual Flemish customers, could not buy goods from the clothiers; the clothiers in consequence dismissed their workmen, and the starving operatives tumultuously demanded "bread or blood."

Wolsey scarcely knew how to account for these riots; he tried force with the workmen, but hunger was stronger than the law; he threatened the clothiers unless they gave employment, but wages could not be paid from empty purses; at length he sent for the merchants, and commanded them to buy cloth as usual! The merchants replied, that they could not sell it as usual; and, notwithstanding his menaces, would give no other answer. At length the true remedy was discovered; an agreement was made that commerce should continue between the two states even during war.

In the reign of Edward VI., an act was passed, by which every one was prohibited from making cloth, unless he had served an apprenticeship of seven years; this law was repealed in the first year of Queen Mary, as the preamble of the act states, "because it had occasioned the decay of the woollen manufactory, and had ruined several towns." It was, however, subsequently restored by Elizabeth.

The persecution of the protestants in France, but more especially in Flanders, drove many eminent manufacturers to seek refuge in England, where they were graciously received by Elizabeth. She passed an act relieving the counties of Somerset, Gloucester, and Wiltshire, from the old oppressive statutes, which confined the making of cloth to corporate towns; and trade, thus permitted to choose its own localities, began to flourish rapidly. In a remonstrance of the Hanse towns to the diet of the empire, in 1582, it is asserted that England exported annually about 200,000 pieces of cloth. In this reign, also, the English merchants, instead of selling their goods to the Hanseatic and Flemish traders, began to export themselves; and their success so exasperated the Hanse towns, that a general assembly was held at Lubeck to concert measures for distressing the English trade. But the jealousy of foreigners was far less injurious to British commerce than the monopolies which Elizabeth created in countless abundance. An attempt, indeed, was made to remove one monopoly; but the experiment was not fairly tried, and its consequent ill-success was used as an argument against any similar efforts. By an old patent, the company of Merchant Adventurers possessed the sole right of trading in woollen goods. This monstrous usurpation of the staple commodity of the kingdom was too bad even for that age of darkness, and Elizabeth opened the trade; but the Merchant Adventurers entered into a conspiracy not to make purchases of cloth, and the queen, alarmed at the temporary suspension of trade, restored the patent.

In the reign of James I. it was calculated that nine tenths of the commerce of the kingdom consisted in woollen goods. Most of the cloth was exported raw, and was dyed and dressed by the Dutch, who gained, it was pretended, 700,000*l.* annually by this manufacture. The king, at the instigation of Cockayne and some other London merchants, issued a proclamation prohibiting the exportation of raw cloths: the Dutch and Germans met this piece of legislation by prohibiting the importation of English dyed cloth; the consequence was, that our export trade was diminished by two thirds, and the price of wool fell from seventy to eighty per cent. The king was forced to recall his proclamation. In the year 1622 a board of trade was erected, as the commission states, "to remedy the low price of wool, and the decay of the woollen manufactory." It is recommended to the commissioners to examine "whether a greater freedom of trade, and an exemption from the restraint of exclusive companies, would not be beneficial." A gratifying proof of the progress of intelligence; but, unfortunately, it led to no practical result.

English commerce increased greatly under the commonwealth, because no regard was paid to the prerogative whence the charters of the exclusive companies were derived, and because the progress of democratical principles led the country gentlemen to bind their sons apprentices to merchants. But with the restoration came the old rage for prohibitions and protections; two thousand manufacturers from Warwickshire, and a great number from Herefordshire, emigrated to the Palatinate; and, in 1662, the company of Merchant Adventurers declared, in a public memorial, that the white clothing trade had abated from 100,000 pieces to 11,000! In 1668, however, some Walloons were encouraged to introduce the manufacture of fine cloths, from Spanish wool only, without the admixture of any inferior wool; but the progress of this branch of trade was very slow, owing chiefly to our municipal laws, which pressed heavily on foreigners.

It is not necessary to bring down the history of our great staple manufactory to a later date. What has been already stated is sufficient to illustrate the evils which arose from legislative interference with the natural course of commerce, industry, and capital, in past ages. It must not, however, be supposed that this impolicy was peculiar to England; on the contrary, English statesmen were generally in advance of the rest of Europe, and monopolies were only supported by corrupt adventurers. The nobility and the country gentlemen of England resisted the imposing of any unnecessary shackles on trade until after the restoration of Charles II., when the system of protection began to be introduced; that system derived its chief support from the short-sighted cupidity of the manufacturers themselves, and the entire blame must not therefore be attributed to the legislature.

The extension of English commerce during the period of history we have been examining was very slow. The long wars with France, and the civil wars of the Roses, diverted attention from the peaceful pursuit of trade. It was not until after the accession of Henry VII. that England began to feel the impulse for maritime discovery and commercial enterprise which had hitherto been confined to southern Europe; the effects of this change belong, however, to a more advanced period of history, and will come under consideration in a future chapter.

Section IV.—*Revolutions of Germany, France, and Spain.*

From the period of the accession of Rodolph, the first emperor of the house of Hapsburgh, the German empire began to assume a constitutional form, and to be consolidated by new laws. Under the government of Albert, the son of Rodolph, an important change took place in Switzerland, which, at the commencement of the fourteenth century, was divided into a number of states, both secular and ecclesiastical. The cantons of Uri, Schwitz, and Underwalden, were immediate dependancies of the empire, while some minor adjoining districts belonged to the dukes of Austria as counts of Hapsburgh. Albert, anxious to found a new kingdom for one of his younger children, resolved to annex the imperial to the Austrian cantons; and in order to reconcile the hardy mountaineers that inhabited them to the intended yoke, he sanctioned and encouraged the cruel tyranny of their German governors. Three brave men resolved to attempt the delivery of their country; they secretly engaged a number of partisans, who surprised the imperial forts on the same day (A. D. 1308), and accomplished a revolution without shedding a drop of blood. The Austrians made a vigorous effort to recover their supremacy, but they suffered a ruinous defeat at Morgarten (A. D. 1315), which secured the independence of the Cantons. Their league of union was renewed at Brunnen, in a treaty that became the base of the federative union of Switzerland. Five other cantons successively joined the former three, and the Helvetic possessions of the house of Austria were conquered by the Swiss during the interval in which the family of the counts of Hapsburgh ceased to wear the imperial crown.

On the death of Albert (A. D. 1308), Henry VII., count of Luxemburg, was chosen emperor; he was a brave and politic prince; taking advantage of the pope's absence at Avignon, and the distracted state of Italy, he made a vigorous effort to restore the imperial authority in the peninsula, and would probably have succeeded but for his premature death.

The troubled reign of the emperor Louis of Bavaria, his contest for the empire with Frederic, duke of Austria, and the wars occasioned by his efforts to restrain the extravagant pretensions of the popes, led the German princes to discover the necessity of having a written constitution. On the accession of Charles of Luxemburg (A. D. 1347), the calamities of a disputed election to the empire were renewed, and after a long series of wars and disorders, a diet was convened at Nuremburg, to form a code of laws, regulating the rights and privileges of the spiritual and temporal authorities. The result of the diet's labors was published in a celebrated edict, called a Golden Bull, from the *bulla*, or seal of gold, affixed to the document (A. D. 1356). This bull fixed the order and form of the imperial elections, and the ceremonial of the coronation. It ordained that the crown should be given by the plurality of votes of seven electors; the prince chosen emperor having a right to give his suffrage. The right of voting was restricted to possessors of seven principalities, called electorates, of which the partition was prohibited, and the regularity of their inheritance secured by a strict law of primogeniture. Finally, the Golden Bull defined the rights and privileges of the several electors, confirming to the princes of the Palatinate and Saxony the administration of the empire during an interregnum.

The next reign, nevertheless, evinced the danger of investing the electors with such preponderating authority. Wenceslaus, the son and successor of Charles, was a supine and voluptuous prince, who paid little attention to the interests of the empire; he was deposed by a plurality of votes (A. D. 1400), and Robert, the elector palatine, chosen in his stead. Several of the states continued to acknowledge Wenceslaus, but Robert is usually regarded as the legitimate emperor. On Robert's death, the empire returned to the house of Luxemburg, Wenceslaus having consented to resign his pretensions in favor of his brother Sigismond, king of Hungary.

A cloud had long hung over the house of Hapsburgh; it was dispelled by the fortunate union of Albert, duke of Austria, with Sigismond's only daughter, queen in her own right of Hungary and Bohemia. On the death of his father-in-law (A. D. 1437), he succeeded to the empire, but survived his elevation only two years. Albert's posthumous son Ladislaus inherited his mother's realms; his cousin Frederic, duke of Stiria, was chosen emperor, and from his posterity the imperial dignity never departed until the extinction of his male issue (A. D. 1740).

The wise policy of Philip Augustus, in weakening the power of the feudal aristocracy and reuniting the great fiefs to the crown, was vigorously pursued by his successors, but by none more effectually than Philip the Fair. On the death of that monarch (A. D. 1314), the king of France was undoubtedly the most powerful sovereign in Europe. Philip left three sons, who successively reigned in France; Louis, surnamed Hutin, Philip the Long, and Charles the Fair; together with a daughter named Isabel, married to Edward II., king of England. The three French sovereigns just mentioned, died without leaving male issue; all had daughters, but Philip and Charles asserted that no female could inherit the crown of France. The claims founded on this law of succession were but slightly questioned; and on the death of Charles IV., Philip, Count de Valois, the nearest male heir, ascended the throne without encountering any immediate opposition (A. D. 1328). Edward III. of England resolved to claim the kingdom in right of his mother Isabel, but the distractions of his native dominions long presented insuperable obstacles to his projects. He even did liege homage to Philip for the province of Guienne, and for several years gave no sign of meditating such a mighty enterprise as the conquest of France.

Aided by his son, the celebrated Black Prince, the English monarch invaded France, and, contrary to the opinions of all the contemporary princes, was everywhere victorious (A. D. 1338). The war was maintained by Philip of Valois, and his son and successor John, with more obstinacy than wisdom; the former suffered a terrible defeat at Crecy, the most glorious field ever won by English valor; King John was taken prisoner at the battle of Poictiers. But these achievements, however glorious, could not ensure the conquest of France, the country was too large, the French nation too hostile to the invaders, and Edward's army too small for such a revolution. Both sides became weary of the contest, a treaty was concluded at Bretigni, by which several important provinces were ceded to Edward, on the condition of his renouncing his claims to the French crown (A. D. 1360). A troubled period of eight years followed, which can scarcely be called a peace, although there was a cessation from open hostilities.

There is scarcely a calamity by which a nation can be afflicted that did not visit France during this disastrous season. A foreign enemy was in the heart of the kingdom; the seditions of the capital deluged its streets with blood; and a treacherous prince of the blood, Charles the Bad, king of Navarre, was in arms against the sovereign authority. Famine devastated the land, and a plague of unparalleled virulence (A. D. 1348) consummated the work of hunger and the sword The companies of adventurers and mercenary troops that remained unemployed during the truce that followed the victory of Poictiers, spread themselves over the land, in marauding troops, which there was no force to withstand. So little scrupulous were they, that they assailed the pope in Avignon, and compelled the pontiff to redeem himself by a ransom of forty thousand crowns. Finally, the peasantry of several districts, impatient of distress, and maddened by the oppressions of their lords, broke out into a fearful insurrection. This was named the Jacquerie, from the contemptuous phrase, "Jacques bon homme," applied by the nobles to their serfs, and it was marked by all the horrors that necessarily attend a servile war, when men, brutalized by tyranny, and maddened by wrongs, seek vengeance on their oppressors.

Edward the Black Prince was intrusted by his father to the government of the French provinces. A brave and adventurous warrior, Edward was deficient in the qualities of a statesman. Having exhausted his finances by an unwise and fruitless invasion of Castile, he laid heavy taxes on his subjects, and they in anger appealed for protection to their ancient sovereigns. Charles V., who had succeeded his father John on the throne of France, gladly received this appeal, and summoned Edward to appear before him as his liege lord (A D. 1368). Though enfeebled by sickness, the answer of the gallant prince to this summons was a declaration of war, but the tide of fortune was changed, and in a few campaigns the English lost all their acquisitions in France, with the exception of a few important seaports.

The weakness of Richard II., and the doubtful title of Henry IV. prevented the English from renewing the war with France during their reigns; indeed they would probably have been expelled from all their continental possessions, but for the deplorable imbecility of the French monarch, Charles VI., and the sanguinary contests of the factions of Orleans and Burgundy. The English nation had been long commercially connected with Flanders, and when that country was annexed to the dutchy of Burgundy, provision had been made for the continuance of trade by separate truces. Encouraged by the promised neutrality if not the active co-operation of the Burgundian duke, Henry V. invaded France, and destroyed the flower of the French chivalry on the memorable field of Agincourt (A. D. 1415). The progress of the English was uninterrupted until the defection of the duke of Bnrgundy (A. D. 1419), an event which seemed to threaten Henry with ruin; but that prince having been assassinated, his partisans in revenge joined the English, and this circumstance, combined with the unnatural hatred of the French queen Isabel to her son the dauphin, led to the treaty of Troyes, by which Henry, on condition of marrying the princess Catharine, was appointed regent of France, and heir to the unconscious Charles VI.

Notwithstanding this arrangement, Charles VII. on the death of his father, was recognised as king in the southern provinces of France, while Henry VI., the infant inheritor of the crowns of England and France, was proclaimed in the northern provinces, under the reign of his uncle, the duke of Bedford (A. D. 1422). At first the fortunes of Charles wore the most unfavorable appearance; and the siege of Orleans (A. D. 1428) threatened to deprive him of hope. A simple country girl overthrew the power of England. Joan of Arc, called also the Maid of Orleans, whether influenced by enthusiasm or imposture, it is not easy to determine, declared herself supernaturally inspired to undertake the deliverance of her country. The English felt a superstitious awe, and lost their conquests one by one, and after a protracted but feeble struggle no memorial of the victories of Edward and Henry remained but the town of Calais and an empty title (A. D. 1449). The destruction of the French nobility in this long series of wars, enabled Charles VII. to mould the government into a despotic form, which was permanently fixed by his crafty successor Louis XI. Scarcely a less important change was made in ecclesiastical affairs; Charles VII. secured the Gallican church from any future encroachment of the holy see, by adopting several decrees of the council of Basil, which were solemnly recognised in a national assembly held at Bourges (A. D. 1438), and published under the name of the Pragmatic Sanction.

Spain, during this period, continued to be divided in several kingdoms; the Christian monarchies of Navarre, Castile, and Aragon, could not be brought to combine against the Moors, whose strength was concentrated in the province of Granada. Alphonso XI. was the only Castilian monarch who distinguished himself in war against the Mohammedans; he defeated the combined forces of the kings of Morocco and Granada, who had united to besiege Tariffa (A. D. 1340), and by this victory, not only delivered his own frontiers, but acquired several important fortresses. The power of Castile was weakened by the unexampled tyranny of Peter the Cruel. He was dethroned by his illegitimate brother, Henry, count of Trastamare, but was subsequently restored by Edward the Black Prince. Proving ungrateful to his benefactor, he provoked a second contest, in which he lost his kingdom and life. The kingdom now passed to the house of Trastamare (A. D 1368), and for a considerable period enjoyed peace and prosperity Though the kingdom of Aragon was inferior in extent to that of Castile, yet the advantages of a better government, and wiser sovereign, with those of industry and commerce, along a line of seacoast, rendered it almost equally important. The Aragonese kings acquired the kingdom of the two Sicilies, the Balearic islands, Sardinia, and the county of Barcelona, with several other Catalonian districts. They would probably have struggled for the supremacy of Spain, had not the crowns of Aragon and Castile been united by the marriage of Ferdinand and Isabella (A. D. 1469).

A similar event had nearly united the crowns of Castile and Portugal. Ferdinand, king of Portugal, having no male heir, wished to secure the succession for his daughter Beatrice, and married her, at the early age of eleven, to John I., king of Castile. On the death of Ferdinand, his illegitimate brother, Don Juan, commonly called John the Bastard, profiting by the national hatred between the Portuguese and Castilians, usurped the regency. A fierce war ensued, the Castilians were overthrown in the decisive battle of Aljubarota (A. D. 1385), and John was proclaimed king by the states of Portugal. The war was continued foi several years, but finally a treaty was concluded, by which the Castilian monarchs resigned all claim to the inheritance of Beatrice.

SECTION V.—*The State of England and the Northern Kingdoms in the Fourteenth and Fifteenth Centuries.*

THE inglorious reign of Edward II. in England was not on the whole unfavorable to the progress of constitutional liberty. After the weakness of the king and profligacy of his favorites had for four years disgusted the nations, the barons compelled the monarch to grant a reform of abuses in full parliament (A. D. 1311). The Great Charter was renewed, and a fresh clause added, of too much importance to be omitted even in this scanty page: "Forasmuch as many people be aggrieved by the king's ministers against right, in respect to which grievances no one can recover without a common parliament; we do ordain that the king shall hold a parliament once in the year, or twice, if need be." But this security against mis-government proved inefficacious, the monarch was deposed, and soon after murdered (A. D. 1327). Edward III. was proclaimed king; and during his minority, the administration was intrusted to Queen Isabella. After the lapse of three years, Isabella, who had disgraced herself by a criminal intrigue with Mortimer, earl of March, was stripped of power, and her paramour beheaded.

Edward III. rendered his reign illustrious, not more by his splendid achievements in France, than by the wise laws he sanctioned in England. These, perhaps, must be ascribed less to the wisdom of the sovereign than the increasing spirit of the commons. It was during this long and prosperous reign that parliament established the three fundamental principles of our government—the illegality of raising money without the consent of parliament; the necessity of both houses concurring in any alteration of the laws; and the right of the commons to investigate public abuses, and impeach the royal ministers for mal-administration. While in the midst of victory, able to boast of his queen having conquered and captured the king of Scotland, and of his son having taken the king of France prisoner, Edward found his parliaments well-disposed to second all his efforts, and gratify all his wishes; but, when the tide of fortune turned, he had to encounter the hostility of a constitutional opposition, at the head of which appeared the prince of Wales. On the death of the heroic Black Prince, the royal favorite the duke of Lancaster became supreme in parliament, but the fruits of the victories acquired by the patriots were not lost, the statute law of the realm was improved, the administration of justice improved, and the great security of ministerial responsibility established. English litera ture began to assume a settled form; Chaucer, the greatest poet that modern Europe had produced, with the exception of Dante, flourished in the time of Edward; and the language had become so far perfect, that it was resolved to have all laws written in English, instead of the Norman French, which had been used since the time of the conquest.

Richard II., son of the Black Prince, succeeded his grandfather (A. D. 1377), ere he had attained his twelfth year. The early part of his reign was troubled by the contests of his ambitious uncles for the regency, and by a dangerous insurrection of the peasants, headed by the celebrated blacksmith, Wat Tyler. About the same time, the zeal with which Wickliffe denounced the corruptions of the church, provoked the hostility of the clergy; his doctrines were condemned by a national synod (A. D. 1382), but they had taken fast hold of the people, and some of his disciples carried them to the continent, more especially into Bohemia, where they continued to flourish in spite of persecution. The continued misgovernment of Richard provoked a revolution, while he was absent in Ireland. Henry of Lancaster, duke of Hereford, enraged at the forfeiture of his paternal estate, headed the revolt; Richard, on his return, finding the royal cause hopeless, surrendered to his haughty cousin, and was forced to abdicate the crown (A. D. 1399).

The throne, thus vacated, was claimed by Henry, as representative of the duke of Lancaster, the third son of Edward III., but the hereditary right belonged to Edmund Mortimer, earl of March, the lineal descendant of Lionel, duke of Clarence, second son of Edward III. The Mortimer claim, at a later period, was vested by marriage in the family of York, descended from the fourth son of Edward. Henry of Lancaster, however, was the idol of the people, and the master of the parliament; his demand passed without question, and the first acts of his reign were well calculated to make the nation acquiesce in his title. The efforts of some discontented nobles to restore Richard, were crushed by the spontaneous exertions of the populace, and the death of the deposed monarch seemed to secure tranquillity. But the fourth Henry found that discontented friends were the most dangerous enemies; the proud Percies, to whom he owed his elevation, dissatisfied with the scanty reward of their services, took up arms, and involved the country in civil war. The Percies were overthrown at Shrewsbury (A. D. 1403), but their Welsh ally, Owen Glendower, maintained a stern resistance to the house of Lancaster for several years.

On the death of Henry IV., his son, Henry of Monmouth, ascended the throne (A. D. 1413). His dissipation in youth gave little promise of a glorious reign, but immediately after his accession he resigned all his follies, and having secured the tranquillity of England by judicious measures of reform, he revived the claims of Edward to the throne of France. The glorious battle of Agincourt left him master of the open field, the crimes and follies of the French court gave him possession of Paris; he died in the midst of victory (A. D. 1422), leaving a son only nine months old to inherit his kingdoms.

The early part of Henry VI.'s reign is occupied by the series of wars that ended in the expulsion of the English from their continental possessions. The loss of trophies so gratifying to popular vanity, alienated the affections of the nation from the house of Lancaster, and this dislike was increased by the haughtiness of Henry's queen, Margaret of Anjou, and the ambition of unprincipled favorites. Richard, duke of York, sure of succeeding to the crown, would probably not have asserted the claims of his house, but for the unexpected birth of a prince, on whose legitimacy some suspicion was thrown. Encouraged by many powerful nobles, he took up arms; the cognizance of the Yorkists was a white rose, that of the Lancastrians, a red rose, and the fierce contests that ensued are usually called the "wars of the roses." After a sanguinary struggle, marked by many vicissitudes of fortune, the white rose triumphed, and Edward IV., son of Richard, duke of York, became king of England (A. D. 1461). Ten years afterward, his triumph was completed, and his rights secured, by the battle of Tewkesbury, in which the Lancastrians were decisively overthrown. Edward's reign was sullied by cruelty and debauchery; after his death (A. D. 1483), the crown was usurped by Richard, duke of Gloucester, who endeavored to secure himself by the murder of his nephews. But the claims of the Lancastrian family were now revived by Henry Tudor, earl of Richmond, the heir to that house by right of his mother, and a proposal, favored by the principal nobles, was made for uniting this nobleman in marriage to the princess Elizabeth, daughter of Edward IV., and thus for ever extinguishing the hostility between the rival houses. At the decisive battle of Bosworth field, Richard was defeated and slain (A. D. 1485); Henry became king of England, and his marriage with Elizabeth united the rival claims of York and Lancaster in the Tudor family.

The wars excited by disputed successions in Scotland, were terminated by the transfer of the crown to the family of the Stuarts (A. D. 1371). Under this dynasty, the royal authority, which had been almost annihilated by the nobles, was greatly extended, and judicious laws enacted for restraining the turbulence of the aristocracy.

Intestine wars long harassed the northern kingdoms, but their tranquillity was restored by Queen Margaret, commonly called the Semiramis of the North, who united Denmark, Norway, and Sweden, into one state, by the treaty of Calmar (A. D. 1397). The predilection shown by Margaret's successors for their Danish subjects, displeased the Swedes, and on the death of King Christopher, without issue, they separated from the union, and chose Charles VIII., one of their native nobles, to be their sovereign. The Danes conferred their crown on Christian I., count of Oldenberg (A. D. 1450), and it has ever since continued in his family.

During the fourteenth and fifteenth centuries, Russia was divided into several principalities, all of which were under the Mongolian yoke, while the western provinces had the additional misery of being ravaged by the Poles and Lithuanians. A diversion in their favor was made by the Teutonic knights, who added several rich provinces to their Prussian dominions, but the oppressive government of the order provoked insurrections, of which the Poles took advantage, not only to regain their former provinces, but also to acquire a considerable portion of Prussia, which was ceded to them by the peace of Thorn (A. D. 1466). A great revolution in the Polish form of government roused the martial enthusiasm, but proved fatal to the tranquillity of the Poles. Casimir he Great, having no male issue, wished to secure the succession for his nephew, Louis, king of Hungary, and convoked a general assembly of the states (A. D. 1339). The nobles, to whom an appeal was thus made, took advantage of the circumstance to render the throne elective, and to place great restrictions on the royal authority. When Louis of Hungary became king of Poland (A. D. 1370), he was obliged to swear fealty to a constitution which changed the monarchy into a republican aristocracy. On his death, the crown of Poland was given to Jagellon, duke of Lithuania (A. D. 1382), who renounced paganism on his election, and established the Christian religion in his hereditary estates. Though the crown continued elective, the Polish kings were always chosen from the Jagellon family, until its extinction in the sixteenth century.

SECTION VI.—*Rise and Progress of the Ottoman Empire.*

UNDER the administration of the Palæologi, the Byzantine empire sunk into hopeless decay; its history presents an unvaried picture of vice and folly; the weakness of the sovereigns, the exorbitant power of the patriarchs and monks, the fury of theological controversy, the multiplication of schisms and sects, would have ruined the state, but for the external pressure of the Mohammedan dynasties; while, on the other hand, the triumph of these enemies was delayed by the revolutions in the sultanies of Anatolia, and the difficulties that the siege of a maritime capital presents to hordes ignorant of navigation. But when the power of the Ottoman Turks became consolidated, it was manifest that the fate of Constantinople could not be averted, though its fall was long delayed.

The power of the Ottoman Turks commenced in Asia Minor; when the Mongolian hordes overthrew the Seljúkian dynasties, a small wandering tribe of Turks sought refuge in Armenia, but after seven years of exile, seized what they deemed a favorable opportunity of returning to their ancient possessions. While fording the Euphrates, the leader of the Turks was drowned, and the tribe was divided into four, by his sons. Ertogrul, the warlike leader of one division, resolved to return into Asia Minor: the sultanies into which the Seljúkian empire had been divided, were harassing each other with mutual wars, and could not be persuaded to combine against either the Mongols or the crusaders, and consequently a band of adventurous warriors might reasonably hope to obtain fame and fortune in such a distracted country. During Ertogrul's retrograde march, he met two armies engaged in mortal combat, and without giving himself the trouble of investigating the cause, he took the chivalrous resolution of joining the weaker party. His unexpected aid changed the fortunes of the day, and he was rewarded by the conqueror, who proved to be a chief of the Seljúkians, with the gift of a mountainous district, forming the frontiers of ancient Bithynia and Phrygia.

Othman, or Ottoman, usually regarded as the founder of the Turkish empire (born A. D. 1258), succeeded his father Ertogrul at an early age. He was fortunate in winning the friendship of a young Greek, who embraced Islamism to please his patron, and instructed the Turkish prince in the art of government. From this renegade descended the family of Mikal-ogli,* which so often appears conspicuous in Turkish history. To the information obtained from this Greek, Othman owed the supremacy which he speedily acquired over his Seljúkian rivals; aided by the surrounding emirs, he wrested several important places from the Byzantine empire, particularly Prusa, the ancient capital of Bithynia, which under the slightly altered name of Brúsa, became his metropolis (A. D. 1327). The new kingdom, thus formed at the expense of the sultans of Iconium and the Greek emperors, increased rapidly, and soon became one of the most flourishing states in the east.

Orkhan, the son and successor of Othman, instituted the military force of the Janissaries, to which the Turks owe the chief part of their success. Having greatly enlarged his dominions, he took the title of sultan and began to expel the Greeks from Anatolia. While Orkhan pursued his victorious career in Asia, his son Soliman crossed the Hellespont (A. D. 1358), captured Gallipoli, and thus laid the first foundation of the Turkish power in Europe.

Amurath, or Morad I., steadily pursued the policy of his father and brother. He captured Adrianople (A. D. 1360), which he made his capital. He subdued Thrace, Macedon, and Servia, but fell at the battle of Cossova, one of the most sanguinary ever fought between Turks and Christians.

Bayezíd, surnamed Ilderín, or the Thunderer, put an end to all the petty Turkish sovereignties in Asia Minor; he subdued Bulgaria, and maintained his conquest by the decisive victory that he gained at Nicopolis over Sigismond, king of Hungary. The pride, the cruelty, and the bravery of Bayezíd have been celebrated in history and romance. Southern Greece, the countries along the Danube, and the western districts of Thrace, submitted to his arms; the empire of Constantinople was bounded by the walls of the city; even this was held blockaded for ten years, and must eventually have fallen, had not Bayezíd's attention been directed to Asia, by the rapid successes of a conqueror, more savage than himself.

Timúr Lenk, that is to say, "Lame Timur," a name commonly corrupted into Tamerlane, was the son of a Jagatay Turk, who ruled a horde, nominally subject to the descendants of Jenghiz Khan. His amazing strength, exhibited even in early infancy, procured him the name Timúr, which signifies "iron." While yet a youth, he resolved to deliver his country from the Mongolian yoke, but at the same time, aware of the high value placed upon illustrious birth, he pretended to be descended from Jenghiz, and on this account he is frequently called Timúr the Tartar; and this error was perpetuated in India, where his descendants, the emperors of Delhi, have been denominated the Great Moguls.

* Sons of Michael.

His empire was rapidly extended from the wall of China to the Meditерranean sea; India in the south, and Russia in the north, acknowledged his sway, and his determination to wrest Syria and Anatolia from the Turks, compelled Bayezíd to abandon the siege of Constantinople, and hasten to the defence of his Asiatic dominions (A. D. 1403). Before he could reach the scene of action, Sivas (the ancient Sebaste) had fallen, and the bravest warriors of the garrison had been buried alive by the ferocious victor. Damascus soon after shared the same fate; it was laid waste by fire and sword, and a solitary tower alone remained to mark the spot that had once been a city.

Bayezíd encountered Timúr in the plains of Angora; he was defeated with great loss, and taken prisoner. The Turkish historians assert that Bayezíd was confined by the conqueror in an iron cage, but Timúr's own companion and historian asserts that the conqueror treated his captive with great lenity; all that can be determined with certainty is that the sultan died in the enemy's camp. Timúr himself fell a victim to disease, while preparing to invade China (A. D. 1405). His empire was dismembered after his death, but Baber, one of his descendants, established an empire at Delhi, in northern India (A. D. 1526), which, sadly shorn of its ancient glories, subsisted almost to our own times, under the name of the empire of the Great Moguls.

After a long fratricidal war, Mohammed I., the youngest of Bayezíd's sons, succeeded to his father's dominions. The greater part of his reign was spent in restoring the Ottoman power in western Asia, and thus the Byzantines obtained a respite, by which they knew not how to profit. Morad, or Amurath II., raised the glory of the Ottomans to a height greater than it had yet attained. He deprived the Greeks of all their cities and castles on the Euxine sea, and along the coasts of Thrace, Macedon, and Thessaly; he even stormed the fortifications that had been constructed across the Corinthian isthmus, and carried his victorious arms into the midst of the Peloponnesus. The Grecian emperors acknowledged him as their superior lord, and he, in turn, accorded them protection. Two Christian heroes arrested the progress of the sultan—John Hunniades, and George Castriot, better known by the name of Scanderbeg. Hunniades was a celebrated Hungarian general; he drove the Turks from Servia, whose possession they eagerly coveted, and long impeded their progress westward. Scanderbeg was an Albanian prince, possessing a small district in the Epirote mountains, of which Croia was the capital. At the head of a small but faithful band of followers, he long resisted the mighty armies of the Ottomans, and compelled Amurath himself to raise the siege of Croia.

At length Mohammed II. ascended the Ottoman throne (A. D. 1451), and from the moment of his accession, directed all his efforts to the capture of Constantinople. At the head of an army of three hundred thousand men, supported by a fleet of three hundred sail, he laid siege to this celebrated metropolis, and encouraged his men by spreading reports of prophecies and prodigies, that portended the triumph of Islamism. Constantine, the last of the Greek emperors, met the storm with becoming resolution; supported by the Genoese, and a scanty band of followers from western Europe, he maintained the city for fifty-three days, though the fanaticism of his enemies was raised to the highest pitch by their confident reliance on the favor of Heaven, while prophecies of impending wo and desolation proportionably depressed the inhabitants of Constantinople. At length, on the 29th of May, A. D. 1453, the Turks stormed the walls, the last Constantine fell as he boldly disputed every inch of ground, multitudes of his subjects were massacred in the first burst of Turkish fury, the rest were dragged into slavery, and when Mohammed made his triumphal entry, he found the city a vast solitude.

The conquest of Constantinople was followed by that of Servia, Bosnia, Albania, Greece, including the Peloponnesus, several islands of the Archipelago, and the Greek empire of Trebizond. All Christendom was filled with alarm; Pope Pius II. convened a council at Mantua, for the purpose of organizing a general association to resist the progress of the Turks (A. D. 1459). A crusade was preached by his order, and he was about to undertake the command of the expedition in person, when death cut short his projects at Ancona (A. D. 1464). The Christian league was dissolved by his death, the Turks were permitted to establish their empire in Europe, and this received a great increase, both of security and strength, by the voluntary tender of allegiance which the khans of the Crimea made to Mohammed II. (A. D. 1478). After the first burst of fanaticism was over, Mohammed granted protection to his Christian subjects, and, by his wise measures, Constantinople was restored to its former prosperity.

CHAPTER VI.

THE REFORMATION, AND COMMENCEMENT OF THE STATES-SYSTEM IN EUROPE.

Section I.—*Progress of Maritime Discovery.*

The scene of the earliest-known navigation was the Mediterranean sea, which naturally seemed to the ancients to be situated *in the middle of the earth;* as is implied by its name. As navigation advanced only at a creeping pace, and as but a small amount of fresh experience was laid up by one generation for the benefit of the next, it took very many ages to explore the Mediterranean, Tyrrhene, Hadriatic, and Ægean seas.

The great natural relief, given to ancient navigation, was the discovery of the trade-winds which prevail in the Indian ocean. These periodical changes of winds, if noticed by the Arabians, were not made to serve their maritime trade, until the keener enterprise of the West, in the person of Hippalus (about A. D. 50), first ventured to steer off from the Arabian and Persian shores, and to be impelled eastward, in the direction of the wind. A voyage which had consumed years, now took up but as many months, by a conformity on the part of the mariner with this invariable law of nature. The means of profit and information were now less monopolized, and the west became better acquainted with the inhabitants and produce of the east.

The navigation to the Indies was continued, when the Romans became masters of Egypt, by sailing down the Arabian gulf, and thence to the mouth of the river Indus, along the southern coasts of Arabia and Persia. But under the emperor Claudius this route was so far changed, that after emerging from the Arabian gulf, they cut across the Indian ocean directly to the mouth of the Indus, by noticing, and taking advantage of, the time when the southwest trade-wind blew.

When the Arabians, in their rapid career of conquest, had reached the Euphrates, they immediately perceived the advantages to be derived from an emporium situated upon a river which opened on the one hand a shorter route to India than they had hitherto had, and on the other an extensive inland navigation through a wealthy country; and Bassora, which they built on the west bank of the river (A. D. 636), soon became a great commercial city, and entirely cut off the independent part of Persia from the oriental trade. The Arabian merchants of Bassora extended their discoveries eastward, far beyond the tracks of all preceding navigators, and imported directly from the place of their growth, many Indian articles, hitherto procured at second hand in Ceylon; which they accordingly furnished on their own terms to the nations of the west.

As an instance of the depressed state of human knowledge during the middle ages, we may mention that Cosmas, a Greek merchant of the sixth century wrote a book called "*Christian Topography*," the chief intent of which was to confute the heretical opinion of the earth being a globe, together with the pagan assertion that there was a temperate zone on the southern side of the torrid zone. He informed his readers that, according to the true orthodox system of cosmography, the earth was a quadrangular plane, extending four hundred courses, or days' journeys, from east to west, and exactly half as much from north to south, enclosed by lofty mountains, upon which the canopy or vault of the firmament rested; that a huge mountain on the north side of the earth, by intercepting the light of the sun, produced the vicissitudes of day and night; and that the plane of the earth had a declivity from north, by reason of which the Euphrates, Tigris, and other rivers running southward, are rapid; whereas the Nile, having to run up-hill, has necessarily a very slow current.

The Feroe islands had been discovered about the latter end of the ninth century, by some Scandinavian pirates; and soon after this, Iceland was colonized by Flok, the Norwegian. Iceland, it appears, had been discovered long before the Norwegians settled there; as many relics, in the nature of bells, books in the Irish language, and wooden crosses, were discovered by Flok, in different parts of the island: so that the Irish seem first to have set foot upon that isle. The Icelandic chronicles also relate that, about these times, the Northmen discovered a great country to the west of Ireland, which account has by many been deemed apocryphal: for, if true, they must be held to be some of the early discoverers of America; but it seems pretty clear that they made their way to Greenland in the end of the tenth century. The settlement effected in Greenland, though comprising but a small population, seems to have been very prosperous in these early times in mercantile affairs. They had bishops and priests from Europe; and paid the pope, as an annual tribute, twenty-six hundred pounds of walrus-teeth, as tithe and Peter's pence. The voyage from Greenland to Iceland and Norway, and back again, consumed five years; and upon one occasion the government of Norway did not hear of the death of the bishop of Greenland until six years after it had occurred; so that the art of navigation, after all, must have been in these times but at a very low pitch.

Greenland seems to have been called Viinland, or Finland, from the vines which were discerned by the early discoverers as abounding in this country; and, in fact, wild vines are found growing in all the northern districts of America. This Viinland is, however, supposed by some persons to have been Newfoundland; and if so, America must in reality have been discovered as much as five centuries before Columbus sailed so far as the West Indies; and moreover, it has been supposed that the many traditions about the west, existing in the time of Columbus, first set him to prosecute the idea of discovering another world.

The impulse which the cultivation of ancient learning had received in Europe was greatly strengthened by the downfall of Constantinople, which drove the most learned Greeks into exile ; they sought refuge for the most part in Italy, and the libraries of that peninsula became the depositories of what remained of the ancient treasures of Greek literature and philosophy. It was hence that the first stimulus was given to the study of the Greek language in Europe. Translators of the Greek authors, and commentators upon them, began to multiply; and the rapid progress of the art of printing gave an additional impulse by the facilities it afforded for the dissemination of learning. The belief that there existed a fourth division of the globe, larger than any yet discovered, had been encouraged by some of the ancient philosophers ; and it had been so generally received, that two eminent fathers of the church, St. Augustine and Lactantius, had zealously labored to refute the theory, believing it inconsistent with the doctrines of Christianity. With the cultivation of Greek literature the old notion was revived, and at the same time the rapid development of the spirit of maritime discovery induced several nations, but especially the Portuguese, to search out new and unknown lands.

The Canaries, or Fortunate islands, were the first discovery that followed the introduction of the mariner's compass ; they became known to the Spaniards early in the fourteenth century, but no regular attempt was made for their colonization.

In the early part of the fifteenth century, John I., king of Portugal, had effected some very important conquests over the Moors ; in which he had been very materially assisted by his son, Prince Henry, who being an able and active-minded cavalier, took delight rather in the more solid glories of learning and science, than in the fame of war, in which he had, however, of late so highly distinguished himself. Upon the cessation of hostilities he retired to the promontory of St. Vincent, and lived at the seaport town of Sagres, which he had himself founded, where he cultivated the science of astronomy, for the purpose of making it available to the mariner, in guiding him over the ocean, when he had quitted the servile tracking of the shore. He, in fact, established a naval college, and an observatory. He engaged to his assistance all the best-informed men of his time ; and the point to which he especially directed his attention, was the practicability of sailing round Africa, and of thus reaching the East Indies. Prince Henry did not live to see the whole of his views accomplished ; but the many minor discoveries which were effected under his auspices, laid up a fund of knowledge and experience for succeeding generations to profit by. Maps were formed under his superintendence : by which means all the geographical knowledge respecting the earth was brought together ; the different parts were marked out ; and the rocks, coasts, and quicksands, to be avoided, were all noted down.

The southernmost cape of Africa known in those days was Cape Non, which received this appellation from the idea that it was utterly impossible to get beyond this cape ; but the officers of Henry having at length doubled it, found Cape Bojador in the distance, whose violent currents and raging breakers, running for miles out to sea, seemed a barrier which could not even be approached with safety by mariners, who were in the habit of coasting along the shore. Seamen now began to be more alarmed than ever at the idea of the torrid zone, and to propagate the notion, that he who should double Cape Bojador would never return. At length this awful cape was passed by; the region of the tropics was penetrated, and divested of its fancied terrors; the river Senegal was observed, the greater part of the African coast, from Cape Blanco to Cape de Verde, was explored, and the Cape de Verde and the Azore islands were discovered; the Madeiras and Canaries having been visited for the first time by the Spaniards some years before. This prince died in the year 1473, after having obtained a papal bull, investing the crown of Portugal with sovereign authority over all the lands it might discover in the Atlantic, to India inclusive.

The passion for discovery languished after the death of Prince Henry, but it was revived by his grand-nephew, King John II., with additional ardor (A. D. 1481). In his reign, the Portuguese, for the first time, crossed the equator, and for the first time beheld the stars of a new hemisphere. They now discovered the error of the ancients, respecting the torrid zone, and practically refuted the common belief that the continent of Africa widened toward the south, for they beheld it sensibly contracting and bending toward the east. The hopes inspired by this discovery, induced the Portuguese monarch to send ambassadors in search of an unknown potentate supposed to profess the Christian religion, by whose aid it was hoped that a lucrative trade might be opened with India, and the progress of the true faith secured.

Early in the thirteenth century, reports were prevalent in Europe of some great potentate in a remote part of Asia having embraced the Christian faith.* In consequence, the pope, Innocent IV., sent two monks to preach Christianity in the Mongolian court (A. D. 1246); and soon after, St. Louis of France employed the celebrated Rubruquis to seek the aid of the supposed Christian sovereign, who was commonly called Prester John, in the crusade that he contemplated. A Venetian, named Marco Polo, visited the most distant parts of Asia (A. D. 1263), and penetrated to Pekin, the capital of China. He was followed by Sir John Mandeville, an Englishman (A. D. 1322), and the narrations of both, though deficient in accuracy of information, contributed to keep alive the feelings of interest and curiosity which had been excited in Europe.

While the Portuguese monarch's emissaries were engaged in a hopeless search for Prester John, and the more useful task of investigating the state of navigation in the Indian seas, an expedition from Lisbon, conducted by Bartholomew Diaz, had actually discovered the southern extremity of the African continent (A. D. 1483). A storm preventing him from pursuing his career, he named the promontory that terminated his voyage "the cape of Tempests;" but King John, aware of the vast importance of the discovery, called it "the cape of Good Hope." At the same time letters were received from the monks who had been sent overland, in which the practicability of reaching the East Indies, by sailing round Africa, was strenuously maintained. But the intervening

* It is probable that this error arose from some inaccurate description of Buddhism. Most persons are aware that the rituals and ceremonials of the Buddhist priests bear a striking resemblance to those of the Roman Catholic church.

discovery of America diverted, for a season, men's minds from this voyage round Africa; and fifteen years had nearly elapsed before Vasco de Gama, having rounded the cape of Good Hope, reached India, and anchored in the harbor of Calicut, on the coast of Malabar (May 22, A. D. 1498).

Among the adventurers who flocked to join the Portuguese from every part of Europe was Christopher Colon, or Columbus, a native of Genoa. The narrative of Marco Polo had led to the belief that the extent of India, beyond the Ganges, was greater than that of the rest of Asia; and, as the spherical figure of the earth was known, he was naturally led to the conclusion that India might more easily be reached by sailing westward, than by the long and tedious circumnavigation of Africa. After enduring many disappointments, Columbus obtained a small armament, from Ferdinand and Isabella of Spain; and, on the third of August, A. D. 1492, sailed from the little port of Palos, in Andalusia, to discover a new world.

During the long voyage, the crew of Columbus was more than once on the point of mutinying and turning back in despair; at length land was discovered on the twelfth of October, and Columbus found himself soon in the midst of that cluster of islands, which, in consequence of the original error about the extent of India, were named the West Indies. On his return to Europe, he was received by Ferdinand and Isabella with the highest honors; a second expedition was prepared to extend and secure his discoveries, but, before his departure, application was made to the pope for a grant of these new dominions, and Alexander VI. shared all the unknown regions of the earth inhabited by infidels between the Spaniards and Portuguese, fixing as their common boundary an imaginary line drawn from pole to pole, one hundred leagues to the west of the Azores, and assigning all west of that line to Spain, and all east of it to Portugal.

The colonies established by the Spaniards differed from those founded by other European countries. The Spaniards were not a trading people, indeed ignorance of the advantages that result from commerce has been always a characteristic of that nation; the precious metals were the only objects that excited their attention, and for a series of years they devoted themselves exclusively to the exploration of mines. It was only when the augmentation of the European population, and the diminished returns from the mines, forced their attention to agriculture, that they began to pay any attention to raising colonial produce. In consequence of these restricted views, the commercial and colonial policy of Spain was always the worst possible; it was fettered by monopolies, exclusions, and restrictions, equally injurious to the parent state and its dependancies; and perseverance in this erroneous system is a principal cause of the low state of civilization both in Spain and its late colonies.

Not only the Dutch, but the English and French, were roused to emulation by the success of the Spaniards and Portuguese. In the reign of Henry VII., Cabot, a mariner of Bristol, made some considerable additions to maritime knowledge; but it was not until the time of Elizabeth that regular plans of colonization were formed.

The growth of commerce in this age was very rapid, but there appeared still room for further discoveries until the globe was circumnavigated by Magellan (A. D. 1521). From that time the attention of nations began to be directed more to completing old discoveries than to the search for new lands. The navies of Europe began to assume a formidable aspect; manufactures multiplied, and states, previously poor, became suddenly rich. Sovereigns and governments began to direct their attention to commerce, justly persuaded that mercantile wealth is equally the source of the prosperity and glory of nations.

SECTION II.—*Origin of the Reformation.*

THE extravagant claims of the popes to temporal, as well as spiritual supremacy, had been resisted by several men of learning, whose works did not die with them, but continued to exercise a powerful, though secret effect, on succeeding generations. This repugnance to ecclesiastical domination was greatly increased by the scandalous schism at the close of the fourteenth and commencement of the fifteenth century. Two or three popes reigning at the same time, excommunicating each other, appealing to the laity for support, compelled men to exercise the right of private judgment, and directed attention to the ecclesiastical abuses that had produced such unhappy fruits. The partial reforms, or rather attempts at reformation, made by the councils of Constance and Basil, spread the disrespect for the Romish see still wider; their deposition of contending pontiffs taught men that there was a jurisdiction in the church superior to the papal power, their feeble efforts to correct abuse brought the evils prominently forward, and left them unamended to meet the public gaze. While this dissatisfaction was hourly increasing, the papal chair was filled successively by two pontiffs, whose career of unscrupulous guilt was sufficient to disgust even a less enlightened age. Alexander VI., profligate in private life, cruel and tyrannical in his public administration, was followed by Julius II., whose overbearing ambition led him to trample on the very semblance of justice and moderation when they interfered with the success of his schemes. The sovereigns of France and Germany, alternately engaged in active hostilities with these heads of the church, could not prevent their subjects from ridiculing papal pretensions, and assailing papal vices. Nor were these scandals confined to the papacy; the licentious lives of the ecclesiastics in Italy and Germany, the facility with which they obtained pardons for enormous crimes, their exorbitant wealth, their personal immunities, and their encroachments on the rights of the laity, had given just offence; and this was the more sensibly felt in Germany, because most of the great benefices were in the hands of foreigners.

When men's minds were everywhere filled with disgust at the existing administration of ecclesiastical affairs, and eager for some change, a dispute, trivial in its origin, kindled a flame, which rapidly spread over Europe, destroying all the strongholds that had been so laboriously erected for the security of tyranny and superstition. Leo X., on his accession to the papal chair, found the treasury of the church exhausted by the ambitious projects of his predecessors, Alexander VI. and Julius II Generous in his disposition, magnificent in his habits of life, eager for the aggrandizement of his family, the princely Medicis, he could not practise the economy necessary to recruit his finances, and he therefore had recourse to every device that his ingenuity could suggest to raise money for the splendid designs he contemplated. Among these he introduced an extensive sale of indulgences, which often had proved a source of large profits to the church.

The origin of indulgences has been sometimes misrepresented by eminent writers; and as we have now reached a period when their abuse produced the most decisive blow which the papacy had yet received, it will be necessary to take a brief survey of their history. In the primitive church it was customary that those who had committed any heinous offence should perform a public penance before the congregation, "that their souls might be saved in the day of the Lord; and that others, admonished by their example, might be the more afraid to offend." In process of time rich and noble offenders became anxious to avoid public exposure, and private penances or a pecuniary compensation were substituted for the former discipline. On this change the popes founded a new doctrine, which, combined with the commutation of indulgences, opened the way for profitable traffic. They taught the world that all the good works of the saints, over and above those which were necessary to their own justification, are deposited, together with the infinite merits of Jesus Christ, in one inexhaustible treasury. The keys of this were committed to St. Peter and his successors the popes, who may open it at pleasure, and by transferring a portion of this superabundant merit to any particular person for service in a crusade, or for a sum of money, may convey to him either the pardon of his own sins, or a release for any one, in whose happiness he is interested, from the pains of purgatory. These indulgences were first issued to those who joined personally in the expeditions for the recovery of the Holy Land; subsequently to those who hired a soldier for that purpose; and finally to all who gave money for accomplishing any work which it pleased the popes to describe as good and pious. Julius II. bestowed indulgences on all who contributed to the building of St. Peter's at Rome, and Leo continued the traffic under the same pretence.

Different orders of monks derived considerable profit from the sale of indulgences, and great indignation was excited among the Augustinian friars when the monopoly of the trade in Germany was granted to their rivals, the Dominicans. Tetzel, the chief agent in retailing them, was a man of licentious morals, but of an active spirit, and remarkable for his noisy and popular eloquence.* He executed his com-

* The following is the form of absolution used by Tetzel:—"May our Lord Jesus Christ have mercy upon thee, and absolve thee by all the merits of his most holy passion; and I, by his authority, that of his blessed apostles, Peter and Paul, and of the most holy pope, granted and committed to me in these parts, do absolve thee first from all ecclesiastical censures, in whatever manner they have been incurred, and then from all thy sins, transgressions, and excesses, how enormous soever they may be, even from such as are reserved for the cognizance of the holy see: and as far as the keys of the holy church extend, I remit to you all punishment which you deserve in purgatory on their account; and I restore you to the holy sacraments of the church, to the unity of the faithful, and to that innocence and purity which you possessed at baptism; so that when you die, the

mission with little regard to discretion or decency, describing the merits of the indulgences in such a blasphemous style of exaggeration, that all men of sense were disgusted, and even the ignorant began to suspect the worth of pardons for sins dispensed by men whose profligacy was notorious and disgusting. The princes and nobles of Germany were enraged by witnessing the large sums of money drained from their vassals to support the lavish expenditure of the pontiff, and many of the higher ranks of the clergy viewed with jealousy the favor displayed to the monastic orders.

MARTIN LUTHER, an Augustinian friar of great learning and indomitable courage, had prepared his mind for the noble career on which he was about to enter by a diligent study of the Holy Scriptures; the question of indulgences early engaged his attention, and he convinced himself that the Bible, which he began to consider as the great standard of theological truth, afforded no countenance to a practice equally subversive of faith and morals. Having vainly sought to procure the suppression of the traffic from the archbishop of Magdeburgh, he appealed to the suffrages of men of letters, by publishing ninety-five theses condemning the sale of indulgences as contrary to reason and Scripture.

Much has been written respecting the personal character of this daring reformer; his boldness frequently degenerated into violence, his opposition to the corrupt discipline of the church sometimes passed the bounds of decency; but these errors arose from the circumstances of his position; he was in fact the representative of the public opinion of his age; and before we pass too severe a censure on the aberrations that sully his career, we must remember that the age had scarcely emerged from barbarism, and that the human mind, as yet unaccustomed to freedom, when suddenly delivered from habitual restraint, necessarily rushed into some extravagances. While hostile writers describe Luther as the vilest of sinners, or the purest of saints, they forget that there is a previous question of some importance, the standard by which his conduct must be measured. We have no right to expect that Luther, engaged in a struggle for life and death, should display the moderation of a modern controversialist, or to look for the intelligence of the nineteenth century at the commencement of the sixteenth. Remembering the school in which he was educated, it is reasonable to believe that many monkish absurdities must long have been perceptible in his words and actions; we need not, therefore, deny that he was sometimes wrong, we need not disguise nor palliate his errors, for the cause which he promoted depends not on the character of him or of any other person. His adversaries, however, have never ventured to deny his courage, his sincerity, his integrity of purpose, and his superiority to all pecuniary considerations. He lived and died poor, though Rome would have purchased his return by wealth and dignity, though the leading reformers were ready to reward his perseverance by any grants he might have required.

gates of punishment shall be shut, and the gates of the paradise of delight shall be opened; and if you shall not die at present, this grace shall remain in full force when you are at the point of death. In the name of the Father, and of the Son, and of the Holy Ghost."

Luther comprehended the state of public opinion; his publications were the manifestation of the revolt of reason against authority, rather than a thesis in his theology. His perseverance, the very violence and grossness of his invectives, showed that he felt human-reason to be on his side. If he had not at first calculated the effect of his first blow, he showed great sagacity in measuring its results. Numerous echoes responded to his summons; Zuinglius began to preach in Switzerland, and the reform engaged the attention of enlightened men of letters; among others, the celebrated Erasmus pointed out corruptions in the church, though he had not moral courage enough to separate himself from it openly. The papal party accepted Luther's challenge, fully believing that the slightest exertion of power would at once stifle opposition (A. D. 1520). Leo X., too indolent to examine the state of the public mind, and too proud to trouble himself about the opposition of a simple friar, published a bull condemning the theses of Luther as heretical and impious (A. D. 1520). The bold reformer at once declared open war against the papacy, by appealing to a general council, and burning the bull of excommunication in presence of a vast multitude at Wittemberg. He treated the volumes of the canon law with the same contumely, and justified his action in a manner more offensive to the advocates of the papacy than the action itself. Having collected from the canon law some of the most extravagant propositions with regard to the plenitude and omnipotence of the papal power, as well as the subordination of all secular jurisdiction to the authority of the holy see, he published these, with a commentary, pointing out the impiety of such tenets, and their evident tendency to subvert all civil governments. From this time, the interests of princes were even more deeply engaged on the side of Luther than popular reason. In fact, as a Romish historian has remarked, "policy became more Lutheran than religous reform!" Sovereigns naturally received with enthusiasm a doctrine which placed at their disposal the enormous wealth of the clergy, and gave them mastery over more riches than could be acquired by the most formidable force, or the most sanguinary combats. Thus, in Germany, Luther, who could at first with difficulty procure a horse when he had to appear before the diet, soon counted princes and entire nations among his disciples. Frederick the Wise, duke of Saxony, was the first among his converts, and the most powerful of his protectors.

It is assuredly very inconsistent in the advocates of the Romish church, to expose the mixture of secular and religious motives in the active supporters of the Reformation; for the abuses which they condemned were equally temporal and spiritual. Indeed, it is very obvious, that the corruptions of doctrine were introduced to serve the political purposes of the papacy; a sordid desire for wealth was the foundation of the system of indulgences, which first provoked the revolt; an ambitious lust for power had caused the subversion of the independence of the national churches, which it was the earliest object of the Lutherans to restore. Politics influenced the enemies of the papacy only because popery was itself a political system, and because in the struggle that now menaced its existence, it had at once recourse to secular auxiliaries

John Calvin, another reformer, was a follower of Zuinglius; he was a native of Noyon, in Picardy, and began first to publish his opinions at Paris (A. D. 1532). Driven thence by the persecutions of the French clergy, he removed to Strasburgh, where he soon rendered himself so eminent by his talents as a writer and a preacher, that the name of Calvinists were given to that section of the reformed congregations which had at first been named Zuinglians.

Calvin was subsequently invited to Geneva, where he organized a system of church-government on the presbyterian principle ; and under the pretence of providing for purity of morals and the continuance of sound doctrine, he contrived to transfer no small portion of the power of the state to the ecclesiastical courts. Unfortunately, these courts soon began to emulate the tyranny of the Romish inquisition, by persecuting those who differed from the standard of religious opinion adopted by the church of Geneva, and an unfortunate Spaniard, named Servetus, was burned alive for publishing some obnoxious doctrines on the subject of the Trinity. The differences which arose between the followers of Luther and Calvin, the obstinacy manifested by each of the parties in support of their own opinions, and the virulence with which they inveighed against each other, sadly checked the progress of the Reformation, and produced a reaction which enabled the court of Rome to recover several countries which it had very nearly lost.

Although much of the early success of the Reformation was owing to the general progress of intelligence and scientific research, there were many among the leading reformers who viewed all secular learning with suspicion, and thus enabled their adversaries to identify their cause with ignorance and barbarism. This was a serious injury to the progress of improvement, for there were many like Erasmus who would gladly have joined in overthrowing the monkish corruptions which had defaced Christianity, but who were alarmed at the prospect of being subjected to the bigoted caprice of the presbyteries and other bodies which began to claim and exercise a power of control over opinion in most of the cities where the reformed religion was established. Whether the Romish church would have displayed a greater spirit of concession, had the reformers exhibited more moderation in their demands for innovation, may be questioned, but it is certain that the papal party could not have made so effectual a struggle as it maintained, had it not taken advantage of the violence, the imprudence, and the dissensions of the reformers themselves.

The rapid progress of the new doctrines was attempted to be checked by the diet of Spires (A. D. 1529), where a decree was promulgated, forbidding any innovation until the assembling of a general council. Luther's friends and followers protested against this decree, and hence the professors of the reformed religion received the common name of Protestants. Soon afterward they presented a general confession of their faith to the emperor at Augsburgh; but unfortunately this celebrated document showed that there were irreconcilable differences between the Calvinistic and Lutheran sections of the reformers.

As the struggle, once begun, was maintained with great obstinacy, it soon led to serious political convulsions. Half of Germany, Denmark, Sweden, Norway, Prussia, and Livonia, adopted the doctrines of Luther, as taught in the confession of Augsburg. England, Scotland

Holland, and Switzerland, embraced the tenets of Zuinglius and Calvin; while efforts to establish similar principles were made in France, Bohemia, Hungary, and Poland.

The means taken to end the controversy only aggravated the evil. It was proposed that the entire matter of dispute should be submitted to a general council, but it was impossible to determine the basis on which it should be convoked. After much delay, a council was assembled at Trent (A. D. 1545), whose sittings were continued, with some interruption, for several years; but when at the close (A. D. 1563), its decrees were published, they were rejected, not only by the protestants, but by many catholic princes, especially the king of France, as subversive of the independence of national churches, and destructive of the lawful authority of sovereigns.

Section III.—*History of the Negotiations and Wars respecting Italy.*

In the midst of the civil and ecclesiastical changes produced by the progress of intelligence, a system of policy for regulating the external relations of states was gradually formed, and attention began to be paid to what was called the Balance of Power; that is, the arrangement of the European states in such a system that the weak might be protected from the aggressions of the powerful and the ambitious. This system first began in Italy, which was divided into a number of petty states; its chief members were the dutchy of Milan, and the republic of Venice, in the north; the republic of Florence, and the states of the church, in the centre; and the kingdom of Naples, in the south. Encouraged by the distracted condition of the peninsula, foreigners were induced to attempt its conquest; and the kings of France and Spain, and the emperors of Germany, made this country the battle-field of rival ambition

After the expulsion of the house of Anjou from Italy, it was established in the petty principality of Provence, where the graces of courtly refinement and light literature were more sedulously cultivated than in any other part of Europe. René, the last monarch of the line, the father of the heroic English queen, Margaret of Anjou, had the prudence not to hazard his security by mingling in the troubled politics of France and Burgundy, but amused himself and his subjects by floral games and poetic contests, heedless of the sanguinary wars that convulsed the surrounding states.

On René's death Provence became a county under the French crown, and was justly deemed a most important acquisition (A.D. 1481). But with the substantial dominions of the house of Anjou, the French monarchs also inherited its pretensions to the thrones of Naples and Sicily Louis XI. was far too prudent a monarch to waste his strength on the assertion of such illusory claims; he directed his attention to a far more useful object, the establishment of the royal power over the great vassals of the crown, several of whom possessed greater real power than the nominal sovereign.

Charles VIII. departed from his father's prudent line of policy; instead of securing the royal authority at home, he directed his attention to foreign conquests, and resolved to assert his imaginary claims to the throne of Naples. He was instigated also by the invitations of Ludovico Sforza, duke of Milan, and by some romantic hope of overthrowing the Turkish empire. A French army crossed the Alps (A. D. 1494), and marched through the peninsula without encountering any effective opposition. Rome, Florence, and Naples, submitted to the conqueror, and Ferdinand II. fled to the island of Ischia. But during the progress of the expedition, a league was formed for the expulsion of all foreigners from Italy; the Venetian republic was the moving power of the confederacy, in which the pope and even Sforza were associated, while the emperor Maximilian, and Ferdinand of Spain, secretly favored its designs. Alarmed by the coming danger, Charles, leaving half his army to protect his conquests, led the remainder back to France. He encountered the Venetians on his road, and gained a complete victory; but the forces he left in Italy were compelled to capitulate, and Ferdinand II. was restored to the throne of Naples.

Charles VIII. was bent on vengeance, and the distracted state of the peninsula gave him hope of success; but before he could complete his arrangements for a second expedition, he was snatched away by a sudden death (A. D. 1498). The duke of Orleans, Louis XII., in addition to his cousin's claims on Naples, inherited from his grandmother a title to the dutchy of Milan. But the French monarch, before undertaking such an extensive conquest, deemed it necessary to strengthen himself by alliances with the republic of Venice, Pope Alexander VI., and Ferdinand, king of Spain. Thus strengthened, he found little difficulty in overrunning Italy; Milan was captured (A. D. 1499), and the turbulent Sforza, after vain attempts to re-establish his power, died in captivity. Naples was next attacked; Ferdinand of Spain had entered into alliance with the Neapolitan monarch Frederick; and his invader, Louis, secretly determined to cheat both. By his aid the kingdom of Naples was subdued, and the dupe Frederic imprisoned for life (A. D. 1501); but no sooner was the conquest completed, than the Spaniard prepared to secure the whole of the spoil. Aided by the abilities of Gonsalvo de Cordova, Ferdinand succeeded in expelling the French from Naples; and the kingdom was finally confirmed to him on his marriage with Germaine de Foix, niece of Louis XII., with whom the French monarch on the receipt of a million of ducats, assigned over his claims on Naples as a dowry (A. D. 1505).

Italy, however, was soon destined to have its tranquillity disturbed by the grasping ambition of Pope Julius II. Anxious to recover the dependencies of the holy see which had been seized by Venice, he organized a confederacy against that republic, of which he was himself the head; while Louis, Maximilian, and Ferdinand, were active members (A. D. 1509). The republic would have been ruined, had the union of the confederates been sincere and permanent; but, owing to the mutual jealousies of its enemies, it escaped when brought to the verge of destruction. The impetuous valor of the French disconcerted all the measures the Venetians had taken to preserve their territories; and the total ruin of their army at Aguadello (A. D. 1509), left them wholly without defence. Julius seized all the towns which they held in the ecclesiastical territories; Ferdinand added all their seaports in Apulia to his Neapolitan dominions; but at the moment when the dismemberment of the republic seemed inevitable, the mutual jealousies of

Louis and Maximilian dissolved the confederacy. The Venetians appeased the pope and Ferdinand, by large concessions, which were the more readily accepted, as Julius had now formed the design of expelling all foreigners from Italy, especially the French, of whose valor and ambition he was justly afraid.

From the fragments of the league of Cambray, a new and stronger confederacy was formed against France, and Henry VIII., who had just ascended the throne of England, was engaged to divert the attention of Louis from Italy, by an invasion of his dominions (A. D. 1511). The master-stroke, however, of the pope's policy was winning over the Swiss, whose mercenary infantry was the best body of troops then used in war. Louis XII. resisted all the efforts of this formidable conspiracy with undaunted fortitude. Hostilities were carried on during several campaigns in Italy, on the frontiers of Spain, and in Picardy, with alternate success. But weakened by the loss of his allies, Florence and Navarre, of which the former having been subjected to the Medicis, joined the league (A. D. 1512), and the latter was conquered and annexed to Spain, Louis would probably have been reduced to great distress, had not the death of Pope Julius (A. D. 1513) come to his relief. Leo, of the princely house of the Medicis, succeeded to the papacy, and immediately made peace with France. Spain, England, and the empire, followed this example, and the war terminated with the loss of everything which the French had acquired in Italy, except the castle of Milan and a few inconsiderable towns in that dutchy.

SECTION IV.—*The History of Burgundy under the Princes of the House of Valois.*

No feudal state was more important in the middle ages than the dutchy of Burgundy, and its history is the best calculated to illustrate the political condition of states, and the relations between powerful princes and their sovereign, produced by the institutions of feudalism. At the same time, the history of Burgundy must in some degree be regarded as an episode in the general annals of Europe, for though its existence was brilliant, it left no permanent trace behind, save the resentment between the houses of France and Austria, arising from the division of its spoils.

The dutchy of Burgundy lapsed to the crown of France soon after the liberation of King John from the captivity in which he had been detained by the English after the battle of Poictiers. He resolved to bestow this rich inheritance upon his third son, Philip, surnamed the Hardy, who had fought gallantly by his side in the unfortunate battle of Poictiers, though only sixteen years of age, and who when John was taken prisoner had accompanied him to England to share his captivity. John's bequest was honorably executed by his son and successor, Charles V. of France ; he gave to Philip the investiture of the dutchy with all legal forms, and on the 2d of June, 1364, the new duke entered upon his inheritance ; he soon afterward married the only daughter of the count of Flanders, and thus became involved in the wars which that nobleman waged against the insurgent citizens of Ghent, and at the same time he actively assisted his brother against the English.

After a long war, in which the burgesses of the free cities of Flan ders sustained with great bravery their municipal franchises against the feudal chivalry of their count and his allies, the insurgents suffered a severe defeat at Rosebecque, in which their gallant leader, the younger Artavelde, was slain. Philip took advantage of the crisis to mediate a peace between the count of Flanders and the revolted cities, which was finally concluded on very equitable conditions. When tranquillity was restored, the duke directed his whole attention to the affairs of France, and during the reign of his unfortunate nephew, Charles VI., took a principal share in the government of that kingdom. While he was thus engaged, ambassadors arrived from the king of Hungary to announce that the Turks not only menaced his territories with ruin, but avowed their determination to subdue the whole of Christendom. Sultan Bayezíd openly vaunted that his cavalry should trample on the cross in every European city, and that he would himself feed his horses on the altar of St. Peter's in Rome.

Duke Philip eagerly seconded the solicitations of the Hungarian ambassadors: under his auspices a crusade was proclaimed; the great body of French chivalry and all the young nobility embraced the project with the greatest ardor, and the young count de Nevers, heir of Burgundy, was appointed to command the expedition (1396).

Sigismund of Luxemburg, king of Hungary, was far from being gratified by the arrival of such auxiliaries. Bayezíd, engaged in suppressing some petty insurrections in his Asiatic dominions, had concluded a truce with the Hungarians, and the prudent king was far from being disposed to revive a war with so dangerous an enemy. His remonstrances were wasted on the proud chivalry of France; the count de Nevers at once crossed the Turkish frontier, and after capturing some places of minor importance, laid siege to Nicopolis. In the hurry of their advance the French had left their battering artillery behind; they were therefore compelled to blockade the place in the hope of reducing it by famine.

So little vigilance was exhibited by the Christians, that the garrison of Nicopolis had intelligence of the near approach of Bayezíd before the Christians knew that he had commenced his march. The news that the sultan was close at hand filled their camp with confusion; the siege of Nicopolis was precipitately raised, and in the first alarm the knights massacred all their prisoners, forgetting that the chances of war might expose them to a terrible retribution. They, however, were all eager to come to an immediate engagement; the Hungarians vainly advised them not to hazard a battle until they had ascertained the number of the Turks, and the tactics which the sultan intended to employ. Some of the more aged and experienced warriors seconded this advice, but they were overborne by the clamors of the young knights, whose ardor was far too great to be moderated by prudence.

Bayezíd had arranged his troops in the form of a crescent, with the convex side turned toward the enemy: he expected thus to induce the Christians to attack his centre, by gradually withdrawing which he might reverse the form of his line, and thus getting his enemies into the concavity of the crescent, avail himself of his vast superiority of numbers to overwhelm them on both flanks. The Christians fell into the snare, and were surrounded. The Hungarian infantry, left exposed by the rapid advance of the French knights, was broken by a charge of a select body of the Turkish cavalry; Sigismund and the grand master of Rhodes escaped in a small boat, leaving their allies to their fate; the palatine of Hungary alone remained with a small body of his countrymen to rescue the French from the consequences of their rashness.

Friends and foes have equally celebrated the desperate valor of the French knights on this fatal day. The Turks at first gave no quarter; it was late in the day before Bayezíd commanded them to make prisoners, and even then he was induced to do so by no feelings of mercy, but by his desire to have an opportunity of revenging the fate of the Turks who had been slaughtered in the camp before Nicopolis.

Bayezíd recognised Sir James de Helly (one of the prisoners) as one of his old companions in arms, and ordered him to be set at liberty by his captors. He then commanded him to point out who were the greatest lords among the Christian captives, that they might be spared for the sake of their ransoms. The count de Nevers and several other princes were pointed out to the sultan as "of the noblest blood in France, nearly related to the king, and willing to pay for their liberty a great sum of money." The sultan said, "Let these alone be spared, and all the other prisoners put to death, to free the country from them, and that others may take example from their fate."

Heavy taxes were laid on the states of Burgundy to raise the enormous sum which the sultan demanded as a ransom for the heir of the dutchy. To increase the difficulty of the transaction, the king of Hungary refused to allow such rich treasures to pass through his dominions for the purpose of strengthening his enemies. It was not until after the lapse of several months that a Genoese merchant, named Pellegrini, in the island of Chios, undertook to arrange the terms of ransom; and the sultan more readily accepted the security of a commercial house, which could only exist by credit, than the plighted oaths of kings and princes, which he knew were too often most flagrantly and shamelessly violated.

While the count de Nevers was thus engaged in the east, his brother-in-law, the count of Ostrevant, aided by his father, Albert, duke of Bavaria, was carrying on a war scarcely less destructive against the Frisons. These barbarous tribes sent out piratical expeditions, which ravaged the coasts of Holland, Flanders, and sometimes of France; the naval forces maintained to keep them in check were found very expensive, and not always efficacious, so that the Flemings and Hollanders supplicated their princes to attack the Frisons in their native fastnesses. An immense armament was prepared for this hazardous enterprise; auxiliaries were obtained from England, France, and western Germany, while crowds of Hollanders and Flemings hastened to volunteer their services against enemies who had been their constant plague.

In about five weeks after the landing, winter set in with unusual severity, and at an earlier period than had been known for many years before. The duke was forced to evacuate the country and disband his army; but about three years after he took advantage of the civil dissensions among the Frisons to reduce the entire country to obedience.

The administration of the government of France by Philip, duke of Burgundy, was on the whole advantageous to the nation. It was chiefly owing to his prudence that the insanity of Charles VI did not produce the calamities of civil war. He had, however, one great fault; his expenditure, both public and private, was most extravagant, and at his death his sons were forced to sell his plate in order to defray the expenses of his funeral. He died of fever (April 27th, 1404), generally regretted, for it was not difficult to foresee the commotions that would ensue when the conduct of the state, which had taxed his talents and energies to the utmost, should be intrusted to a feebler hand.

Section V.—*The History of Burgundy (continued).*

John the Fearless succeeded Philip the Hardy, and immediately began to take measure for procuring to himself the same influence in the government of France which his father had possessed; he was opposed by the queen and the duke of Orleans, who justly dreaded his ambition. In the fury of civil contest he hired assassins to murder the duke of Orleans; and this atrocious crime was perpetrated in the very midst of Paris. Such, however, were the power of the duke and the apathy of the times, that he would probably have obtained a justification of his conduct from the court, had he not been obliged to retire to his territories to quell an insurrection of the citizens of Liege; the partisans of Orleans took advantage of his absence to raise a cry for justice, and being joined by all the enemies of Burgundy, they soon formed a very powerful faction.

The general belief that the duke had committed treason against the state, enabled the faction of Orleans to persuade the dauphin that his death was necessary for the safety of the kingdom, and to join in a perfidious plot for his assassination. Ambassadors were sent to invite John the Fearless to an interview with the dauphin on the bridge of Montereau, in order that they might in common concert measures for the defence of the kingdom. He went to the appointed rendezvous with a very scanty train, armed only with such weapons as gentlemen of the period usually wore on visits of ceremony. So soon as he came into the dauphin's presence, he took off his velvet cap, and bent his knee in token of homage; but before he could rise, he was struck down by the axes and swords of the royal guards, and butchered with such of his train as had entered the saloon (A. D. 1419). The murder of the duke of Orleans was almost the only stain upon the memory of John the Fearless; his Flemish subjects, whose franchises he had protected, and whose trade he had fostered, were most grieved for his loss; but they respected his memory most for his having intrusted the education of his eldest son to the magistrates of the free cities, and in fact the young prince had been educated as a Fleming rather than as a Burgundian.

Philip the Good, immediately after his accession, prepared to take vengeance for the murder of his father; his Flemish education had prevented him from having any very strong sense of the feudal obligations which bound the dutchy of Burgundy to the crown of France, he therefore did not hesitate to enter into alliance with Henry V. of England, and recognised him as the legitimate heir to the crown of France, on condition that Charles VI. should not be deprived of his regal dignity during the remainder of his unhappy existence.

The war between the English and French now became identified with the struggle between the Burgundians and Armagnacs, as the favorers of Orleans were called; the virulence of private animosities was thus added to the horrors of open war, and the atrocities committed on both sides were shocking to human nature.

The death of Henry V. of England, followed speedily by that of Charles VI. of France, produced a great change in the aspect of the war. Henry VI., who was proclaimed king of England and France, was an infant in the cradle, while the dauphin was in the very prime of life, surrounded by the greater part of the French nobility, and warmly supported by the bulk of the nation. Though severely defeated, and apparently brought to the brink of ruin, when his chief city Orleans was besieged, a deliverer suddenly appeared in the person of Joan of Arc, the tide of prosperity which had hitherto flowed in favor of the English, suddenly turned, and the duke of Burgundy opened negotiations with the dauphin. It was at this crisis that Philip instituted the order of the Golden Fleece, on the occasion of his marriage with Isabella of Portugal (A. D. 1430), an order of knighthood which soon became the most illustrious in Europe. Soon after his marriage, the alienation of the duke from the English interest continued to increase, and finally, under the auspices of the pope, he concluded a treaty with Charles VII., whom he consented to recognise as legitimate sovereign of France.

Having disengaged himself from the French wars, the duke of Burgundy devoted himself to the improvement of his dominions in the Low Countries. His brilliant court realized the visions of chivalry; the jousts and tournaments given under his sanction surpassed in magnificence any that had yet been witnessed in Europe; the wealth of the commercial cities in Flanders was freely poured forth to defray the expenses, and noble knights from all parts of Europe flocked to the court of Burgundy to prove their valor in the lists. Philip encouraged this taste for display among his subjects from political motives; he found that luxury diverted the attention of the turbulent municipalities and their magistrates from affairs of state, and suspended, if it did not eradicate, the ancient jealousies between commercial freedom and feudalism.

Nearly a century and a half had now elapsed since the Swiss cantons had emancipated themselves from the yoke of the house of Austria; the free states had become jealous of each other, some leagued with their ancient enemies, others sought alliances with the petty princes of Germany, and the feudal powers, to whom the example of Swiss independence seemed fraught with dangerous consequences, believed that an opportunity was offered for reducing the mountaineers to their former bondage. A league for the purpose was formed by the potentates of western Germany under the direct sanction of the emperor, and application was made to the duke of Burgundy for assistance. He received the proposal very coolly, upon which the imperialists sought the aid of the king of France, who was very anxious, now that the wars were over, to get rid of the Armagnacs, and other companies of soldiers, who lived at free quarters on the peasantry, and prevented the country from enjoying the blessings of tranquillity. An immense army was soon raised and placed under the command of the dauphin.

On the morning of the 24th of August, 1444, Switzers and Frenchmen met for the first time in mortal combat. The advanced guard of the French, which alone was ten times more numerous than the entire Swiss army, occupied the heights on the right bank of the river Pirse, while the main body remained on the left bank, urging forward the siege of Basle. The Swiss were routed, but the dauphin's victory was obtained with the loss of eight thousand of his best soldiers. The French were not willing to fight a second battle with such fearless warriors; in spite of the remonstrances of the Germans, the dauphin resolved to act the part of mediator, and a peace was concluded under his auspices, by which the liberties of the Swiss cantons were formally recognised. The duke of Burgundy took no share in this war; he was too deeply engaged by the troubles of Flanders, where a formidable revolt had been raised by the citizens of Ghent. After a sanguinary struggle, the insurgent Flemings were subdued, and Ghent was deprived of most of its municipal privileges.

The dauphin of France, afterward Louis XI., having provoked his father to war, was obliged to fly from his estates and seek shelter with the duke of Burgundy, who was at the time rendered uneasy by the turbulent disposition of his own son, the count of Charolais, subsequently known in history as Charles the Bold. These family disturbances embroiled the courts of France and Burgundy for several years, but at length the death of Charles VII. rendered the dauphin king of France; the duke escorted him safely to his dominions, rendered him homage as his sovereign, and assisted in the ceremonies of his coronation. Louis was far from being grateful for these benefits; he formed several plots to seize the person of the count of Charolais, foreseeing that he would become his most formidable rival, and he broke all the engagements he had made to restore the towns which had at various times been wrested from the dukes of Burgundy by the monarchs of France. The count of Charolais was not disposed to endure these wrongs with patience; contrary to the wishes of his father, he supported the nobles of France in their revolts against their sovereign, and had just organized a formidable league against Louis, when the death of Duke Philip compelled him to adjourn his warlike designs, until he had secured to himself his inheritance of the dutchy of Burgundy.

Few sovereigns were more generally and justly lamented than Philip the Good; during the fifty years of his reign, Burgundy was the most wealthy, prosperous, and tranquil of all the states of Europe; and had he pleased to assert his independence, he might have become a more powerful sovereign than the king of France himself. The general grief for his loss was increased by the dread which the character of his successor inspired; the rashness, the pride, the obstinacy, and the cruelty of Charles the Bold had stained his entire career as count of Charolais; his subjects and his neighbors were equally filled with alarm, lest the same qualities should be still more signally manifested in the duke of Burgundy.

Section VI.—*The History of Burgundy (concluded).*

Immediately on the installation of Charles the Bold, as duke of Burgundy, an insurrection was organized in Ghent. The duke was forced to yield to the popular demands, but in doing so, he made a secret vow that he would exact deadly vengeance for the insult which had been offered to his authority. His indignation was increased by similar revolts in the cities of Brabant and in Liege, which he justly attributed to the example of Ghent, aided by the secret intrigues of French emissaries.

The troubles of Brabant were easily quieted; but the citizens of Liege, relying on the indistinct promises of aid made by the king of France, not only raised the standard of revolt, but committed such atrocious crimes, that Charles determined to destroy the city. With some difficulty his councillors dissuaded him from executing his design.

In revenge for the incentives to rebellion which the king of France was more than suspected of having supplied to the people of Liege, Charles entered into a close league with the discontented French princes who had taken up arms against Louis XI., while that monarch renewed his intrigues with the discontented burgesses in all the cities subject to the duke of Burgundy. Louis was, however, far the more successful in this species of unavowed warfare; cold, cautious, and cunning, he was able to conduct complicated intrigues, and to await their success with patience, while the violent temper of Charles frequently led him to frustrate the plans on which he had bestowed the most care and attention. In one memorable instance, the reliance of Louis on his own craft had nearly proved his destruction; finding that his envoys did not produce the effect he desired on the mind of his rival, he resolved to try the effect of a personal interview, and unexpectedly presented himself at the duke of Burgundy's court in Peronne, escorted by a feeble company of his personal retainers. The interview between the king and the duke was far from satisfactory; their mutual jealousies soon began to threaten a rupture, when the intelligence of a new revolt in Liege, and the massacre of all the partisans of Burgundy in that city, including the prince-bishop, so roused the fury of Charles, that he made his sovereign a prisoner, and would probably have proceeded to further extremities, but for the interference of his council.

Louis, taken in his own toils, was obliged to submit to the terms of peace dictated by Charles; the most mortifying condition of his liberation was that he should lead an army against the insurgent citizens of Liege, and thus aid his vassal in suppressing a revolt which he had himself secretly instigated. The ducal and royal armies were soon assembled, and they marched together against the devoted citizens of Liege, who had never imagined the possibility of such a combination. They did not however despair, but defended themselves with great courage, until the advanced guard of the Burgundians had forced its way through the breaches of the walls, and made a lodgement in the principal street. All resistance was then at an end; the city became the prey of the barbarous soldiers; it was cruelly pillaged for several days, and those citizens who escaped the sword either perished of hunger as they wandered through the woods and fields, or were delivered over to the executioner. After this scene of massacre had lasted eight days, Charles left the city, after having given orders that every edifice in Liege should be destroyed, except the churches, and the houses belonging to the clergy. As Liege was an episcopal city, the clergy possessed or claimed a very considerable portion of it, and the exception made in their favor saved it from ruin.

Louis never forgave the indignities which he had endured at Peronne, and in his forced march to Liege; without openly declaring war against Burgundy, he secretly raised up enemies against the duke in every quarter, and Charles, by the violence of his passions, constantly exposed himself at disadvantage to the machinations of his rival. Rendered insolent by continued prosperity, he alienated from him the brave chivalry of Burgundy, by bestowing all his confidence on a foreign favorite, the count of Campo-Basso, who flattered his vanity by an absolute submission to his caprices. Louis had the good fortune to win the friendship of the Swiss, whom his rival had changed from friends into foes by the most wanton violation of treaties; and Charles, to whom the very name of freedom was odious, on account of the revolts of Ghent and Liege, resolved to bring the independent mountaineers once more under the yoke of feudal bondage.

Rarely had Europe seen so splendid an army as that which Charles led to the invasion of Switzerland; it consisted of thirty-six thousand soldiers, long inured to military exercises, accompanied by the most formidable train of artillery that had ever yet been brought into the field. The duke advanced to besiege Granson; it was bravely defended, but the walls soon began to crumble under the heavy fire of the Burgundian artillery, and several of the citizens, seduced by promises and bribes, clamored for a capitulation. It was agreed that the governor and the best soldiers of the garrison should present themselves before Charles and demand to be admitted to mercy, as his emissaries had promised. The moment, however, that they appeared, Charles ordered them to be seized; the governor and his officers to be hanged, and all the rest to be hurled as they were, bound hand and foot, into the lake. About two hundred Swiss were thus treacherously massacred.

Intelligence of this event spread rapidly through the cantons; on every side the bold mountaineers flew to arms, while the duke, having formed an entrenched camp at Granson, advanced with a strong detachment toward Neufchatel. Pride had rendered him so regardless of ordinary precautions that he came unexpectedly in presence of the main body of the Swiss in the mountain defiles, when with his usual impetuosity he gave the signal to engage. The Swiss pikemen formed in close line, drove back the Burgundian cavalry, and steadily advancing in close order forced the squadrons of horse before them, destroying some of the bravest knights of the enemy as they got entangled in the press. Every effort which the duke made to extricate his gallant chivalry only added to the confusion, and while he vainly strove to form his lines, fresh troops appeared upon the heights on his left flank, raising the war-cry of "Granson! Granson!" to show that they came to revenge the massacre of their brethren. Soon after the horns of Uri and Unterwalden were heard in the distance; they were two enormous horns, which according to tradition had been bestowed upon these cantons by Pepin and Charlemagne; their sound had often filled invaders with dread during the old wars of Austria, and appeared on the present occasion scarcely less ominous to the Burgundians.

The retreat of the advanced guard of Charles became every moment more disorderly, it was at length converted into a precipitate flight, and the fugitives on reaching the entrenched camp, filled it with the same terror and confusion by which they were possessed themselves. In vain did Charles attempt to remedy the disorder; his artillerymen after a feeble and ineffectual fire abandoned their guns; his Italian auxiliaries fled without striking a blow, and at length, being left almost alone, he quitted his camp with a few attendants, leaving to the Swiss the richest booty that had been gained in war for several centuries. Among the spoils thus abandoned were three celebrated diamonds, of which one now adorns the tiara of the pope, a second is reckoned among the most splendid treasures of the emperor of Austria, and the third, usually called the Souci diamond, was long the richest brilliant in the crown of France.

Grief and rage for his defeat reduced Charles to a state bordering on insanity. It was not until after the lapse of several weeks that he began to take active measures for repairing his losses, and preventing the king of France from profiting by his reverses. All the wealth which he had hoarded during his reign; all the treasures which he could procure from the wealthy commercial cities in Flanders and Brabant, were freely poured forth to recruit his army; the bells of the churches were melted down and cast into cannon to repair the loss of his artillery at Granson; he hired auxiliaries from France, from Italy, and from England. On the other hand the Swiss employed themselves in fortifying Morat, which they regarded as the key of Berne, and sent pressing messages to their confederates to hasten the arrival of their respective contingents.

On the 27th of May, 1476, Charles quitted his camp at Lausaune to commence the siege of Morat; rarely has a place been more vigorously assailed or more obstinately defended; the walls were breached in several places, but every assault of the Burgundians was repulsed, and the duke himself was twice driven back from the ruined ramparts. This marvellous resistance gave the Swiss time to assemble their armies, but Morat was on the point of falling when they advanced to its relief. Several of his officers advised Charles to raise the siege on the approach of the Swiss, and retire to ground more favorable for a field of battle; but he was as obstinately deaf to good counsel as he had been at Granson, and his passions had produced a kind of fever which rendered him so irritable that his dearest friends were afraid to approach him. The Swiss formed their line of battle under the shelter of a line of hills covered with trees, which effectually concealed their movements from their enemies; Charles advanced to dislodge them from this position in a tempest of rain which injured his powder and relaxed the bowstrings of his archers. The Burgundians, finding that they could not get through the wood, nor entice the Swiss from their lines, began to retire toward their camp, drenched with rain and exhausted by their useless march. The Swiss general, Hans de Hallwyll, who had already earned high fame in the wars of Hungary, gave the signal of pursuit; René, the young duke of Lorraine, whom Charles had stripped of his paternal dominions, advanced at the head of the cavalry of the confederates, and the Burgundians were attacked in their intrenched camp. Charles could scarcely be persuaded that the Swiss would have hazarded so perilous an attempt; he hastened to bring up his men at arms to the place where the chief assault was made, and at the same time opened a heavy fire from his batteries on the advancing columns. His best artillerymen however had fallen at Granson; his cannon being ill-served did but little execution, while Hallwyll under cover of the smoke led a body of troops along the Burgundian lines and suddenly falling on their exposed flank, forced his way into the midst of the camp before the manœuvre was discovered. On the other extreme the Burgundians were equally surprised by an unexpected sally from the garrison of Morat; they fell into remediless confusion, the battle was no longer a fight but a carnage, for the Swiss sternly refused quarter, so that "cruel as at Morat," long continued to be a proverb in their mountains.

The states of Burgundy, Flanders, and Brabant, refused to grant the duke the enormous sums which he demanded to raise a third army, and while he was engaged in threatening them with his wrath, and collecting as many soldiers as he could procure from his own resources, he learned that Lorraine was nearly recovered by its young duke Renè, who, after making himself master of several towns, with little or no opposition, had laid siege to Nancy. The city was taken before Charles was ready to march, and Renè having secured it with a faithful garrison, proceeded to the Swiss cantons to solicit aid against their common enemy. Sieges were always unfavorable to the duke of Burgundy; he was unable to reduce Nancy, but he obstinately persisted in remaining before the walls, while his army suffered severely from an inclement winter and the increasing want of pay and provisions. In fact the unfortunate duke was now sold to his enemies by his favorite Campo-Basso, and his rash cruelty had led him to precipitate the execution of the chief agent of the plot, whom he had by chance made prisoner.

On the 4th of January, 1477, Renè of Lorraine, at the head of the Swiss confederates, was seen from the Burgundian camp advancing to the relief of Nancy. In the very beginning of the battle the desertion of the traitor Campo-Basso decided the fate of the day, but the brave chivalry of Burgundy in this, the last of their fields, maintained a desperate resistance until night put an end to the combat. The fate of the duke of Burgundy was for a long time uncertain, but after a tedious search his body was found covered with wounds, some of which had every appearance of being inflicted by assassins. Renè paid every possible respect to the remains of the unfortunate Charles, and he liberated all his Burgundian prisoners that they might attend the funeral.

The history of Mary of Burgundy, the daughter and successor of Charles the Bold, must be related briefly. No sooner was the news of her father's death known, than the king of France prepared to seize on her dominions in Burgundy, and the Flemings rose in insurrection against her authority. Louis at first was disposed to force her to marry the dauphin, and thus reunite Burgundy to France, but the tortuous course of policy which he pursued defeated his object. The Flemings discovered the intrigue; they seized on the favorite counsellors of the unhappy princess, and beheaded them before her eyes in the market-place of

Ghent. Mary was subsequently married to Duke Maximilian of Austria, but he only obtained possession of her dominions in the Netherlands; Burgundy was conquered by the French, and Maximilian had neither the energy nor the wisdom to recover it from Louis. This was the origin of the bitter hostility between the sovereigns of France and Austria, which for a long series of years kept the continent of Europe in almost perpetual war.

SECTION VII.—*The Age of Charles V.*

THE political idea of maintaining a balance of power, which was first formed in Italy, began to spread north of the Alps, in consequence of the rapid and overwhelming increase of the Austrian power. Maximilian of Austria, son of the emperor Frederic III., married Mary of Burgundy, daughter and heiress of Charles the Bold, duke of Burgundy (A. D. 1477), as has been already related, and in her right obtained possession of the fertile and wealthy provinces of the Netherlands. His son, Philip the Fair, was united to Joanna, infanta of Spain, daughter of Ferdinand and Isabella, whose union had joined the kingdoms of Aragon and Castile. The fruit of Philip's marriage with Joanna was two sons, Charles and Ferdinand; and the elder of these, at the age of sixteen, inherited the crown of Spain and its colonies, in addition to his paternal dominions in the Netherlands (A. D. 1516). The death of his grandfather Maximilian transmitted to him the Austrian territories, and the other domains of the house of Hapsburgh, and the electors chose him to fill the vacant throne of the empire. Thus Charles, the first of Spain, and the fifth of the empire, possessed greater power than any sovereign that had flourished in Europe since the days of Charlemagne. In the beginning of his reign, he resigned his hereditary dominions in Germany to his brother Ferdinand, who afterward succeeded him in the empire, and became the founder of the second Austrian line of emperors, which ended with Charles VI. (A. D. 1740). From the emperor Charles descended the Austrian family of Spanish kings, which was terminated by the death of Charles II. (A. D. 1700).

These two branches of the Austrian house, the German and the Spanish, long acted in concert, to procure reciprocal advantages, and were fortunate in strengthening their power by new alliances. Ferdinand married Anne, sister of Louis, king of Hungary and Bohemia; and when that monarch fell in war against the Turks, added both these kingdoms to the hereditary dominions of Austria. Charles V., by his marriage with Isabella, daughter of Emmanuel, king of Portugal, prepared the way for his son Philip's annexation of that country to Spain.

Two monarchs, contemporary with Charles, were almost equally bound by their interests to check the preponderance of the house of Austria—Henry VIII. of England, and Francis I. of France. Henry VII., after the victory of Bosworth-field had given him undisputed possession of the crown, labored diligently and successfully to extend the royal authority, and to raise the commercial prosperity of the nation. On his death (A. D. 1509), he bequeathed to his son a rich treasury and a flourishing kingdom. Possessing such advantages, Henry VIII. might have been the arbitrator of Europe ; but his naturally fine talents were perverted by flattery ; he allowed free scope to all his passions, and his actions were consequently the result of caprice, vanity, or resentment—rarely, if ever, of enlightened policy. Many of the defects in his administration must, however, be ascribed to the pride and ambition of his prime minister, Cardinal Wolsey, who sacrificed the welfare of England and the honor of his sovereign to further his private ends or gratify his idle vanity.

Francis I. was a prince of higher character ; he had many of the noble qualities, and not a few of the faults, usually ascribed to the spirit of chivalry ; bold, enterprising, and personally brave he did not always regulate his actions by prudence, and his rashness lost what his valor had won. Soon after coming to the crown, he undertook to recover Milan, and overthrew Sforza and the imperialists at Marignano. The defeated duke resigned his country for a pension ; the pope and the northern Italian states assented to the arrangement, and the possession of the contested dutchy seemed secured to France by the conclusion of a treaty with the Swiss cantons (A. D. 1516). Nearly at the same time a treaty was made with Charles, who had not yet succeeded to the empire, which seemed to establish peace, but only rendered war more certain.

Henry and Francis were both candidates with Charles for the empire ; the former, however, had no rational hopes of success, while Francis could not hide his anticipations of success, no more than his mortification when he failed. The mutual jealousies of the French and Spanish monarchs were aggravated by hostile claims ; Charles, by right of descent, could demand the ancient possessions of the duke of Burgundy, and he was feudal sovereign, as emperor, over the northern Italian states, the chief dutchy of which had been recently annexed to France. On the other hand, Francis had claims to the thrones of Navarre and Naples, which he was very unwilling to resign. Peace could not long subsist between these potentates, neither were their forces so unequally matched as might at first be supposed. The extensive dominions of Charles were governed by different constitutions ; in none, not even in Spain, was he wholly unfettered, while in Germany, where the Reformation was constantly raising embarrassing questions, and the princes ever anxious to circumscribe the imperial authority, added more to his nominal than to his real strength. His finances were also embarrassed, and he often found it an almost insuperable difficulty to provide for the payment of his troops, most of whom were necessarily mercenaries. On the other hand, Francis inherited almost despotic authority ; his power concentrated, his own subjects were enrolled as his soldiers, and the regular organization of the French government freed him from the financial embarrassments of his rival. Both strengthened themselves by alliances : Charles gained the aid of the pope, and won Henry VIII. to his side by duping the egregious vanity of Wolsey ; Francis, on the other hand, was supported by the Swiss and the Venetians. The war began nearly at the same moment in Navarre, the Netherlands, and Lombardy. The treachery of the queen-mother, who withheld from the French commander, Lautrec, the money necessary to pay the troops employed in Italy, led to the loss of Milan and the greater part of the dutchy. An effort made to recover the lost ground led to the battle of Bicocca (A. D. 1522), in which the French were totally defeated, and finally expelled from Italy; and Genoa, their most faithful ally, was subjected to the power of their enemies. An event of scarcely less importance was the death of Leo, and the elevation of Adrian, a devoted adherent of Charles, to the papal chair; and this was soon followed by the desertion of the Venetians to the imperial side.

Francis might have still recovered the Milanese, where the emperor's troops had been disbanded for want of pay, had not the queen-mother, blinded by passion, induced him to treat the constable of Bourbon with such gross injustice, that this powerful noble entered into a secret intrigue with the emperor, and agreed to raise the standard of revolt. The discovery of the plot delayed the French king's march into Italy; and though he protected his own territories, the Milanese was irrecoverably lost. Encouraged by this success, Charles commanded the imperial generals to invade France on the side of Provence, while the king of England promised to attack it on the north. Had this plan been executed, Francis must have been ruined; but Wolsey, provoked by the elevation of Clement VII. to the papacy, on the death of Adrian, avenged himself for the broken promises of the emperor, abated Henry's ardor for the enterprise, and persuaded him to keep his forces at home, under pretence of resisting the Scots, who had embraced the side of the French king. Charles, unable to command money, could not make a diversion on the side of Spain or the Netherlands; and the imperialists, having uselessly wasted the country, were compelled to retire from Provence.

Elated by his success, Francis hastened to invade Italy; but instead of pressing the pursuit of the shattered imperialists, he laid siege to Pavia, and thus gave his adversaries time to strengthen and recruit their forces. With similar imprudence, he sent a large detachment to invade Naples, hoping that the viceroy of that kingdom would withdraw a large portion of the imperialists from the Milanese for its defence; but Charles's generals, having received a strong reinforcement raised in Germany by the constable of Bourbon, attacked the French in their intrenchments, and gained a decisive victory, in which Francis himself was made prisoner.

This great calamity was principally owing to the romantic notions of honor entertained by the French king: he had vowed that he would take Pavia or perish in the attempt; and rather than expose himself to the imputation of breaking a promise of chivalry, he remained in his intrenchments, though the means of safe retreat were open to him. Never did armies engage with greater ardor than the French and imperialists before the walls of Pavia (February 24, 1525). On the one hand, a gallant young monarch, seconded by a generous nobility, and followed by subjects to whose natural impetuosity indignation at the opposition which they had encountered added new force, contended for victory and honor. On the other side, troops more completely disciplined, and conducted by generals of greater abilities, fought, from necessity, with courage heightened by despair. The imperialists, however, were unable to resist the first efforts of the French valor, and their firmest battal ions began to give way. But the fortune of the day was quickly changed. The Swiss in the service of France, unmindful of the reputation of their country for fidelity and martial glory, abandoned their post in a cowardly manner. The garrison of Pavia sallied out and attacked the rear of the French during the heat of the action with such fury as threw it into confusion; and Pescara, falling on their cavalry with the imperial horse, among whom he had prudently intermingled a consider ble number of Spanish foot, armed with the heavy muskets then in use, broke this formidable body by an unusual method of attack, against which they were totally unprovided. The rout became universal, and resistance ceased in almost every part but where the king was in person, who fought now, not for fame or victory, but for safety. Though wounded in several places, and thrown from his horse, which was killed under him, Francis defended himself on foot with an heroic courage; many of his bravest officers, gathering round him, and endeavoring to save his life, at the expense of their own, fell at his feet. The king, exhausted with fatigue and scarcely capable of further resistance, was left almost alone, exposed to the fury of some Spanish soldiers, strangers to his rank, and enraged at his obstinacy. At that moment came up Pomperant, a French gentleman who had entered, together with Bourbon, into the emperor's service, and placing himself by the side of the monarch against whom he had rebelled, assisted in protecting him from the violence of the soldiers; at the same time beseeching him to surrender to Bourbon, who was not far distant. Imminent as the danger was which now surrounded Francis, he rejected with indignation the thoughts of an action which would have afforded such triumph to his traitorous subject; and calling for Launoy, who also happened to be near at hand, gave up his sword to him; which he kneeling to kiss the king's hand, received with profound respect; and taking his own sword from his side, presented it to him, saying that "it did not become so great a monarch to remain disarmed in the presence of one of the emperor's subjects."

Although Launoy treated his royal captive with all the marks of respect due to his rank and character, he nevertheless guarded him with the utmost precaution. He was solicitous, not only to prevent any possibility of his escaping, but afraid that his own troops might seize his person, and detain it as the best security for the payment of their arrears. In order to provide against both these dangers, he conducted Francis, the day after the battle, to a strong castle, and committed him to the custody of an officer remarkable for the strict vigilance which such a trust required. Francis, who formed a judgment of the emperor's disposition by his own, was extremely desirous that Charles should be informed of his situation, fondly hoping that, from his generosity or sympathy, he should obtain speedy relief. He therefore gave a passport to an imperial officer to carry the intelligence of the battle of Pavia and his own capture through France, as the communication with Spain by land was the most safe and certain at this season of the year.

Charles received the account of this signal success with affected moderation, but at the same time deliberated with the utmost solicitude how he might derive the greatest advantages from the misfortunes of his adversary. His first demands were that Francis should restore the dutchy of Burgundy, which, as we have seen, was dishonorably wrested from his ancestors by Louis XI.; that Provence and Dauphinè should be erected into an independent kingdom for the constable of Bourbon; that satisfaction should be made to the king of England for his claims on France; and that all the pretensions of France to territories in Italy should be renounced for ever. Francis was so indignant at being required to make such ignominious concessions, that he drew his dagger, and made an attempt to commit suicide; he was, of course, prevented, and it was hinted that a personal interview with the emperor would lead to the offer of more equitable conditions. Francis himself was of the same opinion. He was sent in a Spanish galley to Barcelona, whence he was removed to Madrid; but on reaching that city, he was sent to the Alcazar, and guarded more carefully than ever: and it appeared evident that the king's reliance on the emperor's generosity had been wholly misplaced.

But this triumph, which seemed to have made Charles master of Italy and arbiter of Europe, so far from yielding the substantial advantages which might reasonably have been expected, served only to array against him the jealousy of England, of the Italian states, and of the protestant princes of Germany. At the same time, the disorganized condition of his finances, and the consequent difficulty of finding pay, subsistence, or the munitions of war, for his soldiers, reduced his Italian armies to inactivity in the very moment of victory. Henry VIII. was the first of the imperial allies to set the example of defection; he entered into a defensive alliance with Louise, the queen-regent of France, in which all the differences between him and her son were adjusted; at the same time he engaged that he would employ his best offices in order to deliver his new ally from a state of captivity. Imprisonment soon began to produce such injurious effects on the mental and bodily health of Francis, that Charles began to fear that all his plans might be frustrated by the death of his captive, and he therefore sought a personal interview with him, in which he held out a hope of milder conditions of liberation.

The chief obstacle that stood in the way of Francis's liberty was the emperor's continuing to insist so peremptorily on the restitution of Burgundy as a preliminary to that event. But the history of Burgundy while an independent dutchy, as detailed in preceding sections, sufficiently proves that compliance with such a demand would have reduced the monarch of France to a state of complete dependance on his nominal vassals. Francis often declared that he would never consent to dismember his kingdom; and that, if even he should so far forget the duties of a monarch as to come to such a resolution, the fundamental laws of the kingdom would prevent its taking effect. Finding that the emperor was inflexible on the point, he suddenly took the resolution of resigning his crown, with all its rights and prerogatives, to his son the dauphin, determining rather to end his days in prison than to purchase his freedom by concessions unworthy of a king.

Charles was so alarmed by this resolution, that he consented to modify his demands so far as not to insist on the restitution of Burgundy until the king was set at liberty. The remaining conditions of the treaty were sufficiently onerous ; but a few hours before signing them, Francis assembled such of his counsellors as happened to be in Madrid, and having exacted from them a solemn oath of secresy, he made a long enumeration in their presence of the dishonorable acts as well as unprincely rigor which the emperor had employed in order to ensnare or intimidate him. For that reason, he took a formal protest in the hands of notaries that his consent to the treaty should be considered as an involuntary deed, and be deemed null and void. By this disingenuous artifice, for which the treatment he had received was no apology, Francis endeavored to satisfy his honor and conscience in signing the treaty, and to provide at the same time a pretext on which to break it.

About a month after the signing of the treaty, the regent's ratification of it was brought from France, and two princes of the blood sent as hostages for its execution. At last Francis took leave of the emperor, whose suspicion of the king's sincerity increasing as the time of putting it to the proof approached, he attempted to bind him still faster by exacting new promises, which, after those he had already made, the French monarch was not slow to grant. He set out from Madrid, a place which the remembrance of so many afflicting circumstances rendered peculiarly odious to him, with the joy natural on such an occasion, and began the long-wished-for journey toward his own dominions. He was escorted by a body of horse, under the command of Alarçon, who, as the king drew near the frontiers of France, guarded him with more scrupulous exactness than ever. When he arrived at the river Andaye, which separates the two kingdoms, Lautrec, one of his favorite generals, appeared on the opposite bank, with a guard equal in number to Alarçon's. An empty bark was moored in the middle of the stream ; the attendants drew up in order on the opposite banks ; at the same instant Launoy put off with eight gentlemen from the Spanish, and Lautrec with the same number from the French side of the river ; the former had the king in his boat ; the latter the two princely hostages, the dauphin and the duke of Orleans ; they met in the empty vessel ; the exchange was made in a moment ; Francis, after a short embrace of his children, leaped into Lautrec's boat, and reached the French shore. He mounted at that instant a Turkish horse, waved his hand over his head, and, with a joyous voice, cried aloud several times, "I am yet a king!" then, putting spurs to his horse, he galloped at full speed to St. Jean de Luz, and thence to Bayonne. This event, no less impatiently desired by the French people than their monarch, happened on the 18th of March, 1526, a year and twenty-two days after the fatal battle of Pavia.

The states of Burgundy afforded Francis the first opportunity of refusing to fulfil the conditions of his liberation. They represented to the monarch that he had no right to make a transfer of their allegiance without their consent, and that they would rather assert their independence than submit to a foreign dominion. Upon this, Francis, turning toward the imperial ambassadors, represented to them the impossibility of performing what he had undertaken, and offered, in lieu of Burgundy, to pay the emperor two millions of crowns. The ambassadors, who were well aware that the entire scene had been concerted between the king and the states, refused to admit any modification of the treaty, they returned to Madrid, and Charles, who perceived that he had been overreached, exclaimed in the most public manner and in the harshest terms against Francis, as a prince void of faith and honor. The French king, on the other hand, asserted that no promise obtained by force was binding, and easily obtained from the pope a full absolution from all the obligations which he had contracted.

During this period, Germany was cruelly harassed by insurrections of the peasants, goaded to madness by the oppressions of their lords. In Thuringia, where a great part of the population had been converted to Lutheranism, Muncer, a wild fanatic, became the leader of the insurgents, and by stimulating their ignorant zeal, added religious bigotry to the horrors of civil war. Luther sincerely lamented the scandal that these disturbances brought on the cause of the reformation; but his own marriage with a nun who had broken her vows, gave such general offence, that his influence, for a season, was greatly diminished.

Francis was not long at liberty before he not only protested against the treaty of Madrid and refused to fulfil any of its stipulations, but organized a new league against Charles, which was named "Holy," because the pope was its nominal head. The Venetians, the duke of Milan, and the English king, joined the confederacy; but their operations were so slow and feeble, that the imperialists easily maintained their ascendency in the north of Italy. The constable of Bourbon, irritated by the vacillating conduct of the pope, marched against Rome, heedless of the truce that had been granted to the pontiff by the viceroy of Naples. "The eternal city" was taken by assault, and suffered more severely from the soldiers of a catholic king than from the barbarous pagans of an earlier age. Bourbon fell in the assault; but the command of the imperialists devolved on the prince of Orange, who besieged the pope in the castle of St. Angelo, and compelled him to yield himself a prisoner (A. D. 1527). Charles received the intelligence of this success with contemptible hypocrisy; he professed the most sincere sorrow for the captivity of the holy pontiff, and ordered prayers to be offered for his deliverance in all the Spanish churches, instead of sending orders for his liberation. So great was the indignation excited by the harsh treatment of the pope, that Francis was enabled to invade Italy and penetrate to the very walls of Naples. But here his prosperity ended; the pope, liberated from captivity, resolved to conciliate the emperor; the Venetians became jealous of the French power, and, finally, the Genoese hero, Andrew Doria, roused by the wrongs which Francis had inflicted on himself and his country, revolted to the emperor, and turned the scale of the war by making the imperialists superior at sea. Doria's first care was to restore the republic of Genoa; and such was the opinion entertained of his patriotism and disinterestedness, that he was universally called "THE FATHER OF HIS COUNTRY AND THE RESTORER OF ITS LIBERTY" (A. D. 1528). These circumstances, and the defeat of his army in the Milanese, inclined Francis to peace; a treaty was negotiated at Cambray by the emperor's aunt and the king's mother, but the fair diplomatists left enough of disputable points unsettled to furnish grounds for a future war.

Charles having thus prevailed over France, resolved to make a vigorous struggle to crush the reformation in Germany, but the protestant princes, undismayed by his power, formed a league for their mutual protection at Smalkald (A. D. 1530), and applied to the kings of France and England to patronise their confederacy. Henry VIII. was eager to grant them support; he was desirous to be divorced from his wife, Catharine of Aragon, the emperor's aunt, and attributed the pope's reluctance to the intrigues of Charles. Hostilities were for a time averted by the emperor's making some important concessions, for he was anxious to have his brother Ferdinand chosen as his successor, with the title of king of the Romans, and the progress of the Turks, on his eastern frontiers, could only be resisted by the united strength of the empire.

Francis had concluded peace at Cambray, because he was no longer able to maintain war. He sought the earliest opportunity of renewing hostilities, and secured the friendship of the pope, by uniting his son, the duke of Orleans, to the pontiff's niece, Catherine de Medicis. But, though he thus gained one ally, he lost others. Henry VIII., inflamed by love of Anne Boleyn, and enraged by the pope's confirmation of his marriage with Catharine, no longer kept any measures with the court of Rome; his subjects seconded his resentment; an act of parliament was passed, abolishing the papal power and jurisdiction in England (A. D. 1534); by another act, the king was declared supreme head of the church, and all the authority of which the popes were deprived, was vested in him. Henry was thus disinclined to support the pope's ally, and the protestant princes of Germany viewed Francis with some suspicion, because he persecuted the reformed in his own dominions. The death of Clement VII., and the election of Paul III., an adherent of the emperor, suddenly deprived Francis of the papal aid, on which he had confidently calculated, and compelled him to delay his projects for troubling the peace of Europe.

The insurrection of the anabaptists, a new set of fanatics in Germany, and the emperor's expedition against the piratical states of Barbary, employed men's minds for a season. The suppression of the fanatics, and the conquest of Tunis, crowned the emperor with glory, yet it was at this moment that Francis chose to renew the war (A. D. 1535). Savoy was immediately overrun by the French troops, and its unfortunate duke in vain implored the aid of the emperor, whose resources had been exhausted in the African war. It was on this occasion that Charles challenged his rival to single combat, in which proposal he only imitated the former follies of Francis. On the other hand, the death of the dauphin, amid the joy occasioned by the repulse of the imperialists, who had invaded Provence, was absurdly attributed to poison, administered by emissaries of Charles. To complete the exhibition of folly, Francis summoned Charles, as count of Flanders, to appear before the parliament of Paris, and on his refusal, he was declared to have forfeited the Low Countries to his feudal superior. The war itself was languidly conducted, but the pope, alarmed by the progress of the Turks, personally interfered, and a truce for ten years was concluded between the two sovereigns at Nice (A. D. 1538).

The religious disputes in Germany between the princes of the protestant and those of the catholic league, the struggles made by the pope to prevent the meeting of a general council, unless under circumstances that would give him complete control over its deliberations, filled Charles with anxiety, which was not a little increased by the turbulent disposition of his Flemish subjects, and the success of the Turks in Hungary. Notwithstanding all these difficulties, he undertook an expedition against Algiers (A. D. 1541), but his fleet was shattered by a storm, his army wasted by a pestilential disease, and his stores of provision rendered unavailing. He was compelled to return, overwhelmed with loss and disgrace, and his defeat raised the courage of his enemies so high that he had to encounter a new war in Europe.

Francis was eager to take advantage of his rival's distress, and the crime of the imperial governor of the Milanese furnished him with a decent pretext. This imprudent functionary seized two ambassadors, sent from the Parisian court to Turkey, and put them to death, in direct violation of the law of nations. Francis now changed his plan of operations; acting on the defensive in Italy, he invaded the Netherlands and Rousillon (A. D. 1542), but failed to make any permanent impression. Charles found an ally in the king of England: the death of his aunt had removed the great source of enmity between the emperor and Henry, and the close alliance between France and Scotland, recently cemented by the marriage of the Scotch king, James V., to a French princess, Mary of Guise, had excited great jealousy and alarm in England. Henry, with his usual impetuosity, having introduced the reformation into England, became anxious that Scotland should also withdraw its allegiance from the pope, and endeavored to win his nephew James tc adopt his plan, by the most advantageous offers. The influence of the Scottish clergy prevailed over that of the English monarch, and Henry in his fury proclaimed war against Scotland. In the midst of these troubles, James V. died leaving his dominions to his infant daughter Mary, the celebrated and unfortunate queen of Scots. This changed all Henry's plans; he aimed at uniting the two kingdoms, by effecting a marriage between his son Edward and Mary, but he knew that this could only be affected by crushing the French party in Scotland, and eager to accomplish this object he readily entered into the alliance against Francis.

The French monarch, on the other hand, entered into close union with the Turks, and courted the support of the German protestants; but the princes of the empire refused to join so bitter a persecutor of the reformed doctrines, and his only ally, the duke of Cleves, was forced to submit to Charles. The sultan afforded him more effective support; he invaded Hungary in person, and sent the celebrated admiral and pirate, Barbarossa, to join the French in invading Italy. Nice was besieged by their united forces; to the astonishment and scandal of all Christendom, the lilies of France and the crescent of Mohammed appeared in conjunction against a fortress, on which the cross of Savoy was displayed. The allies were finally compelled to raise the siege, and Francis had not even the poor consolation of success, in return for the infamy of having taken as auxiliaries the deadly enemies of Christianity. The battle of Cerisoles (A. D. 1544) gave his arms the fame of useless victory, but it did not prevent the contemporary invasion of France by the emperor on the side of Lorraine, and the English through Calais. Had Charles and Henry acted in concert, Francis must have yielded unconditionally, but he took advantage of their disunion to conclude a separate peace with the emperor at Crespy (A. D. 1544). Henry VIII. continued the war for some time longer, but it did not produce any event of consequence. Charles had now secured his predominance in Italy, and was secretly preparing to restore the imperial authority in Germany. Death removed his two powerful contemporaries, Francis and Henry, in the same year (A. D. 1547), both of whom would nave been dangerous antagonists. Though Henry's motives in favoring the reformation were not very pure, his intense hatred of the popes must have induced him to protect the protestant interest in Germany.

The secularization of Prussia, by Albert of Brandenburg (A. D. 1525), was the first example of the seizure of church property, consequent on the change of religion; but the indignation of the catholic princes, and the ambition of the protestants, were restrained by the Turkish and the French wars. Still the emperor's conduct at the diets of Spires and Augsburg, the pope's anxiety to convene a council subservient to his will, and the intrigues of the ecclesiastics in the states that retained their connexion with Rome, compelled the protestants to renew the league of Smalkald, and assign the fixed contingent of men and arms that should be supplied by the several members. When the council of Trent finally opened (A. D. 1545), its very form and its first decision rendered it impossible for the protestants to take any part in it. But the peace of Crespy left them unprotected, and their want of mutual confidence prevented them from acting in concert. At the very commencement of the war, Prince Maurice of Saxony deserted the league, and joined the emperor; John Frederic, the elector of Saxony, and chief leader of the protestants, was made prisoner at the battle of Mühlberg (A. D. 1547), and his dominions rewarded the treachery of Maurice. The landgrave of Hesse, the last hope of the reformers, was inveigled to visit the emperor, at Halle, and dishonorably detained as a captive.

This rapid success of the emperior alarmed the pope, who began to fear that Charles would prevail upon the council to limit his pontifical authority, and the two potentates, apparently believing the protestant cause crushed, began to seek for their own private advantages. Charles published a code of doctrines called the "Interim," because the regulations it contained were only to be in force until the convocation of a free general council, and this edict, which was strictly conformable to the tenets of the Romish church, he resolved to enforce on the empire (A. D. 1548). Catholics and protestants equally declaimed against this summary mode of settling a nation's faith, but the emperor scarcely encountered any open resistance, except from the free city of Magdeburgh, and an army sent to reduce this disobedient place, was intrusted to Maurice of Saxony.

Maurice was secretly dissatisfied with the conduct of the emperor, and was especially grieved by the detention of his father-in-law, the landgrave of Hesse. He formed a bold plan for compelling the emperor, by a sudden attack, to establish religious freedom, and liberate the landgrave, but concealed his projects until the most favorable moment for putting them into execution. On the surrender of Magdeburgh (A D 1551), he contrived to win the confidence of the garrison and the citizens, without awakening the suspicions of the emperor, and he entered into a secret treaty with Henry II. of France, the son and successor of Francis. No words can describe the astonishment and distress of the emperor, when Maurice, having completed his preparations, published his manifesto, detailing the grievances which he required to be redressed. The active prince proceeded with so much promptitude and vigor, that Charles narrowly escaped being made prisoner at Innspruck. The council of Trent was broken up; the prelates tumultuously voted a prorogation for two years, but more than ten elapsed before its proceedings were renewed. The emperor had the mortification to see all his projects overthrown by the prince whom he had most trusted, and was compelled to sign a treaty at Passau, by which the captive princes were restored to liberty, and a free exercise of their religion secured to the protestants (A. D. 1552). The war with France lasted three years longer; it was conducted without any great battles, but on the whole, proved unfavorable to the emperor. From the hour that the treaty of Passau had wrested from Charles V. the fruits of his whole political career, he felt that his crowns were heavy on his brows. The principles of mutual toleration were formally sanctioned by the diet of Augsburg: Paul IV., who may be esteemed the successor of Pope Julius—for the twenty days' reign of Marcellus produced no political event—was so offended, that he became the avowed enemy of the house of Austria, and entered into close alliance with the king of France. A storm was approaching, when Charles, to the great surprise of the world, abdicated his dominions.

Though a prince of moderate abilities, Charles V. had reigned with more glory than most European sovereigns. A king of France and a pope had been his captives; his dominions were more extensive than those of Alexander, or of Rome. By his generals, or his ministers, he had acquired all the objects which usually excite ambition; he had gained even the distinction of being regarded as the champion of orthodoxy, in an age when toleration was a crime. But the triumph of civilization over the system of the middle ages, of which he was at once the last support and the last representative, was certain and complete, and he could not resist the mortification of finding himself vanquished; the peace of Passau was to him "the hand-writing on the wall;" it announced that his policy was past, and his destiny accomplished. The feebleness of old age overtook him at fifty-six; harassed by vain repinings, overwhelmed by infirmities, he felt that he could no longer appear a hero, and he desired to seem a sage. He became a hermit, removed all his diadems from his head, and sank into voluntary obscurity. He was, however, sure to be regretted, for he bequeathed to the world his successor, the sanguinary Philip, just as Augustus adopted Tiberius.

The protestant religion was first legally established in England by Edward VI., the pious son of the profligate Henry. But the troubles occasioned by his minority, and the ambition of his guardians, prevented the reformed church from being fixed on a permanent foundation. Edward died young (A. D. 1553), and the papal dominion was restored by his bigoted successor and sister, Mary. Charles, having failed to procure the empire for his son Philip, negotiated a marriage between that prince and Queen Mary, which was concluded, much to the dissatisfac tion of the British nation. Mary's cruel persecutions of the protestants failed to reconcile her subjects to the yoke of Rome, and on her death (A. D. 1558), the reformed religion was triumphantly restored by her sister Elizabeth.

The diet which assembled at Augsburg (A. D. 1555), did not secure to the protestants all the advantages they had a right to expect. Maurice had fallen in a petty war, and they had no leader fit to be his successor. With strange imprudence, the Lutherans consented to the exclusion of the Calvinists from the benefits of religious toleration, and left several important questions undecided, the pregnant source of future wars. When the labors of the diet terminated, Charles, mortified at being forced to resign the hope of securing the empire to his son, saddened by his experience of the instability of fortune, and broken down by illness, resolved to abdicate his double authority. He resigned the sceptre of Spain and the Netherlands to his son, Philip II., and the imperial crown some months after to his brother Ferdinand: he then retired to the monastery of St. Justus, in Valladolid, where he died (A. D. 1558).

The long struggle for religious freedom during the reign of Charles V. terminated in the favor of the Reformation; but the Romish church was far from being subdued, and it derived most efficient support from the institution of the Jesuits, a political rather than religious society, admirably organized for the support of the highest and most unyielding assumptions of papal authority. This body became formidable from its unity and the secrecy of its operations, but it at length excited the alarm of catholic princes, and was suppressed in the last century.

In the course of the wars between Charles and Francis, the republic of Venice, which, at the beginning of the sixteenth century, had appeared so formidable that almost all the potentates of Europe united in a confederacy for its destruction, declined from its ancient power and splendor. The Venetians not only lost a great part of their territory in the war excited by the league of Cambray, but the revenues as well as vigor of the state were exhausted by their extraordinary and long-continued efforts in their own defence, and that commerce by which they had acquired their wealth and power began to decay without any hopes of its reviving. All the fatal consequences to their republic, which the sagacity of the Venetian senate foresaw on the first discovery of a passage to the East Indies, by the Cape of Good Hope, actually took place. Their endeavors to prevent the Portuguese from establishing themselves in the East Indies, not only by exciting the Mameluke sultans of Egypt and the Ottoman monarchs to turn their arms against such dangerous intruders, but by affording secret aid to the infidels in order to ensure their success, proved ineffectual. The activity and valor of the Portuguese surmounted every obstacle, and obtained such a firm footing in that fertile country, as secured to them large possessions with an influence still more extensive. Lisbon instead of Venice became the staple for the precious commodities of the east. The Venetians, after having possessed for many years the monopoly of that beneficial commerce, had the mortification to be excluded from almost any share in it. The discoveries of the Spaniards in the western world proved no less fatal to inferior branches of commerce. When the sources from which the state derived its extraordinary riches and power were dried up, its interior vigor declined, and of course its external operations became less formidable. Long before the middle of the sixteenth century, Venice ceased to be one of the principal powers in Europe, and dwindled into a secondary and subaltern state. But as the senate had the address to conceal the diminution of its power under the veil of moderation and caution; as it made no rash effort that could discover its weakness; as the symptoms of political decay in states are not soon observed, and are seldom so apparent to their neighbors as to occasion any sudden alteration in their conduct toward them, Venice continued long to be considered and respected. She was treated, not according to her present condition, but according to the rank which she had formerly held. Charles V., as well as the kings of France, his rivals, courted her assistance with emulation and solicitude in all their enterprises. Even down to the close of the century, Venice remained, not only an object of attention, but a considerable seat of political negotiation and intrigue.

That authority which the first Cosmo de Medici and Lorenzo his grandson had acquired in the republic of Florence by their beneficence and abilities, inspired their descendants with the ambition of usurping the sovereignty in their country and paving their way toward it. Charles V. placed Alexander de Medici at the head of the republic (A. D. 1530), and to the natural interest and power of the family added the weight as well as the credit of the imperial protection. Of these his successor Cosmo, surnamed the Great, availed himself; and establishing his supreme authority on the ruins of the ancient republican constitution, he transmitted that, together with the title of grand duke of Tuscany, to his descendants. Their dominions were composed of the territories which had belonged to the three commonwealths of Florence, Pisa, and Sienna, and formed one of the most respectable of the Italian states.

Section VIII.—*The Age of Elizabeth.*

The accession of Elizabeth was the crisis of the Reformation in Great Britain; as she was the daughter of Anne Boleyn, whose marriage with Henry VIII. had not been sanctioned by the Romish church, her title was not recognised by the catholics, and the king of France permitted his daughter-in-law, Mary, queen of Scots, to assume the arms and title of England. Elizabeth secured herself by entering into secret alliance with the heads of the protestant party in Scotland, who succeeded in withdrawing that kingdom from its allegiance to the pope, and so fettering the royal authority, that the queen dowager, who acted as regent for her daughter, was too much harassed at home to make any hostile attempt on England. Connected with the cause of the Reformation by her own interests, Elizabeth was naturally regarded as the head of the protestants in Europe, while Philip II. was the champion of the catholics. Hence England became the counterpoise to Spain in this age, as France had been in the preceding. But the ancient rivalry between France and Spain was of the highest importance to England; it prevented a cordial union between the catholic powers of Europe for checking the progress of the Reformation, and it secured support for her doubtful title, ere her noble qualities becoming known, earned for her the best of all securities, the affections of the English nation.

Mary, queen of Scots, was the niece of Henry VIII., and next heir to his crown if the illegitimacy of Elizabeth were established; she was wedded to the heir-apparent of the French monarchy; her maternal uncles, the princes of Lorraine, were remarkable for capacity, valor, and daring ambition, and she had reasonable prospects of success at a time when Scotland was divided between the contending communions, Ireland altogether catholic, and while catholics predominated in the north of England. The death of Henry II., by a mortal wound in a tournament, raised Mary's husband, the feeble Francis II., to the French throne, and through the young queen's influence transferred the power of the monarchy to the princes of Lorraine. The bigoted Philip II. was so alarmed at the probable accession of power to his great rivals, that he not only acknowledged Elizabeth's title, but proffered her marriage. She declined the offer, and Philip gave his hand to the princess Elizabeth of France, and concluded a treaty with that power at Château Cambresis. Though no express stipulations were made, it was well known that the extirpation of heresy formed a part of this alliance between the two great catholic powers; it led to a furious war of religion, which ended in the establishment of a new European state.

Before entering on the history of the religious wars in France and the Netherlands, it is of importance to examine the state of England and Scotland during the early part of Elizabeth's reign. On the death of Francis II. (Dec., 1560), Mary was compelled to return to her native dominions by the jealousy of her mother-in-law, Catherine de Medicis, who secretly envied the power of the princess of Lorraine. She left France with a heavy heart, and from the very first moment of her landing had to endure indignities the most mortifying to her proud spirit. Popery had been overthrown in Scotland, but the protestantism erected in its stead was just as bigoted and as intolerant as the ancient creed had been in the worst of times. Still, the winning manners of the queen, and the weakness of her party, prevented any immediate outbreak; and the confidence of the protestants in the earl of Moray restrained the violence of their fanaticism. The marriage of Mary to the young Lord Darnley, in spite of the remonstrances both of Elizabeth and Lord Moray (A. D. 1565), led to the first open breach between the queen and her subjects. Several lords, indignant at the refusal of security to the protestant religion sought safety in England, and they soon gained Darnley himself to join their association. An Italian, of mean birth, David Rizzio, having been appointed private secretary to the queen, gained such an ascendency over her, that Darnley's jealousy was roused; he entered into a conspiracy with the exiled lords, introduced an armed band secretly into the palace, arrested Rizzio in the queen's presence, and murdered him at the door of her chamber. The birth of a son led to an apparent reconciliation between Mary and her husband; but its hollowness was proved by Darnley's being excluded from witnessing the baptism of his own child. The appearance of renewed affection was maintained notwithstanding this insult; Darnley fell sick, Mary visited him with apparent anxiety, and, under the pretence that quiet was necessary to an invalid, removed him to a solitary house called the Kirk of Field. On the 9th of February, 1567, this house was blown up with gunpowder, and the unfortunate Darnley's lifeless body carried to some distance, where it was found without any external mark of violence. The measures taken by Mary to screen Bothwell, universally regarded as the author of this crime, and her subsequent marriage to that nobleman, seemed conclusive evidence that she had countenanced her husband's murder. The Scottish lords flew to arms; Mary was forced to yield herself a prisoner to her irritated subjects, and Bothwell fled into exile.

The unfortunate queen, confined in Lochleven castle, was forced to abdicate in favor of her son, who was crowned with the title of James VI. She escaped from her prison, and soon found herself at the head of a numerous army, but within eleven days from her deliverance she was completely defeated in the battle of Langside, and forced to seek refuge in England (A. D. 1568). Elizabeth placed the fugitive in close custody, a measure which her safety perhaps demanded, but which was scarcely consistent with her honor. The insurrections of the catholic lords in the northern counties, and Mary's intrigues with the duke of Norfolk, combined with the open attempts of the catholic states against Elizabeth, rendered the unfortunate queen's detention a matter of prudent expediency, if not of prime necessity.

The imbecile Francis II. succeeded his father Henry on the throne of France; during his brief reign he was the mere tool of the Guises, whose great anxiety was to establish the inquisition in France. Philip II. was engaged in a similar attempt in the Netherlands, and both provoked a desperate resistance. Like his father Charles V., Philip was ambitious of universal monarchy, but he used different means; he hoped to gain the clergy by his zeal, to win the nobles by the bribes which the wealth of Spanish America enabled him to offer, and to subdue the people by the united efforts of ecclesiastical and aristocratic influence. But in the Netherlands, as in France, the proposal to establish the inquisition was a fatal error of despotism; it provoked the fierce resistance of all who were worthy of their country, it identified the papacy with cruelty and slavery, it gave to the reformed leaders the proud title of deliverers of their country. The election of Pius IV. to the chair of St. Peter precipitated the civil war in France (A. D. 1560). A conspiracy was formed for removing the Guises, in which many ardent catholics joined; it was discovered and defeated, but the sanguinary cruelty of the Lorraine princes rendered their victory injurious to their cause; the memory of the martyrs they slaughtered won proselytes and confirmed opposition. So powerful were the Huguenots, that liberty of conscience was sanctioned in an assembly of the Notables at Fontainebleau; and it was proposed to convoke a national council for regulating the affairs of the Gallican church. Had France been ruled by an energetic sovereign, acquainted with the interests of his crown and the wishes of the nation, the French church at this moment might have been rendered as independent of Rome as the English: the pope saw the danger, and he induced Francis to abandon the national synod, by promising the speedy convocation of a general council. Both the emperor and the king of France objected to reassembling the bishops at Trent, declaring that its name was odious to the protestants; but the ill health of Francis II., who was fast sinking into the grave, induced Pius to quicken his proceedings, and bulls for the continuation of the council were issued. In the meantime the states-general assembled in France. The prince of Condé and the king of Navarre, the great leaders of the Huguenot party, were arrested when they appeared at court, and the former received sentence of death. But the queen-mother, Catherine de Medicis, dreading that the regency would be seized by the Guises when the king died, secretly intrigued with the Huguenots to secure their support, and the life of Condé was the pledge and the reward of their assistance. But while she thus courted the alliance of the protestants, she secretly informed Philip II. that her hatred of the Reformation was unabated, and that she only waited a favorable opportunity to imitate his example of merciless butchery and persecution. She intrigued with both parties, a fatal error; for had she frankly embraced one, she would have stamped the other with the character of revolt; her Italian cunning only served to render civil war inevitable.

The duke of Guise saw clearly that, to sustain the part he designed to act, it was necessary to attempt something of more than ordinary magnitude; he raised the cry "the church is in danger;" ignorance and bigotry responded to the summons; he placed himself at the head of the zealous supporters of papal infallibility, hoping to destroy, by one blow, the queen-regent, who was suspected of culpable indifference to the interests of the faith, the government, which seemed ready to recognise the principles of toleration, and the Huguenots. Like his opponents, he appealed to the people, and attempted to guide public opinion; like them, too, he declared himself the steadfast friend of the monarchy: thus the struggle between the two parties had for its prize the throne of France, and for its pretext the defence of royalty.

In the meantime, the council of Trent continued its deliberations, without showing any symptom of a desire to conciliate the spirit of the age, by improving either the doctrine or the discipline of the church. The bishops wasted their time in scholastic disputations, and proved how delusive were their professions of a desire for peace, by celebrating the victory obtained over the Huguenots at Dreux, by a public thanksgiving. In fact, the council terrified nobody but Pius IV., who saw his power attacked on every side. Maximilian, the son of the emperor Ferdinand, having been elected king of the Romans, refused for a long time to receive the sanction of his election from the pontiff, and finally accepted it as a mere ceremony, venerable on account of its antiquity; it would have been better for the holy see to have abjured such a privilege, than to have it preserved as a subject of ridicule and mockery.

But though the public proceedings at Trent were far from injuring the progress of the Reformation, there were secret plans devised fraught with imminent peril to the protestants. One of these was revealed, by the imprudence of the cardinal of Lorraine. On the 10th of May, 1563, he read a letter from his niece, Mary, queen of Scots, "submitting herself to the council, and promising that when she succeeded to the throne of England, she would subject both her kingdoms to the obedience due to the apostolic see." He added, verbally, that she would have sent prelates, as representatives of Scotland, to the council, had she not been restrained by the necessity of keeping terms with her heretical councillors. The Italians were engaged everywhere alarming monarchs with the republican tendency of the Reformation; a charge which seemed to derive some support from the revolts of the peasants in Germany, the troubles in Flanders, and the confusion of France. Philip II. was not the only sovereign who regarded heretics as rebels, and believed that the papacy would be found an efficient aid to despotism in crushing civil as well as religious liberty.

At length the council of Trent terminated its sittings; eighteen years of debate had produced no plan of reform for ecclesiastical morals, discipline, or doctrine (A. D. 1564). One of the last acts of the assembled fathers was to issue an anathema against heretics, which justified the protestants in their refusal to recognise the acts of the council. But we should commit a great error if we supposed that this last of the general councils produced no change in the constitution of the papacy, it organized the spiritual despotism of the popes, clearly perceiving that the temporal empire was irrecoverably lost, and it placed the holy see in the position of an ally to the monarchs who were eager to maintain despotic power. From the time of this council to the present day, every sovereign of France and Spain, remarkable for hostility to constitutional freedom, has been equally conspicuous for his attachment to the holy see, and the articles of faith ratified by the council of Trent. It was by this assembly that the marriage of priests was definitely prohibited. We have already shown how necessary an element this law has been to the spiritual despotism possessed, and temporal supremacy claimed, by the pope. Family and country had no ties on the bishops of the catholic church; Rome enjoyed exclusive possession of every feeling that can render man a good subject or a good citizen; the infallibility and omnipotence of the pope were made articles of faith, by prelates whose whole heart was engaged in supporting the supremacy of the holy see; the popes could rouse nations to revolt, and trouble empires, because they had obedient emissaries in every parish; the doctrine of implicit submission to the successors of St. Peter was taught by priests, when it could not be enforced by armies, and it was found sufficiently efficacious to harass Europe with a century of war. Pius IV. comprehended the immense value of an unmarried clergy; though he had violently condemned the administration of the eucharist in both kinds, he relaxed the prohibition at the instance of the emperor Maximilian, and permitted the cup to be given to the laity in Germany; but on the point of celibacy he was inflexible, for he was justly convinced that it was the great bond by which all the portions of papal domination were united, and that if it should be relaxed, the entire edifice would fall in sunder.

After the dissolution of the council, a general suspicion was diffused through the protestants of Europe, that a league for their destruction had been formed by some of the leading catholic powers. It is now sufficiently notorious that these suspicions were not groundless, and that Pius IV. was weary of the slow steps by which the members of this pretended holy alliance advanced to the verge of an exterminating war. He earnestly urged a personal interview between Catherine de Medicis and Philip II.; it was declined by the latter on account of his ill health, but he sent a worthy representative, the duke of Alva, to hold a conference with the queen-regent and her son, Charles IX., at Bayonne. The pretext for the meeting was an interview between the young queen of Spain and her mother, Catherine de Medicis; but the presence of the duke of Alva, the avowed enemy of the protestants, whose extirpation he openly proclaimed to be his most solemn duty to God or man, was a clear proof that more important designs were contemplated. The days were spent in all the sports and festivities that are to be found in a luxurious and licentious court. But at the dead hour of midnight, when the courtiers, exhausted by the tournament, the table, and the dance, retired to repose, Catherine held secret conferences with Alva in the apartments of her probably unconscious daughter, Elizabeth. They agreed in their object, the destruction of the Huguenots, and all the parties disposed to place restrictions on the royal authority in the French and Spanish dominions, but they differed very widely as to the means by which this might be most effectually accomplished. Alva recommended the most violent measures, edicts of extermination supported by powerful armies, military execution of all who ventured to offer any opposition, and a general massacre of the Huguenot congregations. But though Catherine would not have shown any scruple in adopting these, or even more atrocious plans, she was well aware that Alva's projects could not be executed without the aid of a Spanish army, and she was too jealous of her own authority to allow a foreign court to exercise any influence in the kingdom which she governed as regent. She relied on her own craft and cunning to retain power, for her zeal for religion was always made subservient to her ambition, and she was infinitely more afraid of any combination of the nobles of France to restrain the royal authority, than of the real or supposed progress of heretical opinions. She hated the Huguenots rather as a political than as a religious body, for the aristocratic leaders of the sect were more bent on rendering the nobles independent of the crown, than of delivering the Gallican church from the power of the pope, and it was the aristocratic character thus imprinted on the principles of the reformation in France, which prevented the protestant movement from ever becoming popular with the great body of the middle and the lower ranks in France. In their minds it was associated with feudalism, which had become so odious to the French people that they would have accepted the worst form of oriental despotism in preference.

Philip began to execute his part of the agreement by a vigorous effort to establish the Inquisition in Flanders; and to put an end to the insurrection which such a measure provoked, he appointed the duke of Alva lord lieutenant of the Netherlands, with almost absolute authority. Many of the Flemish merchants and manufacturers left their country; they brought their industry and their capital to England; a circumstance which had no small share in the rapid growth of England's commercial prosperity. The cruelties of Alva, the noble resistance of the prince of Orange, long the head and hope of the protestant party in Europe, and the final establishment of the independence of the Seven United Provinces, belong to general history; but in this narrative we must not omit to mention, that Philip's brutal obstinacy was frequently blamed by the court of Rome; the crafty Italians would have preferred fraud to violence, and assassination to the perils of open war (A. D. 1572). It must also be mentioned, that the Turks joined in the contest as the protectors of the Flemings, and that their defeat by Don John of Austria, at Lepanto, finally delivered Europe from the perils with which it was menaced by Mohammedan barbarism. Pius V., who ascended the papal throne (A. D. 1566), was disposed to take advantage of the victory at Lepanto, and organize a league against the Turks; but Philip was jealous of the glory acquired by his brother, and he declared that nothing should divert him from the prosecution of the war in Flanders. This pontiff, who was afterward canonized as a saint, was inflexible in his hatred of the protestants but he made some efforts to remedy the evils of the church by founding schools and colleges, and excluding persons of immoral life from ecclesiastical dignities. He was succeeded by Gregory XIII.

In the spring of 1560, the French protestants were detected in a conspiracy for taking the infant king out of the hands of the persecuting Guises, and expelling the entire Lorraine family from France. The massacres with which this crime was punished, produced retaliation; a civil war ensued, which, interrupted by short and unsteady truces, lasted to 1570, when a treaty, favorable to the Huguenots, was concluded at St. Germains. To cement this peace, a marriage was proposed between the young king of Navarre, the hereditary leader of the French protestants, and the princess Margaret, the beautiful sister of the king of France. The proposal diffused such universal joy, that even the more violent of the catholic party were forced to acquiesce, and preparations were made for celebrating the nuptials at Paris with extraordinary magnificence. Admiral Coligni and the other protestant leaders were invited to witness the festivities, and the chief catholic lords, headed by the duke of Guise, came to share in the general reconciliation.

The events which led to the fearful tragedy that accompanied this marriage, have been so misrepresented by party writers on every side, that it is desirable to state the facts at some length, as they have been narrated by the principal actors themselves. At this period the populace of Paris was the most bigoted and sanguinary mob to be found in Europe. They went beyond the most cruel edicts of their rulers in persecuting all who were suspected of heretical opinions, and not unfrequently took the law into their own hands, against the wishes of the court and the clergy. The presence of Coligni and the protestant lords, was, therefore, a source of indignant grief to the fanatical multitude, and nothing but the presence of the royal guards prevented outburst of popular violence. Guise and his friends, opposed to the Huguenots as heretics, and to their leaders as rivals, fostered this general discontent, while the queen-mother, Catherine, negotiated with both parties, believing that she could only retain power by balancing one against the other.

Charles IX., feeble in body, and weak in intellect, had just attained his legal majority, but the real power of the state was wielded by Catherine and her favorite son, Henry, for whom she always showed herself willing to sacrifice the rest of her children. In some of his conversations with the protestant lords, Charles complained very bitterly of the state of thraldom in which he was held, and Coligni, commiserating the unhappy monarch, promised to aid in his deliverance. The king soon began to vaunt of his design to assume the reins of power, and to remove his mother and brother from the court. They took the alarm, and easily discovering by whose counsels the king was influenced, resolved to assassinate the admiral Coligni. Henry hired a man for the purpose, and lent him his own gun; but in order to avert suspicion, he stationed the assassin in the lodgings of a retainer of the duke of Guise. Coligni was shot as he passed the house, but the wound was not mortal; before his friends could break open the door, the assassin had escaped, leaving his gun behind him. At first, the suspicions of the protestants were directed against the duke of Guise, but the gun, and some other circumstances, soon led them to discover the real instigators of the plot, and they very imprudently proclaimed their intention to exact heavy vengeance upon Catherine and her favorite son.

In this emergency, Catherine convoked a secret council of her friends, and there it was resolved to massacre all the Huguenots on the eve of St. Bartholomew (A. D. 1572), and thus crush the entire party at one blow. The conspirators, seven in number, were well aware that they could rely on the royal guards, who were still animated by all the passions of the late religious wars, and they also knew that the Parisian populace waited but a signal to indulge in the excesses of savage bigotry. It was further resolved that the atrocious plot should be kept secret from the king until it was on the eve of execution, but that all arrangements for effectually accomplishing the general slaughter should be made, and everything kept in readiness to begin, the moment that his consent had been obtained.

It was late in the evening when Catherine went to Charles, accompanied by her chosen advisers, and told him that the protestants had formed a plan for the extermination of the royal family, which could only be frustrated by the most immediate and decisive measures. The feeble monarch, who was not many degrees removed from idiotcy, exhibited every sign of helpless alarm. While in this condition, his mother placed before him the dreadful decree of extermination, and demanded his signature; Charles at first refused, and for some time it was doubtful whether his consent could be obtained. At length, in a paroxysm of rage mingled with insanity, he exclaimed, "I consent, provided that you kill them all, and leave no survivor to reproach me."

It was about midnight that the sounding of the tocsin summoned the bands of murderers to commence the work of destruction. Most of the unsuspecting Huguenots were massacred in their beds, or shot on the roofs of their houses while attempting to escape. Charles himself, armed with a gun, stationed himself in a tower, from which he fired upon such fugitives as attempted to escape across the Seine; the palace itself was not respected; several of the attendants of the young king of Navarre were murdered in the royal apartments, and he was himself exposed to considerable danger

The massacre lasted for eight days and nights without any apparent diminution of the fury of the murderers. Several catholics perished, the victims of mistake or of private animosity, and similar atrocities were perpetrated in the principal cities of the kingdom. At first, the court seemed disposed to throw the blame of this fearful atrocity on the duke of Guise and his faction, but finding that the guilt could not be concealed, it was openly avowed, and a royal manifesto issued in its justification. The wish of Charles that none should survive to reproach him was not fulfilled: nearly two millions of Huguenots still survived to avenge the fate of their murdered brethren. The civil war was renewed with greater fury than ever; the protestants felt themselves strengthened by the sympathy of all whom bigotry had not rendered callous to every feeling of humanity; and the authors of this unparalleled crime had the mortification to discover that it had been perpetrated in vain.

While public rejoicings were made at Rome and Madrid, for the supposed overthrow of heresy in France, the horror and indignation excited by the massacre in northern Europe, not only among protestant, but even catholic princes, proved a serious injury to the catholic cause. The prince of Orange placed himself at the head of the revolters in the Netherlands—the Gueux, or Beggars, as they were contemptuously called by their oppressors. Though at first unsuccessful, he gave the insurrection a determinate character by the capture of Brille (A. D. 1572), a conquest which secured him a naval station for his daring cruisers, and encouraged the cities of Holland and Zealand to reject the Spanish yoke. The massacre of St. Bartholomew weakened the insurgents, by depriving them of the aid of the French Huguenots; but instead of quelling their courage, it only stimulated them to perseverance. Defeated by land, and deprived of their strongest cities, they attacked the Spaniards on sea, and captured several rich freights. At length Alva retired in despair, and was succeeded by Zunega y Requesens (December, 1573).

In the very commencement of his administration, Requesens gained a decisive victory over the insurgents at Monher Moor, near Nimeguen. The three brothers of the prince of Orange fell in this fatal battle, which would probably have terminated the war, but for a mutiny of the Spanish soldiers. The turbulence of the royal army, the insolence and licentiousness of the Spaniards, and the pillage of Antwerp by the mutineers, excited the indignation of catholics and protestants. Five of the Batavian and six of the Belgic provinces entered into the pacification of Ghent, which provided for the expulsion of foreigners, the repeal of Alva's sanguinary edicts, and restoration of the ancient power of the states-general (A. D. 1576). Don John of Austria, who had succeeded Requesens in the government, disarmed suspicion by acceding to the league of Ghent; but this confederacy soon fell to pieces, owing to the jealousy between the protestant and catholic states. It now became manifest that freedom could only be attained by a close union of the northern provinces, and a final rupture with Spain. Acting on this belief, the prince of Orange organized the confederacy of Utrecht, the basis of that commonwealth so renowned under the name of the Republic of the United Provinces (A. D. 1579).

But, notwithstanding these precautions, the nomination of the duke of Parma to the regency threatened to ruin all the projects of the prince of Orange. The southern provinces, inspired with a jealousy of the protestant designs on the catholic religion, entered into an alliance with the regent, and levied an army against the insurgents of the north. But the Hollanders, thus deserted, did not lose courage; they formally renounced their allegiance to the Spanish crown, and chose the duke of Anjou, brother to the king of France, for their sovereign (A. D. 1581). But this choice did not produce the expected advantages; and the duke of Anjou, after a brief struggle, abandoned all hopes of competing with the duke of Parma, and returned to France. It is probable that the states would have chosen the prince of Orange for their constitutional sovereign, but that hero was stabbed by a fanatic, whether instigated wholly by bigotry, or partly seduced by Spanish gold, it is now difficult to determine (A. D. 1584). Amid the general gloom spread over the protestant confederates by the loss of their illustrious leader, the Hollanders and Zealanders chose Maurice, his son, a young man of eighteen, their stadtholder and captain-general by sea and land. The war still continued; but though the duke of Parma prevailed in the field, and finally captured the important city of Antwerp (A. D. 1585), the confederates never dreamed of submission. They offered the sovereignty of their republic to Queen Elizabeth on certain conditions; and though she rejected the proffer, she sent the earl of Leicester to their aid with a considerable army. The misconduct of Leicester prevented the Hollanders from gaining all the advantages from the English auxiliaries that might have been expected; but the breaking out of war between England and Spain, the death of the duke of Parma in the civil wars of France, and the heroism of Prince Maurice, gave them such a decided superiority by sea and land, that their independence was secured and finally recognised by Spain (A. D. 1609).

Before entering on the history of the war between England and Spain, it is necessary to take a retrospective view of the state of France. On the death of Charles IX., his brother Henry III., resigned the throne of Poland for that of France (A. D. 1574). This prince, on his return, began a war of persecution, and concluded by an ignominious peace with his own subjects, in less than a year. He then abandoned himself to the lowest debaucheries, strangely combined with the practice of the most degrading superstitions. Opposed to the king, were the princes of Lorraine, whose chief, Henry, duke of Guise, was deservedly regarded as the leader of the violent catholic party in France. Noble in person, polished in demeanor, endowed with superior talents, and animated by grasping ambition, he seemed formed by nature to become the leader of a faction, and art had lent its aid to improve all these advantages. The utter contempt into which Henry III. had fallen, and the rage of the catholics at the tolerance granted to the protestants by the late pacification, encouraged the duke of Guise to raise the cry of religion, and the fanatic populace, roused by this hypocritical pretext, began to take arms to defend their church. The Holy League, drawn up by Guise's uncle, the cardinal of Lorraine, for the defence of the catholic religion, was signed aud sworn to by catholics of all ranks and conditions in Paris and the provinces. The duke of Guise was appointed head of the league ; the pope and the king of Spain declared themselves its protectors, and the wretched Henry was forced to yield to the faction, assemble the states at Blois, and revoke the freedom of conscience granted to the Huguenots. The consequence was a civil war, the ninth which afflicted France since the death of Francis II.

The fate of the unhappy queen of Scots, which had been determined ever since the massacre of St. Bartholomew, was precipitated by the formation of the Holy League. Some enthusiastic English catholics entered into a conspiracy for assassinating Elizabeth ; Mary was cognizant of their plans, but her participation in the plot is very doubtful. However, an act of parliament was passed authorizing her trial ; commissioners were sent for the purpose to Fotheringay castle, the place of her confinement, and after an investigation, in which the forms of law and the principles of justice were little regarded, she was condemned to death. Elizabeth, with much apparent, and some real reluctance, signed the warrant of execution, and placed it in the hands of Davison, her private secretary, enjoining him not to use it without further orders (A. D. 1587). Davison, however, showed the warrant to the members of the council, and they, without further consulting Elizabeth, had the unhappy Mary beheaded. Henry III. of France, soon afterward, had his capital enemies, the duke and cardinal of Guise, assassinated ; but this atrocious crime only roused the leaguers to more vigorous measures. They assembled a parliament, deposed the king, and created the duke of Mayenne lieutenant-general of the kingdom.

Philip II., in the meantime, prepared an expedition which he fondly hoped would conquer England, and thus destroy the great stay of protestantism in Europe. Ships were prepared in all the ports throughout his extensive dominions ; Spain, Portugal, Naples, and those parts of the low countries which still recognised his authority. An army of 30,000 picked men was assembled under the most experienced officers of Italy, Spain, and Germany, and the chief command was intrusted to the celebrated duke of Parma. The pope blessed an expedition that seemed destined once more to restore the supremacy of the holy see ; and the catholics throughout Europe were so confident of success, that they named the armament "The Invincible Armada." Elizabeth undauntedly prepared to meet the danger. She intrusted the command of her fleet to a catholic nobleman, Lord Howard of Effingham, while the land army was placed under the command of the earl of Leicester. Nothing could exceed the enthusiastic determination of the English people to defend their religion and liberties, though the queen had but one ally on whose assistance she could reckon, James, king of Scotland ; she trusted to the attachment of her people, and found that the love of her subjects was the best security of her throne.

On the thirtieth of May, 1588, the armada sailed from Lisbon : but having been shattered by a storm, it was forced to stop at Corunna, and it did not reach the English channel until the nineteenth of July. Here the Spanish admiral, the duke of Medina Sidonia, was surprised to find that the duke of Parma was not prepared to join him with a fleet and army. While he hesitated, the light English squadrons assailed his heavy vessels on all sides, and after seven days, three of which only passed without warm actions, though there was no decisive engagement, the armada was so shattered by English skill and bravery, that it was forced to take shelter in the roads of Calais. The earl of Effingham, following up his advantage, sent in fireships during the night, which destroyed several vessels, and threw the others into such confusion, that the Spaniards no longer thought of victory, but escape. The duke of Medina Sidonia, dreading again to encounter the English fleet, attempted to return home by sailing round the north of Scotland; but dreadful storms overtook the armada, many of the ships were driven on the shores of Norway, Ireland, and the north of Scotland, and out of the triumphant navy that sailed from Lisbon, only a few shattered vessels returned to bring intelligence of the calamity that had overwhelmed the rest.

This glorious success was deservedly regarded, not so much as the triumph of England, as of the protestant cause throughout Europe; it virtually established the independence of the Dutch, and it raised the courage of the Huguenots in France. It completely destroyed the decisive influence that Spain had acquired in the affairs of Europe; ever since the shipwreck of the armada, the Spanish state and people seem to have lost all energy, and sunk into almost hopeless decay.

Henry III. of France, obliged by the violence of the league to seek the aid of his protestant subjects, was murdered by a fanatic monk, just as he was upon the point of driving his enemies from Paris. By his death, the house of Valois became extinct, and the right of inheritance passed to the Bourbon family, descended from Robert, the sixth son of St. Louis. Its representative was Henry of Navarre, who now claimed to be Henry IV. of France, a warlike, chivalrous prince, endowed with many amiable qualities, but disliked by his new subjects on account of his attachment to the protestant religion. After a long struggle, Henry found it necessary to abjure his faith, in order to secure his crown; but he atoned to the Huguenots for his compulsory desertion, by issuing the celebrated edict of Nantes. Still he had to make good his rights by the sword; for his abjuration could not induce either the pope or Philip II. to give up their plans. He received some aid from Elizabeth, but his final success was mainly due to his own eminent abilities; his triumph was virtually completed by the capture of Paris (A. D. 1594), but Spain persevered in its hostility until the peace of Vervins (A. D. 1598).

The close of Elizabeth's reign was clouded by sanguinary wars against her Irish subjects, whose insurrections were too often provoked by the injustice of their rulers, and by the execution of her ill-fated favorite, the earl of Essex. But notwithstanding these domestic calamities, she maintained the war against Spain with great vigor, and encouraged her subjects to undermine the strength of that kingdom by enterprises against its commerce. The annexation of Portugal to the crown of Spain, apparently gave the subjects of Philip II. complete command of the Indian, as well as the South American trade; but the wars of that monarch with England and Holland, raised both countries to a rivalry that terminated to the disadvantage, if not to the ruin of the Spanish commerce. In 1591, the English, for the first time, performed the voyage to India; and in 1600, the year in which the East India company was founded, they took possession of the island of St. Helena. The Hanseatic league, now fast sinking into decay, complained loudly of the encouragement given by the English government to its native merchants, and prohibited the English from trading in Germany; but this unwise attempt to enforce monopoly produced measures of retaliation that speedily proved fatal to their privileges and their power. During Elizabeth's reign, England attained the highest rank among European states, and may be said to have held the balance of power in Christendom; that this was owing, in no small degree, to the personal character of the sovereign, is manifest from the rapid decline of British influence, when the sceptre passed to the feeble house of Stuart.

Section IX.—*The Age of Gustavus Adolphus.*

From the death of Charles V. to the accession of Ferdinand II., there were few events in German history that produced any important result in the general politics of Europe. Ferdinand I. and his son Maximilian II. were sincerely attached to peace, and Rudolph II. was willing to leave the world in quiet, if the world would have left him undisturbed. From the time of his accession (A. D. 1576), Rudolph's great anxiety was to unite the Germanic princes in a firm league against the Turks; but theological discussions, united with political ambition, seemed to prepare the way for fresh convulsions. The influence of the Jesuits in the imperial court so alarmed the protestants, that they formed a new alliance, called "The Evangelical Union," of which the elector-palatine was declared the chief (A. D. 1609), and this was opposed by a catholic league, in which foreign as well as German princes were joined. In this unsettled state of affairs, the competition for succession to a small principality had nearly involved Europe in a general war. Henry IV. of France, after having secured himself on the throne, intrusted the chief management of his affairs to the duke of Sully, under whose wise administration the finances were so improved, and the strength of the kingdom so consolidated, that France began to take the lead in European policy. Henry had formed a great scheme for making all Christendom a federate republic, in which the rights and independence of the several states should be firmly secured. A more immediate project was the humiliation of the house of Austria, whose increasing power in Germany and Spain was deemed dangerous to all the surrounding countries. The vacancy in the dutchies of Cleves and Juliers, which, on the death of the duke without male heirs, had been seized by the emperor as lapsed fiefs, gave Henry a pretext for interfering in the affairs of Germany; he formed alliances with several of his neighbors, and especially with the king of England and the Italian princes. But while preparing to assist at the coronation of his queen, Mary de Medicis, he was stabbed by a fanatic, named Ravaillac (A. D. 1610), and the disturbances that ensued prevented the French from making further exertions in Germany. The dissensions in the Austrian family contributed to avert a general war. Rudolph was gradually driven from his whole dominions by his brother Matthias; deserted by his ancient partisans, he became melancholy and distrustful, shutting himself up in his palace, where grief and want of exercise soon produced a mortal disease, which brought him prematurely to the grave (A. D. 1611).

Matthias succeeded to the imperial crown, and though he had been previously befriended by the protestants, he threw himself into the arms of the catholic party, and thus increased the dissatisfaction which had led to the evangelical union; he procured the crown of Bohemia for his cousin Ferdinand, archduke of Gratz, and this bigoted monarch soon forced his protestant subjects to revolt. While the war was yet in progress, Matthias died, and Ferdinand, to the great alarm of the protestant party, was elected emperor (A. D. 1619). Ferdinand entered into close alliance with the Spanish branch of the house of Hapsburgh, but this family compact was not so formidable as it had been heretofore. The union of the crown of Portugal to that of Spain had not added much real strength to Philip II.; the Portuguese hated the Spaniards, especially as they were compelled to abandon their lucrative commerce with the revolted Hollanders, and were finally deprived of the greater part of their Indian colonies by the successful republicans. The defeat of the armada, followed by these colonial losses, rendered the reign of Philip II. calamitous to the peninsula; but on his death (A. D. 1598) it was destined to suffer still greater losses from the bigotry of his successor. Philip III. expelled the Moriscoes or Moors, who had remained in the peninsula after the overthrow of the last Mohammedan dynasty, and thus deprived himself of the services of more than a million of his most industrious subjects (A. D. 1610). He intrusted the administration of the kingdom to favorites, chosen without discrimination, and made the custom of governing by ministers a maxim of state. On his death (A. D. 1621), Spain, though still respected and even feared, was in reality deplorably weak; but the reign of Philip IV. almost completed its ruin; the Catalans revolted, and placed themselves under the protection of France; the Portuguese, choosing for their monarch the duke of Braganza, achieved their independence (A. D. 1640), and the Neapolitans, harassed by the premier, the count-duke of Olivarez, attempted to form a republic.

These events were not foreseen when Ferdinand became emperor. The Bohemian protestants, dreading his bigotry, chose Frederic, the elector-palatine, son-in-law of the British monarch, for their sovereign, and in an evil hour for himself, Frederic assumed the royal title. James I. was a monarch of much learning and little wisdom; the natural timidity of his disposition, and his anxiety to secure the hand of a Spanish princess for his son, induced him to observe a neutrality in this dispute, contrary to the ardent wishes of his subjects. Duped by vanity, he believed himself a consummate master of diplomacy, and entered into a series of negotiations, which only showed his weakness, and rendered him contemptible in the eyes of Europe. Deserted by his father-in-law, and by many of the protestant princes, on whose assistance he relied, the elector-palatine lost not only Bohemia, but his hereditary dominions, which were shared by his enemies (A. D. 1623).

Circumstances, in the meantime, had occurred to change the neutral policy of England. The young prince Charles, accompanied by his favorite, the duke of Buckingham, had made a romantic journey to

Madrid, which, contrary to general expectation, led to the breaking off of the Spanish match. The discovery of a conspiracy for blowing up the British king and parliament with gunpowder (A. D. 1605), inflamed the English nation against the catholics, because the plot had been devised by some fanatics of that religion, who hoped in the confusion that must have ensued, to restore the supremacy of their church. Finally, Count Mansfelt, the ablest of the protestant leaders, succeeded in convincing James that he had been egregiously duped by the Spaniards. A new protestant union was formed, of which Christian IV., king of Denmark, was chosen the head, and the war burst forth with fresh violence. The imperial generals, Tilly and Wallenstein, were far superior to their protestant adversaries. Wallenstein, having been created duke of Friedland and chief commander of the imperial army raised by himself, acted with so much vigor, that Christian, threatened with the loss of his own dominions, was forced to purchase peace by renouncing all right to interfere in the affairs of Germany, and abandoning his allies, especially the dukes of Mecklenburg (A. D. 1629). Wallenstein obtained the investitute of Mecklenburg, and claimed henceforth a rank among the princes of the empire.

England had borne little share in this arduous contest. On the death of James (A. D. 1625), his son Charles I. ascended the British throne, and was almost immediately involved in a contest with his parliament, which effectually diverted his attention from foreign affairs. The principal causes of this were the growing love of liberty in the English people; the suspicions of danger to religion from the king's marriage with so bigoted a catholic as the princess Henrietta Maria, of France; the unpopularity of Buckingham, the royal favorite; and the increasing hostility of the puritans to the episcopal form of church government. The troubles and distractions by which France was weakened during the minority and the early part of the reign of Louis XIII. began to disappear when Cardinal Richelieu was placed at the head of the administration. His great talents and singular firmness acquired for his country a new and vigorous influence in the political system of Europe, at the very moment when a counterpoise was most wanting to the overgrown power of the house of Austria.

Richelieu's first operations were directed against the Huguenots, whom he completely subdued and rendered utterly helpless by the capture of Rochelle. Scarcely had the reduction of this important city been effected, when the cardinal commenced his war against Austria by endeavoring to secure the dutchy of Mantua for the duke of Nevers, in opposition to the emperor, the king of Spain, and the duke of Savoy. The war was terminated by the treaty of Chierasio (A. D. 1631), which destroyed the Spanish supremacy in Italy, restored the old influence of France, and gave that power possession of several of the most important fortresses on the frontiers. But far more important was the share which Richelieu had in renewing the war in Germany, and bringing forward a protestant leader, able and willing to cope with the imperial generals.

During the war of the Mantuan succession, the emperor Ferdinand published an edict at Vienna, commanding the protestants to restore all the ecclesiastical benefices of which they had taken possession since the treaty of Passau. Some submitted, others remonstrated; imperial commissioners were sent to decide on the claims of the bishops and monks to restitution; the execution of the decree was intrusted to Wallenstein, who acted with so much rigor that the protestants were inflamed with just rage, and even the catholics joined in demanding justice against him from the emperor. So great was the clamor, that the emperor was forced to dismiss his general, and confer the command of the imperial army upon Count Tilly. Scarcely had this important step been taken, when Gustavus Adolphus, king of Sweden, secretly urged by some of the discontented protestant princes, published a declaration of war against the emperor, and after having captured the important island of Rugen, landed in Germany (June 24, 1630). An alliance was formed between the king and the leading protestant princes of Pomerania, Brandenburg, and Hesse; Saxony, after some efforts to preserve neutrality, was forced to accede to the league; and Richelieu, who had no small share in forming the original plan, secured for the confederates the active co-operation of France. The early successes of Gustavus would have been more decisive but for the jealousy of the Saxon princes, who prevented his passage through their dominions, and thus hindered him from relieving the city of Magdeburg, hard pressed by Count Tilly and the imperial forces. The unfortunate city was finally taken by assault; the cruel Tilly would show no mercy, thirty thousand of the inhabitants perished by water, fire, and sword; and of this once flourishing city nothing was left standing except the cathedral and about one hundred and fifty fishing huts on the banks of the Elbe.

This atrocious cruelty cemented the alliance between Gustavus and the protestant princes; the elector of Saxony, justly alarmed by the fate of his neighbors, and irritated by the menaces of Tilly, whom his recent success had filled with presumptuous pride, joined the king with all his forces at Wittemburg. A resolution to try the chances of battle was taken; and at Leipsic the imperialists were so decisively overthrown, that if Gustavus had marched immediately to Vienna, that city would probably have fallen. All the members of the evangelical union joined the king of Sweden; the measures of the catholic confederates were disconcerted, and the whole country between the Elbe and the Rhine was occupied by the protestant forces. Early in the following year Count Tilly was killed in disputing with the Swedes the passage of the Lech, and Gustavus overrun Bavaria.

The emperor, in his distress, had recourse to Wallenstein, who was restored to command with unlimited powers. Gustavus attacked the imperialists in their intrenchments at Nuremberg, and was defeated with some loss; but, anxious to retrieve his fame, he sought an early opportunity of bringing his rival to a second engagement. The armies met at Lutzen (Nov. 16, 1632), the confederates attacked the imperialists in their intrenchments, and after a dreadful contest, that lasted nine hours, put them completely to the rout. But the victors had little cause to triumph; Gustavus fell, mortally wounded, in the middle of the engagement, and died before the fortune of the day was decided. His death produced great changes in the political state of Europe. The elector-palatine, believing all his hopes of restoration blighted, died of a broken heart; the protestant confederates, deprived of a head, were divided into factions; while the Swedes, overwhelmed with sorrow, saw the throne of their heroic prince occupied by a girl only seven years old. But the council of regency, appointed to protect the minority of the young queen Christina, intrusted the management of the German war to the Chanceller Oxenstiern, a statesman of the highest order; under his guidance, the protestant alliance again assumed a formidable aspect, and hostilities were prosecuted with vigor and success by the duke of Saxe Weimar and the generals Banier and Horn. An unexpected event added to their confidence; Ferdinand became jealous of Wallenstein, and suspected him, not without cause, of aiming at sovereign power. The emperor was too timid to bring this powerful leader to a legal trial; he, therefore, had recourse to the dishonorable expedient of assassination (A. D. 1634), and Wallenstein was murdered in his own camp.

The confederates did not gain all the advantages they anticipated from the fall of the duke of Friedland; the emperor's eldest son, the king of Hungary, having succeeded to the command, gained several advantages, and twenty thousand Spaniards arrived in Germany to the aid of the imperialists, under the duke of Feria. The protestant leaders, anxious to stop the progress of the king of Hungary, attacked him at Nordlingen. The battle was one of the most obstinate recorded in history; it ended in the complete rout of the confederates, notwithstanding the most vigorous efforts of the Swedes. The emperor improved his victory by negotiation; he concluded a treaty with all the protestant princes, except the landgrave of Hesse, at Prague (A. D. 1635), and thus the whole weight of the war was thrown on the French and the Swedes.

Section X.—*Administration of the Cardinals Richelieu and Mazarine.*

Richelieu ruled France with a rod of iron; hated alike by the nobility and the people, he continued to hold the reins of government, and all conspiracies formed against him ended in the ruin of the contrivers. Jealousy of Gustavus prevented him from cordially co-operating with that prince, and Oxenstiern afterward was unwilling to give the French any influence in Germany. But the battle of Nordlingen rendered a change of policy necessary, and the Swedish chancellor offered to put the French in immediate possession of Philipsburg and the province of Alsace, on condition of their taking an active share in the war against the emperor. Richelieu readily entered into a treaty so favorable to his projects for humbling the house of Austria. He concluded treaties with the Dutch republic and the duke of Savoy, proclaimed war against Spain, and in a very short space equipped five armies to act at once in Italy, Germany, and the Netherlands. The balance now turned against the imperialists; the duke of Saxe Weimar proved a worthy successor to the king of Sweden, and Banier restored the lustre of the Swedish arms by the victory he gained over the elector of Saxony at Wislock. The death of the emperor Ferdinand II. (A. D. 1637), and the accession of his son Ferdinand III., made little alteration in the state of the war; the victorious leaders of the confederates invaded the hereditary dominions of Austria, but in the midst of their triumphant career, the duke of Saxe Weimar fell a victim to poison (A. D. 1639), said to have been administered by an emissary of Richelieu, for the cardinal had reason o fear that the prince's patriotism would prove a serious obstacle to the aggrandizement of the French power.

The war was still continued, but though the imperialists were generally worsted, disunion crept into the councils of the confederates, and prevented them from improving their advantages. Banier's death might have proved their ruin, had he not been succeeded by Torstenson, a general of scarcely inferior abilities. While the Swedes, under their new leader, maintained their former eminence in Germany, and gained a complete victory at Leipsic, almost on the very ground where Gustavus had triumphed, the French were equally successful in Spain, having reduced Colioure and Perpignan.* The death of Richelieu, and his master, Louis XIII., the accession of the infant Louis XIV. (A. D. 1643), and some changes in Germany, for a time inclined the Swedes to peace; but when it was found that Cardinal Mazarine had resolved to pursue Richelieu's plans, and that France possessed such generals as Condé and Turenne, the hopes of the confederates were once more revived, and the Swedes had even the courage to provoke a fresh enemy by invading the dominions of Denmark. After several vicissitudes, the triumph of the confederates was so decided, that the emperor found it necessary to solicit terms of peace. After long and tedious negotiations, which varied according to the vicissitudes of the war, the celebrated peace of Westphalia was signed at Munster (A. D. 1648), and became a fundamental law of the empire.

While the protestant cause was thus triumphant in Germany, England was convulsed by civil war. The failure of the expedition to relieve Rochelle, and the complete overthrow of the Huguenots in France, had caused great discontent in England, and embittered the dispute between the king and his parliament respecting the extent of the royal prerogative. The Petition of Right, extorted from Charles I., might have laid the foundation of a constitutional monarchy, had the king adhered strictly to its spirit; but he continued to levy taxes by his own authority, and when the remonstrances of the commons became too energetic, he dissolved the parliament (A. D. 1629), with a fixed resolution never to call another until he should see signs of a more compliant disposition in the nation. Religious disputes aggravated these political animosities. When the ecclesiastical jurisdiction was wrested from the see of Rome, the people of England had submitted to a jurisdiction no less arbitrary in the prince, and the sovereign obtained absolute power in all affairs relative to the government of the church and the consciences of the people. An ecclesiastical tribunal, called the high commission court, was established under the immediate direction of the crown. Its judges enforced conformity with established ceremonies by fines and imprisonment. There were many who thought the English reformation incomplete; they deemed that the church had not been sufficiently purified from Romish errors, and they wished for the simpler forms of worship that had been estabished in Scotland and Germany. Many of the puritans, as these reformers were called, had more justifiable reason for discontent; they regarded the ecclesiastical sovereign-

* Richelieu had just detected and punished a conspiracy, when Perpignan was taken. He sent intelligence of both events to Louis XIII., in the following laconic letter: "Sir, your enemies are dead, and your troops in possession of Perpignan."

ty of the monarch as dangerous to general liberty, and they were anxious to transfer a portion of the authority to parliament. About this time, a sect, called from their founder, the Arminians, had rejected the strict doctrines of predestination and absolute decrees, maintained by the first reformers. Their number, in England, was yet small, but by the favor of James and Charles, some who held the Arminian doctrines were advanced to the highest dignities of the church, and formed the majority of the bench of bishops. They, in return for this countenance, inculcated the doctrines of passive obedience and unconditional submission to princes. Hence Arminianism was regarded by the patriots in the house of commons with as much horror as popery, and the preacher of either doctrine was voted a capital enemy to the state.

The success of Charles I. in his struggle with the commons depended very much upon the character of his ministers. The chief of these were Wentworth, earl of Strafford, a deserter from the popular party, and Laud, archbishop of Canterbury; they were both men of arbitrary principles, and Strafford, especially, was very unscrupulous in the use of means to gain a favorite end. Without any regard to the petition of right, which was directly opposed to such measures, tonnage, poundage, and other taxes were levied; the penal laws against catholics were suspended on the payment of stipulated sums; and such extensive jurisdiction given to those arbitrary tribunals, the courts of star-chamber and high commission, that the ordinary constitutional administration of justice almost entirely ceased.

While these innovations spread secret discontent throughout England, Laud's efforts to model the Scottish church after the English form produced a dangerous outbreak in Scotland. The attempt to introduce a liturgy, similar to that used in the English church, provoked a formidable riot; and finally, "The solemn League and Covenant," a bond of confederation for the preservation of the national religion, was signed by a vast number of the higher and lower classes (A. D. 1638). Cardinal Richelieu, fearing that the English government might oppose his designs on the Low Countries, and aware that he was disliked by the English queen, Henrietta, secretly encouraged the Scottish covenanters, and supplied their leaders with money, which, in spite of their exaggerated pretensions to patriotism and sanctity, they did not scruple to accept. Armies were levied, but neither party wished to merit the imputation of commencing civil war. A treaty was concluded at Berwick (A. D. 1639), by which Charles displeased his friends, who thought that he made concessions unworthy of a prince, and did not conciliate his opponents, who were resolved to be satisfied with nothing less than his full acceptance of the covenant.

As might have been foreseen, the treaty of Berwick proved to be merely a suspension of arms. Strafford and Laud considered the rebellion of the Scots to be so manifest, that they deemed the people of England could not entertain a doubt on the subject, and that the king would be supported in its suppression by a parliament. Charles adopted the same opinions, and called a parliament, hoping to obtain a sufficient grant for carrying on the war (A. D. 1640); but the house of commons, postponing all consideration of taxes, applied itself directly to the redress of grievances, and an examination of the recent measures of the government. Incensed by this conduct, Charles dissolved the parliament, and attempted to raise money by new and unconstitutional expedients. The Scotch, not waiting to be attacked, crossed the borders, defeated the earl of Northumberland at Newburn, and occupied Newcastle and Durham. The king was unable to cope with them in the field, and he therefore entered into a treaty by which he agreed to provide subsistence for the hostile army, until terms of pacification could be arranged. A new parliament was convoked, and, on the very first day of its meeting, the house of commons manifested its uncomplying disposition, by choosing as its speaker a vehement opponent of the court. A more important and decisive step, was the impeachment of the earl of Strafford and Archbishop Laud on a charge of high treason; after which, the armistice with the Scottish army was prolonged, and the Scots described not as enemies or rebels, but brethren! Strafford's trial soon engrossed public attention; he was condemned to death by an act of attainder, and Charles, after a long delay, was forced to consent to the public execution of his favorite minister. An attempt was next made to exclude the bishops from parliament; a bill for the purpose passed the commons, but was rejected by the lords; as, however, the public excitement continued, the bishops resolved to abstain from further attending their duty in parliament, and twelve of them published a protest, declaring everything null and void that should be determined during their absence. For this ill-advised proceeding they were accused of high treason, and committed to the Tower (A. D 1641).

Charles, dismayed by the hostility of the English, resolved to seek a reconciliation with his Scottish subjects, and for this purpose undertook a journey to Edinburgh. His measures were not well suited to effect his object, and before anything satisfactory could be done, the insurrection of the Irish catholics produced a change in the position of parties most fatal to the royal interests. Few events have been so much misrepresented as the Irish civil war, and in order to view it correctly, we must go back to an earlier period of history.

The Norman settlers in Ireland paid but a nominal allegiance to the English crown, the most powerful of them acted as independent princes, and adopted the customs of the native Irish. The Tudor monarchs were anxious to break the power of this aristocracy, which was as injurious to the national happiness, as it was opposed to the royal power; but unfortunately, they combined this object with the reform of religion, and with a system of confiscation equally impolitic and unjust. The Irish lords took up arms, to defend at once their religion and their power; they were defeated by Elizabeth's generals, and many of them were deprived of their estates, which were shared among English colonists. James I., under the pretence of a meditated rebellion, confiscated the greater part of the province of Ulster, and deprived all the innocent vassals of their property, for the unproved guilt of their chiefs. Property was rendered still more insecure by an inquisition into titles, on the legal pretence that the right to land belongs primarily to the king, and consequently, that every estate ought to be forfeited for which a royal grant could not be produced. The effect of this principle would be, not only to strip all the native Irish of their estates, but also to confiscate the lands belonging to the greater part of the lords descended from the companions of Strongbow and Henry II. When Strafford became lord-lieutenant of Ireland, he began to enforce the system of confiscation with a rigor which exceeded all former precedent. Every legal pretext was employed to expel the Irish from their possessions, and transfer them to strangers; judges were bribed, juries threatened, and witnesses suborned with the most shameless effrontery. The English nation was induced to countenance this injustice by the belief that it would be useful to substitute a more noble and civilized race of men for the barbarous Irish; though, in fact, the new settlers were for the most part rapacious adventurers, or indigent rabble. Religious intolerance was united to political wrongs; catholics were excluded from all public offices and the acquisition of landed property; their churches and chapels were violently closed, their clergy expelled, and their children given to protestant guardians. They applied to the king for protection, and gave a large sum for a charter of graces, which would secure their persons, property, and religion. Charles took the money, but refused the graces; instigated by Strafford, who had devised a plan for rendering his master absolutely despotic in Ireland, as a preparatory step to his becoming supreme in England.

The success of the Scots in securing their national religion, and placing restrictions on the royal power, induced many of the Irish lords to devise a plan for obtaining similar advantages. Accident precipitated an outbreak; the Ulster Irish, who had been expelled from their lands, hastened to attack the settlers that occupied them as intruders, and they sullied their cause by many acts of violence, which were easily exaggerated by persons who had derived much profit, and expected more, from the trade of confiscation. The English house of commons regarded the Irish as a degraded and conquered people; they deemed their efforts acts of treason, not so much against royal power as English supremacy, while the difference of religion embittered this feeling of national pride, and rendered a peaceful termination of the contest hopeless. It was studiously reported that Charles himself had instigated this revolt in order to obtain unlimited power by aid of the catholics; to refute this suspicion, he intrusted the conduct of Irish affairs to the English parliament; and that body, with inconceivable precipitation, resolved that the catholic religion should no longer be tolerated in Ireland; that two millions and a half of acres should be confiscated to pay the expenses of the war; and that no quarter should be given to the insurgents or their adherents. These ordinances led to a civil war, whose history may be told in a few words: the Irish catholics, after having gained possession of nearly the entire kingdom, were broken into parties more opposed to each other than to the common enemy: in the midst of this disunion, Cromwell, with a mere handful of men, conquered them in detail, and gave their estates to his victorious followers. The new settlers were confirmed in their possession after the restoration of Charles II., and the greater part of the ancient Irish landowners were reduced to beggary.

Charles gained little by sacrificing the Irish to the parliament; finding that his concessions only provoked fresh demands, he attempted to arrest five of the leading members for high treason, but the popular in dignation compelled him to abandon the charge, and soon after to quit the capital. Negotiations were tried to avert the horrors of civil war, but the requisitions of the commons, if granted, would have destroyed all royal authority, and Charles, on the 25th of August, 1642, caused the royal standard to be raised at Nottingham. War immediately commenced; it was conducted with spirit, and was at first favorable to the king. The English parliament, alarmed at the progress of Charles, entered into an alliance with the Scottish covenanters, and on the 15th of January 1644, a Scotch auxiliary army, commanded by General Leslie, entered England. Fairfax, the parliamentary leader in the north, united his forces to those of Leslie, and both generals immediately laid siege to York. Prince Rupert, the son of the unfortunate elector-palatine, hasted to the relief of this important city, and effected a junction with the army of the marquis of Newcastle. Fairfax and Leslie retired to Marston Moor, whither they were followed by the royalists, who were urged to this rash proceeding by the fiery Rupert. Fifty thousand British combatants engaged on this occasion in mutual slaughter; the victory was long undecided; but, finally, the skill of Lieutenant-General Cromwell prevailed over the rash valor of Rupert, and the royalists were signally defeated, with the loss of all their baggage and artillery. A second defeat, at Newbury, so weakened the royal cause, that the king must have been forced to immediate submission, but for the divisions that arose among his adversaries.

The presbyterians and the independents had combined against the church of England as their common enemy; but when episcopacy was abolished, the latter saw with great indignation the presbyterian efforts to establish a system of ecclesiastical tyranny, differing from the papal only in form, the power being lodged in the general assembly of the clergy instead of a single head. The presbyterians had the majority in parliament, but the great bulk of the army favored the views of the independents, which were also supported by some of the most active members of the house of commons. A law, called the Self-denying Ordinance, prohibiting members of parliament from holding military commissions, gave the greater part of the army into the hands of the independents, especially as an exception was made in favor of Oliver Cromwell, their principal leader. The battle of Naseby was decided in favor of the parliamentarians, principally by Cromwell's prudence and valor, an event which gave so much strength to his party, that the presbyterian majority in the house of commons feared to accept the king's proposals for an accommodation, contrary to their open professions and secret wishes. Meanwhile Charles, being unable to keep the field, threw himself on the mercy of his Scottish subjects; and having opened negotiations with their leader, through the French ambassador, ventured on the faith of uncertain promises to present himself in their camp. He had the mortification to find himself treated as a prisoner, while all the towns and fortresses that had hitherto supported his cause fell into the hands of the parliament.

The war was at an end, but civil dissensions raged with more fury than ever. The presbyterians and independents were each anxious to gain the king over to their side; and the former, by a treaty with the Scots, gained possession of his person. Scarcely had they acquired this advantage, when the discontent of the army threatened them with unexpected danger; Cromwell encouraged the soldiers to resist the orders of the parliament, and by a bold measure gave fresh confidence to his party. Cornet Joyce, acting under his orders, removed the king from Holmby house, and brought him to the army. Cromwell and his friends made such a judicious use of the advantage thus obtained, that the presbyterian party soon lost all their influence. The behavior of Charles at this crisis was very injudicious; he negotiated with both parties, and, by his obvious insincerity, displeased all. Finally, he attempted to escape; but seeking shelter in the isle of Wight, he was seized by its governor, Hammond, and from that moment Cromwell became the master of his fate. Another opportunity of escaping from the perils that surrounded him was offered to the king; the Scotch took up arms in his favor, but they were routed by Cromwell with great slaughter, and all hopes from their assistance destroyed. But the parliament having reason to dread Cromwell's ambition, opened negotiations with the king on receiving the news of this victory, and the wisest of the royal counsellors entreated their master to seize this opportunity of concluding a treaty. Unfortunately he hesitated and delayed the arrangements for more than three months, until the army once more took possession of his person, and conveyed him to Hurst. The two houses, indeed, voted that the royal concessions were sufficient grounds for settling the peace of the kingdom; but two days afterward the avenues to the house of commons were beset with soldiers, and all the members supposed favorable to the king forcibly prevented from taking their seats. In this diminished house the resolutions leading to a reconciliation with the king were revoked, and proposals were made for bringing him to a public trial. The final resolution for impeaching the king of high treason before a court of justice constituted for the purpose, was adopted by the house of commons (January 2, 1649): it was at once rejected by the lords; but their opposition was disregarded, and the court regularly constituted. The form of trial was but a solemn mockery; Charles with great spirit refused to acknowledge the jurisdiction of the court, upon which some witnesses were called to prove what everybody knew, that he had appeared at the head of his army, which his judges declared to be treason against the people, and a crime worthy of death. Sentence was pronounced on the 27th of January · and, on the 30th of the same month, the misguided and unhappy Charles was beheaded in front of Whitehall, amid the unaffected sympathy of crowds of spectators.

The death of Charles was followed by the usurpation of Cromwell, and Great Britain was subjected to a despotism more galling and severe than that of any monarch who ever swayed its sceptre.

Section XI.—*Formation of the States-system in the Northern Kingdoms of Europe.*

The revolutions in the northern kingdoms during the progress of the Reformation were scarcely less important than those in central Europe. Norway, Sweden, and Denmark, united by the treaty of Calmar, were never blended into a uniform goverment: the Swedish nobles kept their country in continued agitation; without severing the union, they chose administrators of the kingdom whose allegiance to the crown of Denmark was merely nominal. Christian II., a tyrannical prince, resolved to destroy the Swedish independence, he overthrew the administrator at the battle of Bagesund, and had the ceremony of his coronation performed at Stockholm (A. D. 1520). A few days after this solemnity, Christian perfidiously violated the amnesty he had published; and to gratify the vengeance of the archbishop of Upsal, whom the Swedes had deposed, caused ninety-four of the principal nobles to be publicly executed. This massacre was the signal for a revolution · Gustavus Vasa, son of one of the murdered nobles, escaped to the mountains of Dalecarlia, and supported by the hardy peasants of that province, proclaimed the freedom of his country. Victory crowned his efforts, and he finally became king of Sweden (A. D. 1523). Christian II. was deposed by the Danes, and the crown conferred on his uncle Frederic; he wandered about for some years, vainly seeking support, but was finally seized by his subjects, and thrown into a prison, where he ended his days. The Danish monarchs, for nearly half a century, renewed their pretensions to the Swedish throne; but finding that their efforts only exhausted their own resources, they recognised the independence of Sweden by the treaty of Stettin (A. D. 1570).

Denmark thus lost the ascendency which it had long maintained, and it was further injured by a disastrous change in its internal constitution. The aristocracy established a vicious supremacy over the prerogatives of the crown and the rights of the people. The senate, composed entirely of nobles, seized on all the authority of the state; the national assemblies ceased to be convoked; the elections of the kings were confined to the aristocratic order, and the royal power was restricted by capitulations, which the senate prescribed to the kings on their accession to the throne.

It was in the reign of Frederic I., the uncle and successor of the tyrannical Christian, that the principles of the Reformation were first established in Denmark. The king invited several of Luther's disciples to preach the new doctrines in his kingdom; he openly professed them himself, granted liberty of conscience to all his subjects, and sanctioned the marriages of priests throughout his dominions. Christian III. completed the religious revolution; in a general assembly of the states he procured the abrogation of episcopacy, and the suppression of the Romish worship (A. D. 1536). The castles, fortresses, and vast domains of the bishops, were reunited to the crown; and the rest of their revenues applied to the maintenance of protestant ministers, the purposes of general education, and the relief of the poor. From Denmark the revolution extended to Norway; and about the same time this kingdom, having supported the deposed Christian II., was deprived of its independence, and reduced to a Danish province.

Christian IV. was distinguished among the northern sovereigns by the superiority of his talents, and the zeal that he showed in reforming the different branches of the administration. In his reign the Danes first directed their attention to Asiatic trade, and founded an East India company; a commercial establishment was formed at Tranquebar, on the coast of Coromandel, which was ceded to the company by the rajah of Tanjore. Several large manufactories were established, and many cities founded by this wise monarch, who was also a judicious patron of science and literature. He was less successful in his wars against Austria and Sweden, but this was owing rather to the restrictions which the nobles had placed on his power, than to any want of talent.

Sweden, from having been subject to Denmark, rose to be its successful rival, and even menaced its total overthrow. It owed this preponderance to two of the greatest men of the period, Gustavus Vasa and Gustavus Adolphus. After Vasa had liberated his country, he was raised to the throne, and by his wise government justified the choice of the nation. He directed his attention both to the political and religious reformation of the country; instead of the aristocratic senate, he introduced a diet, composed of the different orders of the state, and by his influence with the commons, introduced Lutheranism, though opposed by the bishops and nobles. He also established the hereditary succession of the crown, which was extended to females in the reign of his son Charles IX.

Gustavus Adolphus, the grandson of Vasa, raised Sweden to the summit of its greatness. Involved in wars at his accession (A. D. 1611), he gained signal advantages over the Russians and Poles, which so extended his fame, that he was chosen, as we have seen, to be the leader of the protestant confederacy against the house of Austria. After a glorious career of two years and a half, he fell in the battle of Lutzen: but the victory which the Swedes won after his death was chiefly owing to his skilful arrangements. The war was continued under the minority of Christina, and brought to a successful issue, as was also the war waged at the same time against Denmark. By the peace of Bromsebro (A. D. 1645), Sweden obtained the free navigation of the Sound, and the cession of several important islands in the Baltic.

Prussia, under the electors of Brandenburg, gradually increased in strength and power, especially during the administration of Frederic William, the true founder of the greatness of his house. His abilities were particularly conspicuous in the protestant wars of Germany; and he obtained such an accession of territory by the treaty of Westphalia, that his son Frederic assumed the title of king of Prussia.

The dismemberment of Livonia led to a fierce struggle between the northern powers, each of which sought a portion of the spoil. Russia, which had slowly acquired consistency, obtained a considerable portion, which, however, it was forced to yield to Poland. After having long submitted to the degrading yoke of the Mongols, the grand-dukes of Moscow, strengthened by the union of several small principalities, began to aspire after independence, which was achieved by Iwan III. This able ruler, having refused to pay the customary tribute to the barbarians, was attacked by the khan of the Golden Horde, as the leading sect of the Mongols was denominated. Instead of acting on the defensive, Iwan sent a body of troops into the very centre of the horde, and ruined all their establishments on the Volga. So great were the losses of the Mongols, that the Golden Horde disappeared, and left no traces but a few feeble tribes. Iwan IV. labored to civilize the empire acquired by the valor of his predecessors: he invited artisans from

England and Germany, established a printing-press at Moscow, and raised the standing army of the Strelitzes to curb his turbulent nobles. It was in his reign that Siberia was discovered and annexed to the Russian dominions, but the complete reduction of that country belongs to the reign of his son Fédor (A. D. 1587), who founded the city of Tobolsk.

On the death of Fédor, without any issue (A. D. 1598), Russia was involved in a series of calamitous civil wars, which ended in the elevation of Michael Fedrowetsch to the crown. He found his dominions exhausted by the late commotions, and could only procure peace from Sweden and Poland by the cession of many valuable provinces (A. D. 1634).

During the reigns of the Jagellons, Poland was one of the most flourishing northern powers. The reformation was favored by Sigismond Augustus II., the last of this dynasty; but the want of a middle order of society, which has ever been the cause of Polish misery, prevented evangelical principles from taking deep root in the country, and producing the benefits that had resulted from them in other states. When the male line of the Jagellons became extinct on the death of Sigismond (A. D. 1572), the throne of Poland became elective (without any restriction),* and the right of voting was given to all the nobles, who met in arms to choose a sovereign. These elections were generally marked with violence and bloodshed; but though the nobles were divided among themselves, they readily united to restrict the royal authority; every sovereign, on his accession, was obliged to sign certain capitulations, which greatly limited his rule, and secured the chief powers of the state to the aristocracy. Under its new constitution, Poland was internally weak and miserable, though some of its monarchs still distinguished themselves by foreign conquests, especially Vladislaus IV., who wrested the dutchy of Smolensko from Russia.

Section XII.—*Progress of the Turkish Power in Europe.*

The successors of Mohammed II. on the throne of Constantinople imitated the vigorous policy of that conqueror, and for nearly a century were the terror of Christendom. Bayezíd II. subdued Bessarabia, and acquired some important provinces in Asia. He was forced to resign the throne by his son Selim (A. D. 1510), and was murdered in prison. Selim I., surnamed Gavúz, or the Savage, was obliged to maintain the throne he had so criminally gained, by a series of sanguinary wars with the other members of his family. Having triumphed over these competitors, he turned his arms against the Persians, and gained a complete victory over Ismael Sofí at Tabríz (A. D. 1514). In consequence of this and other successes, Diarbekr and several other provinces beyond the Tigris were annexed to the Turkish empire. The Mameluke sultans of Egypt having assisted the Persians in this war, Selim led an army into Syria, and encountered Sultan Gaurí near Aleppo. After a sanguinary engagement, the Mamelukes were defeated and their leader slain, upon which Aleppo and Damascus submitted to the Turks. This

* See page 486.

success opened the way for invading Egypt: Túmán Bey, who had been elected sultan in place of Gaurí, assembled the remnants of the Mamelukes under the walls of Cairo, and having procured some auxiliary forces from the Arabs, prepared to meet the enemy. Selim advanced steadily, and attacked the hostile camp. The battle was obstinate and bloody, but the superior fire of the Turkish artillery, which was served principally by Christian gunners, decided the fate of the day; and Túmán Bey, after having done everything that could be expected from an able officer and a brave warrior, was driven into Cairo (A. D. 1517). Selim stormed the city; but Túmán, not yet disheartened, fled across the Nile, and by incredible exertions once more collected an army. The Turks pursued him closely, and forced him to a final engagement, in which the Mamelukes were utterly routed, and their gallant sultan taken prisoner. Selim was at first disposed to spare the captive, but his officers, who feared and envied Túmán, persuaded him that such clemency might inspire the Mamelukes with the hope of recovering their dominions, and the unfortunate sultan was hanged at the principal gate of Cairo.

Soleyman, usually surnamed the Magnificent, succeeded his father Selim, and emulous of the fame acquired by the conquest of Egypt, resolved to turn his arms against the princes of Christendom. Hungary, during the reign of Matthew Corvinus, had become a powerful and flourishing kingdom. Inspired by the example of his father, the renowned Hunniades, Corvinus wrested Bosnia from the Turks, and maintained his supremacy over Transylvania, Wallachia, and Moldavia. But during the reigns of his indolent successors, Uladislaus II. and Louis, who were also kings of Bohemia, Hungary was distracted by factions, and ravaged by the Turks. Soleyman took advantage of the minority of Louis, and the weakness of Hungary, to invade the kingdom. He captured, with little difficulty, the important fortress of Belgrade, justly deemed the bulwark of Christian Europe (A. D. 1521). Inspired by his first success, he returned to the attack; having traversed the Danube and the Drave, without meeting any resistance, he encountered the Christians in the field of Mohatz, and gained over them one of the most signal victories that the Turks ever won (A. D. 1526). King Louis, and the principal part of the Hungarian nobility, fell in this fatal battle, the entire country was laid at the mercy of the invaders; but Soleyman, instead of securing a permanent conquest, laid waste the land with fire and sword, and carried myriads of the inhabitants as slaves to Constantinople.

A triumph of even greater importance was gained by the Turks during the Hungarian war. Rhodes, the seat of the heroic knights of St. John, was besieged by Soleyman's vizier. All the arts of assault and defence that had yet been devised by human ingenuity were used in this siege, which lasted more than five months. The assailants and the garrison fought with such fury that it seemed a contest rather for the empire of the world than the possession of a single city. The sultan himself came in person to superintend the operations of his army, while the knights were not only neglected by the Christian powers, but exposed to the open hostilities of the Venetians. They protracted their resistance until every wall and bulwark had crumbled beneath the over whelming fire of the Turkish batteries, when they surrendered on honorable conditions; and on Christmas day (A. D. 1522), Soleyman made his triumphant entry into what had been a city, but was now a shapeless mass of ruins.

On the death of Louis, Ferdinand of Austria, who had married the sister of the unfortunate monarch, claimed the crowns of Hungary and Bohemia. He received quiet possession of the latter kingdom; but the Hungarians chose for their sovereign John Zapolya, prince palatine of Transylvania. Zapolya, finding himself unable to resist the power of Ferdinand, claimed the protection of the Turks. Soleyman marched in person to his aid, and, not satisfied with expelling the Austrians from Hungary, pursued them into their own country, and laid siege to Vienna (A. D. 1529). He failed in this enterprise, and was compelled to retreat after having lost eighty thousand men.

The emperor Charles V., alarmed at the progress of the Turks, tried to form a general confederation of the German princes against them, but found that the troubles occasioned by the progress of the Reformation would prevent any cordial union. He resolved, however, to check the growth of their naval power in the Mediterrenean, where Khair-ed-dín,* or Barbarossa, a pirate whom Soleyman had taken into his service, captured Tunis and Algiers, and was collecting a formidable naval force. Charles took advantage of Soleyman's being engaged in conquering the pachalic of Bagdad from the Persians, to invade Africa, where he made himself master of Tunis. Soleyman, returning victorious from Asia, was so enraged at his losses in Africa, that he resolved to attempt the conquest of Italy. The imprudence of a Venetian captain turned the wrath of the sultan upon the republic of Venice; he attacked two Turkish galleys in the Adriatic, for some mistake about their signals, and satisfaction being refused, Soleyman proclaimed war.

But while thus engaged in the west, Soleyman did not neglect the enlargement of his eastern dominions. His generals conquered the whole of Arabia, and his admirals issuing from the Red sea, attacked but without success, the Portuguese dominions in India. In the meantime the Venetian senate entered into an alliance with the emperor Charles V., and the pope, Paul III.; their united navies were placed under the command of the celebrated Doria, but his success was far from according with the expectations that the allies had formed. The war, however, led to no decisive result; it was suspended by occasional truces, during which Soleyman took the opportunity of enlarging his Asiatic dominions at the expense of Persia.

The knights of St. John, expelled from Rhodes, obtained a settlement in the island of Malta; they directed their attention to naval affairs, and inflicted severe damages on the Turks by sea. Soleyman, roused by the complaints of his subjects, resolved that Malta should share the fate of Rhodes, and collected all his forces for the siege (A. D. 1565). The knights maintained their character for obstinate valor with more success than on the former occasion: after a sanguinary contest for five months, the Turks were forced to retire, with the loss of twenty-four thousand men and all their artillery. Soleyman prepared to take revenge by com-

* Khair-ed-dín signifies "the goodness of the faith." This terror of the Christians was named Barbarossa, on account of his "red beard."

pleting the conquest of Hungary; but while besieging Sigeth, he fell a victim to disease, produced by old age and fatigue (A. D. 1566), after having raised the Turkish empire to the highest pitch of its greatness.

Selim II., soon after his accession, made peace with the Germans and Persians, but renewed war with the Venetians, from whom he took the important island of Cyprus (A. D. 1571). But while the Turkish army was thus engaged, their fleet was utterly destroyed in the battle of Lepanto, by the allied Venetian, imperial, and papal navy. The allies neglected to improve their victory, and Selim soon repaired his losses. But this sultan sank into the usual indolence of oriental sovereigns, his successors followed his example, and the Ottoman power began rapidly to decline. The Austrian rulers became convinced of the impolicy of harsh measures, and conceded to the Hungarians full security for their political and religious liberties, at the diet of Presburg. Hungary was henceforth united to Austria, and the last war, directly resulting from he Reformation, happily terminated.

CHAPTER VII.

THE AUGUSTAN AGES OF ENGLAND AND FRANCE.

Section I.—*State of the Continental Kingdoms after the Peace of Westphalia.*

Though the treaty of Westphalia restored tranquillity to northern Europe and Germany, France and Spain continued the war in which they had originally but a secondary share, with all the obstinacy of principals. At the same time, France was distracted by civil broils less fatal than those of England, but scarcely less sanguinary. The prime mover in these disturbances was the coadjutor-archbishop of Paris, afterward known as the Cardinal de Retz ; he wished to gain the post of prime minister from Cardinal Mazarine, and he induced several princes of the blood, with a large portion of the nobility, to espouse his quarrel. The parliaments of France resembled those of England only in name ; they were colleges of justice, not legislative assemblies, and the members purchased their seats. This was the body with which Retz commenced his operations ; instigated by the ambitious prelate, the parliament of Paris thwarted all the measures of the queen-regent and her minister, until Anne of Austria, irritated by such factious opposition, ordered the president and one of the most violent councillors to be arrested. Her orders were scarcely executed when the populace arose, barricaded the streets, threatened the cardinal and the regent, and procured the release of the prisoners. Alarmed by the repetition of similar outrages, the queen, attended by her children and her minister, retired from Paris to St. Germains, where their distress was so great that they were obliged to pawn the crown jewels to procure the common necessaries of life. These intrigues led to a desultory civil war, which began to assume a serious aspect after the arrest of the ambitious duke of Condé, who had repeatedly insulted the queen and the cardinal ; the factious took up arms in all the provinces, and the duke of Orleans, uncle to the young king, placed himself at the head of the malcontents (A. D. 1650). Mazarine was unable to resist the confederacy ; he liberated Condé and his associates, in the vain hope of conciliating their favor, but was obliged to fly to Cologne, where he continued to govern the queen-regent as if he had never quitted Paris. By his intrigues, which were now seconded by de Retz, the duke of Bouillon, and his brother Turenne, were detached from the confederates, and by their aid Mazarine was enabled to enter the kingdom at the head of an army, and resume his former authority. Condé, proclaimed a traitor by the parliament of Paris, threw himself upon the protection of Spain, and obtained from that power a body of troops, with which he pursued the court from province to province, and finally entered Paris. Turenne, who commanded the royal forces, brought the young king within sight of his capital; and Louis witnessed a fierce conflict in the suburb of St. Antoine, which terminated in the defeat of his army.

Encouraged by this success, the parliament of Paris proclaimed the duke of Orleans "lieutenant-general of the kingdom," and the prince of Condé, "commander-in-chief of the armies of France." But the danger with which these appointments threatened the monarchy, was averted equally by the rashness of Condé and the prudence of the king. Condé instigated a tumult, in which several citizens lost their lives; Louis conciliated his subjects by sending the cardinal into temporary exile, and was received into his capital with the loudest acclamations. No sooner was the royal authority re-established, than Mazarine was recalled and invested with more than his former power.

During these commotions, the Spaniards had recovered many of the places which they had previously lost to the French, and Louis de Haro, who governed Spain and Philip IV. as absolutely as Mazarine did France and its youthful sovereign, hoped by means of Condé's great military talents to bring the war to a triumphant issue. But the French found a general in Marshal Turenne, who was more than a rival for Condé; he compelled the Spaniards to raise the siege of Arras, and seized all their baggage, artillery, and ammunition (A. D. 1656). He was himself soon after compelled to raise the siege of Valenciennes, but he made a masterly retreat as honorable as a victory, and even took the town of Capelle in the presence of his enemies. Still the fortune of the war was doubtful, when Mazarine, by flattering the passions of the usurper Cromwell, engaged England to take a share in the contest. Dunkirk, the strongest town in Flanders, first engaged the attention of the allies; the English blockaded it by sea; Turenne, with an auxiliary British force united the French army, besieged it by land (A. D. 1656) The Spaniards sent an army to its relief; Turenne did not decline an engagement; the obstinate valor of the English, combined with the impetuosity of the French troops, procured him a decided victory; Dunkirk surrendered in a few days, and was given to the English according to treaty, while France obtained possession of the strongest towns in Flanders.

Peace was now necessary to Spain, and it was also essential to the success of Mazarine's favorite policy; the procuring for the house of Bourbon the eventual succession to the Spanish monarchy, by uniting King Louis to the infanta, Maria Theresa. The preliminaries were adjusted by Mazarine and Louis de Haro, in person, at a conference in the Pyrenees, and France obtained an exten of territory and the prospect of an inheritance, which soon made it formidable to the rest of Europe. About a year after the conclusion of this treaty, Mazarine died (A. D. 1661); and Louis, who had borne the ministerial yoke with secret impatience, took the reins of government into his own hands.

Germany, exhausted by tedious wars, remained undisturbed after the peace of Westphalia until the death of Ferdinand III. (A. D. 1657), when the diet was agitated by fierce debates respecting the choice of uccessor. Recent events had shown how dangerous was the ambition of the house of Austria to the independence of the minor states, and several of the electors wished to have as their head some monarch whose hereditary dominions would not be of sufficient importance to raise him above the control of the Diet. But these considerations were forced to yield to more pressing circumstances; the presence of the Turks in Buda, of the French in Alsace, and of the Swedes in Pomerania, required a powerful sovereign to prevent further encroachments; and Leopold, the son of the late emperor, was unanimously chosen. His first measure was to form an alliance with Poland and Denmark against Sweden, a power which, ever since the victorious career of Gustavus Adolphus, menaced the independence of the neighboring states.

We have already mentioned that the renowned Gustavus was succeeded by his daughter Christina. She was fondly attached to study, and assembled in her court the most distinguished professors of science, literature, and the fine arts. Her favorite pursuits were, however, too antiquated and abstruse for practical life; she was pedantic rather than wise, and her great learning was never applied to a useful end. She consented to the peace of Westphalia, not from any regard for the tranquillity of Europe or her own kingdom, but simply to indulge her passion for study, with which the cares of state interfered. The Swedish senate felt little sympathy in the learned pursuits of their sovereign; they pressed her to marry her cousin, Charles Gustavus, for whom she had been designed in her infancy, but Christina dreaded to give herself a master, and she only nominated this prince her successor. The states renewed their importunity, and Christina offered to resign the crown to her cousin; after some delay, occasioned by reasonable suspicions of her sincerity, she carried her design into execution, and abdicated in favor of Charles Gustavus, who ascended the throne under the title of Charles X. (A. D. 1654). The remainder of Christina's life was disgraceful to her character. Designing to fix her residence at Rome, she renounced Lutheranism, and embraced the catholic faith at Innspruck, not because she deemed it the preferable religion, but because she thought it convenient to conform to the tenets of the people with whom she intended to reside. Her profligate life, her want of any valuable information, and her loss of power, soon rendered her contemptible in Italy; she made two journeys into France, where she was received with much respect, until her infamous conduct excited general abhorrence. In a fit of jealousy, she commanded one of her paramours to be assassinated in the great gallery of Fontainebleau, and almost in her very presence (A. D. 1657). This atrocious violation of the laws of nature and of nations, perpetrated in the midst of a civilized kingdom, and a court that piqued itself on refinement, was allowed to pass without judicial inquiry; but it excited such universal detestation, that Christina was forced to quit France and seek refuge in Italy There the remainder of her life was spent in sensual indulgence and literary conversation, if such a term can be applied to the language of a capricious woman, admiring many things for which she had no taste, and talking about others which she did not understand.

While Christina was thus disgracing her sex and country, Charles

X. indulged the martial spirit of his people by declaring war against Poland. After the death of Sigismond III. (A. D. 1632), his son Ladislaus was elected to the throne, and proved to be a prince of great courage and capacity. He gained several victories over the Russians and the Turks; he forced the Swedes to resign the places which Gustavus Adolphus had seized in Prussia; but unfortunately he combined with his nobles in oppressing the Cossacks, and thus drove those uncivilized tribes to a general revolt. In the midst of this war Ladislaus died (A. D. 1648); he was succeeded by his brother John Casimir, who would gladly have entered into terms with the injured Cossacks, but was forced to continue the war by his turbulent nobles. Alexis, czar of Russia, took advantage of these commotions to capture Smolensko and ravage Lithuania, while Poland itself was invaded by Charles X. The progress of the Swedes was rapid, they obtained two brilliant victories in the field, captured Cracow, and compelled the terrified Casimir to seek refuge in Silesia. But the insulting demeanor of the Swedes, and the cruel massacre perpetrated at the capture of Warsaw, confirmed the Poles in the determined spirit of resistance, of which the burghers of Dantzic set them a noble example; while the chief powers of the north combined to check the dangerous ambition of Sweden. Attacked at once by the czar of Russia, the emperor of Germany, and the king of Denmark, Charles, though deserted by his ally the elector of Brandenburg, did not lose courage. He led an army over the ice to Funen, subdued that and several other Danish islands, and laid siege to Copenhagen. The city was saved by an insincere peace, which proved to be only a suspension of arms; but when Charles renewed his exertions, he was opposed by the republics of Holland and England. Negotiations for peace were commenced under the auspices of these great naval powers; but ere they were brought to a conclusion, Charles died of an epidemic fever (A. D. 1660). The Swedes, deprived of their active and ambitious monarch, were easily brought to resign their pretensions to Poland of the treaty of Oliva; and the general desire of preventing the minority of Charles XI. being disturbed by foreign wars, induced the regency to adjust a pacification with Denmark and the other powers.

SECTION II.—*History of England under the Commonwealth.*

THE civil and religious constitution of England was dissolved by the execution of Charles I.; the great body of the nation was dissatisfied with the result of the civil war, but it was overawed by an army of fifty thousand men, entirely devoted to the service of Cromwell; and the commonwealth parliament, as the inconsiderable remnant of the house of commons was called, found itself in possession of the supreme authority. The state of affairs in Ireland and Scotland soon engaged the attention of the new government, and they were especially interested to maintain the dominion that England claimed over the former country. The revolt of the Irish, like the revolt of the Americans in later days, was regarded as treason against the English people, rather than rebellion against their joint sovereign; the partial successes of the insurgents were viewed as national wrongs, and the use of the phrase "*our* kingdom of Ireland" made every Englishman imagine that he would be robbed of some portion of his hereditary rights, were that island to establish its independence. Cromwell, aware of the great celebrity which might be gained in a war so popular as that undertaken for the recovery of Ireland, successfully intrigued to have himself appointed lord-lieutenant and commander-in-chief of the army.

The state of Ireland could not be more favorable to the purposes of an invader. When Charles I. entered into a treaty with his revolted Irish subjects, he disgusted one party without conciliating the other; for he gave both reason to suspect his sincerity. He appointed the marquis of Ormond lord-lieutenant, a nobleman possessed of many high qualities, but who had imbibed the principles of the unfortunate earl of Strafford, and was bigotedly attached to the support of the royal authority and the episcopal church. Ormond conciliated Inchiquin and some other protestant leaders who had refused to acknowledge the cessation of arms which Charles had granted to the insurgents, but he protracted the negotiations with the catholic confederates until their aid was useless to the royal cause. Alarmed at length by the progress of the parliament, while the confederates were at the same time incensed by the intolerant ordinances of the English commons, he concluded a treaty with the catholic deputies at Kilkenny (A. D. 1646), on the basis of a general pardon and full toleration. The native Irish were dissatisfied with this pacification, which did not restore to them lands of which they deemed themselves unjustly deprived; the bigoted catholics sought the supremacy, not the toleration of their religion, and many of the more moderate entertained suspicions of Ormond's good faith. Under such circumstances they were influenced by Rinuccini, the papal nuncio, to reject the treaty of Kilkenny, and Ormond at once was deprived of all authority. As the king was unable to assist him, he delivered up the fortified towns to an officer of the English parliament, a fatal measure, which rendered the restoration of the royal power impossible.

The Irish soon grew weary of Rinuccini's pride, bigotry, and incapacity; a powerful body of the catholic nobles, headed by the earl of Clanricarde, expelled the nuncio, and invited Ormond to resume the government. The lord-lieutenant returned, and found the royal authority established everywhere except in the towns which he had himself surrendered to the parliament. His first care was to remedy this blunder; he subdued several important garrisons, but he allowed himself to be surprised near Dublin by an inferior force, and was routed with great loss. At this crisis Cromwell landed with an army of enthusiastic soldiers trained to arms, and flushed by recent victories. He besieged Drogheda, took it by storm, and put all the garrison to the sword. The town of Wexford was next assailed, and its defenders similarly butchered; and this cruelty produced such alarm, that thenceforth every town, before which Cromwell presented himself, surrendered at the first summons. The declining season, a failure of provisions, and epidemic disease, soon reduced the invaders to great distress; but they were relieved by a revolution as sudden as it was unexpected. The protestant royalists in Munster, always jealous of their Irish allies, revolted to the parliament at the instigation of the lords Broghill and Inchiquin, and the gates of all the important garrisons in the south of Ireland were opened to Cromwell's sickly troops. The Irish could no longer be brought to pay obedience to a protestant governor, Ormond quitted the country in despair, and the confederates, having no longer any bond of union, were overpowered in detail. Cromwell freed him self from all future opposition, by permitting the Irish officers and soldiers to engage in foreign service. About forty thousand catholics went on this occasion into voluntary exile.

The young king, Charles II., had intended to place himself at the head of the Irish royalists; but when their cause was ruined, he entered into negotiations with the Scottish covenanters, and submitted to terms the most ignominious that ever a people imposed upon its prince. He was forced to publish a proclamation, banishing all malignants, excommunicated persons from his court—that is, the royalists who had perilled their lives and fortunes in the service of his family; to pledge his word that he would take the covenant and support the presbyterian form of government; and promise, that in all civil affairs, he would conform to the direction of the parliament, and submit all ecclesiastical matters to the general assembly of the kirk. Charles did not consent to these disgraceful conditions, until the royal cause in Scotland was rendered desperate by the overthrow of its greatest supporter, the marquis of Montrose. This gallant nobleman, immediately after the execution of Charles I., renewed the war in Scotland, but was made prisoner by the covenanters, and ignominiously put to death as a traitor (A. D. 1650).

Soon after this tragical event, Charles landed in Scotland, and found himself a mere pageant of state in the hands of Argyle and the rigid covenanters, at whose mercy lay his life and liberty. The intolerance of these bigots was not assuaged by the approach of an English army under the command of Cromwell, whom the parliament of England had recalled from the Irish war, so soon as the treaty between Charles and the covenanters was published. Cromwell entered Scotland, but found a formidable competitor in General Leslie, the head of the covenanters. The English were soon reduced to great distress, and their post, at Dunbar, was blockaded by a Scottish army on the heights that overlook tha town. Cromwell was saved by the fanatical and ignorant preachers in the hostile camp; they pretended that a revelation had descended to them, promising a victory over the sectarian host of the English, and forced Leslie, in despite of his urgent remonstrances, to quit his advantageous position. Cromwell took advantage of their delusion; he attacked the Scotch, disordered by their descent from the hills, before they could form their lines, and in a brief space gained a decided victory. Edinburgh and Leith were abandoned to the conquerors, while the remnant of the Scottish army fled to Stirling.

This defeat was by no means disagreeable to Charles; it so far diminished the pride of the bigoted party, that he was permitted to accept the aid of the episcopal royalists, the hereditary friends of his family. Still the king felt very bitterly the bondage in which he was held, and when Cromwell crossed the Forth, he embraced a resolution worthy of his birth and cause, and disconcerting that general by a hasty march, he boldly entered England at the head of fourteen thousand men. But the result disappointed his expectations; the English royalists disliked the Scotch, and detested the covenant; the presbyterians were not prepared to join him, and both were overawed by the militia which the parliament raised in the several counties. At Worcester the king was overtaken by Cromwell with thirty thousand men (Sept. 3, 1651). The place was attacked on all sides: Charles, after giving many proofs of personal valor, saw his cause totally ruined, and sought safety in flight; the Scots were all killed or taken, and the prisoners, eight thousand in number, were sold as slaves to the American plantations. Charles wandered about for forty-five days in various disguises and amid the greatest dangers: more than fifty persons were intrusted with his secret, but they all preserved it faithfully, and he finally escaped to France. In Scotland the presbyterian clergy, formerly all-powerful, found themselves treated with scorn by the English army. Their assembly at Aberdeen was dispersed by a military force, their persons were paraded through the town in insulting mockery, and they were forbidden to assemble in greater numbers than three at a time.

In the meantime, the English republic was engaged in a foreign war. The increase of the naval and commercial power of the Dutch had been viewed with great jealousy by the English nation; but the common interests of religion, and afterward the alliance between the Stuart family and the house of Orange, had prevented a rupture. After the death of William II., prince of Orange, the Dutch abolished the office of stadtholder; and this advance toward a purely republican constitution induced the English parliament to seek a closer alliance with Holland. Their ambassador, however, met but an indifferent reception at the Hague,* and on his return to London it became obvious that the mutual jealousies of the two commonwealths would soon lead to open hostilities.

The English parliament passed the celebrated *Act of Navigation*, which enacted that no goods from Asia, Africa, or America, should be imported into England, except in English vessels; and the prohibition was extended to European commodities not brought by ships belonging to the country of which the goods were the growth or manufacture. This, though apparently general, particularly affected the Dutch, whose commerce consisted chiefly in the carrying trade, their own country producing but few commodities. The war commenced in a dispute on a point of naval etiquette: the English required that all foreign vessels in the British seas should strike their flags to English ships-of-war; Van Tromp, a Dutch admiral, with a fleet of forty sail, met Blake, the commander of the British fleet, in Dover road. Conscious of his superior force, he refused to conform to the degrading ceremony, and answered the demand by a broadside. Though Blake had only fifteen ships, he immediately commenced an engagement, and being reinforced during the battle by eight more, he gained a glorious, though not a very valuable victory. A fierce naval war ensued between the two repub-

* Mr. St. John, the English plenipotentiary, was a stern republican, and a haughty man. He had the presumption to take precedency of the duke of York who was then at the Hague, in a public walk. The prince-palatine, happening to be present, struck off the ambassador's hat, and bade him respect the son and brother of his king. St. John put his hand to his sword, refusing to recognise either the king or the duke of York; but the populace, compassionating fallen royalty, took part with the prince, and forced the stern republican to seek refuge in his lodgings.

lics; it was, on the whole, disadvantageous to the Dutch, though they were commanded by such excellent admirals as De Ruyter and Van Tromp. The death of the latter in an engagement that lasted three days (A. D. 1654), decided the contest, and the Hollanders were forced to beg peace from Oliver Cromwell, who had, in the meantime, dissolved the parliament and usurped the government of England.

When Scotland and Ireland were subdued, the parliament became jealous of Cromwell's power, and resolved to diminish it by disbanding a portion of the army. But the parliament, if such a name could fairly be given to a minority of the house of commons, had lost its sole strength, the confidence of the people, by its obstinacy in retaining the power with which it had been invested by circumstances; it would not dissolve itself, but seemed determined to perpetuate its sovereignty.* An angry remonstrance from the army was rejected, and the soldiers reproved for interfering in public affairs. This brought affairs to a crisis: on the nineteenth of April, 1653, Cromwell turned out the members with military force, locked the doors, put the key in his pocket, and retired to his lodgings at Whitehall. The council of state was similarly dismissed, and so weary were the people of their late rulers, that addresses were sent to Cromwell from almost every part of England, thanking him for his boldness and courage.

It was necessary still to preserve the forms of the constitution, but Cromwell could not venture on an appeal to the people, and allow them their ancient liberty of election, much less a more extended franchise; he therefore adopted a middle course, and by the advice of his officers, nominated one hundred and sixty persons on his own authority, to form a new parliament. This extraordinary body was named the Barebones parliament, from one of its fanatic members, named Praise-God Barebones, who rendered himself conspicuous by his affectation of superior sanctity. Cromwell, finding this convention not so pliant as had been expected, contrived, by his creatures, that a majority should vote for an immediate dissolution, and when about thirty members continued to meet, they were unceremoniously ejected by a file of musqueteers.

A new constitution was formed, by which the legislative power was granted to a lord protector and parliament, and the executive to the protector and a council of state. On the 16th of December, 1653, Cromwell took the oath of fidelity to the new form of government, and was invested with the dignity of lord protector. On the 3d of the following September, the new parliament assembled, but though the strictest regulations consistent with the forms of election had been devised to exclude all but partisans of the government, the protector's authority was menaced on the very first day of debate, and it was resolved, by a majority of five, to refer the examination of the new constitution to a select committee. Cromwell first excluded half the members for refusing to take an oath of allegiance to the protector, and finding that the house, even after this mutilation, continued refractory, he dissolved

* Ludlow asserts, without a shadow of proof, that the parliament was about to dissolve itself, and give the nation a free general election on a reformed plan, when Cromwell interfered. Such a project, indeed, was discussed, but there appear no proofs of its being intended to put it into execution.

the parliament before it had sat the five months required by the constitution, which he had himself framed and sworn to support.

A new parliament was summoned, but notwithstanding the interference of Cromwell and the major-generals that ruled the twelve districts into which England was divided, so many opponents of the government were returned, that Cromwell posted soldiers at the door to exclude those members to whom he had not granted tickets of admission. The parliament, thus modified, proved sufficiently subservient, and on the 26th of March, 1656, it gratified Cromwell's secret ambition, by offering him the title of king. But Fleetwood, the protector's son-in-law, and Desborough, his brother-in-law, disconcerted the entire plan by joining the republicans in the army, and procuring a petition from the officers against royalty, which it would have been dangerous to disregard.* Cromwell was forced to resign his darling object at the moment it seemed within his grasp, and to content himself with the protectorate for life, and the power of nominating his successor.

To divert the attention of the nation from its internal affairs, Cromwell resolved to engage in some foreign war, but was at first undecided whether he should attack France or Spain.† Mazarine's cunning decided the question; he conciliated the protector by banishing the English princes from France, and thus obtained auxiliaries at a critical moment, whose support, as we have already seen, he paid by the cession of Dunkirk. Two formidable fleets were prepared in England; one, under the command of Blake, was sent to cruise in the Mediterranean; the other, intrusted to admirals Penn and Venables, proceeded to the West Indies. To justify hostilities, Cromwell demanded of the Spanish ambassador, that his master should abolish the Inquisition, and open the trade of South America to the English. The ambassador replied, that this was asking for his master's two eyes; indeed, neither demand, under the circumstances, was reasonable. The Spanish Inquisition certainly exercised an unjust tyranny toward protestants, but Cromwell did not treat the Irish catholics with greater mildness; and when England had just given an example of monopoly by passing the navigation act, it showed little regard for consistency to demand free trade from Spain. But both proposals were in accordance with the spirit of the times, and the knowledge of their having been made, brought back to Cromwell a considerable share of the popularity he had forfeited.

Admiral Blake first sailed to Leghorn, and having cast anchor before the town, demanded and obtained satisfaction for the injuries which the duke of Tuscany had done to English commerce. Repairing thence to Algiers, he compelled the dey to restrain his piratical sub-

* "Certain persons," said the petition, "are endeavoring to reduce the nation to the old state of slavery, and urge the protector to assume the royal title, wishing by this means to ruin him. We, therefore, petition the parliament to oppose such intrigues, and to abide by the old cause, for which we are ready to hazard our lives."

† "In order to maintain himself, he, in common with Lambert, and some of the council, wishes for war, and is only revolving whether it were better for him to raise it against France or Spain."—*Report of the French Ambassador, April 20, 1654.*

jects from further depredations on the English. Failing to obtain similar satisfaction at Tunis, he battered its fortifications with his artillery, and burned every ship in the harbor. His fame spread through the entire Mediterranean, and no power dared to provoke his vengeance. Penn and Venables attempted to take Hispaniola, then considered the most valuable island in the West Indies, but failing in this effort, they conquered Jamaica, which has ever since been annexed to the dominions of England. Cromwell, however, was so little satisfied with the conduct of the two admirals, that on their return, he committed them to the Tower. The English, through the entire war, maintained their supremacy by sea; several of the galleons, laden with the precious metals from South America, were taken or destroyed, and an entire fleet burned by the heroic Blake in the bay of Santa Cruz.*

These conquests silenced many opponents for a time, but secret dissatisfaction pervaded the nation, and pamphleteers bitterly assailed the protector, both in verse and prose.† Public attention was roused by the assembling of parliament on the 20th of January, 1658; the house of commons showed its hostility to the government, by admitting the members who had been previously excluded by the privy council, and still more by severely scrutinizing the constitution of the upper house. After a vain effort to conciliate his opponents, Cromwell dissolved the parliament on the 4th of February, and resolved to hazard the perilous experiment of governing alone. But he encountered violent opposition, even in his own family; Elizabeth, his second daughter, keenly reproached him on her dying bed, and the father, who loved her fondly, felt his grief for her loss sharpened by the pangs of conscience. A pamphlet was published, and widely circulated, in which the assassination of the protector was recommended as an act of justice and patriotism; Cromwell read it, and never smiled again. He lived in continual fear, always wore a coat of mail, never slept two successive nights in the same chamber, had guards posted everywhere, and secret avenues contrived, by which he might escape on the least alarm. In such a condition, his death must be considered a happy release; it took place on the 3d of September, 1658, the anniversary of his great victories at Worcester and Dunbar. He was interred with great pomp in Westminster Abbey, but the conduct of the populace evinced anything but sorrow for the loss of their ruler.‡

* April 21st, 1657.—"This was the last and greatest action of this gallant naval commander, who died in his way home. He was, by principle, an inflexible republican, and only his zeal for the interests of his country induced him to serve under the usurper. Though he was above forty-four years of age before he entered into the military service, and fifty-one before he acted in the navy, he raised the maritime glory of England to a greater height than it had ever attained in any former period. Cromwell, fully sensible of his merits, ordered him a pompous funeral at the public expense; and people of all parties, by their tears, bore testimony to his valor, generosity, and public spirit."—*Dr. Johnson's Life of Blake.*

† Satirical poems were published, in one of which is the following passage:—

"A protector! what's that? 'Tis a stately thing
That confesses himself but the ape of a king,
A tragical Cæsar, the actor a clown,
Or a brass farthing, stamped with a kind of a crown."

‡ Evelyn says, "This was the merriest funeral that I ever saw, for no one howled but the dogs, with which the soldiers made sport, amid barbarous noise, parading through the streets, drinking and smoking." Ludlow adds, "The folly

Richard Cromwell had hitherto lived a thoughtless and rather extravagant life, but on his father's death he was acknowledged as protector both at home and abroad, without opposition. He had, however, soon to contend against a powerful republican minority in parliament, while still greater dangers menaced him from the discontent of the army, which was equally dissatisfied with the protector and the parliament.* The officers urged Richard to dissolve the refractory commons, and when he had taken this imprudent step, seized the reins of government into their own hands. Having deliberated on several projects, the military junta came to the resolution of re-assembling the Long parliament. About ninety members were hastily collected, but those who displeased the new rulers were excluded, and the deliberations of the rest were fettered, by what was called "an humble petition and address from the officers to the parliament of the commonwealth of England." Richard, weary of his situation, resigned the protectorate, and the chief power of the state passed to the cabal of officers, at whose head were Lambert, Fleetwood, and Desborough. In the contests that followed between the parliament and the council of officers, the nation generally took no interest. It was a period of complete anarchy; principle was forgotten, every one was guided by his caprice, or by some prospect of private advantage. All true friends of their country were heartily tired of this confusion, and the illusion of the republicans had so completely vanished, that if we except those who wished for a protector, or expected the personal reign of Christ, not more than a few hundreds could be found anxious to restore the commonwealth. In this state of affairs, George Monk, afterward duke of Albemarle, resolved to act a decided part. He had been intrusted by Cromwell with the government of Scotland, and the command of the army: though suspected of a secret attachment to the royal cause,† he continued to hold his place during the protectorates of Oliver and Richard. On the abdication of the latter, he professed the utmost anxiety for a reconciliation between the parliament and the English army; but if that could not be effected, he declared that he would support the former, because the establishment of a commonwealth was dear to his heart. This declaration gave so much confidence to the opponents of the officers, that Fleetwood found it necessary to permit the parliament to assemble; and the Rump parliament, as the house of commons so often mutilated was ignominiously termed, met amid the loudest acclamations of the soldiers, who only two months before had dispersed it by military violence. The house promptly made use of the power which it had

and profusion (of the lying in state) so far provoked the people, that they threw dirt in the night on his escutcheon that was placed over the great gate of Somerset house."

* Richard derided the fanatical pretensions of his father's officers; when a remonstrance was made against his granting commissions to "the ungodly," he replied, "Here is Dick Ingoldsby, who can neither pray nor preach, and yet I will trust him before ye all." "These imprudent, as well as irreligious words," says Ludlow, "so clearly discovering the frame and temper of his mind, were soon published in the army and city of London, to his great prejudice."

† Cromwell once wrote to him, "I have been informed that there is in Scotland, a certain cunning fellow, George Monk by name, who has a scheme for restoring Charles Stuart; endeavor to catch him, and send him hither."

regained; the members and officers of whom it did not approve were removed; Desborough, with some others, fled to Lambert. Fleetwood was overwhelmed with consternation.

On the 1st of January, 1660, Monk, at the head of six thousand men, commenced his march toward London; he was received everywhere with the greatest enthusiasm; in all the towns on his road the people rang the bells, lighted bonfires, and declared their ardent wish for a free parliament. Lambert's army melted away as he advanced; but Fleetwood's soldiers excited so much alarm, that the speaker wrote to Monk to hasten his march. On the 6th of February he appeared in parliament, and first excited some suspicions of his real designs by refusing to take the oath of abjuration against the Stuarts. The parliament tried to embroil him with the citizens of London, by sending him to arrest some members of the common council for resolving that no taxes should be paid until the parliament was filled. Monk performed this disagreeable duty; but immediately after reconciled himself to the city, and sent a letter to the speaker, demanding a dissolution of parliament and a new election. While this letter was fiercely debated, Monk took the decisive step of introducing the old excluded members, by which he gained a triumphant majority.

On the 17th of March the Long parliament concluded its sittings, to the great joy of the nation, and a new house of commons met on the 25th of April. In the interval, Lambert made a desperate effort to place himself at the head of a new army, but by Monk's promptitude and vigor he was taken prisoner and sent to the Tower.

When the new parliament, consisting both of upper and lower house, met, it was manifest that the royalists had such a preponderance that the only question remaining to be decided was, whether Charles II. should be restored with or without conditions. The latter course was unfortunately chosen, perhaps because it would have been impossible to frame terms, the discussion of which would not have roused the slumbering feuds of hostile parties.

On the 29th of May, the day on which he completed his thirtieth year, Charles triumphantly entered London. He was accompanied by the members of parliament, the clergy, the civic authorities, and about twenty thousand persons on foot or horseback. The streets were strewed with flowers, the houses decorated with tapestry, the bells rung in every church, the air resounded with acclamations. The monarch, so recently a hopeless exile, might well ask, as he witnessed the tumult of universal joy, "Where then are my enemies?"

SECTION III.—*History of England, from the Restoration to the Revolution; and Rise of the Power of Louis XIV.*

FEW monarchs ever had such an opportunity of rendering himself popular, and his subjects happy, as Charles II.; there is scarcely one who failed more lamentably. His first measures promised well; a few of the regicides and their adherents were indeed excepted from the act of indemnity, and executed; but pardon was granted to the chief parliamentary leaders, and many of them received into favor. Ecclesiastical affairs, however, began to disturb the harmony of the nation, when a new parliament was assembled, in which the episcopal and royalist party had a triumphant majority. An act was passed, requiring that every clergymen should possess episcopal ordination, declare his assent to everything contained in the book of common prayer, take the oath of canonical obedience, abjure the solemn league and covenant, and the right of taking up arms against the king under any pretence whatever. About two thousand of the clergy rejected these conditions, and resigned their benefices, rather than do violence to their religious opinions. The ejected clergymen were persecuted with unwise rigor; severe laws were enacted against conventicles, and a non-conformist minister was prohibited from coming within five miles of a corporation.

The marriage of the king to Catherine of Portugal, when his subjects hoped that he would make a protestant princess his queen, and the sale of Dunkirk to the French monarch, tended still further to diminish the royal popularity; and a war, equally unjust and impolitic, undertaken against the Dutch, completed the public dissatisfaction. Hostilities were commenced without a formal declaration of war; the English seized several of the Dutch colonies in Africa and America, especially the province of Nova Belgia, which Charles, in honor of his brother, named the state of New York. Holland was at this time ruled by the Louvestein, or violent republican party; its head, the celebrated John de Witt, who, with the title of pensionary, enjoyed almost dictatorial power, feared that Charles might make some effort to restore William III., prince of Orange, to the office of stadtholder, which his ancestors had enjoyed; and to avert this danger, entered into close alliance with France. The pensionary found, however, that he must rely upon his own resources; he fitted out a powerful fleet; the English exerted themselves with equal diligence, and a furious engagement took place upon the coast of Holland (A. D. 1665). Victory declared in favor of the English; more than thirty of the enemy's ships were taken or destroyed, and the whole would probably have fallen had not the pursuit been stopped by the oversight or cowardice of the duke of York, who had been created lord high-admiral of England by his brother.

The joy occasioned by this victory was diminished by the ravages of the great plague, which swept away seventy thousand citizens of London in the course of a year. De Witt, in the meantime, exerted himself to restore the naval power of the Dutch; he formed an alliance with the king of Denmark, procured aid from France, and soon sent out a more powerful fleet than that which had been defeated. But the English still maintained their wonted superiority; and the Dutch, disheartened by repeated defeats, began to murmur against the government of the grand pensionary. Scarcely had the plague ceased, when London was subjected to a second calamity; a dreadful fire, which raged for four days, destroyed four hundred streets and lanes, including thirteen thousand houses; but it is remarkable that not a single life was lost by the conflagration. Great discontents were excited by the severity with which the non-conformists were treated in England and Scotland; about two thousand of the discontented, in the western counties of Scotland, had recourse to arms, and renewed the covenant but they were overpowered by the royal forces, and their insurrectior punished with remorseless cruelty. One of the first stipulations made with Charles on his accession was, that he should not disturb the grants which Cromwell had given to his followers in Ireland. But as many, if not most, of these estates had been forfeited for the attachment of the proprietors to the royal cause, it was necessary that some compensation should be made to the sufferers. After a long struggle, the best arrangement that was perhaps possible, under the circumstances, was effected by the act of settlement; and though many of those who had been dispossessed complained of injustice, the island was restored to tranquillity. It was fast recovering its prosperity, when the unwise jealousy of the English parliament produced considerable distress, by prohibiting the importation of Irish cattle.* While these circumstances embarrassed the British government, the pensionary, De Witt, sent out a new fleet, which destroyed several vessels at the mouth of the Thames, reduced Sheerness, insulted Portsmouth and Plymouth, and for several week rode triumphant in the channel (A. D. 1667). The conclusion of a peace at Breda dissipated the alarm, but at the same time increased the discontent, of the English nation; it was felt that the prodigality of the king had exhausted the treasury and left the kingdom exposed to insult and disgrace.

The ambitious projects of Louis XIV. began now to excite general alarm; his personal qualities won him the affections of his people; the splendor of his court dazzled the nobility, and changed the factious lords of France into a body of the most subservient courtiers that had ever been seen in modern Europe. On the death of Philip IV. of Spain, Louis claimed the Spanish Netherlands in right of his wife, the daughter of Philip by his first marriage, asserting that females could inherit according to the custom of Brabant, and that his queen should have precedence of her infant brother, the offspring of a second marriage. Anna Maria of Austria, queen-regent of Spain, was a weak woman, entirely governed by her confessor, a German jesuit, named Nithard, who was more anxious to check the growth of heresy than to protect the monarchy.† Louis entered Flanders at the head of a powerful army, and found the Spaniards almost wholly unprepared for resistance. The principal towns surrendered immediately; Lisle, though a place of considerable strength, capitulated after a siege of nine days, and Louis secured his conquests by intrusting the repair of their fortifications to the celebrated Vauban, and garrisoning them with his best troops. The Dutch were alarmed at the prospect of having their frontiers exposed to such a powerful neighbor; they received succor from an

* The discussion of this act, in the house of lords, gave rise to some singular debates. It was secretly opposed by the king, who felt its obvious impolicy; it was urged forward by the eccentric duke of Buckingham, who hoped to force himself into power by means of the house of commons. The commons declared the importation of Irish cattle "a nuisance." The lords rejected a term so revolting to common sense, and substituted "a grievance." The duke of Buckingham insisted on retaining the obnoxious phrase; another noble lord moved that the importation of Irish cattle should be deemed "a felony," or a "præmunire:" a third, with more wit and as much reason, proposed that it should be accounted "adultery."

† His arrogance and ignorance were displayed in his reply to a nobleman who had addressed him in a tone of disrespect. "You ought," said he, "to revere the man who has every day your God in his hands and your queen at his feet."

unexcepted quarter. Charles II., either jealous of Louis, or eager to acquire popularity, concluded a defensive alliance between England and Holland (A. D. 1668); and Sweden soon after concurred in the treaty. Louis found it necessary to stop short in his career; he made peace with Spain, retaining a great portion of his conquests, which, however, were not sufficient to console him for the brilliant prospects he was compelled to resign. He had to endure another mortification; the Turks one more became formidable, under the administration of the vizier Kuproeli, and compelled the German emperor to conclude peace on terms highly favorable to their interests; and they wrested the important island of Candia from the Venetians, in spite of the efforts made by the French monarch to save the place.

Louis saw that his designs on the Netherlands, and his revenge against Holland, could not be accomplished without the active participation of England. Knowing the profligate habits of Charles, whose court was a scene of extravagance and dissipation, he concluded a secret treaty with that monarch, in which it was agreed that Charles should receive a large pension from Louis, in return for which he should co-operate in the conquest of the Netherlands, propagate the catholic faith in his dominions, and publicly announce his conversion to that religion. France and England commenced the war by atrociously outraging the laws of nations; Louis, without the shadow of a pretext, seized the dutchy of Lorraine; Charles attempted the capture of a rich Dutch fleet, before he had announced his dissatisfaction with the recent treaty. The Dutch were wholly unable to resist this storm; at sea they maintained their equality, but the armies of France bore down all opposition; Louis crossed the Rhine, advanced to Utrecht, and had he not delayed there, might have conquered Amsterdam. The Dutch populace vented their rage on the unfortunate pensionary, to whom they unjustly attributed all their calamities. John de Witt and his brother Cornelius were arrested, but ere they could be brought to trial, a furious mob burst into their prison and tore them to pieces. William III., prince of Orange, was immediately chosen stadtholder; his exhortations revived the sinking spirits of the Dutch; they resolved, that rather than submit to disgraceful terms, they would abandon their country, seek their settlements in the East Indies, and re-establish their republic in southern Asia.* Louis soon found the results of this determined spirit; the emperor, thoroughly alarmed, sided with the Dutch, and many of the northern German states followed his example. Indecisive engagements were fought at sea; but the conquest of Cologne by the Dutch and Germans, intercepted the communication between France and the United Provinces, in consequence of which Louis was compelled to withdraw his forces and abandon his conquests. A more important change was the secession of England; Charles, distressed for want of money, loaded with debt, and rendered anxious by the progress of public discontent, concluded peace with Holland on very equitable conditions (A. D. 1674). He then offered his mediation to the contending powers.

* Several efforts were made to corrupt the prince of Orange, but he sternly rejected them. When told that the ruin of his country was inevitable, he replied, "There is one way by which I can be certain not to see the ruin of my country; and that is, to die disputing the last ditch."

Louis surprised all Europe by the magnitude of his efforts, but they did not produce any corresponding result; and the desolation of the Palatinate by Marshal Turenne excited such general indignation, that Louis bribed Charles to dissolve the parliament, lest it should force its sovereign to declare war against France. The war was maintained with great fury during the ensuing campaigns; it was on the whole favorable to the French, but the rapid progress of Louis, in the year 1677, excited so much alarm, that the English parliament addressed the king to conclude an offensive and defensive alliance with Holland. Charles, however, had sold his neutrality, and would not abandon his pension to promote either the honor or advantage of his kingdom; but he tried to conciliate the nation by giving his niece, the daughter of the duke of York, in marriage to the prince of Orange. Louis continued his victorious career uninterrupted by England, until the Dutch sought peace on any terms, and a treaty was concluded at Nimeguen (A. D. 1678), by which France acquired an increase of power dangerous to all the neighboring states.

The jealousy of the English nation at the exaltation of a rival, long regarded as their natural enemy, the feeling that the national honor had been sacrificed, and the fear of the design of the court to establish the Romish religion and arbitrary power, spread a deep gloom over England, and disposed the people to suspicions that led them to become the dupes of the vilest impostors. Just as the account of the cruelties practised on the covenanters in Scotland excited most alarm and indignation, the three kingdoms were roused to sudden phrensy by the announcement of a popish plot. A wicked impostor, named Titus Oates, framed a tale of a conspiracy by the jesuits for the subversion of the protestant religion and the murder of the king; his narrative was improbable, confused, and contradictory, but it suited the temper of the nation, and it was favorable to the ambition of some designing men, anxious to obtain power at any hazard. Before censuring too severely the credulity of the nation, we must remember that a plot for the re-establishment of the Romish religion really existed, but it was formed by the king, not against him; many catholics, aware of the king's secret attachment to their religion, and encouraged by the duke of York's open profession of it, indulged hopes of the speedy reconciliation of the British kingdoms to the holy see, and several enthusiastic phrases in their letters were capable of being distorted into confirmation of a plan formed to accelerate such a consummation.* The inexplicable murder of Sir Edmondbury Godfrey, an active magistrate who had taken Oates's depositions, completed the delusion: to deny the reality of the plot was now to be reputed an accomplice; even to doubt of it was criminal. Several catholics were brought to trial; the evidence against them was a tissue of palpable falsehoods, but, in the phrensy of the moment, every absurdity received credence; they were condemned and executed. The parliament at the same time passed a law excluding from both houses all who would not swear that "the sacrifice of the

* This is especially the case with the letters of the first victim to the national delusion, Edward Coleman, secretary to the duke of York. Dryden has well described the plot in a single line:—

"Some truth there was, but dashed and brewed with lies"

mass was damnable and idolatrous," and it was with great difficulty that an exception was made in favor of the king's brother, the duke of York. The covenanters in Scotland were driven to such desperation by the severities of the royal government, that they murdered Archbishop Sharpe, and broke out into open rebellion. Their revolt was suppressed, and those who had shared in it, or who were suspected of favoring the views of the covenanters, were punished with remorseless cruelty. It deserves to be remarked that, during this turbulent period, Ireland, to the great discredit of the popish plot, continued perfectly tranquil. Still its name was dragged into the controversy, and it lent a title to a party. The supporters of the court were named tories, from the Irish robbers, who, under that name, harassed the Cromwellian settlers; the leaders of the opposition were denominated whigs, the appellation of the fiercest of the Scottish covenanters (A. D. 1681). A bill to exclude the duke of York from the succession passed the commons, but was rejected by the lords; Charles seized the moment when the violence of his adversaries disgusted the sound part of the nation, to dissolve the parliament, and to summon a new one to assemble at Oxford. This second parliament proving refractory, it was suddenly dissolved, and a declaration vindicating the king's proceedings was ordered to be read in all churches and chapels.

Charles won the support of the clergy by vigorously enforcing the act of uniformity and persecuting sectaries, and at the same time chose some of the most pliant lawyers to be judges. By these means the doctrines of passive obedience and non-resistance were revived, and the bench and the pulpit seemed to contend with each other which should show most zeal for the unlimited power of the crown. He next assailed his opponents with their own weapons; the spies, the informers, and false witnesses, who had been employed by the popular party to establish the reality of the popish plot, were now enlisted against their former patrons, and gave their perjured support to one party as freely as they had done to another. The spirit of independence still reigned in the hearts of the citizens of London, but, on the most flimsy legal pretexts, the capital was deprived of its charter, and the power of the corporation virtually transferred to the king. The popular leaders, not disheartened, formed a plan of insurrection; they were betrayed by one of their party: Lord Howard, who had been a leader, became a witness against his associates; several of them were tried, condemned, and executed; but the victims whose fate excited the most sympathy were the popular Lord Russell and the virtuous Algernon Sydney. The duke of York was now placed at the head of the royal councils, but Charles soon became weary of his brother's violence and bigotry; he is even said to have meditated a change in the government, and the adoption of popular measures, when he died suddenly (A. D. 1685), not without strong suspicions of poison. It was supposed that some of the violent catholics attached to the duke of York perpetrated the crime without that prince's knowledge or participation.

While England was thus convulsed at home, its foreign interests were wholly neglected by its profligate sovereign, who continued to be the pensioner of the French king. Louis XIV. thus had full scope to gratify his ambition; he continually enlarged his frontiers on the most frivolous pretences, while Spain and Holland were too weak, and the Germanic empire too much harassed by other enemies, to check his progress. The emperor Leopold, by flagrantly violating the privileges of his Hungarian subjects, provoked a formidable revolt; it was headed by Count Tekeli, a leader possessing great courage and resolution, and he called the Turks to the assistance of his countrymen. While these allies were ravaging Silesia, the sultan Mohammed IV. was preparing one of the most formidable armies that the Ottoman empire had ever sent against Christendom. Leopold, convinced that his own resources were not equal to the crisis, entered into close alliance with the celebrated John Sobieski, who, in the year 1674, had been raised to the throne of Poland.

Before the Polish levies could be completed, the Turkish army, commanded by the grand vizier, Kara Mustapha, entered Austria; the duke of Lorraine, who commanded the imperialists, was unable to resist the progress of the invaders; they advanced rapidly, and at length laid siege to Vienna. During several weeks the city was vigorously defended, but, at length, its fortifications crumbled under the heavy fire of the Turkish artillery; the suburbs were destroyed, and the final assault was expected every moment (A. D. 1683). The garrison, reduced to despair, was about to resign all thoughts of resistance, when the banners of John Sobieski, approaching to their relief, were seen on the hill of Schellenberg. Kara Mustapha led the main body of his forces to meet the Poles, while a body of twenty thousand men attempted to storm the city. But the courage of the garrison was now revived, and the confidence of their enemies abated; the assailants were repelled; a panic seized the Turks; they broke at the first charge of the Polish cavalry, and fled in such confusion, that they abandoned their artillery, baggage, and treasures. Even the consecrated banner of Mohammed became the prize of the victors, and was sent as a trophy to the pope. Leopold, in consequence of this decided triumph, recovered possession of Hungary, but his ingratitude to his deliverers was as signal as their merits.

Louis XIV. had raised the siege of Luxemburg when he heard of the advance of the Turks, declaring that he would not attack a Christian prince while Christendom itself was endangered by the invasion of the infidels. No sooner, however, had Sobieski's valor crushed the Mohammedans, than he renewed his aggressions. Spain was thus provoked into a war which it had not strength to support, and a hasty peace confirmed Louis in his conquests. His naval power was steadily increased at the same time; he humbled the Algerines, compelled the republic of Genoa to submit to the most degrading humiliations, and did not even spare the pope. But while his ambition was provoking the resentment of Europe, he weakened his kingdom by a display of ferocious bigotry, at the moment when all its strength was required to resist justly-provoked hostility. The religious toleration of the Huguenots had been secured by the edict of Nantes, which was designed to be perpetual; Louis, after the death of his wisest minister, the virtuous Colbert, revoked this edict, and attempted to impose his religion on his subjects by the sword. He began by issuing an edict, authorizing Huguenot children, above seven years of age, to change their religion without the consent of their parents; this pernicious law introduced dissension into the bosom of families; children were enticed to ingratitude and disobedience by the arts of clerical kidnappers who overspread the country. The parents were next persecuted; they were excluded from all public employments and the incorporations of the trades. Bribes were offered on the one hand, punishments were menaced on the other; apostacy was assured of reward, and the payment of conversions became a heavy charge on the state. Finally, a brutal and licentious soldiery was let loose on the hapless protestants; dragoons were sent as missionaries among them, and the edict of Nantes, their last security, was formally revoked. Exposed to all the cruelties and horrors that bigotry could dictate, or brutality execute, nearly four hundred thousand of the Huguenots abandoned their country, and carried into lands hostile to France, their wealth, their commercial intelligence, their manufacturing industry, and their desire of vengeance. The accounts of their sufferings published by the exiled Huguenots in England, Holland, and Germany, aggravated the hatred of France, which was spreading through these countries, and accelerated a general war. A league was formed by all the princes of Germany to restrain the encroachments of Louis; Spain and Holland joined it as principals; Sweden, Denmark, and Savoy, were afterward gained: and a sudden revolution in England placed that country at the head of the confederacy.

James II. succeeded to the English crown on the death of his brother Charles; he commenced his reign by liberal promises, which procured him general popularity, notwithstanding his open adhesion to the Romish church, and his going to mass with all the ensigns of regal dignity. But there were many discontented spirits who lamented his accession, and these secretly instigated the duke of Monmouth, the natural son of Charles II., to assert his mother's marriage, and his own consequent claim to the throne. Monmouth was a weak, vain man; he readily adopted the scheme, and in concert with the earl of Argyle, prepared for the simultaneous invasion of Scotland and England. Argyle, who was the first, readily effected a landing in Scotland, but soon found that the country was not so ripe for revolt as he had believed. Surrounded by superior forces, he attempted to force his way into the disaffected part of the western counties, but his followers gradually abandoned him; he was taken prisoner and sent to Edinburgh, where he expiated his imprudence on the scaffold. In the meantime, Monmouth had landed in the west of England, where he was received with great enthusiasm. Encouraged by the proofs of attachment he received, he ventured to attack the royal army encamped at Sedgemoor, near Bridgewater. But the cowardice of Lord Grey, who commanded the horse, and the incapacity of Monmouth himself, proved fatal to the insurgents; they were routed with great slaughter, and their unfortunate leader, after wandering about several days in great distress, was taken prisoner.

James II. induced the unhappy Monmouth to degrade himself by a mean supplication for life,* and then informed him that his offence was

* Monmouth displayed great firmness and intrepidity on the scaffold. The exe-

too great to be pardoned. The cruelties exercised on all suspected of having shared in the insurrection, by the inhuman Colonel Kirke, and the still more infamous Judge Jeffries, were shocking to human nature; they spread general consternation through the western counties, but at the same time they excited a spirit of secret hostility to the tyrannical king. Encouraged by his success, James resolved to dispense with the test acts, by which catholics were excluded from the public service, and, finding the parliament opposed to his views, he dissolved that body. Eleven out of the twelve judges asserted that the dispensing power was an essential part of the royal prerogative; and the king, fortified by their opinion, gave several places of trust to catholic lords and gentlemen. The lord-lieutenancy of Ireland was intrusted to the earl of Tyrconnell, a zealous adherent of the Romish church; many of the catholics, who felt that their religion was the cause of their being deprived of their estates, began to look forward to the repeal of the Act of Land Settlement, and several of the more timorous protestants sought refuge in England. Their representations, and the tales of horror related by the exiled Huguenots, filled the nation with a general hatred of popery; the king, however, unconscious of his increasing unpopularity, unwisely deprived himself of his chief security by quarrelling with the church. He commenced by endeavoring to open the doors of the universities to catholics; more opposition was offered than had been anticipated, but the king persevered, and a catholic, named Parker, was installed into the presidency of Magdalen college, Oxford.

Although there was much discontent in England, no project had as yet been formed against the king; it was believed that Mary of Modena, James's queen, would never have any children, and the nation was disposed to wait quietly for the accession of one of his daughters by his former marriage, both of whom were known to be strongly attached to the church of England. Mary, the eldest daughter of James by Anne Hyde, was married to the prince of Orange, who was engaged in supporting the liberties of Europe, and the protestant religion against the ambition and bigotry of Louis XIV.; she was less popular in England than her husband, to whom she was known to be fondly attached, and it was generally believed that she would relax the laws against protestant dissenters, if ever she came to the throne, in order to gratify the attachment of her husband to presbyterian principles. She was, however, childless, and the national hope of a protestant successor to the throne centred in her sister.

The princess Anne, afterward queen, had been educated in the strictest principles of the Anglican church by her maternal grandfather, the celebrated earl of Clarendon. She was married to Prince George of Denmark, by whom she had several children, all of whom, except the duke of Gloucester, either died in their infancy, or were still-born. She was the favorite child of her father, and nothing had ever occurred to interrupt their affection, until nearly at the same time James's queen

cutioner, touched with pity, or respect for the victim's noble bearing, struck him three times without effect, and then threw aside the axe, declaring he was unable to perform his office. The sheriff compelled him to renew his efforts, and the head of the unhappy duke was at length severed from his body.

appeared likely to give an heir to the throne, and he himself became involved in a contest with the church of England.

Anxious to relieve the catholics from the civil disabilities under which they labored, as a monarch of the same religion as themselves must naturally have been, and at the same time desirous to obtain the support of so powerful a body as the protestant dissenters, in the new course of policy which he meditated, James published a new declaration of indulgence, suspending all the penal laws against every species of dissent, and soon after issued a proclamation commanding it to be read in churches. The legality of such a command was questioned by the prelates, for though royal declarations had been read in churches with their sanction during the preceding reign, considerable doubts were entertained of the king's power to suspend the penal laws, and in fact, such an exercise of the royal authority had been pronounced unconstitutional by the best lawyers of the kingdom. Had the declaration related to a less obnoxious matter than the virtual abrogation of the laws against non-conformity, which had been only procured by the most vigorous exertions of the hierarchy, it is probable that the king's orders might have been obeyed: but it was unwise to call upon the English prelates to undo their work, and to proclaim in the churches that they had hitherto pursued an erroneous course of policy. It was also known that the great majority of the English dissenters, far from being grateful for the king's favor, viewed his edict of toleration with suspicion, believing that it was not intended to serve them, but to advance the cause of popery.

Under these circumstances six bishops, in concert with Sancroft the primate, prepared a remonstrance in the form of a petition to the king, which stated, in firm but respectful language, their reasons for refusing to comply with his injunctions. When this document was presented to James, he was so violently enraged, that he ordered the prelates to be arrested on the charge of having uttered a seditious libel, and as they all refused to find bail, they were committed to the Tower.

At this crisis the queen gave birth to a prince of Wales, and the absence of the archbishop, imprisoned in the Tower, who ought in virtue of his office to have been present on the occasion, gave rise to a report that he had been purposely removed out of the way, lest he should detect the king and queen in their attempts to impose a spurious child on the nation. This monstrous tale was studiously circulated; and though the queen's delivery had been as public as decency would permit, the story that the prince of Wales was supposititious was received with equal credulity in England and Holland. James at first paid no regard to the reports which were in circulation, but when he learned that the prayers for the young prince were discontinued in his daughter's chapel at the Hague, he remonstrated very strongly on the subject, but was forced to rest satisfied with excuses so disingenuous that their fallaciousness was transparent.

As the king, according to the constitution as settled at the Reformation, was the head of the English church, it was impossible to avoid some collision when the monarch professed a religion at variance with that of the establishment; and though such an evil might be endured for a season, the members of a protestant establishment naturally shrunk from the prospect of being governed by a continued succession of Romish sovereigns. The birth of a prince of Wales forced men to take into serious consideration the position of the church and the country, especially as it took place at a time when seven prelates of the church were persecuted by its head for defending what they believed to be the proper privileges of the established religion. Such an anomaly was too glaring to escape notice, and James exhibited extraordinary weakness in forcing it on the consideration of the country. There never, perhaps, was a trial which excited such interest as that of the seven bishops for the pretended libel contained in their petition to the king. The best lawyers in England were engaged on each side, and the question between prerogative and privilege was never more ably debated. The trial lasted during the whole of the day. In the evening the jury were desired to retire and consider their verdict. They remained together in close consultation all night, without fire or candle: great difference of opinion appears to have prevailed among them, for it was not until ten o'clock on the following morning that they pronounced the acquittal of the prelates.

"The moment the verdict was pronounced," says the earl of Clarendon, who was present, "there was a wonderful shout, that one would have thought the hall had cracked."—"The loud shouts and joyful acclamations were," as Sir John Reresby expresses, "a rebellion in noise, though not in intention." From London the tumultuous sounds of joy extended rapidly into the country, and a well-known expression of James is preserved, on hearing acclamations, even among the soldiers in his camp at Hounslow. He was told by his general, Lord Faversham, of whom he had inquired the cause of the noise, that it was nothing but the rejoicing of the soldiers for the acquittal of the bishops. "Do you call that nothing?" he replied, "but so much the worse for them." Bonfires were made, and the bells of the churches rung not only in London, but in the greater part of the country towns, as soon as the news of the acquittal reached them, although the strictest orders were given to prevent such proceedings. So strong was the general feeling, that though several persons were indicted at the next sessions for Middlesex for riotous behavior, yet the grand jury would not find bills against them, though they were sent out no less than three times. It is stated further, that the churches of London were crowded on that forenoon with multitudes, eager to pour forth their gratitude to God for this great deliverance. "O what a sight was that," says Nichols, "to behold the people crowding into the churches to return thanks to God for so great a blessing, with the greatest earnestness and ecstacy of joy, lifting up their hands to heaven; to see illuminations in every window and bonfires at every door, and to hear the bells throughout all the city ringing out peals of joy for the wonderful deliverance."

It was in the midst of this popular excitement, and most probably in consequence of it, that the project of a revolution was first formed. In order to form a right estimate of this great event, which for nearly half a century became the great turning point of European policy, it will be necessary to take a brief retrospect, in order to explain the position of parties in England. From the time of the restoration, a party, consisting of a few nobles and a very large body of country gentlemen, labored to introduce so much of the principles of the old commonwealth as consisted in restraining the power of the crown, and the ecclesiastical privileges of the establishment. They were at first called the puritanical, and afterward the whig party; they were animated by a perfect horror of popery, or of anything which seemed approaching to it, but they were more favorable to the protestant non-conformists than to the episcopal clergy, and their main strength rested on the support of the protestant dissenters. Except in hatred of popery, the English people of that day had little community of feeling with the whig leaders; the rigid rule of the presbyteries in the time of the commonwealth and Cromwell, when the most innocent amusements were strictly prohibited, had alienated the lower orders, and though they were rallied round the whigs for a time when the perjuries of Titus Oates and his associates had filled the nation with senseless terror, the reaction against this delusion had reduced the party to more than its former weakness, and it had found little support out of doors when an attempt was made to exclude James from succeeding to the throne on account of his obnoxious religion. Another reason for the small amount of popular favor enjoyed by the whig party was the notorious fact that many of the leaders, in spite of their loud professions of patriotism, accepted bribes from foreign powers. Some took money from Holland, others from France, and not a few from both governments, excusing such conduct to themselves by the necessity of obtaining foreign support to resist the prerogatives of the crown, and the many advantages of position enjoyed by the court party. The more ardent whigs had raised a rebellion against James, to give the crown to the duke of Monmouth, and the ease with which that rebellion was crushed seemed to prove the extinction of their power as a party. James certainly undervalued them, and had he not taken measures which constrained a coalition between them and their rivals, he might have continued to despise the English whigs with impunity. Matters were very different in Scotland: presbyterianism was there the favored religion of the nation, and prelacy was scarcely less hated than popery. So far as the important question of church government was concerned, the Scotch were whigs and something more, but James and his court made little account of Scotland; they had taken no warning from the fate of Charles I., which had been decided by a Scottish army.

A far more powerful party was known by the names of prelatists, cavaliers, or tories; it included the great majority of the nobility, the entire body of the clergy, a large proportion of the country gentlemen and in general the masses of the agricultural and laboring population, so far as the latter were capable of forming any opinion, or selecting a party. Their great principle of union was to support the exclusive supremacy of the church of England, and to extend the influence of that sovereign in his capacity of head of that church; their rallying cry was "church and king," in which church came first not only in name but in reality. From the very moment of James's accession, the tories found themselves in an awkward and false position. They had long taught the doctrines of the divine right of kings and passive obedience to the will of the sovereign, denouncing all resistance as sinful; but when the monarch began to exercise his prerogatives as head of the church, in a spirit of direct hostility to the principles on which the church had been established, they found themselves involved in difficulties which every day became more embarrassing. The trial of the bishops was the crisis of their loyalty; it was not unjustly regarded as a kind of declaration of war by the monarch against the national establishment, and all the friends of that establishment felt themselves coerced to take measures for its defence and protection. It is true that the adoption of such measures was a virtual abandonment of the doctrine of non-resistance, and so far a concession to the principles of their old adversaries the whigs; hence the first movements of the tories to join in inviting the prince of Orange to England were slow and unsteady, and the most for which they looked was that the prince might act as mediator between the king, the church, and the nation.

We have next to examine the connexion between the position of the king of England in relation to the general politics of Europe. At this period the arbitrary designs of Louis XIV. had excited universal distrust, and alliances were secretly formed to resist his designs, whether covert or avowed, to the different districts and territories over which he sought to extend his sway. England was prevented from joining in this coalition only by the strict alliance between its monarch and Louis, and hence the reign of James was odious to the princes of Germany, the houses of Spain and Austria, and even to the pope himself, who had been harshly treated by the French monarch, stripped of his territory of Avignon, and menaced with further injuries. Holland was still more deeply interested in detaching England from the French alliance: Louis had openly avowed his intentions to destroy its independence, and if he had procured the promised support of the naval power of England, the Dutch would in all probability have become subjects of France. The combination of parties by which the prince of Orange was invited into England, had little unity in itself, and might have been dissolved in a moment if James had shown a disposition to adopt conciliatory measures and regain the friendship of the tories and churchmen. William was well aware of these circumstances, and made the most vigorous exertions to take immediate advantage of the crisis. While he was thus engaged, the invasion of western Germany by Louis XIV. without the formality of a declaration of war, and the fearful ravages perpetrated by the French in the palatinate, excited universal alarm and indignation throughout Europe. The states of Holland immediately placed their fleets and armies at the disposal of William; he set sail with a powerful armament, and on the 5th of November, 1688, landed safely at Torbay.

The perplexity into which all parties were thrown by the landing of William was almost ludicrous. At first he was joined by so few partisans, that he began to think of returning; then on a sudden the nobles and leading men of England flocked to him from all quarters; the favorite officers of James, those who were solely indebted to him for rank and fortune, even his favorite daughter Anne, joined in the general defection—while he, sinking at once into despondency, abandoned his army, and after a brief delay in London, fled to France. It is unfortunately true that the prince of Orange made use of many dishonorable artifices to terrify the unfortunate monarch, and induce him to seek safety in flight; but James seems to have adopted the fatal resolution of abandoning his kingdom, in the belief that the complicated embarrassments of parties would lead to his recall; and that returning at the head of a French army, he might yet triumph over all his enemies. Confidence in the power of Louis XIV. had been his bane from the beginning, and his connexion with that detested monarch was the principal cause of his dying in exile.

William assumed so much of royal power as to summon a convention to regulate the affairs of the nation. Three proposals were made to this body: first, that terms should be made with James, and the chief administration intrusted to the prince of Orange as lieutenant-general of the kingdom; secondly, that the flight of James should be taken as an abdication, and a regency proclaimed, with the prince of Orange at its head; and thirdly, that the throne should be declared vacant, and William and Mary declared king and queen of England. The first proposal was the most acceptable to the consistent tories, including the primate, Sancroft, and several of the bishops whom James had so recently prosecuted, but the great majority felt the absurdity of turning a king out for the mere purpose of calling him back, and it had already passed into a proverb that "the worst of all revolutions was a restoration."

In the consideration of the second proposition was involved the question of the legitimacy of the prince of Wales, which nobody really doubted, but almost everybody affected to deny. There were, however, great practical difficulties in recognising the infant prince as heir to the crown. It was tolerably certain that James would not consent to reside in France, and send his son to be educated as a protestant in England; the princesses Mary and Anne were naturally opposed to a plan which would have deprived them of their fondly-cherished hopes of wearing a crown, and William had taken pains to make it known that if a regency should be determined upon, somebody else must be sought to exercise the functions of regent.

In fact, the circumstances of the time rendered the third plan the only one possible to be adopted; but the majority of those who voted for conferring the crown on William and Mary did so with undisguised reluctance, as men submitting to a painful necessity. The subsequent efforts of James to recover his dominions by the aid of French armaments completed the alienation of the English people from his cause, while the cowardice and incapacity he displayed in Ireland, particularly at the battle of the Boyne, led to the utter ruin of his unfortunate partisans in that country. Louis was himself injured by his efforts in favor of the dethroned king: his futile attempts to invade England, his intrigues to provoke insurrections, and his continued menaces of conquest, provoked and kept alive against him the flame of popular indignation in Great Britain, and induced the people to bear the brunt of expensive continental wars, in which England was very remotely and indirectly concerned, for the mere purpose of restraining his ambition. It was in the same way at a later period that Napoleon's menace of invading England, excited a spirit among the people which led them similarly to fight the battle of continental Europe, and pay its sovereigns for maintaining their own independence.

Section IV.—*General History of Europe, from the League of Augsburg to the Formation of the Grand Alliance.*

The domestic history of England, during the reign of William III., is so remotely connected with the progress of the war to restrain the ambition of Louis XIV., that it will be convenient to limit our attention to the former before commencing the narrative of the latter. Several parties, as we have seen, joined in effecting the revolutiun; scarcely had they succeeded, when their old jealousies were renewed with aggravated fury. The Scottish convention made the establishment of presbyterianism an essential part of the settlement of the crown; the protestant sectarians in England were thus encouraged to hope for some modifications in the discipline of the English church; they did obtain a general toleration, to the great disgust of the tory or high-church party. Ireland remained faithful to James, though William not only offered wealth and dignity to the lord-lieutenant, Tyrconnell, but promised to secure the catholics in their civil rights, and give them one third of the churches.

But the protestants, who had so recently been secured in their lands by the acts of Settlement and Explanation, conscious that the justice of their titles would not bear a very rigid scrutiny, and dreading that, under a catholic monarch and a catholic parliament, these acts might be repealed, boldly took up arms, and atoned for their deficiency of number by martial vigor and a daring spirit. They felt that under Cromwell they had won their possessions by the sword, and by the sword they were resolved to retain them. Some of them formed guerilla bands, and scoured the country; others threw themselves into Londonderry, Enniskillen, and other garrison towns, resolved to hold out until aid could arrive from England. James, with a small French force, proceeded to Ireland, and convened a parliament in Dublin. The act of Settlement was repealed, and all the protestants who favored, or were supposed to favor, the prince of Orange, were declared guilty of high treason. But in the meantime, the adherents of the abdicated monarch had been ruined in Scotland by the loss of their leader, the brave Viscount Dundee, who fell in the arms of victory. The Highlanders who followed his standard dispersed, and the jacobite party had no person of sufficient influence to collect another army. James began his operations in Ireland by the siege of Londonderry; it was nobly defended by the inhabitants, whose religious enthusiasm more than supplied their deficiency in martial discipline. They were, however, on the point of sinking under the joint sufferings of fatigue and famine, when a reinforcement arrived from England, with provision and ammunition, upon which the besiegers abandoned their undertaking.

Ere James could recover from this disaster, the duke of Schomberg landed at Carrickfergus with ten thousand men; but as the operations of this general were too slow for the impatience of the people of England, William followed with a considerable reinforcement, and hasted to meet his father-in-law. The hostile armies met on the 1st of July, 1690, on the banks of the river Boyne; the skill of William procured him a victory, which the cowardice of James rendered decisive; he fled from the field of battle, and scarcely halting in Dublin hasted to take shipping at Waterford for France, abandoning his faithful subjects to their fate. The Irish, though forsaken, did not despair; they threw themselves into Limerick, which William immediately invested, but was finally forced to raise the siege. This failure was, however, compensated by the success of the earl of Marlborough, in Munster, who with five thousand men reduced Cork, Kinsale, and some other places of less importance. But Ireland was not yet subdued, and William intrusted the completion of the task to Baron Ginckle, who took Athlone almost in the presence of the Irish army, chiefly through the negligence of St. Ruth, whom Louis had sent over at the request of James. Stung with remorse, St. Ruth hazarded a battle at Aughrim, but he was defeated and slain. The Irish a second time sought shelter in Limerick, which Ginckle once more besieged. All parties were now weary of the war, and a treaty was concluded at Limerick, by which it was stipulated that the catholics should enjoy the same toleration as in the reign of Charles II.; that they should be restored to the privileges of subjects, on taking the oath of allegiance; and that as many as chose to follow the fortunes of the late monarch should be transported to the continent at the expense of the government. About ten thousand men took advantage of the last article, and, under the name of the Irish brigades, were taken into the service of the king of France.

William had, in the meantime, become disgusted with the constitutional jealousy of the whigs, and had sought the friendship of the tories, who were remarkable for their zealous support of the royal prerogative. But a sanguinary act of vengeance, the massacre of the Macdonalds of Glencoe, under circumstances of great treachery, brought so much odium on the new government, that James began to entertain some hopes of a restoration. The Macdonalds had recognised the new government a day later than that named in the act of parliament, but as their allegiance was formally accepted by the authorities, they believed themselves in perfect security. A military force was received into their glens without distrust or suspicion. But in the dead hour of the night, the soldiers, pursuant to previous orders, rose upon their hosts, set fire to the houses, and shot down the wretched inhabitants as they attempted to escape from the flames.

This atrocity excited universal indignation throughout Europe; the French king hoped that it would enable him to replace James on the throne; and had he been able immediately to transport his forces across the channel, the liberties of England and the crown of William would have been exposed to serious danger. A camp was formed between Cherbourg and La Hogue; twenty thousand Irish and French soldiers were prepared to invade England, and a powerful navy was equipped to support the expedition. The whole was frustrated by the valor of the British seamen; Admiral Russell having formed a junction with a Dutch squadron, attacked the French fleet off La Hogue, burned several of their men-of-war and transports, and drove the rest into their harbors. James beheld from the shore this annihilation of his hopes, but could not forbear expressing his admiration of the valor of his former subjects.*

The death of Queen Mary revived the hopes of the jacobites, as the

* When he saw the French fleet set on fire, he exclaimed, "Ah! none but my brave English tars could have performed so gallant an action!"

partisans of the Stuarts were called ; but instead of open rebellion, they resolved to remove the king by assassination. The plot was discovered, and the nation was so disgusted with the intended treachery, that William was restored to all his former popularity. From this time to the accession of Queen Anne, there is little worthy of note in the domestic history of England. On the death of the duke of Gloucester, the last protestant heir to the crown, an act was passed by which the eventual succession was settled on Sophia, dutchess dowager of Hanover, and her heirs, being protestants (A. D. 1701). She was the grand-daughter of James I., by the princess Elizabeth, married to the unfortunate elector-palatine. Party animosities between the whigs and tories were occasionally violent, and William III. was not always on the best of terms with his parliament.

The emperor Leopold, the head of the league of Augsburg, was a prince of great abilities, sullied, however, too often, by cruelty and bigotry. Though the chief of a confederacy for maintaining the liberties of Europe, he trampled on the privileges of his Hungarian subjects, and persecuted the protestants. But the overthrow of the Turks at Vienna, and the subsequent capture of Belgrade, left the discontented without an ally, and they were forced to submit in silence. Louis was not daunted by the power of the league ; he assembled two armies in Flanders, sent a third to check the Spaniards in Catalonia, and, to form a barrier on the side of Germany, ravaged the Palatinate with fire and sword (A. D. 1688). This barbarous policy filled Europe with horror ; men, women, and children, driven from their habitations, in the inclement month of February, wandered by the light of their own burning houses over the frozen fields, and fell victims by thousands to cold and hunger. Nor did this detestable expedient produce the desired effect ; the German armies, in the ensuing campaign, gained several important triumphs. Louis sought to recover his former superiority by nobler means ; he intrusted his armies to new generals of approved talent, and the fortune of the war instantly changed. Savoy was overrun by the French marshal Catinat ; Marshal Luxemburg gained a brilliant victory over the allies in Flanders ; the united Dutch and English fleets were defeated off Beachy Head, and the Spaniards were scarcely able to defend Catalonia (A. D. 1690). Little was done on the side of Germany, for the emperor was once more assailed by Tekeli and the Turks, whose progress threatened the ruin of his hereditary dominions. Had this course of fortune continued, Louis must have become the master of Europe, but in the following campaigns, the Turks, deprived of all their advantages, left the emperor at leisure to watch his western frontiers, and Catinat was driven from Italy by the duke of Savoy. But in Flanders the French continued to be eminently successful. Mons and Namur were taken in spite of all the efforts which the united forces of the English and Dutch could make for their relief, and the allies were defeated in two great general engagements by the duke of Luxemburg. But William III. was never daunted by ill success, and he adopted such prudent measures, that Luxemburg was unable to derive any important advantages from his victories. Similar success attended the armies of Louis in Savoy, Spain, and Germany ; but the triumphs were equally unproductive. Even at sea, notwithstanding the recent loss at

La Hogue, the French navy rode triumphant, and gained a decided superiority over the English and Dutch fleets. But France was exhausted by these efforts; a dreadful famine ravaged the country, arising partly from an unfavorable season, and partly from the want of hands to till the ground; and the finances of the state were fast falling into confusion. The allies, aware of these circumstances, made vigorous efforts to recover their losses, but they were generally unsuccessful, except on the side of Flanders, where William recaptured Namur, and thus, in some degree, retrieved his military reputation. All parties became weary of a war in which much blood was shed, much treasure expended, and no permanent acquisitions made. Negotiations were commenced under the mediation of Charles XI., of Sweden, at Ryswick (A. D. 1697), and a treaty concluded, in which Louis made many important concessions, to purchase an interval of tranquillity for his future projects. The French king's renunciation of the Spanish succession, which it had been the main object of the war to enforce, was not even mentioned in the articles of pacification, and several other omissions left abundant grounds for a renewal of the war at no distant period.

The emperor, though severely harassed by the Turks, consented to the peace with great reluctance, and complained bitterly of the desertion of his allies. But no one of the confederates derived more advantage from the treaty; he was enabled to direct his whole force against the Ottomans, who, under their new sultan, Mustapha II., became, for a brief space, formidable to Europe. The danger was averted by the celebrated Prince Eugene, of Savoy, who now began to attract admiration. After the peace of Ryswick, he took the command of the imperialists, and encountered Mustapha at Zenta, a small village on the banks of the river Theysse, in the kingdom of Hungary. The battle was brief, but, for its duration, one of the most sanguinary on record; fifteen thousand Turks were slain, and eight thousand more drowned in their flight across the river; their artillery, baggage, and ammunition, the sultan's magnificent pavilion, countless standards, and the great seal of the Ottoman empire, remained the prize of the victors; the grand vizier, the aga of the janissaries, and twenty-seven paçhas, were among the victims of this fatal field. Mustapha, having vainly attempted to retrieve his losses in a new campaign, was forced to consent to the peace of Carlowitz, by which several provinces were resigned to the Austrians, Azof ceded to the Russians, now fast rising into importance under the administration of the Czar Peter, and the Venetians gratified by the cession of the Morea, anciently called the Peloponnesus.

The declining health of the king of Spain, Charles II., engaged the general attention of Europe after the peace of Ryswick: three princes were candidates for the succession, Louis XIV., the emperor Leopold, and the elector of Bavaria. It is unnecessary to canvass their several claims, but it is manifest that the general interests of Europe pointed to the electoral prince as the most eligible of the competitors. A secret treaty of partition was concluded between William and Louis, but Charles II. received information of the transaction, and enraged that his dominions should be shared during his life, proclaimed the electoral prince of Bavaria sole heir. Scarcely, however, had this arrangement been made, when that prince died suddenly, not without strong suspicions of poison (A. D. 1699). A new treaty of partition was arranged by Holland, France, and England, but the emperor Leopold refused his concurrence, expecting to obtain for his family the inheritance of the whole Spanish monarchy. During these negotiations, the affections of the Scotch were alienated from William, by his sacrificing the settlement which they had established at a great expense, on the isthmus of Darien, to quiet the fears of the Spaniards, and the commercial jealousy of the English. Could they have found leaders, they would probably have had recourse to arms, but fortunately they were contented to vent their rage in violent language, and furious invective. Charles II. was long disposed to favor the Austrian claimant to his crown, but the arrogance of his queen and her German favorites, alienated the nation from the court of Vienna, while the Spanish nobility and clergy urged the dying monarch to bestow the sovereignty on the house of Bourbon. Charles applied to the pope for advice; Innocent XII., who then filled the pontifical chair, was very jealous of the progress of the Austrian power in Italy; he therefore strenuously recommended the choice of a French prince; a new will was made, and Philip, duke of Anjou, second son of the dauphin, was nominated heir to the crown of Spain. Not long after Charles died (A. D. 1701), and Louis, after some hesitation between the will and the partition treaty, proclaimed his grandson king of Spain and the Indies, under the title of Philip V.

Though England and Holland were equally alarmed at this proceeding, both powers were obliged to acquiesce for a season. William found his parliament reluctant to engage in a new war, and Louis, by an unexpected movement against the barrier towns, had secured a great portion of the Dutch army. The emperor, however, commenced a war, claiming the dutchy of Milan as a fief of the imperial crown, and his army, under the command of Prince Eugene, gained several advantages over Marshal Catinat, in Italy. During this campaign, the states-general and William, having failed to make any satisfactory explanations of his designs from the French king, concluded a treaty, called the Grand Alliance, with the emperor. Its avowed objects were "to procure satisfaction to his imperial majesty in the case of the Spanish succession; obtain security to the English and Dutch for their dominions and commerce; prevent the union of the monarchies of France and Spain, and hinder the French from possessing the Spanish dominions in America." But this treaty would probably have been frustrated by the English parliament, but for the imprudence with which Louis hazarded an insult to the British nation (A. D. 1701). On the death of James II., he caused his son, commonly called the Old Pretender, to be recognised king of Great Britain and Ireland, under the title of James III. The parliament at once entered heartily into the war, which they had hitherto disapproved, and their martial ardor was not abated by the death of William, who fell a victim to a fall from his horse, and the unskilfulness of an inexperienced surgeon (A. D. 1702). The intelligence of this event filled the allies with consternation; but their fears were of short duration, for Queen Anne, who next ascended the throne, declared her resolution to adhere steadily to the policy of her predecessor.

SECTION V.—*The War of the Spanish Succession.*

THE accession of Queen Anne gave great satisfaction to the English people; William was disliked as a foreigner, who was more strongly attached to Holland than to his adopted country, and his coldness of manner had greatly tended to increase his unpopularity. He was suspected by the tories of secret designs against the church, on account of his attachment to presbyterianism, and the whigs had ceased to respect him, because he had not shown himself sufficiently grateful for their services in raising him to the throne. Though his military talents were great, he had not been a very successful general, and it was studiously circulated, that he endeavored as much as possible to keep back the earl (afterward duke) of Marlborough, through envy of his superior abilities. He had, at first, recognised the duke of Anjou to the crown of Spain, and therefore when he joined the grand alliance formed to prevent what he had previously sanctioned, he was exposed to suspicions of insincerity, and it was generally believed that if Louis made any large sacrifices to conciliate the Dutch, the English monarch would not persevere in his resistance. It is scarcely necessary to say that it was of very little importance to England, whether an Austrian or a French prince became monarch of Spain; the war of the succession, in which this country bore the principal share, was that in which its interests were the least involved; and this country lavishly poured forth its blood and treasure to accomplish objects which had no connexion with its real position. It was the indignation excited by the attempt of Louis to impose upon the English people a sovereign of his choice, which induced the queen and her people to enter on a bloody and expensive war, for no other purpose than humiliating the insolence of a despot. They subsequently found out that they had to pay too dear a price for the luxuries of war and vengeance.

Queen Anne infused vigor into the grand alliance, not only by the prompt declaration of her adhesion, but by her judicious choice of ministers; Lord Godolphin was placed at the head of the treasury, and the earl of Marlborough, who was connected with the premier by marriage, was appointed commander-in-chief of the English army in Flanders, and appointed ambassador extraordinary to the states-general. War was declared against France on the same day, at London, the Hague, and Vienna; and the campaign was simultaneously opened in Italy, Germany, and Flanders (A. D. 1702). The earl of Marlborough, who commanded in Flanders, was the only one of the allied generals who obtained success; he captured several important towns, and would probably have defeated the French in the open field, had not his motions been fettered by the presence of the Dutch field-deputies, who were too cautious or too timorous to allow of his hazarding an engagement At sea the ancient renown of the English navy was re-established; Sir George Rooke sailed against Cadiz with a fleet of fifty sail, having with him the duke of Ormond and an army of twelve thousand men. Cadiz was too strong to be taken, and Rooke sailed to Vigo, where the galleons, laden with the treasures of Spanish America, lay protected by a French fleet and a formidable castle and batteries. The English admiral broke the boom that protected the narrow entrance into the inner harbor, Ormond stormed the castle, and the French losing all hope, set fire to their ships. But the English and Dutch were at hand to extinguish the flames; six ships of the line and nine galleons became the trophies of the conquerors.

These losses, and the defection of the duke of Savoy, did not abate the courage of Louis; and the confederates, though joined by the king of Portugal, did not improve their advantages (A. D. 1703). The elector of Bavaria, the firm ally of France, being joined by Marshal Villars, gained a great victory over the imperialists at Hochstet, by which a road was opened to Vienna. The armies of Louis retained their superiority in Italy; even at sea the French disconcerted the plans of the confederates, and these disasters were poorly compensated by the acquisition of a few fortified towns in Flanders, which were captured by Marlborough. Even these slight successes gave courage to the allies; the English parliament voted liberal supplies for continuing the war and the emperor, though menaced on one side by the Hungarian insurgents, and on the other by the French and Bavarians, ordered his second son, Charles, to assume the title of king of Spain, and to proceed to Portugal, for the purpose of invading that country.

Marlborough had hitherto been greatly impeded by the timid caution of his Dutch colleagues; he concerted the plan of his next campaign with a more congenial spirit, Prince Eugene. As his Flemish conquests, in the preceding campaigns, had secured a good barrier for the united provinces, Marlborough now advanced to the title of duke leaving the defence of the fortresses to the Dutch garrisons, concentrated his forces, with the professed design of invading France, and then suddenly marched into Germany. A junction was effected with the imperialists, the elector of Bavaria's lines at Donawert were forced, and the allies advanced to the Danube. The Bavarian prince having been reinforced by thirty thousand French under the command of Marshal Tallard, resolved to hazard a battle, and the duke having been joined by Prince Eugene, with an equal number, eagerly sought for an engagement (August 13, A. D. 1704). The French and Bavarians were advantageously posted on a hill between the Danube and the village of Blenheim; but their line was weakened by detachments, and Marlborough, taking advantage of their error, charged through, and won a decisive victory. Thirty thousand French and Bavarians were killed, wounded, or taken; their camp-equipage, baggage, artillery, and standards, became the prize of the conquerors; Tallard was taken prisoner, and the Bavarian prince narrowly escaped the same fate. The allies, however, suffered very severely; their loss amounted to no less than five thousand killed and seven thousand wounded.

The consequences of this brilliant but bloody victory were, the immediate liberation of the emperor from all danger; the Hungarian insurgents were terrified into submission, Bavaria was abandoned by its sovereign to the ravages of the imperialists, and the shattered relics of the French army were driven to seek shelter within their own frontiers. The moral influence of the victory was even of more importance than the immediate results: it not only compensated for the ill success of the allies in Italy and Spain, but changed the whole complexion of the war. At sea the English navy began to retrieve its fame; though Sir George Rooke failed in an attack on Barcelona, he stormed Gibraltar, a fortress hitherto deemed impregnable, and gained a glorious but unprofitable victory over the French fleet off Malaga.

Had all the allies exhibited the same vigor as the English, Louis must have been speedily ruined; but the Germans were sluggish; the death of the emperor Leopold, and the accession of his more enterprising son Joseph, made no change in their policy (A. D. 1705): the prince of Baden, the general of the imperialists, obstinately refused to join Marlborough on the Moselle, and the allies could attempt no conquest of importance in Flanders. In Italy the French obtained so many advantages that the duke of Savoy was forced to shut himself up in his capital, where he was besieged, with but little prospect of relief; but on the side of Spain the allied arms were crowned with brilliant success. Sir John Leake defeated a French fleet off Gibraltar, and thus forced the marshal de Tessè to raise the siege of that fortress; the confederates, entering Spain on the Portuguese side, captured several places in Estremadura, while the earl of Peterborough, having been convoyed by Sir Sir Cloudesly Shovel to the coast of Catalonia, took the important city of Barcelona, and established the authority of Charles III. in the whole province of Catalonia, and the greater part of the kingdom of Valencia.

These variations of success inflamed the courage and obstinacy of the belligerant powers. Louis was so elated that he ordered Marshal Villeroy to act on the offensive in Flanders, while his Italian army besieged Turin, and the forces he sent into Germany drove the prince of Baden and the imperialists before them (A. D. 1706). The English parliament, now composed principally of whigs, showed the greatest eagerness for the prosecution of the war, and voted liberal supplies for the ensuing campaign. Marlborough joined the united army of Holland and England in May, and soon after received a subsidiary Danish force. Villeroy, relying on his superior strength, advanced to attack the allies, and the two armies met near the village of Ramillies. The French marshal posted his left wing behind a morass, where it could not be attacked, but where it was equally incapable of advancing against the enemy. Marlborough took immediate advantage of this error; amusing the French left wing by a feigned attack, he poured his infantry in masses on the centre; they encountered a brave resistance, but the duke, bringing up the cavalry just as the French lines began to waver, broke through them with a headstrong charge, and in an instant Villeroy's army was a helpless mass of confusion. Seven thousand of the French were slain, six thousand taken prisoners, and a vast quantity of artillery and ammunition abandoned to the victors. The loss of the allies, in killed and wounded, did not exceed three thousand five hundred men.

The results of this brilliant victory were the immediate conquest of Brabant, and almost all the Spanish Netherlands; but its consequences were felt even in Italy. Marshal Vendome having been recalled to remedy, if possible, Villeroy's disaster, Prince Eugene resolved to raise the siege of Turin, and baffled the efforts of the duke of Orleans to obstruct his march. Orleans therefore joined the besieging army, and as a battle was manifestly inevitable, the French marshals anxiously de liberated whether they should wait for the enemy in their intrenchments. The majority voted against the measure, but Marshal Marsin produced an order, signed by the king, immediately after receiving the account of his defeat at Ramillies, commanding his generals not to offer, but to wait for battle. This order hurt the pride and confused the measures of the duke of Orleans. While the French generals were angrily debating what arrangements should be made, Prince Eugene and the duke of Savoy fell upon their lines; the French got entangled in their extensive intrenchments, the river Doria running through their camp prevented one part of their army from coming to the assistance of the other; they were speedily routed, and fled with precipitation, not halting until they had passed their own frontiers. In men, the loss of the French army was not great, but they abandoned all their cannon, baggage, ammunition, and military chest. By this single blow, the house of Bourbon lost the dutchies of Milan and Mantau, the principality of Piedmont, and eventually the kingdom of Naples.

That the success of the allies was not equally decisive in Spain must be attributed to the want of energy and Austrian sluggishness of the archduke Charles. Philip besieged his rival in Barcelona, but was forced to retire by the appearance of Sir John Leake, with an English squadron, before the town. The retreat was made in great disorder, partly occasioned by an eclipse of the sun, which the superstitious Spaniards regarded as an omen of their ruin. Forty thousand English and Portuguese, under the command of the earl of Galway and the marquis de las Minas, advanced through Estremadura toward Madrid, and Philip was forced to abandon his capital; at the same time, the count de Santa Cruz surrendered Carthagena and the galleys to the allied powers. Had the archduke gone immediately to Madrid, and closely pressed his rival, the crown of Spain would probably have been lost to the house of Bourbon; but he lingered unaccountably in the neighborhood of Barcelona, until Philip and the duke of Berwick,* having collected a superior army, compelled the English and Portuguese to abandon Madrid. Carthagena was soon after recovered, but this was more than compensated by the loss of the islands of Majorca and Ivica, which surrendered to the English fleet under Sir John Leake. Louis was so disheartened by his losses, that he sought for peace on very humble conditions, but the allies, intoxicated with success, demanded such humiliating terms, that he resolved to try the hazards of another campaign.

While the English ministers were lavishing blood and treasure to support foreign wars, they did not neglect the internal affairs of the nation. A treaty for uniting England and Scotland under one legislature, was ratified by the parliaments of both countries; but the Scottish nation generally was opposed to a union that galled their national pride, and the advantages of which time alone could develop (A. D. 1707). Louis derived one advantage from his recent misfortunes; the expulsion of his force from Italy enabled him to send powerful succors into Spain, where the allies were acting with the greatest negligence and misconduct. The earl of Galway and the marquis de las Minas, having ex-

* The duke of Berwick was the natural son of James II., and one of the ablest generals in the service of France.

hausted all their provisions in Valencia, attempted to pass into New Castile; the duke of Berwick, having received large reinforcements, and aware that the allies had been weakened by the departure of the archduke, did not hesitate to attack them at Almanza, and won a victory as complete as any that had been obtained during the war. This great triumph restored the cause of the Bourbons in Spain, and similar success attended the French army in Germany, where Marshal Villars penetrated to the Danube, and laid the dutchy of Wirtemberg under contribution. Nothing of importance occurred in Flanders, and the only naval enterprise was the siege of Toulon. Prince Eugene, and the duke of Savoy, marched through France to besiege this great port, while Sir Cloudesly Shovel appeared off the coast to second their operations. But unfortunately, the garrison of Toulon had been reinforced two hours before the appearance of the allies; they retreated through Provence, wasting the country as they passed, and diffusing consternation almost to the gates of Paris. Nor was this the only evil that Louis suffered from the invasion; the detachments withdrawn from the army of Marshal Villars so weakened that general, that he was forced to relinquish his high projects in Germany, and repass the Rhine, instead of advancing beyond the Danube.

Great expectations had been formed in England, which the results of the campaign miserably disappointed; Godolphin and Marlborough lost a considerable share of their popularity; they were opposed even by the members of the cabinet, and though they persuaded the queen to dismiss Mr. Secretary Harley, and Mr. St. John, they saw that their influence with her majesty, and their power in parliament, had been considerably diminished (A. D. 1708). Marlborough felt that a vigorous campaign was essential to his future interests, especially as the duke le Vendome had, by treachery, gained possession of Ghent and Bruges; he therefore resolved to risk a general battle, and crossing the Scheldt, came up with the French army strongly posted at Oudenarde. The British cavalry broke their opponents at the first charge, the French lines fell into confusion, and though the approach of darkness prevented the allies from completing their victory, the enemy fled in such disorder, that nine thousand were taken prisoners, and nearly six thousand deserted. Marlborough, being reinforced by Prince Eugene, undertook the siege of Lisle, the principal city in French Flanders, and though it was vigorously defended by Marshal Boufflers, it was forced to surrender after a siege of two months, while Ghent and Bruges were recovered ere the close of the campaign. Nothing of importance occurred in Italy, Germany, or Spain; but the English fleet conquered the island of Sardinia, and terrified the pope into the acknowledgment of the archduke Charles as lawful king of Spain.

The confidence of the allies now rose to the highest pitch; Godolphin and Marlborough found the English parliament ready to grant additional supplies; the Dutch agreed to augment their troops, and the imperialists promised to lay aside their inactivity. Louis, on the contrary, disheartened by defeat, his treasury exhausted, his councils distracted, and his kingdom suffering from famine, offered to purchase peace by every concession that could reasonably be demanded (A. D. 1709). Once more his proffers were rejected, except upon conditions inconsistent with his personal honor and the safety of his kingdom, and once more he appealed to the hazards of war. The confederates in Flanders, finding that Marshal Villars had taken a position from which he could not be dislodged, laid siege to Tournay, and on the surrender of that place invested Mons. Villars, unable to relieve the place, took possession of a strong camp at Malplaquet, whence he trusted that he could harass the besiegers. The confederates, elated with past success, resolved to attack the French in their intrenchments. Few battles, since the invention of gunpowder, have been more obstinate and bloody; victory finally declared in favor of the allies, but it was dearly purchased by the loss of fifteen thousand men; while the French, who had fought under cover, lost only ten thousand. Mons was now closely invested, and the surrender of that important place closed the campaign Nothing of importance occurred in Germany, Italy, or Spain; but Louis, finding his resources exhausted, once again made an unsuccessful effort to obtain peace.

Conferences were opened at Gertruydenberg (A. D. 1710), but the allies, influenced by Marlborough and Prince Eugene, rejected the propositions of the French king; he was, however, unwilling to break off the negotiations, and the conferences were continued even after the hostile armies had actually taken the field. The duke of Marlborough took several fortified places in Flanders; but nothing of importance was done in Germany or Piedmont; and the misfortunes of the allies in Spain more than counterbalanced their other successes. The archduke Charles, aided by the English general, Stanhope, twice defeated his rival, and a second time gained possession of Madrid; instead of improving these advantages, he loitered in the capital until forced to retire by the united forces of the French and Spaniards, under the duke of Vendome. The allies retired toward Catalonia, and marched, for the sake of subsistence, in two bodies. Stanhope, who commanded the rear division, allowed himself to be surrounded at Brihuega, and was forced to surrender at discretion. Staremberg, who led the principal division, was soon after forced to engage at a disadvantage, but he made such able dispositions, that Vendome was compelled to retreat, and the imperialists continued their march in safety. They were, however, so weakened and dispirited by Stanhope's misfortune, that they could not check the victorious progress of Philip.

A revolution in the English cabinet proved of more consequence to Louis than even the success of his arms in Spain. The queen, a woman of feeble mind, had long been under the influence of the dutchess of Marlborough, who did not always use her power with discretion. A new favorite, Mrs. Masham, supplanted the dutchess, and was gained over, by Harley and St. John, to induce the queen to make a total change in the administration. This would have been impossible if the whigs had continued to enjoy the confidence of the nation; but many circumstances contributed to diminish their popularity. The weight of taxes, occasioned by the expenses of the war, began to be felt as a burden, when victories, from their very frequency, ceased to excite joy; the conduct of the allies, who contrived that "England should fight for all and pay for all," gave just dissatisfaction; and the rejection of the French king's offers at Gertruydenberg was justly regarded as the triumph of private ambition over public policy. In addition to these grounds of discontent, the tories raised the cry that the "church was in danger," on account of the favor shown to the dissenters; and the whigs, instead of allowing the imputation to refute itself, unwisely attempted to silence the clamor by force. Dr. Henry Sacheverell preached a sermon before the lord mayor, in which he bitterly attacked the dissenters, and advocated the exploded doctrines of passive obedience and non-resistance. Though it was but a poor contemptible production, such is the violence of party, that it was printed, and forty thousand copies are said to have been sold in a week. In another week, it would probably have been forgotten, had not Godolphin, who was personally attacked in the commons, persuaded his friends to make it the subject of a parliamentary impeachment. Common sense revolted from such an absurdity; the generous feelings of the nation were enlisted on the side of the preacher, and this sympathy was soon transferred to his cause. During his trial, the populace showed the liveliest zeal in his behalf; and when he was found guilty, the house of lords, dreading popular tumults, passed a sentence so lenient, that it was hailed by the tories as a triumph.

The persecution of Sacheverell was the ruin of the whigs; the queen, aware of their unpopularity, dismissed all her ministers except the duke of Marlborough; and a new cabinet was formed under the auspices of Mr. Harley, who was soon after created earl of Oxford. A new parliament was summoned, in which the tories had an overwhelming majority (A. D. 1711), but the ministers did not abandon the foreign policy of their predecessors, and copious supplies were voted for the maintenance of the war.

At this crisis an unexpected event changed the situations and views of all parties. The emperor Joseph died without issue; his brother Charles, the claimant of the Spanish crown, succeeded to the empire, and the liberties of Europe were thus exposed to as much danger from the aggrandizement of the house of Austria, as from that of the Bourbon family. The campaign was languidly conducted in every quarter, and ere its conclusion, the English ministers were secretly negotiating with France.

After many disgraceful intrigues, in which all the actors sacrificed the interests of the nation to party purposes, the duke of Marlborough was stripped of all his employments, and conferences for a general peace commenced at Utrecht. The successive deaths of the dauphin of France, his son the duke of Burgundy, and his grandson the duke of Bretagne, left only the sickly duke of Anjou between Philip and the throne of France. The union of the French and Spanish monarchies filled the confederates with no unreasonable apprehension, and the English ministers were obliged to threaten that they would renew the war, unless Philip renounced his right of succession to the throne of France (A. D. 1712). When this important point was obtained, the English and French agreed upon a cessation of arms; the Dutch and the imperialists continued the campaign, but with such ill success, that they were induced to renew the conferences for peace. On the 31st of March, 1713, the treaties between the different powers were signed at Utrecht by the plenipotentiaries of France, England, Prussia (recently exalted into a kingdom), Savoy, and the United Provinces The emperor held out until the following year, when he signed a treaty at Radstadt, less favorable than that which had been offered at Utrecht; and the king of Spain, with more reluctance, gave his adhesion to the general arrangements.

Few subjects have been more fiercely contested than the conduct of the English ministers in relation to the treaty of Utrecht. The reason is perfectly obvious: both the political parties that divided the nation had acted wrong; the whigs continued the war after all its reasonable objects had been gained; the tories concluded a peace in which the advantages that England might have claimed, from the success of her arms, were wantonly sacrificed. The people of England generally disliked the peace, and the commercial treaty with France was rejected by a majority of nine votes in the house of commons. The whigs now began to pretend that the protestant succession was in danger, and the alarm spreading rapidly, brought back to their party a large share of its former popularity. Nor were these apprehensions groundless; through the influence of the jacobites, the earl of Oxford was removed from his office, and a new administration, more favorable to the house of Stuart, formed under the auspices of St. John, Lord Bolingbroke. But before the court of St. Germains could derive any advantage from this change, the queen, harassed by the intrigues and quarrels of her servants, sank into a lethargy, and her death disappointed the hopes of the Pretender and his adherents (August 1, 1714). Several whig lords, without being summoned, attended the council, which was of course held at the demise of the crown; and the tories, overawed, concurred in issuing an order for the proclamation of the elector of Hanover, as George I., king of Great Britain and Ireland.

SECTION VI.—*Peter the Great of Russia.—Charles XII. of Sweden.*

IN the last two sections, we have confined our attention to the wars which the ambition of Louis XIV. excited in the south and west of Europe. During this period, the northern and eastern divisions of Christendom were occupied by the rivalry of two of the most extraordinary men that ever appeared on the stage of human life—Peter the Great of Russia, and Charles XII. of Sweden. Before entering on their history, we must take a brief retrospect of the affairs of the north after the accession of the Czar Alexis, and the resignation of Queen Christina.

Under the administration of Alexis, Russia began rapidly to emerge from the barbarism into which it had been plunged by the Mongolian invasion and subsequent civil wars. He reformed the laws, encouraged commerce, and patronised the arts; he recovered Smolensko from the Poles, and prevented the Turks from establishing their dominion over the Cossack tribes. His son Theodore, though of a weak constitution, steadily pursued the same course of vigorous policy. "He lived," says a native Russian historian, "the joy and delight of his people, and died amid their sighs and tears. On the day of his decease, Moscow was in the same state of distress which Rome felt at the death of Titus." John, the brother and successor of Theodore, was a prince of weak intellect; his ambitious sister, Sophia, seized for a time on the sovereignty, excluding her young brother Peter, to whom Theodore had bequeathed the crown. During seven years of boyhood Peter endured Sophia's galling yoke; but when he reached his seventeenth year, he took advantage of the general indignation excited by the misconduct of the government, to shut that princess up in a nunnery, and banish her favorite into a distant part of the empire.

Denmark was the scene of an extraordinary revolution (A. D. 1661). The tyranny of the aristocracy arose to such a height, that the clergy and commons voted for the surrender of their liberties to the king, and Ferdinand III., almost without any effort of his own, was thus invested with absolute power. On his death (A. D. 1670), his successor, Christian V., commenced war against Charles XI., king of Sweden, who, though assailed by a powerful league, defended himself with great ability and success. Charles XI., after the restoration of peace, tried to make himself as absolute as the kings of Denmark, but he died prematurely (A. D. 1697), leaving his crown to his son Charles XII., who has been deservedly styled the Alexander of the North.

Peter the Great commenced his reign by defeating the Turks, from whom he wrested the advantageous port of Azof, which opened to his subjects the commerce of the Black sea. This acquisition enlarged his views; he resolved to make Russia the centre of trade between Europe and Asia, to connect the Dwina, the Volga, and the Don, by canals, thus opening a water communication between the northern seas and the Black and the Caspian seas. To complete this magnificent plan, he determined to build a city on the Baltic sea, which should be the emporium of northern commerce, and the capital of his dominions. A still greater proof of his wisdom, and of his anxiety to secure the prosperity of his subjects, was his undertaking a tour through Europe, for the purpose of acquiring instruction, and bringing back to his subjects the improvements of more civilized nations. In 1698, having established a regency to direct the government during his absence, he departed from his dominions as a private gentleman, in the train of the ambassadors that he had sent to the principal courts of Europe. Amsterdam, at that time one of the most flourishing commercial cities in Europe, was the first place that arrested his attention; he entered himself as a common carpenter in one of the principal dockyards, laboring and living exactly like the other workmen. Thence he went to England, where he examined and studied the principal naval arsenals. King William presented the czar with a beautiful yacht, and permitted him to engage several ingenious artificers in his service. After a year's absence, Peter returned home, greatly improved himself, and accompanied by a train of men well qualified to instruct his subjects.

Anxious to extend his dominions on the eastern side of the Baltic, he entered into an alliance against Sweden with Frederick Augustus, elector of Saxony, who had succeeded John Sobieski on the throne of Poland, and Frederick IV., king of Denmark (A. D. 1700). The Danes commenced the war by invading the territories of the duke of Holstein-Gottorp, brother-in-law and ally of the king of Sweden. Their progress was slower than they expected, and, in the midst of their career, they were arrested by intelligence of the dangers which menaced their own capital. Charles XII., undaunted by the power of the league, resolved to carry the war into the dominions of Denmark. While his fleet, strengthened by an English squadron, blockaded Copenhagen, he suddenly embarked his troops at Carlscrona, and having easily effected a passage, laid siege to the city, by land. Frederic, cut off from his dominions by the Swedish cruisers, and alarmed by the imminent danger of his fleet and capital, concluded a peace highly honorable to the Swedes, leaving his Russian and Polish allies to continue the contest.

No sooner had Charles concluded the treaty, than he resolved to turn his arms against the Russians, who were besieging Narva with a force of eighty thousand men; though his own army did not exceed ten thousand, the heroic king of Sweden boldly resolved to attack his enemies in their intrenchments. As soon as his artillery had opened a small breach, he commanded his men to advance to the charge with fixed bayonets. A storm of snow, that blew full in their faces, added to the confusion into which the undisciplined Russians were thrown by this daring assault; the very superiority of their numbers added to their confusion; after a contest of three hours' duration they were totally routed; eighteen thousand of the besiegers fell in the battle or flight, thirty thousand remained prisoners, all their artillery, baggage, and ammunition, became the prey of the conquerors. The czar was not disheartened by this defeat, which he attributed to the right cause, the ignorance and barbarism of his subjects; "I knew," he said, "that the Swedes would beat us, but they will teach us to become conquerors in our turn." Though at the head of forty thousand men, he did not venture to encounter his rival, but evacuated the provinces that he had invaded.

Having wintered at Narva, Charles marched against the Poles and Saxons, who were encamped in the neighborhood of Riga; he forced a passage across the Duna, and gained a complete victory. Thence he entered as a conqueror into Courland and Lithuania, scarcely encountering any opposition. Encouraged by this success, he formed the project of dethroning King Augustus, who had lost the affection of the Poles by the undisguised preference which he showed for his Saxon subjects. With this design he entered into a secret correspondence with Radzrewiski, the cardinal primate, by whose means such a spirit of opposition was raised in the diet and senate, that Augustus sought peace as his only means of safety. Charles refused to treat unless the Poles elected a new king; and Augustus, convinced that he could only protect his crown by the sword, led his army to meet the Swedes, in a spacious plain near Clissau (A. D. 1702). The Polish monarch had with him about twenty-four thousand men, the forces of Charles did not exceed half that number; but the Swedes, flushed by recent conquests, gained a complete vtctory; and Augustus, after having made in vain the most heroic efforts to rally his troops, was forced to fly, leaving the enemy in possession of all his artillery and baggage. A second triumph at Pultusk, in the following campaign, gave such encouragement to the enemies of Augustus, that he was formally deposed by the diet (A. D. 1704), and the vacant crown given to Stanislaus Leczinski, who had been nominated by the king of Sweden.

Peter had not been in the meantime inactive; though he had not given much assistance to his ally Augustus, he had made a powerful diversion by invading Ingria, and taking Narva, so recently the scene of his misfortunes, by storm. At the same time he founded his projected capital in the heart of his new conquests, and by his judicious measures protected the rising city from the attacks of the Swedish generals. St. Petersburgh, founded on a marshy island in the river Neva, during a destructive war, and surrounded by countries recently subdued or still hostile, rose rapidly into importance, and remained in perfect security while all around was in confusion. Augustus had not yet resigned all hopes of recovering his crown; he concerted a scheme of operations with Peter, and sixty thousand Russians entered Poland to drive the Swedes from their recent acquisitions. Charles was not daunted by the numbers of his enemies; he routed the Russian divisions successively, and inspired such terror by the rapidity of his movements, which seemed almost miraculous, that the Russians retreated to their own country (A. D. 1706). In the meantime a victory obtained by a division of the Swedish army over the Saxons, opened to Charles a passage into the hereditary dominions of his rival, and crossing the Oder, he appeared in Saxony at the head of twenty-four thousand men. Augustus was forced to conclude peace on the most humiliating conditions. Charles wintered in Germany, where his presence created considerable alarm. He demanded from the emperor toleration for the protestants of Silesia, and the relinquishment of the quota which Sweden was bound to furnish for its German provinces. Involved in the war of the succession, Joseph submitted,* and the fears with which the presence of Charles filled the allied powers were soon dispersed by his departure in quest of new adventures.†

From Saxony Charles marched back into Poland, where Peter was making some ineffectual efforts to revive the party of Augustus. Peter retired before his rival, who had, however, the satisfaction of defeating an army of twenty thousand Russians, strongly intrenched. Intoxicated by success, he rejected the czar's offers of peace, declaring that he would treat at Moscow;‡ and without forming any systematic plan of operations, he crossed the frontiers, resolved on the destruction of that ancient city. Peter prevented the advance of the Swedes, on the direct line, by destroying the roads and desolating the country; Charles, after having endured great privations, turned off toward the

* The pope was greatly displeased by the emperor's restoring the Silesian churches to the protestants; Joseph facetiously replied to his remonstrances: "Had the king of Sweden demanded that I should become a Lutheran myself, I do not know what might have been the consequence."

† The duke of Marlborough went into Saxony to dissuade the Swedish monarch from accepting the offers of Louis XIV. Marlborough was too cautious a politician to enter immediately on the object of his mission. He complimented Charles on his victories, and even expressed his anxiety to derive instruction in the art of war from so eminent a commander. In the course of the conversation, Marlborough perceived that Charles had a rooted aversion to, and was not, therefore, likely to form an alliance with Louis. A map of Russia lying open before the king, and the anger with which Charles spoke of Peter, revealed to the duke the real intentions of the Swedish monarch. He, therefore, took his leave without making any proposals, convinced that the disputes of Charles with the emperor might easily be accommodated, as all his demands would be granted.

‡ When Peter was informed of this haughty answer, he coolly replied, "My brother Charles affects to play the part of Alexander, but I hope he will not find in me a Darius."

Ukraine, whither he had been invited by Mazeppa, the chief of the Cossacks, who, disgusted by the conduct of the czar, had resolved to throw off his allegiance. In spite of all the obstacles that nature and the enemy could throw in his way, Charles reached the place of rendezvous; but he had the mortification to find Mazeppa appear in his camp as a fugitive rather than an ally, for the czar had discovered his treason, and disconcerted his schemes by the punishment of his associates.

A still greater misfortune to the Swedes was the loss of the convoy and the ruin of the reinforcement they had expected from Livonia. General Lewenhaupt, to whose care it was intrusted, had been forced into three general engagements by the Russians; and though he had eminently distinguished himself by his courage and conduct, he was forced to set fire to his wagons to prevent their falling into the hands of the enemy. Undaunted by these misfortunes, Charles continued the campaign even in the depth of a winter* so severe that two thousand men were at once frozen to death almost in his presence. At length he laid siege to Pultowa, a fortified city on the frontiers of the Ukraine, which contained one of the czar's principal magazines. The garrison was numerous and the resistance obstinate; Charles himself was dangerously wounded in the heel while viewing the works; and while he was still confined to his tent he learned that Peter was advancing with a numerous army to raise the siege. Leaving seven thousand men to guard the works, Charles ordered his soldiers to march and meet the enemy, while he accompanied them in a litter (July 8, 1709). The desperate charge of the Swedes broke the Russian cavalry, but the infantry stood firm, and gave the horse an opportunity of rallying in the rear. In the meantime, the czar's artillery made dreadful havoc in the Swedish line; and Charles, who had been forced to abandon his cannon in his forced marches, in vain contended against this formidable disadvantage. After a dreadful combat of more than two hours' duration, the Swedish army was irretrievably ruined; eight thousand of their best troops were left dead on the field, six thousand were taken prisoners, and about twelve thousand of the fugitives were soon after forced to surrender on the banks of the Dnieper, from want of boats to cross the river. Charles, accompanied by about three hundred of his guards, escaped to Bender, a Turkish town in Bessarabia, abandoning all his treasures to his rival, including the rich spoils of Poland and Saxony.

* This catastrophe is powerfully described by Campbell:—

> "Oh! learn the fate that bleeding thousands bore,
> Led by their Charles to Dnieper's sandy shore.
> Faint from his wounds, and shivering in the blast,
> The Swedish soldier sank and groaned his last;
> File after file the stormy showers benumb,
> Freeze every standard sheet and hush the drum;
> Horseman and horse confessed the bitter pang,
> And arms and warrior fell with hollow clang.
> Yet, ere he sank in Nature's last repose,
> Ere life's warm current to the fountain froze,
> The dying man to Sweden turned his eye,
> Thought of his home, and closed it with a sigh.
> Imperial pride looked sullen on his plight,
> And Charles beheld, nor shuddered at the sight."

Few victories have ever had such important consequences as that which the czar won at Pultowa; in one fatal day Charles lost the fruits of nine years' victories; the veteran army that had been the terror of Europe was completely ruined; those who escaped from the fatal field were taken prisoners, but they found a fate scarcely better than death, for they were transported by the czar to colonize the wilds of Siberia; the elector of Saxony re-entered Poland, and drove Stanislaus from the throne; the kings of Denmark* and Prussia revived old claims on the Swedish provinces, while the victorious Peter invaded not only Livonia and Ingria, but a great part of Finland. Indeed, but for the interference of the German emperor and the maritime powers, the Swedish monarchy would have been rent in pieces.

Charles, in his exile, formed a new plan for the destruction of his hated rival; he instigated the Turks to attempt the conquest of Russia, and flattered himself that he might yet enter Moscow at the head of a Mohammedan army. The bribes which Peter lavishly bestowed on the counsellors of the sultans, for a time frustrated these intrigues; but Charles, through his friend Poniatowski, informed the sultan of his vizier's corruption, and procured the deposition of that minister. Pupruli, who succeeded to the office of vizier, was averse to a Russian war, but he was removed at the end of two months, and the seals of office given to the pacha of Syria, who commenced his administration by sending the Russian ambassador to the prison of the Seven Towers.

The czar made the most vigorous preparations for the new war by which he was menaced (A. D. 1711). The Turkish vizier, on the other hand, assembled all the forces of the Ottoman empire in the plains of Adrianople. Demetrius Cantemir, the hospodar of Moldavia, believing that a favorable opportunity presented itself for delivering his country from the Mohammedan yoke, invited the czar to his aid; and the Russians, rapidly advancing, reached the northern banks of the Pruth, near Yassi, the Moldavian capital. Here the Russians found that the promises of Prince Cantemir were illusory; the Moldavians, happy under the Turkish sway, treated the invaders as enemies, and refused to supply them with provisions; in the meantime, the vizier arriving, formed a fortified camp in their front, while his vast host of light cavalry swept round their lines and cut off all foraging parties. The Russians defeated three successive attempts to storm their intrenchments; but they must have yielded to the effects of fatigue and famine, had not the emperess Catherine,† who accompanied her husband during the campaign, sent a private message to the vizier, which induced him to open negotiations. A treaty was concluded on terms which, though severe, were more favorable than Peter, under the circumstances, could reasonably have hoped; the Russians retired in safety, and Charles

* The Danish monarch invaded Schonen, but his troops were defeated by the Swedish militia, and a few regiments of the line, commanded by General Steenbock. When intelligence of this victory was conveyed to Charles, he exclaimed, "My brave Swedes! should God permit me to join you once more, we will beat them all."

† Catherine was a Livonian captive, of low condition, whom the emperor first saw waiting at table. Her abilities and modesty won his heart, he raised her to his throne, and never had reason to repent of his choice.

reached the Turkish camp, only to learn the downfall of all his expectations.

A new series of intrigues in the court of Constantinople led to the appointment of a new vizier; but this minister was little inclined to gratify the king of Sweden; on the contrary, warned by the fate of his predecessors, he resolved to remove him from the Ottoman empire (A. D. 1713). Charles continued to linger; even after he had received a letter of dismissal from the sultan's own hand, he resolved to remain, and when a resolution was taken to send him away by force, he determined, with his few attendants, to dare the whole strength of the Turkish empire. After a fierce resistance, he was captured and conveyed a prisoner to Adrianople; on his road, he learned that Stanislaus, whom he had raised to the throne of Poland, was likewise a Turkish captive; but, buoyed up by ardent hopes, he sent a message to his fellow-sufferer, never to make peace with Augustus. Another revolution in the divan revived the hopes of Charles, and induced him to remain in Turkey, when his return to the North would probably have restored him to his former eminence. The Swedes, under General Steenbock, gained one of the most brilliant victories that had been obtained during the war, over the united forces of the Danes and Saxons, at Gadebusch, in the dutchy of Mecklenburg; but the conqueror sullied his fame by burning the defenceless town of Altona, an outrage which excited the indignation of all Europe. This, however, was the last service that Steenbock could perform to his absent master; unable to prevent the junction of the Russians with the Danes and Saxons, he retreated before superior numbers, and, by the artifices of Baron Goertz, obtained temporary refuge in a fortress belonging to the duke of Holstein. The allies, however, pursued their advantages so vigorously that Steenbock and his followers were forced to yield themselves prisoners of war. Goertz, however, in some degree averted the consequences of this calamity by a series of political intrigues, which excited various jealousies and discordant interests between the several enemies of Sweden

The czar in the meantime pushed forward his conquests on the side of Finland; and the glory of his reign appeared to be consummated by a naval victory obtained over the Swedes near the island of Oeland (A. D. 1714). This unusual success was celebrated by a triumphal entry into St. Peterburgh, at which Peter addressed his subjects on the magnitude of the advantages they had derived from his government. Charles heard of his rival's progress unmoved; but when he learned that the Swedish senate intended to make his sister regent, and to make peace with Russia and Denmark, he announced his intention of returning home. He was honorably escorted to the Turkish frontiers; but though orders had been given that he should be received with all due honor in the imperial dominions, he traversed Germany incognito, and toward the close of the year reached Stralsund, the capital of Swedish Pomerania.

Charles, at the opening of the next campaign, found himself surrounded with enemies (A. D. 1715). Stralsund itself was besieged by the united armies of the Prussians, Danes, and Saxons, while the Russian fleet, which now rode triumphant in the Baltic, threatened a descent upon Sweden. After an obstinate defence, in which the

Swedish monarch displayed all his accustomed bravery, Stralsund was forced to capitulate, Charles having previously escaped in a small vessel to his native shores. All Europe believed the Swedish monarch undone; it was supposed that he could no longer defend his own dominions, when to the inexpressible astonishment of every one, it was announced that he had invaded Norway. His attention, however, was less engaged by the war than by the gigantic intrigues of his new favorite Goertz, who, taking advantage of a coolness between the Russians and the other enemies of Sweden, proposed that Peter and Charles should unite in strict amity, and dictate the law to Europe. A part of this daring plan was the removal of the elector of Hanover from the English throne, and the restoration of the exiled Stuarts. But while the negotiations were yet in progress, Charles invaded Norway a second time, and invested the castle of Frederickshall in the very depth of winter. But while engaged in viewing the works, he was struck by a cannon-ball, and was dead before any of his attendants came to his assistance (A. D. 1718).* The Swedish senate showed little grief for the loss of the warlike king; on the first news of his death, his favorite, Baron Goertz, was arrested, brought to trial, and put to death on a ridiculous charge of treason. The crown was conferred upon the late king's sister, but she soon resigned it to her husband, the prince of Hesse, both being compelled to swear that they never would attempt

* Dr. Johnson's character of Charles XII. is the best comment on the life of that adventurous warrior:—

"On what foundation stands the warrior's pride,
How just his hopes, let Swedish Charles decide;
A frame of adamant, a soul of fire,
No dangers fright him, and no labors tire;
O'er love, o'er fear, extends his wide domain,
Unconquered lord of pleasure and of pain;
No joys to him pacific sceptres yield,
War sounds the trump, he rushes to the field;
Behold surrounded kings their powers combine,
And one capitulate, and one resign;
Peace courts his hand, but spreads her charms in vain:
'Think nothing gained,' he cries, 'till naught remain:
On Moscow's walls, till Gothic standards fly,
And all be mine beneath the polar sky.'
The march begins in military state,
And nations on his eye suspended wait;
Stern famine guards the solitary coast,
And winter barricades the realms of frost;
He comes, nor want, nor cold, his course delay;
Hide, blushing Glory, hide Pultowa's day:
The vanquished hero leaves his broken bands,
And shows his miseries in distant lands;
Condemned a needly supplicant to wait
While ladies interpose, and slaves debate.
But did not chance at length her error mend?
Did no subverted empire mark his end?
Did rival monarchs give the fatal wound?
Or hostile millions press him to the ground?
His fall was destined to a barren strand,
A petty fortress, and a dubious hand;
He left the name, at which the world grew pale,
To point a moral, or adorn a tale."

the re-establishment of arbitrary power. Negotiations for peace were commenced with all the hostile powers, and treaties concluded with all but Russia (A. D. 1720). The appearance of an English fleet in the Baltic, coming to aid the Swedish squadron, however, finally disposed the czar to pacific measures ; and he consented to grant peace, on condition of being permitted to retain Ingria, Livonia, and part of Finland (A. D. 1721). Thus the great northren war terminated, just as it was about to be connected with the politics of southern Europe

CHAPTER VIII.

GROWTH OF THE MERCANTILE AND COLONIAL SYSTEM.

SECTION I.—*Establishment of the Hanoverian Succession in England.*

DURING the wars that had been waged against Louis XIV., the funding system was established in England; it commenced by the founding of a national bank (A. D. 1694), which lent its capital to the government at a lower rate of interest than was then usual. Further loans were contracted to support the exigences of the wars; parliament guarantied the payment of the interest, without entering into any obligation to restore the capital, which was transferable to any one. The gradual extension of the wealth of the nation facilitated the growth of this system, which soon gave England commanding influence on the continent. The facilities of raising money possessed by the English government enabled it to conclude subsidiary treaties, and set the armies of allied states in motion. Internally the funding system wrought a still greater change; a great portion of the political influence previously possessed by the landed aristocracy was transferred to large capitalists and manufacturers; the banking and funding systems afforded great facilities for accumulating the profits of industry, and thus fostered the growth of an intelligent and opulent middle class, whose strength was soon displayed in the increasing importance of the house of commons. Even at the treaty of Utrecht, the mercantile system began to manifest itself in all its strength. Grants of commercial privileges were made the conditions of peace with the maritime powers, and territorial concessions were made with a regard to the interests of trade rather than power. Justly as the British negotiators at Utrecht may be blamed for not taking sufficient advantage of the position in which their country was placed by the victories of Marlborough, it is undeniable that the treaty they concluded laid the foundation of the commercial superiority of England; it also contained the germes of two future wars, but these consequences were slowly developed; and at the commencement of the eighteenth century, the republic of Holland was still the first commercial state in Europe.

The accession of George I. produced a complete change in the English administration; the tories were dismissed with harshness, the whigs were the sole possessors of office, and on the new election consequent on the demise of the crown, they obtained a decided majority in parliament. Unfortunately they used their power to crush their political adversaries; the chiefs of the late ministry were impeached for high treason, and their prosecution was hurried forward so vindictively, that Lords Bolingbroke and Ormond fled to the continent. This seemed a favorable moment to make an effort in favor of the exiled Stuarts, but Louis XIV., broken down by age, infirmities, and misfortune, was unwilling to hazard a new war, which might disturb the minority of his great-grandson, for in consequence of the mortality in the royal family, this remote descendant was destined to be his successor. The death of Louis (Sept. 1, 1715) further disconcerted the projects of the Pretender and his adherents; the duke of Orleans, who was chosen regent by the parliament of Paris during the minority of Louis XV., adopted every suggestion of the English ambassador, the earl of Stair, for counteracting the designs of the jacobites; and he did them irreparable injury by seizing some ships laden with arms and ammunition, at a time when it was impossible for them to purchase any fresh supply. The jacobites, however, persevered, and a plan was formed for a general insurrection; but this was defeated by the Pretender's imprudence, who prematurely gave the earl of Mar a commission to raise his standard in Scotland. The earl of Mar possessed considerable influence in the highland counties; no sooner had he proclaimed the Pretender, under the title of James III., than the clans crowded to his standard, and he was soon at the head of nine thousand men, including several noblemen and persons of distinction. Thus supported, he made himself master of Perth, and established his authority in almost all that part of Scotland which lies north of the Frith of Forth. In the meantime the government was alarmed; the jacobite leaders who had agreed to raise the west of England were taken into custody, and the duke of Argyle was sent against Mar with all the forces of North Britain. An ill-contrived and worse executed insurrection of the jacobites exploded in the north of England; its leaders, the earl of Derwentwater, Lord Widdrington, and Mr. Foster, a Northumbrian gentleman of great influence, were joined by several Scottish lords and a body of Highland infantry. But being unable to agree upon any rational plan of operations, they were surrounded by the royal forces in the town of Preston, and forced to surrender at discretion. It would have been better for the character of the government had lenity been shown to these unhappy men, but unfortunately most of the leaders were doomed to suffer the penalties of high treason.

In the meantime the earl of Mar had fought an indecisive battle with the duke of Argyle, which proved nevertheless ruinous to the Pretender's cause. Many who had been previously in doubt, declared for the royal cause, and several of the insurgent leaders returned to their allegiance. In this desperate state of his affairs, the Pretender landed with a small train in Scotland; but finding his cause hopeless, he returned to France with such of the leaders as did not expect pardon, and the whole country quietly submitted to the duke of Argyle.

Before entering on the singular changes wrought by the policy of the duke of Orleans in Europe, it will be convenient to cast a brief glance at the affairs of Russia and Turkey. No sooner had Peter the Great concluded peace with Sweden than he assumed the title of emperor, with the consent of all the European powers. By sending an auxiliary force to aid the lawful sovereign of Persia against an Afghan usurper, he obtained the cession of the provinces on the south and west of the Caspian sea; and, while he thus extended his dominions, he did not neglect their internal improvement, but constructed canals, planned roads, and established manufactories. But Peter's own character retained many traces of barbarism, and his treatment of his eldest son, Alexis, excited general horror. This unfortunate prince is said to have been induced by some of the Russian priests and boyars to promise, that in the event of his accession, he would restore the old state of things, and abolish the new institutions of his father. He was arrested and forced to sign an abdication of the crown; soon after this, he died in prison, but whether violent means were used to accelerate his end, has never been satisfactorily ascertained. The second son of the Russian emperor died in infancy, and Peter chose his emperess as his successor. He assisted at her coronation after his return from the Persian war; and on his death (A. D. 1725) she became empress of all the Russias, and by the excellence of her administration justified the choice of her illustrious husband.

The Turks were enraged at the diminution of their national glory in the war that was terminated by the treaty of Carlowitz, and eagerly longed for an opportunity of retrieving their lost honor. Ahmed III., the most warlike sultan that had recently filled the throne, was far from being displeased by their martial zeal, and he took the earliest opportunity of declaring war against the Venetians, whom he expelled from the Morea in a single campaign (A. D. 1715). The emperor, Charles VI., was solicited by the pope to check the progress of the Mohammedans; he therefore interfered, as protector of the treaty of Carlowitz; but finding his remonstrances disregarded, he assembled a powerful army, and published a declaration of war (A. D. 1716). Prince Eugene, at the head of the imperialists, crossed the Danube, and attacked the forces of the grand vizier, near Peterwaradin. He gained a complete victory, twenty-five thousand of the Turks were either killed or drowned, while the loss of the Austrians did not exceed one fifth of that number. In the ensuing campaign, the prince laid siege to Belgrade, and having defeated with great slaughter the vast Turkish army that marched to its relief, became master of that important fortress. The consequence of these victories was the peace of Passarowitz (A. D. 1718) by which Austria and Russia gained considerable acquisitions; but the republic of Venice, for whose sake the war was ostensibly undertaken, did not recover its possessions in Greece, and found its interests neglected by its more potent allies.

These wars were very remotedly connected with the political condition of southern Europe, which now depended entirely on the maintenance of the terms of the peace of Utrecht. Several powers were interested in their preservation; England's flourishing commerce depended in many essential particulars on the articles of the treaty; they were the best security to Austria, for the provinces lately ceded in Italy; and the Dutch, unable or unwilling to garrison the barrier towns, felt that peace was necessary to their security. But above all, the regent of France believed that this treaty was the sole support of his power, since it involved the Spanish king's renunciation of his claims to the French crown. Altogether opposed to these views were the designs of the court of Spain; the marriage of Philip to Elizabeth Farnese, heiress to the dutchies of Parma, Placentia, and Tuscany, inspired him with the hope of recovering the provinces that had been severed from the Spanish monarchy; his prime minister, Cardinal Alberoni, flattered him with hopes of success, and at the same time diligently labored to improve the financial condition of the country. Alberoni's projects included an entire change in the political system of Europe; he designed to reconquer Sardinia and Sicily for Spain; to place James III. on the throne of England by the aid of the Russian emperor and the king of Sweden; to prevent the interference of the emperor, by engaging the Turks to assail his dominions. Pope Clement XI., a weak and stupid pontiff, could not comprehend the merits of Alberoni's schemes; he refused to pay the ecclesiastical subsidies to Philip V., and before the ambitious cardinal could further develop his schemes, the Quadruple Alliance was formed by the alarmed potentates of Europe, and Philip V., was forced to dismiss his intriguing minister. The pope had the mortification to find that his interests were totally disregarded in the new arrangements made for preserving the tranquillity of Europe; his superiorities in Parma and Placentia formed part of the bribe tendered to the court of Spain by the rulers of France and Germany; he remonstrated loudly, but, in spite of his efforts, they were accepted and retained.

On the death of Clement XI., Alberoni became a candidate for the papacy, and was very near being elected. Fortunately for the permanency of Romish power, this violent prelate was excluded from the chair of St. Peter, and Innocent XIII. was chosen. During his pontificate the society of freemasons began to be regarded with suspicion by the heads of the church, especially as several other secret associations were formed in Germany and Italy for the propagation of what were called philosophical tenets; but these doctrines were, in reality, not only hostile to popery, but subversive of all religion and morality. Though Austria, France, England, and Holland, united against the dangerous schemes of Alberoni, and formed the Quadruple Alliance (A. D. 1716), yet the cardinal steadily pursued his course, and war was proclaimed against Spain by France and England.

The strength of Spain, exhausted by the war of the succession, could not resist this powerful combination; the English fleet rode triumphant in the Mediterranean; a German army expelled the Spaniards from Sicily; the French, under the command of the duke of Berwick, invaded Spain, and captured several important fortresses; the duke of Ormond failed in his attempt to land a Spanish army in Great Britain; and Philip, completely subdued, dismissed Alberoni (A. D. 1720), and acceded to the terms of the Quadruple Alliance.

During this war, France and England were involved in great financial difficulties, by the Mississippi scheme in one country, and the South sea speculation in the other. A Scotch adventurer, named Law, proposed a plan to the regent of France for speedily paying off the vast national debt, and delivering the revenue from the enormous interest by which it was overwhelmed. He effected this by an extraordinary issue of paper, on the security of the Mississippi company, from whose commercial speculations the most extravagant results were expected. So rapid was his success, that in 1719, the nominal value of the funds was eighty times greater than the real value of all the current coin of the realm. This immense disproportion soon excited alarm; when the holders of the notes tried to convert them into money, there was no specie to meet the demands, and the result was a general bankruptcy. Some efforts were made by the government to remedy this calamity, but the evil admitted only of slight palliation, and thousands were completely ruined.

The South sea scheme, projected by Sir John Blount, in England, was a close imitation of Law's plan. He proposed that the South sea company, to which great commercial advantages had been secured by the treaty of Utrecht, should become the sole creditor of the nation; and facilities were offered to the owners of stock to exchange the security of the crown for that of the South sea company. Never did so wild a scheme meet such sudden success; South sea stock in a short time rose to ten times its original value; new speculations were started, and for a time had similar popularity; but when suspicion was excited and some cautious holders of stock began to sell, a universal panic succeeded to the general delusion. By the prompt interference of parliament a general bankruptcy was averted, and the chief contrivers of the fraud, including many individuals of rank and station, were punished, and their estates sequestrated for the benefit of the sufferers.

The confusion occasioned by the South sea scheme encouraged the jacobites to make another effort in favor of the Stuarts (A. D. 1722). But their plans were discovered, a gentleman named Layer was capitally punished for enlisting men in the service of the Pretender, and Dr. Atterbury, bishop of Rochester, the soul of his party, was exiled.

Fortunately for the repose of Europe, the prime ministers of France and England, Cardinal Fleury, who succeeded to power soon after the death of the duke of Orleans, and Sir Robert Walpole, were both bent on the preservation of peace, and for nearly twenty years they prevented any active hostilities. Walpole's administration, however, began to lose its popularity, on account of his not gratifying the national hatred against Spain. A powerful opposition was formed against him, composed of the old tories, and some disappointed courtiers, which he contended against by unbounded parliamentary corruption. The death of George I. (A. D. 1727) made no change in the position of parties, for George II. intrusted Walpole with the same power he had enjoyed under his father.

The emperor Charles, having no prospect of male issue, was naturally anxious to secure the peaceful succession of his daughter, Maria Theresa, to his hereditary dominions; and for this purpose he prepared a solemn law, called the Pragmatic Sanction, and procured its confirmation by the principal states of Europe. The guarantee of France was not obtained without war. Stanislaus Leczinski, father-in-law to the French monarch, was elected king of Poland, but was dethroned by the influence of the German powers (A. D. 1733). To avenge this insult, the French king formed a league with the courts of Spain and Sardinia against the emperor; and, after a brief struggle, the court of Vienna was forced to purchase peace by considerable sacrifices. The success of the Russians under the reign of the emperess Anne, niece to Peter the Great, against the Turks, induced the German emperor to commence a second unfortunate war. Scarcely was it concluded, when the death of Charles (A. D. 1740) involved Europe in the contentions of a new disputed succession.

Sir Robert Walpole had long preserved England at peace; but the interested clamors of some merchants engaged in a contraband trade with the Spanish colonies, compelled him to commence hostilities (A. D. 1739). Admiral Vernon, with a small force, captured the important city of Porto Bello, on the American isthmus. This success induced the minister to send out large armaments against the Spanish colonies. Vernon with a fleet, and Lord Cathcart with a numerous army, undertook to assail Spanish America on the side of the Atlantic, while Commodore Anson sailed round Cape Horn to ravage the coasts of Chili and Peru. The death of Lord Cathcart frustrated these arrangements. he was succeeded by General Wentworth, an officer of little experience, and very jealous of Vernon's popularity. An attack was made on Carthagena, but it failed lamentably, owing to the disputes between the naval and military commanders. Both were reinforced from England, but they effected nothing of any importance, and returned home after more than fifteen thousand of their men had fallen victims to the climate. Anson, in the meantime, encountered such a severe storm in rounding Cape Horn, that two of his ships were forced to return, and one was lost. His diminished squadron, however, took several prizes off the coast of Chili, and plundered the town of Paita, in Peru. His force was finally reduced to one ship, but with this he captured the Spanish galleon, laden with treasure, that sailed annually from Acapulco to Manilla. He then returned to England triumphant; but the loss at Carthagena was so severely felt, that the English would not venture to renew their enterprises against Spanish America.

Scarcely had Maria Theresa succeeded her father, the emperor Charles, when she found herself surrounded by a host of enemies. The elector of Bavaria laid claim to Bohemia; the king of Sardinia revived some obsolete pretensions to the dutchy of Milan; while the kings of Poland, Spain, and France, exhibited claims to the whole Austrian succession. An unexpected claimant gave the first signal for war. Frederic III., who had just ascended the Prussian throne, inherited from his father a rich treasury and a well-appointed army. Relying on the goodness of his troops rather than the goodness of his cause, he entered Silesia, and soon conquered that fine province (A. D. 1741). At the same time he offered to support Maria Theresa against all competitors, on the condition of being permitted to retain his acquisition. The princess steadily refused, though she knew that France was arming against her, and that her enemies had resolved to elevate Charles Albert, elector of Bavaria, to the empire. The forces of the king of France entered Germany, and being joined by the Bavarian army, made several important conquests, and even threatened Vienna: but Maria Theresa, repairing to Presburg, convened the states of Hungary, and appearing before them with her infant son in her arms, made such an eloquent appeal, that the nobles with one accord exclaimed, "We will die for our KING, Maria Theresa." Nor was this a momentary burst of passion; they raised a powerful army for the defence of their young and beautiful princess, and a subsidy was at the same time voted to her by the British parliament. So great was the attachment of the English people to her cause, that the pacific Sir Robert Walpole was forced to resign, and a new administration was formed by his political rivals.

The new ministers had been raised to power by a sudden burst of popular enthusiasm, but they soon showed themselves unworthy of the nation's confidence. They took the lead in suppressing the measures which they had themselves declared necessary to the security of the constitution, and they far outstripped their predecessors in supporting German subsidies, standing armies, and continental connexions, which had been so long the theme of their severest censure. They augmented the army, sent a large body of troops into the Netherlands under the command of the earl of Stair, and granted subsidies to the Danes, the Hessians, and the Austrians. The French had some hopes of gaining the support of the Russians, who were now ruled by the emperess Elizabeth. On the death of the emperess Anne, her niece, the princess of Mecklenburgh, assumed the government, as guardian of her son John. But the partiality that the regent showed for her German countrymen displeased the Russian nobles; their discontents were artfully increased by a French physician named Lestocq; a bloodless insurrection led to the deposition of the Mecklenburgh princess, and Elizabeth, the daughter of Peter the Great, was raised to the throne. She found the country involved in a war with Sweden, which she brought to a successful issue, and secured the inheritance to the Swedish crown for her favorite, Adolphus, bishop of Lubeck. Though the czarina owed her elevation in a great degree to French intrigue, she was inclined to support the Austrian cause; but she did not interfere in the contest until she had completed all her arrangements.

The republic of Holland showed still more reluctance to engage in the war; and the English army in the Netherlands, deprived of the expected Dutch aid, remained inactive. In Germany, the Bavarian elector was driven not only from his conquests, but from his hereditary dominions,* while the king of Prussia took advantage of a brilliant victory to conclude a treaty with Maria Theresa, by which he was secured in the possession of Silesia. The French army, thus deprived of its most

* Dr. Johnson has powerfully described the fate of this unfortunate prince:—

"The bold Bavarian, in a luckless hour,
Tries the dread summits of Cæsarean power,
With unexpected legions bursts away,
And sees defenceless realms receive his sway:
Short sway! fair Austria spreads her mournful charms,
The queen, the beauty, sets the world in arms;
From hill to hill the beacons' rousing blaze
Spreads wide the hope of plunder and of praise;
The fierce Croatian and the wild hussar,
With all the sons of ravage, crowd the war;
The baffled prince, in honor's flattering bloom,
Of hasty greatness finds the fatal doom;
His foes' derision, and his subjects' blame,
And steals to death, from anguish and from shame."

powerful ally, must have been ruined but for the abilities of its general, the count de Bellisle, who effected one of the most masterly retreats recorded in history, from the centre of Bohemia to the frontiers of Alsace. The Spaniards failed in their attacks on the imperial territories in Italy, chiefly owing to the activity of the English fleets in the Mediterranean; and the court of Versailles, disheartened by these repeated failures, made proposals of peace. Maria Theresa, intoxicated with success, rejected all the proffered eonditions (A. D. 1743). She urged forward her armaments with such vigor, that the French were driven to the Rhine, and the unfortunate elector of Bavaria, abandoned by his allies, and stripped of his dominions, sought refuge in Frankfort, where he lived in indigence and obscurity. The errors of the French in Flanders led to their defeat at Dettingen, just when a little caution would have insured the ruin of the English and Austrians. But the allies made no use of their victory, owing to the irresolution of George II., who took the management of the campaign into his own hands, and superseded the earl of Stair. The war lingered in Italy, but the haughtiness and ambition of the emperess began to excite the secret jealousy of the German princes; and the French and Spanish courts, alarmed by her treaty with the king of Sardinia, drew their alliance closer by the celebrated Family Compact, which bound them to maintain the integrity of each other's dominions.

England had now become a principal in the war, and the monarchs of France and Spain resolved to invade that country, and remove the Hanoverian dynasty. A powerful army was assembled, and a fleet prepared to protect the transports; but the French ships were shattered in a storm, and forced to take refuge in Brest from a superior English force (A. D. 1744). The English navy was less successful in the Mediterranean: the combined fleets of France and Spain were met by the British admirals, Matthews and Lestock; but owing to the misconduct of some captains, and Lestock's remaining aloof with his whole division, the result of the engagement was indecisive. It is a sad proof of the violence and injustice of faction, that when these officers were brought to trial, Matthews, who had fought like a hero, was condemned, and Lestock acquitted. The war in Italy was sanguinary, but indecisive. In Germany, however, the king of Prussia once more took up arms against Maria Theresa, and invaded Bohemia. He was defeated with great loss, and forced to retire precipitately into Silesia. Soon afterward, the death of the elector of Bavaria removed all reasonable grounds for the continuance of hostilities; his son, who had no pretensions to the empire, concluded a treaty with Maria Theresa, and promised to support the election of her husband, the grand duke of Tuscany, to the imperial dignity.

But the national animosity between the French and English prevented the restoration of peace (A. D. 1745). The Austrians were completely vanquished in Italy by the united forces of the French and Spaniards, whose vast superiority of numbers could not be resisted; and on the side of the Netherlands, the misconduct of the allies gave a signal triumph to the Bourbons. The French army under Marshal Saxe was strongly posted at Fontenoy, but was, notwithstanding, attacked by the English, Dutch, and Germans In few battles has the valor of the

British infantry been displayed more signally or more uselessly. Forming themselves into a column, they bore down everything before them, until, deserted by their Dutch and German auxiliaries, they were outflanked and driven back by the entire force of the French army. The loss on both sides was nearly equal; but though the victory was not decisive, it enabled Marshal Saxe to reduce some of the most considerable towns in the Netherlands. Tranquillity was restored to Germany by the election of the grand duke of Tuscany to the empire, under the name of Francis I.; and about the same time Maria Theresa, as queen of Hungary, concluded the treaty of Breslau with the king of Prussia, and thus quieted her most dangerous enemy.

The discontent occasioned by the loss at Fontenoy induced the grandson of James II., commonly called the Young Pretender, to attempt the restoration of his family. He landed in Scotland with a small train, but being soon joined by the enthusiastic Highland clans, he descended from the mountains and marched toward Edinburgh. The city surrendered without any attempt at resistance, but the castle still held out. Sir John Cope, the royal commander in Scotland, had marched northward to raise the loyal clans; having collected some reinforcements, he proceeded from Aberdeen to Dunbar by sea, and hearing that the insurgents were resolved to hazard a battle, he encamped at Preston Pans. Here he was unexpectedly attacked by the Young Pretender, at the head of about three thousand undisciplined and half-armed soldiers. A panic seized the royal troops; they fled with the most disgraceful precipitation, abandoning all their baggage, cannon, and camp-equipage, to their enemies.

The reduction of the French colony of Cape Breton, in North America, had revived the spirit of the English; and the time that the Pretender wasted in idle pageantry at Edinburgh afforded the ministers an opportunity of bringing over some regiments from Flanders. Notwithstanding the formidable preparations thus made, the Pretender, probably relying on promised aid from France, crossed the western borders, and took Carlisle. But the vigilance of Admiral Vernon prevented the French fleet from venturing out; and the Pretender having failed to raise recruits in Lancashire, and unable to force a passage into Wales, baffled the royal armies by an unexpected turn, and suddenly marched to Derby. Had he continued to advance boldly, London itself might have fallen; but he delayed at Derby until he was nearly enclosed between two powerful armies, and was forced either to retreat or to hazard a battle on very disadvantageous terms. It was finally determined that they should return to Scotland, and this retrograde movement was effected by the Highlanders with extraordinary courage and expedition.

This retreat did not produce the dispiriting effect on the insurgents that had been anticipated. The Pretender's forces were greatly augmented after his return to Scotland; but finding that Edinburgh had been secured by the royal army during his absence, he marched to Stirling, captured the town, and besieged the castle. General Hawley was sent with a strong force to raise the siege, but despising the undisciplined Highlanders, he acted so imprudently that he suffered a complete defeat near Falkirk (A. D. 1746). The Pretender, instead of following up his advantage, returned to the siege of Stirling castle, while the royal army, reinforced by fresh troops, was placed under the command of the duke of Cumberland, a prince of the blood, who, though by no means a skilful general, was a great favorite with the soldiery. The insurgent army retired before the royal troops until they reached Culloden Moor, where they resolved to make a stand. Warned by the errors of Cope and Hawley, the duke of Cumberland took the most prudent precautions to meet the desperate charge of the Highlanders; they rushed on with their usual impetuosity, but being received by a close and galling fire of musketry, while their ranks were torn by artillery, they wavered, broke, and in less than thirty minutes were a helpless mass of confusion. The victors gave no quarter: many of the insurgents were murdered in cold blood, and their unfortunate prince was only saved from capture by the generous devotion of one of his adherents, who assured the pursuers that he was himself the object of their search.

The cruelties of the royalists after their victory were perfectly disgraceful; the country of the insurgent clans was laid waste with fire and sword; the men were hunted like wild beasts on the mountains, the women and children, driven from their burned huts, perished by thousands on the barren heaths. When all traces of rebellion, and almost of population, had disappeared, the duke of Cumberland returned to London, leaving a large body of troops to continue the pursuit of the surviving fugitives. During five months the young Pretender remained concealed in the Highlands and Western isles of Scotland, though a reward of thirty thousand pounds was set on his head, and more than fifty persons were intrusted with his secret. At length he escaped on board a French privateer, and, after enduring incredible hardships, arrived safely in Brittany. The vengeance of the government fell heavily on his adherents: numbers of the leaders were tried and executed, and though they died with heroic firmness, their fate excited little commiseration.

In the meantime the French, under Marshal Saxe, had overrun the greater part of the Netherlands; Brussels, Antwerp, and Namur, were captured, while the confederate army was defeated in a sanguinary but indecisive engagement at Raucoux. In Italy, the allies were more successful; taking advantage of the mutual jealousies between the French and Spaniards, the Austrians, reinforced by the king of Sardinia, drove their enemies from Italy, and pursued them into France. The death of their monarch had abated the vigor of the Spaniards, for the designs of Ferdinand VI., Philip's son and successor, were for some time unknown; but when he declared his resolution to adhere to the Family Compact, the hopes of the partisans of the house of Bourbon were revived. About the same time the imperialists were compelled to evacuate the south of France by the judicious measures of the marshal de Bellisle; and the Genoese, irritated by the severity with which they were treated, expelled the Austrian garrison, and baffled every attempt that their oppressors made to recover the city. The national animosity between the French and English was aggravated by commercial jealousy; they mutually fitted out armaments against each other's colonies; but these expeditions, badly contrived and worse executed, led to no decisive results, and all parties began to grow weary of a war which produced no consequence but a lavish waste of blood and treasure.

Conferences were commenced at Breda, but the demands of the French appeared so exorbitant to the allies, that the negotiations were abruptly terminated, and the hostile powers made the most vigorous preparations for a decisive struggle (A. D. 1747). The exertions of the allies were long paralyzed by the indecision of the Dutch rulers; even when their own country was invaded, they could not be induced to adopt more vigorous councils, until a popular revolt compelled them to revive the office of stadtholder, and confer that dignity on the prince of Orange.

Though this revolution gave more vigor to the operations of the allies, the whole weight of the war was ungenerously thrown upon the English. The obstinate and bloody battle of Val would have been won by British valor, but for the timidity and slowness of the Dutch and Austrians; in consequence of their misconduct it terminated to the disadvantage of the confederates. Soon after, the fortress of Bergen-op-Zoom, generally believed to be impregnable, was captured by the French, who thus became masters of the whole navigation of the Scheldt. In Italy, the allies, though forced to raise the siege of Genoa, were generally successful, while the British navy gained several important triumphs at sea. A valuable French convoy was attacked by Admirals Anson and Warren, off Cape Finisterre, and, after an obstinate engagement, six ships-of-the-line and several armed Indiamen were taken. Seven weeks after, a fleet laden with the rich produce of St. Domingo fell into the hands of Commodore Fox; and at a later period of the year, Admiral Hawke, after a sharp battle, took six ships-of-the-line in the latitude of Bellisle. These reverses, and the sailing of a powerful British armament to the East Indies, so alarmed the court of Versailles, that negotiations for peace were once more commenced.

While conferences were opened at Aix-la-Chapelle (A. D. 1748), Marshal Saxe continued to carry on the war with great vigor: he laid siege to Maestricht, which was obstinately defended, but before the contest could be decided, intelligence was received that the preliminaries of peace had been signed. The basis of the treaty was a restitution of all conquests made during the war, and a mutual release of prisoners without ransom. It left unsettled the clashing claims of the Spaniards and British to the trade of the American seas, and made no mention of the right of search which had been the original cause of the war; the only advantage, indeed, that England gained, was the recognition of the Hanoverian succession, and the general abandonment of the Pretender, whose cause was henceforth regarded as hopeless. This result, from so expensive a contest, gave general dissatisfaction; but the blame should fall on the authors of the war, not of the peace; England had no interest in the contests for the Austrian succession; under the peaceful administration of Sir Robert Walpole, her commerce and manufactures had rapidly increased; but through an idle ambition for military glory, and a perverse love of meddling in continental affairs, the prosperity of the country received a severe check, and an enormous addition was made to the national debt.

SECTION II.—*The Colonial Struggle between France and Great Britain.*

THE peace of Aix-la-Chapelle was soon discovered to be little better than a suspension of arms. Two causes of a very different nature united to produce a new and fiercer struggle, which no arts of diplomacy could long avert. The first of these was the jealousy with which the court of Austria regarded the great increase of the Prussian monarchy; the extorted renunciation of Silesia could neither be forgiven nor forgotten, and its recovery had long been the favorite object of the court of Vienna. The Prussian monarch was not popular with his neighbors—all new powers are naturally objects of jealousy—and the selfish policy which Frederic displayed, both in contracting and dissolving alliances, prevented him from gaining any permanent friend; he was the personal enemy of Elizabeth, emperess of Russia, and of Count Bruhl, the leading minister in the court of Saxony, and both readily joined in the plans formed for his destruction.

But with these confederates, the Austrian cabinet was reluctant to engage in hostilities, while France might at any time turn the balance, by renewing its former relations with Prussia. Prince Kaunitz, the real guide of the court of Vienna, and, during four reigns, the soul of the Austrian councils, resolved to unite the empire and France in one common project for sharing the rule of Europe. Louis XV., who had sunk into being the slave of his mistresses, was induced, by this able diplomatist, to depart from the course of policy which for two centuries had maintained the high rank of France among the continental powers; from being the rivals and opponents of the Austrian dynasty, the house of Bourbon sank into the humble character of assistants to that power—a change which eventually brought the greatest calamities on themselves and their country.

The commercial jealousy with which the English regarded the French, was the second cause for the renewal of the war. During the late war, the French navy had been all but annihilated, and the exertions made for its restoration were viewed with secret anger. Owing to incapacity or defective information, the negotiators at Aix-la-Chapelle had left most of the colonial questions at issue between England and France wholly undecided. The chief subjects contested were, the limits of the English colony of Nova Scotia, the right claimed by the French to erect forts along the Ohio, for the purpose of connecting the Canadas with Louisiana, the occupation of some neutral islands in the West Indies by the French, and, finally, the efforts of both nations to acquire political supremacy in Hindústan.

The maritime war between England and France had no immediate connexion with the struggle between Prussia and Austria. But when the French king, at the commencement of the contest, menaced Hanover, George II., who preferred the interests of this petty principality to those of the British empire, entered into a treaty with Frederic for its defence. Thus these two wars, so distinct in their origin and nature, were blended into one; but before their termination, they were again separated and concluded by distinct treaties of peace.

The empire which the descendants of Baber had established in Hindústan, touched the summit of its greatness in the reign of Aurungzebe; under his feeble successors the imperial power rapidly declined, and after the successful eruption of Nadír Shah (A. D. 1738), it was almost annihilated. The governors of provinces and districts became virtually independent sovereigns, and the allegiance they paid to the court of

Delhi was merely nominal. Both the French and the English East India companies took advantage of this state of things to extend their influence and enlarge their territories. Dupleix, the French governor of Pondicherry, had long sought an opportunity of interfering in the troubled politics of India; it was afforded him by the contests which arose on the vacancies in the souhbadary of the Deccan, and the nabobship of the Carnatic. He supported the claims of Chundah Saheb to the latter post, and endeavored to make Murzafa Jing souhbadar, or viceroy of the Deccan. He succeeded in these objects, but his favorites did not long retain their elevation; still, however, a precedent was established for the interference of the French in the contests between the native powers, and their aid was purchased by fresh concessions in every revolution. The rapid progress of their rivals roused the English from their supineness, and, fortunately, they found a leader whose abilities, both as a general and statesman, have scarcely been surpassed by any European that ever visited the east. Mr. Clive, the son of a private gentleman, had been originally employed in the civil service of the East India company; but war no sooner broke out than he exchanged the pen for the sword, and the union of courage and skill which he displayed at the very commencement of his career, excited just expectations of the glory which marked its progress. He gained several brilliant advantages over the allies of the French, and greatly strengthened the English interest in the Deccan or southern division of Hindústan. But the French East India company had begun to distrust the flattering promises of Dupleix; they found that his plans of territorial aggrandizement involved them in expensive wars, and were, at the same time, destructive of their commerce. A similar feeling, though to a less extent, prevailed in England, and the rival companies prepared to adjust their differences by the sacrifice of Dupleix. No regard was paid by his countrymen to his defence; he was loaded with obloquy, as a selfish and ambitious man, though it was notorious that he had sacrificed his entire private fortune to the support of what he believed to be the true interests of France.

The successor of Dupleix concluded a treaty with the English authorities, in which all the objects of that able governor were abandoned. Mohammed Ali, the friend of the English, was recognised as the nabob of the Carnatic; the claims of the French upon the northern Circars were relinquished, and it was agreed that the colonists from each nation should, for the future, abstain from all interference with the affairs of the native princes. It was scarcely possible that these stipulations could be strictly observed; indeed, the treaty had scarcely been signed, when mutual complaints were made of infractions; but, in the meantime, events had occurred in another part of the globe, which frustrated it altogether.

After the peace of Aix-la-Chapelle, the British ministry, anxious to secure the province of Nova Scotia, as a barrier for the other American colonies, induced many disbanded soldiers and sailors to settle in that country. The town of Halifax was built and its harbor fortified, and Nova Scotia began to rise rapidly in importance. The French, who had hitherto viewed the province as little better than a barren waste, began now to raise disputes concerning its limits; and the settlers from both countries, did not always arrange their controversies by peaceful discussion. Still more important were the differences which arose in the interioi of North America. The French were naturally anxious to form a communication between the Canadas in the north and Louisiana in the south. This could only be effected by depriving the English of their settlements west of the Allegany mountains, and seizing the posts which the British settlers in Virginia and the Carolinas had established beyond that chain for the convenience of trade with the Indians. Hostilities were commenced by the colonial authorities, without the formality of a declaration of war; the Virginian post of Logs' town was surprised by a French detachment, and all its inhabitants but two inhumanly murdered; the North American Indians were stimulated to attack the British colonists, and large supplies of arms and ammunition were imported from France (A. D. 1755). The British ministers immediately prepared for hostilities; all the French forts within the limits of Nova Scotia were reduced by Colonel Monckton; but an expedition against the French forts on the Ohio was defeated, owing to the rashness of General Braddock, who refused to profit by the local knowledge of the provincial officers. He fell into an ambuscade of French and Indians, and instead of endeavoring to extricate himself, attempted to make a stand. At length he was slain, while vainly striving to rally his troops, and the regular soldiers fled with disgraceful precipitation. It deserves to be remarked, that the provincial militia, commanded by Major Washington, did not share the panic of the royal army, but displayed great coolness, courage, and conduct.

Two other expeditions, against the forts of Niagara and Crown Point, failed, though General Johnson, who commanded the latter, gained a victory over the hostile army. But at sea the British strength was more effectually displayed; two sail-of-the-line were captured by Admiral Boscawen, off Newfoundland; and more than three hundred merchant-ships were brought as prizes into the ports of Great Britain. Notwithstanding these hostilities, a formal declaration of war was delayed; its publication was the signal for one of the fiercest struggles in which modern Europe had been involved. Before, however, we enter on this part of our history, we must briefly notice the important events that for a time threatened the total ruin of the English in Bengal, but whose final results made their power paramount in northern India.

The privileges which the emperor of Delhi had granted to the English settlers in Calcutta excited great jealousy among the provincial governors, and were violently opposed by Jaffier Khan, the souhbadar of Bengal. Means were taken, however, to conciliate this powerful feudatory, and peace was preserved until the accession of the ferocious Suraja Dowla, who was enraged at the shelter which the English afforded to some of his destined victims (A. D. 1756). He advanced against Calcutta, when most of the local authorities were seized with a scandalous panic; the governor and the military commanders escaped in boats, leaving Mr. Holwell, Mr. Perks, and about one hundred and ninety more, to provide for their own safety as they best might.

After endeavoring vainly to bring back even one vessel to aid their removal, this handful of men, after a vigorous defence, fell into the power of the ferocious Suraja. They were all thrust into a room twenty feet square, where, from the heat and foulness of the atmosphere, all but twenty-three died before the morning. The news of this catastrophe reached Madras just when Colonel Clive and Admiral Watson, flushed by their recent victory over the celebrated pirate Angria, had arrived at Madras to aid in the destruction of the French influence in the Deccan. The troops assembled for that purpose were now sent to recover Calcutta, and this object was effected by the mere appearance of the fleet before the city. Several of the Suraja's own places were taken and plundered, and the French fort of Chandernagore reduced; conspiracies were formed against Suraja Dowla, and that haughty chieftain felt that the sovereignty of Bengal must be decided by a battle. Contrary to the opinion of all his officers, Clive resolved to hazard an engagement, and took up a position in the grove of Plassy (June 23, 1757). The British force consisted of three thousand two hundred, not more than nine hundred of whom were Europeans; their artillery consisted of eight six-pounders, and two howitzers. On the other hand, Suraja Dowla had with him fifty thousand foot, eighteen thousand horse, and fifty pieces of cannon. Though the engagement continued the greater part of the day, the British did not lose more than seventy in killed and wounded; they owed the victory, indeed, more to the errors of their adversaries than to their own merits; for the contest seems to have been little better than an irregular cannonade, occasionally relieved by ineffectual charges of cavalry. Its consequences were not the less decisive from the ease with which it was won; Suraja Dowla, after wandering for some time as a fugitive, was murdered by one of his personal enemies; and the viceroyalty of Bengal was given to Jaffier Khan, who purchased the favor of the British by large public grants and larger private bribes. This brief campaign established the supremacy of the English in northern India, where their power has never since been shaken.

Section III.—*The Seven Years' War.*

When the French government received intelligence of the events that had taken place in India and America, vigorous preparations for war were made throughout the kingdom, and England itself was menaced with invasion (A. D. 1756). Never was the national character of the British nation so tarnished as it was by the panic which these futile threats diffused; Hessians and Hanoverians were hired to protect the kingdom, while the presence of these mercenaries was justly regarded as dangerous to public liberty. It is more honorable to Britain to relate, that when Lisbon, on the very eve of this war, was almost destroyed by an earthquake, parliament voted one hundred thousand pounds for the relief of the sufferers. But the French government menaced an invasion only to conceal its project for the reduction of Minorca; a formidable force was landed on the island, and close siege laid to Fort St. Philip, which commands the principal town and harbor. Admiral Byng, who had been intrusted with the charge of the English fleet in the Mediterranean, was ordered to attempt the relief of the place; he encountered a French squadron, of equal force, but instead of seeking an engagement, he would not even support Admiral West, who had thrown the French line into confusion. After this indecisive skirmish, he returned to Gibraltar, abandoning Minorca to its fate General Blakeney, the governor of Fort St. Philip, made a vigorous defence, though his garrison was too small by one third; but finding that he had no prospect of relief from England, he capitulated. But his conduct was so far from being disapproved of, that he was raised to the peerage by his sovereign, and welcomed as a hero by the people.

The rage of the people at the loss of Minorca was directed against the unfortunate Byng; popular discontent was still further aggravated by the ill-success of the campaign in America, where a second series of expeditions against the French forts signally failed; while the marquis de Montcalm, the governor of Canada, captured Oswego, where the British had deposited the greater part of their artillery and military stores. Our ally, the king of Prussia, displayed more vigor; unable to obtain any satisfactory explanation from the court of Vienna, he resolved to anticipate the designs of the Austrians, and invade Bohemia. For this purpose it was necessary that he should secure the neutrality of Saxony, but the elector was secretly in league with Frederic's enemies, and the Prussian monarch, finding pacific measures ineffectual, advanced against Dresden. The elector Augustus, who was also king of Poland, fortified himself in a strong camp at Pirna, where he resolved to wait for the junction of the Austrian forces. Frederic blockaded the Saxon army and cut off its supplies; the imperialists, who marched to the relief of their allies, were defeated at Lowositz, and the Saxons, thus left to their own resources, were forced to lay down their arms. Augustus fled to his kingdom of Poland, abandoning his hereditary dominions to the Prussians, who did not use their success with extraordinary moderation.

But the victories of their ally only exasperated the rage of the English people against their rulers; the king was forced to yield to the storm, and dismiss his ministers. William Pitt (afterward earl of Chatham), the most popular man in the kingdom, was appointed head of the new administration, though the duke of Devonshire was nominally premier; a spirit of confidence was spread abroad, and abundant supplies voted for the war. Unfortunately, as a concession to popular clamor, the unhappy Byng, whose worst fault appears to have been an error of judgment and the dread of the fate of Admiral Matthews,* was brought to trial, found guilty of a breach of the articles of war, and sentenced to death. Great exertions were made to save the life of the unhappy admiral, but all in vain; he was ordered to be shot on board the Monarque, and he met his fate with an intrepidity which effectually clears his memory from the stain of cowardice (A. D. 1757). In France, the attention of the court was engaged by an attempt on the king's life. A maniac, named Damien, stabbed Louis with a penknife as he was entering his carriage; the wound was not dangerous, but it was supposed that the assassin might have accomplices in his treason. Every refinement of cruelty that scientific ingenuity could devise was exhausted in the tortures of this unhappy wretch, whose manifest lunacy made him an object of compassion rather than punishment.

The danger to which Louis had been exposed did not prevent him from making vigorous exertions to continue the war. Two armies

* See page 606.

were sent into Germany, one destined to invade Hanover, the other to join the imperial forces against Prussia. George II., anxious to save Hanover, wished to send over a body of British troops for the defence of the electorate, but being opposed by the Pitt administration, he dismissed his ministers, and tried to form a new cabinet. The burst of national indignation at the removal of the popular favorite was, however, so great, that Pitt was soon recalled to power, but not until he had evinced a desire to make some concession to the royal inclinations.

At the commencement of the campaign, the prospects of the king of Prussia were very gloomy; the Russians were advancing through Lithuania, the Swedes threatened him in Pomerania, the united forces of the French and imperialists were advancing through Germany, and the emperess-queen, Maria Theresa, covered her hereditary dominions with four armies, whose united strength amounted to one hundred and eighty thousand men.

Frederic, baffling the Austrians by a series of masterly movements, opened a passage into Bohemia, where he was joined by the prince of Bevern and Marshal Schwerin, who had defeated the Austrian divisions that opposed their progress. Confident in the excellence of his troops he resolved to engage without delay, though his enemies were posted in a camp strongly fortified by nature (May 6). The memorable battle of Prague was vigorously contested, and success continued doubtful until the Austrian right wing, advancing too rapidly, was separated from the left. Frederic poured his troops through the gap, so that when the Austrian right was forced back by the intrepidity of Marshal Schwerin, it suddenly found itself surrounded, and fled in confusion. The centre and left, thus abandoned, could not resist the successive charges of the Prussians, and sought shelter in Prague. Frederic ventured to besiege this city though the numbers of the garrison nearly equalled those of his own army; and his delay before the walls gave the Austrians time to recover their courage and recruit their forces. Count Daun began soon to menace the Prussian communications; Frederic sent the prince of Bevern to drive him back; Daun, though his forces were superior, retreated before the prince, until he could procure such additional strength as to render victory certain. When this was effected, he resumed the offensive, and Frederic was forced to hasten to the prince's assistance. A junction was effected at Kolin, and Frederic marched to attack the imperial camp (June 18). The Prussians charged their enemies with their usual vigor, but they were unable to force the Austrian lines, and were finally driven from the field.

In consequence of this defeat, the Prussians were forced, not only to raise the siege of Prague, but to evacuate Bohemia. Nor were the arms of Frederic and his allies more successful in other quarters. The Russians having defeated General Lehwald, invaded the Prussian dominions on the side of Germany, and committed the most frightful devastations; the British and Hanoverian troops, under the duke of Cumberland, were forced to accept the disgraceful convention of Closterseven, by which thirty-eight thousand soldiers were reduced to a state of inactivity; and the French, thus released from an enemy that might interrupt their communications, advanced to join the Austrians in the invasion of Prussia; finally, an Austrian army, by a rapid march, arrived at the very gates of Berlin, and laid that city under contribution.

An expedition, planned by Mr. Pitt soon after his restoration to power, was defeated by the weakness and indecision of the officers intrusted with its execution. The object of attack was the French port and arsenal of Rochefort, which would have fallen an easy prey, had it been assailed when first the fleet arrived before the place. But the time which ought to have been employed in action was wasted in deliberations, and the expedition returned ingloriously home. The conduct of British affairs in America was equally disastrous; an armament was sent against Louisbourg, but it returned without having made any effort to effect its object; while the French, under the marquis de Montcalm, captured the strong fort William Henry, the bulwark of our northern frontier, without meeting the slightest interruption from a British force posted in its immediate neighborhood.

These disasters would have proved fatal to the new ministry, had it not been generally understood that the officers, whose cowardice or incapacity had led to such inglorious results, were the choice of their predecessors, and were maintained in their posts by court favor. This conviction proved favorable to Mr. Pitt, the king was compelled to grant full powers to his ministers, and the secret intrigues by which the cabinet was controlled were rendered powerless for a season. An unexpected change of fortune on the continent brightened the prospects of the British and Prussians toward the close of the year. Frederic, hough his dominions were invaded by three hostile armies, never lost courage; though his army did not exceed half the number of his enemies, he resolved to give battle to the united forces of the French and Austrians (Nov. 5). Frederic, by a series of judicious movements, led his enemies to believe that he dreaded an engagement; confident of victory, they hasted to force him to action, near the village of Rosbach. They advanced so precipitately, that their lines were thrown into disorder; and before they could remedy the error, they were broken by the headlong charge of the Prussian horse. Every effort made by generals of the combined army to retrieve the fortunes of the day was anticipated by the genius of Frederic; they were forced to retreat in great confusion, having lost nearly nine thousand men in killed, wounded, and prisoners, while the total loss of the Prussians did not exceed five hundred.

From this field Frederic hasted to another scarcely less glorious. The Austrians and Hungarians, under Prince Charles of Lorraine, entered Silesia, captured the important fortress of Schweidnitz, drove the prince of Bevern from his intrenchments, and made themselves masters of the greater part of the province. Frederic, by a rapid march, formed a junction with the relics of the prince of Bevern's army, and thus reinforced, attacked the Austrians at Lissa (Dec. 5). Pretending tc direct all his force against the Austrian right, Frederic suddenly poured his chief strength against their left wing, which was speedily broken; Prince Charles attempted to restore the courage of his flying soldiers by sending reinforcements from the centre and right, but these fresh troops were unable to form under the heavy fire of the Prussians, and thus the Austrian battalions were defeated one after another. Night alone prevented the total ruin of the vanquished army. About five thousand men were killed and wounded on each side; but within a week after the battle the Prussians pressing vigorously the pursuit of their retiring foes, captured twenty thousand prisoners, three thousand wagons, and two hundred pieces of cannon. The Austrians abandoned all Silesia except the town of Schweidnitz, which surrendered in the following spring. The effects of the victories of Rosbach and Lissa were felt throughout Europe; the French had flagrantly violated the convention of Closterseven; it was now disavowed by the British and Hanoverians (A. D. 1758). Prince Ferdinand of Brunswick was chosen by George II. to command his electoral forces, and this able general in a short time not only recovered Hanover, but drove his adversaries across the Rhine. Mr Pitt changed his policy, and consented to reinforce Prince Ferdinand with a body of British troops, while liberal supplies were voted to subsidize the German princes. The campaign was honorable to Prince Ferdinand's abilities, but its most important result was the diversion it made in favor of the king of Prussia, by compelling the French to employ their chief force on the Rhine.

Frederic in this campaign endured several vicissitudes of fortune. Having taken Schweidnitz, he unexpectedly entered Moravia, which had hitherto escaped from the ravages of war, laid that fine province under contribution, and even menaced Vienna. He failed, however, at the siege of Olmutz, but he effected a retreat as honorable as a victory, and suddenly directed his march against the Russians, whose ravages in Brandenburgh were shocking to humanity. He gained a complete victory over the invaders at Zomdorff, and then, without resting a moment, hasted to relieve his brother Henry, who was almost surrounded with enemies in Saxony. Count Daun, the commander of the imperialists, was a worthy rival of Frederic; he surprised and routed the Prussian right wing at Hochkirchen; but the judicious measures of the king saved the rest of his army, and Daun was unable to pursue his advantages. Indeed so little was Frederic affected by the reverse, that he drove the Austrians a second time from Silesia, and then returning, compelled Daun to raise the sieges of Dresden and Leipsic, and even retreat into Bohemia.

The enterprising spirit of Mr. Pitt, freed from the trammels which secret intrigues had formed, diffused itself through the British empire, and particularly animated the officers of the army and navy. Several French ships-of-war were captured by the British; an armament, destined for North America, was dispersed and driven on shore by Sir Edward Hawke, whose fleet rode triumphant in the channel. From apathy and despair the nation passed at once to the opposite extreme of overweening confidence. It was resolved to carry the war into France itself, and two successive expeditions were sent against the French coast. As might reasonably have been anticipated, these armaments produced no important result; the only consequence arising from such a waste of blood and treasure, was the destruction of Cherbourg, a triumph dearly purchased by the subsequent loss of some of the best of the troops in the hurried embarkation.

But in North America, where the British arms had been tarnished by delay, disaster, and disgrace, the removal of the earl of Loudon from the command, led to a complete change in the fortune of the war. His successor, General Abercrombie, planned three simultaneous expedition, two of which produced triumphant results. General Amherst laid siege to Louisbourg, and aided by the talents of Brigadier Wolfe, who was fast rising into eminence, forced that important garrison to surrender. This was followed by the entire reduction of the island of Cape Breton, and the inferior stations which the French occupied in the gulf of St. Lawrence. Brigadier Forbes was sent against Fort du Quesne, which the French abandoned at his approach, and fled down the Mississippi. Abercrombie marched in person against Ticonderoga, which he found better fortified than he had anticipated, and after a useless manifestation of desperate valor, he was forced to retire with considerable loss. The French were, at the same time, deprived of all their settlements on the coast of Africa; but the count de Lally not only preserved their East Indian possessions, but wrested from the English, Fort St. David and Cuddalore.

Great anxiety was felt at the opening of the next campaign (A. D. 1759). Early in the year, the Prussians destroyed the Russian magazines in Poland, laid Bohemia under contribution, and reduced the imperial armies to inactivity. But Prince Ferdinand was unable to prevent the French from sending succors to the Austrians; and his ill-success once more exposed Hanover to an invasion. Had Ferdinand wavered, the British and Hanoverians might have been forced to a second convention as disgraceful as Closterseven, but his courage rose with the crisis, he engaged the French at Minden, and gained a complete victory. Minden, indeed, would have been as illustrious and decisive a battle as Blenheim, but for the unaccountable conduct of Lord George Sackville, who commanded the cavalry, and either misunderstood or disobeyed the order to charge the discomfited French. There had been some previous disputes between the prince and Lord George; they threw the blame mutually on each other, but which ever was in fault, it is certain that on this occasion the best opportunity that could have been desired for humbling the power of France was irretrievably lost.

The victory of the British, at Minden, was more than counterbalanced by the defeat of the Prussians by the united forces of Austria and Russia, at Cunersdorff. But the heroic Frederic soon retrieved this disaster, and he would probably have triumphed in his turn, had he not exposed a large division of his troops in the defiles of Bohemia, which was surrounded and taken by Count Daun. Still the only permanent acquisition that the Austrians made was Dresden, for Frederic's vigor and rapidity of movement rendered even their victories fruitless.

This indecisive campaign greatly diminished the ardor of the English for their ally, the king of Prussia, while their victories in North America and the West Indies, directed their attention to their colonial interests. Immediately after the conquest of Louisbourg, which was justly considered the key of Canada, an expedition was planned against Quebec. The colonists were prepared to submit to a change of masters by the politic protection granted to the French settlers in Gaudaloupe, which had been subdued early in the year (A. D. 1758); and by the guarantee given to the inhabitants for the enjoyment of religious freedom. When General Wolfe, therefore, proceeded up the St. Lawrence, he did not encounter any serious opposition from the Canadians, who seemed to view the struggle with indifference. While Wolfe advanced toward Quebec, General Amherst conquered Ticonderoga and Crown Point, and Sir William Johnson gained possession of the important fortress of Niagara. But Amherst, as had been originally intended, was unable to form a junction with General Wolfe, who was thus employed in a hazardous enterprise, with very inadequate means. Though he almost despaired of success, Wolfe resolved to persevere; he adopted the daring plan of landing at night under the Heights of Abraham, leading his men up the steep, and securing this position, which commanded the town. The stream was rapid, the landing-place narrow, and the precipices formidable even by day, but the soldiers, animated by their heroic commander, triumphed over these difficulties; and when morning dawned, the marquis de Montcalm was astonished to learn that the British army occupied those heights which he had deemed inaccessible. A battle was now inevitable, and both generals prepared for the contest with equal courage. The battle was brief but fierce; the scale of victory was just beginning to turn in favor of the British, when Wolfe fell mortally wounded. This loss only roused the English regiments to fresh exertion, their bayonets broke the French lines, and a body of Highlanders, charging with their broad swords, completed the confusion. The French fled in disorder; the intelligence was brought to Wolfe, he collected his breath to exclaim, "I die happy!" and instantly expired (September 13).

The marquis de Montcalm fell in the same field; he was not inferior to his rival in skill and bravery, nor did he meet death with less intrepidity. When told, after the battle, that his wounds were mortal, he exclaimed, "So much the better: I shall not live to witness the surrender of Quebec." Five days after the battle, that city opened its gates to a British garrison, and this was soon followed by the complete subjugation of the Canadas, which have ever since remained subject to the crown of Great Britain.

The success of the English in the East Indies was scarcely less decisive than in America. Lally, the French general, possessed more courage than prudence; he engaged in enterprises beyond his means, and especially wasted his limited resources in a vain attack on Madras. Colonel Coote, the commander of the English forces, was inferior to his adversaries in numerical strength, but he enjoyed ampler pecuniary resources, and was far superior to Lally, both as a general and a statesman. Coote and Lally came to an engagement at Wandewash (Jan. 21, 1760), in which the French were completely overthrown, and their influence in the Carnatic destroyed. During the campaign, Admiral Pococke defeated a French fleet off the coast of Ceylon; the English, in consequence, became masters of the Indian seas, and began to form reasonable expectations of driving their rivals from Hindústan. A Dutch armament arrived in Bengal, under suspicious circumstances, but Clive ordered that it should be immediately attacked by land and sea;* the

* Clive was engaged in a rubber of whist, when an express from Colonel Forde brought him intelligence of the advance of the Dutch. He replied by the following pencil-note, on a slip of paper torn from the colonel's letter: "Dear Forde—Fight them immediately, and I'll send you an order of council to-morrow."

Dutch were forced to surrender, and ample apologies were made by the authorities of Holland for this infraction of treaties.

The French court threatened to take revenge for the destruction of Cherbourg, by invading Great Britain and Ireland; but the ports were so strictly blockaded by the English squadrons, that no vessel could venture to appear in the channel. Admiral Boscawen pursued a squadron from Toulon, that tried to slip unnoticed through the straits of Gibraltar, overtook it off Cape Lagos, on the coast of Portugal (August 18), destroyed two ships-of-the-line, and captured two more. A still more important triumph was obtained by Sir Edward Hawke, between Belleisle and Quiberon (November 20). Conflans, the French admiral, taking advantage of the gales that drove the blockading squadrons off the coast, put to sea, but was soon overtaken by Hawke. Conflans, unwilling to hazard a battle, sought shelter among the rocks and shallows of his own coast. Hawke unhesitatingly encountered the perils of a stormy sea and a lee shore; he gained a decisive victory, destroying four ships-of-the-line, and compelling another to strike her colors. A tempestuous night alone saved the French fleet from destruction. Though this victory delivered the English from all fears of the invasion, some alarm was excited by the enterprises of Commodore Thurot, who sailed from Dunkirk with five frigates, and hovered round the coasts of North Britain. Having failed to make any impression on Scotland, he entered the Irish sea, and landing at Carrickfergus, stormed and pillaged that town.* Having heard the news of Conflans' defeat, he steered homeward, but was swiftly pursued by a squadron under Commodore Elliot, and overtaken near the Isle of Man (February 28, 1760). After a fierce engagement, Thurot was killed, and all his vessels forced to surrender.

Vigorous preparations were made by all parties for the maintenance of the war in Germany, although the people of England had become weary of continental connexions, and the French finances had fallen into a state of lamentable disorder (A. D. 1760). The conduct of the people of France to their sovereign was, indeed, truly generous; the principal nobility and gentry sent their plate to the treasury to be coined for the public service; an army of nearly one hundred thousand men was assembled in Westphalia, under the duke de Broglio, while an inferior army was formed upon the Rhine, under Count St. Germain. Prince Ferdinand could not have coped with such an overwhelming force, had not the French generals quarrelled with each other. Several battles were fought, but they were all more or less indecisive; and rarely has there been a campaign in which such numerous and well-appointed armies were opposed that produced so few memorable events.

The king of Prussia resolved to act on the defensive in Saxony, while his brother Henry opposed the Russians and Austrians in Silesia.

* An interesting example of humanity softened the horrors of war during the attack on Carrickfergus. While the French and the garrison were engaged in the streets, a beautiful child, unconscious of its danger, ran between both parties. A French grenadier, moved with compassion, threw down his musket, rushed into the midst of the fire, took up the child, and having placed it in safety, returned to his companions, who with loud shouts applauded the heroic deed.

But his plans were deranged by the enterprise of Marshal Laudohn, who surrounded the Prussian general, Fouquet, slew three thousand of his army, and compelled the remainder to surrender at discretion. Frederic attempted to retrieve his affairs by a sudden advance on Dresden, but he failed to capture the city; his brother, Prince Henry, was more fortunate in raising the siege of Breslau, which Laudohn had invested after his victory. But Frederic's ruin seemed unavoidable, as the Russians were advancing with overwhelming forces, and he was himself surrounded by three Austrian armies at Lignitz. Count Daun marched to storm the Prussian camp, in full confidence of victory; but, to his astonishment, he found it deserted, Frederic having marched that very night to meet the army of Marshal Laudohn, who was eagerly pressing forward to share, as he fondly believed, in assured victory. The heights of Pfaffendorff, judiciously protected by a formidable array of artillery, prevented Daun from marching to the assistance of his colleague; Laudohn was completely defeated, and the Austrian grand army driven from Silesia. But this victory did not prevent the success of the enemy in other quarters; the Russians, being joined by a considerable body of Austrians, under General Lascy, pushed forward through Brandenburgh, and made themselves masters of Berlin. They levied a heavy contribution on the city, and destroyed its arsenals, foundries, and public works.

The Prussians were equally unfortunate in Saxony, but Frederic resolved to run every risk to recover a country that had hitherto supplied the chief support to his armies. Daun, equally convinced of the importance of Saxony, protected the electorate with a force of seventy thousand men, advantageously posted in a fortified camp, near Torgau. Frederic, with only fifty thousand men, resolved to attack the Austrians in their intrenchments, and to stake his life and crown on the hazard of the engagement (November 3). The battle was furious, but the ardor of the Prussians, who felt that they fought for the very existence of their country, was irresistible. Dunn was borne from the field severely wounded; the Austrians were broken by separate charges, and night alone saved them from total ruin. The result of this glorious victory was, that Frederic recovered all Saxony except Dresden, and compelled the Russians, Austrians, and Swedes, to evacuate his dominions.

The Canadian war was not terminated by the capture of Quebec; the French had still formidable forces in the country, and they made a vigorous effort to recover that city. They were baffled by the intrepidity of General Murray; and General Amherst soon after having obtained reinforcements from England, advanced to Montreal, and compelled the entire French army to capitulate. The savage tribes of Indians who had been induced by French gold to attack the British settlements, were now severely chastised, and compelled to make the most humiliating submissions.

Not less complete was the success of the English arms in India; Pondicherry and Mahie were reduced by Colonel Coote, the French power in the east completely subverted, and the English rendered masters of the commerce of the vast peninsula of Hindústan. These important acquisitions made the English very impatient of the German war; they complained of the inactivity of the navy, and asserted tha the French islands in the West Indies, more valuable to a commercial people than half the German empire, might have been gained with far less risk and loss than attended the protection of the useless electorate of Hanover. In the midst of these disputes, George II. died suddenly, in the seventy-seventh year of his age (October 25). He was succeeded by his grandson, George III., a young prince in his twenty-third year, who had hitherto taken no active part in public life.

The death of George II. produced little change in European politics; but that of the peaceful Spanish monarch, Ferdinand VI. (A. D. 1759), led to some important results. His successor, Charles III., was king of the Two Sicilies, and by the treaty of Aix-la-Chapelle, it had been agreed, that on his accession to the throne of Spain, his former kingdom should devolve to Don Philip, duke of Parma and Placentia, and that these dutchies should be resigned to the empire. By the mediation of France with Austria, Charles was enabled to procure the Neapolitan throne for his third son, Ferdinand, while Philip was permitted to retain Parma and Placentia. Grateful for such a benefit, Charles signed the family compact, which bound the Bourbon princes to afford each other mutual assistance, and secretly prepared to join France in the war against Great Britain. The haughty conduct of the English diplomatists, which was not unjustly offensive to Spanish pride, greatly contributed to strengthen the resolution of the court of Madrid, especially as the naval superiority of the English menaced the communications of Spain with her American colonies.

Negotiations for peace were commenced by the courts of France and Great Britain, soon after the accession of George III., but with little sincerity on either side (A. D. 1761). Mr. Pitt was firmly resolved to humble the house of Bourbon; the duke de Choiseul, the French minister, relied on the secret promises of Spanish aid, and thus it was impossible to arrange preliminaries. The war languished in Germany; Prince Ferdinand succeeding in protecting Hanover, but he could not prevent the French from ravaging Westphalia and East Friesland. The king of Prussia, exhausted even by his victories, was forced to act on the defensive; though he lost no battle, he had the mortification to see the Russians make themselves masters of Colberg, and the Austrians surprise Schweidnitz. The possession of these important places enabled the Russians to establish their winter-quarters in Pomerania, and the Austrians in Silesia. On sea, the honor of the British flag was maintained in several actions between single ships and small squadrons. The island of Belleisle, on the coast of France, was captured by a British armament, but at a very disproportionate cost of blood and treasure.

This languid campaign seemed to prove that all parties were weary of the war, and negotiations were resumed In their progress, Mr. Pitt discovered the intimate connexion that had been formed between the courts of Versailles and Madrid; and he proposed to anticipate the hostile designs of the latter by seizing the plate-fleet, laden with the treasures of Spanish America. But the colleagues of Mr. Pitt, already dissatisfied with his imperious manners, refused to adopt such bold measures, and he instantly resigned the seals of office. The king, anxious to introduce his favorite, the earl of Bute, into the cabinet, adopted the opinions of the majority of his council, and accepted th resignation. Fierce political disputes arose, whose effects were felt throughout Europe; the hopes of the French court were raised, and the German allies of Great Britain were greatly dispirited.

But the new ministry showed no want of alacrity in maintaining the honor of the country. One of their earliest measures was a declaration of war against Spain, the conduct of the court of Madrid having amply justified Mr. Pitt's anticipations of its hostile designs (A. D. 1762). The superiority of the British navy over the combined fleets of France and Spain, hindered these powers from making any attempt at colonial conquests; but they believed themselves equally superior by land, and therefore resolved to attack Britain through the side of its ancient ally, Portugal.

Few kingdoms had sunk into such a state of degradation as Portugal at this period. Trusting to the protection of England, and enriched by the treasures of Brazil, the court of Lisbon reposed in ignorance and indolence; its fortresses were neglected, its army mouldering away, its subjects destitute of martial spirit. The earthquake that laid Lisbon in ruins was followed by a dangerous conspiracy against the life of Joseph, the reigning sovereign. This monarch, less superstitious than most Portuguese kings, had banished the jesuits from his court, and had resented with spirit the encroachments of his nobles. Some of the dissatisfied jesuits and nobles formed a plot to murder the king, and he was dangerously wounded by assassins while on his road from his country-seat to Lisbon. The principal conspirators were arrested and punished by cruel deaths; and all the jesuits banished from the kingdom (A. D. 1759). But the nobles continued discontented; the pope and the clergy resented the expulsion of the jesuits, while the superstitious Portuguese seemed ready to renounce their allegiance to a sovereign who had incurred the resentment of the church. Such was Joseph's situation, when the ministers of France and Spain presented a joint demand that he should instantly renounce his alliance with Britain, under pain of incurring their resentment, and allowing him only four days to deliberate on his answer. Joseph at once returned a spirited refusal to such an insolent memorial, and the Spanish army crossed the frontiers. An auxiliary British force of eight thousand men was sent to Portugal, together with a large supply of arms and ammunition. Joseph intrusted the command of his army to the count de la Lippe, who had already distinguished himself in Germany. The skill of this commander, and the valor of the British officers, compelled the Spaniards to evacuate the kingdom with loss and disgrace, before the close of the campaign.

The French hoped that the invasion of Portugal would facilitate the progress of their arms in Germany; but Prince Ferdinand, and the marquis of Granby, not only protected Hanover, but recovered the greater part of Hesse. An unexpected event delivered the king of Prussia from the ruin that seemed to threaten him at the close of the last campaign. Elizabeth, emperess of Russia, died, and was succeeded by her nephew, Peter III., who entertained a romantic admiration of Frederic. The new emperor not only put an end to hostilities, but entered into alliance with the Prussian monarch; and Europe saw with astonishment the unprecedented spectacle of an army marching off from its former allies to the camp of its enemies. Sweden followed the example of Russia in concluding peace; and Frederic, taking advantage of these favorable circumstances, recovered Schweidnitz and drove the Austrians from Silesia.

A new revolution in Russia compelled the Prussian king to halt in his victorious career. The reforms of Peter III. had given offence to a great body of his subjects; he was dethroned by his wife, who usurped the throne, with the title of Catherine II. Peter died in prison a few days after his deposition, but it has not been ascertained whether he was the victim of disease or violence. Catherine did not renew the war against Prussia, as had been at first expected, but she withdrew her forces, and resolved to observe a strict neutrality. Frederic's victories had in the meantime, so seriously alarmed the Austrians, that they consented to a cessation of hostilities for Silesia and Saxony. This impolitic truce laid Bohemia open to Frederic: one division of his army advanced to the very gates of Prague and destroyed a valuable magazine; another laid the greater part of Egra in ashes, while detachments ravaged Franconia, and even Suabia. The princes of the empire hasted to conclude treaties of neutrality, and the war was left to be decided by the powers of Prussia and Austria, between which the contest had begun.

In the meantime the English conquered the chief islands that the French still retained in the West Indies, Martinique, St. Lucie, Grenada, and St. Vincent; while the Spaniards suffered the more severe loss of Havana, the capital of Cuba, and the large fleet that lay in its harbor. Nor was this the least alarming of the consequences that resulted to the court of Madrid from its unwise interference; an armament from Madras, under the command of Admiral Cornish and General Draper, captured Manilla, and the fall of this city involved the fate of the whole range of the Philippine islands.

France and Spain, heartily tired of a war which threatened ruin to the colonies of both, became desirous of peace, and they found the earl of Bute, who now ruled the British cabinet, equally anxious to terminate the war. Indeed, so anxious was that minister to avoid a continuance of hostilities, that he not only stopped the career of colonial conquest, but consented to sacrifice several acquisitions that Britain had already made. Still the British nation gained by the war the whole of Canada and part of Louisiana, the chief settlements on the western coasts of Africa, and a decided superiority in India; had the war lasted another year, had even the fair claims of Britain's position been supported by her negotiators, these gains would have been more extensive and more secure. Contrary to all expectation, the preliminaries were sanctioned by a majority of the British parliament, and soon after the definite treaty was signed at Paris (Feb. 10, 1763). The king of Prussia and the emperess of Austria, deserted by their respective allies, agreed to a reconciliation about the same time, on the basis of a restitution of conquests and an oblivion of injuries.

The result of the continental war was, that Prussia and Austria became the principal European powers, France lost her political preeminence when united to the empire, and England abandoned her influence in the European system, maintaining an intimate relation only with Portugal and Holland. Britain, by the colonial war, obtained complete maritime supremacy; she commanded the entire commerce of North America and Hindústan, and had a decided superiority in the West Indian trade. But during the seven years' war a question arose which led to very important discussions; France, unable to maintain a commercial intercourse with her colonies, opened the trade to neutral powers; England declared this traffic illegal, and relying on her naval superiority, seized neutral vessels and neutral property bound to hostile ports. The return of peace put an end to the dispute for a season, but it became the subject of angry controversy in every future war. The internal condition of England improved rapidly during the contest by the extension of the funding system; the pecuniary affairs of the government became intimately connected with those of the nation; by far the greater part of the loans required for the war was raised at home, so the increase of the national debt more closely united the rulers and the people in the bonds of a common interest. This altered state of things scarcely excited notice, though it was the chief source of the permanence and stability displayed by the British government when revolutionary movements threatened to subvert the other dynasties of Europe.

CHAPTER IX.

THE AGE OF REVOLUTIONS.

SECTION I.—*Change in the Relations of the Catholic Powers to the Holy See. Dismemberment of Poland.*

No country had suffered so severely as France during the late war; the finances had long been in confusion, and the profligate expenditure of a demoralized court aggravated the indignation produced by national distress. Louis XV., though not destitute of abilities, was the slave of his sensual appetites; ruled by his mistresses, and other unworthy favorites, he connived at glaring abuses, and sanctioned the grossest acts of tyranny and rapacity. A spirit of opposition spread through the kingdom, several of the parliaments refused to register the edicts for the continuance of war-taxes, and others remonstrated in a tone of censure to which the French monarchs had been long unaccustomed. This unusual liberty of the parliaments had been in some degree fostered by the court itself; the king permitted these bodies to set bounds to ecclesiastical tyranny, and to suppress the order of the jesuits in France (A. D. 1762); and their spirit was further increased by the intrigues of the duke de Choiseul, who persuaded the king to allow the Parisian parliament to pass sentence on Lally, the unfortunate commander of the French in India, whose only crime was failure under circumstances that rendered success impossible.

Popular discontent was at the same time rapidly spreading in Spain, where the reforms of the prime minister, Squillacé, offended the obstinate prejudices of an ignorant and bigoted nation. Charles III. yielded to the clamors of his subjects and dismissed the minister, but he firmly resolved to take vengeance on the jesuits, who were supposed to have secretly instigated the insurrection. A reforming minister in Portugal maintained his post in spite of opposition; the marquis of Pombal ruled the land with iron sway, and confident in the rectitude of his intentions, scorned all opposition. But though he removed all impediments, including the higher order of nobility and the society of jesuits, his reforms took no root in the land, and the institutions which he established by force perished when that force was taken away.

The enmity of Pombal and Choiseul to the jesuits was felt in the Spanish cabinet; the king was indignant at their share in the late disturbances, his minister, Count d'Aranda, regarded the order as hostile to all existing governments. Both took their measures with profound secresy (A. D. 1767). The houses of the jesuits in Madrid were surrounded at night, and the inmates commanded to set out instantly for the coast. An edict was then issued for the banishment of the regulars of that community from Spain and its colonies, and the confiscation of their temporalities. The jesuits in Mexico and Peru were similarly seized; and in Paraguay, where they had established an almost independent empire, they were suddenly deposed and transported to Europe The king of Naples and the duke of Parma followed the example of the court of Spain, in spite of the urgent remonstrances of Pope Clement XIII.; they also placed new restrictions on the pontiff's jurisdiction in their states, and when Clement made a vigorous effort to support the ancient privileges of the holy see, he found himself opposed to all the Italian powers, except the king of Sardinia, to the remonstrances of Spain and Portugal, and the active hostility of France.

While these disputes between the catholic powers and the head of their church proved that the supremacy of the papacy no longer existed, but in name, the struggles of a small insular people to maintain their national independence excited general sympathy. The Genoese transferred their nominal claims over the island of Corsica to the crown of France, and Choiseul sent a large army to occupy this new acquisition. But the Corsicans, justly enraged at the transfer of their allegiance without the formality of asking their consent, boldly flew to arms, and under the command of the heroic Paoli, prepared for an obstinate resistance. Had the British ministry interfered, the result of the contest would have been very doubtful; but Paoli could not resist the entire force of France, he was driven by the vast superiority of numbers from post to post, until every strong place had yielded to the invaders, when he cut his way through the enemy, and embarked for Leghorn (A. D. 1769). The island submitted to Louis, but many of the Corsicans long continued to harass the French by a guerilla war in their mountain fastnesses.

Choiseul, finding his influence with Louis XV. on the decline, sought to strengthen it by cementing the alliance between the courts of Paris and Vienna. He effected a marriage between the king's grandson and heir and Marie Antoinette, daughter of the emperess-dowager. These ill-omened nuptials were celebrated with extraordinary splendor during a season of great public distress: during the festivities a fatal accident cast a shade of melancholy over all parties; some confusion arose in the crowd of spectators, and nearly two hundred persons lost their lives in the tumult. Choiseul involved the king in a quarrel with the parliaments, which precipitated the fall of that able minister; the king reluctantly consented to abandon the new forms of jurisdiction which were proposed, and allow the old courts to resume their functions. This unfortunate and dishonorable proceeding completed the abasement of France; it was notorious that the duke de Choiseul owed his disgrace to the intrigues of the king's profligate mistress;* and whatever may have been the faults of that minister, he would certainly never have permitted the influence of his country to sink so low as it did during the administration of his successor, the duke d'Aguillon.

While France was thus declining, the Russian empire was rapidly acquiring a preponderating influence in eastern Europe. The emperess

* Madame du Barri. She was subsequently one of the victims of the French revolution.

Catherine procured the throne of Poland for one of her favorites, Stanislaus Augustus (A. D. 1765), having sent a Russian army to overawe the diet, when it assembled to choose a sovereign. Frederic of Prussia, anxious to remedy the calamities which the seven years' war had brought upon his country, did not venture to oppose the schemes of the ambitious czarina; on the contrary, he was gained over by some commercial concessions to aid her projects with all his influence. The new sovereign of Poland, opposed by a licentious aristocracy and a bigoted people, was unable to remedy the disorders of the state, or control the events that soon furnished a pretext for the interference of his powerful neighbors. Poland had long been agitated by religious disputes; the oppressions of the catholics compelled the dissidents, as the dissenting sects were called, to seek foreign protection; those of the Greek church appealed to the emperess of Russia, while the Lutherans sought aid from the kings of Prussia and Denmark. Catherine, with great promptitude, sent an army to enforce the claims of the dissidents, and paying little regard to the remonstrances of Stanislaus, acted as if Poland had been one of her own provinces. The catholic lords formed a confederacy to maintain the purity of their religion, and the independence of their country, but they were unable to compete with the overwhelming forces of Russia; Cracow, where they attempted to make a stand, was taken by storm, the fugitives were pursued beyond the Turkish frontiers, and the country that had afforded them refuge was cruelly devastated.

Mustapha III. was more peacefully inclined than most of the sultans that have filled the throne of Constantinople, but he felt that the power which Russia was acquiring in Poland would be dangerous to the security of his northern provinces; he was indignant at the violation of his dominions, and he was secretly instigated by the French court. The king of Prussia vainly remonstrated with the sultan;* Mustapha had formed an extravagant estimate of his military resources, and he is said to have been animated by a personal dislike of Catherine. The war was commenced by the Turks (A. D. 1769); their irregular troops entered southern Russia, and committed the most frightful ravages; but when they hazarded a regular engagement at Choczim, they suffered a severe defeat. Catherine prepared to strike a decisive blow against the Turkish power; she sent a fleet from the Baltic round to the Mediterranean, to support an insurrection which her emissaries had excited in Southern Greece (A. D. 1770). The insurgents, aided by a Russian force, at first gained some advantages, but on the first reverse they were abandoned by their allies to the brutal retaliations of their Turkish masters. Soon after, the Turkish fleet of fifteen ships-of-the-line was burned by a Russian squadron in the bay of Chesmé, with the exception of a single vessel that was captured. This was followed by the defeat of the grand Ottoman army near the Pruth, the capture of Bender, Akerman, and Ismail, and the occupation of the entire province of Bessarabia.

Stanislaus was forced to join in the war against the Turks, though he knew that one of the chief causes of their taking up arms was to

* Frederic, who loved to indulge in sarcasm, said that a war between the Russians and the Turks would be a contest between the one-eyed and the blind.

defend the independence of Poland. But Joseph, who had succeeded his father in the German empire (A. D. 1765), began to dread the dangerous ambition of Russia; and even his mother, Maria Theresa, began to court the friendship of her old rival, Frederic, as a counterpoise to the governing power of the czarina. It was obviously the interest of the northern states, Denmark and Sweden, to adopt a similar course of policy; but the governments of both countries were too deeply engaged by their domestic affairs to attend to the state of their foreign relations.

Frederick V., one of the best monarchs that ever occupied the throne of Denmark, was succeeded by Christian V., a prince of weak intellect and dissipated habits (A. D. 1766). Soon after his accession, Christian married Caroline Matilda, one of the sisters of the queen of England, and the engaging manners of this princess won her the favor of the Danish king and people. To maintain her ascendency over the mind of her husband, Caroline favored the ambition of Struensee a foreign adventurer, who was raised to the office of prime minister, or rather, sole ruler of Denmark. Struensee's administration was vigorous and useful, but his haughtiness gave great offence to the Danish nobles; a conspiracy was formed against him, of which the king's step-mother and her son Frederic were the principal instigators, and it was resolved to involve the unfortunate queen Caroline in his fate. Struensee and his friend Brandt were arrested at midnight, by virtue of an order which had been extorted from the imbecile Christian; they were insulted with the mockery of a trial, and put to a cruel death. The queen was also arrested and sent a prisoner to Cronenberg castle; dread of British vengeance, however, saved her from personal violence. She was permitted to retire to Hanover, where the remainder of her life was spent in comparative obscurity. The queen dowager, having removed her rival, usurped the royal authority; a young nobleman named Bernstorff was appointed prime minister, and the court of Copenhagen became remarkable for its subserviency to that of St. Petersburgh.

Gustavus III., a young prince of great vigor and sagacity, ascended the Swedish throne on the death of his father, Adolphus Frederic (A. D. 1771); he had early formed a project for removing the restrictions which the senate had imposed on the royal authority after the death of Charles XII., and his efforts were seconded by the bulk of the nation, long weary of aristocratic tyranny. The senate, suddenly surrounded by armed bands, was intimidated into assenting to the instrument of government which Gustavus had prepared, and a revolution which changed Sweden from one of the most limited into one of the most absolute monarchies of Europe, was effected without spilling a drop of blood. Dread of a counter-revolution, and the necessity of providing some remedy for the distress which prevailed in Sweden, prevented Gustavus from interfering in the affairs of Poland, a country that had often occupied the anxious cares of his predecessors.

Stanislaus was sincerely anxious to confer the blessings of tranquillity and good government on Poland; but all his judicious measures were frustrated by the Polish nobles, who clung to their tyrannous and absurd privileges, though they were known to be as pernicious to themselves as they were ruinous to the country. An attempt on the persona liberty of the unhappy king gave Catherine a pretext for sending a Russian army into the country, and suggested to the Prussian king a scheme for the dismemberment of Poland. A treaty was concluded between Austria, Russia, and Prussia, for dividing the Polish provinces between them. Their armies instantly occupied their several shares; and the diet, overawed by the united forces of the three powers, was forced to acquiesce in an arrangement that left Poland a merely nominal existence (A. D. 1773). The unhappy Stanislaus, reproached for calamities which it was not in his power to avert, could not avoid retorting on his accusers, and attributing the national calamities to the bigotry, the factious spirit, and the incessant contentions, of the turbulent nobles. By the intervention of Prussia, a treaty was subsequently concluded between Russia and Turkey, by which the emperess gained several important fortresses, a large acquisition of territory, and permission for her subjects to navigate the Black sea (A. D. 1774). Great as these gains were, they were less valuable in themselves than as means for obtaining other objects of Catherine's secret ambition.

Degraded as Louis XV. was, he could not receive, without emotion, intelligence of events which showed the low ebb to which the influence of France was reduced. When informed of the partition of Poland, he could not refrain from exclaiming, "Had Choiseul been still in the cabinet, this disgraceful transaction might have been averted." The duke d'Aguillon merited this reproach, but he resolved to atone for his negligence by gratifying the national hatred against the Jesuits, though he had long been suspected of secretly favoring that order. The death of Clement XIII. favored his projects (A. D. 1769). Ganganelli, who succeeded to the papacy under the title of Clement XIV., felt that the time was for ever gone by when the extravagant claims of the pontiffs could be maintained, and he therefore sought a reconciliation with the catholic sovereigns by making reasonable concessions. After a long but not unjustifiable delay, he issued a bull suppressing the order of jesuits; and most of the catholic prelates, who had long been jealous of that fraternity, eagerly enforced the papal edict (A. D. 1773). Little opposition was made by the jesuits to this decree, but the insurrection in Sicily and the deaths of Louis XV. and Pope Ganganelli (A. D. 1774) were attributed to their secret practices, though not a shadow of proof could be adduced to support such severe accusations. Indeed, it is notorious that Louis died of small-pox, and Ganganelli of a constitutional disease to which he had long been a martyr. Louis XVI., of whom his subjects had long been taught to form the most favorable expectations, ascended the throne of France: Angelo Braschi was elected to the papacy, under the title of Pius VI., by the influence of the more bigoted cardinals, who believed that he would be a more zealous supporter of the church than his predecessors.

SECTION II.—*History of England from the Peace of Paris to the Commencement of the American War.*

WHEN the British ministry concluded a separate treaty with France, they dissevered their country from its expensive connexion with the continent, but at the same time they diminished its influence in European politics. Extensive colonies, rapidly increasing commerce, and improving manufactures, afforded the nation ample amends for this loss; but a spirit of faction began to appear in the national councils, which produced a pernicious influence on the growing prosperity of the nation. While there was any reason to apprehend danger from the house of Stuart, the Brunswick dynasty was necessarily thrown for support on the whigs, for the tories were from principle more or less disposed to favor the claims of the exiled house; but when all fears from the Pretender had disappeared, the zeal which the tories had ever shown for the maintenance of the royal prerogative naturally recommended them to royal favor. Personal friendship induced George III. to introduce the earl of Bute into his cabinet; his influence excited the jealousy of the whigs, who had long monopolized the favor of the king and the nation; they accused him of an attachment to toryism, of partiality to his Scottish countrymen, and of having sacrificed the interests of the nation at the peace. Unable or unwilling to face popular clamor, the earl of Bute resigned his office, but it was believed he privately retained his influence in the cabinet; and thus no small portion of his unpopularity was inherited by his successors.

John Wilkes, member of parliament for Aylesbury, assailed the ministers with great bitterness in a paper called the North Briton. The forty-fifth number of this periodical contained a fierce attack on the king's speech at the opening of the parliamentary session; and the ministers, forgetting discretion in their rage, issued a general warrant against the authors, printers, and publishers of the libel. Wilkes was arrested, but was soon liberated, on pleading privilege of parliament. The house of commons, in opposition to the legal authorities, voted that privilege of parliament did not extend to the case of libel; but it subsequently joined with the lords in voting the illegality of general warrants. Wilkes, in the meantime, quitted the country, and not appearing to take his trial, was outlawed. So much was the nation engrossed by this dispute between the government and an individual, that little attention was paid to colonial affairs; but during this period the East India company acquired several rich districts in Bengal, and displayed a grasping ambition, which threatened the independence of the native powers.

A more dangerous prospect was opened in the American states. The French being removed, and the Indians driven into the backwoods, the colonies began to increase rapidly in wealth, and their prosperity suggested to Mr. Grenville a scheme for making them share in the burden of taxation. The late war had been undertaken principally for the security of the colonists, they had been almost exclusively the gainers by its successful termination, and it was therefore deemed equitable that they should pay a portion of the cost. But the Americans were not represented in the British parliament, and they, together with a large party in Britain, maintained that they could not be constitutionally taxed without their own consent. Mr. Grenville, supported by his royal master, disregarded opposition, and an act was passed imposing stamp-duties on a multitude of articles (A. D. 1765).

The dispute seemed to be allayed by a change in the British ministry; the marquis of Rockingham, much against the king's will, repealed the obnoxious Stamp Act; but he was forced to assert, in strong terms, the right of the king and parliament to enact laws, binding the colonies in all cases whatsoever. The marquis of Rockingham was soon obliged to give way to Mr. Pitt, who had been created earl of Chatham; but the cabinet constructed by this once-popular minister had no principle of union, and soon fell to pieces. The appointment of Lord North to the chancellorship of the exchequer aggravated party animosities (A. D. 1767); the new minister was suspected of hostility to the American claims, and had taken a prominent part against Wilkes. That demagogue returned to England; he was chosen member for the county of Middlesex at the general election, after which he surrendered himself to justice, obtained the reversal of his outlawry, and was sentenced to imprisonment for the libel he had published. When parliament met, it was supposed that Wilkes would take his seat for Middlesex, and a crowd assembled to escort him to the house; some rioting occurred, the military were called out, and a scuffle ensued, in which some lives were lost. Wilkes stigmatized the employment of the soldiers on this occasion in the most unmeasured terms; the ministers took advantage of this second libel to procure his expulsion from the house of commons, but the electors of Middlesex re-elected him without any hesitation. The commons resolved that an expelled member was incapable of sitting in the parliament that had passed such a sentence upon him, and issued a writ for a new election. Once more Wilkes was unanimously chosen, and once more the commons refused to admit him. A new election was held, and Wilkes was returned by a great majority over Colonel Luttrell, the ministerial candidate. The house of commons persevered in its declaration of Wilkes's incapacity, and resolved that Colonel Luttrell should be the sitting member.

In their anxiety to crush a worthless individual, the ministers had now involved themselves in a contest on an important point of constitutional law, with all the constituencies of the nation. A fierce opposition was raised against them in England, and this not a little encouraged the Americans to persevere in their resistance.

The resignation of the duke of Grafton, who wished to conciliate the colonies, the removal of Earl Camden, who disapproved of the decision respecting the Middlesex election, and the appointment of Lord North as premier, added to the exasperation of parties (A. D. 1770). The imposition of a light duty on tea kept alive the dispute with America, while the concessions made to the court of Spain, in a dispute respecting the Falkland islands, were represented as a deliberate sacrifice of the honor of the country. The only beneficial result from these disputes was, the indirect license given to the publication of the parliamentary debates, which had hitherto been deemed a breach of privilege. The commons sent a messenger to arrest some printers and publishers, but the execution of their orders was opposed by the civic magistrates, Crosby, Oliver, and Wilkes. The two former were sent to the Tower; but Wilkes refused to attend, unless permitted to take his seat for Middlesex, and the commons gave up the point by adjourning over the day on which he had been summoned to appear. Since that time the debates have been regularly published in the newspapers.

The abuses in the government of the dominions of the East India company having attracted considerable attention, a law was passed for bringing the affairs of that commercial association in some degree under the control of government; but to reconcile the company to such interference, a loan was granted on favorable terms; and also permission to export teas without payment of duty. A quantity of tea was shipped for Boston, and Lord North hoped that the low price of the commodity would induce the New Englanders to pay the small duty charged on importation; but when the vessels arrived at Boston, they were boarded during the night by a party of the townsmen, and the cargoes thrown into the sea. This outrage, followed by other acts of defiance, gave such offence in England, that acts were passed for closing the port of Boston, and altering the constitution of the colony of Massachusetts (A. D. 1774). It was hoped that the other colonies would be warned by this example; but, on the contrary, they encouraged the people of Massachusetts in their disobedience, and signed agreements against the importation of British merchandise, until the Boston port bill should be repealed, and the grievances of the colonies redressed. But though the colonists acted firmly, they showed the greatest anxiety for reconciliation; they prepared addresses to the government and their fellow-subjects, and they sent a memorial to the king, couched in terms equally spirited and respectful. The address to his majesty was not received, as it had emanated from an illegal assembly; and the determination evinced by the new parliament, which met in 1775, to support ministerial measures, defeated all hopes of an accommodation.

The continental powers, jealous of the maritime and commercial prosperity of England, exulted in the contest thus unwisely provoked. Even the moderate king of France, though severely harassed by the disordered state of his finances, and the embarrassing disputes which had been raised by his grandfather between the court and the parliaments, seemed disposed to favor the revolted colonies; several of his ministers urged him to offer them support, but the opinion of Turgot, the wisest of the French cabinet, prevailed for a season; he strenuously condemned such interference as impolitic and unjust. Spain, involved in a disastrous war with the piratical states of Barbary, and in a less formidable dispute with Portugal, respecting the boundaries of their South American colonies, was slow to engage in fresh hostilities, and was resolved to imitate the example of France. The king of Prussia, indignant at the desertion of his interests in the peace of 1763, openly rejoiced in the embarrassment of the British ministry; and Catherine of Russia exulted in the hope of seeing the naval power most likely to oppose her ambitious schemes preparing to destroy what was believed to be the secret source of its strength. Undervaluing the power and the fortitude of the provincials, the king and his ministers resolved to force them into obedience, parliament seconded these views, and the great bulk of the people applauded their determination. It is useless to conceal that the American war was popular at its commencement. The vague notion of dominion over an entire continent flattered English pride, and the taxes which the ministers demanded, promised some alleviation to the public burdens. The colonial revolt was regarded by many as a rebellion, not against the British government, but the British people, and the contest was generally looked upon in England as an effort to establish, not the royal authority, but the supremacy of the nation.

Section III.—*The American War.*

Blood having once been shed, it was manifest that the dispute between Britain and her American colonies could only be decided by the sword. Both parties, therefore, prepared for the struggle, but apparently with some lingering hope of a restoration of peace. Mutual forbearance was exhibited by the hostile generals, when the English were compelled to evacuate Boston; Howe, the British commander, made no attempt to injure the town, and Washington permitted the royal army to retire unmolested. But the employment of German mercenaries, by the English ministry, completed the alienation of the colonists; they resolved to separate themselves wholly from the mother-country, and on the 4th of July, 1776, the congress published THE DECLARATION OF INDEPENDENCE OF THE THIRTEEN UNITED STATES.

The first campaign, after some important successes gained by the British forces under General Howe, terminated in the entire destruction of the army of the north commanded by General Burgoyne. But this did not abate the confidence of the British ministers or the British people. Conciliatory acts were, indeed, passed by the parliament, but before intelligence of this altered policy could be received in America, France had entered into a treaty recognising the independence of the United States (A. D. 1778). There were already some in Britain who advocated this extreme measure; the earl of Chatham vehemently opposed the dismemberment of the empire, but while addressing the lords, he was struck down in a fit, and died within a few days. The nation mourned his loss, but it did not the less prepare vigorously to meet impending dangers. A declaration of war was issued against France, and a respectable fleet, commanded by Admiral Keppel, sent to cruise in the channel. Keppel met and engaged the French fleet off Ushant, but being badly supported by Sir Hugh Palliser, the second in command, he was unable to make any use of the slight advantage he obtained.

The peace of the continent was momentarily menaced by the efforts of the emperor Joseph to obtain possession of Bavaria, but the prompt interference of the king of Prussia, the remonstrances of the empress Catharine, and the unwillingness of France to second the ambitious designs of Austria, compelled Joseph to relinquish his prey when it was almost within his grasp (A. D. 1779). France alone, of the continental powers, had yet interfered in the American contest, but the intimate connexion between that country and Spain, led to a general belief that the latter would not long remain neutral. Nor was the expectation groundless; the court of Madrid, after an insincere offer of mediation, threw off the mask, and openly prepared for active hostilities. Washington adopted a cautious defensive policy, by which his adversaries were more exhausted than by a loss of a battle. The English subdued Georgia, and made some progress in the Carolinas; but the French captured several islands in the West Indies, and a Spanish fleet, for a time rode triumphant in the channel, and even insulted Plymouth.

Serious riots in London tended more to lower the character of the English, among foreign nations, than these reverses. Some of the penal laws against the catholics having been repealed, an association was formed by some ignorant fanatics for the protection of the protestant religion; they stimulated the passions of the mob, and roused an immense multitude to acts of outrage. For several days, London was at the mercy of an infuriate populace; some catholic chapels were burned, and many private houses destroyed. Tranquillity was at length restored by the interference of the military, and several of the rioters capitally punished. These disgraceful transactions alienated the court of Madrid at a time when it was disposed to negotiate, and the promise of the French to aid in the reduction of Gibraltar, confirmed the hostile dispositions of the Spaniards.

The English had reduced all the French settlements in the East Indies in 1778, and humbled the Mahrattas; but a new and formidable enemy now appeared. Hyder Ali, a soldier of fortune, raised by chance to the throne of Seringapatam, resolved to drive the European intruders from Hindústan, and entered the Carnatic with overwhelming forces. The local government of Madras was unprepared for this event, and the resources at its command were wasted by the obstinacy and incapacity of the council. Owing to this mismanagement, the English forces, commanded by Baillie and Fletcher, were all either slain or taken by Hyder and his son Tippoo.

The maritime glory of England was ably maintained by Sir George Rodney; he captured four Spanish ships-of-the-line off Cape St. Vincent, drove two more on shore, and burned another: thence proceeding to America, he thrice encountered the French fleet, under the count de Guichen, and though he obtained no decisive success, he prevented Washington from receiving naval aid in his meditated attack on New York. But the progress of the war now threatened to involve England in a new contest with all the maritime powers, respecting the trade of neutral vessels. The emperess of Russia took the lead in demanding freedom of trade for neutral vessels not laden with the munitions of war, to all ports not actually blockaded; she proposed that the northern powers should unite to support this right; a confederacy, called the Armed Neutrality, was formed by Russia, Denmark, and Sweden; Holland promptly acceded to the league; the courts of Vienna, Berlin, and Naples, adopted its principles; the republic of Venice, and even Portugal, the oldest ally of England, joined the association. The British ministry temporized, they expected, probably, that the smothered jealousy between Austria and Prussia might lead to a war that would divert the attention of the continental powers, but these hopes were frustrated by the death of Maria Theresa, whose inveterate hatred of the Prussian monarch was not inherited by her successor.

The conduct of the Dutch government had long been suspicious; but proof was at length obtained of its having concluded a treaty with the American congress, and the remonstrances of the British minister were treated with disdain. War was instantly declared, and several of the Dutch colonies in the South American seas were subdued by the English forces. Nor was this the only calamity that befell the Dutch republic; no sooner had the emperor Joseph succeeded to the ample inheritance of Maria Theresa, than he commanded a series of important reforms, among which was included the dismantling of the barrier towns in the Netherlands, which had been fortified at a vast expense to save Holland from the encroachments of France (A. D. 1781). A Dutch fleet, under Zoutman, was defeated by Admiral Parker, at the Doggers' bank; but the English had less success in the American seas, where Sir Samuel Hood was reduced to inactivity by the superior force of Count de Grasse.

The defeat of Lord Cornwallis, and the loss of the second British army that had been forced to surrender, led to a general feeling in England that any further protraction of the contest would be hopeless (A. D. 1782). The ministers, indeed, seemed at first resolved to continue the war, but they could no longer command a parliamentary majority, and were forced to resign. A new ministry, formed by the marquis of Rockingham and Mr. Fox, commenced negotiations for peace, without at all relaxing in their efforts to support the war; but before the results of the change could be fully developed, the ministry was dissolved by the death of the marquis. But ere this event produced any effect on the political aspect of affairs, two signal triumphs shed lustre on the arms of Britain. Admiral Rodney gained a decisive victory over the French fleet under Count de Grasse, between the islands of Martinique and Guadaloupe; and General Elliott, who had long been besieged in Gibraltar, defeated the formidable attack of the combined French and Spanish forces on that fortress, and burned, by showers of red-hot balls, the floating batteries, which the besiegers had fondly believed irresistible. In the East Indies, Sir Eyre Coote partly retrieved the fortunes of the company; he recovered the Carnatic, and totally routed Hyder's army at Porto Novo (A. D. 1781); and again at Pollalore. All the Dutch settlements were captured (A. D. 1782), but this success was interrupted by the defeat of Colonel Braithwaite, whose forces were surprised, surrounded, and cut to pieces by Tippoo and an auxiliary French force under M. Lally. Several indecisive engagements took place between Suffrein and Hughes, the French and English admirals, in the Indian seas; and the operations of the British by land were impeded by the jealousies of the civil and military authorities (A. D. 1783). The death of Hyder, and the restoration of peace between France and England, induced Tippoo to listen to terms of accommodation, and the English terminated this most unfortunate and disgraceful war, by submitting to humiliations from the son of Hyder, which greatly diminished the respect that had hitherto been paid to their name in Asia.

The changes of ministry in England protracted the negotiations for peace. The earl of Shelburne succeeded the marquis of Rockingham; but he was forced to yield to the overwhelming parliamentary strength of Lord North and Mr. Fox, who formed an unexpected coalition. The independence of America was recognised by the signature of preliminaries at Versailles (November 30, 1782); little difficulty was found in arranging terms with France and Spain; but the English wished to gain some compensation for their losses from Holland, and this circumstance occasioned a delay in the final arrangement of the treaty.

SECTION IV.—*The British Empire in India.*

THE British empire in India was, as we have already stated, founded on the ruins of the empire of Delhi. The French were the first who aimed at acquiring sovereignty by interfering in the contests of the local governors who had established their independence; they gained a decided superiority in the Carnatic and on the Coromandel coast, until the naval supremacy of England, in the seven years' war, intercepted their communications, and enabled their rivals to seize all their settlements. It was soon discovered that Coromandel cost more than it was worth, and that the territorial acquisitions most desirable were the countries round the Ganges. Under the government of Lord Clive, the English obtained the sovereignty of Bengal, Bahar, and Orissa, on the condition of paying twelve lacs of rupees annually to the emperor of Delhi. No sooner had the company acquired the sovereignty of this rich and opulent country, than an opposition of interest arose between the directors at home and their officers in India. The former were anxious to augment their commercial dividends by the territorial revenues, the latter were as obstinate in applying the surplus income to their own advantage. The want of control over the subordinate authorities in India led to most calamitous results; the officers of the company established monopolies in all the principal branches of domestic trade, rendered property insecure by arbitrarily changing the tenure of land, and perverted the administration of justice to protect their avarice. The injustice with which the native princes were treated, roused a formidable enemy to the English in Hyder Ali, sultan of Mysore; and had he been supported by European aid as effectively as he might have been, the company's empire in Hindústan would soon have ended. Some improvements were made in 1774, by concentrating the power of the three presidencies in the governor-general and council of Bengal, and the establishment of a supreme court of judicature. But Warren Hastings, the first governor-general, by a series of oppressions and extortions, provoked a second war with Hyder and the Mahratta states, the general results of which have been stated in the preceding chapter.

Notwithstanding the fortunate termination of the Mysorean and Mahratta wars, and the extension of the company's territory in Bengal, by the capture of Negapatam from the Dutch, the aspect of affairs was very gloomy and threatening. All the exactions of the company did not enable it to fulfil its engagements with the government; and its affairs were considered as fast approaching bankruptcy. It had also been found very inconvenient to have a mercantile association existing as a state within the state, and all parties agreed that the company ought to be placed more directly under the control of the government.

Under the administration of the marquis of Rockingham, Mr. Fox had taken the lead in arranging the affairs of Ireland. That country had been left unprotected during the late war; the inhabitants, menaced by invasion, armed in their own defence, and the volunteers thus raised, resolved, while they had the power, to secure the legislative independence of their country. The prudence of their leaders averted the horrors of a civil war, which would probably have ended in the separation of the islands; but they could not long have restrained the impatience of their followers, had not the Rockingham administration showed early its desire to comply with their demands. The legislative independence of Ireland was acknowledged (A. D. 1782), and a federal union of the two governments arranged, which promised to produce permanent advantages to both countries. His success in Ireland induced Mr. Fox to prepare a measure for regulating the complicated affairs of India; and a bill was introduced, on whose success he staked the existence of the coalition ministry. The principle of Mr. Fox's measure was to place the whole civil and military government of India under a board of nine members, chosen for four years, and not removable without an address from either house of parliament. Such a board would manifestly be an independent authority in the state; and it was said that its design was to make the power of a party rival that of the king. When the bill had passed the commons, his majesty, through Earl Temple, intimated to the peers his hostility to the measure, and the lords rejected it by a considerable majority. A new ministry was formed under the auspices of Mr. Pitt, second son to the great earl of Chatham; and as it was impossible to resist the strength of the coalition in the house of commons, the parliament was dissolved at the earliest moment that the state of public business would permit (A. D. 1784). The success of this measure surpassed the expectations of the new minister; the nation had been disgusted by the coalition of parties, that had been so long and so bitterly opposed to each other as those of Mr. Fox and Lord North; their friends were in most places beaten by the supporters of the new cabinet, and Mr. Pitt found himself firmly established in the plenitude of power. A new bill was framed for the government of India, which transferred to the crown the influence which Mr. Fox had designed to intrust to parliamentary commissioners; but some share of power, and the whole management of commercial affairs, was allowed to remain with the court of directors. The most important branch of commerce monopolized by the company was the tea trade with China, and this was thrown completely into their hands by a reduction of the duty, which removed all temptation to smuggling.

This change in the government of India was followed by the memorable impeachment of Mr. Hastings, whose trial lasted several years. It ended in the acquittal of that gentleman, at least of intentional error; but his fortune and his health were ruined by the protracted prosecution. A wise selection of rulers greatly improved the condition of the British empire in India; under the administration of Lord Cornwallis, the situation of the natives was greatly ameliorated; but the seeds of corruption, arising from ancient misgovernment and internal wars, could not be wholly eradicated.

The great extension of the British colonies gave a fresh stimulus to the spirit of maritime discovery, and the English penetrated into the remotest seas, stopping only where nature had interposed impenetrable barriers of ice. The three voyages of Captain Cook awakened a spirit of enterprise scarcely inferior to that which had been roused by the discoveries of Columbus. The islands of the south Pacific ocean became soon as well known as those of the Mediterranean sea, and their natural productions speedily formed articles of trade. Cook himself suggested the expediency of forming a settlement on the coast of New Holland; in less than half a century this colony has risen into great importance as an agricultural community; it promises, at no very distant day, to outgrow the fostering care of the mother-country, to afford her a rich reward, and become one of her most flourishing descendants.

From the period of Mr. Pitt's accession to power until the commencement of the French revolution, there was little beyond the strife of parties remarkable in the domestic history of England. The illness of the king (A. D. 1787), gave indeed alarming proof that the federal union of the English and Irish legislatures was by no means sufficient to secure the permanent connexion of the countries; for, while the British parliament adopted a restricted regency, the Irish offered the entire royal power to the prince of Wales. The speedy recovery of the king averted the evils that might have resulted from so marked a discrepancy, but from that time Mr. Pitt seems to have determined on his plan for uniting the two legislatures. The chief parliamentary struggles were for a repeal of the disqualifying laws that affected the dissenters, and the abolition of the infamous slave-trade; but the success of both these measures was reserved for later times.

Section V.—*History of Europe, from the end of the American War to the commencement of the French Revolution.*

During the progress of the American war, a gradual improvement in the science of government began to be manifested in the European states. Many of the German princes began to moderate the stern exercise of their despotic authority, to reform their expenditure and military establishments, and to adopt new institutions suited to the advanced state of civilization. The emperor Joseph was the most enterprising of the royal reformers; his measures for regulating the church involved him in a contest with Pope Pius VI., who hated and dreaded innovation, and was bigotedly attached to the ancient pretensions of the Romish see. Persuaded that his personal influence would be sufficient to dissuade Joseph from pursuing his course of change, the pontiff undertook an expensive journey to Vienna, but the emperor only gave him an abundance of compliments, and persevered in his resolutions. His failure covered the pontiff with ridicule, especially as he had to endure similar disappointments in his negotiations with the courts of Russia and Prussia. Joseph was willing to join the empress Catherine in the dismemberment of Turkey, and permitted that princess to seize the Crimea; but the principal western powers still dreaded the aggrandizement of Austria, and the threat of their confederacy saved the Ottoman empire. The king of Prussia was foremost in checking the encroachments of the emperor; he secretly instigated the Dutch to refuse the free navigation of the Scheldt to the ships of the Austrian Netherlands, and he planned a confederacy for maintaining the integrity of the Germanic states. Frederic died when he had completed the consolidation of a kingdom which his conquests had nearly doubled (A. D. 1786); he was succeeded by his nephew Frederic William, whose attention was early directed to the affairs of Holland.

The success of the Americans in establishing a commonwealth, induced many of the Dutch to aim at restoring their old republican constitution, and abridging or destroying the power of the stadtholder, which had become in all but name monarchical. The French secretly encouraged the opponents of the prince of Orange, hoping to obtain from the popular party an addition to their East Indian colonies, or at least such a union of interests as would counterpoise British ascendency in Asia; but the new king of Prussia, whose sister was married to the stadtholder, resolved to prevent any change, and the English ambassador vigorously exerted himself to counteract the intrigues of the French. An insult offered to the princess of Orange brought matters to a crisis; Frederic William immediately sent an army to redress his sister's wrongs; the republicans, deserted by France, made but a feeble resistance, and the stadtholder was restored to all his former authority.

The disordered state of the French finances was the cause of this desertion of their party by the ministers of Louis; through mere jealousy of England, they had involved their country in the American war, and had thus increased the confusion in which the prodigality of the preceding year had sunk the treasury. Minister after minister had attempted to palliate the evil, but M. de Calonne, who owed his elevation to the unwise partiality of the queen, Marie Antoinette, aggravated the disorder by a series of measures formed without prudence, and supported with obstinacy. Opposed by the parliaments, Calonne recommended the king to convene an assembly of the notables, or persons selected from the privileged orders (A. D. 1787); but these orders had hitherto paid far less than their fair proportion of the imposts, and an equitable system of taxation could not be expected from such an interested body. Necker, a Swiss banker, who had been for a short time the French minister of finance, joined in the opposition to Calonne, and it must be confessed that he demonstrated the total inadequacy of the proposed measures to remedy the decline of public credit. Louis dismissed Calonne, but he would not gratify his subjects by recalling Necker to the cabinet; and he dismissed the notables, whose uncomplying disposition rendered all hopes of aid from that assembly fruitless.

But the derangement of the finances was not the only evil that the French court suffered from its interference in the American war; the officers and soldiers who had fought for liberty in one hemisphere became dissatisfied with despotism in the other. A general desire for the establishment of a free constitution, like that of England, was diffused through the nation, and some more ardent spirits began to speculate on a republic. The connexion of the court with Austria was the cause of much secret discontent; the decline of the influence and the power of France was traced to its unfortunate alliance with the court of Vienna during the seven years' war, and the queen, who was naturally inclined to perpetuate this unpopular union, became an object of suspicion and dislike. It was mortifying to find that France no longer held the balance of power on the continent; that she could not save Turkey from the aggressions of the ambitious Catherine, nor protect the republican party in Holland from punishment for acts done in her service.

While France was thus disturbed, the progress of reform in other states was unimpeded; the rulers of Spain and Portugal improved their kingdoms by institutions for the protection of trade, and by placing checks on the exorbitant powers of the clergy. They joined in an effort to chastise the piratical powers in the Mediterranean, but the strength of the Algerine capital frustrated the attempt. The emperor Joseph and his brother Leopold, grand duke of Tuscany, distinguished themselves by enacting new and salutary codes of law; they abolished the use of torture to extort confessions, and they greatly limited the number of offences to which the penalty was affixed. Their example was followed by the emperess Catherine, whose code was the greatest blessing that her glorious reign conferred on Russia; and even the sultan evinced a desire to improve the institutions of Turkey.

But the course of events in France soon inspired all the sovereigns of Europe with a horror of innovation. After the dismissal of the notables, M. de Brienne, archbishop of Toulouse, had become minister of finance, and he soon involved himself in a dispute with the parliaments, by refusing to produce the accounts, which they insisted on examining before registering any new edicts of taxation. The great object of the parliament was to maintain the immunities of the privileged orders; the minister justly recommended a less partial system, when his opponents, yielding to temporary irritation, demanded the convocation of the states-general. The nobles and the clergy joined in the demand, without any expectation of its being granted, but merely to annoy the court; the people, however, took up the matter in earnest, and determined to enforce compliance. Various schemes were tried by the archbishop to overcome this powerful opposition, but all his plans were disconcerted by the obstinacy of the parliaments, and the king, finding every expedient fail, consented to recall Necker (A. D. 1788). At the same time, a solemn promise was given for the speedy assembly of the states-general, a body that had not been convened since the year 1614.

Before the assembling of this legislative body, it was necessary to determine the number of representatives that should be sent by each of the three orders, the nobles, the clergy, and the people; the majority of the notables voted that an equal number of deputies should be sent by the respective classes, but it was subsequently determined that the representatives of the third estate should equal in number those of the nobles and clergy conjoined. The king declared that the three estates should form separate chambers, but this very important matter was not so definitely fixed as to prevent future discussion. On the 5th of May, 1780, the states-general met at Versailles, and the democratic party, confident in its strength, demanded that the three orders should sit and vote together. After a short struggle, the court was compelled to concede this vital point, and the united bodies took the name of the National Assembly.

A spirit of insubordination began to appear in Paris, caused in some degree by the pressure of famine; artful and ambitious men fanned the rising flame, and directed the popular indignation against the king and his family. The arms in the Hospital of Invalids were seized by the mob, and the insurgents immediately proceeded to attack the Bastile, or state-prison of Paris. After a brief resistance, the governor, having an insufficient garrison, capitulated, but the conditions of the surrender were not observed by the infuriate multitude; the governor was torn to pieces, and many of the soldiers inhumanly massacred. Louis, greatly alarmed, tried by every means to conciliate his subjects; he removed the regular troops from Paris and Versailles, intrusting the defence of the capital to a body of civic militia, called the National Guards. The command of this new force was intrusted to the marquis de la Fayette, who had acquired great popularity by his liberal sentiments and his services to the cause of freedom in the American war. But all the king's concessions failed to conciliate the democratic, or rather, as we may henceforth call it, the republican party; relying on the support of the Parisian populace, the leaders of this band resolved that the legislature should be removed to the capital, and a mob was secretly instigated to make the demand. A crowd of the lowest rabble, accompanied by some of the national guards, proceeded to Versailles, the palace was violently entered, several of its defenders slain, and the king compelled instantly to set out for Paris, a prisoner in the hands of a licentious crowd, whose insults and indecencies were revolting to human nature.

This atrocious outrage may fairly be regarded as the commencement of the French Revolution; thenceforth the royal authority was an empty name, and all the ancient forms of government set aside; visionaries indulged in speculations on a new order of things, ardent patriots hoped to establish a constitution more perfect than the world ever yet had witnessed, but the base and the depraved sought to gain their own selfish ends by stimulating popular violence; and the last class was the only one whose expectations were realized.

Section VI.—*The French Revolution.*

From the moment that Louis XVI. was brought a prisoner to his capital, the ancient constitution of France was overthrown; the monarchy continued to exist only in name, and the abolition of feudal rights, the extinction of hereditary titles, and the secularization of ecclesiastical property, established popular sovereignty on the ruins of the ancient structure. Several German princes, who had possessions in Alsace, protested against these violent changes, but the popular rulers would not listen to any proposal of a compromise, and thus the leaders of the revolution were embroiled with the empire in the very outset of their career. A club, called from its place of meeting, the Jacobin Association, was formed by the leading democrats, and from this body denunciations were issued against all who were believed favorable to the ancient institutions of the country. Through the machinations of the Jacobins, popular hatred was directed against the court, and violent tumults excited in various parts of France. Infinitely more dangerous to the repose of Europe were the emigrations of the nobles, who were dissatisfied with the revolution; instead of remaining at home and organizing a constitutional resistance, they resolved to seek the restoration of the old government, with all its abuses, by the intervention of foreign powers. A meeting and conference took place at Pilnitz, between the emperor of Germany, the king of Prussia, and the elector of Saxony; the Count d'Artois, brother to the French monarch, and head of the emigrants, came uninvited, and he engaged the sovereigns to issue a vague declaration in favor of the rights of kings. Louis, wearied by the violence of the Jacobins, the licentiousness of the Parisian mob, and the disappointments he was daily forced to meet, resolved to escape from the captivity in which he was detained, and seek refuge on the frontiers. He fled from Paris, accompanied by his queen and children, but was unfortunately discovered at Varennes, seized, and brought back a prisoner to his capital. This failure exposed the royal family to suspicions of which the Jacobins took advantage; but the more moderate of the patriots were for a time sufficiently powerful to restrain their violence; and after a long deliberation, hey prepared a constitutional code, which was tendered to the king for acceptance. The readiness with which Louis assented to this instrument of government, and his frank communication of his satisfaction with the arrangement to his ambassadors at the different European courts, for a time restored his popularity. The emperor Leopold notified to the other powers that all danger of war was averted, and the external and internal tranquillity of France seemed to be assured.

But the constitution, thus established, could not be permanent; it was itself defective; and the minds of the French people, once animated by the desire of change, could not rest satisfied with any fixed form of government. The assembly by which it had been framed was dissolved, and a new legislative body chosen, according to the system recently established, and in this assembly the more violent partisans of democracy had more influence than in the preceding. It was the great object of the revolutionary party to involve the kingdom in foreign war; and the suspicious proceedings of the emigrants, their intrigues in the German courts, and the avowed determination of the emperor to maintain the feudal rights of the German princes in Alsace, furnished plausible pretexts for the commencement of hostilities. The death of the emperor Leopold accelerated a rupture; his successor, Francis II., continued to make alarming military preparations, and on his refusal to give any satisfactory explanation, Louis was compelled to declare war against him (A. D. 1792). But the strife of parties in the royal cabinet and the national assembly, led to such confusion in the councils of the French, that their armies, though superior in number, were defeated with loss and disgrace; while the Jacobins, whose intrigues were the real cause of these misfortunes, ascribed them to royalist treachery, and to the influence that Austrian councils possessed over the court from its connexion with the queen. These malignant slanders, industriously circulated, and generally believed, stimulated the Parisian mob to disgraceful acts of violence and disorder, against which La Fayette and the friends of rational liberty protested in vain.

A new incident gave fresh strength to the Jacobin party; Frederic William, king of Prussia, engaged to co-operate with the emperor Francis to restore the royal authority in France; their united forces were placed under the command of the duke of Brunswick; and this prince issued a sanguinary and insulting manifesto, which had the effect of uniting all the French factions in the defence of their common country. A declaration issued soon after by the emigrant brothers and relatives of Louis, in which the revolution was bitterly condemned, proved still more injurious to the unfortunate king; scarcely did intelligence of the publication reach Paris, when the palace was attacked by an infuriate mob, the Swiss guards ruthlessly massacred, and Louis with his family, forced to seek shelter in the hall of the national assembly. The deputies protected his person, but they suspended his regal functions, and committed him a prisoner to a building called the Temple, from having been once a monastery of the knights of that order.

La Fayette was equally surprised and indignant at these outrages of the Jacobins; he tried to keep the army firm in its allegiance; but all his exertions not being sufficient to accomplish this result, he fled into the Netherlands, when he was seized and imprisoned by the Austrians for his former opposition to the royal power. He was succeeded in the command of the army by Dumouriez, who made energetic preparations to resist the coming invasion. Confident in their strength, the allied armies entered France with the proudest anticipations, and their rapid progress in the beginning seemed to promise the most decisive results. To diminish the number of their internal enemies, Robespierre, Marat, and other chiefs of the Jacobins, planned the massacre of all the suspected persons confined in the prisons of Paris, and this diabolical plot was executed by the licentious populace. Similar horrors were perpetrated in other parts of France; a reign of terror was established, and no man dared to remonstrate against these shocking excesses. In the meantime the invaders had met with unexpected rereverses; trusting to the representations of the emigrants, that the revolution had been the work of a few agitators, not of the nation, and that there was a general reaction in favor of royalty, the allies had advanced without providing adequate stores, and when they received a check at Valmy, their camp was attacked by famine and disease; they were soon compelled to retreat, and to purchase an inglorious security by resigning the fortresses they had occupied. Dumouriez pursued the Austrians into the Netherlands, and gained a decisive victory, which encouraged the Belgians to throw off the imperial yoke; Flanders and Brabant were soon in possession of the victors, and their arms had made considerable progress in the reduction of Luxemburg. The convention, as the national assembly began to be called, having made their own country a republic, resolved to extend the revolution into other states; they offered their alliance to every nation that desired to recover its liberties, and they ordered the ancient constitutions of all the countries occupied by the French troops to be subverted. As the republican arms had conquered Savoy, and were fast gaining ground in Germany, the adoption of such a decree was virtually a declaration of war against all the kings of Europe.

The Jacobins, aided by the Parisian mob, and still more by the cowardice and indecision of their opponents, were now masters of the convention, and the first use they made of their power was to bring the unfortunate king to trial, on the ridiculous charge of his having engaged in a conspiracy for the subversion of freedom. Louis defended himself with great spirit and energy, but his judges were predetermined on his conviction: six hundred and eighty-three deputies pronounced him guilty of treason against the sovereignty of the nation, while there were only thirty-seven who took a more favorable view of his conduct. A motion for an appeal to the people was rejected; but the sentence of death was passed by a very inconsiderable majority, and this probably induced the Jacobins to hasten the execution. On the twenty-first of January, 1793, the unfortunate Louis was guillotined in his capital city; and the severity of his fate was aggravated by the insults of his cruel executioners.

This judicial murder excited general indignation throughout Europe; Chauvelin, the French ambassador, was dismissed from the British court, and many persons in England, who had hitherto applauded the efforts of the French people, became vehement opposers of revolutionary principles. A similar result was produced in Holland, where the government had been justly alarmed by the progress of the French in the Netherlands.

The convention did not wait to be attacked; a vote was passed that the republic was at war with the king of England and the stadtholder of Holland, by which artful phraseology it was intended to draw a marked distinction between the sovereign and the people of both countries. Spain was soon after added to the enemies of France, and the new republic had to contend against a coalition of all the leading powers of Europe. None of the allies threatened more loudly than the empress Catherine; she had just concluded a successful war against Turkey, in which her general, Suwaroff, had won a large addition of territory for his mistress, and the power of Russia in the Black sea was secured; she had also triumphed over the king of Sweden, more, however, by the insubordination of her rival's officers, than by the valor of her own troops. Poland was in everything but name subjected to Russia, and the empress was secretly maturing a plan to blot that country from the list of nations. As the coalition against the French republic was regarded as a war in the defence of the rights of kings, it was intended that a king should be placed at the head of the allied armies; and Gustavus, who had subverted the free constitution of Sweden, offered his services; but while he was preparing for the expedition, a conspiracy was formed against him by his discontented nobles, and he was murdered at a masked ball by Ankarstrom, an officer who believed himself personally injured by the king (A. D. 1792). After the death of Gustavus, the insincerity of Catherine became more manifest; she issued violent proclamations against the French, but carefully abstained from active hostility; indeed, it was manifestly her purpose to involve the continental powers in a war, which would prevent them from watching too jealously the aggrandizement of Russia.

The English and Prussians, deeming the defence of Holland a matter of primary importance, combined to check the progress of Dumouriez, who had overrun Dutch Brabant, with little opposition (A. D. 1793). But the progress of the Austrians, on the side of Germany, stopped the French in their career of conquest. Dumouriez quitted Holland to defend Louvain; he suffered a complete defeat at Neer-winden, by which his soldiers were so discouraged, that they deserted in great numbers. Dumouriez, finding himself suspected by the two great parties which divided the republic, and weary of the disorganized state of the French government, entered into negotiations with the allied generals, and arrested the deputies sent by the convention to watch his movements. But the army did not share the anti-revolutionary feelings of Dumouriez, and he was forced to seek shelter in the Austrian camp.

Custine, the successor of Dumouriez, was unable to check the progress of the allied armies; being reinforced by a British force under the duke of York, they captured the important fortress of Valenciennes, and seemed to have opened a way to Paris. The revolutionary government punished Custine's failure by a public execution, and employed the terrors of the guillotine as an incentive to patriotism. But the separation of the allied forces was more serviceable to the cause of the convention than the cruelties of the "Committee of Public Safety," to which the supreme power in France was intrusted. Austria, Prussia, and England, had separate interests, in the pursuit of which the common cause was forgotten; the imperialists laid siege to Le Quesnoi, while the English and Dutch proceeded to invest Dunkirk. The duke of York attacked Dunkirk with great spirit, but not receiving the support by sea that he had expected, and the Hanoverian force that covered his operations having been routed by Houchard, he was obliged to raise the siege and abandon the greater portion of his artillery and military stores. The Austrians were for a time more successful, but when Hoche, the defender of Dunkirk, was promoted to the command of the republican armies, they were driven from all their conquests in Alsace, and forced to seek shelter within the imperial frontiers. In Italy, the French maintained their hold of Savoy, but they experienced some severe reverses on the Spanish frontier.

The revolutionary excitement produced the most dreadful effects beyond the Atlantic; the colored population in the French division of St. Domingo took arms to force the whites to grant them equal privileges; their claims were supported by the three deputies sent by the convention to regulate the affairs of the colony, the negroes were seduced, by offers of liberty, to revolt against their masters, and St. Domingo, which had been one of the most flourishing islands in the West Indies, was devastated by a civil war, scarcely to be paralleled for its sanguinary fury and the wanton destruction of life and property.

The wars of southern and western Europe permitted Catherine of Russia to accomplish the favorite object of her policy, the dismemberment of Poland. Austria and Prussia joined in this iniquitous scheme, for the purpose of sharing the plunder, but the Poles made a gallant struggle to maintain their independence. Kosciusko, who had served in America, under Washington, was the chief of the patriots, and his heroic efforts protracted a struggle which from the first was hopeless. Kosciusko, severely wounded, fell into the hands of his enemies, Warsaw was stormed by the brutal Suwaroff, and the kingdom of Poland, erased from the list of nations, was divided between the three confederates (A. D. 1795). The king of Prussia, more anxious to secure his new acquisitions than to support the objects of the coalition, made peace with the French, and offered to mediate between the republic and Austria.

Scarcely had the Austrians been driven from France, when tha country was convulsed by civil war (A. D. 1793.) The jacobins having, by the aid of the Parisian populace, triumphed over the rival faction in the convention, mercilessly proscribed their political adversaries as traitors, and after a mockery of trial, hurried them to execution. Among the victims to their fury was the unfortunate queen of France, Marie Antoinette, but death was to her not a punishment, but a release from suffering. The tyranny of the Jacobins provoked formidable insurrections in the south of France, and encouraged the royalists of La Vendée to take up arms in the cause of their church and their king. Nothing could exceed the fury of the Jacobins when they heard of these revolts; severe decrees were passed against the cities which had resisted their authority, but no place was so cruelly punished as Lyons, which had continued for four months in a state of insurrection. After having endured a furious bombardment, it was forced to surrender at discretion, five deputies, of whom Callot and Fouché were the chief, received a communication from the convention to punish the Lyonese revolters by the summary process of military law, and about four thousand victims were shot or guillotined after the mockery of trial before this savage tribunal. But, in the midst of their butcheries, the Jacobins did not neglect the military defence of their country; a decree of the convention declared, that all the French were soldiers, and a levy of the population, *en masse*, was ordered. To support such numerous armies, private property was seized and paid for in promissory notes, called *assignats*, whose value was speedily depreciated, a circumstance which ruined public credit in France.

Toulon having revolted, an English garrison, strengthened by Spanish and Neapolitan detachments, occupied that important seaport. It was soon besieged by the troops of the convention; the artillery of the besiegers was directed by a young Corsican, Napoleon Bonaparte, who had risen by his merits from an inferior station. Owing to his exertions, the English soon found the place untenable; they evacuated Toulon, without loss, after having destroyed the arsenal and shipping, but they abandoned the inhabitants to the fury of the conquerors, who punished their revolt with indiscriminate severity.

In the Netherlands and Germany, the French, under Pichegru and Jourdan, gained many important advantages over the imperialists and their allies; but though many battles were fought, nothing of any consequence was effected in the early part of the campaign (A. D. 1794). A more important event was the downfall of the sanguinary faction which had so long deluged France with the blood of its best citizens; Robespierre's enormities were too numerous and too shocking to be borne, even by many of the Jacobin party; a conspiracy was formed against him; the convention was induced to resume its authority, and order his arrest, and, after a brief struggle, he and his accomplices were hurried before the revolutionary tribunal, which they had themselves organized, and sent to the scaffold. This revolution did not produce the beneficial results that had been expected; Robespierre's successors were little better than himself, and they were confirmed in their hostility to Britain by the recent defeat of their navy. Lord Howe, who had been distinguished as a naval commander in the two preceding wars, encountered a French fleet of rather superior force (June 1), and having broken the enemy's line, took six ships-of-war and sank two This success revived the declining spirits of the English nation, discouraged by the ill success of the war in Holland. Corsica was soon after annexed to the dominions of England, but the French were victorious on the Spanish frontier, and Holland was completely subdued by Pichegru and Moreau. The prince of Orange and the English forces escaped by sea; the Dutch abolished the office of stadtholder, and adopted a new form of government, similar to that of the French republic. If there were any in Holland who expected to derive advantage from this revolution, they were grievously disappointed; the French despised their new confederates, and treated them as a conquered people, while the English seized the colonies and destroyed the remains of the once unparalleled commerce of Holland.

The alarm which the French revolution excited in England, led the government to prosecute some enthusiastic advocates of reform in parliament for high treason; three of them were brought to trial and acquitted, upon which the prosecutions of the others were abandoned. There were few in the country anxious to make a change in the established institutions, the crimes and follies of the French Jacobins had rendered innovation unpopular, and many who had hitherto been in opposition to the court, tendered their aid to the minister; the most remarkable of these converts was the eloquent Burke, whose denunciations of French principles, produced a powerful effect on the national mind.

The dismemberment of Poland, and the desertion of the coalition by the king of Prussia, gave great dissatisfaction to the British parliament, and the character of our faithless ally was made the theme of severe and not unmerited censure. He had accepted a large subsidy from England, and employed the money lavishly granted him, against the Polanders instead of the French. But the defection of Prussia did not dishearten the English or the Austrians, who were encouraged to continue the war by the distracted state of France. In Paris, the convention partially succeeded in throwing off the yoke of the Jacobins, but the city was frequently endangered by their machinations, and the insurrections of the ferocious populace who supported them. The royalist war was renewed in La Vendée, and the south of France continued discontented. But the allies profited little by these commotions. The Spaniards, completely humbled, were forced to make peace with the republicans; the Austrians barely maintained their ground in Italy, and success was evenly balanced on the side of Germany. Great Britain, however, maintained its supremacy at sea; Admiral Cornwallis compelled a fleet of very superior force to retire, and Lord Bridport, with ten sail-of-the-line, attacked twelve of the enemy, three of which were compelled to strike their colors. The French were deprived of Martinique, Gaudaloupe, and St. Lucie, in the West Indies, and their reluctant allies, the Dutch, lost their settlements at the Cape of Good Hope, and in the island of Ceylon.

The convention, by an attempt to perpetuate its authority, provoked a formidable insurrection in Paris; Bonaparte had a considerable share in subduing the revolters, more than two thousand of whom were mercilessly slaughtered. Soon afterward, France had a new constitution, consisting of a legislative assembly, an upper house, called the council of ancients, and a directory of five members, intrusted with the executive functions of government. The directors soon began to limit the powers of the legislative body, and the new constitution was found to be a delusion. But an approach had been made to regular government, and the war was carried on with fresh vigor by the directory (A. D. 1796). Marshals Jourdan and Moreau made successful irruptions into Germany, but they encountered a formidable antagonist in the archduke Charles of Austria. He stopped the invaders in their mid-career of victory, completely routed Jourdan at Kornach, and then suddenly marching against Moreau, he nearly succeeded in surprising and overwhelming that general. Moreau's celebrated retreat was more honorable to his abilities than the most brilliant victory; he led his forces through the black forest, from position to position, often compelled to yield his ground, but never thrown into confusion, until he safely crossed the Rhine with all his artillery and baggage.

The campaign in Italy, where the French were commanded by Napoleon Bonaparte, was more eventful. The king of Sardinia, completely routed and cut off from his communications with the Austrians, was forced to purchase a dishonorable peace from the republic, by the cession of his most important fortresses. Napoleon then led his forces against the Austrians, forced, but with great loss, a passage over the bridge of Lodi, and gained possession of Milan and the principal cities of Lombardy. The victors made a harsh use of their triumph, the unfortunate Lombards were treated with great cruelty, the duke of Tuscany was compelled to exclude the English from the port of Leghorn, and the pope was forced to purchase the forbearance of the republicans by ceding to them Bologna, and several other towns, paying a heavy ransom, and sending three hundred precious manuscripts and pictures to enrich the national museum at Paris. The dukes of Modena and Parma were subjected to similar exactions, but the king of Naples had providently made a truce with the French before they approached his frontiers. Mantua, the last stronghold of the Austrians in Italy, was closely besieged, but the court of Vienna made vigorous preparations for its relief. Marshal Wurmser twice pushed forward against the French, but was each time defeated with great loss, a calamity owing to his unwisely dividing his forces. Alvinzi, who succeeded to the command of the Austrians, committed the same fault, and was compelled to retire; Mantua, however, was still obstinately defended, but the garrison ceased to entertain sanguine hopes of success.

In the meantime, the Corsicans grew weary of their connexion with Great Britain, drove the English from the island, and placed themselves under the protection of France. Ireland was exposed to the horrors of an invasion; a formidable squadron, having a large body of troops on board, appeared in Bantry Bay. Hoche, who had acquired considerable fame by his suppression of the insurrection in La Vendée, commanded the expedition, and, could he have effected a landing, the safety of the British empire would have been perilled; but a violent storm dispersed the ships, most of which were subsequently either sunk or captured. The death of the emperess Catherine inspired the English minister with the hope of gaining more effective assistance from Russia; but her successor, the emperor Paul, disregarded all the solicitations addressed to him by the courts of London and Vienna.

A new enemy appeared against England; the Spanish government, always jealous of British naval power, and overawed by the French directory, entered into alliance with the republic, and began to increase its navy (A. D. 1797). At this moment, when the existence of England depended on its sailors, a formidable mutiny broke out in the fleet at Spithead; the officers were suspended from their authority and dismissed from their ships; the malcontents blockaded the mouth of the Thames, and committed several acts of depredation. Fortunately the sailors grew alarmed themselves and hastened to return to their allegiance; a few of the ringleaders were hanged, but the great body of the revolters was conciliated by an act of amnesty.

The war in Italy was not discontinued during the winter; Alvinzi made a desperate effort to retrieve the fortunes of Austria, but he was again defeated, and Mantua soon capitulated. Having very severely punished the pope for his attachment to the imperial interests, Napoleon resolved to carry the war into the hereditary states of Austria. The territory of Friuli was quickly subdued, and a great part of the Tyrol occupied by the French; the archduke Charles made a bold defence, but the emperor Francis, terrified by the advance of Hoche and Moreau in Germany, sued for peace, in spite of the remonstrances of his English allies. While the terms of pacification were under discussion, Napoleon subverted the ancient constitution of Genoa and Venice, and made both republics virtually dependant on France.

Spain suffered severely in the war she had so rashly commenced. Admiral Jervis encountered a Spanish fleet of very superior force off Cape St. Vincent, and by a dexterous manœuvre cut off nine of their ships from the line, so that he could engage the rest on more equal terms. Four ships-of-the-line were taken in this brilliant engagement, to the success of which Nelson, who was now commencing his brilliant career, mainly contributed. The Spaniards lost also the valuable island of Trinidad, but an attack made by the British on Teneriffe was unsuccessful. The Dutch, too, were punished for their alliance with France. Three ships-of-the-line and four frigates were taken by the British, after an unsuccessful attempt to recover the cape. But they suffered a more severe loss on their own coast; an English squadron, commanded by Admiral Duncan, got between their ships and the shore, and took eleven out of fifteen sail-of-the-line. Two of the prizes, however, in consequence of the difficulties of the navigation, were abandoned.

A new revolution in France invested the directory with supreme power, and their opponents were banished to the unhealthy swamps of Guiana, where they were treated with great rigor. Negotiations for peace were commenced, but those with England were broken off abruptly by the extravagent demands of the French plenipotentiaries. This did not prevent the conclusion of a treaty between the republic and Austria, when the emperor was renumerated for the loss of Mantua by the cession of Venice, which he meanly accepted, and the frontiers of France were extended to the Rhine.

Great Britain was now the only power at war with France, and the directory prepared a large army for its invasion. This threat produced a noble display of patriotism throughout the country, volunteer associations for defence were formed, and every man was ready to act as a soldier. But while the British navy rode triumphant in the channel, the menace of invasion was an idle boast, and Bonaparte only used it as a pretext to cover his ulterior designs. While the French were modelling, at their pleasure, the governments of Italy, Switzerland, and Holland, Napoleon planned an expedition to Egypt, with the hope of rendering the French influence as predominant in the east as it was in western Europe (A. D. 1798). Convoyed by a fleet, under Admiral Brueys, he sailed first to Malta, which was betrayed by the French knights. A garrison was left to secure the forts of this important island; the rest of the expedition escaping the vigilance of the English fleet, safety reached Egypt, and having effected a landing, took Alexandria by storm. The Mameluke beys, who were then masters of the country, led their brilliant cavalry to check the progress of the invaders; but these undiscipl ied warriors were unable to break the firm squares of the French infantry, and they were almost annihilated in the battle of Embaba.

But the hopes inspired by such success were soon dashed by the ruin of the French fleet. After a long search, Admiral Nelson discovered Brueys, in the bay of Aboukir, and immediately formed a bold plan of action. He led a part of his fleet between the French and the shore, so as to place his enemies between two fires. The victory was complete, nine sail-of-the-line were captured, L'Orient, a ship of uncommon size, blew up with the greater part of her crew; another ship-of-the-line and a frigate were burned by their respective captains.

But Great Britain was not equally fortunate in other quarters; an armament sent against the Belgic coast signally failed, and the island of St. Domingo was evacuated by the British troops. Ireland was distracted by an insurrection, planned by some enthusiastic admirers of French principles, but put into execution by an ignorant peasantry, whose excesses their leaders were unable to control. Many acts of atrocity were committed by the insurgents, and the conduct of the royal army was frequently very disgraceful. The insurrection was finally quelled; but scarcely was tranquillity restored, when a small party of French landed in Connaught, and through the cowardice of the troops first sent o oppose them, penetrated into the heart of the country. Lord Cornwallis, who had just been appointed lord lieutenant, soon overtook the French, and forced them to surrender. Judiciously tempering severity with clemency, he conciliated the discontented; and Sir John Warren, by capturing the greater part of a French fleet, averted the dangers of a future invasion.

The victory of Nelson at the Nile produced a powerful effect throughout Europe. The sultan made preparations for a vigorous defence of his dominions; the Russians sent an armament into the Mediterranean, and captured the Ionian islands, which the French had wrested from the Venetians; the king of Naples took arms to recover the Roman territories for the pope; and the emperor of Austria yielded to the suggestions of Mr. Pitt, and commenced hostilities.

The French were not daunted by this powerful coalition; they easily repelled the Neapolitans, but they found a more formidable foe in the Russians, who entered Italy under the command of Suwaroff, and being there joined by the Austrians, gained several important advantages in spite of Marshals Moreau and Macdonald. But these successes were so dearly purchased, that the allies resolved to try a new plan of operations. Suwaroff undertook to drive the French from Switzerland; Kray and Melas were to direct the Piedmontese and Austrian troops in Italy; while the archduke Charles protected Germany with all the forces of the empire. Victory in general favored the allied powers: the French lost all their posts in Italy except Genoa, and that was closely besieged; Suwaroff made rapid progress in Switzerland; and in Germany the French arms suffered several but not very important reverses. In the meantime Napoleon invaded Syria; but being foiled at Acre, chiefly through the heroic exertions of Sir Sydney Smith, he returned to Egypt, and having provided for the security of that country, secretly embarked for France. He escaped the vigilance of the English cruisers, and arrived at Paris just as the directory were indulging in extravagant joy for the defeat of the joint invasion of Holland by the English and Russians. It had been confidently asserted that the Dutch were anxious to throw off the yoke of France, but these representations were proved to be fallacious; and the duke of York, who commanded the English forces, was compelled to purchase a safe retreat by restoring eight thousand French prisoners without ransom or exchange.

Bonaparte soon perceived that the French people had grown weary of the directory. Trusting to his popularity with the army, he drove the legislative council from their chamber at the point of the bayonet, and formed a new constitution, by which the executive power was intrusted to three consuls, of whom he was the chief. The first consul, in everything but name a monarch, attempted to commence negotiations; the English ministers repulsed him rather harshly, and preparations were made for a decisive campaign.

An important and necessary change was made in the constitution of the British empire (A. D. 1800). Some difficulties had arisen from the existence of independent legislatures in England and Ireland; the two parliaments had already divided differently on the important question of the regency, and there was reason to fear that some future discrepancy might lead to the dismemberment of the empire. To prevent such an evil, it was resolved that the two legislatures should form one imperial parliament, and the terms of the union were warmly canvassed in both countries. The measure was very unpopular in Ireland, and when first proposed, was rejected by the parliament; but, during the recess, the minister found means to increase the number of his supporters, and in the following session the Act of Union was passed by considerable majorities.

It was expected that the first consul would attempt the invasion of England or Ireland; but Napoleon was too well aware of his naval weakness to undertake such a hazardous enterprise. He formed a daring plan of a campaign in Italy, and led his army like Hannibal over the Alps. The Austrians could scarcely have been more surprised if an army had fallen from the clouds, than they were by the appearance of the French columns descending from Mount St. Bernard; but, encouraged by their recent acquisition of Genoa, they prepared to make a vigorous resistance. The battle of Montebello, in which the French had the advantage, was the prelude to the decisive battle of Marengo. The Austrians commenced the fight with unusual spirit; both wings of their opponents were beaten, and the centre shaken; but some fresh divisions arriving to the support of the French at the last moment of the crisis, Napoleon pierced the lines of the imperialists, which were too much extended, and Murat's furious charge completed the rout of the Austrians. So disheartened was the imperial general, Melas, that he purchased a truce by resigning Genoa, and the principal fortresses in Piedmont and the Milanese, to the conquerors.

The influence of the British cabinet, and some slight successes in Germany, induced the emperor Francis to continue the war; but his rising hopes were crushed by the battle of Hohenlinden, in which the French and Bavarians under Moreau completely defeated the imperialists, and opened a passage into Upper Austria. The emperor, alarmed for his hereditary dominions, consented to a truce, and this was soon followed by the treaty of Luneville, which annihilated for a season the Austrian influence in Italy. Scarcely had Great Britain lost one ally, when she was threatened with the active hostility of another. The Russian emperor, Paul, had been chosen patron of the order of St. John of Jerusalem; and when the English, after having reduced Malta by blockade, refused to restore the island to the degenerate knights, the chivalrous potentate ordered the British ships in the Russian ports to be detained, and prevailed upon Sweden and Denmark to unite with him in an armed neutrality (A. D. 1801). In the meantime Mr. Pitt, who had so long presided over the councils of Great Britain, resigned his office as premier. When he was urging forward the great measure of the union with Ireland, he had endeavored to conciliate the catholics of that country by a promise of his aid in procuring a repeal of the laws which excluded them from parliament and office; but the king's repugnance to catholic emancipation was invincible, and Mr. Pitt retired from the cabinet. Mr. Addington, his successor, had scarcely been installed, when the gratifying intelligence was received of a great triumph obtained by the British navy in the Baltic. When Mr. Pitt received intelligence of the armed neutrality, he sent a large fleet into the northern seas, under the command of Sir Hyde Parker and Lord Nelson. The latter, with twelve sail-of-the-line and some small vessels, attacked the Danish fleet, moored in a formidable position before their capital, and after a desperate contest, took or destroyed every Danish ship that had a share in the engagement. The Danes were humbled by this loss but they were still more disheartened by the death of the Russian emperor, Paul, who was the founder and head of the northern confederacy. This potentate's incapacity provoked the indignation of the nobles and the people, and he was murdered by a party of conspirators, who placed his son Alexander upon the throne The young prince concluded a treaty with the British on equitable terms, and the other northern powers imitated his example.

A British army, under Sir Ralph Abercrombie, had been sent to drive the French from Egypt, and it succeeded in this object, but with the loss of its gallant commander. Some naval enterprises were less successful: and as there was now a stable government in France, the English minister consented to commence negotiations for peace. The terms were soon arranged: France retained her acquisitions in Germany and the Netherlands, and her supremacy in Holland, Switzerland, and Italy. England consented to resign Malta to the knights, to make the Ionian islands an independent republic, and to restore all her colonial conquests except Ceylon and Trinidad. The treaty was signed at Amiens, and for a short time Europe was deceived with a hope of continued tranquillity.

During this war the maritime and commercial supremacy of England had been completely established, and her colonial empire in India extended and secured. When the French invaded Egypt, Tippoo, the sultan of Mysore, inheriting his father's hostility to the English, meditated an attack on the company's territories, but he was anticipated by the vigor of the earl of Mornington, the governor-general, who, instead of waiting for an attack, invaded Mysore. Seringapatam, Tippoo's capital, was taken by storm, and that unfortunate prince fell in the assault. This conquest made the British power supreme in southern India, and led to the establishment of the company's paramount authority over the whole peninsula of Hindústan.

France had gained a vast accession of territory, but the freedom which the French had taken arms to defend was no more. The revolution, whose progress had been so strangely marked by savage crime and cruel suffering, was now fast finding its consummation in a military despotism, more arbitrary and crushing than the iron rule even of the feudal monarchs; but the French, weary of the many vicissitudes that their government had undergone, submitted to a change that promised future stability, and consoled themselves with dreams of glory for the loss o' freedom.

CHAPTER X.

THE FRENCH EMPIRE.

SECTION I.—*Renewal of the War between England and France.*

WHEN peace was restored, Napoleon directed all his energies to consolidate the power he had acquired. Permission was granted to those whom the violence of the revolution had driven from their country, to return, on certain conditions. Christianity, abolished in the madness of the preceding convulsions, was restored, and arrangements were made with the pope for the future government of the Gallican church; and finally, the consular power was conferred upon Napoleon for life, while a representative constitution preserved for the nation a mere shadow of freedom. His interference in foreign states was less honorable: he moulded the Italian and Ligurian republics at his pleasure; but the Swiss proving more refractory, Marshal Ney entered their territory with a large army, to enforce submission to the imperious dictates of the first consul. The British ministers remonstrated against this interference, but they could not prevent the French from extending their influence in Germany and Italy, as well as the Swiss cantons. Napoleon was less successful in his efforts to recover the island of Hispaniola or St. Domingo. A large French army was sent to the island, and the proceedings of its commanders were marked by gross cruelty and treachery; but these abominable means failed to crush the spirit of the insurgent negroes, and the unfortunate colony was exposed to all the horrors of a servile war. Great Britain did not interfere in this contest; the example of a successful revolt of slaves was deemed of dangerous consequence to our West Indian islands, and the reduction of St. Domingo was desired rather than deprecated.

But the encroachments of France on the independence of the neighboring states, and the determination of England to retain the island of Malta, gave rise to angry discussions, which, it was soon obvious, would only terminate in a renewal of hostilities (A. D. 1803).

The English commenced the war by issuing letters of marque, authorizing the seizure of French vessels; Napoleon retaliated, by seizing the persons of all the British whom pleasure or business had induced to visit France during the brief interval of peace. The threats of invasion were renewed, but the English people evinced a spirit of loyalty which quelled all fear of danger. In Ireland an unmeaning insurrection was raised by two enthusiasts, Russell and Emmett, but it was suppressed almost the instant it exploded, and a few of the leaders were capitally punished. Hanover, however, was occupied by a French army, and the Dutch republic joined in the war against Britain. On the other hand, the English conquered the French islands of St. Lucie and Tobago, and the Dutch settlements of Demerara and Essequebo. In Asia, the English broke the dangerous power of the Mahrattas, who were supposed, at the instigation of the French, to have formed plans for the subversion of the company's power. The earl of Mornington, who had recently been created marquis of Wellesley, disconcerted their schemes by his vigor and promptitude ; and the formidable Scindiah was forced to purchase peace by the cession of a large portion of his dominions. The king of Kandi, who had assailed the British power in Ceylon, was also subdued, and the English colonial empire in Asia was at once enlarged and secured. The French colonial power was at the same time nearly annihilated : the island of St. Domingo was wrested from them by the insurgent blacks, and erected into an independent state, under its ancient Indian name of Hayti. These results might have been reasonably anticipated, for without a navy it was impossible for France to retain its colonies.

Mr. Pitt had retired from office just before the conclusion of the peace, his friends became anxious that he should return to the administration on the renewal of war, and Mr. Addington was forced to yield to their superior influence (A. D. 1804). The premier encountered many difficulties in constructing a cabinet, and had to resist a more formidable opposition in parliament than he had been accustomed to meet. While Mr. Pitt was laboring to strengthen his ministry, Napoleon was more successfully engaged in securing the supreme power in France. He accused his rivals, Moreau and Pichegru, of having plotted his destruction, in conjunction with Georges, a royalist leader, and charged the English ministers with having hired assassins to destroy him. A more atrocious crime was the murder of the most amiable of the Bourbon princes. The young duke D'Enghien was unjustifiably seized in the neutral territory of Baden, hurried to the castle of Vincennes, and shot by the sentence of a court-martial, contrary to all forms of law, as well as principles of justice. Immediately after the perpetration of this ruthless deed, Napoleon obtained the title of emperor from his servile senate ; the dignity was declared hereditary in his family, and the principal powers of Europe, with the exception of Great Britain, recognised the new sovereign.

The emperor of Russia was anxious to avenge the fate of the duke D'Enghien, his remonstrances against the usurpations of Napoleon were very warm, but none of the other continental sovereigns seconded his zeal, and the storm, which threatened to burst forth, soon subsided Having no ally on the continent, England had no means of employing her military strength, and the operations of the war were confined to a few naval enterprises. Napoleon offered terms of peace ; but the British minister, relying on the probable co-operation of Russia, refused to negotiate (A. D. 1805). At the same time war was commenced against Spain, by sending out a squadron to intercept the Plate fleet, laden with the treasures of Spanish America. This attempt was made before hostilities were formally declared ; but the British minister justified it by referring to the intimate connexion that had been formed between the courts of Paris and Madrid. Mr. Pitt's conduct was approved by large parliamentary majorities; but he received a harsh proof of the decline of his influence, in the impeachment of his friend Lord Melville, for official delinquency. When the charge was made in the house of commons, Mr. Pitt vindicated the conduct of Lord Melville; but, notwithstanding the minister's exertions, the impeachment was carried by the casting vote of the speaker. The premier was more successful in his foreign policy; the emperor of Russia concluded a treaty with England for restraining the ambition of France, and Napoleon's encroachments in Italy induced Austria to accede to the league.

Napoleon, at the request of the constituted authorities of the Italian republic, assumed the title of king of Italy; and in the cathedral of Milan placed upon his head the ancient iron crown of the Lombard monarchs, and with less ceremony, annexed the territories of the Ligurian republic to the French empire. The Austrian emperor vainly remonstrated; and at length, relying on the aid of the Russians, published a declaration of war. Unfortunately, Francis commenced hostilities by an action as unjustifiable as any of which he accused Napoleon. The elector of Bavaria, whose son was in the French capital, declared himself neutral, upon which the Austrian troops entered his dominions, treated them as a conquered country, and compelled him to seek refuge in Franconia. Napoleon eagerly seized the opportunity of branding his enemies as the aggressors in the contest, and declaring himself the protector of the liberties of Europe.

The naval war was maintained by Great Britain with equal vigor and success. The French and Spanish fleets having formed a junction, sailed for the West Indies, but they were soon pursued by Lord Nelson, the terror of whose name induced them to return to Europe. Off Ferrol they encountered an inferior squadron, under Sir Robert Calder, and lost two of their ships, but the rest reached the bay of Cadiz, where they were strongly reinforced. Lord Nelson, with twenty-seven sail-of-the-line, appeared off the coast, and the French admiral Villeneuve, relying on his vast superiority of force, resolved to hazard an engagement. The allied fleets of France and Spain, amounting to thirty-three ships-of-the-line, besides frigates and corvettes, appeared near Cape Trafalgar, ranged in order of battle; Nelson gave immediate orders for an attack, and the English fleet, advancing in two divisions, soon broke through the adverse line. In the heat of the engagement, the heroic British commander fell mortally wounded; but he lived to know that his plans had been crowned with success, twelve of the enemies' ships having struck before he expired. A dreadful storm, which arose just after the battle closed, prevented the English from retaining all the fruits of their victory; but four prizes reached Gibraltar, fifteen French and Spanish vessels were destroyed or sunk; out of the fourteen which fled, six were wrecked, and four taken at a later period by Sir Robert Strachan. The joy which so brilliant a victory diffused throughout England was chastened by grief for the loss of the gallant Nelson; he was honorably interred at the public expense, and monuments were erected to his memory by a grateful nation.

Napoleon consoled himself for his losses at sea by the prospect of

42

gaining some decisive advantage over the Austrians before they could be joined by their Russian auxiliaries. He treated with contempt the threats of Gustavus, king of Sweden ; and it must be confessed that the pompous boasts of that eccentric monarch, combined with his vacillating conduct, did not entitle him to much respect. The French army crossed the Rhine, and disregarding the neutrality of the king of Prussia, passed through the Franconian territories of that monarch, and having passed the Danube, began to menace the rear of the Austrians. In spite of the remonstrances of the archduke Charles, the cabinet of Vienna had intrusted the chief command of their armies to General Mack, whose talents and fidelity were both suspicious. Mack in a short time permitted himself to be surrounded by the French at Ulm ; he had ample means for a protracted defence, having twenty thousand men under his command, but through cowardice or incapacity, he consented to a capitulation, by which he and his soldiers became prisoners-of-war. Intelligence of the battle of Trafalgar came to abate Napoleon's triumph, while the courage of Francis was revived by the arrival of the Russian auxiliaries. The French, pushing forward, made themselves masters of Vienna ; but the Russians, encouraged by the presence of their emperor, though they had been severely harassed in Moravia, showed so much spirit, that the allies resolved to hazard an engagement. In the beginning of December, the hostile armies met near the village of Austerlitz ; Kutuzoff, who directed the movements of the allies, injudiciously extended his lines, with the intention of outflanking the French ; Napoleon at once saw and took advantage of the error, he separated the enemies' central divisions from those of both wings, and pouring his columns through the gaps, overwhelmed his foes in detail. After a desperate resistance, the Russians were forced to retreat ; a large body attempted to escape over a frozen lake, but the French artillery poured a storm of shot from a neighboring eminence, which broke the ice around the fugitives, and the greater part of them perished in the waters. This severe defeat humbled the emperor Francis ; he accepted peace on the terms dictated by the conqueror, but the emperor Alexander refused to be a party to the treaty, and returned to his own country.

During these transactions, the selfish conduct of the king of Prussia was as injurious to the allies as it was ultimately ruinous to himself. On the violation of his Franconian territories, he had taken arms, and entered into treaties with Great Britain and Russia ; but Napoleon, aware that the prompt movement of a third power might disconcert all his plans, contrived to keep awake the ancient jealousy between the sovereigns of Austria and Prussia, and he finally won the tacit approbation of the latter power by offering Hanover as a bribe. Thus the Prussian sovereign was induced to favor the alarming extension of French power by a share of the plunder of his own allies.

The battle of Austerlitz was a fatal blow to Mr. Pitt ; he had been the chief agent in forming the coalition—he had loudly and boldly prognosticated its success, and had despised the warnings of his political adversaries ; the failure of all his hopes proved too much for his shattered constitution, and he died at the commencement of the parliamentary session (A. D. 1806). His parliamentary friends procured him a splendid funeral, and the payment of his debts at the national cost, and a monument was erected to his memory in Westminster Abbey.

Section II.—*Progress of Napoleon's Power.*

While Napoleon was establishing his supremacy over the continent of Europe, the marquis of Wellesley was further extending and securing the British empire in India, by humbling the Mahratta powers. Jesswunt Holkar, a formidable chief, made a vigorous resistance, but he soon found that his soldiers could not cope with the disciplined troops of the company, and was forced to beg a peace. He obtained better terms than he could have expected, from the marquis Cornwallis, who succeeded the marquis of Wellesley, for the court of directors had found that conquests were very expensive, and that every new acquisition of territory became an additional source of expense. At this time the English nation generally took little interest in the affairs of India; men's minds were more occupied by the change of ministry consequent on the death of Mr. Pitt. It was generally desired that as large a share of the talent of the country as possible, without reference to party, should be included in the new administration; and Lord Grenville, to whom the arrangements were confided, overcame the king's reluctance to Mr. Fox, and made that gentleman one of the secretaries of state. The first measures of the ministers won them a considerable share of public favor; Lord Henry Petty introduced order into the financial accounts, which were in such a state of confusion as to afford protection to fraud and peculation; Mr. Fox proposed and carried the abolition of the infamous slave-trade, which had been so long a disgrace to England and to Christianity. The acquittal of Lord Melville by the house of peers was received with some surprise; but the ministers appear to have acted impartially in avoiding any interference that might influence the result of an official investigation.

The war was still prosecuted with great vigor; the Dutch colony of the Cape was subdued, and a small force under Sir Home Popham and General Beresford, captured the important city of Buenos Ayres in South America. The provincials, however, disappointed in the hope of obtaining freedom and independence by British aid, took up arms, and the conquerors of Buenos Ayres were forced to capitulate, while a British armament was on its way to maintain the supposed conquest.

Hastening to secure the reward of his perfidy, the king of Prussia occupied Hanover, ceding to the French the dutchy of Cleves, and some other districts, as a reward for yielding him the electorate. Gustavus of Sweden joined the British court in remonstrating against this proceeding; but as that monarch's actions were not very consistent with his menaces, the Prussians treated him with contempt. An ally of Britain was about the same time driven from his dominions. During the Austrian war, the king of Naples, encouraged by the withdrawal of the French troops from his territories, and instigated by his queen, an Austrian princess, received an army of Russians and English into his capital. Napoleon, provoked by this unexpected war, declared that the Bourbon dynasty had ceased to reign in Naples, and assembled an army to execute his threats just as the Russian and English forces were withdrawn. The invaders scarcely encountered any resistance except in Calabria, where the peasants made a brief stand. The king of Naples fled to Sicily, and Napoleon conferred the vacant throne on his brother, Joseph Bonaparte. The peasants in Calabria and the Abruzzi, harassed the French by desultory attacks, and they were supported by Sir Sydney Smith, who commanded the British naval force on the Sicilian station. The queen of Naples and Sir Sydney Smith prevailed on Sir John Stuart, the commander of the British force in Sicily, to transport his troops into Calabria; the natives did not join the invaders in such force as had been expected, and they would have immediately returned, had not an opportunity offered of engaging the French general Regnier. The armies met at Maida, and the French, though greatly superior in number, were completely defeated. But the victory had no result except to raise the character of the British army, which had been for some time depressed. The French poured large bodies of soldiers into Calabria, and in a short time established their authority over the whole of the south of Italy.

Having procured the throne of Naples for his brother Joseph, Napoleon resolved to place his brother Louis on that of Holland. The Dutch submitted to the change without remonstrance, though their country thus became a mere province of France; but they consoled themselves by reflecting on the mild character of their new sovereign, who was sincerely anxious to promote the prosperity of his subjects His efforts, were, however, controlled by his imperial brother, who was anxious of becoming the arbiter of Europe, and rendering everything subservient to the military sway of France. Still Napoleon professed an anxious desire for peace, and made overtures to Mr. Fox, for whose character he professed and probably felt the highest veneration. The negotiations were broken off by the refusal of the French to admit the Russians to a share of the treaty, and by Napoleon's perseverance in retaining power inconsistent with the independence of the other European states. While the subject was under discussion, Mr. Fox died, and was succeeded in office by Mr. (afterward Earl) Grey: the conferences were continued, but M. Talleyrand, who was the representative of France, insinuated that the change in the British cabinet blighted the hope of restoring tranquillity to Europe.

The frustration of this negotiation led to a new war; during the conferences, Napoleon's agents averred that the restoration of Hanover would not be refused; the king of Prussia was indignant at the readiness with which this pretended friend sacrificed his interests; Hanover had been the reward of subserviency, if not treachery, and he now found that he retained the bribe by a very insecure tenure. A more justifiable ground of indignation was the opposition which Napoleon gave to the efforts of the Prussians, in forming an association which might counterbalance the Confederation of the Rhine, an alliance that transferred to France the supremacy over Germany, that had formerly belonged to the house of Austria; finally, it was more than suspected that Napoleon had offered to win the favor of the Russian emperor at the expense of his Prussian ally. Frederic William was further stimulated by his queen and his subjects; the Germans generally were enraged by the military tyranny of the French, especially by the judicial murder of two booksellers, who were shot pursuant to the sentence of a court-martial for circulating libels against Napoleon.

Anger is an evil counsellor to nations as well as individuals; yielding to the suggestions of indignation rather than prudence, the king of Prussia commenced hostilities before his own arrangements were complete, or his allies ready to give him effective assistance; and he intrusted the command of his army to the duke of Brunswick, who possessed the personal bravery of a soldier, but not the prudence and abilities requisite for a general. Louis, the king's cousin, impetuously advancing to seek the French, encountered a vastly superior force; he was defeated and slain, a calamity that greatly dispirited the Prussian army. This was only the preliminary to the fatal battle of Jena; the Prussians injudiciously posted, and badly commanded, were routed with great slaughter, and what was even worse than defeat, a dispute arose between them and their Saxon allies, which induced the latter to conclude a separate peace with Napoleon. The success of the French was uninterrupted, Berlin opened its gates to the conquerors, and the division of the Prussian army, which had been long preserved unbroken by the heroic exertions of Marshal Blucher, was forced to capitulate. The fugitive king still preserved his courage, relying on the approaching aid of his Russian ally. Napoleon's forces advanced into Poland, where they were joined by many of the inhabitants, who were taught to hope that the French emperor would restore the independence of their native country; but he was incapable of such generous policy, and in after-life, he lamented too late that he sacrificed the hopes of a brave and grateful people to the temporary gain of selfish ambition. The Russians successfully engaged the French at Pultusk, but they were unable to retain their advantages, and were forced gradually to retreat.

Encouraged by his rapid success, Napoleon resolved to crush, if possible, the commercial prosperity of Great Britain; he issued a series of edicts from Berlin, declaring the British islands in a state of blockade, and excluding British manufactures from all the continental ports. Every country that refused obedience to these decrees was threatened with immediate vengeance, and Portugal, so long the faithful ally of England, was marked out as the first victim (A. D. 1807). Great indignation was excited throughout Britain by the French emperor's adoption of this unparalleled system; but it proved eventually more injurious to himself than to his enemies: British manufactures and colonial produce were smuggled to the continent in various ways, and Napoleon was finally compelled to connive at the illicit traffic. But the menaces of the French had roused the spirit of the English people, and complaints were made of the want of vigor and success with which the war was supported. A second expedition against Buenos Ayres, under General Whitelock, disgracefully failed, though it must be confessed that the hatred of the Spanish provincials to the English, as strangers and heretics, would probably have prevented any permanent success in South America. An armament sent against Constantinople, to gratify our Russian ally by enforcing his demands on Turkey, was equally unsuccessful; and an attempt to occupy Egypt, badly contrived, and worse executed, terminated in loss and disgrace. But the ministers might have overcome the unpopularity occasioned by these failures, had they not displeased the king by introducing a bill for opening the highest dignities of the army and navy to Roman catholics. His majesty entertained religious objections to the measures; he demanded that the cabinet should not only abandon it for the present, but give a promise that it should not be proposed at any future period. The ministers refused to give a pledge which they regarded as unconstitutional, and resigned their offices. A new administration was formed under the auspices of the duke of Portland and Mr. Perceval; an appeal was made to the country by a dissolution of parliament, and the tide of popular prejudice ran so strong against the preceding cabinet, that many, if not most of its supporters, were rejected by the electors.

Russia vigorously maintained the war against Turkey, and gained some important advantages. The Turks, enraged by their losses, directed their vengeance against Sultan Selim, whose attempts to introduce European reforms had offended their inveterate prejudices. The Janissaries deposed their unfortunate sovereign, and raised his cousin Mustapha to the throne; but this revolution did not change the fortune of the war, for the Russians soon after gained a signal naval victory off the island of Tenedos.

But the Turkish war did not divert the attention of Alexander from the more important object of checking French ambition. Military operations were renewed during the winter, and a sanguinary battle at Eylau, in which each army lost more than twenty thousand men, led to no decisive result. In some minor engagements the allies had the advantage, but their gains were more than outbalanced by the loss of Dantzic, which, after an obstinate resistance, surrendered to the French. Napoleon, on the fall of Dantzic, hastened to terminate the war by the decisive battle of Friedland; the Russians fought with great bravery, but their generals were inferior in ability and experience to those of the enemy, and they were completely defeated. Köningsberg was surrendered immediately after this battle, and the existence of the Prussian monarchy now depended on the discretion or moderation of the conquerors. An armistice having been concluded, Napoleon sought a personal interview with the Russian emperor, and arrangements were soon made for a conference of the two potentates on a raft in the river Niemen. In this and some subsequent interviews, Bonaparte won over the emperor Alexander to his interests, by stimulating that monarch's ambition for eastern conquest, and promises of support. Peace was restored by the treaty of Tilsit, all sacrifices were made at the expense of the Prussian monarch, by whose distress even his Russian ally did not refuse to profit; and when Frederic ventured to remonstrate, he was contemptuously informed that he owed the preservation of the miserable remnant of his kingdom to Napoleon's personal friendship for Alexander.

The eccentric king of Sweden refused to be included in this pacification, but he was unable to prevent the French from occupying Stralsund and the island of Rugen. Terms were arranged for a peace between Russia and Turkey, but so many points remained open for dispute, that it was manifest war would be renewed at no distant period The king of Prussia was forced, not only to accede to the Berlin decrees, and exclude British manufactures and colonial produce from his dominions, but had also to receive French garrisons into his principal fortresses, and these troops treated the unfortunate Germans with such arrogance and cruelty, that they were almost reduced to despair. Napoleon's power had now nearly touched the summit of its greatness, and had he been contented with what he had already acquired, it might have been permanent; but his restless ambition hurried him soon into an unprincipled contest, which terminated in his overthrow.

Section III.—*The French Invasion of Spain.*

After the treaty of Tilsit, it was generally believed that Napoleon would endeavor to enforce the Berlin decrees by excluding the British from the navigation of the Sound, and that he would probably avail himself of the Danish navy to execute his old project of an invasion. To prevent such an enterprise, a powerful armament was sent against Denmark, which had hitherto remained neutral in the contest. An imperious demand for the instant surrender of the Danish fleet and naval stores, to be retained as a deposite by the English until the conclusion of the war, being peremptorily rejected, the Danes were briskly attacked by land and sea. After Copenhagen had been furiously bombarded for four days, the Danish court was constrained to submit to the demands of the British, and the fleet was removed, while the indignant people could scarcely be prevented from avenging the national insult even by the presence of a superior force.

The attack on Denmark furnished the Russian emperor with a pretext for fulfilling the promises he made to Napoleon at Tilsit, and breaking off his connexion with Great Britain. He complained in strong language of the disregard which England had ever shown for the rights of neutral powers, and the unscrupulous use that had been made of her naval supremacy, and many of the maritime states seconded his remonstrances. A second fleet was saved from the grasp of the French by a less unjustifiable proceeding than the attack on Denmark. Napoleon issued one of his imperious edicts, that "the house of Braganza had ceased to reign," and to enforce it, sent an army to occupy Portugal. The prince-regent of that country, at the instigation of the British, sailed with the Portuguese fleet for Rio Janeiro, where he resolved to hold his court until peace was restored. As a retaliation for the Berlin decrees, the British government issued orders in council, restraining the trade of neutrals with France, and all countries subservient to its power. Against these regulations the government of the United States of America protested loudly, and their remonstrances assumed a very angry character, which threatened speedy hostilities. An attack made on an American frigate, whose captain refused to submit to having his ship searched by an English vessel of inferior force, was resented as a national insult; a proclamation was issued, excluding all armed British ships from the harbors and waters of the United States; and an embargo was laid on British commerce.

While the policy of the orders in council, and the proffered mediation of Austria to effect the restoration of tranquillity, were warmly discussed in the British parliament, events were occurring in Spain which gave the war an entirely new character and direction.

The annals of the world could scarcely supply a parallel to the picture of degradation which the Spanish court presented at this period. Charles, the imbecile king, was the dupe of a faithless wife and an unprincipled minister; this unworthy favorite had been raised, by the queen's partiality, from an humble station to the highest rank; Godoy, Prince of the Peace, as he was called, had neither abilities for the high office with which he was invested, nor strength of mind to support his elevation; he excluded Ferdinand, the heir apparent, from all share in the government, and thus provoked the resentment of a prince who was as ambitious of power as he was unfit to possess it. But Ferdinand's evil dispositions were as yet unknown to the Spaniards, and when Godoy attempted to ruin him by an accusation of treason, the people showed such discontent that Charles was forced to consent to his son's liberation. Napoleon won Godoy's support by proposing a partition of the peninsula, part of which should be assigned to the royal minion, as an independent sovereignty, and he thus obtained the means of pouring a large body of troops into Spain, and occupying the principal fortresses. Charles, intimidated by these proceedings, meditated flight to Spanish America, but finally resolved to resign his crown to Ferdinand (A. D. 1808). By the intrigues of the French, Charles was induced to disavow his abdication, while Ferdinand was led to expect a recognition of his royal title from the emperor Napoleon. Deluded by such representations, he proceeded to Bayonne, where he was contemptuously informed that "the Bourbons had ceased to reign;" and on his refusal to resign his claims for the petty kingdom of Etruria, he was guarded as a prisoner. A fierce riot in Madrid, occasioned by preparations for the removal of the Spanish princes to France, was cruelly punished by Murat, who massacred multitudes of the unarmed populace. Soon after, Charles, accompanied by his queen, proceeded to Bayonne, and formally abdicated his crown in favor of Napoleon. Ferdinand, daunted by intelligence of the massacre at Madrid, pursued the same course; and the French emperor summoned his brother Joseph from the throne of Naples, to occupy that of Spain. The Neapolitan kingdom was given to Murat, whose eminent services to the French emperor were not overpaid, even by the splendid donation of a crown. Many of the Spanish nobles tamely acquiesced in this arrangement, but the great bulk of the nation rejected the intruding sovereign, and preparations to maintain Spanish independence were made in the principal provinces. Andalusia took the lead: Ferdinand VII. was proclaimed in Seville, war declared against Napoleon, and a junta, or council, chosen to direct the affairs of the government. A French squadron, which had been stationed in the bay of Cadiz, was forced to surrender to a Spanish flotilla; but this would not have happened if the port had not been at the same time blockaded by the British fleet.

In every province not occupied by French troops, the adult population offered military service to the different juntas; the English sent large supplies of arms and ammunition, and released all their Spanish prisoners-of-war, a seasonable reinforcement to the patriotic armies. In their first contests with the invaders, the Spaniards obtained considerable success; Marshal Moncey was repulsed from Valencia with great loss, and Marshal Dupont, with eight thousand men, was forced to surrender to the patriot general, Castanos (July 20). On the very day that this unfavorable event occurred, the intrusive monarch made his triumphal entry into Madrid. Joseph Bonaparte, however, had neither the firmness nor courage of his brother Napoleon; the moment he heard of Dupont's surrender, he plundered the treasury and royal palaces of their most valuable contents, and fled to Burgos.

A bold example of Spanish heroism directed the attention of all Europe to the struggle in the peninsula. The citizens of Saragossa, distrusting the fidelity of the captain-general of Aragon, deposed him, and chose for their leader Don Joseph Palafox, a nobleman of dauntless courage, though destitute of military experience. Their city was almost destitute of defences, they had only a mere handful of regular soldiers in the garrison, and they had a very limited supply of arms and ammunition. Notwithstanding these disadvantages, they sternly refused to admit the French, and prepared for a desperate resistance. All classes were animated with the same spirit; the monks manufactured gunpowder and prepared cartridges, the women shared the toil of raising fortifications—even the children lent their feeble aid in such labor as was not beyond their strength. It is not wonderful that the French soldiers were daunted by such an heroic population. After a long and sanguinary contest they abandoned the siege, leaving Saragossa in ruins, but immortalized by the patriotic courage that had enabled its undisciplined citizens to triumph over a regular army.

The spirit of resistance soon extended to Portugal: the people of Oporto rose in a body, seized and imprisoned all the French they could find, and formed a junta under the superintendence of the bishop. A British force commanded by Sir Arthur Wellesley, stimulated and protected these patriotic exertions. A French division, posted at Roleia to terrify the insurgents, was driven from its position by the allied forces, and the north of Portugal delivered from the invaders. Marshal Junot collected all the forces at his disposal to drive back the English; he found Sir Arthur Wellesley at Vimiera, and immediately attacked his lines (August 21). After a brief but vigorous struggle, the French were defeated and driven in confusion toward Lisbon. Scarcely had the victory been won, when Sir Arthur Wellesley was superseded by Sir Hugh Dalrymple, who concluded a convention with Junot for the evacuation of Portugal, on terms that were generally regarded as too favorable to the French after their recent defeat.

While Napoleon was pursuing his ambitious designs against Spain, Alexander of Russia was engaged in a war with Sweden, undertaken in an equally unjust and aggressive spirit. The English sent an army under Sir John Moore to assist their ally, but that general refusing to submit to the dictates of the eccentric, or perhaps the insane Gustavus, soon returned home. Though the Swedes fought with great courage, they were unable to resist the overwhelming force of the Russians, especially as the limited resources of Sweden were wasted by Gustavus in senseless and impracticable enterprises. At length the Swedes grew weary of a sovereign whose conduct threatened the ruin of their country. He was arrested by some of his officers, deposed, and the crown transferred to the duke of Sudermania, who took the title of Charles XIII. (A. D. 1809). The new monarch was forced to purchase peace from

Russia by the cession of Finland, and the exclusion of British vessels from the ports of Sweden.

The Spaniards soon found that a central government was necessary to the success of their operations; the different juntas, therefore, chose deputies who formed a supreme junta for the general conduct of the war. The marquis de la Romana, who had commanded a large body of Spaniards employed by the French in Holstein, was enabled to return home with his troops, by British aid, and take a share in the defence of his country. But the want of concert among the Spanish leaders, and of discipline among the soldiers, rendered them unable to cope with the French; they were severely defeated at Durango, Reynosa, and Tudela, and Napoleon soon appeared in Spain at the head of one hundred and fifty thousand men (A. D. 1808).

A very exaggerated notion of the capabilities of the Spaniards appears to have been formed by the English ministers. They ordered Sir John Moore to advance with the British forces in Portugal to the aid of the patriot armies, but do not seem to have sufficiently investigated the obstacles by which his march was impeded. When Sir John Moore entered Spain, he found that the French were everywhere victorious, and that it was hopeless to expect such active co-operation from the Spaniards as would enable him to turn the scale. After some hesitation, finding himself in danger of being surrounded, he retired rather precipitately into Gallicia. The English soldiers, in their retreat, displayed great courage whenever they were attacked by the French; but in other respects, their conduct was so disorderly that it was stigmatized by the general himself as disgraceful. At length a halt was made at Corunna, where the troops remained until the transports prepared for their embarkation could arrive from Vigo. In this position they were attacked by the French; but the English soldiers, though dispirited by their late retreat, and worn down by fatigue, compelled the enemy to retire. Sir John Moore was mortally wounded in this battle, and was buried on the field. The embarkation of the army was very feebly resisted, and though the British gained no honor by the campaign, its conclusion impressed the enemy with greater respect for English patience and valor than they had previously been accustomed to entertain.

At the beginning of the year 1809, the possession of Spain seemed assured to Napoleon, but neither the Spaniards nor the British despaired of final success. The English parliament readily voted the necessary supplies for the defence of Spain and Portugal, and reinforcements were sent to the peninsula. About the same time, his royal highness the duke of York was accused of having connived at some abuses in the command of the army; he was acquitted by a great majority of the house of commons, but he deemed it prudent to resign his situation, and Sir David Dundas was appointed commander-in-chief.

Austria once more resolved to try the hazards of war. The emperor Francis was induced to take this precipitate step by the harsh remonstrances and menaces of Napoleon. Taking advantage of the absence of the large body of French troops employed in Spain, the archduke Charles entered Bavaria and took possession of Munich. But the rapid measures of Bonaparte baffled the Austrian calculations; he speedily collected a large army and defeated the archduke at Eckmuhl, so severely, that he was compelled to cross the Danube. Vienna was thus opened to the conqueror, and Napoleon took possession of that capital. The archduke was still undismayed; he attacked the French in their positions at Asperne and Essling. The battle was very sanguinary and obstinate; it terminated to the advantage of the Austrians, but they had suffered such severe loss that they were unable to profit by their victory. The failure of the archduke John, in Italy, more than counterbalanced the success of the Austrians at Asperne, and was the chief cause of their final overthrow at Wagram (July 5). It would be impossible to describe within reasonable limits the various conflicts that terminated in this result; suffice it to say, that the Austrians were driven from all their positions, forced to retreat in confusion, and only saved from total ruin by an armistice.

The Tyrolese and Voralbergers had been transferred to the king of Bavaria by the treaty of Presburg, but their national privileges and immunities had been guarantied by the articles of pacification. But Maximilian Joseph was as regardless of a compact as his master Napoleon; he violated the Tyrolese constitution without scruple, crushed the peasants with severe taxes, and punished remonstrances as seditious. The Tyrolese seized the opportunity of the Austrian war to raise the standard of revolt; success attended their early operations, and the Bavarians were expelled from the principal towns. A French army entered the country and laid it waste with fire and sword; but the Tyrolese, animated by an heroic peasant named Hoffer, expelled the invaders once more, and secured a brief interval of tranquillity. When the total defeat of the Austrians at Wagram compelled the emperor Francis to accept peace on any terms, the Tyrolese were assailed by overwhelming forces; they made a desperate resistance, but the French and Bavarian columns penetrated their fastnesses, desolated the land with fire and sword, and punished the leading patriots as rebels. Hoffer was taken prisoner and put to death by the sentence of a court-martial; Mayer, another gallant chieftain, shared the same fate, and the green hills of Tyrol were again subjected to Bavarian tyranny.

Several efforts were made in Germany to shake off the French yoke. Schill, who commanded a regiment in the Prussian service, collected a considerable force and harassed the French detachments in Saxony and Westphalia, but he was defeated and slain by some Dutch and Danish troops, near Stralsund. The duke of Brunswick made a bold effort to recover his hereditary dominions, but after the overthrow of the Austrians he despaired of success, and sought refuge in England. The archduke Ferdinand invaded Saxony, while Napoleon's brother Jerome trembled for the security of his Westphalian throne, in consequence of the progress of General Kienmayer. But the success of Napoleon in Austria frustrated the exertions of the patriots in the north of Germany, especially as no effort was made to send them support from England.

The attention of the British ministry was occupied by an expedition of a very different nature, for which the most ample preparations were made. A fleet of thirty-seven sail-of-the-line, twenty-nine ships of inferior rate, besides small craft, and an army of forty thousand men, were sent to the island of Welcheren, on the coast of Holland. After many delays, the fort of Flushing was besieged and taken; but Antwerp which was the great object of attack, had, in the meantime, been secured, and the commanders despaired of success. Soon afterward the pestilential climate of Walcheren spread disease through the British army and navy; the greater part of the forces returned to England; the progress of the disease soon rendered the removal of the remainder necessary, and the only result of this costly armament was the destruction of the fortifications of Flushing. Their naval successes in some degree consoled the English for this disappointment. Lord Cochrane destroyed four vessels, forming part of a French squadron, in Basque-roads, and irreparably injured several others; Lord Collingwood was similarly successful in the Mediterranean, and the French were deprived of their remaining colonies in the West Indies.

Some European islands, especially those called the Ionian, were added to the British dominions, a proceeding which gave some offence to the new sultan of Turkey, Mahmoud II., who had been elevated to the throne on the deposition of his cousin Selim and his half-brother Mustapha. But the progress of the Russian arms induced Mahmoud to court an alliance with Great Britain, and jealousy of the same power inclined the Persian shah to renew his former friendly connexions with England.

Though the Russian emperor did not join Napoleon in the war against Austria, he received a share of the provinces which Francis was forced to resign, in order to purchase peace. But though the Austrian emperor was compelled to make many great and painful sacrifices, he obtained more favorable conditions than had been anticipated; and Napoleon received general praise for the moderation with which he used his victory. The secret cause of this affected generosity was subsequently revealed, and proved that it resulted from a plan for more effectually securing his despotism over Europe.

After the retreat of the British from Corunna, the French seemed to have permanently secured possession of Spain. Though the marquis de la Romana and the duke del Infantado held out against the invaders yet Saragossa was taken, in spite of the heroic resistance of its inhabitants; and Soult having invaded Portugal, made himself master of Oporto. Victor also advanced toward the same country, and, on his march, overthrew the Spanish army of Estremadura. But Oporto was soon recovered by a British force under Sir Arthur Wellesley; and the removal of a large body of the French to take part in the Austrian war revived the courage of the Spaniards. Sir Arthur Wellesley, believing it possible to strike an important blow before the French grand army could be reinforced, boldly, and perhaps rashly, advanced into Spain. He was attacked at Talavera (July 28), by the united forces of Jourdan, Victor, and Sebastiani, who were rather the masters than the servants of the nominal king, Joseph Bonaparte. British valor has rarely been more nobly displayed than in this engagement; the French were beaten back at every point, and had the Spaniards displayed the same courage and zeal as their allies, the retreat might have been changed into a total rout. The misconduct of the Spaniards, indeed, deprived the English of the chief fruits of their victory; they were soon compelled to act only on the defensive, and to retreat slowly toward the frontiers of Portugal. Nor were the patriots more successful in other quarters; they did not, however, despair, and the supreme junta published a spirited proclamation, animating the national courage, and convoking an assembly of the cortes or estates of the realm, to form a fixed constitutional government.

The celebration of the fiftieth anniversary of the king's accession diffused joy through England. About the same time the death of the duke of Portland, and some dissensions in the cabinet, led to a partial change in the ministry. Mr. Perceval was appointed premier, and several angry debates ensued in both houses of parliament. The opponents of the ministry failed in procuring a condemnation of the Walcheren expedition; but, during the discussion, party spirit raged with great violence, and Sir Francis Burdett, having assailed the privileges of the house of commons in very unmeasured terms, was ordered to be committed to the Tower. He declared his intention to resist the warrant, but was arrested and committed to the Tower by a military force. The soldiers, on their return, were assaulted by the mob, and a riot ensued, in which several lives were lost. At the close of the session, the popular baronet was liberated, as a matter of course; he brought actions for what he regarded as an illegal arrest, against the speaker and the serjeant-at-arms, but the court of King's Bench disallowed his claims, and supported the privileges of the house of commons.

These ebullitions of party violence did not weaken the British cabinet, though they induced the enemies of England to believe the country on the verge of a convulsion. France was apparently tranquil, and Napoleon revealed the secret of his moderation at Vienna, by procuring a divorce from the emperess Josephine, the faithful companion of his former fortunes, and offering his hand to the archdutchess Maria Louisa, daughter of the emperor Francis (A. D. 1810). This marriage, which seemed permanently to establish Bonaparte's power, became eventually the principal cause of his ruin, for it alarmed all the northern powers, and especially the Russians, who justly feared that Napoleon, secured by the Austrian alliance, would strive to make himself absolute master of Europe. His arbitrary conduct to Holland justified these suspicions; he removed his brother from the throne of that country, and annexed it as a province to France.

The disputes respecting the trade of neutrals, between England and America, began to assume a very hostile aspect, and it was feared that war could not long be delayed. But public attention was diverted from this subject to the struggle in Portugal, where Sir Arthur Wellesley, who had recently been created Lord Wellington, nobly sustained the honor of the English arms. The French army, strongly reinforced, was placed under the command of Massena, prince of Essling; the fortresses of Astorga, Ciudad Rodrigo, and Almeida, were captured; Lord Wellington retired slowly before a superior force, and Massena flattered himself that he would soon obtain possession of Lisbon. His presumption was first checked at Busaco, where the British made a stand and inflicted a severe check on their assailants; but the hopes of the French were completely destroyed when they saw Lord Wellington take up his position in the formidable lines of Torres Vedras. Not daring to advance, and ashamed to retreat, Massena remained for more than a month watching his cautious adversary, and losing thousands of his men by disease or desertion. He at length retreated to Santarem, but though he received a large reinforcement, he did not venture to resume offensive operations.

A desultory war was maintained in Spain; the patriot armies were usually defeated in regular engagements, but the invaders were severely harassed by the incessant attacks of the guerilla parties; convoys were intercepted, stragglers cut off, and outposts exposed to constant danger. Cadiz, the residence of the supreme junta and the seat of government, was besieged, but the strength of its works and the ease with which relief was obtained by sea, prevented the French from making any progress in its reduction. The cortes assembled in this city and framed a form of constitutional government, which, however, had many violent opponents among the higher orders of the nobility and clergy.

Most of the French and Dutch colonies in the Indian seas were subdued, under the direction of Lord Minto, the governer-general of India, a nobleman whose judicious administration of affairs in the east, not only extended the British dominions in the east, but suppressed a dangerous mutiny in the presidency of Madras, occasioned by the adoption of economical regulations, which curtailed the allowances made to officers in the company's service.

In the north of Europe, little of moment, in war, occurred; the Danes and Russians had some trivial naval engagements with English vessels; but Sweden was the theatre of a most extraordinary revolution, which, for a time, added her to the enemies of England. The crown prince died suddenly, not without some suspicion of poison, and the Swedish senate tendered the succession to Charles John Bernadotte, one of Napoleon's most celebrated marshals, who had won their favor by the leniency and prudence he displayed some years before in the north of Germany. Bernadotte accepted the offer, to the secret annoyance of Napoleon, who had long been jealous of his military fame and independent spirit.

Civilized Europe might now be said to be arrayed against Great Britain, but the spirit of its inhabitants did not sink. Its sovereign, afflicted by grief for the loss of his favorite daughter, was seized by the disease under which he had formerly suffered, and fell into a state of mental derangement, from which he never afterward recovered (A. D. 1811). The prince of Wales was appointed regent, under restrictions similar to those proposed by Mr. Pitt in 1789, but these were subsequently removed when it was found that he intended steadily to pursue his father's system of policy.

It was not long before Lord Wellington reaped the fruits of his prudent arrangements for the defence of Portugal. Massena was forced to retreat from Santarem, but before he evacuated the country, he ravaged it in the most frightful manner, destroying many noble monuments of architecture in mere wantonness. The British parliament voted the sum of one hundred thousand pounds for the relief of the Portuguese, and a liberal subscription for the same purpose was formed by private liberality. Almeida was the only town in Portugal retained by the French; it was blockaded by the allies, and Massena's efforts to relieve it led to the battle of Fuentes d'Onor. The engagement was severe, but British valor triumphed; the garrison of Almeida, disheartened by the defeat of their countrymen, evacuated the place, and Portugal was delivered from the presence of an enemy.

The liberation of Spain was a more difficult task, and it was rendered still more so by the surrender of Badajoz to Marshal Soult, after a very brief and ineffective defence. Lord Wellington sent Sir William Beresford to recover this important place, but the advance of the French from Seville, compelled that general to raise the siege. The united forces of the British and Spanish encountered the French at Albuera, and gained an important victory; Badajoz was once more invested, but the approach of Soult on one side and Marmont on the other, induced Lord Wellington to retire beyond the Tagus. But in his anxiety to save Badajoz, Soult had so much weakened the force which blockaded Cadiz, that the Spaniards resolved to hazard an expedition against the invading armies in Andalusia. General La Pena, aided by the British lieutenant-general, Graham, undertook to direct these operations, and great hopes were entertained of success. But though Graham obtained a brilliant victory at Barossa, over Marshal Victor, no efforts were made to follow up his success. In the other Spanish provinces, the patriotic armies were still more unfortunate; Mina, indeed, from his mountains, threatened and harassed the invaders, but the other Spanish leaders showed themselves equally deficient in courage and conduct. Neither did all the expected advantages result from the assembling of the cortes; they prepared, indeed, a constitutional code, which, however, was scarcely suited to the Spanish people; but they maintained the onerous restrictions on the colonial trade, and thus gave deep offence to the South American provinces, and drove them to organize plans for self-government.

In other quarters the war was more favorable to British interests; the island of Java was wrested from the Dutch; several flotillas were destroyed by English frigates in the Italian seas, and an attempt made by the Danes to recover the island of Anholt, in the Baltic, was defeated by the gallant garrison. Sweden could scarcely be said to be at war with Great Britain; Bernadotte soon discovered that subserviency to France was inconsistent with the interests of his adopted country, and he secretly entered into negotiations with the Russian emperor for restoring their mutual independence. But Alexander was still too deeply engaged in pursuing the favorite policy of the czars, and establishing the supremacy of Russia on both sides of the Black sea, at the expense of Turkey and Persia. His success was far from answering his expectations; the wild tribes of the Caucacus severely harassed the invaders of Asiatic Turkey; and though Kutusoff was more successful on the European side, his acquisitions were obtained by a very disproportionate expenditure of blood and treasure. The disorganized state of the Turkish provinces prevented the sultan from effectively defending his dominions; in most of them a military aristocracy had usurped the chief power of the state, and in Egypt especially, the Mameluke beys acted as independent princes. Mohammed Ali, pacha of Egypt, finding that the beys would not submit to his power, and fearing the hazards of civil war, invited them to a banquet, where they were all ruthlessly massacred. The sultan applauded this perfidy, but ere long he found Mohammed Ali a more dangerous subject than the turbulent lords whom he had removed.

The mental disease of George III. showed no symptoms of improvement, and as the time approached when the restrictions imposed on the authority of the prince regent would expire, some anxiety was felt about the probable fate of the ministry. But the prince regent had become reconciled to the cabinet, and after a faint effort to gain the support of Lords Grey and Grenville, it was resolved that no change should be made in the government (A. D. 1812). At a later period in the year, negotiations were resumed, in consequence of the murder of Mr. Perceval; the premier was shot in the lobby of the house of commons, by Bellingham, a merchant, who believed that the ministers had shown indifference to his fancied claims on the Russian government. After some delay, the old cabinet was reconstructed, under the auspices of the earl of Liverpool, and the plans for forming a united administration were abandoned.

Lord William Bentinck, the British minister in Sicily, strenuously exerted himself to remedy the evils which the imbecility of the king and the tyranny of the queen had introduced into the government of that island. He succeeded in procuring the establishment of a constitution similar to that of Britain; and the island began to enjoy peace and prosperity in a greater degree than had been experienced for several centuries.

A change in the Spanish constitution revived the courage of the nation; a new regency, the promulgation of the constitutional code, and various reforms in the different branches of the administration, gave fresh spirit to the Spaniards, and inspired hopes of final success. Lord Wellington opened the campaign with the siege of Ciudad Rodrigo; the capture of this important fortress was followed by that of Badajoz, but the victors suffered severe loss of both places. Wellington, who had been created an earl for these exploits, next marched against Marmont, and took the important city of Salamanca. Marmont, strengthened by large reinforcements, hoped not only to defeat the British, but to intercept their retreat. As he extended his lines for this purpose, Wellington seized the favorable opportunity, and, pouring his whole force on the weakened divisions, gained the most complete victory that the allies had yet won in the peninsula. Indeed if the Spaniards had displayed the same energy as the British and the Portuguese, Marmont's entire army would have been ruined. Still the immediate results of the battle of Salamanca were very great; Madrid was evacuated by the intrusive king Joseph; the blockade of Cadiz was raised; and the city of Seville was taken by Colonel Skerret and the Spanish general La Cruz.

The failure of the British at the siege of Burgos, the want of concert in the Spanish councils, and the great reinforcements received by the French, compelled Wellington to resign the fruits of his victory; he retired leisurely to the frontiers of Portugal, and firmly waited an opportunity for renewing his efforts. But events in other parts of the globe were producing the most important results in favor of Spanish independence, the South American colonies, alarmed by an earthquake which was superstitiously believed to be a visitation of Providence, returned to their allegiance, and the Russian emperor prepared to measure his strength with the colossal power of Napoleon.

SECTION IV.—*The Russian War.*

No long time after the conclusion of the peace of Tilsit, Alexander began to doubt the prudence of the compact he had made with the French emperor, and the subsequent marriage of Napoleon to an Austrian princess gave him fresh grounds of alarm. The Austrian emperor, however, was not very sincerely attached to his son-in-law, Napoleon had given his infant son the title of king of Rome, a very plain intimation of his design to retain his hold on Italy. The interests of his subjects, many of whom were almost ruined by the suspension of the trade with Great Britain, compelled Alexander to seek for some relaxation of the restrictive system established by the Berlin decrees; but Napoleon would not abandon his favorite policy, and the discussions between the courts of St. Peterburgh and Paris began to assume an angry and even hostile tone. Both parties, however, professed an anxious desire for peace, and Napoleon even made overtures to the British government, but as he refused to restore Spain to its legitimate sovereign, or to withdraw his troops from Prussia, negotiations were fruitless, and both sides prepared for war.

Alexander entered into alliance with Sweden and England: Napoleon arrayed under his banners the military strength of western and southern Europe. But the selfishness of the French emperor in the very outset deprived him of the best security for success; to secure the aid of Austria, he refused to restore the independence of Poland, and thus lost the hearts of a brave and enthusiastic race of warriors, who would have powerfully aided his advance, or effectually covered his retreat. Trusting to the vast number of his victorious legions, Napoleon crossed the Niemen, routed a division of Cossacks at Kowno, and directed his march to the capital of Lithuania. The Russians retired before the French deliberately, wasting the country as they retreated Several sharp battles were fought without any important result; but the hopes of the Russians were raised by the conclusion of a treaty with the Turks, which enabled them to direct all their energies to repel the invaders. Napoleon with his main body directed his march toward Moscow, while a large division of his forces menaced the road to St. Petersburgh. The Russians repelled the latter, but the main force of the invaders advanced to Smolensko, which was justly regarded as the bulwark of Moscow. A dreadful battle was fought under the walls of Smolensko; it terminated in favor of the French, but they purchased their victory very dearly, and the Russians made an orderly retreat.

Kutusoff now assumed the command of the Russians, and resolved to hazard another battle for the protection of Moscow; he fixed upon a position near the village of Borodino, and there firmly awaited the enemy. The battle was furious and sanguinary, nearly seventy thousand of the combatants fell without giving to either side a decisive victory. The Russians indeed maintained their ground; but the French having been joined by new reinforcements, Kutusoff was forced to retreat and abandon Moscow to its fate. This ancient capital of the czars is revered by the Russians, as Jerusalem was by the Jews; they give it the fond name of Mother Moscow, and regard it as the sanctuary of their nation. But when the invaders approached, the citizens resolved not only to abandon their beloved metropolis, but to consign it to the flames. Napoleon entered Moscow, and took up his residence in the Kremlin, the ancient palace of the czars ; but while he was holding a council, fires broke out in various parts of the city, and though many of the incendiaries were shot, it was found impossible to check the conflagration.

When the greater part of the city was destroyed, its stores consumed, and all supplies cut off, Napoleon found himself in a very embarrassing position. With great reluctance he gave orders for a retreat, and the French obeyed with so much precipitation, that they were unable to complete the demolition of Moscow. Before the fugitives had proceeded far on their route, they began to experience the horrors of a Russian winter ; thousands became the victims of cold and hunger, while their pursuers, taking courage from their calamities, harassed them severely at every step. It had been Napoleon's intention to make a stand at Smolensko, but the magnitude of his losses, the disorganized state of his army, and the increasing want of provisions, rendered such a course impossible. Once more the French had to undertake a perilous march, amid the rigors of the severest winter ever known, pursued by enraged enemies, deprived of food, of clothing, and of shelter. Language fails to describe the horrors of such a retreat · every hour added to the miseries of the sufferers ; they lost the discipline of soldiers, and almost the semblance of men. The passage of the Borodino was one of the most terrific scenes recorded in history ; in their eagerness to place the river between themselves and their pursuers, the French rushed in a disorderly crowd over the bridges, under a heavy fire of artillery from the heights behind them. Eight thousand were killed or drowned in this calamitous passage, and long before all had crossed over, Napoleon ordered the bridges to be set on fire, abandoning twelve thousand of his followers to the mercy of the irritated Russians. Napoleon at length resolved to provide for his personal security, and fled to Paris, where indeed some revolutionary attempts rendered his presence necessary ; the miserable remnant of his once mighty host found a precarious shelter in Poland.

In the meantime Great Britain was engaged in active hostilities with the United States. The Americans twice invaded Canada, but were defeated ; they were more successful at sea, where the superiority of their frigates in size and weight of metal to the British vessels of the same denomination, secured their victory in some engagements between single ships. But this war attracted comparatively but little attention ; every mind was too deeply occupied with the great struggle on the continent of Europe.

The domestic affairs of England, though of importance, did not divert attention from the contest with Napoleon. An unfortunate publicity was given to the discords between the prince regent and his consort ; a bill for emancipating the catholics was rejected, after having passed several stages, in the house of commons, and the charter of the East India company was renewed for twenty years. Notwithstanding his recent reverses, Napoleon found that he still possessed the confidence of the French nation, a large conscription was ordered to supply the losses of the late campaign; and the emperor having provided for the internal security of his dominions, hasted to the north of Europe, where he had to encounter the hostility of a new enemy.

It was with great reluctance that the king of Prussia sent an army to serve under Napoleon, and the officers and soldiers of the contingent were far from being anxious for the success of the cause in which they were engaged. During the retreat, one Prussian corps separated itself from the division to which it was attached, and concluded a convention of neutrality; as the Russians advanced, the Prussian monarch took courage to assert his independence, and he entered into alliance with Alexander. But notwithstanding his recent losses, Napoleon had assembled an army numerically superior to those of his adversaries; in three sanguinary battles the French gained the advantage, but they were unable to obtain a decided victory; and Napoleon, alarmed by the magnitude of his losses, and the obstinacy of his enemies, consented to an armistice. During the truce the British government encouraged the allies by large subsidies, and the aid of Sweden was purchased not only by money, but by a promise to aid that power in the acquisition of Norway. But what was of far greater importance, the emperor of Austria was induced to abandon the cause of his son-in-law, and take an active part in the confederation for restraining the power of France.

Napoleon, establishing his headquarters at Dresden, commenced a series of vigorous operations against his several foes. They were at first successful; but the tide of fortune turned; several of his divisions were defeated, the Bavarians joined the allies, and at length the baffled emperor retired to Leipsic. Under the walls of this ancient city the battle was fought which decided the fate of Europe (Oct. 18). While the result of the engagement was yet undecided, the Saxon troops in the French service deserted in a body to the allies, and the position thus abandoned was immediately occupied by the Swedish forces. Napoleon's soldiers, driven from their lines in every direction, were compelled to seek shelter in Leipsic, but, as the city was incapable of defence, a further retreat became necessary. The French emperor gave the requisite orders, but did not wait to see them executed; the evacuation of the city was not completed when the allies forced an entrance; the French, entangled in the streets, suffered very severely, and many were drowned as they crowded over the narrow bridge, which was their only path of safety. The bridge was blown up before the whole of the fugitives could pass, and this obstruction of the retreat swelled the number of the slain and the captives.

The battle of Leipsic liberated Germany; Napoleon fled to France, his followers were severely harassed in their retreat, especially as the Bavarians made a vigorous effort to intercept them at Hanau; their sufferings were very great, and multitudes were made prisoners by the allied armies, as they advanced to the Rhine. Bernadotte was naturally reluctant to join in the meditated invasion of France, but he undertook the task of expelling the enemy from the circle of Lower Saxony. At his approach, the Hanoverians eagerly seized the opportunity of delivering themselves from a foreign yoke, and returning once more under the paternal government of the Guelphs. The flame of independence spread to Holland, and kindled even the cold bosoms of the Dutch. Insurrections broke out in the principal towns, the hereditary claims of the house of Orange were rapturously acknowledged, and when the stadtholder arrived from England, he found the Hollanders eager, not only to acknowledge his former power, but to extend it by conferring on him the title of royalty.

While the allies were thus triumphant in Germany, Wellington was now gloriously occupied in the liberation of Spain. Early in the spring, he concentrated his forces near Ciudad Rodrigo, and by a series of able movements, compelled the French not only to abandon their positions on the Douro, but to retire beyond the Ebro. Marshal Jourdan, who exercised the real authority, for Joseph was king only in name, resolved to make one vigorous effort for the maintenance of the French power, and chose a strong position near Vittoria, as the theatre of a decisive engagement. The allied army advanced with an eagerness that insured success ; the heights that protected the hostile lines were successively stormed, and at length the French were forced to retreat in such disorder, that they abandoned their artillery, baggage, and military chest. In the east of Spain the allies were less successful ; Sir John Murray, on the approach of Marshal Suchet, abandoned the siege of Tarragona with unnecessary precipitation ; but the arrival of Lord William Bentinck prevented the enemy from profiting by this partial success.

When the news of the battle of Vittoria reached Napoleon, he sent Marshal Soult from Germany to take the command of the army in Spain, where Pampeluna and St. Sebastian had been invested by Wellington, now raised to the dignity of marquis. Soult's operations were vigorous, but unsuccessful ; his forces were unable to make any impression on the British lines, and so severe was their repulse, that they fled to their own frontiers. St. Sebastian was soon after taken by storm, but not without a very severe loss to the conquerors, and the British now prepared to invade France.

The allies crossed the Bidassoa, and advanced slowly but steadily toward Bayonne : Soult showed great courage and talent in his arrangements, but his efforts were foiled by the superior valor of the British soldiers, and two regiments of Dutch and Germans quitting his lines, went over to the camp of his allies. Spain was now free, but the efforts of the enlightened portion of the cortes to secure its future happiness, by the establishment of a constitutional government, were frustrated by the interested opposition of the clergy, and the ignorant bigotry of the people.

The war between Great Britain and the United States continued to be maintained with the obstinacy that characterizes the quarrels between " foes who once were friends ;" but it was not productive of any important event. The Americans were unsuccessful in their repeated invasions of Canada, but they established their naval superiority on the lakes, while the honor of the British flag was nobly maintained in the engagement between the frigates Chesapeake and Shannon.

The memorable year 1814 opened with the invasion of France ; the Russian, Prussian, and Austrian armies forced an entrance through the eastern frontiers, while Wellington was making an alarming progress on the western side. Never, in the hours of his greatest success, did Napoleon display more promptitude and ability; but he had beaten his enemies into the art of conquering, and even partial success was injurious, because it inspired hopes which prevented him from embracing the proffered opportunities of negotiation. Several furious but indecisive battles were fought: the allied armies had moved at too great a distance from each other, and it was not until they had suffered severely for their error, that they learned the necessity of a combined plan of operations. But in other quarters the success of the allies was more decided; Bernadotte completed the liberation of the north of Germany, and not only intimidated the Danish court into an abandonment of the French alliance, but enforced its consent to the transfer of Norway; thence he marched to the Netherlands, where the allies had made considerable progress, though General Graham had been baffled, with much loss, in an attempt to surprise Bergen-op-Zoom.

But Napoleon was much more alarmed by the progress of Wellington in the southwest of France. The English general having driven the French from their posts, crossed the Adour, and invested the citadel of Bayonne. As he advanced, the old partisans of the Bourbons began to revive, the exiled family was proclaimed, and the white flag hoisted at Bordeaux. More mortifying was the defection of Murat; eager to secure his crown, the king of Naples entered into a secret treaty with Austria, and lent his aid in the expulsion of the French from Italy.

But in the meantime the fate of France was decided; Napoleon moved his main army eastward, hoping to intimidate the allies into a retreat, by threatening their communications. Blucher and Prince Schwartzenberg immediately decided on marching to Paris, and having defeated the forces of Marmont and Mortier, who guarded the road, soon came in sight of that metropolis. The outworks that defended Paris were stormed, and the intimidated citizens hastened to secure their persons and property by a capitulation. The allied sovereigns, Frederic and Alexander, made a triumphant entry into the city (March 31), and were hailed as liberators by the fickle populace.

When Napoleon heard that the Austrians had effected a junction with the Prussians, he hasted back to defend his capital, but before he reached Fontainebleau the capitulation had been signed, and a provisional government installed, without any regard to his authority. On the 2d of April he was formally deposed; and on the 6th of the same month, Louis XVIII. was invited to ascend the throne of his ancestors. A constitutional charter was framed for the protection of the French people, and Napoleon was promised the sovereignty of the island of Elba, and a pension. Before intelligence of these events was received in the south, a sanguinary battle had been fought between the armies of Soult and Wellington at Toulouse, which ended in the complete discomfiture of the former; but the British general sincerely lamented a triumph which had been purchased by a useless expenditure of human life.

On the 3d of May, Louis XVIII. returned from his tedious exile, and landed at Calais. The preliminaries of a general peace were signed at Paris ; and it was arranged that the details and the adjustment of the claims of the different European princes should be referred to a future convocation at Vienna.

SECTION V.—*History of Europe from the dethronement of Napoleon to the Conclusion of the Treaty of Vienna.*

BEFORE his final overthrow, Napoleon liberated the captive Ferdinand, well aware that Spain would have little reason to rejoice in the restoration of such a sovereign. No sooner had he obtained his freedom than he annulled all the proceedings of the cortes, re-established the old despotism with all its abuses, and even revived the horrors of the inquisition. Several of those who had most strenuously resisted the French invasion were punished by imprisonment or exile, their attachment to constitutional freedom being deemed to outweigh their former services. The allies could not be blamed for the perfidy and tyranny of Ferdinand, but they incurred just censure by aiding in the forcible annexation of Norway to Sweden, against the earnest remonstrances of the inhabitants, and they displayed little policy in uniting Belgium to Holland, for the countries were opposed to each other in their religious creeds and commercial interests.

The American war was protracted more in a spirit of revenge than sound policy ; a sanguinary but indecisive struggle took place in Canada ; an English armament captured Washington, the capital of the United States, and destroyed the public buildings ; but similar attacks on Baltimore and New Orleans were repulsed with great loss. Peace was at length concluded at Ghent, and we may confidently hope that hostilities will never again be renewed between two nations so closely united by the ties of language, religion, and blood. Before this war was terminated, the emperor Alexander, and Frederic, king of Prussia, accompanied by their most distinguished marshals and statesmen, personally visited England, and were received with great enthusiasm. But the convulsion produced in the commercial world by the sudden transition from war to peace, was necessarily followed by numerous bankruptcies and great distress, which threw a shade of gloom over the general joy.

The conduct of Louis XVIII. immediately after his accession to the throne, was calculated to win popularity ; but the establishment of a censorship over the press, his anxiety to restore the power and influence of the clergy, and to remunerate the loyal emigrants who had shared the calamities of his exile, gave general offence, and revived the courage of the friends of Napoleon. A secret conspiracy was formed for restoring the emperor, and he, dreading that the allied powers, whose plenipotentiaries were assembled at Vienna, would remove him from Elba to a place of greater security, resolved to make a bold effort for the recovery of his throne. Accompanied only by eleven hundred men, he landed at Frejus (March 1, 1815), and advanced into the interior of the country. At first he received little encouragement ; but being joined by the garrison of Grenoble, and supported by secret promises of aid from other divisions of the army, he proceeded to Lyons, where he held his court. Louis made a spirited appeal to the loyalty of the

French nation; but Marshal Ney having set the example of defection all the soldiery declared in favor of the emperor; and Louis, compelled to abandon his kingdom, sought safety in Ghent.

Though the allied powers had shown a great want of vigilance and caution in not preventing, as they easily might have done, the escape of Napoleon, they were not for a moment undetermined in resolving on the course of action rendered necessary by that event. A proclamation was issued by the congress of Vienna, denouncing him as the common enemy of Europe, and excluding him from the pale of civil and social relations. A treaty was concluded, by which each of the four powers, Russia, Prussia, Austria, and England, engaged to maintain an army of 150,000 men until they had rendered Napoleon incapable of disturbing the tranquillity of Europe; and the Prussians and the English at once began to assemble their forces on the northern frontiers of France

Napoleon, disappointed in his hope of procuring the acquiescence of the allied powers in his usurpation, prepared boldly to meet the danger by which he was menaced. He gratified the vanity of the Parisians by the splendid ceremonial of proclaiming a new constitution in the Champ de Mars, and at the same time he made the most vigorous exertions to recruit his armies and supply his military stores. In a short time, far shorter than had been anticipated, his troops were ready for action, and instead of waiting for the attack of his enemies, he resolved to become the aggressor. The first brunt of the war fell on the Prussians, who were driven from their advanced posts. Blucher immediately concentrated his forces at Ligny; while the duke of Wellington, with the British and subsidiary troops, occupied a parallel position at Quatre Bras. The main body of the French attacked the Prussian lines, and, after a sanguinary battle, compelled Blucher to abandon Ligny (June 16); but his retreat was effected in good order, and in a very few hours his troops were ready to renew the fight. In the meantime the British had defeated the enemy at Quatre Bras, but the retreat of the Prussians rendered a corresponding movement necessary on their part; and Wellington led his army to the memorable position of Waterloo.

Flushed by his recent victory over the Prussians, Napoleon, on the morning of the 18th of June, appeared in front of the English position, and commenced an attack, in full assurance of success. His first effort was directed against Hougoumont, a post which protected the English right; but after a murderous conflict, the French were baffled, and the place maintained. The emperor's next effort was to turn the left wing so as to intercept the communication with the Prussians, but this still more signally failed; Sir Thomas Picton's division, though with the loss of their brave commander, repulsed the French infantry, while the Scotch Greys, aided by a corps of dragoons, routed the French cavalry, particularly the cuirassiers, who fondly deemed themselves invincible

A third great effort was made against the centre, and at first some advantages were gained. The French seized the farm of La Haye Sainte, which covered the position, and poured masses of cavalry and infantry on the British lines. But Wellington, forming his troops in hollow squares, maintained a steady resistance, and the efforts of the baffled assailants gradually relaxed. At this moment the Prussian troops began to appear on the right flank of the French, and to take a share in the engagement. Napoleon now mustered his guard for one decisive engagement, but did not, as was expected, place himself at their head. The imperial guard advanced under a perfect storm of artillery and musketry from the British lines, which had been gradually advanced after the defeat of the former attacks. They attempted to deploy, under this formidable fire, but their lines were shaken, and they began to fall into confusion. Wellington seized the decisive moment to charge; the effect was instantaneous, not a single French soldier remained to cross a bayonet; and as the British pressed forward, the retreat was soon a perfect rout. As the English were too much fatigued to pursue the fugitives, that duty devolved upon the Prussians, and they executed it with the vigor of men who felt that they had the wrongs of their country to avenge. Out of the entire French army not more than forty thousand men could again be imbodied.

Napoleon continued his melancholy flight to Paris, where he soon found that his reign was at an end. He abdicated the crown in favor of his son, but while his resignation was received, the acknowledgment of Napoleon II. was evaded. He lingered so long in the hope of some favorable change, that his opportunities of escape were cut off, and he was forced to seek refuge on board a British man-of-war. After some discussion respecting his destination, it was resolved that he should be imprisoned for life, in the island of St. Helena; and to this rock, in the Atlantic ocean, he was sent, with a small train of attendants.

Murat's fate was still more calamitous; no sooner had he heard of Napoleon's landing in France, than he renounced his alliance with Austria, and endeavored to unite all the Italians in a league against that power. His efforts completely failed; his forces were routed at Ferrara, the cowardly Neapolitans could not be induced to make any effective resistance, and finally he fled disguised from his kingdom. His restless ambition induced him, with only thirty followers, to make an effort to recover his dominions; he landed on the Calabrian coast, but he was made a prisoner, and shot by sentence of a court-martial.

After the victory at Waterloo, the Prussians and the British advanced toward Paris, without encountering any serious opposition. The two legislative chambers were reluctant to restore the king, at least unconditionally, but their appeal to the nation was disregarded, and on the nearer approach of the allies, a convention was concluded by which Louis was restored. A few of Napoleon's most strenuous supporters were excluded from the act of amnesty; Ney and Labedoyère were shot, but Lavalette escaped by the aid of his wife and some British officers.

The future peace of Europe now depended on the congress of Vienna, but the decrees of this body were guided more by the convenience of sovereigns, than the wishes of nations. The ancient republics of Venice and Genoa were abolished; the territories of the former were given to Austria, while the latter were assigned to the king of Sardinia; Poland was annexed to the territories of Russia, and the Prussian dominions enlarged at the expense of Saxony. When these arrangements were completed, the sovereigns of Austria, Russia, and Prussia, entered into a solemn compact called the Holy Alliance; the professed object of the treaty was to preserve the peace of Europe, on the principles which God, in his revelation, has pointed out as the source of tranquillity and prosperity. But the contracting parties understood by these principles the maintenance of despotic power, and made their engagement a pretext for resisting the efforts made subsequently, by several nations to establish constitutional freedom.

CHAPTER XI.

HISTORY OF THE PEACE.

SECTION I.—*State of Europe at the Close of the War*

WHEN the sanguinary and expensive wars arising out of the French revolution terminated, the different nations of Europe that shared in the contest were so enfeebled and harassed, that they sank at once into inactive repose. But the transition from war to peace made such a complete change in all commercial transactions, that credit was shaken, trade injured, manufactures checked, and thousands suddenly deprived of employment. These evils were more sensibly felt in England than in any other country; for while the tide of war swept over every other European state, England, protected by her insular situation, enjoyed internal tranquillity, and was enabled to sell with profit, not only her manufactures, but her agricultural produce to less favored countries. Peace permitted the people of the continent to supply themselves with many of the articles which they had previously been forced to import; and the jealousy with which the continental sovereigns began to regard the commercial prosperity of England, induced them to encourage native manufactures; hence the demand for British goods and produce suddenly slackened, and distress was felt by every portion of the community. Several serious riots occurred in the agricultural distress; but still more alarming symptoms of dissatisfaction were displayed in the metropolis, where meetings were held under pretence of procuring a reform in the constitution, but which threatened to end in revolution. Several strong restrictive statutes were passed by parliament, and energetic, if not severe measures adopted by the government; it was not, however, until the commercial crisis had passed over, and the embarrassments of transition disappeared that the public tranquillity was restored.

There were not, however, wanting more cheering occurrences which relieved the gloom; the piratical states of Algiers were humbled; Lord Exmouth, with a united squadron of English and Dutch, attacked the city of Algiers, destroyed its fortifications, and compelled the dey to abolish Christian slavery (A. D. 1816). Great joy was also diffused by the marriage of the princess Charlotte, the pride and the hope of England, to Prince Leopold of Saxe Coburg. But the expectations of the nation were fatally disappointed; the princess died on the 6th of November, 1817, after having been delivered of a dead child. The national sorrow was general and profound, and there never was an occasion in which the British nation showed greater regret for the loss of an individual. But this was only the beginning of a series of deaths in the royal family; Queen Charlotte died during the ensuing year, she was soon followed to the grave by the duke of Kent, and finally, the aged monarch George III., without having enjoyed one lucid interval during his long illness, sank quietly into the tomb.

France, much to the surprise of the neighboring states, enjoyed the blessings of tranquillity under the mild and conciliatory government of Louis XVIII. The revolution, and its consequent wars, had given the chief property of the country, and consequently the elements of political power, to the middle classes of society; their interests could only be secured by the preservation of peace, and they became zealous royalists, because they regarded the monarchy as the surest pledge for the maintenance of public order. Some of them carried their zeal to such extravagant lengths that they provoked resistance, and the king was forced to interfere, to prevent the ill consequences that were likely to result from the indiscretion of those who claimed to be his best friends.

The united kingdom of the Netherlands, though apparently tranquil, was secretly shaken by the national antipathy between the Belgians and the Dutch. Gratitude induced the sovereign to accede to the holy alliance, a circumstance which gave great offence to many of his subjects, especially in Flanders, where a republican spirit, fostered by municipal institutions, had prevailed from the time of the Middle Ages.

Great disappointment was felt in Germany, by the delay or refusal of the constitutions, which the several states had been taught to expect during the war of independence. But the principal sovereigns, especially the emperor of Austria and the king of Prussia, alarmed by the remembrance of the calamities that political innovations had produced in France, steadily opposed every change in the forms of government, but, at the same time, zealously labored to secure to their subjects the benefit of a just and enlightened administration.

Spain was far more unfortunate; the imbecile Ferdinand was the tool of the courtiers and the priests; at their instigation he revived the ancient principles of despotism and bigotry, punishing with remorseless severity every expression of liberal sentiments in politics or religion. The arbitrary conduct of the court was not the only cause of the misery that prevailed in the Peninsula; the South American colonies, which had long been regarded as the chief and almost the only source of the small share of commercial prosperity which the Spaniards retained, openly revolted, and raised the standard of independence. Ferdinand made some faint efforts to subdue the insurgents, but he was badly supported by his subjects, and the troops he had assembled refused to embark. Finally, the liberals having gained over a great portion of the army, compelled the king to establish a democratic constitution, by which the royal power was almost annihilated (A. D. 1820). Similar revolutions took place in Portugal, Naples, and Piedmont; alarm seized the minds of the European sovereigns, and they secretly combined to check popular movements. But experience soon proved that those who had framed the Spanish constitution were ignorant of the wants and wishes of the Spanish people. Louis XVIII. alarmed for the safety of France by the revolutionary movements in Spain, sent an army, under the command of the duke of Angouleme, to restore the royal authority; the invaders encountered no effective opposition; the cortes fled before them to Cadiz, and when the French approached that city, they permitted the king to resume his former despotic authority (A. D. 1823). The revolutions of Naples and Piedmont ended similarly; the liberals laid down their arms on the approach of the Austrian armies, and the new constitutions were abolished.

The accession of Charles John Bernadotte, to the crown of Sweden, made no change in the politics of the northern nations; his right of inheritance had been solemnly recognised by the allied sovereigns, at the congress of Vienna, and his conduct as a crown-prince had taught the Swedes to respect and love the monarch they had chosen. Even the Norwegians became reconciled to their fate, and learned to console themselves for the loss of national independence by the blessings that result from paternal government.

No sooner was peace restored between Great Britain and the United States than the old feelings of friendship and kindred revived between the two countries, and the leading statesmen, in both, showed an earnest desire to have former animosities buried in oblivion. But far different were the feelings between Spain and her revolted colonies; the South American states vigorously maintained their struggle for independence, and finally succeeded. The English government delayed acknowledging these republics until the duke of Angouleme had crossed the Pyrenees, when consuls were sent out to the chief states, and commercial treaties formed with their governments.

From this rapid sketch, it will be seen that throughout the greater part of the civilized world there was a struggle between the principles of monarchy and democracy, and that even England, though it had long enjoyed the blessings of a free constitution, was not wholly exempt from the agitation.

SECTION II.—*History of Europe during the reign of George IV.*

GEORGE IV. had so long wielded the supreme executive power in England, under the title of regent, that no political change was made or expected when he assumed the royal dignity. A month had not elapsed after his accession, when a plot was discovered for the murder of all his majesty's ministers, and thus facilitating a revolution, which had been planned by a few obscure enthusiasts. The conspirators used to assemble in Cato street, an obscure place near the Edgeware road; they were arrested in their rendezvous, just as they were preparing to execute their project, all their plans having been betrayed to government by a spy who had pretended to join in the conspiracy. Such were the insanity and misery of these wretched men, who proposed to subvert a powerful government, that when they were searched, not even a shilling was found among the whole party. The government pitying their delusion, punished only the ringleaders, and this clemency had a beneficial effect in calming political agitation.

Preparations were now made for the king's coronation, when they were suspended by an event which excited more public interest, and stimulated more angry passions than any other which had occurred for several years. This was the return of Queen Caroline to England, and her subsequent trial before the house of lords. Her marriage had been unfortunate almost from the commencement; she was early separated from her husband; after the lapse of some years, her conduct was made the subject of official inquiry; at the commencement of the regency she was excluded from court, and these indignities induced her to quit England. She visited the most celebrated spots along the coast of the Mediterranean, and then selected a permanent residence in that part of Italy subject to the Austrian government. Reports injurious to her character were circulated; commissioners were sent to Milan to investigate them, and the ministers, in consequence of the evidence thus collected, excluded her name from the liturgy, on the king's accession. Irritated at such an insult, she resolved to return to England, though a pension of fifty thousand pounds annually was offered to purchase her submission, and though she was informed that her landing would be the signal for the commencement of a prosecution.

No sooner had the queen landed, than messages were sent to both houses of parliament, recommending that her conduct should be investigated. "A Bill of Pains and Penalties" was introduced, to deprive her of royal rights and dignities, and a trial commenced which lasted forty-five days, when the bill was read a second time by a majority of forty-five. On the third reading, however, the ministers could only command a majority of nine, and the bill was abandoned. During these proceedings, the agitation of the public mind knew no bounds; addresses to the queen poured in from all sides, and when the bill was abandoned, her friends celebrated her escape as an acquittal. The remainder of her melancholy history may be briefly told: her popularity sank as rapidly as it had risen; she was refused a share in the ceremonial of the coronation; her appeals to the nation were disregarded, and the sense of disappointment and degradation produced a mortal disease which terminated her unhappy life. Her funeral was marked by a disgraceful riot: the mob determined that her remains should pass through the city of London, and triumphed over the troops that tried to carry the hearse by a different route.

Soon after his coronation the king visited Ireland, Scotland, and Hanover; he was everywhere received with the greatest enthusiasm, but the permanent results expected from these visits were not realized. In Ireland, party spirit blazed more furiously than ever, and the depreciation of agricultural produce rendering it difficult for tenants to pay their rents, led to a series of agrarian outrages which could only be checked by severe coercive laws. The distress of the lower classes, which indeed almost exceeded credibility, was relieved by a general and generous subscription in England, which arrested the progress of a pestilential disease, produced by famine and distress.

England suffered severely from the financial difficulties produced by the immense expenditure of the late war. While statesmen were engaged in devising means to alleviate the pressure of taxation, Napoleon Bonaparte, the cause of so many calamities, died almost unnoticed in his place of exile at St. Helena. During the king's visit to Scotland, Lord Londonderry, who had so long directed the foreign affairs of England, committed suicide; his place was supplied by Mr. Canning, who was supposed to be favorable to what was called a more liberal line of policy than that of his predecessor.

The distracted condition of Spain at this period engaged the attention of Europe. Ferdinand had been compelled to grant his subjects a free and almost a republican constitution, but the ministers forced upon him by the cortes, showed little wisdom or moderation, and the proceedings of the cortes themselves were unworthy the dignity of a deliberative assembly. In consequence of these errors, a large party was formed in the Peninsula to restore absolute monarchy; several bodies of insurgents were raised by the monks and friars, who feared that the estates of the monasteries and the church would be confiscated; they called themselves the "Army of the Faith," and were zealously supported by the lower ranks of the populace. Under these circumstances, a congress of the European powers was held at Verona, and a resolution was adopted for subverting the Spanish constitution, and restoring the absolute power of the king. The duke of Wellington, on the part of England, refused to sanction this design, and the execution of it was intrusted to the king of France, who was naturally anxious to check the progress of revolutionary principles, before his own throne was endangered by the contagion.

Early in the year 1823, the duc d'Angouleme entered Spain at the head of a powerful army; the constitutionalists made but a feeble resistance, and the king was restored to absolute authority with little trouble. Ferdinand made a bad use of his power; he persecuted all whom he suspected of liberal principles with the utmost severity, and revived all the ancient abuses which had so long disgraced the government of Spain. Though the English ministers maintained a strict neutrality during this contest, they severely censured the conduct of the French government, and as a counterpoise, they recognised the independence of the South American republics, which had withdrawn themselves from their allegiance to Spain.

During the Spanish war, which excited little interest, the sympathies of civilized Europe were engaged in the Greek revolution, which, however, was a barbarous and sanguinary struggle, that for many years seemed to promise no decisive result. The principal members of the Holy Alliance viewed the Greek insurrection with secret dislike, for they regarded it as a rebellion against legitimate authority; but the young and enthusiastic spirits throughout Europe viewed it as a just revolt against Turkish tyranny, and hoped that its success would restore the classical ages of Greece. Among the many volunteers who went to aid the insurgents was the celebrated poet, Lord Byron; before, however, they could profit by his services, he was attacked by fever, and died prematurely at Missolonghi.

Commercial embarrassments and political disputes diverted the attention of England from foreign affairs; a sudden rage for speculation seized the people; projects and joint-stock companies were multiplied without number, but suddenly the bubbles burst, and a terrible reaction ensued. The panic in the money-market was equal to the overweening confidence which had led to these extravagant speculations. But the evil was transitory, and it had perhaps some beneficial influence in limiting attention to those branches of trade best suited to the condition of the country. Political agitation was not so easily cured; the leaders of the Irish catholics formed an association to procure the repeal of the restrictive laws by which members of their church were excluded from parliament and offices of state. This body assumed all the forms and some of the functions of a legislative assembly, and though an act of parliament was passed for its suppression, the statute was eluded by he legal skill of the popular leaders in the association.

Soon after Mr. Canning's accession to power, the attention of all Europe was excited by an event which seemed to prove that England had not only deserted the principles of the Holy Alliance, but was about to take her position at the head of a more liberal political system. On the death of John VI., king of Portugal (March 10, 1826), the crown devolved to his eldest son, Don Pedro, who reigned, with the title of emperor, over the old Portuguese colonies in Brazil. Compelled to choose between his empire and his kingdom, Pedro selected the former; but he sent to Portugal a constitutional charter, and a formal resignation of the crown in favor of his daughter Donna Maria. Pedro's brother, Don Miguel, the queen dowager, and the most bigoted portion of the clergy, labored hard to frustrate this arrangement, and their machinations were encouraged by the French and Spanish cabinets. Several Portuguese regiments were induced to desert across the frontier and proclaim Don Miguel absolute king. As the Spanish government notoriously supplied the rebels with military stores and arms, the Portuguese minister applied to the British government for aid, and a message was sent to both houses of parliament, calling on them to aid in maintaining the independence of Portugal. Mr. Canning introduced the subject in the house of commons, describing the situation and policy of Great Britain, placed as a mediator between the conflicting opinions that convulsed Europe; and such was the effect of his eloquence, that only four persons in a full house could be got to oppose the address. A British armament was sent to the Tagus: its effect was instantaneous and decisive. The French diplomatic agent was recalled, the Spanish cabinet forced to desist from its intrigues, and Portugal restored to temporary tranquillity

Death and disease among the great and noble of the land produced some important changes in the councils of Great Britain. In the beginning of the year 1827, the duke of York, who had solemnly pledged himself to oppose the claims of the catholics to the utmost, sank under disease. He was sincerely lamented even by his political opponents; for his conduct in the management of the army, ever since he had been restored to the office of commander-in-chief, had deservedly won for him the honorable appellation of "the soldier's friend." Soon afterward the earl of Liverpool, who by his conciliating conduct as premier, had held together the friends and the opponents of catholic emancipation in the cabinet, was seized with a fit of apoplexy, which terminated his political existence, though his natural life was protracted for several months. Mr. Canning, who had long been a distinguished advocate of the catholic claims, was appointed his successor, upon which all the members of the cabinet, opposed to concession, resigned in a body. The fatigues and anxieties imposed upon him proved too much for the new premier; he sank under them, and was succeeded by Mr. F. Robinson, who was at the same time raised to the peerage, with the title of Lord Goderich. Before relating the overthrow of this feeble ministry, we must turn our attention to the events in another part of the globe, which accelerated its downfall.

Notwithstanding the horrid atrocities committed on both sides during the Greek war, the sympathies of Christendom in favor of the insurgents continually increased; it was expected that Alexander, emperor of Russia, would have taken some measures in their favor, but he died rather suddenly while engaged in a survey of his southern provinces. At this crisis, the sultan, unable to crush the revolt by his own strength, sought the aid of his powerful vassal, Mohammed Ali, the pacha of Egypt. This provincial governor, who had acted for some time more like an independent monarch than a tributary, readily sent his adopted son, Ibrahim Pacha, with a powerful army, into the Morea. The excesses of the Turks and Egyptians were so shocking to humanity, that the European powers felt bound to interfere, especially as the protracted contest was very pernicious to the commerce of the Levant. A treaty for the pacification of Greece was concluded in London between Russia France, and England, by which it was stipulated that Greece should enjoy a qualified independence under the sovereignty of Turkey, and that measures should be taken to coerce the sultan if he refused his consent to these arrangements.

The Austrian cabinet refused to share in this treaty. Dread of a similar insurrection in Italy, which was scarcely less oppressed, and which could equally appeal to classical sympathies and reminiscences, induced the court of Vienna to oppose anything that seemed like sanctioning a revolt. But not content with refusing to join the allies, the Austrians secretly urged the sultan to reject the proffered compromise, and the court of Constantinople, already bent on the extermination of the Greeks, made more vigorous exertions than ever. The fleets of England, Russia, and France, which had been sent to support the negotiations, when it was known that the sultan's answer was unfavorable, blockaded the Turco-Egyptian fleet in the harbor of Navarino, and Sir Edward Codrington, who commanded the allied squadrons, concluded an armistice with Ibrahim Pacha, in order to alleviate the horrors of war. This armistice was flagrantly violated by the Turks and Egyptians in every particular, and the allied squadrons entered the harbor of Navarino, in order to enforce compliance with its stipulations. A shot fired from a Turkish ship at an English boat, was the signal or the pretext for a general engagement, which ended in the utter annihilation of the Turco-Egyptian armament. The independence of Greece was thus virtually secured, and its completion was secured soon after by the arrival of a small military force from France, which compelled the Turks to evacuate the Morea.

In Russia and in France the victory of Navarino was regarded as a national triumph; in England it only increased the embarrassments of Lord Goderich's distracted cabinet, the members of which were at variance on almost every point of policy, foreign and domestic. Finding themselves unable to determine in what manner the event should be noticed in the king's speech, the ministers resigned their situations before the meeting of parliament, and the task of forming a new administration was intrusted to the duke of Wellington.

The sultan was not daunted by the intelligence of the destruction of his fleet; it seemed, indeed, rather to confirm him in his obstinacy After many ineffectual efforts to change his resolution, the ambassadors of France, England, and Russia, demanded their passports, and quitted Constantinople, a proceeding which was of course equivalent to a declaration of war. But the allies were no longer united in their policy: France and England were not unreasonably jealous of Russian ambition; France limited her exertions to protecting the Morea, the new ministers of England declared the victory of Navarino "an untoward event"—a phrase which led to the belief that they were disposed to look favorably on the pretensions of Turkey. This error precipitated what all wished to avoid, a war between Russia and Turkey. Still more unfortunate, the events of the first European campaign led many European statesmen to believe that Turkey could defend herself from her own resources; though the Russians had taken Varna by the treachery of its governor, they were forced to raise the siege of Shumlah, and retire with some precipitation. It was unnoticed or forgotten that this failure was more than compensated by the decisive success of the Russians in the Asiatic provinces, where the real strength of the Turkish empire lies; they conquered the greater part of ancient Armenia, occupied the fortresses which command the principal lines of march, and thus laid the foundation of decisive success in the next campaign.

In consequence of the general misapprehension respecting the position and resources of the belligerant parties, Turkey narrowly escaped being blotted from the map of Europe. The Russians opened the campaign by surprising Sizopoli, and laying siege to Silistria. The grand vizier advanced to the relief of the fortress, but he was surprised on his march by Marshal Diebitsch, and defeated. In this battle the Turks behaved so courageously that the Russians almost despaired of success, and made an attempt to open negotiations. Their offers were rejected; the vizier, trusting to his impregnable position at Shumlah, remained quietly in his intrenchments, while the Russians pressed forward the siege of Silistria. That city surrendered on the last day of June, but it was the middle of July before Diebitsch could concentrate his forces for the bold enterprise which decided the fortune of the war. Having masked Shumlah with one division of his forces, he forced a passage through the defiles of the Balkan, and took Aidos by storm. The vizier, alarmed by this unexpected movement, determined to remove his quarters to Salamno. He was encountered by Diebitsch on his march, and irretrievably defeated. The very soldiers who had so recently fought the Russians for seventeen hours, now scarcely withstood them for as many minutes; they fled at the first onset, abandoning arms, ammunition, artillery, and baggage. Adrianople, the second city in the Turkish empire, was captured without firing a shot; Stamboul itself must have fallen, had not the sultan consented to the terms of peace dictated by the conquerors. He signed a treaty on the 14th of September, by which he recognised the independence of Greece, and granted to Russia very considerable advantages, and a guarantee for the payment of the expenses of the war. Greece indeed was already virtually free; the French expedition had recovered the fortresses of the Morea from the Turks and Egyptians, while the Greeks themselves had gained considerable advantages in the north. It was resolved that the final destinies of the country should be arranged by a congress of the great powers in London. The crown of Greece was first offered to Prince Leopold, the relict of the late princess Charlotte, but after a long negotiation he rejected it, and it was finally bestowed on Prince Otho, the son of the king of Bavaria.

A revolution of a very different character took place in Portugal. When Don Pedro resigned the throne of that kingdom in favor of his daughter, Donna Maria de Gloria, he appointed his brother, Don Miguel regent, reasonably hoping that he might thus secure his daughter's rights, and the constitutional privileges which he had given to the Portuguese. Before quitting Vienna to assume the reins of power, Don Miguel took an oath of fidelity to the charter; when he visited England, on his way to Portugal, he repeated his protestations of attachment to the constitution and the rights of his niece so warmly, that the British statesmen, assured of his fidelity, consented to withdraw their troops from Lisbon. Unfortunately, after his return, he resigned himself to the guidance of the queen-mother, an unprincipled woman, who seemed to think that a bigoted zeal for what she believed to be the cause of religion would atone for every other crime. At her instigation, he induced the fanatic rabble, by means of an artful priesthood, to proclaim him absolute king, and to denounce the charter as inconsistent with the purity of the Roman faith. The friends of the constitution organized a resistance at Oporto and in the island of Madeira; but their efforts were badly directed, and worse supported. They were finally defeated and driven into exile, while Don Miguel commenced a bitter persecution against all who had been conspicuous for their advocacy of liberal opinions. The principal powers of Europe manifested their detestation of such treachery, by withdrawing their ambassadors from the court of Lisbon.

France during this period was greatly agitated by political strife. Charles X. was more bitterly opposed to revolutionary principles than his brother, and he yielded to the counsels of the bigoted priests, who persuaded him that it was his duty to restore to the church all the power which it had possessed in the dark ages. On the other hand, the French people became persuaded that a plot was formed to deprive them of the constitutional privileges which they had gained after so long a struggle; thus the nation became gradually alienated from the court, and the court from the nation; while some turbulent spirits endeavored to aggravate this hostility, in the hope of profiting by a future convulsion. A new ministry was forced upon the king by the popular party; the members of it professed moderate principles, but they wanted the abilities and the influence necessary for steering a safe course between the extremes of royal prerogative on one side, and popular encroachment on the other. They were driven, by the majority of the chambers, to make larger concessions to the demands of the people than they had originally intended, and the reluctance with which they yielded, deprived them of popular gratitude. Even their sending an armament to aid the Greeks in the Morea, their recalling the French army of occupation from Spain, and their acknowledging the independence of the South American republics, failed to conciliate the support of the democratic party, while these measures rendered them perfectly odious to he royalists. They were suddenly dismissed, and the formation of a cabinet was intrusted to Prince Polignac, whose appointment was studiously represented as a declaration of war by Charles X. against his subjects.

Interesting as these events were, they excited little attention in England, where the public mind was intently fixed on the struggle in parliament, between those who sought to effect important constitutional changes, and those who were resolved to resist all innovation. The duke of Wellington's cabinet had been placed in office mainly by the influence of that portion of the aristocracy which was anxious to check the progress of change, and resist certain proposed measures, which they deemed inconsistent with the supremacy, if not the safety, of the established church. One of these measures was the repeal of the Test and Corporation acts, by which dissenters were excluded from office; it was proposed in the house of commons, and on a division the ministers were left in such a minority, that they not only withdrew further opposition, but adopted the measure as their own, and carried it successfully through both houses of parliament.

This event gave fresh vigor to the efforts made by the Irish catholics to procure the concessions which they usually called emancipation. The rejection of a bill for the purpose by the house of lords in 1828, only roused them to greater exertion; and on the other hand, the partisans of protestant ascendency in Ireland began to form clubs for the protection of their peculiar privileges. An unexpected event exasperated the strife of parties, and threatened to bring matters to a dangerous crisis. Mr. Vesey Fitzgerald, having accepted office under the duke of Wellington, vacated his seat for the county of Clare, reasonably expecting that there would be no obstacle to his re-election. Mr. O'Connell, an Irish catholic, who had been long recognised as the popular leader, offered himself as a candidate for the vacant seat, and in spite of the disqualifying laws, was elected by an overwhelming majority. It was considered disputable whether he might not take his seat, but on all hands it was allowed that he was the legal representative of the county.

This was a state of things which could not with safety be permitted to continue; the ministers felt that they should either increase the severity of the exclusive laws, which the temper of the times would hardly have permitted, or that they should remove the few restrictions which prevented catholics from enjoying the full benefits of the constitution. They chose the latter alternative, and after some difficulty in overcoming the king's reluctance, they had the concession of the catholic claims recommended in the royal speech, at the opening of the session of parliament. The bill for giving effect to this recommendation was strenuously opposed in both houses, but as it was supported by the united strength of the ministers and the party by which they were most commonly resisted, it passed steadily through both houses, and received the royal assent on the 13th of April, 1829.

From the time that this important measure was carried, the domestic condition of England presented an aspect of more tranquillity than had been witnessed for many years. Party strife seemed hushed within and without the walls of parliament, as if both parties had been wearied out by the protracted discussion of the question they had just settled. This calm was increased by the gloom which the illness of the king diffused over the nation. Early in 1830 the symptoms of the disease became alarming, and for many weeks before its termination, all hopes of a favorable result were abandoned. On the 26th of June, George IV. died at Windsor castle, after having borne the agonies of protracted sickness with great firmness, patience, and resignation.

SECTION III.—*History of Europe during the Reign of William IV.*

FEW monarchs ever obtained such immediate popularity on their accession as William IV. He had been educated in the navy, always a favorite branch of service with the British people; he was eminent for the domestic virtues, which are the more readily comprehended by a nation, as their value is felt in every walk of life; his habits were economical, and his manners familiar; he exhibited himself to his people, conversed with them, and shared in their tastes and amusements. As he had been intimately connected with some of the leading whigs before his accession to the throne, it was generally believed that the policy by which that party had been jealously excluded from power during the two preceding reigns would be abandoned, and it was hoped that a new cabinet would be formed by the coalition of ministers with their opponents. The parliamentary debates soon put an end to these expectations; the opposition to the ministry, which had been almost nominal since the settlement of the catholic question, was more than usually violent in the debate on the address; the formal business of the house was indeed despatched with all possible expedition, preparatory to a new election; but before parliament could be prorogued, the whigs were virtually pledged to irreconcilable war with the administration.

It is now time to turn to the affairs of France, which had for two years been fast hastening to a crisis. Never had a ministry in any country to encounter such a storm of virulence and invective, as that which assailed the cabinet of Prince Polignac; though he was perhaps justly suspected of arbitrary designs, yet his first measures were dignified and moderate; some of them even seem to have been framed in a spirit of conciliation. But nothing could purchase the forbearance of his opponents; they scrupled not to have recourse to downright falsehood, and in some cases accused him of designs so exquisitely absurd, that they appeared to have been invented for the express purpose of measuring the extent of popular credulity. Charles X. more than shared the odium thrown on his obnoxious favorite; his patronage of the Jesuits and monastic orders, his revival of austere and rigid etiquette in his court, and his marked dislike of those who had acquired eminence in the revolution, or under Napoleon, were circumstances which rendered him unpopular with the great bulk of the nation so long estranged from the Bourbons and their policy.

Polignac defied the storm; but unfortunately, as the contest continued, he departed from the course of caution and prudence, probably because injustice had driven him into anger, and he soon furnished his adversaries with just grounds for continued hostility. When the chambers assembled, the royal speech was a direct attack on the first principles of the constitution, concluding with a threat of resuming the concessions made by the charter, which was notoriously impotent, and therefore supremely ridiculous. A very uncourtly reply was voted by the chamber of deputies, after a very animated debate, by a majority of forty. The only alternative now left was a dissolution of the chambers, or a change of the ministry; Charles X. chose the former, trusting that events might turn the popular current, and give him a more manageable chamber at a new election.

Charles and his ministers appear to have hoped that their unpopularity would be overcome, and their future projects facilitated, by gratifying the taste of the French people for military glory. An armament was therefore prepared with extraordinary care, and sent against Algiers, under the pretext that the dey had insulted the honor of France. The success of the expedition corresponded with the exertions made to ensure it; the city of Algiers was taken after a very slight resistance, the dey was sent prisoner to Italy, and his vast treasures remained at the disposal of the conquerors. It was reasonable that the maritime powers should feel jealous at the establishment of French garrisons and colonies in northern Africa; to allay their suspicions, a promise was made that the occupation of Algiers should be merely temporary; but the French nation formed such an infatuated attachment to their conquest, that they have kept it ever since, though it causes an annual waste of life and treasure, without conferring any appreciable advantage either on Africa or on France.

Polignac, relying on the moral effect which the conquest of Algiers would produce, dissolved the chambers, but, with the same infatuation which seems to have directed all his movements, he at the same time dismissed the only two moderate members of his cabinet, and supplied their places by the most unpopular men in France. Such a course, as ought to have been foreseen, more than counterbalanced any benefit which the ministers might have gained from the conquest of Algiers; the elections left them in a miserable minority, and matters were consequently brought to a crisis.

The majority of the commercial classes and landed proprietors in France dreaded the renewal of civil commotions; they knew that there was an active republican party in the country, which though not very numerous, was very unscrupulous and energetic; they feared, and not without reason, tha the triumph of this party, which was no unlikely termination of a revolutionary struggle, would lead to the renewal of the horrors perpetrated during the reign of terror, when the Jacobins were in power. But at the same time, these classes were equally hostile to the restoration of the ancient despotism, which they believed to be the object of the king and his ministers. Had Charles X. declared that he would be contented with the prerogatives of a constitutional monarch, dismissed his obnoxious ministers, and formed a cabinet of moderate men, the crisis would have passed over without danger; unfortunately, more arbitrary counsels prevailed; Polignac and his colleagues resolved to terminate the struggle by subverting the constitution.

On the morning of the 26th of July, three ordinances were published, which virtually subverted the constitutional privileges granted by the charter. The first dissolved the newly elected chamber of deputies before it assembled: the second changed the law of elections and disfranchised the great body of electors; and the third subjected the press to new and severe restrictions which would completely have annihilated its liberties.

It was late in the day before intelligence of these events was generally circulated through Paris, and the news, at first, seemed to excite astonishment rather than indignation; the ministers passed the day in quiet at their hotels, receiving the visits of their friends and congratulating themselves upon the delusive tranquillity. But their opponents were not inactive; expresses were sent to summon all the deputies of their party within reach, and those who had already arrived in Paris held a private meeting to concert measures of resistance. The principal journalists acted with still greater promptitude; they prepared and published a protest against the restrictions on the press, whose daring language would probably have exposed them to the penalties of treason had the contest terminated differently.

On the morning of the 27th, few of the journals appeared, for the publication of those which were not sanctioned by the minister of the interior was prohibited by the police. The printers, thus suddenly deprived of employment, formed a body of vindictive rioters, and their numbers were increased by the closing of several large factories in the suburbs of Paris. The proprietors of two journals printed their papers in defiance of the ordinance, and the first disturbance was occasioned by the police forcing an entrance into their establishments, breaking the presses, scattering the types, and rendering the machinery unserviceable. So little was an insurrection anticipated, that Charles, accompanied by the dauphin, went on a hunting match to Rambouillet; and his ministers neglected the ordinary precaution of strengthening the garrison of the capital. It was only on the morning of the 27th that Marmont received his appointment as military governor of Paris, and it was not till after four in the afternoon that orders were given to put the troops under arms.

Between six and seven o'clock in the evening some detachments of troops were sent to the aid of the police; this was the signal for commencing the contest; several smart skirmishes took place between the citizens and the soldiers, in which the latter were generally successful, so that Marmont wrote a letter to the king, congratulating him on the suppression of the riot, while the ministers issued their last ordinance, declaring Paris in a state of siege. When night closed in, the citizens destroyed every lamp in the city, thus securing the protection of darkness for their preparations to renew the struggle.

On the morning of the 28th, Marmont was astonished to find that the riots which he had deemed suppressed, had assumed the formidable aspect of a revolution. The citizens were ready and organized for a decisive contest; they were in possession of the arsenal and the powder magazine; they had procured arms from the shops of the gunsmiths and the police stations; they had erected barricades across the principal streets, and had selected leaders competent to direct their exertions. Under these circumstances, the marshal hesitated before taking any decisive step; it was noon before he had resolved how to act, and he then determined to clear the streets by military force. He divided his troops into four columns, which he directed to move in different directions, thus unwisely separating his forces, so that they could not act in concert. Every step taken by the columns was marked by a series of murderous conflicts; they were assailed with musketry from the barricades, from the windows and tops of houses, from the corners of streets, and from the narrow alleys and passages which abound in Paris. When the cavalry attempted to charge, they were overwhelmed with stones and articles of furniture flung from the houses; their horses stumbled in the unpaved streets, or were checked by the barricades, while the citizens, protected by their dwellings, kept up a heavy fire, which the disheartened horsemen were unable to return. Though the royal guards performed their duty, the troops of the line showed great reluctance to fire on the citizens, and hence the insurgents were enabled to seize many important posts with little or no opposition. When evening closed the troops had been defeated in every direction; they returned to their barracks, weary, hungry, and dispirited; by some inexplicable blunder, no provision was made for their refreshment, while every family in Paris vied in supplying the insurgents with everything they wanted.

Marmont was now fully sensible of the perils of his situation; he wrote to the infatuated king, representing the dangerous condition of Paris, and soliciting fresh instructions; the orders he received in reply, urged him to persevere, and indirectly censured his former conduct, by directing him "to act with masses."

The contest was renewed on the morning of the third day, the soldiers evincing great feebleness, while the populace seemed animated by a certainty of success. While the issue was yet doubtful, two regiments of the line went over to the insurgents in a body; the citizens thus strengthened, rushed through the gap which this defection left in the royal line, took the Louvre by assault, and soon compelled the troops that remained faithful to the royal cause, either to lay down their arms or evacuate Paris. The revolution was speedily completed by the installation of a provisional government; measures were adopted for the speedy convocation of the chambers, and in a few hours the capital had nearly assumed its ordinary aspect of tranquillity.

Charles and his ministers appear to have believed that the country would not follow the example of Paris. They were speedily convinced of their error; the king was abandoned, not only by his courtiers, but even by his household servants; he was forced to wait helplessly in his country-seat, until he was dismissed to contemptuous exile by the national commissioners. His ministers attempted to escape in disguise, but were most of them arrested, a circumstance which occasioned great perplexity to the new government. In the meantime, the duke of Orleans, far the most popular of the royal family, was chosen lieu tenant-general of the kingdom, and when the chambers met, he was elected to the throne, with the title of Louis Philippe I., king of the French.

This revolution produced an extraordinary degree of political excitement throughout Europe; even in England the rick-burnings and other incendiary acts gave formidable signs of popular discontent but the personal attachment of the nation to the sovereign, and the prudent measures of the government, prevented any attempt at revo lution. When parliament assembled, the duke of Wellington took an early opportunity of declaring that he would resist any attempt to make a change in the representative system of the country, and this declaration, which was wholly unexpected, or rather, which was contrary to very general expectations, at once deprived the ministers of the popularity they had hitherto enjoyed. An event of trifling importance in itself, but very grave in its consequences, proved still more injurious to the Wellington administration. The king had been invited to dine with the lord-mayor of London on the 9th of November, and his ministers were of course expected to accompany him. All the preparations were complete, when a city magistrate, having heard that some persons intended to insult the duke of Wellington, in consequence of his late unpopular speech, wrote to his grace, recommending him not to come without a military escort. The riots in Paris and Brussels, which had commenced with trifling disturbances, and ended in revolutions, were too recent not to alarm the ministers; they resolved that the king's visit to the city should be postponed to some more favorable conjuncture.

This announcement produced a general panic; business was suspended; the funds fell four per cent. in a few hours: the city of London continued in the greatest anxiety and alarm, for every one believed that some dreadful conspiracy was discovered at the moment it was about to explode. A day sufficed to show that no substantial grounds for apprehension existed, and people excused their vain terrors by throwing all the blame upon the government. The ministers were overwhelmed with a storm of indignant ridicule, which was scarcely merited, for they could not have anticipated such an extensive and groundless panic, and there could be little doubt of the propriety of removing any pretext for a tumultuous assembly in the long nights of November.

This strange occurrence proved fatal to the ministry, which indeed had previously been tottering. On a question of confidence, the ministers were defeated by a majority of twenty-nine in the house of commons, upon which the duke of Wellington and his colleagues immediately resigned their offices. A new ministry was formed under the auspices of Earl Grey, composed of the old whig opposition, and the party commonly called Mr. Canning's friends; it was recommended to the nation by the premier's early declaration, that the principles of his cabinet should be reform, retrenchment, and peace.

But to preserve the peace of Europe was now a task of no ordinary difficulty. The excitement produced by the late French revolution had aroused an insurrectionary spirit in every country where the people had to complain of real or fancied wrongs; and the continental sovereigns, alarmed for their power, looked with jealousy on every movement that seemed likely to lead to a popular triumph. The emperor of Russia went so far, as to hesitate about acknowledging the title of Louis Philippe to the throne of France, and when he at length yielded to the example and influence of the other European states, his recognition of a king elected by the people was so reluctant and ungracious, as to be deemed an insult by the French nation.

Nowhere did the insurrectionary spirit thus excited produce more decisive effects than in Belgium, whose compulsory union with Holland was one of the most unwise arrangements of the congress of Vienna. The Dutch and Flemings differed in language, in habits, and in religion; their commercial interests were opposed, their national antipathies were ancient and inveterate. In the midst of these anxieties produced by the events in Paris, the Dutch ministers continued to goad the Belgians by restrictive laws, and at length drove them into open revolt. On the night of the 25th of August, a formidable riot began in Brussels; the Dutch authorities and garrison, after having exhibited the most flagrant proofs of incapacity and cowardice, were driven out, and a provisional government installed in the city. The king of Holland hesitated between concession and the employment of force; he adopted a middle course of policy, and sent his sons to redress grievances, and an army to enforce the royal authority; at the same time he convoked the states-general. The Dutch princes were received with such coolness at Brussels, that they returned to the army; soon after, Prince Frederick, having learned that the patriots were divided among themselves, led the royal troops to Brussels, and at the same time published an amnesty, but unfortunately, with such sweeping exceptions, that it should rather be called an edict of proscription. For four days the Dutch and Belgians contested the possession of the city with equal want of skill and courage, but with somewhat more of energy on the part of the insurgents. Finally, the Dutch were driven out, and a provisional government established. Proposals of mediation were made by the prince of Orange, which were disavowed by his father, the king of Holland, and equally rejected by the Flemings; thus refused by both parties, he allowed matters to take their course, and Belgium became an independent state. Many tedious negotiations and discussions were necessary before this disarrangement of the European powers could be adjusted so as to avert the danger of a general war. At length Leopold, prince of Saxe Coburg, nearly connected with the royal family of England, was elected sovereign of the new kingdom, and to conciliate his subjects and strengthen his throne, he formed a matrimonial alliance with the daughter of the king of the French.

Germany was not exempt from the perils of popular commotion. In the year 1813, the sovereigns of the principal German states had promised popular constitutions to their subjects, as a reward for their exertions in delivering the continent from the tyranny of Napoleon. These promises had not been fulfilled; there were many discontented persons anxious to profit by the example of France and Belgium, but fortunately, in the principal states, the personal character of the sovereigns had so endeared them to the people, that no insurrection was attempted. In some of the minor states there were slight revolutions; the duke of Brunswick was deposed by his subjects, and the throne transferred to his brother; the king of Saxony was forced to resign in favor of his nephew; and the elector of Hesse was compelled to grant a constitutional charter.

Spain continued to languish under the iron sway of Ferdinand VII.;

the people generally seemed to have no wish for liberty, and the abortive efforts to establish the constitution again were easily quelled, and cruelly punished. The condition of Portugal appeared to be similar; Don Miguel, who had usurped the throne, was so strenuously supported by the priests and monks, that every attempt to effect a change seemed hopeless. Italy shared in the excitement of the time, but the jealous watchfulness of Austria, and the formidable garrisons which that power had established in northern Italy, effectually prevented any outbreak. Insurrectionary movements took place in several of the Swiss cantons, but the disputes were arranged with promptness and equity, so speedily as to avert the horrors of civil war.

Poland was one of the last countries to catch the flame of insurrection, but there it raged most furiously. Provoked by the cruelties of the archduke Constantine, who governed the country for his brother, the emperor of Russia, the Poles took up arms, at a time when all the statesmen of Europe were intent on maintaining peace, and were therefore compelled to withhold their sympathies from the gallant struggle. Unaided and unsupported, the Poles for nearly two years maintained an unequal struggle against the gigantic power of Russia; they were finally crushed, and have ever since been subjected to the yoke of the most cruel despotism.

France, which had scattered these elements of discord, was far from enjoying tranquillity itself. The republican party deemed itself betrayed by the election of a king, and several who had consented to that arrangement were dissatisfied with the limited extension of popular privileges gained by the revolution. A great number of idle and discontented young men were anxious to involve Europe in a war of opinion, and they denounced the king as a traitor to the principles which had placed him on the throne, because he refused to gratify their insane wishes. The total separation of the church from the state alienated the French clergy; while the royalists recovered from their first terror, began to entertain hopes of a restoration. Thus surrounded by difficulties and dangers, Louis Philippe was far from finding his throne a bed of roses; but he evinced firmness and talent adequate to the occasion, and he was zealously supported by the middle classes, who looked upon him as their guarantee for constitutional freedom and assured tranquillity.

His success, however, would have been doubtful but for the efficient support he received from the national guard, whose organization was rapidly completed in Paris and the provinces. This civic body repressed the riots of the workmen and artisans, broke up the meetings of revolutionary clubs, and frustrated the attempts of republican fanatics, without incurring the odium which would have been attached to the exertions of the police and military. The severest test to which the stability of the new government in Paris was exposed, arose from the trials of the ministers who had signed the fatal ordinances. Louis Philippe made no effort to seize these delinquents, and would probably have been rejoiced at their escape; four of them were, as we have said, arrested by some zealous patriots, at a distance from Paris, as they were endeavoring to escape under the protection of false passports; the government had no option, but was forced to send them for trial before the chamber of peers. The partisans of anarchy took advantage of the popular excitement to raise formidable riots, which might have terminated in a new and sanguinary revolution, but for the zeal and firmness of the national guard. After an impartial trial, Polignac and his companions were condemned to perpetual imprisonment and civil death, and were quickly removed from the capital to a distant prison. Tranquillity was re-established on the morning of the third day after the trial, and the citizens of Paris demonstrated the extent of their late alarms by the brilliant illuminations with which they celebrated the restoration of order.

England was deeply engaged in an attempt to remodel her constitution. Early in 1831, the new premier declared that "ministers had succeeded in framing a measure of reform, which they were persuaded would prove efficient without exceeding the bounds of that wise moderation, with which such a measure should be accompanied." On the 1st of March the measure was introduced to the house of commons by Lord John Russell, andfrom that moment to its final success it almost wholly engrossed the attention of the country. The debate on the first reading of the bill lasted the unprecedented number of seven nights; the discussion on the second reading was shorter, but more animated; it was carried only by a majority of one. Ministers were subsequently defeated on two divisions, and at their instigation the king hastily dissolved the parliament. The elections took place amid such popular excitement, that ardent supporters of the ministerial measure were returned by nearly all the large constituencies, and the success of the reform bill, at least so far as the house of commons was concerned, was secured.

The reform bill passed slowly but securely through the house of commons, it was then sent up to the lords, and after a debate of five nights, rejected by a majority of 41. Great was the popular disappointment, but the promptitude with which the house of commons, on the motion of Lord Ebrington, passed a vote of confidence in ministers, and pledged itself to persevere with the measure of reform, calmed the agitation in the metropolis and the greater part of the country. Some serious riots, however, occurred at Derby and Nottingham, which were not suppressed until considerable mischief was done; Bristol suffered still more severely from the excesses of a licentious mob, whose fury was not checked until many lives were lost, and a great amount of valuable property wantonly destroyed.

While the excitement respecting the reform bill was at the highest, a new pestilential disease was imported into the country. It was called the Asiatic cholera, because it first appeared in India, whence it gradually extended in a northwestern direction to Europe. Its ravages in Great Britain were not, by any means, so great as they had been in some parts of the continent, yet they were very destructive; they were met by a bold and generous offer of service from the physicians throughout the empire, and their conduct, while the pestilence prevailed, reflected the highest honor on the character of the medical profession in Great Britain.

A new reform bill was introduced into the house of commons immediately after the assembling of parliament; it passed there with little opposition, and was sent up to the house of lords. As no change had been made in the constitution of that body, great anxiety was felt respecting the fate of the measure; but some peers, who had formerly opposed it, became anxious for a compromise, and the second reading was carried by a majority of nine. But these new allies of the ministry were resolved to make important alterations in the character of the measure, and when the bill went into committee the ministers found themselves in a minority. Earl Grey proposed to the king the creation of a sufficient number of peers to turn the scale, but his majesty refused to proceed to such extremities, and all the members of the cabinet resigned. The duke of Wellington received, through Lord Lyndhurst, his majesty's commands to form a new administration, and he undertook the task in the face of the greatest difficulties that it had ever been the fate of a British statesman to encounter. The nation was plunged into an extraordinary and dangerous state of excitement; the house of commons by a majority of eighty, virtually pledged itself to the support of the late ministry; addresses to the crown were sent from various popular bodies, which were by no means distinguished by moderation of tone or language; associations were formed to secure the success of the reform measure, and the country seemed brought to the verge of a revolution. Under such circumstances, the duke of Wellington saw that success was hopeless, he resigned the commission with which he had been intrusted, and advised his majesty to renew his communications with his former advisers. Earl Grey returned to office; a secret compact was made that no new peers should be created if the reform bill were suffered to pass; and the measure having been rapidly hurried through the remaining stages, reeeived the royal assent on the 7th of June. The Irish and Scotch reform bills attracted comparatively but little notice; a law for enforcing the collection of tithes in Ireland was more vigorously opposed, and the ignorant peasants of Ireland were encouraged by their advocates to resist the payment of the impost.

While England was engrossed by the discussions on the reform bill, the new monarchy established in France was exposed to the most imminent dangers from the republicans on the one hand, and the partisans of the exiled family on the other. The republican party was the more violent and infinitely the more dangerous, because, in the capital at least, there was a much greater mass, to whom its opinions and incentives were likely to be agreeable. There was also a spirit of fanaticism in its members, which almost amounted to insanity; several attempts were made to assassinate the king, and his frequent escapes may be justly regarded as providential. When any of the apostles of sedition were brought to trial, they openly maintained their revolutionary doctrines; treated the king with scorn and derision; inveighed against the existing institutions of the country; entered into brutal and violent altercations with the public prosecutor; menaced the juries and insulted the judges. The very extravagance of this evil at length worked out a remedy: the bombast of the republicans was carried to such an excess of absurdity, that it became ridiculous; the republicans were disarmed when they found that the nonsense of their inflated speeches produced not intimidation, but shouts of laughter. Moderate men took courage;

the middle classes, to whose prosperity, peace abroad and tranquillity at home were essentially necessary, rallied round the monarchy, and the republicans were forced to remain silent, until some new excitement of the public mind would afford an opportunity for disseminating mischievous falsehoods.

An insurrection of the Carlists, as the partisans of the exiled family were called, in the south of France, injured the cause it was designed to serve. It was easily suppressed, but the government learned that the dutchess de Berri, whose son, the duke of Bourdeaux, was the legitimate heir to the crown, had made arrangements for landing in La Vendée, and heading the royalists in the province. Such preparations were made, that when the dutchess landed, she found her partisans disheartened, and their movements so closely watched, that it was scarcely possible for them to assemble in any force. Still she resolved to persevere, but the enterprise degenerated into a series of isolated and insignificant attacks, made by small bodies in a strong country, and the proceedings of the royalists, consequently, resembled those of brigands. The dutchess continued five months in the country, though actively pursued by the military and police ; she was at length betrayed by one of her associates, and made prisoner. The government of Louis Philippe treated the royal captive with great clemency ; she had not been long in prison when it was discovered that she was pregnant, having been privately married some time before her arrest. This unfortunate circumstance threw such an air of ridicule over the entire enterprise, that the royalists abandoned all further efforts against the government.

While the south of France was thus agitated by the royalists, Paris narrowly escaped the perils of a republican revolution. The funeral of General Lamarque afforded the opportunity for this outbreak, which lasted about five hours, and was attended with great loss of life. The entire body of the military and all the respectable citizens supported the cause of monarchy and good order, or else the consequence would have been a new revolution. The revolt had the effect of strengthening the ministerial influence in the chambers ; when they met, the opposition could not muster more than half the number of votes that supported the cabinet.

A treaty had been concluded by the representative of the five great powers, Austria, Russia, Prussia, and England, arranging the conditions on which Belgium should be separated from Holland ; to these terms the Belgians had acceded, but they were declined by the Dutch, who still retained the citadel of Antwerp. A French army entered Belgium, and proceeded to besiege this fortress ; it was taken after a sharp siege, and was immediately given up to a Belgian garrison, the French retiring within their own frontiers in order to avert the jealousies and suspicions of the European powers.

Turkey was exposed to the greatest danger, by the rebellion of its powerful vassal, the pacha of Egypt. Mohammed Ali was anxious to annex Syria to his territories, a dispute with the governor of Acre furnished him a pretext for invading the country ; the sultan commanded him to desist, and on his refusal treated him as a rebel ; Mohammed Ali was so indignant, that he extended his designs to the whole empire ; his forces routed the Turkish armies in every battle ; Syria and a great part of Asia Minor were subdued with little difficulty, and Constantinople itself would have fallen but for the prompt interference of Russia. The sultan was thus saved from his rebellious vassal, but the independence of his empire was fearfully compromised.

The declining health in King Ferdinand directed attention to the law of succession in Spain: his only child was an infant daughter, and the Salic law, introduced by the Bourbon dynasty, excluded females from the throne. Ferdinand had repealed this law, but when he was supposed to be in his mortal agonies, the partisans of his brother, Don Carlos, who was looked upon as the surest support of the priesthood and of arbitrary power, induced him to disinherit his daughter, and recognise Don Carlos as heir to the crown. The very next day Ferdinand was restored to consciousness and understanding; the queen instantly brought before him the injustice he had been induced to commit, and the king was so indignant that he not only dismissed his ministers but threw himself into the arms of the liberal party. A general amnesty was published; those who had been exiled for supporting the constitution were invited home, and the Carlist party was so discouraged that it sank without resistance. Don Carlos himself, his wife, and his wife's sister, the princess of Beira, were compelled to quit Madrid; they sought and found shelter with Don Miguel, the usurper of Portugal.

On the 20th of September, 1833, Ferdinand died: his daughter was proclaimed at Madrid, but Carlist insurrections broke out in several parts of Spain, and have continued, with little interruption, almost ever since.

The excitement produced by the French revolution extended beyond the Atlantic. Don Pedro, emperor of Brazil, was compelled by his subjects to abdicate the throne in favor of his infant son; an event the more singular, as he had some time before resigned the crown of Portugal in favor of his daughter, Donna Maria de Gloria. When Pedro returned to Europe, he resolved to assert his daughter's rights, which had been usurped by Don Miguel; soldiers were secretly enlisted in France and England, the refugees from Portugal and Brazil were formed into regiments, and, after some delay, a respectable armament was collected in the Azores, which had remained faithful to Donna Maria. Pedro resolved to invade the north of Portugal; he landed near Oporto, and made himself master of that city; but his further operations were cramped by the want of money, and of the munitions of war; Oporto was invested by Don Miguel, and for several months the contest between the two brothers was confined to the desultory operations of a siege. At length, in the summer of 1833, Don Pedro intrusted the command of his naval force to Admiral Napier; this gallant officer, after having landed a division of the army in the province, sought Don Miguel's fleet; though superior in number of ships, men, and weight of metal, he attacked it with such energy, that in a short time all the large vessels belonging to the usurper struck their colors. This brilliant success, followed by the capture of Lisbon, which yielded to Pedro's forces with little difficulty, and the recognition of the young queen by the principal powers of Europe, proved fatal to Miguel's cause. After some faint attempts at protracted resistance, he abandoned the struggle, and sought shelter in Italy.

Don Pedro's death, which soon followed his triumph, did little injury to the constitutional cause. His daughter retains the crown; she was married first to the prince at Leuchtenberg, who did not long survive his nuptials; her second husband is Prince Ferdinand of Saxe Coburg, nearly allied to the queen of Great Britain.

Several disturbances in the papal states gave the French a pretext for seizing the citadel of Ancona, which gave just grounds of offence to Austria. But neither party wished to hazard the perils of war. The pope excommunicated all the liberals in his dominions, but was mortified to find that ecclesiastical censures, once so formidable, were now ridiculous. When the French evacuated Ancona, he was obliged to hire a body of Swiss troops for his personal protection, and the pay of these mercenaries almost ruined his treasury. To such a low estate is the papal power now reduced, which was once supreme in Europe, and exercised unlimited sway over the consciences and conduct of potentates and nations.

The attention of the first reformed parliament of Great Britain was chiefly engrossed by domestic affairs. In consequence of the continued agrarian disturbances in Ireland, a coercive statute was passed, containing many severe enactments; but at the same time, the Irish church was forced to make some sacrifices, a tax for ecclesiastical purposes was levied on its revenues, and the number of bishoprics was diminished.

But measures of still greater importance soon occupied the attention of parliament; the charter of the bank of England was renewed, on terms advantageous to the country; the East India company was deprived of its exclusive commercial privileges, and the trade to Hindústan and China thrown open; but the company was permitted to retain its territorial sovereignty. Finally, a plan was adopted for the abolition of West India slavery; the service of the negro was changed into apprenticeship for a limited period, and a compensation of twenty millions was voted to the planters. There was a very active though not a very large section of the house of commons dissatisfied with the limited extent of change produced by the reform bill; they demanded much greater innovations, and they succeeded in exciting feelings of discontent in the lower classes of the community. Popular discontent was not confined to England, it was general throughout Europe, but fortunately no serious efforts were made to disturb the public tranquillity.

The second session of the reformed parliament was rendered memorable by the passing of an act for altering the administration of the poor laws, which was very fiercely attacked outside the walls of parliament. It was, however, generally supported by the leading men of all parties; though its enactment greatly weakened the popularity of the ministers. The cabinet was itself divided respecting the policy to be pursued toward Ireland, and the dissensions respecting the regulation of the church, and the renewal of the Coercion bill, in that country, arose to such a height, that several of the ministry resigned. Lord Melbourne succeeded Earl Grey as premier, but it was generally believed that the king was by no means pleased with the change; and that on the Irish church question, he was far from being satisfied with the line of conduct pursued by his ministers. In the month of November, the death of Earl Spencer removed Lord Althorp, the chancellor of the exchequer, to the house of lords, and rendered some new modifications necessary. The king took advantage of the opportunity to dismiss the ministers, an express was sent to summon Sir Robert Peel from the continent, to assume the office of premier; and the duke of Wellington, who had administered the government in the interim, was appointed foreign secretary. Parliament was immediately dissolved, and the three kingdoms were agitated by a violent explosion of party spirit. A tithe-affray in Ireland, which ended with the loss of life, supplied the opponents of the ministry with a pretext for rousing the passions of the peasantry in that country, and of this they availed themselves so effectually, that the ministerial candidates were defeated in almost every election.

While the country was anxiously waiting the result of the struggle between the rival political parties, both houses of parliament were burned to the ground. This event at first excited some alarm, but it was soon allayed, for the cause of the fire was clearly proved to be accidental. When parliament met, Sir Robert Peel's cabinet was found to be in a minority in the house of commons. The premier, however, persevered in spite of hostile majorities, until he was defeated on the question of the Irish church, when he and his colleagues resigned. The Melbourne cabinet was restored, with the remarkable exception of Lord Brougham, whose place as chancellor was supplied by Lord Cottenham.

On the death of his brother, Don Carlos, after a vain attempt to assert his claims, was driven from Spain into Portugal, and so closely pursued that he was forced to take refuge on board an English ship-of-war. He came to London, where several abortive efforts were made to induce him to abandon his pretensions. But in the meantime his partisans in the Biscayan provinces had organized a formidable revolt, under a brave leader, Zumalacarregui, and a priest named Merino. Don Carlos secretly quitted London, passed through France in disguise, and appeared at the head of the insurgents. A quadrupartite treaty was concluded between Spain, Portugal, France, and England, for supporting the rights of the infant queen. It was agreed that France should guard the frontiers, to prevent the Carlists from receiving any aid by land; that England should watch the northern coasts; and that Portugal should aid the queen of Spain with a body of auxiliary troops if necessary.

Notwithstanding these arrangements, the Carlists were generally successful, and, at length, the court of Madrid applied to England for direct assistance. This was refused; but permission was given to raise an auxiliary legion of ten thousand men in the United Kingdom, the command of which was intrusted to Colonel Evans. But the effect produced by this force was far inferior to what had been expected; in the dilapidated state of the Spanish finances, it was found difficult to supply the legion with pay, provisions, and the munitions of war. A revolution at Madrid, which rendered the form of government very democratic, alienated the king of the French from the cause of the Spanish queen, and the war lingered, without any prospect of restored tranquillity. At the end of its second year of service, the British legion was disbanded, and the Spanish government and its auxiliary force parted with feelings of mutual dissatisfaction.

After the departure of the legion, the Carlists, weary of the war, entered into negotiations with the queen regent, and returned to their allegiance. Carlos was again compelled to become an exile; but defeat could not break his spirit, and he continued to declare himself the rightful heir to the Spanish crown, though rejected by the people, and disavowed by the other sovereigns of Europe. Spain, however, was too disorganized for tranquillity to be easily restored; the queen regent endeavored, with more good will than ability, to reconcile contending factions; but her efforts proved unavailing, and, wearied of her situation, she resigned the regency in the summer of 1840.

The people of England generally felt little interest in the affairs of Spain; public attention was principally directed to the state of Ireland and Canada. The great Irish questions discussed in parliament were, the reform of the corporations on the same plan that had been adopted in the reform of the English and Scotch corporations; the regulation of tithes, and the establishment of a provision for the poor; but the different views taken by the majorities in the houses of commons and lords, prevented the conclusion of any final arrangements. In Canada, the descendants of the old French settlers, for the most part bigoted and ignorant, viewed with great dissatisfaction the superiority to which the English settlers had attained, in consequence of their knowledge, spirit, and enterprise; they attributed this pre-eminence to the partiality of the government, and, instigated by designing demagogues, clamored for constitutional changes, little short of a recognition of their independence. Their demands were refused, and the deluded Canadians were persuaded to hazard a revolt. After a brief struggle, the insurgents were reduced, and since the termination of the revolt, Upper and Lower Canada have been united into one province by an act of the British legislature.

Great embarrassment was produced in the commercial world by the failure of the American banks, which rendered many leading merchants and traders unable to fulfil their engagements. The crisis was sensibly felt in England, where it greatly checked the speculations in railroads, which perhaps were beginning to be carried to a perilous extent; the manufacturing districts suffered most severely, but the pressure gradually abated, and trade began to flow in its accustomed channels. Parties were so nicely balanced in the British parliament, that no measure of importance could be arranged; a further gloom was thrown over the discussions by the increasing illness of the king, and the certainty that its termination must be fatal. William IV. died on the morning of the 20th of June, 1837, sincerely regretted by every class of his subjects. During the seven years that he swayed the sceptre, England enjoyed tranquillity both at home and abroad; it was the only reign in British history in which there was no execution for high treason, and no foreign war.

CHAPTER XII.

HISTORY OF COLONIZATION.

In order to avoid frequent interruptions in the course of the narrative, it has been deemed advisable to reserve the account of the principal European colonies for the close of the volume, and thus to bring before the reader one of the most remarkable features in modern history. The discovery of a new world gave an extraordinary impulse to emigration, and produced one of the most striking series of events in the annals of mankind. The subject naturally divides itself into two great parts—the European colonies in the western, and those in the eastern world; and to the former we shall first direct our attention.

Section I.—*The Establishment of the Spaniards in Mexico.*

Immediately after the discovery of America, the first Spanish colony was established in Hispaniola, better known by the more modern name of St. Domingo. The queen Isabella had given strict orders to protect the Indians, and had issued a proclamation prohibiting the Spaniards from compelling them to work. The natives, who considered exemption from toil as supreme felicity, resisted every attempt to induce them to labor for hire, and so many Spaniards fell victims to the diseases peculiar to the climate, that hands were wanting to work the mines or till the soil. A system of compulsory labor was therefore adopted almost by necessity, and it was soon extended, until the Indians were reduced to hopeless slavery. The mines of Hispaniola, when first discovered, were exceedingly productive, and the riches acquired by the early adventurers attracted fresh crowds of greedy but enterprising settlers to its shores. The hardships to which the Indians were subjected, rapidly decreased their numbers, and in the same proportion diminished the profits of the adventurers. It was therefore resolved to seek new settlements; the island of Puerto Rico was annexed to the Spanish dominions, and its unfortunate inhabitants were subjected to the same cruel tyranny as the natives of Hispaniola. The island of Cuba was next conquered; though it is seven hundred miles in length, and was then densely populated, such was the unwarlike character of the inhabitants, that three hundred Spaniards were sufficient for its total subjugation.

More important conquests were opened by the intrepidity of Balboa, who had founded a small settlement on the isthmus of Darien.

At length the Spaniards began to prepare an expedition for establishing their empire on the American continent. An armament was organized in Cuba, and the command intrusted to Fernando Cortez, a commander possessing great skill and bravery, but avaricious and cruel even beyond the general average of his countrymen at that period. On the 2d of April, 1519, this bold adventurer entered the harbor of St. Juan de Uloa, on the coast of Yucatan. By means of a female captive, he was enabled to open communications with the natives; and they, instead of opposing the entrance of these fatal guests into their country, assisted them in all their operations with an alacrity of which they too soon had reason to repent. The Mexicans had attained a pretty high degree of civilization; they had a regular government, a system of law, and an established priesthood; they recorded events by a species of picture-writing, not so perfect as the Egyptian system of hieroglyphics, but which, nevertheless, admitted more minuteness and particularity than is generally imagined; their architectural structures were remarkable for their strength and beauty; they had advanced so far in science as to construct a pretty accurate calendar; and they possessed considerable skill, not only in the useful, but also in the ornamental arts of life. Cortez saw that such a nation must be treated differently from the rude savages in the islands; he therefore concealed his real intentions, and merely demanded to be introduced to the sovereign of the country, the emperor Montezuma.

The Indian caziques were unwilling to admit strangers possessed of such formidable weapons as muskets and artillery into the interior of their country; and Montezuma, who was of a weak and cowardly disposition, was still more reluctant to receive a visit from strangers, of whose prowess he had received an exaggerated description. He therefore resolved to temporize, and sent ambassadors to Cortez with rich presents, declining the proposed interview. But these magnificent gifts served only to increase the rapacity of the Spaniards. Cortez resolved to temporize; he changed his camp into a permanent settlement, which subsequently grew into the city of Vera Cruz, and patiently watched from his intrenchments the course of events. He had not long continued in this position, when he received an embassy from the Zempoallans, a tribe which had been long discontented with the government of Montezuma. He immediately entered into a close alliance with these disaffected subjects, and sent an embassy to Spain to procure a ratification of his powers, and set fire to his fleet, in order that his companions, deprived of all hope of escape, should look for safety only in victory. Having completed his preparations, he marched through an unknown country to subdue a mighty empire, with a force amounting to five hundred foot, fifteen horsemen, and six pieces of artillery. His first hostile encounter was with the Tlascalans, the most warlike race in Mexico; their country was a republic, under the protection of the empire, and they fought with the fury of men animated by a love of freedom. But nothing could resist the superiority which their firearms gave the Spaniards; the Tlascalans, after several defeats, yielded themselves as vassals to the crown of Spain, and engaged to assist Cortez in all his future operations. Aided by six thousand of these new allies, he advanced to Cholula, a town of great importance, where, by Montezuma's order, he was received with open professions of friendship, while plans were secretly devised for his destruction. Cortez discovered the plot, and punished it by the massacre of six thousand of the citizens the rest were so terrified, that, at the command of the Spaniard, they returned to their usual occupations, and treated with the utmost respect the men whose hands were stained with the blood of their countrymen.

As a picture of national prosperity long since extinct, we shall here insert the description given by Cortez in his despatches to the Spanish monarch of the ancient city of Tlascala, which still exists, though much decayed: "This city is so extensive, so well worthy of admiration, that although I omit much that I could say of it, I feel assured that the little I shall say will be scarcely credited, since it is larger than Granada, and much stronger, and contains as many fine houses and a much larger population than that city did at the time of its capture; and it is much better supplied with the products of the earth, such as corn, and with fowls and game, fish from the rivers, various kinds of vegetables, and other excellent articles of food. There is in this city a market, in which every day thirty thousand people are engaged in buying and selling, besides many other merchants who are scattered about the city. The market contains a great variety of articles both of food and clothing, and all kinds of shoes for the feet; jewels of gold and silver, and precious stones, and ornaments of feathers, all as well arranged as they can possibly be found in any public squares or markets in the world. There is much earthenware of every style and a good quality, equal to the best of Spanish manufacture. Wood, coal, edible and medicinal plants, are sold in great quantities. There are houses where they wash and shave the heads as barbers, and also for baths. Finally, there is found among them a well-regulated police; the people are rational and well disposed, and altogether greatly superior to the most civilized African nation."

From Cholula, Cortez advanced toward the city of Mexico, and had almost reached its gates before the feeble Montezuma had determined whether he should receive him as a friend or as an enemy. After some hesitation, Montezuma went forth to meet Cortez, with all the magnificence of barbarous parade, and granted the Spaniards a lodging in the capital.

But notwithstanding his apparent triumph, the situation of Cortez was one of extraordinary danger and perplexity. He was in a city surrounded by a lake, the bridges and causeways of which might easily be broken; and his little band, thus cut off from all communication with its allies, must then have fallen victims to superior numbers. To avert this danger, he adopted the bold resolution of seizing Montezuma as a hostage for his safety, and he actually brought him a prisoner to the Spanish quarters. Under pretence of gratifying the monarch's curiosity to see the structure of European vessels, the Spaniards built two brigantines, and launched them on the lake, thus securing to themselves the means of retreat in case of any reverse of fortune.

The ostensible pretext for this act of violence was that a cazique, named Qualpopoca, had slain several Spaniards in the city of Nautecal or Almeira. The account which Cortez gives of the transaction is too singular to be omitted, especially as his despatches are utterly unknown in this country. It will be seen that he never gives Montezuma, or as he writes his name, Muteczuma the title of king or emperor, but speaks of him as if his right to royalty had been sacrificed from the moment that the Spaniards had landed in his country.

The offending cazique, Qualpopoca, was brought to the capital, as our readers are probably aware, and, with his followers, was burnt alive. Cortez tells this part of the story with much *naïveté:* " So they were publicly burnt in a square of the city, without creating any disturbance; and on the day of their execution, as they confessed that Muteczuma had directed them to kill the Spaniards, I caused him to be put in irons, which threw him into great consternation." All this was manifestly done merely from the motives above intimated, namely, " to subserve the interests of your majesty and our own security;" yet Cortez had some apprehension lest he might offend royal sympathies, and so, in respect of his demeanor toward Montezuma, he writes to the emperor:—

" Such was the kindness of my treatment toward him, and his own contentment with his situation, that when at different times I tempted him with the offer of his liberty, begging that he would return to his palace, he as often replied that he was well pleased with his present quarters, and did not wish to leave them, as he wanted nothing that he was accustomed to enjoy in his own palace; and that in case he went away, there would be reason to fear the importunities of the local governors, his vassals, might lead him to act against his own wishes, and in opposition to your majesty, while he desired in every possible manner to promote your majesty's service; that so far he had informed them what he desired to have done, and was well content to remain where he was; and should they wish to suggest anything to him, he could answer that he was not at liberty, and thus excuse himself from attending to them."

Cortez thus describes the original city of Mexico, which he soon afterward totally destroyed: " This great city of Temixtitan [Mexico] is situated in this salt lake, and from the main land to the denser parts of it, by whichever route one chooses to enter, the distance is two leagues. There are four avenues or entrances to the city, all of which are formed by artificial causeways, two spears' length in width. The city is as large as Seville or Cordova; its streets (I speak of the principal ones) are very wide and straight; some of them, and all the inferior ones, are half land and half water, and are navigated by canoes. * * * This city has many public squares, in which are situated the markets and other places for buying and selling. There is one square twice as large as that of the city of Salamanca, surrounded by porticoes, where are daily assembled more than sixty thousand souls, engaged in buying and selling; and where are found all kinds of merchandise that the world affords, embracing the necessaries of life, as, for instance, articles of food, as well as jewels of gold and silver, lead, brass, copper, tin, precious stones, bones, shells, snails, and feathers. There are also exposed for sale wrought and unwrought stone, bricks burnt and unburnt, timber hewn and unhewn, of different sorts. * * * Every kind of merchandise is sold in a particular street or quarter assigned to it exclusively, and thus the best order is preserved. They sell everything by number or measure; at least so far we have not observed them to sell anything by weight. There is a building in the great square that is used as an audience-house, where ten or twelve persons, who are magistrates, sit and decide all controversies that arise in the market, and order delinquents to be punished. In the same square there are other persons who go constantly about among the people, observing what is sold, and the measures used in selling; and they have been seen to break measures that were not true. This great city contains a large number of temples, or houses for their idols, very handsome edifices, which are situated in the different districts and the suburbs: in the principal ones religious persons of each particular sect are constantly residing, for whose use beside the houses containing the idols there are other convenient habitations. All these persons dress in black, and never cut or comb their hair from the time they enter the priesthood until they leave it; and all the sons of the principal inhabitants, both nobles and respectable citizens, are placed in the temples, and wear the same dress from the age of seven or eight years until they are taken out to be married; which occurs more frequently with the first-born who inherit estates than with the others. The priests are debarred from female society, nor is any woman permitted to enter the religious houses. They also abstain from eating certain kinds of food, more at some seasons of the year than others. Among these temples there is one which far surpasses all the rest, whose grandeur of architectural details no human tongue is able to describe; for within its precincts, surrounded by a lofty wall, there is room enough for a town of five hundred families. Around the interior of this enclosure there are handsome edifices, containing large halls and corridors, in which the religious persons attached to the temple reside. There are full forty towers, which are lofty and well built, the largest of which has fifty steps leading to its main body, and is higher than the tower of the principal church at Seville. The stone and wood of which they are constructed are so well wrought in every part, that nothing could be better done, for the interior of the chapels containing the idols consists of curious imagery, wrought in stone, with plaster ceilings, and woodwork carved in relief, and painted with figures of monsters and other objects. All these towers are the burial-places of the nobles, and every chapel in them is dedicated to a particular idol, to which they pay their devotions."

But danger impended over Cortez from an unexpected quarter. The governor of Cuba, anxious to share in the plunder of Mexico, of whose wealth, great as it really was, he had received very exaggerated statements, sent a new armament, under the command of Narvaez, to deprive the conqueror of the fruits of his victory. Cortez, leaving a small garrison in Mexico, marched against Narvaez, and by a series of prudent operations, not only overcame him, but induced his followers to enlist under his own banners. This reinforcement was particularly valuable at a time when the Mexicans, weary of Spanish cruelty and tyranny, had resolved to make the most desperate efforts for expelling the invaders. Scarcely had Cortez returned to Mexico, when his quarters were attacked with desperate fury; and though thousands of the assailants were slain, fresh thousands eagerly hurried forward to take their place. At length Cortez brought out Montezuma in his royal robes on the ramparts, trusting that his influence over his subjects would induce them to suspend hostilities. But the unfortunate emperor was mortally wounded by a missile flung by one of his own subjects; and Cortez, having done everything which prudence and valor could dictate, was forced to abandon the capital. The Spaniards suffered severely in this calamitous retreat; they lost their artillery, ammunition, and baggage, together with the greater part of the treasure for which they had encountered so many perils. A splendid victory at Otumba, over the Mexicans, who attempted to intercept them, restored the confidence of the Spaniards, and they reached the friendly territories of the Tlascalans in safety. Having collected some reinforcements, and by judicious arts revived the courage of his men, Cortez once more advanced toward Mexico, and, halting on the borders of the lake, he began to build some brigantines, in order to attack the city by water. While thus engaged, he succeeded in detaching many of the neighboring cities from their allegiance to the new emperor, Guatimozin; and having obtained some fresh troops from Hispaniola, he prepared for a vigorous siege by launching his brigantines on the lake. Guatimozin made a gallant resistance, and repulsed the Spaniards in an attempt to take the city by storm; but being unable to resist the slower operations of European tactics, he attempted to escape over the lake, when his canoe was intercepted by a brigantine, and the unfortunate emperor remained a prisoner. As soon as the fate of their sovereign was known, the resistance of the Mexicans ceased, and all the provinces of the empire imitated the example of the capital. Guatimozin was cruelly tortured to extort a confession of concealed treasure, and his unfortunate subjects became the slaves of their rapacious conquerors. Cortez himself was treated with gross ingratitude by his sovereign, whose dominions he had enlarged by the conquest of an empire, and he died in comparative obscurity.

The first thought of the conquerors was to propagate the Christian faith in their new dominions, not only from motives of bigotry, but in obedience to the soundest dictates of prudence. Missionaries were invited from Europe to aid in the great work of civilization; between the years 1522 and 1545, numbers of monastics came from various parts of the world to aid in the conversion of Mexico. Many practices unknown to the Roman ritual were admitted and consecrated.

It must not be omitted that the missionaries honorably exerted themselves to protect the Mexicans from the sanguinary cruelty of the Spaniards; Sahagun and Las Casas were particularly famous for their exertions in behalf of the vanquished; they obtained bulls from the pope, and edicts from the Spanish government, fully recognising the claims of the Indians to the rights of humanity, and though they failed to obtain a full measure of justice for the native Mexicans, they saved them from the wretched fate which swept away the native population in almost every other colony of Spain. In consequence of the protection thus accorded them, both by the secular and regular clergy, the attachment of the native Mexicans to the Romish religion became more ardent and passionate than that of the Spaniards themselves, and it still continues to be felt, though the country has been restored to independence.

The edicts of the Spanish monarchs in favor of the Indians were disregarded; the population began to decrease rapidly, and a new system was adopted by which oppression was reduced to an organized form, and ameliorated by being placed under the control of the government. It was determined that the native Americans should be regarded as serfs attached to the soil, and distributed into *encomiendas*, a kind of fiefs or estates established in favor of the Spanish settlers, who took the name of *Conquistadores*. Slavery, which had previously been arbitrary, was thus invested with legal forms; the Indian tribes divided into sections, some of which contained more than a hundred families, were assigned either to the soldiers who had distinguished themselves in the war of invasion, or to the civilians sent from Madrid to administer the government of the provinces. It was fortunate for the Mexicans that their masters did not erect fortified castles, like the feudal barons of the middle ages; instead of these they established *haciendas*, or large farms, which they had the wisdom to govern according to the old forms of the Mexican proprietary. There was no change or interruption in the cultivation of plants indigenous to the soil; the serf cultivated the soil according to hereditary routine, and so identified himself with his master, that he frequently took his name. There are many Indian families of the present day bearing Spanish names, whose blood has never been mingled with that of Europeans. Another fortunate circumstance contributed to the preservation of the native Mexicans; the Spanish settlers in that country did not enter into any of those mining speculations which led their brethren in Hispaniola and other islands of the Antilles to sacrifice the natives by myriads to their grasping cupidity. The *Conquistadores* had neither the capital nor the intelligence necessary for such enterprises; they contented themselves, in imitation of the natives, with washing the earth, silt, and sands, brought down from the mountains by rivers and winter torrents, to extract the grains of gold which they contained. The mines of Mexico, which have spread so much of the precious metals over the surface of the globe, were not discovered until after the conquest, and brought very trifling profits to those who first attempted their exploration. The loss of these speculators was a positive gain to humanity.

Up to the eighteenth century the condition of the Mexican peasants was very little different from that of the serfs in Poland or Russia. About that period their condition began to be sensibly ameliorated. Many families of *Conquistadores* became extinct, and the *encomiendas* were not again distributed by the government. The viceroys and the provincial councils, called *Audiencias*, paid particular attention to the interests of those Indians who were liberated by the breaking up of the *encomiendas;* they abolished every vestige of compulsory labor in the mines, requiring that this employment should be voluntary, and fairly remunerated. Several abuses, however, prevailed in the colonial administration, from the monopolies established by the agents of the Spanish governments; they conferred upon themselves the exclusive privilege of selling those articles most likely to be used by an agricultural population, and fixed whatever price they pleased upon these commodities. Having thus, by a system of force and fraud, got the Indians deeply into their debt, they established a law by which insolvent debtors became the absolute slaves of their creditors. Many edicts were issued to check these abuses, but they were not effectually remedied until after the revolution which gave independence to Mexico.

We shall now briefly state the circumstances which led to the assertion of Mexican independence. On the 8th of July, 1808, a corvette from Cadiz brought intelligence of the dethronement of the Spanish Bourbons, by Napoleon, and the transfer of the monarchy to Joseph Bonaparte. The viceroy at first published the news without a word of comment, but soon recovering from his first surprise, he issued a proclamation declaring his intention to preserve his fidelity to King Ferdinand, and exhorting the Mexican people to maintain the rights of their legitimate sovereign. It was the first time that "the people" had been named in any act of state, emanating from the colonial government, and this was among the chief causes of the extraordinary enthusiasm with which the viceroy's appeal was received. It was proposed to establish a provisional government on the model of the juntas, which had been formed by the patriots in Spain. This proposition, favorably received by the viceroy, was rejected by his council as inconsistent with the ascendency which had hitherto been enjoyed by all pure Spaniards; three months were spent in controversy, until at length the council or *audiencia* took the bold measure of arresting the viceroy, and throwing him into the prisons of the inquisition on a charge of heresy. As, however, there was some danger that the populace might rise in his favor, the *audiencia*, having first invested itself with the functions of regency, sent the governor a prisoner to Cadiz, where he was long confined in a dungeon.

The Creoles and Indians were indignant at this usurpation, and they were still more enraged by the undisguised contempt with which their claims were treated by the Spanish oligarchy. Bataller, one of the leading members of the council, was accustomed to say that "no native American should participate in the government, so long as there was a mule-driver in La Mancha, or a cobbler in Castille to represent Spanish ascendency." The juntas of Spain, though engaged in a desperate struggle for their own freedom, were obstinate in their resolution to keep the colonies in dependance, and they sent out Venegas as viceroy, with positive orders to maintain the ascendency of the Spaniards, and keep the Creoles and Indians in their own condition of degradation.

A pries of Indian descent, Hidalgo, the curate of Dolores, raised the standard of revolt; he declared to his congregation that the Europeans had formed a plot to deliver up the country to the French Jacobins; he exhorted them to take up arms to defend their liberties and their religion, and to march boldly to battle in the name of King Ferdinand and the blessed Virgin. On the 18th of September, 1810, he made himself master of San Felipe, and San Miguel el-Grande; he confiscated the property of all the Europeans, declaring that the soil of Mexico belonged of right to the Mexicans themselves. Several other cities were conquered, and in all of them the Indians and Creoles sacrificed every European without mercy, their commander seeming to wink at their excesses, which he trusted would prevent terms of peace from being offered or accepted.

Venegas, the viceroy, made the most vigorous efforts to check the progress of this rebellion; he conciliated the Creoles by investing one of their body with high military rank; he caused Hidalgo to be excommunicated by the ecclesiastical authorities, and he paraded an image of the Virgin, to which superstition attached miraculous powers, through the streets of Mexico. This last expedient caused Hidalgo to stop short in the midst of his victorious career, and at a time when he was joined by several regiments of provincial militia, and by the curate Morelos, whose abilities were equivalent to a host. Hidalgo retired from before the walls of Mexico, which could not have resisted a vigorous assault. He was overtaken and defeated by an army of Spaniards and Creoles; several of the towns which had submitted to him were recaptured, and the victors more than retaliated the sanguinary excesses of the insurgents. The royal army continued to pursue Hidalgo and his half-armed associates: a second victory completed their ruin; Hidalgo and two of his principal officers endeavoring to escape to the United States were betrayed to the Spaniards, March 21, 1811, and after a long confinement, in which they were vainly tortured to obtain a confession of the extent of the conspiracy, they were publicly executed.

The dispersed army of Hidalgo divided itself into separate bands and maintained a ruinous guerilla warfare against their oppressors Rayon and Morelos resolved to unite them once more in a grand scheme of patriotic warfare. Rayon caused a national junta to be established in the district where the Spaniards had least power; and in its name an address was sent to the viceroy requiring him to convoke a national cortes, similar to that which had been assembled in Spain, and insisting on the equality of the American and the European Spaniards in all political rights. The tone of this manifesto was equally firm and respectful, but it gave such offence to the viceroy Venegas, that he ordered it to be burned by the common hangman in the market-place of Mexico.

Morelos, who had succeeded to the influence of Hidalgo, prudently initiated his troops to habits of discipline in skirmishes and petty enterprises before venturing on any decisive engagement with the regular armies of Spain. His defence of Cuantha, where he was besieged by the royalists for several weeks, gave lustre to his very defeat. Yielding to famine, he evacuated the town, and led his army to Izucar, with the loss of only seventeen men. The barbarous cruelties perpetrated by the Spanish General Calleja in the town after the garrison had withdrawn, rendered the royalist cause so odious, that many who had hitherto supported the viceroy passed over to the ranks of the insurgents. It would be tedious to enumerate the battles, skirmishes, and sieges which filled the next two years; we must limit ourselves to saying that Morelos was continuously successful until the close of the year 1813, when he was decisively defeated by Iturbide. Thenceforward his career was one continued series of misfortunes, until, on the 5th of November, 1815, he was surprised by an overwhelming force, and made prisoner after a desperate resistance. He was carried in chains to Mexico, degraded from his clerical rank, and executed. The Mexican junta, or congress, was soon after dissolved, and the revolt became once more a confused series of partial and desultory insurrections which the Spaniards hoped to quell in detail. In 1817 the younger Mina attempted to rekindle the flames of insurrection in Mexico; but, as he refused to assert the absolute independence of the country, he did not receive such enthusiastic support as Hidalgo or Morelos. After a brilliant career, in which he displayed the most extraordinary bravery and resources of genius, he was overthrown, made prisoner, and shot as a traitor.

The insurrection in Mexico was virtually at an end, when news arrived that the army which had been assembled in Spain to restore the absolute authority of the sovereign in America, had revolted at Cadiz, proclaimed the constitution, and demanded the convocation of the cortes. The viceroy, Apodaca, was a devoted partisan of absolute power; he formed a plan for inviting Ferdinand to Mexico, and there restoring him to his despotic authority, and he employed as his chief agent Don Augustin Iturbide, who had shown himself a bitter enemy of Mexican liberty during the entire course of the preceding insurrection. Iturbide drew up a very different plan from that which Apodaca had contemplated; it asserted the civic equality of all the inhabitants of Mexico, established a constitution, proclaimed the country independent, invited Ferdinand to become its sovereign with the title of emperor, and in case of his refusal declared that the crown should be proffered to some other prince of the blood. The old Spaniards of Mexico, in a storm of mingled rage and fear, deposed Apodaca, and chose Francisco Novello viceroy in his place. This false step rendered Iturbide irresistible; the Creoles and Indians flocked to his standard; several Spanish officers, disliking the new viceroy, joined him with their regiments; and on the 27th of November, 1821, the royalist army surrendered the capital, and consented to evacuate Mexico. The treaty which the viceroy had concluded with the insurgents was annulled by the cortes of Madrid, and the effect of this imprudence was the utter ruin of the party which clung to the hope of seeing a Bourbon prince placed at the head of the new state.

The congress which assembled in Mexico seemed disposed to form a federative republic; but the partisans of Iturbide suddenly proclaimed their favorite emperor, and the deputies were constrained to ratify their choice. He did not retain the sovereignty for an entire year; he was dethroned, as he had been elevated, by the army; the congress pronounced upon him sentence of perpetual exile, but with laudable generosity granted a considerable pension for his support. Iturbide, after the lapse of rather more than a year, returned to Mexico, July 16th, 1824, in the hopes of reviving his party. He fell into the hands of the republicans, and was immediately put to death. A republic was then established; soon after the fortress of St. Juan d'Ulloa, the last possession of the government, was surrendered by capitulation, and the standard of Castile, after an ascendency of more than three hundred years, disappeared for ever from the coasts of Mexico.

The progress of the Mexican republic since the establishment of its independence has not been prosperous. Conspiracies, insurrections, and civil wars, have kept every part of the territory in misery and confusion. Texas, one of the richest provinces, has separated from the Mexican union, and established its independence. All European Spaniards have been compelled to quit the territories of the republic, which thus drove away some of the most wealthy, intelligent, and industrious of its citizens. The Mexican finances have fallen into confusion, and the army seems to be the sole ruling power in the state.

Section II.—*The Establishment of the Spaniards in Peru.*

The discovery of a passage round the South American continent into the Pacific ocean, by Magellan, and the establishment of a colony at Panama, soon after Balboa had ascertained the nature of the isthmus, incited the Spanish adventurers to undertake new conquests. Pizarro, one of the most enterprising men that ever visited the New World, having with great difficulty prepared a small armament, landed in Peru (A. D. 1531), and though at first disappointed by the barren appearance of the coast, he found so much treasure at Coague as to convince him that the accounts which Balboa had received of the riches of the country were not exaggerated. When the Spaniards first appeared in Peru, the nation was divided by a civil war between the sons of the late inca, or sovereign; Huascar, the elder, was dethroned by his brother Atahualpa, and detained in captivity, while his partisans were secretly maturing plans for his restoration. Pizarro advanced into the country with the professed design of acting as mediator, but with the perfidious purpose of seizing Atahualpa, as Cortes had the unfortunate Montezuma. He prepared for the execution of his scheme with the same deliberation, and with as little compunction, as if he had been engaged in the most honorable transaction. When the Spaniards approached the capital, the inca was easily persuaded to consent to an interview; and he visited the invaders with a barbarous magnificence, and ostentatious display of wealth, which inflamed the cupidity of the Spaniards, almost beyond the power of restraint. When Atahualpa reached the Spanish camp, he was addressed by Valverde, the chaplain to the expedition, in a long, and what must to the inca have appeared an incomprehensible discourse. The priest, after a brief notice of the mysteries of creation and redemption, proceeded to explain the doctrine of the pope's supremacy. He then dwelt upon the grant which Pope Alexander had made to the crown of Spain, and by virtue of it called upon Atahualpa at once to embrace Christianity, and acknowledge himself a vassal of the Spanish monarch. The inca, completely puzzled, demanded where Valverde had learned such wonderful things. "In this book," replied the priest, presenting the monarch with his breviary. The inca took the book, turned over the leaves, and then put it to his ear. "This tells me nothing!" he exclaimed, flinging the breviary on the ground. "Blasphemy! blasphemy!" exclaimed Valverde; "to arms, to arms, my Christian brethren! avenge the profanation of God's word by the polluted hands of infidels."

This solemn farce appears to have been preconcerted. Ere Valverde had concluded, the trumpets sounded a charge; a dreadful fire of artillery and musketry was opened on the defenceless Peruvians; and, in the midst of their surprise and consternation, they were charged by the cavalry, whose appearance to men who had never before beheld a horse, seemed something supernatural. Atahualpa was taken prisoner and conveyed to the Spanish camp, while the invaders satiated themselves with the rich spoils of the field. The unfortunate inca at tempted to procure his liberation by the payment of an enormous ransom, but Pizarro, after receiving the gold, resolved to deprive the credulous monarch of life. He was brought to trial under the most iniquitous pretences, and sentenced to be burned alive; but on his consenting to receive baptism from Valverde, his sentence was so far mitigated that he was first strangled at the stake. The Spaniards quarrelled among themselves about the division of the spoils; the Peruvians took advantage of their discord to raise formidable insurrections, and the new kingdom seemed likely to be lost almost as soon as it was gained. Pizarro himself was murdered by Almagro, the son of one of his old companions, whom he had put to death for treason, and but for the arrival of Vara de Castro, who had been sent as governor from Spain, the confusion produced by this crime would probably have been without a remedy. De Castro conquered Almagro, and by his judicious measures restored tranquillity to the distracted province. Fresh disturbances were excited by the ambition of Gonzalo Pizarro, and it was not until more than a quarter of a century after its conquest, that the royal authority was firmly established in Peru.

The government established by the Spaniards in Peru was far more iniquitous and oppressive than that of Mexico, because the Peruvian mines were, from the first moment of the conquest, almost the only objects which engaged the attention of the Spanish and the provincial governments. A horrible system of conscription was devised for working these mines; all the Indians between the ages of eighteen and fifty were enrolled in seven lists, the individuals on each list being obliged to work for six months in the mines, so that this forced labor came on the unfortunate Indians at intervals of three years and a half; four out of every five were supposed to perish annually in these deadly labors, and to add to the misery of the natives, they were not allowed to purchase the necessaries of life except from privileged dealers, who robbed them of their earnings without remorse or scruple. Toward the close of the last century two serious insurrections of the native Peruvians filled the Spaniards with terror; they were not suppressed until the rebellion had taxed the resources and power of the provincial government to the utmost, and the sanguinary massacres of all who were suspected of having joined in the revolt, left the country in a state of helplessness and exhaustion from which it had not recovered at the commencement of the revolution.

As it was impossible to gratify the rapacious cupidity of all the Spaniards who sought to share in the produce of the Peruvian mines, it became a principle of colonial policy to keep alive the spirit of adventure, by sending divisions to wrest new tracts of land from the natives, without organizing any new system of conquest. It was thus that Chili became finally annexed to the Spanish dominions; but the efforts made for its conquest were desultory and separated by long intervals, so that over a great part of the country the sovereignty of Spain was merely nominal. The colonists and natives, however, seem never to have wished for independence, until the desire of nationality was pressed upon them by the irresistible force of circumstances, and in fact their first revolutionary movements were made in the name of loyalty and obedience.

When Joseph Bonaparte was proclaimed king of Spain by Napoleon, all the Spanish colonies of South America resolved to remain faithful to the ancient dynasty. It was suspected that the European Spaniards were disposed to make terms with the French emperor, and therefore native juntas were elected to maintain the rights of Ferdinand. In September, 1810, the Chilians formed a junta in Santiago; the Spanish general of the district attempted to disperse this body; a smart skirmish ensued, and the Chilians, having obtained the victory, became desirous to establish a perpetual system of self-government. The struggle for independence in Chili and Peru resembled the Mexican war in its general outlines: at first the patriots, after gaining advantages of which they did not know how to make use, were reduced to temporary submission. But the Spanish yoke, always heavy, proved intolerable to men who had obtained a brief experience of freedom; new insurrections were raised in every quarter, the superior discipline which had previously given victory to the royalists was acquired by the revolters; several European officers joined them, the Spanish government feebly supported its defenders, and the viceroys showed themselves destitute of talent either as generals or statesmen. The independence of the Spanish colonies in South America was nearly completed in the year 1823, but the last Spanish garrison was not surrendered until the 26th of February, 1826, when Rodil, the only royalist leader who had exhibited courage, fidelity, and talent, surrendered the citadel of Callao to the patriots.

Before the revolution the provinces of upper Peru formed part of the viceroyalty of Buenos Ayres; but as the manners, habits, and even the language of the Peruvians, differed materially from those of the people on the Rio de la Plata, the latter, after forming themselves into the Argentine republic, left their neighbors free to pursue any course they pleased. A general assembly of the Peruvian provinces solemnly proclaimed that upper Peru should henceforth form an independent nation, that it should be named Bolivia in honor of Bolivar, the chief agent in its liberation, and that the rights of person and property should form the basis of its republican constitution. A million of dollars was voted to Bolivar as a tribute of national gratitude, but that chivalrous general refused to receive the money, and requested that it should be expended in purchasing the freedom of the few negroes who still remained slaves in Bolivia.

In lower Peru the Bolivian constitution was far from being so popular as it had been in the upper provinces. It was indeed at first accepted, and Bolivar chosen president, but when he went to suppress an insurrection in Columbia, advantage was taken of his absence to set aside the system he had established. Since that period Columbia, Bolivia, and Peru, have suffered severely from intestine wars and civil commotions, which have greatly deteriorated the vast natural resources of these states. Bolivia has indeed regained tranquillity, and its rulers appear desirous to extend its commerce and encourage those branches of industry most likely to benefit the community. It is the only one of the new republics in which the finances are in a wholesome condition; its revenues are not only sufficient for the necessary expenses of the state, but there is a considerable surplus, which is wisely expended on the maintenance and construction of roads, and on facilitating the means of communication internally among the inhabitants themselves and externally with strangers.

Previous to the expeditions of Cortez and Pizarro, Florida had been discovered by Juan Ponce de Leon. Its verdant forests and magnificent flowering aloes seemed so inviting, that a colony was formed with little difficulty. But the Indians of Florida were the most warlike of the native races in America, and they severely harassed the settlers. Soto, a companion of Pizarro, led an expedition into the interior, where he discovered the Mississippi. He died on the banks of the river, and his followers, anxious to conceal his death from the Indians, sank his body in the stream. A plan was formed by the leaders of the French Huguenots for emigrating to Florida, and an exploring party was sent out, but the jealousy of Spain was roused; the adventurers were closely pursued, made prisoners, and put to death. Florida remained subject to Spain until the year 1818, when, in consequence of the depredations of the Indians, which the governors pleaded their inability to restrain, the Americans, under General Jackson, entered the province and annexed it to the United States. The Spanish government remonstrated, but had not the means of obtaining redress; and it finally acceded to the cession (A. D. 1821).

Section III.—*Portuguese Colonies in South America.*

Brazil was accidentally discovered by a Portuguese admiral bound to the East Indies, in the year 1501, but he did not ascertain whether it was an island or part of the continent, a subject which long remained a matter of doubt. No effort was made to colonize the country for nearly half a century; this apparent neglect arose from the reluctance of the Portuguese to interfere with the pretensions of the court of Spain, for the papal grant of newly-discovered countries to the Spanish monarch was held by the court of Madrid to include the whole American continent. At length the king of Portugal, envious of the wealth acquired by the Spaniards, sent out a small body of colonists, who founded St. Salvador (A. D. 1549). These settlers reported that the native Brazilians were far lower in the scale of civilization than the Mexicans or Peruvians; they were divided into a number of petty tribes or states, constantly at war with each other, and the invaders, though few in number, were easily able to subdue the Indian tribes in detail, by fomenting their animosities and cautiously holding the balance between their contending interests. This course of policy was rendered necessary by the personal bravery of the native Brazilians; though ignorant of discipline and unable to act in masses, they displayed great individual courage in battle; they were skilful in the use of bows, darts, wooden clubs, and shields, and frequently were victorious in petty skirmishes. But they were unable to resist European tactics and European policy, and hence they were finally reduced under the yoke, with which they soon appeared to be contented. The facility with which the Portuguese made themselves masters of this rich territory excited the cupidity of other powers, and they were successively attacked by the Spaniards, the French, and the Dutch. The latter were the most dangerous enemies, they had just effected their deliverance from the iron despotism of Spain, under which the Portuguese themselves groaned at the period, and hence they had such a party in the country that their conquest would have been certain had they not alienated their supporters by attempting to establish odious monopolies. From the time of the expulsion of the Dutch, the Portuguese made it their object to keep everything connected with Brazil a profound secret, and little was known of the country until it asserted its independence.

For more than three centuries one of the most beautiful and fertile regions of the globe was thus, by the policy of Portugal, restricted from all intercourse and commerce with the other nations of Europe, and even the residence or admission of foreigners was equally prohibited. The vessels of the allies of the mother-country were occasionally permitted to anchor in its ports, but neither passengers nor crew were allowed to land excepting under the superintendence of a guard of soldiers.

Previously to the year 1808, though the viceroy resident in Rio de Janeiro was nominally the highest functionary of the government, yet this personage was, in reality, invested with but little political power except in the province of Rio, where alone he acted as captain-general, the virtual administration of the colony being intrusted chiefly to similar officers, one of whom was appointed to each province. They were nominated for three years only, and received their instructions from the court of Lisbon, to which they were compelled to render an account of their proceedings. They were not only prohibited from marrying within the sphere of their jurisdiction, but also from the transaction of any commercial pursuits, as well as from accepting any present or emolument, in addition to the stipend allotted them by the government. For the management and application of the public finances bodies were appointed denominated "Juntas de Fazenda," Juntas of Finance; of which the captains-general of the respective provinces were the presidents.

The highest functions of the judicial power were confided to a court of appeal composed of disembargadores, or chief judges, to whom succeeded the onvidores, or itinerant judges, who were under the obligation of making an annual circuit to the districts committed to their charge, for the purpose of passing judgment in criminal cases. For the adjudication of certain cases, judges termed "Juizes de Fora," who were selected from among such as had taken their degree in Coimbra as bachelors of law, were appointed, who, as well as the officers of the higher tribunals, were all nominated by the court of Portugal. In the less populous and inferior districts, "Juizes ordinarios," with the same attributes as the "Juizes de fora," were also occasionally selected by the votes of individuals denominated "Bous de pivo," the qualification for which title was to have held office in the municipalities. From the sentence of these "Juizes" appeal could be made to the court of disembargadores in Rio, and from this again, ultimately, to the "Disembargo do Baco" in Lisbon. Unless, however, the appellant were possessed either of great interest at court, or, in default of it, could bribe higher than his antagonist, these final appeals were seldom of any real utility.

The statutes on which the decisions of the judicial power were founded, was the Portuguese code framed during the reigns of the two Philips, and entitled "Ordnacoens do Reino," to which were appended all the "Cartas de Lei" and decrees issued since the accession of the house of Braganza, forming altogether about nine volumes.

Though in ordinary cases the decision of both civil and criminal causes was left exclusively to the judicial authorities, the mandate of the captains general was at any time sufficient either to suspend or set aside the ordinary operation of the law.

The municipalities were close corporations, formed on the model of those of Portugal; where those bodies had formerly been intrusted with the nomination of deputies to the supreme cortes: though this as well as many other important privileges, had latterly fallen into desuetude.

On occasions of public ceremony the national banner was still carried in their processions, and they were still recognised, in appearance at least, as the representatives of the people. In Brazil also their power was once considerable, and instances have occurred of the deposition of the captains general by the municipalities, and of this exercise of authority having been sanctioned by the entire approbation of the government of Lisbon, though toward the end of the last century their powers had been restricted almost exclusively to the improvement of roads, the construction of bridges, the control of the markets, and other objects of minor importance. Their executive officers, who were entitled "Juizes Almotaceis" were nominated by the municipalities themselves every three months, and were charged with the power of exacting fines and enforcing imprisonment according to certain established regulations.

The regular troops were recruited according to the direction, and placed entirely at the disposition of the captains-general, but the officers were nominated by the court of Lisbon. The militia, or troops of the second line, were enlisted by the officers of each respective corps, and the officers themselves were also appointed in Lisbon, at the proposition of the captains-general. Though serving gratuitously, this latter force was often employed in very laborious and odious services, and its members as well as the regular troops were amenable to martial law in all matters relative to their military duty.

In addition to the preceding were the Ordenanças, or troops of the third line, who by the regulations of their institution ought to have been composed exclusively of such individuals as were incapacitated by physical defects or otherwise from serving in the militia. Their duty was to defend the country in cases of emergency, but this service was merely nominal, and, by a perversion of the real objects of the institution, it became customary for all possessed of sufficient patronage to obtain a post in the Ordenanças for the express object of avoiding enrolment in the militia. The fidalgos, or Portuguese noblemen of the first rank, were exempt from personal service altogether.

The orders of knighthood were those of Santo Iago, San Bento de Aviz, and the order of Christ, of all of which the sovereigns of Portugal were the grand masters and perpetual administrators. Among the privileges appertaining to the office of grand master of the order of Christ, a pontifical bull had conferred that of an entire ecclesiastical jurisdiction over ultra-marine conquests, and by virtue of this title, the crown of Portugal shortly after the discovery of Brazil appropriated to its own use all the tithes levied in the country; with however a proviso binding the monarch to provide for the celebration of public worship and to pay a stipulated sum for the adequate maintenance of the various clergy. By the same authority the presentation of ecclesiastial benefices was also constituted one of the exclusive privileges of royalty, though, at the proposition of the bishops, with an injunction that the natives of the respective captaincies, and more especially the descendants of the ancient nobility who were among the first emigrants to Brazil, should on all occasions be preferred, the right of presentation still being restricted to the sovereign.

The stipulations made for the maintenance of the established religion, and the due support of the clergy, were nevertheless but very imperfectly complied with.

Many priests came to be dependant on the mere fees of their office for subsistence, and the stipend paid to the highest dignitaries of the church was but trifling when compared with what would have accrued to them, had they been allowed to retain possession of their tithes. The revenue of the archbishop of Bahia, the head functionary of the Brazilian church, never amounted to more than ten contos of rees per annum, at par, 2,812*l.* 10*s.* sterling; nor was the bishopric of Rio de Janeiro, embracing within its limits, the provinces of Rio Grande, Espirito Santo, and Santa Catherine, ever worth to its incumbent more than six contos of rees, or, 1,687*l.* 10*s.* per annum. These peculiarities in the condition of the clergy are perhaps worthy of more particular note than the circumstances of any other class, since they will be found to have exercised a most important influence during the period of the subsequent revolution.

The jealousy of the Portuguese government constantly led them to dread the growth of every power or corporation which might hereafter militate against the exercise of its authority; and on this account not only were the civil and ecclesiastical functionaries brought more immediately under control than in the mother-country, but even the increase of capitalists and large proprietors was systematically prevented. The entailment of landed property could be effected only by virtue of an express permission from the sovereign; and all manufactures, excepting the preparation of sugar, were most rigidly prohibited.

During the year 1769 a conspiracy was formed by a few influential individuals in Villa Rica, not so much, however, with the design of proclaiming an independent republic, as from a desire to ascertain what co-operation they were likely to meet with in case that step should subsequently be adopted. From a diminution in the product of the coal-mines in this district, several of the individuals working them were in considerable arrear for taxes. These arrears the government in Lisbon had ordered to be paid up, with but little regard to the practicability of the demand. Much irritation had in consequence been excited, and a military officer of the name of Joaquim Jozé da Silva Xavier, commonly termed "Tiradentes," or the Tooth-drawer, was sent off for the purpose of ascertaining the disposition of the inhabitants of Rio Janeiro. Here the imprudence of Tiradentes led to an immediate discovery of the association, the members of which were forthwith arrested. Altogether, however, their numbers did not amount to forty, yet, though little could be urged in evidence against them, they were all sentenced to death, banishment, or the galleys, according to the different degrees of their supposed guilt.

These sentences were nevertheless mitigated in favor of all, except the unfortunate Tiradentes, who, though but an instrument in the hands of others, was, after the lapse of two years, condemned to be hanged, decapitated, and quartered; by the same sentence it was, among other ignominious provisions, enacted that his head should be exposed in the public square in Villa Rica, his house razed to the ground, and his children and grandchildren declared infamous. A conspiracy, originating exclusively among the people of color, was also organized in Bahia during the year 1801, but like the former, it was discovered before any attempt had been made to put it into execution. The communication between the different provinces was neither sufficient to facilitate a general revolt, nor indeed were the free population disposed to it. Their condition, as contrasted with that which is the result of European civilization, was wretched; yet the tyranny exercised over them was of a negative rather than of a positive character. Their wants were few, and from the almost total absence of nobility, large proprietors, or powerful ecclesiastical dignitaries, there was an equality throughout their entire association which prevented their being sensible of any undue privations. Could they have been exempted from all extraneous impulse, ages might have rolled away, and Brazil have been known to Europe, only as the colossal, yet submissive, and unaspiring dependancy of Portugal. But events were occurring elsewhere, about the close of the eighteenth century, the effects of which were fated to extend their influence to the very ends of the earth. The young republic of France emerged from amid the storms of the revolution, and the crowned heads of all the surrounding states entered into one mighty coalition to crush the intruder. In this attempt their efforts were partially successful, yet their aggressive policy was, ere long, followed up by a fearful and overwhelming counteraction. They raised up a spirit which they afterward in vain attempted to exorcise. They called forth a conqueror who for a while scattered all their armaments before him, and who burst and riveted at will the manacles of many nations. The results of his victories were not bounded by the hemisphere wherein they were achieved. They gave birth to the immediate independence of all the Spanish colonies in South America, and by compelling the royal family of Portugal to seek refuge in Brazil, they created as it were a new era in her history.

The royal family of Portugal sailed from Lisbon under the escort of a British squadron, and reached Rio Janeiro on the 7th of March, 1808. As Portugal was occupied by a French army, it would have been absurd to maintain the ancient monopoly of trade, and the ports of Brazil were thrown open to foreigners of every nation by a royal decree. As the dowager-queen of Portugal was in a state of mental imbecility, the government was administered by her son, Don John, with the title of regent; he introduced several great improvements into the government; Brazil was no longer treated as a colony it was raised to the dignity of a nation, and the progress of amelioration in its financial and commercial condition was unusually rapid.

The first cause of discontent was the preference which the court naturally showed for officers of Portuguese birth; and this jealousy was increased by the contempt with which the Europeans treated every one of Brazilian birth. Indeed, a Portuguese general formally proposed that all Brazilians should be declared incompetent to hold a higher rank than that of captain, and though no such law was formally enacted, its spirit was acted upon in every department of the administration. Dissatisfaction was silent, but it was deeply felt and rapidly extending, when in October, 1820, intelligence arrived of the revolt in Portugal in favor of a constitutional government. On the 26th of February, 1821, the king was compelled to proclaim the constitution in Rio de Janeiro, and to promise that he would convoke a Brazilian cortes.

In the meantime the cortes at Lisbon began to form projects for securing to Portugal its ancient monopoly of Brazilian commerce, and to render its provinces once more colonies dependant on the mother-country. These projects were eagerly supported by the Portuguese in Brazil, who trusted to revive their ancient ascendency over the colonists and natives. Violent disputes, frequently ending in bloodshed, arose between the Portuguese and the Brazilians; Don John, who had assumed the title of king on his mother's death, returned to Lisbon, leaving his son, Don Pedro, at the head of the Brazilian government, which he clearly saw would not long remain dependant on Portugal. The cortes of Lisbon assumed the right of legislating for the colonies without consulting their inclinations; they abolished the tribunals which had been created in Rio Janeiro, and passed a decree recalling Don Pedro to Europe. These decrees were resisted by the Brazilians, and after some delay they took the decisive step of declaring their independence, and establishing a constitutional monarchy under Don Pedro as emperor.

We have elsewhere noticed the revolution in which Pedro was dethroned and a regency established in the name of his son. Since that period Brazil has enjoyed more tranquillity than any of the other South American states, and but for the difficulties which arise from the continuance of negro slavery in the country, it would seem to have every fair prospect of advancing rapidly in social prosperity and political importance.

Paraguay can not with propriety be reckoned among the colonies either of Spain or Portugal, though both governments have claimed it as their own. It was first brought under European control by the jesuit missionaries, who professed a nominal obedience to the crown of Spain. Their success in making converts was greater than that of their brethren in any other quarter of the globe; they instructed the Indians who embraced Christianity in agriculture and the arts of social life; the surrounding tribes were not slow in perceiving the advantages which their countrymen had derived from the change, and they came voluntarily to seek instruction. In a very short time the jesuits became complete masters of the country; in order to perpetuate their dominion, they carefully excluded all foreigners from Paraguay, and infused into the minds of the natives a suspicious jealousy, or rather hatred of foreigners, which has never since been eradicated.

When the order of the jesuits was abolished, Paraguay was all but left to itself, and its name was scarcely mentioned in Europe, until it took a share in the revolutionary movement which established so many new states in South America. Doctor Francia headed the revolution of Paraguay, and obtained absolute power for himself, with the title of dictator. He established as rigid a system for excluding foreigners as the jesuits themselves, and his successors appear to continue the same course of policy.

Section IV.—*The English in America.*

England had shared in the ardor for discovery which the successful enterprise of Columbus diffused throughout Europe. Newfoundland was visited by Sebastian Cabot, in the reign of Henry VII.; and two unsuccessful voyages were made to the southern seas, by the same navigator, in the reign of Henry VIII. But the object which long continued to be the favorite one of the English adventurers, was the discovery of a passage through the northern seas to India and China. Sir Hugh Willoughby, and Richard Chancellor, hoped that this might be attained by sailing to the northeast; the latter reached Archangel, a port then unknown in western Europe, and though he failed in his principal object, he laid the foundation of an active commerce between Great Britain and Russia. The company of Merchant Adventurers, incorporated by Edward VI., were indefatigable in their efforts to open new courses of trade, by encouraging maritime and inland discovery; while their navigators penetrated to Nova Zembla and the river Oby, several of their factors accompanied some Russian caravans into Persia, by the route of Astrachan and the Caspian sea; and the accounts which they published on their return, first gave British merchants accurate intelligence concerning the state of the remote regions of the east. These enterprises were renewed under the reign of Elizabeth; a commercial treaty was concluded with the shah of Persia, and such information obtained respecting India, as greatly increased the national ardor for opening a communication with that country by sea. But every effort to discover a northwest or northeast passage failed; Martin Frobisher, like every navigator from his days to those of Sir John Ross, found the seas blockaded with fields of ice, through which no opening could be made. This disappointment might have damped the spirit of the English, but for the successful enterprise of Sir Francis Drake, who circumnavigated the globe with a small squadron, and returned home with an account of many important discoveries in the Pacific ocean. War with Spain rendered this information peculiarly important; and the English resolved to attack their enemies through their colonies, and thus cut off the sources of the wealth which rendered Philip II. formidable to Europe.

In the sketch of the history of the United States will be found an account of the colonies planted by the English within the limits of that country.

Canada was the first colony established by the French in Canada but the early settlers suffered so many misfortunes, that the country was several times on the point of being abandoned. It began, however, to prosper after the foundation of Quebec, by Champlain (A. D. 1608), and the formation of a new colony at Montreal. The contests of the French with the Iroquois and the Hurons were less perilous than those of the New Englanders with the Pequods and Narragansets, but they were less ably conducted, and more injurious to the prosperity of the colony.

At a much later period, the French colonized Louisiana (A. D. 1686), with the hope of securing the fertile countries watered by the Mississippi. The settlement was more valued by the government than Canada, because it was supposed to contain mines of gold, and for the same reason possession of it was equally coveted by the English and the Spaniards. Having two colonies, one at the northern and one at the southern extremity of the British settlements, the French government prepared to connect them by a chain of forts which would have completely hemmed in the English. A furious war ensued between the two nations in the back woods, which ended in the complete overthrow of the French. Canada and Louisiana were ceded to England by the peace of 1763; but the latter is now joined to the United States, while the former still continues under British government. In the history of the other British American colonies there is nothing of sufficient importance to deserve a place in this summary. The most important of them now form a great republic, which must for the future occupy a conspicuous position in Modern History; and among the best guides to a correct estimate of their future career, is a knowledge of the circumstances attending their foundation.

SECTION V.—*Colonization of the West Indies.*

WE have already mentioned the settlements of the Spaniards in Hispaniola, Puerto Rico, and Cuba, and shall now briefly give a sketch of the colonization of the other principal islands. Barbadoes, one of the earliest English settlements, was totally uninhabited when the English took possession of it (A. D. 1623). Its prosperity first began to attract notice when some of the Dutch, who were expelled from Brazil by the Portuguese, introduced the manufacture of sugar, and the cultivation of the cane, from which that useful article is extracted. Negroes were not imported as slaves until about the year 1630; previously to which time the planters are said to have been frequently guilty of kidnapping the Caribs. The negroes multiplied so fast, that they frequently conspired to massacre all the white inhabitants, and take possession of the island, but their plots were discovered and punished with remorseless severity.

St. Lucia was first settled by the English (A. D. 1637), but the colonists were soon massacred by the Caribs, after which it was seized by the French, who are said to have instigated the revolt of the native tribes. The island frequently changed masters in the wars between France and England, but it now belongs to the latter power. St. Vincent and the Grenadine islands were similarly contested, and now belong to England.

Martinico and Guadaloupe were colonized by the French, in the beginning of the seventeenth century. Their prosperity received very severe checks in the frequent wars between France and England. At the late treaty of peace they were restored to France. The other Caribbee islands are possessed by the Dutch, the Danes, the Swedes, and the English, but the largest share belongs to the English. Antigua is, perhaps, the most flourishing of these islands, but there is nothing remarkable in its history.

Tobago was colonized by the Dutch, conjointly with the Courlanders (A. D. 1632). It was wrested from them by the French, who subsequently ceded it to the English (A. D. 1737).

Trinidad is a large and fertile island on the coast of South America, remarkable for a lake of asphaltum, or mineral pitch. It was early colonized by Spain, but was captured by the English in 1797, and is still retained by them. It is one of the very few of these islands which contains any portion of its ancient population.

The Bahama islands, though discovered by Columbus, were completely neglected until they were accidentally visited by an Englishman named Sayle (A. D. 1667), who was driven to seek shelter among them by stress of weather. The account which he gave of their climate and productions, on his return home, induced some spirited adventurers to combine for their colonization. The early settlers suffered very severely from hurricanes and the hostility of the Spaniards, but they surmounted these difficulties, and laid the foundation of communities which are now flourishing and prosperous.

The Bermudas, or Summer islands, were discovered but never colonized by the Spaniards. An Englishman named May was shipwrecked on one of them; he and his companions built a vessel of the native cedar, and returned to Europe, where they published a very exaggerated account of the beauty and fertility of these islands, which gave rise to many poetic fictions. A colony was planted on St. George's island, by the Virginia company, but it narrowly escaped destruction in its infancy from a very singular visitation. Some rats, imported in European vessels, multiplied so prodigiously, that they covered the ground and built nests in the trees. Their devastations were continued during five years, when they suddenly disappeared, but from what cause is uncertain. Since that period the prosperity of these islands has been uninterrupted; and of late years vast works for the purpose of establishing here a naval arsenal have been in progress, and are now near completion.

Jamaica was discovered by Columbus, and soon after colonized by the Spaniards, who massacred the greater part of the native inhabitants. As there were no mines in the island, it was neglected by the Spaniards, and was easily wrested from them by a British armament, under the command of Penn and Venables, during the protectorate of Cromwell. The position of Jamaica afforded many facilities for attacking the Spanish settlements, and it was therefore the great rendezvous of the formidable combination of pirates called the bucaniers. This confraternity was composed of adventurers from various nations, and the Spanish ships and colonies were their chief objects of attack. They were not, however, very scrupulous in ascertaining to what nation any richly-laden vessel belonged; and, to prevent any discovery of their crimes, they generally massacred the crews. Morgan was their most noted leader; he conquered Panama, and several other rich towns belonging to the crown of Spain; and having by his continued successes gained the command of a large force, appears to have meditated the establishment of an independent sovereignty. Subsequently he abandoned his piracies, submitted to the English government, and received the honor of knighthood. The bucaniers being no longer protected in Jamaica, removed to the French settlement in Hispaniola, and long continued to be the terror of the American seas. Jamaica has often been harassed by negro insurrections, but since the mountains have been opened by roads, the insurgents, deprived of any place of shelter, have found themselves unable to make considerable stand.

To the north of the river Amazon, on the eastern coast of South America, lies a vast level tract, known by the general name of Guiana, possessed by the Portuguese, the French, Dutch, and English. The land is exuberantly fertile, but the climate unhealthy. Formerly the Dutch settlements were the most considerable, but the chief of them were captured in 1797 by the English, and are now in their possession. This is the only portion which bears the appearance of regular colonization, the other tracts being either held by the natives, or mainly used by the European rulers as penal settlements.

Hispaniola, or St. Domingo, after having been long an object of contention between the French, Spaniards, and English, is now an independent negro state, and has resumed its old native name of Hayti.

Section VI.—*The Portuguese in India.*

The colonies we have just described owe their origin to the discoveries of Columbus; we must now direct our attention to those in the opposite division of the globe, which were consequent on the discovery of a passage round the Cape of Good Hope, by Vasco de Gama. The first enterprises of the Portuguese, when a way was opened for them to Hindústan, were limited to securing their commerce; but under the guidance of the illustrious Albuquerque, they procured a grant of ground from one of the native sovereigns, and founded a strong fortress. The Mohammedans, who had hitherto engrossed the entire commerce of India, formed a league to expel the intruders, in which they were encouraged by the Venetians, who purchased Indian spices and other goods from the Arabs, with which they supplied the principal markets of Europe. This enterprise was defeated, and soon after Don Alphonzo Albuquerque laid the foundation of the future supremacy of the Portuguese by reducing Goa, which afterward became the seat of government, and was also erected into an archbishop's see by the pope. This was the first commencement of territorial acquisition by European powers in India, a system strongly deprecated by Vasco de Gama, and which it is impossible to defend on any principles of national justice. Albuquerque defended himself by declaring that it would be impossible for Portugal to command the trade unless it shared in the empire of India, a pretext whose obvious weakness it is not necessary to expose. Albuquerque also subdued the city of Malacca, and the island of Ormuz, in the Persisn gulf. The efforts of his successors were principally directed to the maintenance of Albuquerque's acquisitions, and to checking the progress of the Turks, who, after the conquest of Egypt, made several attempts to establish themselves on the coast of Malabar. Had they succeeded, it is probable that the Christians would never have occupied India, for the Mussulmans spread over the peninsula would have united to support a power equally favorable to their religious prejudices and their temporal interests. In about sixty years the Portuguese had established an empire in the east, whose extent and power were truly wonderful. On one side, their authority extended as far as the utmost limits of the coast of Persia, and over all the islands in the Persian gulf; some of the Arabian princes were their tributaries, others their allies, and through the whole Arabian peninsula none dared to confess themselves their enemies. In the Red sea, they were the only power that commanded respect, and they had considerable influence over the emperor of Abyssinia and the rulers of eastern Africa. They possessed the whole coast of Malabar, from Cape Ramoz to Cape Comorin; they were masters also of the Coromandel coast, the bay of Bengal, the city, fortress, and peninsula of Malacca. The potent islands of Ceylon, Sumatra, and Java, paid them tribute, as did the Moluccas; and they had obtained a settlement in China (Macao), and a free trade with the islands of Japan.

The ruin of this empire arose chiefly from the union of Portugal with Spain (A. D. 1580). Immediately after that event, Philip II. issued an edict, prohibiting the Dutch from trading with Lisbon, and thus compelled them to seek for the spices and wares of India in other quarters. The enterprising republicans were then hardy and necessitous, and had everything to gain and nothing to lose; the Portuguese, on the other hand, were divided in their counsels, depraved in their manners, and detested by their subjects and neighbors. The Dutch first established themselves in some distant islands, whence, being joined by new settlers from home, partly by force of arms and partly by taking advantage of the errors committed by the Portuguese, they finally supplanted them everywhere, and stripped them of their dominions in far less time than they had acquired them.

The most remarkable of the Portuguese settlements was the island of Ormuz. It is nothing more than a salt and barren rock in the Persian gulf, destitute of water, save where rain, which rarely falls, is collected in natural or artificial cavities; but its commodious situation rendered it the most flourishing commercial mart in the eastern seas. Its roadstead was frequented by shipping from all parts of the Indies, from the coasts of Africa, Egypt, and Arabia, while it possessed an extensive caravan trade with the interior of Asia, through the opposite ports of Persia. The wealth, the splendor, and the concourse of traders at Ormuz, during its flourishing condition, gave the world a memorable example of the almost omnipotent power of commerce: in the trading seasons, which lasted from January to March, and from the end of August to the beginning of November, not only was there an unparalleled activity of traffic, but a display of luxury and magnificence which seemed to realize the extravagances of fiction. The salt dust of the streets was concealed and kept down by neat mats and rich carpets; canvass awnings were extended from the roofs of the houses to exclude the scorching rays of the sun; the rooms next the street were opened like shops, adorned with Indian cabinets and piles of porcelain, intermixed with odoriferous dwarf trees and shrubs, set in gilded vases, elegantly adorned with figures. Camels laden with water-skins stood at the corner of every street, while the richest wines of Persia, the most costly perfumes and the choicest delicacies of Asia, were poured forth in lavish profusion. The Portuguese, in the insolence of prosperity, provoked the hostility of Shah Abbas, the most powerful of the Persian monarchs, and quarrelled with the English, just as they were beginning to obtain consideration in the east. A league was formed between Shah Abbas and the English; their united forces assailed Ormuz (A. D. 1622); it was taken with little difficulty, and the value of its plunder was estimated at two millions. Thenceforward the trade of Ormuz rapidly declined: its merchants transferred their capital and enterprise to other quarters, the very materials of its splendid edifices were taken away by the Dutch ships as ballast, and it soon relapsed into its original condition of a barren and desolate rock. Scarcely the smallest remains are now left to vindicate the records of history, or to prove that this was once the flourishing capital of extensive commerce, and the principal magazine of the east.

Section VII.—*The Spaniards in the East Indies.*

We have before stated that the object of the first voyage of Columbus was to discover a western passage to the East Indies, and this project was not forgotten by the Spaniards, even after a new world had been opened to their ambition. After the discovery of the passage round the extremity of South America by Magellan, they prepared to occupy some of the Moluccas, but were prevented by the papal division of newly-discovered countries between them and the Portuguese. But when Portugal was united to Spain, under Philip II., Lopez de Legaspi resolved to form a settlement in a valuable cluster of these islands, which he called the Philippines, in honor of his sovereign. The city of Manilla was speedily built and fortified; scarcely were its defences complete, when it was attacked by the native islanders, instigated by the Chinese, who appear to have been, at some remote period, masters of the country. With some difficulty the insurrection was suppressed; but more formidable rivals soon appeared: the Dutch occupied the most valuable of the Moluccas, and the Spanish court seriously contemplated the abandonment of the Philippine islands. But though these settlements have been frequently attacked both by the Dutch and English, they have been preserved to the crown of Spain, and are now almost the only remnant of the extensive colonial empire once possessed by that monarchy.

Section VIII.—*The Dutch in the East Indies.*

It was the intolerable cruelty of the Spanish government that drove the Dutch to revolt; and the incurable bigotry of Philip II. prevented the insurgents from ever seeking an accommodation. But the same sanguinary and short-sighted policy laid the foundation of the future prosperity of Holland, and enabled the Dutch to attain, in a very short period, an unrivalled ascendency in commerce. To check the growing spirit of freedom in the Netherlands, the Spaniards destroyed the trade of Antwerp, discouraged every effort made for its restoration, and thus drove its merchants to increase the establishments and the trade of Amsterdam. Desirous of humbling the Portuguese, Philip's ministers laid the most vexatious restraints on the commerce of Lisbon, and thus compelled the Dutch, whose subsistence almost wholly depended on the carrying-trade, to seek out means for the direct importation of Indian commodities. It was still hoped that a northeast passage to the Indian seas might be discovered, and three fruitless expeditions were sent out on this hopeless inquiry. In the meantime, Cornelius Houtman, who had been made prisoner by the Spaniards at Lisbon, obtained such information from the Portuguese respecting the course of their voyages round the cape of Good Hope, that on his escape to Amsterdam, he induced some of the leading merchants to form a company for sending him out with an expedition; and a fleet, well provided, sailed from the Texel (A. D. 1595). The Spaniards first attempted to defeat the enterprises of the Dutch by main force, but being soon convinced of their inferiority at sea to the hardy republicans, they sent emissaries to the principal eastern sovereigns, describing the new adventurers as pirates. But the Dutch admiral, Heemskirk, having captured a rich Portuguese vessel, on her way from Macao, treated his prisoners with so much generosity, that letters of thanks were addressed to him from the principal Spanish authorities in the east; these letters he produced in every port at which he touched, and thus satisfactorily refuted the calumnies which had been heaped upon his nation. A company was soon incorporated in Holland for managing the Indian trade; and the rest of the subjects of the United Provinces were prohibited from trading with Asia, either by the cape of Good Hope or Cape Horn. They first occupied the Moluccas, or Spice islands, from which they were driven by the Spaniards, but soon retrieved their losses. Ere long, the Dutch and English East India companies, excited by mutual jealousy, began to assail each other's possessions. The island of Java was the chief object of their mutual ambition; after a long struggle, the Dutch prevailed, and immediately secured their acquisition by building the city of Batavia. Soon afterward, all the English merchants resident at Amboyna were massacred, and by this act of treachery the Dutch succeeded in securing for a long time the monopoly of the spice trade. They also wrested the Japanese trade from the Portuguese, and continue even now to be the only Europeans admitted to trade with the empire of Japan.

The next great object of the Dutch was to gain possession of the island of Ceylon, from which they not only expelled the Portuguese, but reduced the native princes under their dominion, and thus gained the monopoly of the cinnamon trade. They long kept possession of this valuable island, but during the wars of the French revolution it was wrested from them by the English, under whose power it still continues.

The influence of the jesuits at the court of Pekin baffled all the efforts of the Dutch to open a trade with the Chinese empire; but they succeeded in establishing a flourishing settlement on the island of Formosa, which opened to them a lucrative traffic with the Indo-Chinese nations. But soon after the conquest of China by the Mantchew Tartars, the Formosans, joined by a large army from China, besieged the Dutch settlement and compelled the garrison to surrender. Since that period, Formosa has been annexed to the empire of China, and is no longer visited by Europeans.

The Dutch adopted a more exclusive system of policy than the Spaniards or Portuguese, and this was the principal cause of the ruin of the empire they had acquired. Their harsh conduct to the natives produced frequent civil wars or insurrections, which greatly weakened their settlements. In Java especially, their dominion was maintained only by an enormous expenditure of blood and treasure; and as other European nations began gradually to obtain a share in the spice trade, the Dutch East India company found the profits of its monopoly rapidly diminishing. During the wars of the French revolution, most of the Dutch colonies were occupied by the English, but some of them were restored at the general peace. England, however, kept the two of greatest importance, the cape of Good Hope and the island of Ceylon; but Holland still possesses the island of Java, and the monopoly of the trade with Japan.

Section IX.—*The Danes in the East Indies.*

An association was formed at Copenhagen for opening a trade with the East Indies (A. D. 1612), in consequence of the riches which so lucrative a branch of commerce seemed to have brought into the neighboring nations. A small expedition was sent out to the Coromandel coast, where the adventurers were hospitably received by the rajah of Tanjore, from whom they received permission to establish a settlement at Tranquebar. Many circumstances contributed to check the prosperity of the Danish East India company, but none more than the pertinacious jealousy of the Dutch, who excluded them from the most profitable branches of trade. But though the Danes did not attain to any remarkable eminence in East Indian commerce, they were honorably distinguished by their zeal for the propagation of the Christian religion; and, notwithstanding their limited means, they have succeeded in diffusing the principles of true religion through a considerable portion of the south of India.

Section X.—*The French in the East Indies.*

Maritime affairs were long neglected in France; and though Francis I. and Henry III. issued edicts, exhorting their subjects to undertake long voyages, yet either a want of enterprise in the people, or the inability of the government to afford pecuniary assistance, prevented any effort being made meriting notice. After some attempts to form an association of merchants, productive of little advantage, an East India company was founded (A. D. 1616), but meeting with some misfortunes, the members resolved to abandon the Indian trade, and to direct their attention to the establishment of a settlement in the island of Madagascar. Toward the close of the seventeenth century, the French purchased the town of Pondicherry from the king of Visapúr, and began to form a settlement there with every reasonable prospect of success. It was, however, wrested from them by the Dutch (A. D. 1693), but was subsequently restored by the treaty of Ryswick (A. D. 1697). Thenceforward, the prosperity of the colony progressively increased, and the subsequent acquisition from the Dutch of the islands called the isles of France and Bourbon, but previously the Mauritius and the Mascarenhas, led the French to hope that they might acquire an important share in eastern commerce. A new career of ambition was opened to them by the sanguinary struggles which arose between the new states formed out of the fragments of the empire of Delhi; M. Dupleix, the governor of Pondicherry, hoped by embroiling the natives with each other, to obtain territorial acquisitions as the price of his assistance to some of the combatants. The English adopted the same course of policy, and thus the ancient hostility between the two nations extended its influence to India. The talents of Clive, however, carried the English triumphantly through an arduous struggle, which ended in the almost total expulsion of the French from the peninsula, and the cession of most of their settlements, by the peace of 1763. They afterward intrigued with the native princes, Hyder Ali and Tippoo Sultan, against their successful rivals, but they have been utterly unable to regain any portion of their former influence.

SECTION XI.—*The English in India.*

A HUNDRED years have not elapsed since the possessions of the British East India company were limited to three settlements of narrow extent, inhabited by a few hundred Europeans, who were scarcely able to defend themselves against pirates and banditti, much less compete with the power of the native princes. Now this association of merchants, from its court in Leadenhall street, rules over an empire containing a hundred millions of subjects, raises a tribute of more than three millions annually, possesses an army of more than two hundred thousand rank and file, has princes for its servants, and emperors pensioners on its bounty. Calcutta, from a miserable village, has become the metropolis of the east; Bombay possesses more trade than Tyre, in the days of its glory; and Madras, in spite of its perilous surf, rivals the commercial prosperity of Carthage. There is no parallel to such a career in the annals of the world; conquerors, indeed, have acquired a more extensive dominion in a shorter space of time, but they failed to establish a permanent empire; after a few years, the traces of their tempestuous passage were as completely effaced as the track of a vessel in the waves of the ocean.

In the preceding chapters, we have incidentally noticed the progress of the company's empire in its relation to the general politics of Europe, but it is of importance to mark more definitely the successive steps by which such vast acquisitions have been won and secured. The history of the East India company, indeed, has more than ordinary claims on our attention; it is intimately connected with our national character and national welfare, and all must desire to know whether our eastern empire has advanced the great cause of civilization, and whether our domination is likely to endure, or to meet at some time or other a precipitate overthrow.

The London company for trading with the East Indies was incorporated by Queen Elizabeth (A. D. 1600), and remained without a rival for nearly a century, when the necessities of the state led to the formation of the English company (A. D. 1698) ; it was soon found that the rivalry between these bodies was prejudicial to the interests of both, and at the recommendation of his majesty King William III., the two companies agreed to form one association, to be designated "*The United Company of Merchants of England, trading to the East Indies.*" The first English settlement of importance was Bantam, in the island of Java ; but in 1658, they obtained a grant of land on the Coromandel coast, near Madras, where they erected a stronghold, Fort St. George. In 1668, the island of Bombay, ceded by the crown of Portugal to Charles II., as a part of the dowry of the infanta Catharine, was granted by the king, and appointed the capital of the British settlements in India. Bengal was not at first estimated at its true value, but toward the close of the seventeenth century (A. D. 1698), the English had a settlement at Calcutta, the French at Chandernagore, and the Dutch at Chinsura, all situated on the river Hooghly. An embassy was sent to the court of Delhi with presents ; fortunately one of its members was an eminent physician, and his professional aid was required by the emperor Ferrokshir. In gratitude for the services of Dr. Hamilton, Ferrokshir granted valuable *firmáns*, or patents of privileges to the company, which gave them great advantages over their European rivals The viceroy of Bengal, jealous of the privileges granted to the English, advanced against Calcutta, took the town, and confined one hundred and forty-six in a dungeon called the Black Hole, so narrow and confined, that only twenty-three of the captives survived till the morning (A. D. 1756). Colonel Clive, who had already given proofs of his military talents in the Madras presidency, was sent into Bengal. He soon recovered Calcutta, and took Chandernagore from the French. Finding that the viceroy of Bengal, Suraj-u-Dowlah, was obstinate in his opposition to the company's interest, Clive adopted the bold resolution of deposing him without waiting for, or indeed asking the emperor's sanction, although the company was at peace with the court of Delhi. Acting promptly on this determination, Clive attacked the viceroy's troops at Plassey (June 23, 1757), and gained a decisive victory. Suraj-u-Dowlah was deposed, and his post given by the conquerors to Jaffier Ali Khan.

After Clive's return to England, the government of Calcutta was intrusted to a council, of which Mr. Vansittart was appointed president. The rapidity with which the English had acquired supremacy in Bengal, inspired them with feelings of contemptuous superiority, which involved them in angry disputes with the new viceroy. At length, the council of Calcutta, induced by a bribe of 200,000*l*., resolved to depose Jaffier, and confer the viceroyship on Cossim Ali Khan. But Cossim was soon as odious as his predecessor. The servants of the East India company claimed an exemption from all duties on commerce and thus ruined the native merchants; Cossim, after many remonstrances to the council of Calcutta, abolished the transit duties altogether; and this act of justice to his own subjects, though extorted by necessity, was loudly exclaimed against as an infringement of his engagements with the company, and two agents were sent to demand the repeal of the decree. While negotiations were pending, the English resident seized the citadel of Patna, and though it was immediately retaken by Cossim Ali, his rage was so excited by what he regarded a deliberate act of treachery, that he put all the English prisoners to death. War was instantly declared, Cossim Ali was defeated and deposed, and Jaffier Khan was once more declared viceroy of Bengal. It is not known at what price Jaffier purchased his restoration, but he did not long enjoy it; he died a few months before Clive, who had been recently elevated to the peerage, returned as governor-general to Calcutta.

Lord Clive found the affairs of the presidency in a deplorable condition: their troops, goaded to madness by the insolence and rapacity of their officers, were in open mutiny; the fertile province of Bengal was "marred to a wilderness" by the most corrupt of all the corrupt bodies ever intrusted with its destinies; friendly native powers were estranged by systematic extortion; hostile princes were confirmed in their enmity by witnessing such excesses of profligacy and peculation; and, to complete his lordship's difficulties, his proceedings were controlled by a subordinate committee, wholly unused to subordination. Clive's zeal in reforming such crying abuses, procured him a host of enemies, whose resistance was encouraged by their friends and patrons in the court of directors at home. The first outbreak of opposition was a general mutiny of the military officers, supported by a large subscription from the civilians in Calcutta. Through a defect in the mutiny act, the governor-general was not able to sentence any of the criminals to death, not even those who were found guilty of planning his assassination. Sir Robert Fletcher, the general in command of the army, was subsequently proved to be the instigator of the whole plot, and having been convicted by a court-martial, he was cashiered. But it must be added, that this very officer was subsequently appointed commander-in-chief of the army of Madras, where he headed the mutinous opposition by which Lord Pigot was removed from that government. Another of the mutineers, sent home by Clive, on charges that affected his life, obtained a very high appointment in the civil service of Bengal by his party interest in the court of directors.

Clive's firmness restored order in Calcutta; and soon after, the substitution of British rule for the native viceroyalties in Bengal, removed the chief source of intrigue and peculation. But in the meantime, the presidency at Madras was brought to the brink of ruin by the arms of Hyder Ali, whose abilities had raised him from the rank of a private soldier to that of an independent sovereign. After a protracted war, Sir Eyre Coote retrieved all the losses of the English, and, on the death of Hyder (A. D. 1782), concluded a treaty with his son, Tippoo, on terms very advantageous to the company.

The charters granted at various times to the company, only secured to it the exclusive right of trade; when, therefore, it began to make territorial acquisitions, it became a serious constitutional question whether the British crown did not possess an inherent right to all provinces conquered by its subjects. The ministers, and especially Lord North, already embarrassed by the American war, were unwilling to attempt the decision of a matter encumbered with so many difficulties; but the right of the British parliament to interfere in the affairs of India, was virtually asserted, by passing various acts of regulation, and the establishment of a custom of time-bargains with the company, which were, in fact, mere expedients to escape from difficulties becoming more complicated every hour.

The administration of Mr. Warren Hastings greatly extended the company's territories, and rendered its influence paramount in northern India; but the means which he employed were not always consistent with European notions of equity; and the disputes which arose between him and his council, fixed the attention of the British parliament and the British nation on the affairs of India. Mr. Fox, who was then in power, introduced a bill for transferring the government of India from the court of directors to a parliamentary committee, but the measure was frustrated by the reluctance of the king, and the dismissal of the ministry. We have already noticed the impeachment of Mr. Hastings and his acquittal, after a trial of unparalleled duration, by the house of lords.

At length an important change was made in the government of India, by the establishment of a board of control, according to a plan proposed by Mr. Pitt (A. D. 1784). The principal object of the new measure was to secure the obedience and responsibility of the company's servants to the authorities in England, and to remedy the most glaring abuses of patronage by the court of directors. This measure, though not so stringent as it was originally intended to be, produced very beneficial effects, and introduced a system of subordination, in which the presidencies had long been deficient.

Lord Cornwallis was sent out as governor-general, under the new system; he exerted himself to remedy some of the most flagrant abuses in the administration, and, though opposed by a majority of the supreme court at Calcutta, he partially succeeded. He soon began to look with suspicion on the ambitious projects of Tippoo Sultan, who had inherited his father Hyder's hostility to the English. Tippoo's intrigues were secretly encouraged by the French government, for sufficiently obvious reasons. The French had been the first to try the plan of acquiring territorial possessions by interference in native wars, often excited by themselves; and they had been completely defeated, while the English had as completely succeeded. Anger at this failure, too high an estimate of the injury which the British power had received from the loss of the American colonies, and a confident belief that our empire in the east was as insecure as it had proved in the west, were popular feelings in France, and were just as rife in the court of Versailles as they were at a later period in the jacobin clubs of Paris. The danger which Lord Cornwallis anticipated, seemed more formidable to Mr. Pitt than to the court of directors, and led to a serious dispute between the ministry and the company. The premier, through the board of control, insisted on sending regular British troops to India, and compelling the company to pay for their support. This was regarded by the court of directors as an indirect effort on the part of the crown to grasp the patronage of the Indian army, and was, of course, strenuously resisted. Mr. Pitt settled the matter by forcing through parliament, with all the influence at his command, an act of explanation; but he had the mortification to encounter a fierce opposition from many who were generally his stanchest supporters. The war with Tippoo, which rendered the English authority supreme from the river Krishna to Cape Comorin, soon followed. Lord Cornwallis having brought it to a prosperous termination, returned home, and was succeeded by Sir John Shore, afterward Lord Teignmouth.

During Sir John Shore's peaceful administration, the organization of the internal government of India was considerably improved; but its most remarkable events were the interference of the English, as arbitrators, in the disputed succession to the throne of Oude; and the commencement of discontents, almost amounting to mutinies, among the officers of the Indian army, in consequence of the reduction of their field allowances by the court of directors. The latter subject soon became one of increasing annoyance, and even danger; but the calamities which it threatened were fortunately averted by judicious measures of conciliation.

Lord Mornington, afterward marquis of Wellesley, was next appointed governor-general. His first efforts were directed to lessen the growing influence of the French in Hindústan; finding Tippoo indisposed to form new engagements with the British government, war was declared against him, which, as we have already stated, ended in the defeat and death of that turbulent monarch. A subsequent war with the Mahratta powers completely established British supremacy in India, and made the company supreme in the Peninsula. But notwithstanding his brilliant services, the marquis of Wellesley was thwarted in many important points of policy by the court of directors. The chief of these were, the employment of India-built ships, the establishment of a college for the education of civil servants at Calcutta, and the patronage of certain appointments, which the court wished to reserve for its favorites. This last difference led to very angry remonstrances, both from the marquis of Wellesley and Lord Clive, who was governor of Madras. Lord Clive resigned his situation; and on quitting Madras, addressed a spirited remonstrance to the court of directors, in which the inefficiency, insubordination, and delinquency of many of their servants, were directly traced to the abuse of patronage, and to the encouragement which the idle and the dissolute, possessing interest with the court, received from authority superior to the local government. Lord Wellesley, supported by the board of control, retained his place in defiance of the court, and, by his successful management of the Mahratta war, bore down all opposition.

The great extent of country gained in the Mahratta war, gave rise to serious embarrassments after the marquis of Wellesley had returned to Europe; his successor, Lord Cornwallis, died before completing the requisite arrangements, and Sir George Barlow, who acted as vice-governor, adopted a line of policy directly contrary to that which had received the sanction of his predecessor. This change led to an angry controversy with the English ministers (Lord Grenville and Mr. Fox) respecting the appointment of a successor to the marquis of Cornwallis. The ministers nominated Lord Lauderdale to the vacant office, the court of directors insisted that Sir George Barlow should retain his power. After a very long negotiation, both parties agreed to withdraw the rival candidates, and they finally concurred in selecting Lord Minto as governor-general.

When Lord Minto reached Madras, his attention was directed to certain transactions in that presidency, too important to be omitted even in this brief outline of Indian history. Lord William Bentinck succeeded Lord Clive (afterward earl of Powis) in the government of Madras, and, like his predecessor, was involved in serious disputes with the local council and the subordinate servants of the company. In the midst of these discussions, a dangerous mutiny of the native Indian army at Vellore, furnished a pretext for recalling the obnoxious governor with something like censure. In the Indian army no native could attain the rank of commissioned officer; many of the sepoys were Mohammedans, and they could not forget how very recently the whole peninsula of India was their own; the deposed dynasty of Mysore, including Tippoo's family and several of his ministers, were on the spot, to aggravate these feelings of natural discontent; and the *fakirs*, or preaching friars of Mohammedanism, lent their aid to fan the flame. A regulation respecting the head-dress of the troops was the pretext for revolt; though the shape of the sepoy turban had no more connexion with the real cause of the mutiny, than the color of the roses with the rival claims of the houses of York and Lancaster. The insurrection was suppressed, but the leniency which Lord William Bentinck was disposed to show toward the mutineers, though sanctioned by Lord Minto, gave such displeasure to many influential persons, that the governor returned home.

When Lord Minto reached Calcutta (A. D. 1809), he prepared to adopt a system of policy, which had long been a favorite scheme with the court of directors and indeed with the great majority of the people of England. This was simply to introduce the European principle of a balance of power in India;—no plan could be more excellent in theory, but it was impossible to reduce it to practice, for no materials existed in the disorganized governments of India, from which such a system could be constructed. The company had ever opposed the colonization of India by Europeans, and had therefore rather occupied than possessed its successive acquisitions; with the exception of its hired servants (and not all of them), there was not a single individual interested in maintaining its sway; its soldiers were mere mercenaries, its subjects utterly indifferent to the continuance of its rule. In pursuit of this favorite but hopeless project, the establishment of a balance of power, Lord Minto committed many serious errors, but his administration was on the whole very beneficial to England, especially as he was among the first to appreciate the value of the Indian archipelago, with which our commerce is so rapidly increasing, both in extent and importance. His prudence terminated a very serious dispute between the civil and military authorities at Madras, which had nearly produced the most calamitous results: he tried the experiment of neutral policy with greater success than could have attended such a system in less able hands; and when he at length perceived that "balance of power" was inapplicable to the state of society in India, he acknowledged the change in his opinions with a manly candor which is too rarely met with among modern statesmen.

The earl of Moira, afterward marquis of Hastings, succeeded Lord Minto in the government. He was forced to abandon the neutral line of policy, by which the Goorkas, or wild tribes of the mountains of Nepaul, had been encouraged to encroach upon the territories both of the British and their allies. War was declared; the Goorkas proved more formidable enemies than the company's troops had yet encountered, but they were finally overcome, and the provinces ceded by the Nepaulese, as the price of peace, brought the English dominions into close contact with the frontiers of the Chinese empire. In the meantime central India was devastated by ferocious bands of freebooters, known by the name of Pindarries, and extensive combinations were formed for their suppression. The treachery and duplicity of several of the native powers on this occasion compelled the marquis of Hastings to demand from them considerable cessions of territory; and, at the conclusion of the war, the company felt itself bound to retain those acquisitions, not only as essential to its own interests, but to those of the native inhabitants. Of greater importance than all these provinces was the establishment of a British settlement at Singapore (A. D. 1819), by which its present share in the lucrative commerce of the Indian archipelago was secured to Great Britain.

The earl of Amherst, who had previously been sent on an embassy to China, was the next governor-general (A. D. 1823). In a few months after his arrival, he found himself constrained to adopt active measures for repressing the insults and encroachments of the Burmese. The war was one of more than ordinary difficulty, but it finally terminated to the advantage of the British, who obtained possession of many new and valuable provinces. Scarcely less important was the capture of Bhurtpore, a fortress which, having been on two former occasions assailed in vain by the British, was fondly believed impregnable by the natives of Hindústan (A. D. 1826); its conquest therefore tended not a little to increase that general sense of British superiority on which the security of our Indian empire mainly depends.

Earl Amherst was succeeded by Lord William Bentinck, whose generally peaceful administration is principally remarkable for a series of financial reforms in every department of the government. But the expiration of the company's charter, and the arrangements for its renewal, led to a total change of system (A. D. 1833). The company was deprived of its exclusive right of trade; the commerce with India and China was opened freely to all British subjects: the political government of Hindústan was continued to the company for twenty years, but all its other rights and possessions were ceded to the nation for an annuity of six hundred and thirty thousand pounds, secured by a guarantee fund of two millions sterling.

The East India company was not the only power that profited by the overthrow of the Mogul empire; two new kingdoms, that of the Afghans and that of the Síkhs, were founded on the northwest of Hindústan, and both have risen to great importance. The Afghans were originally subject to Persia, but toward the close of the seven teenth century they revolted against their rulers and nearly conquered the whole Persian empire. Nadir Shah restored the Persian supremacy, but on his death an Afghan leader proclaimed the independence of his country, and while the Persians wasted their strength in civil wars, founded a new kingdom at Cabul. The Afghan monarchy continued to prosper until the commencement of the present century, when it was distracted by the wars arising out of a disputed succession. Three brothers, Zemán, Mahmúd, and Sujáh, contended for the crown, and each prevailed in turn, according to the will of the chief vizier, who was head of the Baurikzye tribe. At length Zemán was blinded, Sujáh driven into exile, and Mahmúd placed on the throne. Unfortunately he permitted his son Kemrân to assassinate the vizier, upon which the Baurikzye brothers revolted, and compelled Mahmúd to seek shelter in Herat.

Under the Baurikzye brothers, Afghanistan was divided into a number of petty independent states, each governed by one or more chieftains of this powerful family; the principal being Dost Mohammed, the ruler of Cabul, whose supremacy was nominally recognised by all the rest. Soon after Lord Auckland had succeeded Lord William Bentinck as governor-general of India, an embassy was sent to Cabul for the purpose of forming a commercial treaty which might open the markets of central Asia to British manufactures. When the Persian court, yielding to Russian suggestions, had determined to advance against Herat, the mission to Cabul was changed from a commercial to a political legation, and a treaty was proposed to Dost Mohammed which it was believed might avert the danger of Russian influence being established on the banks of the Indus. The ruler of Cabul demanded as the price of his adhesion that the territory of Peshawer, recently seized by the king of Lahore, should be restored to the Afghans, and when this was refused he manifested a disposition so hostile to English interests that the envoy was recalled, and a resolution formed to restore Shah Sujáh to his throne by the aid of a British army.

The army of the Indus having surmounted all the toils and difficulties of its march through previously untraversed countries, soon arrived at the capital of Afghanistan, and Shah Sujáh was reinstated upon the throne of his ancesters.

Shah Sujáh's government was not popular, and indeed did not deserve to be so; general dissatisfaction continued to exist, but had not begun to show itself in a dangerous shape when General Elphinstone took the command of the occupying force, in April, 1841. In the following November a formidable insurrection unexpectedly exploded in Cabul; Sir Alexander Burnes, and several other Englishmen, were treacherously massacred, while the most deplorable want of energy and decision was displayed, both by the envoy and the military authorities. The fort in which the provisions for the troops were stored was permitted to fall into the hands of the enemy, without an effort being made to relieve its feeble garrison; and after the means of holding out in Cabul, until relief could be obtained from the other divisions of the army, had been sacrificed, it was resolved to commence a retreat.

The only result from this calamitous war, is the occupation of the territories of Scinde, which have been formally annexed to the British dominions. These districts command the navigation of the lower Indus, and would possess some value and importance if that river could be rendered available for the purposes of commercial navigation, but in the present distracted condition of central Asia, it does not appear probable that the peaceful pursuits of trade will be found lucrative for many years to come, and it is therefore very doubtful whether the accupation of Scinde will produce such a demand for British manufactures as to defray the heavy expenses which its retention will necessarily involve.

CHAPTER XIII.

HISTORY OF CHINA.

THE Chinese, like the ancient Egyptians, lay claim to a most extravagant antiquity, but their authentic history does not commence till the age of Confucius, who flourished about five centuries before the Christian era. At the time of his birth, China was divided into a number of independent states, which harassed each other by mutual wars, and his earliest efforts as a reformer were directed to unite them in one great confederation. He collected the old traditions of the country, and from them deduced a series of moral and political lessons, designed to form the basis of good government. His main principle was, that outward decorum is both the emblem and the test of goodness of heart; he therefore constructed a ritual strictly regulating every relation of life, both public and private, which was gradually received as a standard authority by the nation.

Ching-whang, the founder of the Tsin dynasty, was the first who united all the Chinese under one sovereign; and it is probable that the name China was adopted from that of his family. He is said to have erected the Great Wall, to restrain the incursions of the Tartars (B. C. 240), but this service was overbalanced by his cruelty and inveterate hostility to men of letters. Under the Han dynasty, which arose B. C. 202, the Huns began to invade China and frequently devastated the country; they at length were induced to direct their march westward, and burst like a torrent into the Roman empire, while China continued tranquil. Under the Han dynasty, foreigners came to China for the first time; literature was zealously cultivated, the art of printing invented, and the laws collected into an orderly system. For these reasons the memory of the Hans is still cherished in China; their dynasty ended A. D. 264.

No very important event occurred in the history of China from the extinction of the Han dynasty until the invasion of the empire by the Mongols, under the celebrated Zingis Khan (A. D. 1234). The sovereign who then ruled was cruel and cowardly; town after town submitted to the invaders, and at his death the Mongols possessed the greater part of the country, though the conquest was not completed till the year 1279, by Kublai Khan, the grandson of Zingis. Ze-ping, the infant son of the last emperor, sought shelter in the fleet, but the Mongols soon prepared a navy and pursued him. The Chinese and Mongol fleets met, and after an engagement which lasted an entire day, the former was totally defeated. When the Chinese admiral saw that escape was impossible, he went to the prince, who stood on the deck, and said, "It is better to die free than to dishonor our ancestors by an inglorious captivity," then, without waiting for a reply, he caught the prince in his arms and jumped into the sea, where they both perished.

The Mongols, though foreigners, were wise and beneficent rulers; Kublai Khan constructed several canals, and made every possible exertion to restore the agricultural prosperity of China; his grandson, Timur Khan, extirpated the bands of robbers that infested the country, and both labored to promote commercial intercourse with foreign nations. But on the failure of the direct royal line, the Mongols were so weakened by a war of disputed succession, that the Chinese easily drove them from the country, and placed a native dynasty on the throne (A. D. 1388).

Choo-quen-chang, the conqueror of the Mongols and founder of the Ming dynasty, was the son of a poor laborer. In early life he was destined for the priesthood, but his martial spirit induced him to enlist as a soldier. He very soon became so distinguished for courage and conduct that he was promoted to high rank; his marriage to a lady of great wealth strengthened his influence, and he soon began to be regarded as the leader of a party. So great was the hatred of the Chinese to their barbarian conquerors, that it required only a few months to drive the Mongols beyond the Great Wall; they were pursued in their retreat and slaughtered without mercy. The new emperor was a wise and prudent ruler; his early death was a national misfortune, especially as it involved the country in the calamities of a disputed succession.

The last of the Ming dynasty was Hwae-tsung. Very soon after his accession the king of the Mantchew Tartars advanced toward the frontiers, and issued a proclamation, declaring that he had been divinely summoned to assume the empire of China. There would have been, however, little reason to fear this invasion, had not rebellions in other quarters distracted the attention of the emperor. Bands of robbers infested the roads, and uniting themselves together under favorite chiefs, bade defiance to the imperial army. One of these, named Lè, gained the favor of the populace by promising a remission of taxes; crowds flocked to his standard, and entire battalions of the imperial army deserted to him. Lè no longer scrupled to declare himself emperor; he marched to Pekin, the soldiers intrusted with its defence threw down their arms, and the emperor was abandoned even by his domestic servants. In his despair, he slew his children, and then strangled himself, leaving behind him a written request that the conqueror would be satisfied with the destruction of the royal family, and not inflict any cruelty on the people.

Woo-san-kivei, a celebrated general, was stationed with a large army on the frontiers of Mantchew Tartary, when he received intelligence of these events. He resolved to avenge his master, and punish the usurper; for this purpose he had not only made peace with the Mantchews, but solicited their active assistance. The Tartars gladly assented to a proposal which opened them a passage into China; and acting with a rapidity of which their opponents had no idea, their progress was irresistible. The usurper Lè was defeated in three great battles, but when the general wished to dismiss his allies, they not only refused to return, but took possession of Pekin, and proclaimed a Mantchew prince emperor. For many years the Chinese in different provinces sternly resisted the domination of the Tartars, but there was no harmony in their councils and no concert in their actions; they were therefore successively subdued, but not until the entire country had been so devastated that it almost became a desert (A. D. 1644). During this calamitous period, a pirate, named Coxinga, kept the entire coast of China in constant alarm; he expelled the Dutch from the island of Formosa, which for a time flourished as an independent kingdom: but after his death, his son submitted to the Mantchews, and this noble island was annexed to the empire of China.

Kang-he, the second of the Mantchew emperors, was very anxious to make his subjects acquainted with the arts and sciences of Europe; he patronised the jesuit missionaries who came to his court, and profited so much by their instructions, as to become himself the author of a clever treatise on geometry. All his wishes, however, to give a new turn to Chinese literature were frustrated; the native men of letters refused to quit the tracks of their ancestors, and nothing new was consequently produced. Equally able in the cabinet and in the field, Kang-he was unquestionably, next to Kublai Khan, the greatest prince who ever sat on the throne of China. He revived the empire, distracted by repeated rebellions, impoverished by long and ruinous wars, and oppressed by vicious administration. When he died (A. D. 1722), peace and tranquillity pervaded all the provinces, and the unruly barbarians on the frontiers had been reduced to obedience.

Yung-ching succeeded his father on the throne, but did not pursue the same enlightened policy. He put an effectual stop to improvement, by banishing the missionaries who had spread themselves over all the Chinese provinces, and only retained a few individuals at court, with whose services he could not dispense. It must, however, be confessed, that the intriguing spirit of the jesuits had given some reasonable grounds for alarm, and that their extravagant assertions of papal supremacy might have infused suspicions of their designing to render the emperor dependant on the pope. In other respects Yung-ching was a good sovereign; he preserved peace during his reign, and by prudent precautions he averted the horrors of those famines that periodically devastated China. He died A. D. 1735, and was succeeded by his illegitimate son, Keën-lung.

The long reign of Keën-lung was almost wholly spent in wars with the various barbarous races on the whole western frontier of China. There is no interest in the record of these savage contests, which were for the most part a series of ruthless massacres. He cruelly persecuted the Christians, whom he accused of treasonable designs without a shadow of reason; and the relentless fury he displayed was eagerly seconded by the mandarins, who had been jealous of the superior intelligence of the missionaries. Keën-lung always thought that he had a just cause when he butchered whole tribes. After the defeat and massacre of the Kalmuks, he erected a stone tablet at Ele, with the following inscription: "The tree which Heaven plants, though man may fell it, can not be unrooted: the tree which Heaven fells, though man may replant it, will never grow."

The fame of Keën-lung extended to Europe, and missions from Hol land, England, and Russia, were sent to his court. These embassies did not produce the good expected from them: the Chinese, with all the conceit of ignorance, believed or pretended to believe themselves the only enlightened nation in the universe, and claimed homage from all others as barbarians. The emperor himself appears to have been free from these prejudices, but all the officers of state were opposed to an increase of foreign intercourse, which they feared would be fatal to their privileges.

After a reign of sixty years, Keën-lung abdicated the throne in favor of his fifth son, Kia-king (A. D. 1795), and died three years afterward at the age of eighty-eight. His successor had all his vices, without any of his redeeming qualities; his misconduct provoked frequent insurrections, while his feeble administration encouraged the pirates to renew their depredations in the Chinese seas. Unfortunately the greatest maritime power in the world submitted to receive laws from this feeble government. In 1808, a British squadron commanded by Admiral Drury was sent to take possession of the Portuguese settlement of Macao, and prevent it from falling into the hands of the French. The Chinese authorities at Canton became alarmed, and threatened to stop all trade unless the English garrison was withdrawn from Macao; their demands were granted with a precipitation which closely resembled cowardice, and the Chinese erected a pyramid to commemorate what they were pleased to call their victory over the English. It must be acknowledged that the concessions then made to their arrogance have been the chief cause of the repeated insults they have since offered to the British flag.

Kia-king's bitter hatred of Europeans was supposed by many to have arisen from the misrepresentations of the Canton authorities, and it was therefore resolved to send Lord Amherst as an ambassador to Pekin, for the purpose of establishing amicable relations between England and China. This embassy completely failed; the officers of the imperial court prevented Lord Amherst from obtaining an audience, and he returned to Canton. In the meantime the Chinese had shown a disposition to insult the naval forces that had conveyed the embassy, but a few shots from one of the frigates brought them to their senses, and the mission returned in safety.

Kia-king died in 1820, and was succeeded by the reigning emperor, Tao-kwang, who is even more prejudiced against Europeans than his predecessor. Proclamations against the importation of opium were issued by the Chinese government, but the prohibited article continued to be largely smuggled into the country. At length Captain Elliot, the English resident at Canton, was compelled by the Chinese authorities to consent to the destruction of several cargoes of opium, and his protests against the restraint to which he was subjected, were disregarded. War was declared against the emperor of China by the English government, and a large naval and military force sent against Canton. Canton and Ningpo, two of the most important cities in China, were taken by mere handfuls of British troops, and the immense masses collected in the imperial armies were unable to withstand an organized force rarely amounting to the tenth of their numbers. A treaty was at length negotiated, in which great concessions were very reluctantly made to the

English demands: the island of Hong-kong was ceded to them in perpetuity, five ports were freely opened to their trade, and the emperor consented to pay a large sum to defray the expenses of the war, and compensate for the large quantities of opium, the property of the British subjects, which had been destroyed at the commencement of the war.

A nation so completely isolated by natural boundaries as the Chinese, having no neighbors but the barbarous tribes of Tartary, is of course disposed to indulge in national vanity. They believe that their country occupies the centre of the globe, and that "the middle kingdom," as they therefore call it, is unequalled on the earth. Their own laws and usages, the origin of which is lost in remote antiquity, appear to them perfect, and every successive government has shown itself a decided foe to innovation. But the Chinese are the only people that have persevered in treating all foreigners as barbarians, and even when compelled to abate their absurd claims for the time, have invariably revived them on a more favorable opportunity. Hence it is impossible to negotiate with them according to the rules of European diplomacy, for until intimidated by defeat or terror, they will look upon attempts to form a treaty as signs of submission. It is singular that the Tartar conquerors of China have invariably adopted the institutions and prejudices of the vanquished; but they have not succeeded in winning the affections of the nation. During the greater part of a century, insurrections have followed each other with frightful rapidity, and the Mantchew domination has been more than once on the point of ruin. Secret societies exist at the present moment, formed to restore the ancient supremacy of the native Chinese, and it is not improbable that any signal humiliation of the imperial forces may lead to a revolution.

CHAPTER XIV.

HISTORY OF THE JEWS.

In the "*Manual of Ancient History*," we sketched the history of the Jews from the days of the patriarchs to the suppression of the revolt of Bar-Cochab (A. D. 136): it now remains to trace the fortunes of this singular race down to our own times, and briefly to exhibit their condition at the present day.

Though the number of Jews who perished in the successive overthrows of their nation was doubtless very great, we are by no means to believe that on any of these occasions the whole body fell into the hands of the victor; in proof of the contrary, we may refer to the Jewish colonies which we early find in places to which their conquerors would not have transported them, and where, consequently, we must look upon them as located by their own choice. Beside other places of less importance, we have mention of a flourishing Jewish community in Rome before the Christian era; and the travels of the apostles furnish evidence that shortly after that period they were to be met with in almost every part of Asia, Greece, and northern Africa. Though their fathers in their own land had been noted for a proud contempt for all literature but their own, these colonists did not neglect the opportunities of mental culture thus laid open to them, and accordingly we find that many of the most learned philosophers of Alexandria were either Jews, or in habits of such intimacy with them, as imply that the sciences were pursued with equal ardor by both parties. Indeed, it was only under such circumstances that that strange mixture of pagan, Jewish, and Christian dogmas, called Gnosticism, could have originated; and this we know to have taken its rise in the schools of Alexandria.

Though the Jews who spread over the east seem chiefly to have resorted to the more polished regions of Egypt or Babylon, circumstances induced many of them to repair to Arabia, and others penetrated even to China, where their reception seems to have been favorable. In the days of Mohammed, great numbers of Jews, wealthy, and possessed of political power, were found settled in the peninsula, whom the impostor endeavored in vain to conciliate. His successors granted them toleration, and both parties being animated by a like hatred of the Christians, we often find them acting in concert, especially during the Saracen conquest of Africa and Spain.

The Abbaside khaliphs, who seized the throne of Islám from the Ommiade dynasty, were generally tolerant of the Jews; the khaliph Almanzor, indeed, went so far as to restore their academies, and evinced some taste for Hebrew literature himself. In the beginning of the ninth century, the khaliph Mamun caused the best of the Jewish books to be translated into Arabic, for the purpose of diffusing a taste for literature and science among his subjects. Several eminent men of Jewish race flourished at his court; they were particularly famous for their skill in astronomy and medicine, which had up to this period been very slightly cultivated by the Saracens. The fame of the Jewish physicians was spread over all the Mohammedan countries, so that few of any other race could find employment; but the wealth acquired by this lucrative profession excited the cupidity of several of the later khaliphs, who availed themselves of religious prejudices to gratify their avarice. During this season of persecution the Jews were frequently duped by false prophets and pretended messiahs, who induced them to raise partial insurrections, which only served to furnish a pretext for renewed persecutions. In the midst of their difficulties the khaliphate was overthrown by the barbarous Mongols, and the Jews were exposed to renewed persecutions from the Saracens, who attributed to their impiety all the calamities of the empire.

From the death of Timúr Lenk to the accession of Shah Abbas, the Jews, like the other inhabitants of Media and Persia, had to endure all the calamities arising from a violent war, a rapid conquest, and the long series of sanguinary wars for succession between the conqueror's descendants. At the accession of Shah Abbas, Persia was almost uninhabited; and in order to obtain subjects, that monarch granted large privileges to all strangers willing to settle in his dominions. Numbers of Jews who were oppressed in other eastern countries accepted his offers, but their wealth soon excited suspicions, and the shah issued an edict that they should either embrace Islamism or prepare for death. The remonstrances of the Mohammedan priests prevented the execution of this sanguinary edict, but legal protection was withdrawn from the persecuted race, and has not been again restored in the provinces subject to Persia.

The Jews from Africa crossed into Spain, and thence to Gaul, Germany, and even Britain. In Spain they were often subject to persecution under the Gothic monarchs, which induced some to dissemble their faith, and others to leave the country. Of these latter, many retired to Africa, whence they returned with the Saracens, whom they materially assisted in the conquest of the country. Under the rule of the Spanish Moslems, the condition of the Jews was highly prosperous; they cultivated science, were intrusted with the highest offices of the state, and enjoyed complete toleration; indeed to this era belong the names of Rabbi Hasdai, Benjamin of Tudela, Isaac of Cordova, and numerous others, whose works have been preserved, and which prove their proficiency in almost every art or science then known.

In more northern countries their state was materially different. Though their industry and abilities rendered them valuable to their rulers, and some few are to be found even in the courts of princes, they were as a body subject to the most galling restrictions, being in the eye of the law mere chattels of the superior lord, not human beings. Charlemagne, and his immediate successors, employed many of the Jews as their physicians, or as bankers, and even despatched them on important embassies; but about the year 870, by a decree of the council of Meaux, they were declared incapable of filling any civil offices, and under Philip Augustus (A. D. 1180) they were stripped of their property, and banished from France. They soon returned, but were exposed to the most rigorous and unjust treatment; Louis IX., whose right to the title of Saint appears more than questionable, began the career of renewed persecution by forbidding the legal officers to seize the persons or estates of Christians indebted to Jews in default of payment; catholics were strictly prohibited from employing Jewish physicians; it was ordained that they should have only one synagogue and burial-ground in each diocese, that they should not exercise any of the higher industrial arts, and that they should wear some distinctive mark on a conspicuous part of their dress. In 1288 the parliament of Paris fined the Jews for singing too loud in their synagogues. Philip the Long pronounced sentence of banishment against them, but granted charters of protection to a few who were able to gratify his cupidity by large bribes. A strict search was made for those who dared to remain in the kingdom; several were burned alive, and, as an additional insult, dogs were thrown on the funeral pile. A great number were slain with less ceremony by the populace, who practised all sorts of cruelty upon the unfortunate sufferers. In 1350 John revoked the edicts of banishment, and the Jews, grateful for his kindness, cheerfully aided him in raising the large ransom with which he purchased his deliverance from captivity in England. This tranquillity was disturbed by the renewal of persecution under Charles VI., but the edicts of intolerance were found so difficult of execution that they were permitted soon to sink into oblivion.

Many of the popes commiserated the sufferings of the Jews, and endeavored to restrain the fanaticism of their persecutors. Honorius III. issued a bull, forbidding the use of force in converting them to Christianity, and menacing excommunication against those who insulted or injured them on account of their religion. Gregory IX., when a sudden burst of bigotry threatened the extermination of the Jews in every country in which they had settled, not only protected them in his own states, but wrote urgent letters in their behalf to all the monarchs of Europe. When the holy see was transferred to Avignon at the commencement of the fourteenth century, the favor shown to the Jews in Italy was continued, and the lot of those in France greatly alleviated. Avignon itself became the chief residence of the wealthy Jews, and their riches contributed not a little to the splendor of the pontifical court.

After the popes had returned to Rome, several pontiffs exhibited less wise and humane policy toward the Jewish race. Gregory XIII., who celebrated the atrocious massacre of St. Bartholomew with public thanksgivings, was of course a persecutor of the Jews. He ordained that they should be subject to trial before the inquisition, for blasphemy, for ridiculing the ceremonies of the catholic religion, or for reading the Talmud and similar prohibited books. He further enjoined that all the Jews in Rome, above twelve years of age, should be assembled once a week to listen to a sermon in condemnation of their religion. Sixtus V. was a pontiff of a different character; on the 22d of October, 1586, he re-established the Jews in all their municipal privileges, allowed them full right of citizenship in the Roman states, with power to hold houses and lands; he restored their synagogues and burial-grounds, imposing on them only a very moderate tribute, and promising them exemption for the future from all arbitrary exactions. Subsequent popes revoked the tolerant edicts of Sixtus, but they did not revive the cruel code of Gregory XIII., and in general the Jews have been permitted to enjoy greater freedom and to hold their property with greater tranquillity in the papal states, than in most other countries of Christendom. Hence while the Spanish Jews generally favored the reformation, those of Italy regarded the progress of protestant opinion with complete indifference, and sometimes with avowed hostility.

In the tenth and eleventh centuries, most of the great German cities had among their inhabitants numerous Jews, wealthy, intelligent, and polished in their manners, but their prosperity was at all times at the mercy of their rulers, and it was only by means of their purchased and precarious protection that even their lives were secure. At length arose the crusading spirit, and the Jews in Germany, to the number of many thousands, were its first victims. Again the fanatics who were preparing to march to the third crusade (A. D. 1188), butchered all the Jews they met with in Germany and Italy, and similar barbarities were exercised in this and other countries, so that the annihilation of the devoted race seemed inevitable; but this, like other storms, passed away. After a while the Jews again arose from the dust, some returned to their ancient habitations, and others pushed forward into the then almost unknown regions of Poland, where they at length became, and still continue, a very influential part of the population.

At what period the Jews first reached Britain does not distinctly appear; but in the eighth century we find them reckoned among the property of the Anglo-Saxon kings, who seem to have exercised absolute power over both their lives and goods. In this state they remained under the Norman princes and the early Plantagenets, as is sufficiently testified by their butchery in the reign of Richard I.; the conduct of John, who drew out a tooth daily till he obtained a large sum of money from a rich Jew; the enormous fines levied on them by Henry III.; and their expulsion by Edward I. (A. D. 1290), after the confiscation of all their property. The conduct of the monarchs was of course imitated by the nobles to the extent of their power, and the hatred of all classes was excited by marvellous stories of the crucifixion of Christian children, the profanation of the sacraments, and other improbable outrages, of which they were said, but never proved, to be guilty.

As the Arabs lost their hold on Spain the Jews found themselves exposed to all the horrors of persecution. The inquisition was introduced, and after great numbers had been burnt, all who refused to be come Christians were expelled the kingdom, being allowed to retain only their moveable property (A. D. 1492); their number is said to have exceeded 800,000, and they chiefly took refuge in Africa and Turkey. They were treated in a similar manner in Portugal. But it soon appeared that Judaism, though suppressed, was by no means extinguished in the peninsula, and the severity of the inquisition was then exercised upon the nominal Christians; such was the case also in Italy. Thus persecuted in every country under the influence of the see of Rome, the Jews at the era of the reformation eagerly flocked toward the rising protestant states, where they were at least sure of personal safety. This was more especially the case in Holland, where they were equitably treated, and where they are now exceedingly numerous.

Although no repeal of the edict for their banishment had taken place, the Jews entered into some negotiations with Oliver Cromwell for their return to England, but which do not appear to have led to any result. At the time of the restoration they came in, in small numbers, without exciting any particular notice, and have ever since remained unmolested. In 1753, an act was passed to facilitate their naturalization, but it was speedily repealed, and though popular feeling is less strong at present on the subject, the attempt to place them upon the same footing as other British subjects, though several times made, has been unsuccessful.

In the course of the last and the present centuries the condition of the Jews in European countries has been greatly ameliorated. Maria Theresa of Austria, and, after her, most of the German states, have granted them equal privileges with Christians; in France they enjoy every civil right; in Poland they form the only middle class, and are found engaged in agriculture and manufactures; in Italy, Spain, and Portugal, they now reside unmolested, and in many of the British colonies (as Malta, Gibraltar, and Jamaica), they are among the principal merchants and traders. Indeed, Russia is the only civilized state where they are now subject to anything like their former restrictions, or are looked upon with much of the antipathy of former days. In Mohammedan countries, however, they are still an obnoxious sect, against whom the most improbable charges are readily credited, a circumstance frequently taken advantage of by the local governors.

As might be expected with regard to a people so widely scattered, the most contradictory statements of the number of the Jews have been made, few of them being anything more than mere conjecture. The most probable statement seems to be that of the *Weimar Almanac*, which gives a total of about 3,200,000, reckoning near 2,000,000 in Europe, 740,000 in Asia, 500,000 in Africa, and 5,000 in America.

CHAPTER XV.

HISTORY OF THE UNITED STATES OF AMERICA.

SECTION I.—*Colonial History.*

SEVERAL unsuccessful attempts to plant colonies within the limits of the United States were made in the sixteenth century; but no permanent settlement was effected until the beginning of the seventeenth Before the close of that century, however, all the colonies composing the original thirteen states were established except one, that of Georgia

In the reign of Elizabeth of England, the whole country between the thirty-fourth and forty-fifth degrees of north latitude, received the name of *Virginia*, in honor of the queen. In the next reign it was granted by royal charter to two companies formed for the purpose of settling it, the southern portion, called South Virginia, to the *London* company, and the northern, called North Virginia, to the *Plymouth* company.

In 1607, one hundred and fifteen years from the discovery of San Salvador by Columbus, the first permanent settlement was made at *Jamestown* under the auspices of the London company: and thus commenced the planting of the colony of *Virginia.*

In 1613 the settlement of *New York* was begun by the Dutch, on the island of New York, then called Manhattan. The same year, a naval force from Virginia compelled the Dutch to acknowledge the sovereignty of the king of England: but it was not until 1664 that the colony was finally conquered and occupied by the English.

In 1620 the colony of *Plymouth* was planted by English independents, who had for some years been settled in Holland. Two unsuccessful attempts had been previously made to form settlements in New England, one by the Plymouth company in 1607, at the mouth of the Kennebec river; the other, a little later by the celebrated Capt. John Smith, the father of the Virginia colony.

In 1628 the *Massachusetts* colony was established by a company under a grant of lands from the Plymouth company. The first settlement was at *Salem.* Shortly after Charlestown, Boston, and the towns adjacent, were settled. In 1692, the Plymouth colony was incorporated with that of Massachusetts. Up to this time it had remained a voluntary association, governed by regulations made by the settlers among themselves.

In 1623, the settlement of *New Hampshire* was begun at the mouth of the Piscataqua river, and subsequently at *Dover*, *Portsmouth*, and *Exeter.* These three settlements continued distinct and independent governments until 1641, when they united in coming under the government of Massachusetts. In 1679 New Hampshire was by a royal ordinance erected into a separate province.

New Jersey was first settled by the Danes about the year 1624; and shortly after some Dutch families planted themselves in the vicinity of New York. In 1655, Peter Stuyvesant, the Dutch governor of New York, conquered the country, which was finally occupied by the English on the conquest of New York in 1664.

Delaware was first occupied by the Swedes in 1627. The Dutch, however, disputed the possession of it with them, from the first, and in 1655 obtained and held it until it fell into the power of the English along with New York and New Jersey in 1664. Most of the Swedes, after the Dutch conquest, left the country.

Maine was settled in 1639. The first town founded was York. This province was united to Massachusetts in 1652, and so continued until 1820.

Maryland was settled in 1634 by English Roman catholics, under a patent to Cecil Calvert, Lord Baltimore, by whom a colony was planted at the mouth of the Potomac, at a place called St. Mary.

The first settlement in *Connecticut* was begun in 1635 at Hartford and its vicinity, by a company from Massachusetts. In 1638, *New Haven* was settled, and with the towns around it was called the colony of New Haven; but in 1662, it was united to the colony of Connecticut.

The settlement of *Rhode Island* dates from 1636, when Roger Williams, banished from Massachusetts on account of his religious principles (which were those of the baptists), established the town of *Providence*. Rhode Island itself was occupied in 1638, by persons also driven from Massachusetts by religious persecution. Roger Williams was a man far in advance of his time. To him belongs the eminent glory of giving the first practical example of religious toleration. The Providence and Rhode Island colonies were politically united in 644.

North Carolina was occupied by settlers from Virginia between the years 1640 and 1650. They established themselves on lands north of Albemarle sound. It became a distinct colony in 1729.

In 1670 the settlement of *South Carolina* was begun at Port Royal; but the colony removed the next year, and founded a town which was called Charleston; but in 1680 this place was abandoned, and the settlement of the present city of Charleston commenced.

Pennsylvania was settled in 1682, under a royal grant to William Penn. Thi colony had a more rapid and prosperous growth than any of the other colonies, owing partly to the later date of its settlement when the obstacles to colonization had become less, and partly to the mildness and equity of its laws and administration.

Georgia was not colonized till 1733. It was then settled under a patent granted to twenty-one trustees, for the purpose of giving land gratuitously to indigent subjects of Great Britain. Liberal donations were made by benevolent persons to defray the expense of transporting and providing for the settlers. The first place founded was Savannah.

The limits of this sketch will not permit any details in regard to the history of the separate colonies, the dates of whose settlement have now been given A few matters of more general interest can only be noted.

In 1643, the colonies of Massachusetts, Connecticut, and New Haven, formed a union by articles of confederation, under the style of "The United Colonies of New England." To protect themselves against the Indians, and against the claims and encroachments of the Dutch of New Netherlands (as New York was then called), were the motives of this confederation. Rhode Island, refusing to merge her political existence under the jurisdiction of Massachusetts, was excluded from the union. The conquest of New York, New Jersey, and Delaware, in 1664, brought the whole country, from Maine to Carolina, under the dominion of the English.

In 1675 New England was afflicted by a memorable war with the Indians, called *King Philip's war*, from the name of an Indian sachem of great abilities, who combined the Indian tribes against the English. The capture and death of Philip the following year put an end to the war, in which New England suffered the loss of six hundred men, the flower of her strength, twelve or thirteen towns destroyed, and six hundred dwellings consumed.

In 1676 a rebellion broke out in Virginia, known as "Bacon's rebellion" from the name of the leader, an able and ambitious man, who seized, and for some months maintained, the supreme authority. His death put an end to the civil war. The causes of this rebellion were oppressive restrictions on commerce, and heavy taxes imposed by Governor Berkley.

During the reign of James II. the New England colonies were severely oppressed. The king revoked the charters and assumed the government into his own hands, appointing Sir Edmund Andros governor. Under his arbitrary and tyrannical administration the colonies suffered until the accession of William and Mary in 1689.

The news of the abdication of James, and the accession of William and Mary to the English throne was the signal for a revolution in New England. Sir Edmund Andros was deposed and imprisoned. Connecticut and Rhode Island resumed their charters and were allowed to retain them. Massachusetts obtained a new charter, in some respects preferable to its former one.

In New York, where Sir Edmund Andros had formerly been the tyrannical governor, and where his successors had generally followed his example, the discontents of the people led likewise to a revolution, which at length resulted in a constitution; but the collisions between the colonial assemblies and the royal governors retarded the restoration of peace and prosperity to the colony.

It will be proper here to advert to the forms of government which prevailed in the several colonies. These were of three sorts—the charter; the royal; and the proprietary.

1. The CHARTER governments. These were confined to New England. By their charters the people of these colonies were expressly entitled to all the privileges of British born subjects; and invested with the legislative, judicial, and executive powers of government. They chose their governors and legislative bodies, and established their own

courts. Their legislatures were, however, restrained from passing any laws contrary to those of England. The crown claimed the right of revoking the charters; but this was denied by the colonists, unless they were forfeited for cause. They were sometimes declared forfeited, or forcibly revoked, as we have just seen in the reign of James II. The disputes arising on this subject were one of the causes of the revolution.

2. The ROYAL governments. These were Virginia, New York, and subsequently, North and South Carolina and New Jersey. In these colonies, the people had legislative assemblies of their own choosing; but the governor and council were appointed by the crown, who had a negative on all proceedings of the popular assemblies, and also the appointment of the judges and most of the administrative officers. The sources of grievance in these colonies were the arbitrary conduct of the governors, and the claim of absolute power by the crown to negative the acts of the assemblies.

3. The PROPRIETARY governments. These were Maryland and Pennsylvania, and, at first, the Carolinas and Jerseys. In these colonies, the proprietors, or individuals to whom the territories had been granted by the crown, were empowered, under certain limitations reserved by the crown, to establish civil governments and to make laws. There were in most cases colonial assemblies, partly summoned by the proprietors, and partly chosen by the people. Perpetual quarrels arose between the people and the proprietors, chiefly respecting the prerogative exercised by the latter of repealing or negativing the acts of the assemblies.

At the time of the accession of William III., in 1689, the population of the colonies is estimated to have exceeded two hundred thousand. There was but little trade or commerce except with England, whence the colonists derived all their merchandise, sending thither in return tobacco, peltry, some pork, and fish. Agriculture was the principal employment; and the manufactures in use were principally limited to the most common articles of necessity and convenience, and these were mostly imported from England.

The year 1692 is signalized in the annals of New England by the commencement of the trials for *witchcraft*. This fanatic delusion went on increasing until about twenty persons were publicly executed; one hundred and fifty were in prison, and two hundred more were accused. The phrensy then subsided as suddenly as it had sprung up and spread. The principal theatre of these deplorable scenes was in Salem, Massachusetts, and the neighboring towns, though there were some cases in Connecticut.

The English revolution, which placed William III. on the throne, while it freed the colonies from the oppressions they endured during the reign of his predecessor, involved them in the calamities of the war between France and England, which lasted from 1690 to the peace of Ryswick in 1697. The French in Canada directed an expedition against the English colonies, instigating the Indians to join them in their hostilities. In return, an armament was fitted out by Massachusetts for the invasion of the French settlements. Port Royal in Nova

Scotia was taken. A second expedition was undertaken by the colonies of New York, Connecticut, and Massachusetts, for the reduction of Montreal and Quebec. It failed in its object, and had the effect of producing dissatisfaction among the Indian tribes in New York, who were the allies of the English. This war, commonly called *King William's war*, was marked by the most savage atrocities on the part of the French and Indians.

Scarcely had the colonies begun to recover from this war, when in 1702 they were plunged into another with the French, Indians, and Spaniards, commonly called *Queen Anne's war*, arising from disputes about the boundaries, which had been left unsettled at the peace of Ryswick. The colonies of Massachusetts and New Hampshire were the chief sufferers, being most exposed to the devastating and murderous incursions of the French and Indians from Canada. Several expeditions were sent into Canada; but the only success that attended the English arms was the taking again of Port Royal, which had been restored to the French at the close of the former war. It was now named *Annapolis*. The peace of Utrecht, in 1713, put an end to the war in the northern colonies; but South Carolina continued to be annoyed for some time by the Indians. By the treaty of Utrecht, France ceded Newfoundland and Nova Scotia to England.

In 1744, England again declared war against France and Spain, which again involved the colonies in hostilities with the enemies of the mother-country and with their Indian allies. The principal event of this war, in America, was the capture of Louisburg from the French by forces from New England. The treaty of Aix-la-Chapelle in 1748 again gave peace to the colonies. Prisoners were to be released on both sides without ransom, and all conquests to be mutually restored.

This war was extremely disastrous to the colonies. Many lives were lost; the growth of population was checked; great losses were sustained in the commercial interests of the country; and finally a burdensome debt of several millions had been incurred to defray the expenses of the war. With the return of peace, however, commerce revived; the settlements began to extend, and public credit was restored.

But only a brief interval of repose was allowed to the colonies. In 1756, eight years from the peace of Aix-la-Chapelle, Great Britain again declared war against France, on the ground of the encroachments of the French upon the English territories in America.

Some years previous to this war the French had commenced a chain of posts, designed to extend from the head of the St. Lawrence to the Mississippi, with a view to maintain a communication between their northern possessions and Louisiana.

In 1750, the English government granted a large tract of land on the Ohio river to a company called the *Ohio company*, formed for the purpose of settling the country, and carrying on a trade in furs with the Indians. The French governor of Canada, apprehending both the loss of the fur-trade and the interruption of his communications with Louisiana, claimed the whole country between the Ohio and the Alleganies, and prohibited the further encroachments of the English. He also opened a new communication between Lake Erie and the Ohio, and stationed troops at posts along the line. The Ohio company, thus threatened in their trade, persuaded Governor Dinwiddie of Virginia, in 1753, to send a remonstrance to the French commandant. George Washington was the bearer. The commandant returned for answer that he had taken possession of the country by order of the governor-general of Canada, whose orders alone he could regard.

The British government, on learning the claim set up by the French, directed the Virginians to resist it by force. In 1754, an expedition was conducted against the French by Washington; but the superior force of the French obliged him to capitulate, with the privilege of returning with his troops to Virginia. This was properly the commencement of what is commonly styled the *French war*, although the formal declaration was not yet made.

In the meantime, the British government recommended the colonies to unite for their common defence. A convention of delegates from all the northern colonies accordingly met at Albany in 1754, and adopted a plan of union; but it was rejected, both by the provincial assemblies and by the home government: by the former because it gave too much power to the crown, and by the latter because it gave too little.

In the spring of 1755, vigorous preparations were made for carrying on the war. An expedition was sent against *Nova Scotia*, which met with entire success: the colonial forces, with trifling loss, subdued the French, and gained complete and permanent possession of the whole country.

An expedition under General Braddock, directed against the French on the *Ohio*, was unfortunate. Owing to the arrogance and rashness of the commander, the British troops were surprised and defeated with great loss by a very inferior force of French and Indians. General Braddock was mortally wounded, and the conduct of the retreat devolved on Washington, who was in command of the colonial militia, and by whom the army was saved from total destruction.

The American arms were more successful in the north. The French were signally defeated on the borders of Lake George, and their commander, Baron Dieskau, was mortally wounded. The moral effect of this victory, following within a few weeks the discomfiture of Braddock, was very great and salutary in its influence upon the colonies.

The next year, 1756, war was formally declared between Great Britain and France; and in Europe began what is called the *seven years' war*, in which Prussia was united with England against France. In America the campaign of 1756 was very disastrous to the colonists; they were unable even to attempt gaining possession of *Niagara* and *Crown Point*, places of great importance in the hands of the French, and the reduction of which was in the plan of operations. The French, under Montcalm, took Fort Oswego, thus gaining entire command of Lakes Ontario and Erie, besides inflicting upon the English a very severe loss, amounting to sixteen hundred men made prisoners, one hundred and twenty cannon, with fourteen mortars, two sloops-of-war, and two hundred bateaux.

The British government made great preparations for the campaign of 1757. A large force was destined for the reduction of Louisburg; but the indecision and incapacity of Lord Loudon, the commander-in-chief, caused the expedition to be abandoned. Meantime, Montcalm, the

French commander, besieged and took Fort William Henry, on Lake George, after a most spirited defence by Colonel Munroe. The English troops, after being admitted to honorable capitulation, were treacherously massacred by the Indians attached to Montcalm's army.

The campaign of 1758 was more prosperous. Lord Chatham had now become prime minister, and infused new energy into the prosecution of the war. In answer to a call made by him upon the colonies, Massachusetts, Connecticut, and New Hampshire, united in raising fifteen thousand men. The tide of success now turned in favor of the English. Three expeditions had been planned : one against Louisburg, another against Ticonderoga, and the third against Fort du Quesne on the Ohio. Louisburg was taken, with great loss to the French in prisoners, ships, and munitions of war. Fort du Quesne was abandoned by the French, taken possession of by the English, and named *Pittsburgh*. The expedition against Ticonderoga failed, but the failure was compensated by the capture of *Fort Frontinac*, an important fortress at the outlet of Lake Ontario.

The campaign of 1759 commenced with a nearly simultaneous attack upon all the French strongholds in Canada, namely, Ticonderoga, Crown Point, Niagara, and Quebec. One division of the army, under General Amherst, the commander-in-chief, proceeded against Ticonderoga and Crown Point, which were successively taken. Another division, under General Prideaux, advanced and took Niagara. General Wolfe was no less successful in the great enterprise of conquering Quebec. The French, under Montcalm, were defeated on the plains of Abraham, and Quebec fell into the hands of the British. General Wolfe died upon the field of battle.

In 1760, the French made an unsuccessful attempt to recover Quebec. In less than a year from the capture of that city, Montreal, Detroit, and all other places in the possession of the French, were surrendered to the British, and the conquest of Canada was completed.

By the treaty of peace definitively concluded at Paris in 1763, Nova Scotia, Canada, Cape Breton, and all other islands in the gulf and river St. Lawrence, were ceded to the British crown.

Thus it appears that in the seventy-one years from 1689 to 1760, the colonies were involved in *four* wars, occupying in all *twenty-seven* years. Yet during this period the population had increased from two hundred thousand to about three millions. The arts and manufactures, being opposed by the mother-country, made but little progress ; but there was a steady advancement in agriculture. Trade and commerce had gone on very greatly increasing—so much, that in the ten years preceding the revolutionary war, the average annual exports to Great Britain and elsewhere amounted to four million pounds sterling, and the imports to three and a half millions.

In the meantime, colleges and other superior institutions of learning had been established in nearly all the colonies, and popular instruction provided for, especially in New England ; the country was advancing in intellectual culture ; and more than all, the necessity of uniting for the common defence, and the intercourse between the colonies that grew out of it, had tended to create a *national* spirit, which the events of the twelve years succeeding the peace of Paris still further developed and strengthened.

SECTION II.—*Revolutionary History.*

IN 1775, twelve years from the peace of Paris, began the war which terminated in the final separation of the United States from the British empire. We will briefly glance at the causes of this revolution.

The colonists, from the first, always cherished a jealous sense of their rights: as early as the middle of the seventeenth century, it was a settled doctrine among them that the authority of parliament was limited to the regulation of trade, and that taxes could not be imposed upon them without their own consent. Previous, indeed, to the peace of Paris, the home government had never attempted to interfere with internal taxation. For a century, however, before that event, a variety of restrictions had from time to time been imposed upon the trade of the colonies, the object of which was to oblige the colonists to buy and sell exclusively in the English markets. Colonial manufactures were also in every possible way discouraged. These restrictions produced much discontent and ill-blood.

In 1764, the first act avowedly for the purpose of raising a revenue in America was passed in parliament. This was followed the next year (March 22, 1765) by the famous *Stamp Act*, making void all bonds, notes, and such like instruments, unless written on stamped paper, upon which a duty to the crown was imposed. These acts excited great displeasure throughout the colonies; and in October a congress of delegates from Rhode Island, Massachusetts, Connecticut, New York, New Jersey, Maryland, and South Carolina, met at New York, and passed several resolutions, acknowledging the rightful authority of parliament, but denouncing the stamp act and other acts, as subversive of the just rights and liberties of the colonists as natural-born English subjects. The proceedings of this body were sanctioned by all the colonies. The public indignation, inflamed by newspapers, pamphlets, and popular meetings, rose to the highest pitch; combinations were everywhere formed to abstain from using articles of British merchandise, and in every way to oppose the measures of the home government. The officers appointed under the stamp act were in many places insulted, abused, and forced to resign; and when the first of September, the day for the act to go into operation, arrived, neither stamps nor stamp-officers were to be found. Business of all kinds requiring stamps was for a time suspended; law proceedings were stayed, the courts shut, and marriages ceased to be celebrated.

The next year (March 18, 1766) the stamp act was repealed, though the repeal was accompanied by a declaration of the "*right of parliament to bind the colonies in all cases whatsoever.*" In a few months from this time, a new ministry came into power, and a new plan for taxing America was introduced into parliament, namely, by laying a duty on glass, paper, pasteboard, painters' colors, and tea, imported into the colonies. The bill imposing these duties and providing for their collection by a new customhouse system, was passed June 29, 1767. A body of troops was soon after sent out and quartered in Boston. These measures produced great exasperation in the colonies, and led to combinations against using the articles subjected to duty. In 1770, this act was repealed, with the exception of the duty on tea. The colonists were only the more decided in renouncing the use of that article. An act of parliament was passed in 1773, allowing the East India company such a drawback of duties on teas exported to America that they could afford to sell them there cheaper than in England. This was done with the hope of inducing the colonists to return to the use of the article. Large shipments were accordingly made; but the Americans refused to pay the slight duty upon it; the cargoes sent to New York and Philadelphia were not suffered to be landed; in Charleston it was not allowed to be put to sale; and at Boston it was thrown into the sea by a party of men disguised as Indians. These proceedings excited the fierce displeasure of the British government, especially against Boston; and in March, 1774, the "*Boston Port Bill*," so called, was passed, prohibiting all commercial intercourse with that town. Another bill subverted the charter government of Massachusetts, vesting the appointment of the council and judges in the crown; and a third shortly after empowered the governor to send persons indicted for capital offences to another colony or to Great Britain for trial.

These violent proceedings awakened the greatest indignation throughout the colonies. All made common cause with Massachusetts. On the 5th of September a general congress met at Philadelphia, and adopted a declaration of rights and grievances, and agreed to an entire suspension of all commercial intercourse with Great Britain until the repeal of the acts of which they complained. They likewise voted an address to the king, another to the people of Great Britain, and a third to the inhabitants of Canada. These peaceful measures for redress proving ineffectual, the feeling of the necessity of resisting by force became quite general in the colonies. Preparations began to be made; warlike stores were collected, and the citizens began to arm.

In Massachusetts Governor Gage had convoked the legislative assembly for the 5th of October, 1774, but afterward judged it expedient to countermand the writs. The assembly notwithstanding convened, and the governor not appearing, organized themselves and adopted a plan for the defence of the province. In November they met again and resolved to raise a force of twelve thousand men, and to request the other New England states to increase the number to twenty thousand.

Early the next year, 1775, parliament, in spite of the conciliatory counsels of the Earl of Chatham, proceeded to pass a bill restraining still further the trade of New England. Soon after they imposed restrictions upon the middle and southern colonies, except New York, Delaware, and North Carolina. This exception was made with a view to produce dissension among the colonies: but it failed of its object.

This brings us to the commencement of actual hostilities. General Gage, the royal governor of Massachusetts, sent a detachment of eight hundred soldiers to destroy some military stores deposited at Concord. On their way, they arrived at *Lexington* on the morning of the 19th of April, 1775, where they found a company of provincial militia assembled on parade. This company, not instantly obeying an order to throw down their arms and disperse, were fired upon and eight of their number killed. The detachment proceeded to Concord and destroyed the stores, though not without opposition and bloodshed. But the spirit of the people was up, and on their return to Boston the British were harassed the whole way, and continually fired upon from behind walls, buildings, and fences. The British loss, in killed, wounded, and missing, amounted to nearly three hundred: the American to less than a hundred.

The war was now begun in good earnest. The important fortresses of Ticonderoga and Crown Point were taken by the Americans; and soon after (June 17, 1775) the memorable battle of *Bunker's Hill* was fought. The result of this engagement, though the Americans, from failure of ammunition, were obliged to retreat, was in its moral effect equal to a victory. The British loss was wo hundred and twenty-six killed, and eight hundred and twenty-eight wounded. The Americans lost one hundred and thirty-nine killed, and three hundred and fourteen wounded and missing.

The second continental congress was at this time in session, having met at Philadelphia on the 10th of May, and resolved to organize an army. On the 15th of June, GEORGE WASHINGTON was appointed commander-in-chief. He proceeded at once to the American army amounting to about 14,000 men, posted in the environs of Boston. The British occupied Boston, Bunker's and Breed's hill, and Boston Neck. The first cares of the commander-in-chief were directed to introducing discipline, order, and system, into the army.

Meantime, an expedition against Canada was planned. St. John's and Montreal were successively taken; Quebec was unsuccessfully besieged. General Montgomery, the commander of the expedition, fell beneath its walls. The Americans, for want of adequate forces, were obliged to retire from Canada.

In March, 1776, General Washington executed a plan for driving the British from Boston, by seizing and fortifying Dorchester heights, and thus getting command of the harbor and British shipping. On the 17th the British forces evacuated the town and sailed for Halifax.

In the month of June, General Clinton and Sir Peter Parker made an attack on Fort Moultrie, near Charleston, South Carolina; but were repulsed with considerable loss.

Congress meanwhile continued in session, and on the 4th of July adopted the memorable *Declaration of Independence.* This declaration was received with every demonstration of joyous enthusiasm throughout the colonies. The royal authority had been everywhere entirely subverted the year before: the revolution was now in a political sense completed; but the war for its establishment was yet to be waged.

Shortly after the evacuation of Boston by the British, General Washington removed to New York, making that place his headquarters. The American forces in and around the city were about 17,000 men, of whom a part were encamped near Brooklyn, on Long Island, under the command of General Sullivan. In June following, General Howe with the forces from Halifax, arrived near New York, and was shortly after joined by his brother Admiral Lord Howe, with a reinforcement of troops, a strong naval force, and abundant military stores. The army under General Howe now amounted to twenty-four thousand.

On the 27th of August, the Americans on Long Island were attacked and defeated with the loss of upward of a thousand men. Generals Sullivan, Woodhull, and Lord Sterling, were taken prisoners. General Washington crossed over from New York during this engagement and witnessed the defeat of his best troops with indescribable anguish. He immediately withdrew the American forces from Long Island and shortly afterward from New York, which was taken possession of by the British. Washington at first took position at Harlem heights, but soon retired to White Plains. Here on the 28th of September a battle was fought, but without any decided advantage to either side. General Washington had adopted the policy of wearing out the enemy by keeping them in perpetual pursuit, and avoiding any general engagement for the present, and by engaging in skirmishes whenever he could do so with decided advantage. In pursuance of this policy he withdrew from White Plains, leaving part of his army in a position a few miles from there, crossed the Hudson, and took post near Fort Lee. The British general having been thus far baffled in his attempts to draw on a general engagement, turned his forces against Fort Washington and Fort Lee. The former was first attacked, and after a spirited defence was taken, with between 2,000 and 3,000 men made prisoners. The garrison of Fort Lee abandoned the place and joined Washington, who was now at Newark.

The forces with the commander-in-chief were now reduced to three thousand men, and they were destitute of tents, blankets, and even of utensils to cook their provisions. Pursued by the enemy, Washington retreated successively to Brunswick, Princeton, Trenton, and finally across the Delaware into Pennsylvania. So hot was the pursuit that the rear of the American army was often in sight of the van of the enemy.

This retreat through New Jersey was the darkest hour of the revolutionary struggle. On the same day that Washington was driven across the Delaware, the British took possession of Rhode Island. They were already in possession of New York and New Jersey. The division of the army with Washington was continually diminishing by the discharge of the militia whose term of service expired, and by desertion of the regulars. The militia of New Jersey and Pennsylvania disregarded the call made upon them; and the handful of men that remained with Washington were exposed in an open country, without tools to intrench themselves, suffering the greatest hardships and privations in the midst of a population of whom many were hostile and all disheartened. A general gloom and despondency hung over the country. But nothing could shake the constancy of Washington. Being at length reinforced by some militia and by the second division of the regular army that had been left in New York under General Lee, but which (in consequence of that general being surprised and taken prisoner by the British) was then in command of General Sullivan, his forces now amounted to about 7,000 men. Feeling the absolute necessity of doing something to rouse the army and the country from the depression that was weighing down all minds, Washington crossed the Delaware with a detachment of his army, surprised and took prisoners a body of a thousand Hessians, with the loss of but nine men on his own side.

Soon after evading by night the British who were encamped at Trenton in the confident expectation of forcing him to a general engagement the next day, he marched upon Princeton where a part of the British force had been left, routed and put to flight two regiments which he met on his way, and captured nearly the whole of another. These brilliant affairs turned the tide. The British immediately evacuated Trenton, and retreated to New Brunswick; the inhabitants, stung to revenge by the brutalities they had suffered, took courage, and the enemy were driven from every post in New Jersey, except Amboy and New Brunswick: and Washington went into secure winter quarters at Morristown. Thus closed the campaign of 1776.

During the darkest period of this campaign the American congress showed no sign of dismay. They adopted articles of confederation for a perpetual union of the states; took measures for raising a new army with a larger term of enlistment; created a paper currency; and solemnly proclaimed that they would listen to no terms of peace short of independence. They sent commissioners to France to treat for the acknowledgment of their independence and for aid in their struggle. The cause of America was popular at the French court; countenance and assistance were at once in various ways secretly given. Many French officers became desirous of enlisting in the struggle, among whom was the young Marquis de la Fayette, who arrived in season to take part in the next campaign.

The campaign of 1777. In May, Washington broke up his winter encampment at Morristown. His army now amounted to little more than 7,000 men. The British also removed from New Brunswick. No decided movement was made till August, when General Howe, the British commander, sailed for the Chesapeake with 16,000 men. Washington immediately put his army in motion to save Philadelphia from falling into the enemy's hands. The two armies met at *Brandywine*, September 11, and the Americans, after fighting nearly all day, were forced to retire. In this battle La Fayette was wounded in the leg After another ineffectual attempt to save Philadelphia, Washington was obliged to withdraw his force, and General Howe entered the city. Congress adjourned to Lancaster.

On the 4th of October, Washington attacked a part of the British army posted at *Germantown*, but was repulsed with a loss double that of the enemy. After this the British remained for some time inactive at Philadelphia.

But while the southern army under Washington accomplished so little, brilliant success crowned the army of the north. As a part of the plan formed by the British, General Burgoyne invaded the states from the north, with a view to form a communication between Canada and New York, and cut off New England from the more southern states. After various movements—in the course of which Ticonderoga was abandoned by the Americans, and a detachment of the British was defeated at *Bennington*—the two armies met at Saratoga, where, after two severe engagements, General Burgoyne, finding himself hemmed in without chance of escape, and his provisions reduced to a three days' supply, found himself under the necessity of surrendering to General

Gates, with his whole army, consisting of five thousand and seven hundred effective men.

This event was hailed throughout the country with transports of joy. Its moral effect was every way important. Among its consequences was the acknowledgment of the independence of the United States by France, and the conclusion of a treaty of alliance and commerce between the two nations. The campaign was terminated by the British army going into winter quarters at Philadelphia, and the American at Valley Forge, about fifteen miles distant. The hardships and sufferings of the American army this winter, from badness of shelter, destitution of clothing, and scarcity of food, with consequent sickness, were intense.

Campaign of 1778. The intelligence of the alliance between America and France, determined the British to evacuate Philadelphia. They began their retreat to New York on the 18th of June. General Washington crossed the Delaware in pursuit, and on the 28th an engagement took place at Monmouth, in New Jersey. Night broke off the battle, but the Americans on the whole gained the advantage, passing the night on the field, intending to renew the attack in the morning. But under cover of the night, the British general made good his retreat.

Toward the close of this year, the southern states became the theatre of the operations of the enemy. Savannah was taken, and with it the whole state of Georgia fell into the hands of the English.

The campaign of 1779 was marked by nothing memorable or decisive. An attempt was made to recover Savannah and Georgia by the combined forces of the Americans, under General Lincoln, and the French, under Count D'Estaing, who had arrived the year before with twelve ships-of-the-line and six frigates. Several British vessels-of-war were taken, but the attempt to reduce Savannah failed. D'Estaing left the continent.

The enemy limited their efforts this year chiefly to predatory expeditions, fitted out from New York, with a view to distress and impoverish the country. An expedition of this kind was sent to Virginia; New Haven, in Connecticut, was plundered; and Fairfield, Norwalk, and some other towns in the same state, were wantonly burnt.

With the exception of taking Stony Point (July 15), and sending an expedition against the Six Nations of Indians, little was done or attempted by the Americans. This is attributable partly to the disappointment of the country with respect to the advantage they expected from the aid of D'Estaing and the French, but still more to the embarrassments and difficulties which resulted from the depreciation of the "continental currency," as the bills of credit issued by Congress were called. The amount in circulation had now risen to nearly two hundred millions of dollars; and so great was the depreciation, that it is said "four months' pay of a private would not procure his family a single bushel of wheat, and the pay of a colonel would not purchase oats for his horse." Under circumstances like these, the wisdom and prudence of Washington were tasked to the utmost to keep an army together

The campaign of 1780 was marked by more important events. Sir Henry Clinton, leaving General Kniphausen in command at New York, conducted a force of between seven and eight thousand men against Charleston, South Carolina. General Lincoln, who was in command of the army of the south, attempted to defend the place, but was obliged to capitulate, and his army, amounting to five thousand men, became prisoners. Sir Henry Clinton soon returned to New York, leaving Lord Cornwallis with four thousand men in South Carolina.

General Gates succeeded General Lincoln in command of the American army of the south. On the 16th of August, a bloody battle was fought at *Camden*, in which the Americans were defeated.

Meanwhile, at the north, the British continued their system of impoverishing the country by marauding expeditions sent out from New-York.

In July, arrived at Rhode Island a French fleet of seven sail-of-the-line, five frigates, and five smaller armed vessels, and several transports, with six thousand men, under the command of Count de Rochambeau. Great was the joy and great were the hopes inspired by this event; but the British naval force was still the greatest; and both the French fleet and army were for some time prevented from aiding the Americans, by being blocked up at Rhode Island.

This year is memorable in the annals of the war, for the treachery of General Arnold, and the sad fate of Major Andre. Arnold was in command of the important fortress of West Point, and engaged to betray it into the hands of the enemy. Major Andre was the agent employed by the British general in conducting the negotiation. The plot was discovered; Arnold fled to the British, and Andre was taken and hung as a spy.

The campaign of 1781 was opened by an inauspicious event, the revolt of the Pennsylvania line-of-the-army, occasioned by want of pay, clothing, and provisions. Their grievances were considerately examined and redressed by congress, and the mutiny subsided.

Virginia was meanwhile suffering from the marauding incursions of the British, commanded by the traitor Arnold.

In the south, General Greene succeeded General Gates. Lord Cornwallis was preparing to invade North Carolina, but unwilling to leave an enemy in his rear, sent Colonel Tarleton to engage General Morgan, whom Greene had put in command of one division of his army, and stationed in the western part of South Carolina. They met at *Cowpens*, on the 17th of January, and more than one thousand of the choicest veterans of the British army were defeated by scarcely five hundred Americans, chiefly militia. This was the most brilliant affair of the war.

Hereupon Lord Cornwallis went in pursuit of Greene, who evaded him until the 8th of March, when, having received a reinforcement, he marched against the British, and a general engagement took place at *Guilford* Courthouse, which was decided in favor of the enemy. General Greene then led his forces to South Carolina, to attack Lord Rawdon at *Camden*. A battle was fought, March 25, and Greene was obliged to retreat. Meanwhile General Lee, with a detachment despatched for that purpose, took possession of a post at Mottes, near the junction of the Santee and Congaree rivers. This led the British to evacuate Camden and their whole line of posts, except Ninety-six and Charleston. Not long after, Ninety-six was abandoned, and the British encamped at *Eutaw Springs*, forty miles from Charleston. Here, on the 8th of September following, an indecisive battle was fought. The British now retired to Charleston.

After the battle of Guilford, Lord Cornwallis began his march to Virginia, where he arrived on the 20th of May. General Lafayette hastened to oppose him, and to cut off the reinforcements which were marching to join him. In this he failed. Cornwallis's force now amounted to eight thousand men. Lafayette was obliged by inferiority of numbers to avoid a battle, and continued to retreat, manœuvring with great prudence and skill. Cornwallis at length retired to Yorktown, near the mouth of York river, and fortified himself there.

The plan of the campaign, as first formed by Washington, had for its main project the siege of New York, in concert with a French fleet under Count de Grasse, expected to arrive in August. Being advised, however, that De Grasse would arrive at the Chesapeake, instead of New York, Washington changed his whole plan of operations, and began to move upon Yorktown with a combined force of Americans and French amounting to twelve thousand, while Count de Grasse with his fleet occupied the mouth of York river, and thus cut off the retreat of Cornwallis in that direction.

The siege of Yorktown commenced on the 6th of October, and on the 19th Lord Cornwallis was obliged to capitulate, surrendering his whole force, amounting to seven thousand men, and one hundred and sixty pieces of artillery.

With so much skill had Washington arranged his measures for withdrawing his army from New York, and combining his forces for the blockade of Yorktown, that Sir Henry Clinton, the British commander-in-chief, then at New York, did not suspect his designs till he was far on his way to Virginia. On the very day that Cornwallis surrendered Clinton left New York with a reinforcement of seven thousand men; and five days after, arrived off the capes of Virginia. Receiving intelligence of the fate of Cornwallis, he returned to New York.

This great and important victory filled the country with joy and exultation. Congress passed resolutions of thanks to the generals, officers, and soldiers, and went in procession to church to render solemn thanks to Almighty God: and appointed the 30th of December as a festival of national thanksgiving.

Thus ended the campaign of 1781, and with it the war was substantially ended. The British held a few posts of importance—New York, Charleston, and Savannah—but the country at large was wrested from their possession.

On the 4th of March, 1782, the British house of commons passed a resolution that "the house would consider as enemies to his majesty and to the country all those who should advise or attempt the further prosecution of offensive war on the continent of North America." The government immediately appointed Sir Guy Carleton commander-in-chief, in place of Sir Henry Clinton. In obedience to his instructions,

Sir Guy made advances for negotiations, but congress refused to negotiate except in concert with the French government. Not long after, at the instance of the French court, commissioners were appointed to negotiate a peace. These were John Adams, Benjamin Franklin, John Jay, and Henry Laurens. The commissioners on the part of England were Mr. Fitzherbert and Mr. Oswald. Provisional articles of peace were signed on the 30th of November, 1782. The definitive treaty was not signed until September 30, 1783. A formal proclamation of the cessation of hostilities was made to the army on the 19th of April, 1783. In July, the British evacuated Savannah; in November, New York; and in December, Charleston.

On the 3d of November, the army of the United States was disbanded; and on the 23d of December, Washington appeared in person in the hall of congress, and resigned his commission as commander-in-chief. The moral grandeur of that act and of that scene is without parallel in history. Washington concluded his address on that occasion as follows:—

"I consider it an indispensable duty to close the last solemn act of my official life by commending the interests of our dearest country to the protection of ALMIGHTY GOD, and those who have the superintendence of them to his holy keeping.

"Having now finished the work assigned to me, I retire from the great theatre of action; and, bidding an affectionate farewell to this august body, under whose orders I have long acted, I here offer my commission, and take my leave of all the employments of public life."

Mr. Mifflin, president of congress, in behalf of that body, replied to this address, expressing their high sense of his wisdom and ability in the conduct of the war; concluding in these words:—

"We join you in commending the interests of our dearest country to the protection of ALMIGHTY GOD, beseeching him to dispose the hearts and minds of its citizens to improve the opportunity afforded them of becoming a happy and respectable nation.

"And for *you*, we address to HIM our earnest prayer that a life so beloved may be fostered with all his care; that your days may be as happy as they have been illustrious; and that he will finally give you that reward which this world can not give."

Well for the nation if it always remember the example and the lesson here presented!

During the war, the trade and commerce of the country were nearly destroyed. Agriculture was greatly interrupted and depressed; but the necessity of providing articles which could no longer be imported, led to a greater progress in manufactures than at any former period. The population of the country at the close of the war was about three millions and a quarter.

SECTION III.—*Constitutional History.*

THE return of peace found the country burdened with more than forty millions of dollars of debt, due partly to foreign holders, and partly to the officers and soldiers of the revolutionary war. By the articles of confederation, under which the general government of the country had been carried on since 1777, congress had exclusive right to declare war, make peace, borrow money, issue bills of credit, and make requisitions upon the states for men and money: but it had no power to discharge the national debt. It could only recommend the states to raise money. Various plans were proposed, to redeem the credit of the country, among which was that of the states granting congress power to impose a duty of *five per cent.* on foreign goods. But this was defeated by the opposition of Rhode Island and New York. The interest of the public debt remained unpaid; the certificates of it depreciated every day, and many of the poor officers and soldiers who held them were obliged to sell them for almost nothing. Some of the states made attempts to maintain their credit; Massachusetts imposed a heavy tax to this end, but it produced an armed insurrection (A. D. 1786), which was with some difficulty put down.

In this disturbed and distressed condition of affairs, it became obvious that the common danger from foreign war being over, the confederation was an insufficient basis for the government of the country. Accordingly, in the month of May, 1787, a convention of delegates from all the states, except Rhode Island, assembled at Philadelphia, and after about four months' session, adopted the present constitution of the United States, with a resolution that as soon as it should be ratified by nine states, it should be carried into operation by congress. July 14, 1788, ten states having acceded to it, it was declared ratified and adopted by congress. The other states subsequently assented to it: New York, July 26, 1788; North Carolina in November, 1789; and Rhode Island in May, 1790.

GEORGE WASHINGTON was unanimously elected the first president under the new constitution: John Adams vice-president. The first congress assembled at New York, March 4, 1789; and on the 30th of April, Washington was inaugurated. The most important affairs pressed upon the attention of congress: the government was to be organized; the administrative and judiciary departments to be established; and a revenue to be provided. These measures occupied the first session of congress, which terminated on the 29th of September.

The second session of the first congress began January 8, 1790. Agreeably to a plan submitted by Mr. Hamilton, secretary of the treasury, congress proceeded to make provision for discharging in full the foreign and domestic debt, and assumed also the debts incurred by the several states in carrying on the war. To this object the proceeds of the public lands lying in the western territory, the surplus revenue from the duties on imports, and a loan of two millions, were appropriated. This measure immediately restored public credit; certificates of public debt rose to par; and those who had purchased low, realized immense fortunes. Business of all kinds revived, and the country entered upon a career of prosperous activity and enterprise.

At the next session of congress, after a protracted debate, a bill was passed imposing a tax on domestic spirits, for the purpose of paying the interest on the state debts assumed by the Union. A national bank was also established, not without opposition, mainly on the ground of its unconstitutionality. The party lines between the federalists and anti-federalists (as they were called), which had begun to appear when the adoption of the new constitution was under discussion, became this session more broad and clear. A regular opposition to the administration began to be organized.

Meantime the hostilities of the Indians northwest of the Ohio made it necessary to send an expedition against them. General Harmar was put in command, but he was defeated with considerable loss in a battle near Chilicothe. General St. Clair, who succeeded in command, was also totally defeated. A bill then passed congress for raising an additional force to the army. The measure was bitterly resisted by the opposition, chiefly on the ground that standing armies were dangerous, and that the proposed increase showed the existence of monarchical designs on the part of the administration. An unsuccessful attempt was made the next session to reduce the military establishment; and the opposition introduced various resolutions, evincing their hostility to the administration. The public press became also the vehicle of vehement attacks, particularly upon the secretary of the treasury, Mr. Hamilton; and party spirit, from day to day, grew stronger throughout the country.

On the expiration of his first term of office, Washington was nevertheless unanimously re-elected president, March, 1793; Mr. Adams again vice-president. Beside the still unsettled condition of Indian affairs, this term of Washington's administration was embarrassed by new difficulties, growing out of the French revolution. The French republic had just declared war against England and Holland; and so strong in the United States was the hatred of the people to the British, and so lively their sympathy with the French, that the opinion was entertained in many quarters that America was bound by every consideration, both of gratitude to an old ally, and sympathy with the cause of republicanism, to make common cause with France.

Immediately on receiving intelligence of the declaration of war, Washington convened a cabinet council, and by their unanimous advice, issued a proclamation, enjoining strict neutrality to be observed on the part of the United States toward the belligerant powers, April 22, 1793. The opposition (anti-federalist) party, through the press, bitterly inveighed against this proclamation, denouncing it as a high-handed assumption of power on the part of the president, "a royal edict," evincing his monarchical disposition, and also as dishonorable and ungrateful toward France.

In this state of things, Mr. Genet, the new minister appointed by the French republic, arrived in the country, with the object of engaging the co-operation of the United States against England. Misled by the flattering reception he met with at Charleston, where he landed, he immediately began, even before he had been recognised as minister, to excite the people against the government; and carried his audacity so far, as to set at defiance the proclamation of neutrality, fitting out expeditions, and giving commissions to American vessels to cruise against the enemies of France, and assuming the power to hold admiralty courts, for the trial and sale of prizes thus made. In these measures he was supported by the opposition, or as it began to be called, the DEMOCRATIC party, which now began, under the influence of the French minister, and in imitation of the affiliated clubs in France, to form democratic societies throughout the country.

Washington demanded the recall of Mr. Genet. The French government complied, and instructed his successor to express its entire disapproval of Genet's conduct.

When congress assembled in December following, the proclamation of neutrality, and the conduct of Washington toward Genet, were approved by that body, as they were finally by the great body of the nation.

1794. Congress this year passed a bill providing for a naval force to protect American commerce against the Algerines. The slave-trade was likewise prohibited.

There seemed now reason to apprehend the necessity of another war with England. In addition to severe and unjust commercial restrictions imposed by that government, she had proceeded to capture and condemn neutral vessels having on board French goods, or carrying corn and other supplies to France. In anticipation of a war, congress passed several bills—for imposing an embargo; for organizing the militia; and for increasing the standing army. Meanwhile information was received that the British government was disposed to redress the grievances complained of, and amicably adjust all differences. John Jay was accordingly nominated and approved as envoy to Great Britain.

All attempts to make peace with the Indians having failed, the war was renewed. General Wayne was appointed to succeed General St. Clair. On the 20th of August, he gained a decisive victory over a large body of the Miamies, and then proceeded to lay waste their country. This victory prevented a general war with the Six Nations and with the tribes northwest of the Ohio.

The "Whiskey Insurrection" in Pennsylvania is one of the events of this year. It grew out of the duty on domestic spirits; this tax pressed heavily on the inhabitants of the west, and was besides considered unjust in principle. The proclamation of the president being disregarded, a considerable force of militia (fifteen thousand men), under Governor Lee of Maryland, was ordered out. On their approach, the insurgents laid down their arms, and promised submission to the laws.

1795. This year Mr. Jay having concluded a treaty of amity, commerce, and navigation, with Great Britain, the senate was convoked to consider it. Meanwhile, its contents having been disclosed, the most violent opposition was made to it; public meetings were held, and petitions against it were sent from all quarters of the country. The partisans of France and the enemies of England denounced it in the most unmeasured terms. The objections to it "were, generally, that it wanted reciprocity; that it gave up all compensation for negroes carried away contrary to the treaty of peace, and for the detention of the western posts; that it contravened the French treaty, and sacrificed the interest of our ally to that of Great Britain; that it gave up in several important instances the law of nations, particularly in relation to free ships making free goods, cases of blockade, and contraband of war; that it improperly interfered with the legislative powers of congress . . . . . . and that the commercial part gave few advantages to the United States."* The treaty was, however, ratified by the senate, and signed by the president, August 14, 1795.

* Pitkin, Civil History of the United States.

In October, after a long negotiation, a treaty was made with Spain, settling some questions of boundary, and acquiring for the United States the right of navigating the Mississippi. Treaties were also concluded with Algiers, and with the Indians in the west.

1796. On the assembling of congress this year, it became necessary to make appropriations and pass resolutions for carrying these treaties into effect. This gave occasion for a new display of hostility to the British treaty; and it was only after a debate of seven weeks, that the necessary resolutions passed the house of representatives, and then only by a majority of three. Public opinion at length gradually settled in favor of this treaty, as the only means of saving the country from becoming involved in the wars of the French revolution; and in the sequel it proved of great advantage to the United States.

The close of the second term of Washington's administration was now approaching. Signifying his intention to retire from public life, the Father of his country took occasion to issue a *farewell address* to his countrymen, replete with maxims of political wisdom, and sentiments of patriotism and virtue. If anything in this incomparable document may be signalized, where all should be profoundly weighed, the conclusion may justly claim attention: "Of all the dispositions and habits which lead to political prosperity, RELIGION and MORALITY are indispensable supports . . . . . . Whatever may be conceded to the influence of refined education on minds of peculiar structure, reason and experience both forbid us to expect that *national morality* can prevail in exclusion of *religious principle.*" This was said, let it be considered, at a time when the infidel spirit, the sneering spirit, of French atheism, was fashionable, almost the prevailing spirit, among the higher classes throughout the land.

The personal influence of Washington, due alike to his wisdom, his virtues, and his eminent services, was of the utmost importance in the first working of the new government. During the eight years of his administration, all differences with foreign nations had been peaceably settled, except those with France; and at home the Indian tribes had been pacified. "Public and private credit was restored; ample provision made for the security and ultimate payment of the public debt; American tonnage had nearly doubled; the exports had increased from nineteen to more than fifty-six millions of dollars; the imports in about the same proportion; and the amount of revenue from imposts had exceeded the most sanguine calculations."* The population had increased from three and a half to five millions; and agriculture and all the industrial interests of the country were in a flourishing state.

The only drawback to this picture of prosperity were the difficulties with France. Discontented at the neutral policy of America, the French republic continued to make demands upon the gratitude of the United States, which could be yielded to only by surrendering the right of self-government. Finding all attempts to involve America in its wars with Europe ineffectual, and feeling aggrieved at the treaty with its enemy, the French government proceeded to retaliate, by adopting certain resolutions injurious to American commerce, under the operation of which, moreover, several hundred American vessels were seized and confis-

* Pitkin.

cated. Just before his retirement from office, Washington had recalled Mr. Monroe, and despatched Mr. Charles Cotesworth Pinckney to France, as minister plenipotentiary, to settle the difficulties between the two nations.

Such was the state of the country at the close of Washington's administration.

On the 4th of March, 1797, JOHN ADAMS became president. The French republic refusing to receive Mr. Pinckney; a subsequent mission extraordinary to that government having also totally failed; and spoliations upon American commerce continually increasing; congress began to adopt vigorous measures for defence and retaliation. The treaties with France were declared no longer obligatory on the United States; an army was raised; and Washington was appointed commander-in-chief. Several engagements at sea took place between French and American vessels. The French government now signified indirectly a willingness to treat, and envoys were again sent from the United States. Before their arrival, the revolution of the 18th *Brumaire* (November 10, 1799) had taken place; the directorial government was overthrown, and Bonaparte was at the head of affairs as first consul. This event changed the policy of the French government; negotiations were commenced, and a treaty was concluded September 30, 1800.

On the 14th of December, 1799, died GEORGE WASHINGTON, mourned by the nation as no other man was ever mourned by any people. There have been great men superior perhaps to him in particular qualities and endowments: but in the perfect proportion and harmony of all the qualities of his nature, intellectual and moral, in the entireness and unity of his character, he is distinguished above all the great men whom history presents to our contemplation. In this consisted the secret of the repose, dignity, and grandeur, that through his whole life made so strong an impression upon all who approached him, and gave him such power over them.

Party spirit ran high during Mr. Adams's administration. Its measures were violently assailed by the opposition, particularly the "alien" and "sedition" laws: by the former of which, any alien considered dangerous might be ordered to depart from the country; and by the latter, combinations to oppose the government, libellous publications, &c., were made penal. The unpopularity of these and some other measures gave great strength to the democratic party, and defeated the re-election of Mr. Adams.

On the 4th of March, 1801, THOMAS JEFFERSON succeeded Mr. Adams as president of the United States.

At the next session of congress, several of the most important acts of the preceding period were repealed, particularly those imposing internal taxes, and reorganizing the United States courts.

Among the most important events of this period was the purchase of *Louisiana* from the French for fifteen millions of dollars.

Mr. Jefferson's term of office expiring, he was re-elected, and commenced a second term, March 4, 1805. The same year a war, which had been carried on for several years with Tripoli, was brought to a close by a treaty of peace.

The close of the year 1806 is marked by the explosion of *Aaron Burr's* plot for revolutionizing the western and southwestern territory. This ambitious and unprincipled man was engaged in the western country ostensibly with the purpose of settling a tract of country on the Washita, in Louisiana; but the nature of his preparations, the character of the men he was collecting, &c., excited suspicions—which the indiscreet disclosures of some of his associates confirmed—that his real object was to seize New Orleans, and establish himself at the head of a new empire in the southwestern territory of the United States; or, failing that, in Mexico. He was seized and brought to trial the next year, but no overt act being in proof against him, he was discharged. He was, however, generally believed to be guilty; and under the odium thus incurred, joined with that which attached to him for his murderous duel with General Hamilton in 1804, he sunk to abject contempt and wretchedness.

The interests of the United States were now becoming complicated with policy of the belligerant powers of Europe. The peace of Amiens (A. D. 1802) gave but a short repose from war; hostilities were soon renewed between France and England, and all the powers of Europe became involved in them. The United States maintained a strict neutrality, and engaged in an extensive and profitable carrying-trade.

But in 1806, the English government, by an *order of council*, declared the blockade of all the ports and rivers from the Elbe to Brest. Napoleon retaliated by the famous "*Berlin decree*," declaring all the British islands in a state of blockade. This was met by another British order of council, prohibiting all coasting-trade with France.

While these measures, which were partly in contravention of the law of nations, operated very injuriously upon the commerce of America, and tended to embroil her with both the belligerant powers, an old difficulty with England was aggravated by a special outrage. Great Britain had always claimed the right of searching American vessels, and of impressing from them native-born British subjects. They had also impressed some thousands of American seamen, under the pretext that they were British born. In this course the English government persisted in spite of the remonstrances of the United States. In June, 1807, Commodore Barron, commanding the American frigate Chesapeake, refusing to deliver three men claimed by the British, the Chesapeake was attacked by the British frigate Leopard off the capes of Virginia, very much injured and crippled, and the men in question forcibly taken away.

The public mind was greatly exasperated by this outrage. The president, by proclamation, ordered all British armed vessels off the waters of the United States, until satisfaction should be made, which the American minister, Mr. Monroe, was instructed to demand forthwith, as well as security against future impressments from American vessels. The British government declined to treat concerning the general question of *search and impressment*, but sent a special envoy to the United States, to settle the particular injury in the case of the Chesapeake. Mr. Rose was instructed, however, not to treat until the president's proclamation was revoked. This being refused, the matter rested; and was not finally adjusted until four years later, when satisfactory reparation was made by the British government.

Meantime, on the 17th of December, 1807, Bonaparte, in retaliation for the British order in council, issued "*the Milan decree,*" declaring every vessel denationalized that should submit to search by the British, and every vessel a good prize taken sailing to or from Great Britain or its colonies, or any place occupied by British troops.

The embargo failing to compel the belligerant powers to revoke measures so injurious to American commerce, and so subversive of the rights of neutrals, it was repealed on the 1st of March, 1809, and a law passed prohibiting all trade and intercourse with France and England.

Mr. Jefferson declining a re-election, was succeeded, March 4, 1809, by JAMES MADISON.

The state of the country was gloomy. Her commerce was suffering both from foreign and domestic restrictions; and it seemed that she must indefinitely submit to this condition of things, or make war with the belligerants.

In passing the *non-intercourse act* of March 1, congress had empowered the president to repeal it by proclamation in regard to either of the hostile parties revoking their edicts. The British minister at Washington engaged for his government the repeal of the orders of council, so far as the United States were concerned. The president accordingly notified the renewal of commercial intercourse with Great Britain. But the English government disavowed the engagement of its minister, and non-intercourse was again proclaimed.

On the 23d of March, 1810, Napoleon retaliated the non-intercourse act of congress by issuing the "*Rambouillet decree*"—ordering all vessels arriving in French ports, or the ports of countries occupied by French troops, to be seized and condemned. On the 1st of May, congress passed an act excluding British and French armed vessels from the waters of the United States—with a provision for renewing intercourse with whichever nation should within a given time cease to violate the commercial rights of neutral nations. In consequence of this act, the French decrees were revoked, and intercourse with France was renewed.

It had been made a condition on the part of the French government, in revoking its decrees, that the English orders of council should be also revoked. But England, affecting to question the fact of the actual revocation of the French decrees, continued to enforce its orders, stationing vessels-of-war just out the harbors of the United States, searching, and in many instances capturing and condemning American merchant-vessels. In the period between 1803 and the close of 1811, nine hundred American vessels had been thus captured.

On the 3d of April, 1812, an act was passed by congress laying an *embargo* for ninety days on all vessels within the jurisdiction of the United States. And on the 4th of June following, WAR WAS DECLARED against Great Britain. The grounds of war alleged were the impressment of American seamen, and the violation of neutral rights.

The feeling of the nation was by no means unanimous in favor of the war. It was protested against by a strong minority in congress, as unnecessary, impolitic, and immoral; and was generally condemned by the federal party throughout the country.

Thus the United States were again at war with England. The contest lasted for nearly three years. The limits of this history forbid anything but a slight sketch of its events.

In the campaign of 1812, nothing of any importance was achieved by land. The invasion of Canada was planned : forces were drawn to the northern frontier of the Union, and naval preparations made upon the lakes. No footing was, however, gained in the British territory ; on the contrary, Detroit and all the forts and garrisons in Michigan fell into the hands of the British, together with a considerable force under the command of General Hull, who surrendered without a battle, August 19 ; and the Americans were repulsed in an attack on *Queenstown*, and obliged to surrender, October 13.

But on the ocean the American arms were more successful. The series of brilliant naval victories which distinguished the war was commenced by the capture of the British frigate *Guerriere* by the *Constitution*, Captain Isaac Hull, August 10. This was followed (August 13) by the capture of the *Alert* by the *Essex*, Captain Porter ; of the *Frolic* by the *Wasp* (October 17) ; of the *Macedonian* by the *United States*, Commodore Decatur (October 25) ; and of the *Java* by the *Constitution*, then commanded by Commodore Bainbridge.

On the 4th of March, 1813, Mr. Madison was re-elected president.

The military operations of this year extended along the whole line of the northern frontier. The Americans were signally defeated at *Frenchtown* by a body of British and Indians, and five hundred men made prisoners, who were nearly all massacred by the Indians after their surrender. York (now Toronto), the capital of Upper Canada, was taken by the Americans, with a large quantity of military stores.

On the 1st of June, this year, the American navy suffered a severe loss in the capture of the frigate *Chesapeake*, Captain Lawrence, by the British frigate *Shannon*. In the engagement, Captain Lawrence and several brave officers were killed. This was followed (August 14) by the loss of the *Argus*.

These losses were counterbalanced by the capture of the British brig *Boxer* by the *Enterprise*, on the 5th of September, and by a brilliant victory gained (September 10) by the fleet on Lake Erie, under the command of Commodore Perry. This made the Americans masters of the lake, and opened the way to Detroit, which was soon after taken ; its fall being preceded by the battle of the *Thames*, in which the British and Indian forces, under the command of General Proctor, were totally defeated by General HARRISON. This victory had the effect of putting an end to the Indian war in the northwest, and of giving security to that frontier.

The invasion of Canada was again attempted ; but unexpected circumstances concurred to disarrange the plan of operations, and at length the northern army went into winter-quarters, without having effected anything toward the accomplishment of the object. High expectations had been formed of the success of this campaign, and the public disappointment was proportionably great.

At the south, the Creek Indians, instigated by the British, had taken up arms against the United States, and a sanguinary war was carried on in that quarter during the year 1813, and until in the summer of 1814, when General Jackson, having reduced the enemy in several engagements, at length inflicted upon them an almost exterminating defeat at *Horseshoe Bend.* The remnant of the tribe submitted, and the war was at an end. General Jackson was soon after appointed to the command of the forces at New Orleans.

In the spring of 1814, the American frigate *Essex* was captured by a superior British force in the bay of Valparaiso. But about the same time, the British brigs *Epervier* and *Reindeer* were captured, the former by the United States sloop-of-war Peacock, the latter by the sloop Wasp.

After some ineffectual movements at the north by General Wilkinson, little was attempted by either nation until midsummer, when the British government, freed from the burden of the European war by the abdication of Napoleon, augmented their armies in America by the addition of fourteen thousand of the veteran troops of Wellington, and at the same time sent a strong naval force to blockade the harbors, and ravage the towns upon the coast.

On the 3d of July, General Brown crossed the Niagara river from Buffalo, and took the British fort Erie; and on the 4th, after an obstinate and bloody engagement, gained a victory over the British at *Chippewa.* On the 25th, was fought the battle of *Bridgewater,* near the falls of *Niagara,* one of the most bloody battles of modern times. The British force amounted to nearly five thousand men; the American was one third less. The loss of the English was eight hundred and seventy-eight; of the Americans, eight hundred and sixty. The Americans were left in possession of the field.

About the middle of August, a large British fleet arrived in the Chesapeake bay. Six thousand men, under the command of General Ross, landed and proceeded to Washington, burnt the capitol, the president's house, and the buildings of the executive departments; and then by rapid marches retired to the ships, having lost about one thousand men in the expedition.

On the 12th of September, an attack was made on Baltimore; but the place was so gallantly defended by militia and the inhabitants, that the enemy abandoned the attempt. General Ross, the commander-in-chief of the British forces, was among the killed.

While the English were thus repulsed from Baltimore, signal success attended the American arms at the north. The naval force of the enemy on Lake Champlain was annihilated by Commodore M'Donough. The engagement took place off Plattsburgh; and while it was raging, Sir George Provost, with a force of fourteen thousand men, commenced an assault on the American works at Plattsburgh: but he met with such a destructive fire from the Americans under General Macomb, that he was compelled to retire, with the loss of twenty-five hundred men, abandoning his military stores, his sick and wounded.

The close of the year 1814 is memorable in the annals of the country on account of the celebrated *Hartford convention.* The federal party, as has been said, was from the first opposed to the war, as unjust and impolitic. The opposition was particularly strong in the New England states. As the war advanced, the opposition became still more decided, and serious apprehensions were expressed that the measures of the general government would involve the country in ruin. The opposition was aggravated by a misunderstanding between the governors of those states and the president in relation to the requisitions made by the latter for the militia to be placed under the command of officers of his appointment. Massachusetts, Rhode Island, and Connecticut, were at this time unprotected by any national troops against the enemy's forces hovering on the coast.

In this state of things, a convention of delegates from the New England states met at Hartford on the 15th of December, 1814; and after a session of three weeks, published a statement of grievances, and recommendations for redress. "The convention recommended—1. That the states they represent take measures to protect their citizens from 'forcible drafts, conscriptions, or impressments, not authorized by the constitution of the United States;' 2. That an earnest application be made to the government of the United States, requesting their consent to some arrangement, whereby the states separately, or in concert, may assume upon themselves the defence of their territory against the enemy, and that a reasonable portion of the taxes collected within the states be appropriated to this object; 3. That the several governors be authorized by law to employ the military force under their command in assisting any state requesting it to repel the invasions of the public enemy; 4. That several amendments of the constitution of the United States, calculated in their view to prevent a recurrence of the evils of which they complain, be proposed by the states they represent for adoption . . . . .; 5. Lastly, that if the application of these states to the government of the United States should be unsuccessful, and peace should not be concluded, and the defence of these states be still neglected, it would, in their opinion, be expedient for the legislatures of the several states to appoint delegates to another convention, to meet at Boston, in June, with such powers as the exigency of a crisis so momentous may require.

"The effect upon the public mind in the aggrieved states was alike seasonable and salutary . . . . . served greatly to allay the passions, and to inspire confidence and hope. Nor was the influence of this body upon the national councils less perceptible. Within three weeks after the adjournment of the convention, and the publication of their report, an act passed both houses of the national legislature, and received the signature of the president, authorizing and requiring him to 'receive into the service of the United States any corps of troops which may have been or may be raised, organized, and officered, under the authority of any of the states,' to be 'employed in the state raising the same, or an adjoining state, and not elsewhere, except with the consent of the executive of the state raising the same.' Before the commissioners who were sent to confer with the government could reach Washington, a bill passed the senate, providing for the payment of the troops and militia already called into service under the authority of the states. The arrival of the treaty of peace, at this juncture, arrested all further proceedings."*

While the Hartford convention was in session, on the 24th of De-

* Holmes's Annals.

cember, a treaty of peace was signed at Ghent. But before its arrival, the last and most memorable battle of the war was fought at *New Orleans.* On the 8th of January, 1815, the American forces, amounting to about *six thousand*, chiefly militia, under the command of General Jackson, intrenched before the city, were attacked by *fifteen thousand* British troops, commanded by Sir Edward Packenham. After three charges, in which they were swept down with incredible slaughter, the British fled in confusion, leaving their dead and wounded on the field of battle. General Packenham was killed while rallying his troops to the second charge; General Gibbs, who succeeded in command, fell mortally wounded in the third charge. The loss of the British in killed was *seven hundred;* in wounded, *fourteen hundred;* in prisoners, *five hundred:* in all, *twenty-six hundred.* The Americans lost *seven* killed and *six* wounded.

The joy excited by this victory was merged in the still livelier joy with which the news of the treaty of peace was soon after received. On the 17th of February, the treaty was ratified by the president and senate. This treaty made no allusion to the causes of the war, and settled none of the matters in dispute, and for which it was professedly declared. All parties, however, welcomed the return of peace. At a subsequent convention, signed by plenipotentiaries of the two countries appointed for the purpose, various articles for the regulation of commerce between England and the United States were adopted.

Before the expiration of the time, within which, by the treaty, all vessels taken by either party were to be held good prizes, several engagements at sea were fought, and several captures made. Among them the American frigate *President* was captured by a British squadron; and the British ships *Cyane*, *Levant*, and *Penguin*, were taken by the Americans.

At the next session of congress, a bill was passed incorporating the "*bank of the United States*," with a capital of thirty-five millions of dollars. The charter was to continue in force until the 3d of March, 1836. This measure was the subject of a very earnest and protracted debate, both as to its constitutionality, and as to the principles on which the bank should be established.

Mr. Madison was succeeded in the office of president by James Monroe, March 4, 1817.

The country was now at peace, but its condition was by no means prosperous. Commerce had not yet revived, and the manufactures which had been carried on during the war were entirely broken down by the influx of foreign merchandise.

In 1818, a war broke out between the Seminoles and the United States, occasioned by the removal of some Indians from lands ceded to the United States by the Creeks in 1814. The Indians were entirely subdued by General Jackson.

In 1819, another convention was made between Great Britain and the United States, granting to American citizens the right to fish on the banks of Newfoundland; establishing a portion of the northern boundary; and extending for ten years longer the commercial convention concluded four years before.

A treaty was also this year concluded with Spain, by which East and West Florida, with the islands adjacent, were ceded to the United States.

On the 4th of March, 1821 Mr. Monroe was unanimously elected to a second term of office. Much less unanimity, however, was displayed in the deliberations of the next congress. Some important commercial acts were passed ; revolutionary soldiers were provided for by pensions ; and the ratio of population and representation fixed at one representative to forty thousand inhabitants.

The year 1824 is signalized in the annals of the country by a visit from La Fayette, the friend and companion-in-arms of Washington, to whose services in the dark day of the revolutionary war the nation owed so much. He passed about a year in the country, visiting every part of it, and receiving everywhere the most enthusiastic tokens of homage and gratitude. He returned to his own country in a national frigate prepared for the purpose, and named, in honor of him, the *Brandywine*—the name of the battle in which he was wounded nearly fifty years before. During his visit, congress appropriated two hundred thousand dollars, and a township of land in Florida, as an acknowledgment of his eminent services.

Mr. Monroe retired from office with the respect and good will of all parties. His administration of affairs, both foreign and domestic, had been uninfluenced by party spirit, and characterized by uprightness, prudence, and good sense. The country was everywhere peaceful and prosperous.

No choice of a successor to Mr. Monroe having been made by the electors, the choice devolved upon the house of representatives.

On the 4th of March, 1825, JOHN QUINCY ADAMS was inaugurated president of the United States.

Among the noticeable events during this administration, the first to be mentioned is a controversy between the general government and the executive of Georgia, in relation to certain lands held by the Cherokees and Creeks in that state. The general government had agreed to extinguish, for the benefit of Georgia, the Indian title to those lands—" whenever it could be peaceably done, upon reasonable terms." But the Creeks, at a national council, refused to alienate their territory. After the council had broken up, and a majority of the chiefs had departed, a few who remained were induced to make a treaty, ceding the lands in question to the United States. This treaty was repudiated by the Creek nation. But the governor of Georgia determined to act upon it as valid. To prevent a war, the president ordered General Gaines to repair to the Creek country, for the protection of the Indians ; and directed Governor Troup of Georgia to suspend his intended measures. Congress approved the course of the president ; and at length a treaty was formed with the Creeks, which gave satisfaction to all parties except the state of Georgia.

The fiftieth anniversary of the Declaration of Independence (July 4, 1826) was rendered memorable by the death of ex-presidents ADAMS and JEFFERSON.

The most important among the measures which occupied the first session of the twentieth congress, was the revision of the *tariff*, with a view to afford protection to American manufactures. The principle of a *protective* tariff was warmly opposed by the south, and by a large portion of the commercial body at the north; while the details of the bill which was passed were far from satisfactory to the friends of protection.

During the last year of Mr. Adams's administration, the most absorbing subject of public interest was the approaching election; and never before had party spirit displayed itself in such virulent and unjustifiable attacks upon private life and character. Mr. Adams was defeated. During his administration the prosperity of the United States had increased to an unexampled height. Agriculture, commerce and manufactures, were everywhere flourishing. The public debt, which at the close of the war, amounted to nearly one hundred and fifty millions of dollars, was almost extinguished. The annual revenue largely exceeded the demands of government; and at the close of Mr. Adams's term, there was a surplus of more than five millions in the treasury.

On the 4th of March, 1829, ANDREW JACKSON was inaugurated president of the United States.

The new president signalized his accession to office by a sweeping removal from office of the functionaries of the general government appointed by his predecessors. Besides the principal officers of the treasury, marshals, district attorneys, revenue and land officers, nearly five hundred postmasters were removed from office. During Mr. Adams's administration there were but *two* removals, both for cause.*

Among the most important measures which engaged the attention of the twenty-first congress, were, the modification of the tariff; Indian affairs; internal improvements; and the renewal of the charter of the United States bank.

It was not until 1832 that a memorial came before congress for a renewal of the charter of the United States bank. A bill to that effect passed both houses of congress; but on the 10th of July it was returned by the president with objections.

The policy of making appropriations for *internal improvements* was adopted during Mr. Jefferson's term of office, and had continued through all the succeeding administrations. To this policy General Jackson was opposed, and accordingly returned, with his veto, several bills making such appropriations.

In 1832, the hostility of the south to the protective tariff assumed in South Carolina an attitude dangerous to the peace of the country. A convention of delegates assembled at Columbia, November 24; pronounced the acts of congress imposing duties for protection unconstitutional, and of no binding force in that state; and that it was the duty of the state legislature to pass laws to prevent the payment or enforcement of such duties. The remedy thus proposed received the name of *nullification*.

President Jackson immediately issued a proclamation, containing an

* Washington removed from office *nine*; John Adams, *ten*; Jefferson, *thirty-nine*; Madison, *five*; Monroe, *nine*: making, with the *two* removed by John Q. Adams, *seventy-four* in all.

admirable exposition of the principles and powers of the general government, and expressing a firm determination to maintain the laws. This only increased the exasperation in South Carolina: the governor of the state, by the authority of the legislature, issued a counter-proclamation, urging the people to be faithful to their primary allegiance to the state, and to resist the general government in any attempt to enforce the tariff laws. General orders were also issued to raise volunteers for repelling invasion, and supporting the rights of the state.

General Jackson hereupon addressed a message to congress, recommending such measures as would enable the executive to suppress the spirit of insubordination, and sustain the laws of the United States.

Everything thus betokened a civil war. But an appeal to South Carolina by the general assembly of Virginia, and the passage of a bill modifying the tariff (introduced by Henry Clay, and commonly known as the "compromise act"), joined with the manifestation of firmness and energy on the part of the executive, served to allay the ferment in South Carolina, and lead to a repeal of the *nullifying* ordinances.

On the 4th of March, 1833, Andrew Jackson entered on a second term of office.

The charter of the United States bank being about to expire, the president, who had before expressed to congress his doubts of the expediency of continuing that institution the depositary of the funds of the United States, directed the secretary of the treasury, Mr. DUANE, to remove the government "deposites" from the bank. This Mr. Duane declined to do. He was immediately removed from office by the president; and Mr. TANEY was appointed in his place, by whom the deposites were removed, and placed in the custody of several state banks. This measure was strongly censured by a resolution which passed the senate, June 9, 1834.

The country was now disturbed with serious apprehensions of a collision with France. By a treaty, negotiated in 1831, by Mr. Rives, the French government had agreed to make indemnity for spoliations committed on American commerce during the reign of Napoleon; but it had failed to fulfil its stipulations. In December, 1834, the president recommended reprisals upon French commerce. This was deemed by congress not expedient at present. Happily, however, the danger of hostile collision was removed in the course of the next year by the action of the French government in making provision to fulfil its stipulations.

The most important act of the first session of the twenty-fourth congress, which began December 7, 1835, was a law directing the deposite, under certain regulations, of the moneys of the United States in several of the state banks, and distributing the surplus revenue among the several states.

In December, 1835, one of the most destructive fires on record occurred in the city of New York. The amount of property destroyed is computed not to have fallen much short of *twenty millions* of dollars, without estimating the injury and loss from suspension and derangement of business.

Near the close of this year, the *Seminole* Indians, refusing to remove from Florida to the lands appropriated for them west of the Mississippi, the country became involved in a war with them; and it was not until 1842 that they were finally subdued and sent west.

On the 11th of July, 1836, the receivers of public money were instructed, by a circular from the treasury department, to receive nothing but gold and silver in payment for public lands.

On the 16th of January, 1837, the "expunging resolution" (so called) introduced by Mr. Benton, passed the senate by a small majority. By this act, the resolution of the senate passed June 9, 1834—censuring the president for removing Mr. Duane, and ordering the withdrawal of the United States deposites from the bank of the United States—was expunged from the journal of the senate. Against this proceeding, Mr. Webster, of Massachusetts, in behalf of himself and his colleagues, read a solemn protest.

On the 4th of March, 1837, MARTIN VAN BUREN became president of the United States.

Mr. Van Buren's administration was, in its general policy, a continuation of that of his predecessor. Scarcely, however, had he entered upon office, when the country was overwhelmed by one of the most severe commercial revulsions ever known.

For several years previous, the wildest spirit of speculation had prevailed throughout the country. Vast public works were undertaken by states and chartered companies; immense importations of foreign goods were made; and real estate, especially lots in cities and towns, went up a hundred fold, not to say in many cases a thousand fold, beyond its intrinsic value. The multitude of state banks that had been chartered, after the expiration of the charter of the United States bank, and the consequent excessive expansion of the paper currency, had contributed to increase the spirit of speculation. At length a crisis came; and the revulsion was proportionably severe. Some idea of it may be formed from the fact that a list of failures in the city of New York (including only the more considerable, and omitting hundreds of less importance) shows a total amount of more than *sixty millions* of dollars. All credit, all confidence, was at an end.

On the 10th of May, all the banks of the city of New York suspended specie payments, and the suspension became general throughout the country. The general government became involved in the universal embarrassment—the banks in which its deposites were placed having stopped in the general suspension. The government still insisted, however, upon all postages and duties being paid in specie or its equivalent, and even refused its own checks and drafts when offered in payment of customhouse bonds.

In this state of things, the president convoked an extra session of congress, which began on the 4th of September. Agreeably to the recommendation of the executive, as measures for the immediate relief of the general government, congress passed a law postponing to the 1st of January, 1839, the payment to the states of the fourth instalment of the surplus revenue; and authorizing the issue of ten millions of treasury notes, to be receivable in payment of public dues. The president also recommended the "separation of the fiscal operations of the government from those of corporations or individuals." A bill in accordance with this recommendation—commonly called the *sub-treasury bill*, placing the public money in the hands of certain receivers-general, subject to the order and control of the treasurer of the United States—passed the senate, but was lost in the house.

At the next regular session of congress (December, 1837—July, 1838), a reissue of treasury notes was authorized. The *sub-treasury* system was again urged upon the attention of congress, but was not adopted.

On the 13th of August, 1838, the banks throughout the country generally resumed specie payments : but in October following, the banks of Philadelphia again suspended, and their example was followed by the banks in Pennsylvania, and in all the states south and west. The banks of New York and New England continued to pay specie.

The twenty-sixth congress commenced its first session December 2, 1839. Among its acts, two only need be mentioned : one for taking the *sixth census* of the United States ; the other, "for the collection, safe keeping, transfer, and disbursement, of the public revenue"—being the *sub-treasury* system so earnestly recommended by the president.

At the second session of this congress, nothing was done of sufficient importance to find a place in this sketch.

The administration of Mr. Van Buren was drawing to a close. He was a candidate for re-election ; William Henry Harrison, of Ohio, was the candidate of the opposition. After a contest unprecedented for intensity of political excitement, Mr. Van Buren was defeated.

On the 4th of March, 1841, WILLIAM HENRY HARRISON was inaugurated president of the United States.

Scarcely had the new president entered upon his office, and organized his administration by the appointment of his cabinet, when he was stricken with sickness ; and on the 4th of April, one month from the day of his inauguration, he expired. "In death, as in life, the happiness of his country was uppermost in his thoughts."

By the death of General Harrison, JOHN TYLER, of Virginia, the vice-president, became, according to the constitution, president of the United States.

The passage of a general bankrupt law was one of the earliest measures passed by congress. This law was, however, subsequently repealed. The tariff was modified with a view to further protection of American industry. To the influence of this measure, the friends of protection mainly attribute the return of the country to a state of prosperity as great as ever before. It has, however, created great dissatisfaction in some of the southern states, where it is considered an infraction of the compromise act.

Among the most memorable events of this administration is the *treaty of Washington*, concluded in September, 1842, between Great Britain and the United States, by Lord Ashburton and Daniel Webster, by which the differences about the boundary line between Maine and Lower Canada, long a matter of dispute and ill-blood, were amicably and satisfactorily adjusted.

The disturbances in Rhode Island are a less agreeable subject of record; though happily the apprehensions they excited have been dispelled. In 1841, a convention of inhabitants of Rhode Island framed a new constitution, giving the right of suffrage (which under the existing government was extremely limited) to all free white inhabitants; and proceeded to organize a new government under this constitution. They elected a legislative body, and chose Thomas W. Dorr governor of the state. All these proceedings were considered as unlawful and revolutionary by those opposed to them, inasmuch as they had taken place without any legal warrant, and without being in any way initiated by the lawful and actual government. A civil war seemed inevitable. The legal government applied to the president of the United States, who detached several companies of troops to Newport to await events. Dorr mustered a considerable force of armed men, with two pieces of artillery, and made an ineffectual attempt to gain possession of the arsenal at Providence. Shortly after, he took a position at *Chepachet*, where his force was increased by volunteers from New York and other states. Upon the approach of a body of the state militia, under General M'Neil, Dorr and his party broke ground and fled, June 25, 1842. His government fell to pieces. After two years, Dorr returned to Rhode Island; was tried and convicted of treason, and sentenced to the state-prison for life. This sentence, however, the government of the state have signified their readiness to revoke, whenever Dorr shall acknowledge his allegiance to the existing government—which now rests upon a new constitution, legally formed and adopted by the people of the state since the commencement of the disturbances, making the right of suffrage as extensive as in that proposed by the revolutionary party, except that two years' residence in the state is required instead of one.

During the last session of congress, Mr. Tyler communicated to the senate a treaty formed with the republic of *Texas*, by which that state was to become a member of the Union. The treaty was not ratified by the senate.

During the summer and autumn of 1844, the election of president was the absorbing subject of public interest. The candidates of the rival parties were HENRY CLAY, of Kentucky, for president, and THEODORE FRELINGHUYSEN, of New Jersey,* for vice-president, on the one side; and JAMES K. POLK, of Tennessee, and GEORGE M. DALLAS, of Pennsylvania, on the other.

Thus have been briefly sketched the leading events, political and civil, of the history of the United States, from the first feeble and scattered colonial establishments to the formation of a great and prosperous nation. The great problem of the possibility of a permanent and well-ordered republic, on so extensive a scale, doubtless yet remains to be solved. It depends on the INTELLIGENCE and VIRTUE of the people, whether it shall be solved as the friends of free institutions desire. Theoretically the most perfect of all forms of human government, it requires, beyond any other, the presence of these conditions to preserve it from being practically the worst. May the Almighty Ruler of nations

*** Mr. Frelinghuysen has for five years past resided in New York, as chancellor of the university of that city.**

dispose the hearts and minds of the people to such a religious observance of his holy commandments, that the history of the nation in all coming ages may be as glorious as its rise and progress have been wonderful! "Blessed are the people who have the Lord for their God yea, happy are the people that are in such a case!"

CONTEMPORARY DYNASTIES,

FIFTH

Sarmatians.	Germans.	Franks and Gauls.	Italy.
General movement of the Sarmatian tribes toward Southern and Western Europe; for six centuries their history obscure.	Movements of the Saxons to England; the Franks to Gaul; the Goths to Italy; the Lombards to Pannonia, and in the next century to Italy; the Alemanni to the Roman provinces on the Rhine, &c.	420 Pharamond. 449 Merovæus. 481 Clovis, who, by the defeat of Syagrius, established the power of the Franks in Gaul.	476 End of Western empire. — Odoacer becomes king of Italy. 493 Establishment of the Gothic kingdom of Italy, by Theodoric.

SIXTH

France.	Italy.	Spain.
511 Thierry I. Clotaire I. 534 Theodobert. 561 Caribert. Gontram, Sigibert. Chilperic. 593 Childebert. 596 Theodobert II. Thierry II.	*Ostragoths.* 526 Athalaric. 534 Theodobalus. 536 Vitiges. 540 Heldibadus. 541 Elaric. 551 Theia, conquered by *Lombards.* 568 Alboinus. 573 Clephes. 586 Antharis. 590 Agilulphus. 569 Longinus, Exarch of Ravenna; his successors tributary to the Lombards.	*Visigoths.* 507 Gesalric. 526 Amalaric. 531 Theudis. 548 Theodogesil. 549 Agila. 554 Athanagild. 572 Leovigild. 586 Recared I.; he renounces Arianism and establishes orthodox Christianity.

SEVENTH

France.	Italy.	Spain.	England.
614 Clotaire II. 628 Dagobert I. 638 Sigebert II. — Clovis II. 660 Clotaire III. 669 Childeric II. 672 Dagobert II. (Pepin Heristal.) 673 Thierry III. 690 Clovis III. 695 Childebert II. The kingdom frequently divided.	*Lombards.* 616 Adaloaldus. 626 Arioaldus. 638 Rotharis. 654 Rodoaldus. 659 Aribertus. 662 Gundebertus 672 Garibald 673 Pertharit. 691 Cunibertus. The Exarchate of Ravenna nominally held by the Eastern Empire, but tribute paid by its governors to the Lombards.	*Visigoths.* 603 Witeric. 610 Gondomar. 612 Sisebad. 621 Recared II. — Suintilla I. 631 Sisenaud I. 636 Sisenaud II. 640 Tulca. 642 Chindaswind. 649 Recheswind. 672 Wamba. 680 Ervig. 687 Egiga. Toward the close of the century the Moors begin to threaten the South of Spain.	*Heptarchy.* 617 Rodoald. East Anglia. 624 Edwin. Northumberland. 643 Oswyn unites several kingdoms. 656 Ceadwalla, Sussex and Wessex. 688 Ina, Wessex. The native Britons seek shelter in Scotland and Wales from the Saxon invaders

FROM A. D. 400, TO A. D. 1840.

CENTURY.

SPAIN.	BRITAIN.	EASTERN EMPIRE.	PROGRESS OF CIVILIZATION.
Under the Vandals. 438 Rechilda. 448 Rechiarius. 456 Maldias. 460 Fumarius. 463 Regismund. *Under the Visigoths.* 451 Therismond. 452 Theodoric II. 466 Euaric. 484 Alaric. The Vandals conquered by the Visigoths.	426 Relinquished by the Romans. *Under the Britons.* 445 Vortigern. 454 Vortimer. 465 Ambrosius. *Saxons.* 454 Hengist in Kent. 491 Ella in Sussex.	408 Theodosius III. and Pulcheria. 450 Marcian. 457 Leo I. (Thracian). 474 Leo II. — Zeno. 491 Anastasius I. Rise of the factions of the Circus.	Bells used in Churches. Commencement of the middle or dark ages. Establishment of the Salic Law. Introduction of Christianity into France.

CENTURY.

ENGLAND.	SCOTLAND.	EASTERN EMPIRE.	PROGRESS OF CIVILIZATION.
519 Cerdic, Kingdom of Wessex. 527 Erchenwin, Kingdom of Essex. 547 Ida, Kingdom of Northumberland. 575 Uffa, Kingdom of East Anglia. 582 Cridda, Kingdom of Mercia. The Saxons were joined by the Angles and Jutes from Germany.	501 Goran. 535 Eugene III. 558 Congal II. 569 Kinathal. 570 Aidan.	518 Justin I. 527 Justinian I. (Belisarius. Narses). 565 Justin II. 578 Tiberius II. 582 Maurice.	Silk worms brought to Europe. Code of Civil Law formed. Water-mills erected at Rome. The Anglo-Saxons converted to Christianity.

CENTURY.

SCOTLAND.	EASTERN EMPIRE.	SARACENS.	PROGRESS OF CIVILIZATION.
604 Kenneth I. 605 Eugene IV. 622 Ferchard I. 636 Donald IV. 650 Ferchard II 668 Maidrum. 688 Eugene V. 692 Eugene VI.	602 Phocas. 610 Heraclius I. 641 Constantine III. — Heraclius Heraclianus. — Constans II. 668 Constantine IV. 685 Justinian II. 695 Leontius. 698 Tiberius II.	622 Hejira, or Flight of Mohammed from Mecca. 632 Abu Bekr. 634 Omar. 644 Othman. 656 Ali. 660 Hassan. 661 Moawiyah, founder of the Ommiade dynasty. 679 Yezid I. 683 Merwan I. 684 Abdalmater.	Latin disused as a living language. Pens made from quills. Glass manufactured in England. The Alexandrian Library destroyed. The Greek fire invented.

EIGHTH

FRANCE.	ITALY.		SPAIN.
	Lombards	*Popes.*	
711 Dagobert III. 715 Chilperic II. Charles Martel. 717 Clotaire IV. 720 Thierry IV. 741 Pepin (regent). 742 Childeric III. 752 Pepin (king) 768 Charlemagne. The Merovingian dynasty set aside by Pepin, father of Charlemagne, and founder of the Carlovingian dynasty.	700 Luitpertus. 701 Arimbertus. 712 Ausprandus. — Luitprandus. 743 Hildebrand. 744 Rachisius. 750 Astolphus. 756 Desiderius. The dynasty of the Lombards subverted by Charlemagne.	The Popes raised to the rank of temporal princes by Pepin, king of France. 752 Stephen III. 757 Paul I. 768 Stephen IV. 772 Adrian I. 795 Leo III.	712 Dynasty of the Visigoths subverted by the Saracens under Tarik and Musa. 755 Abderrahman, independent khaliph. The power of his successors, who reign in Spain until A. D. 1051, is gradually weakened both by internal discords and continued wars with Chiistian insurgents. 718 Pelagius founds a petty Christian kingdom in the Asturian mountains.

NINTH

NORTHERN NATIONS.	AUSTRIAN. DOMINIONS.	WESTERN EMPIRE.			POPES.
762 Regular government established in Russia by Ruric. Denmark formed into a kingdom. Sweden formed into a kingdom. The petty principalities of Norway formed into a kingdom by Harold Harfager.	794 The Magyars occupy Hungary, the ancient Pannonia. The Moravians become a formidable nation. Bohemia formed into a regular state, and Christianity introduced. It was generally governed by dukes tributary to the emperors of Germany.	800 Charlemagne, emperor of the West. 814 Louis the Pious. 843 Empire divided.			816 Stephen V. 817 Pascal I. 824 Eugenius II. 827 Valentine. 828 Gregory IV. 844 Sergius II. 847 Leo IV. 855 Benedict III. 858 Nicholas I. 867 Adrian II. 872 John VIII. 882 Martin II. 884 Adrian III. 885 Stephen VI. 891 Formosus. 896 Boniface VI. — Stephen VII. 898 Theodore II. — John IX. 900 Benedict IV.
		Germany.	*Italy, &c.*	*France.*	
		843 Louis the German. 876 Carloman and Louis III. 881 Charles the Fat. 887 Arnulph. 899 Louis the Child.	843 Lothaire I. 855 Lothaire II. 879 Boson, duke of Burgundy. The great feudatories of the crown assume the power of sovereign princes in various parts of the empire.	843 Charles the Bald. 877 Louis the Stammerer. 879 Louis III. Carloman. 887 Eudes. 898 Charles the Simple. The family of the Capets begins to usurp the royal authority.	

TENTH

SCANDINAVIA.	RUSSIA AND POLAND.	HUNGARY, &c.	GERMANY.	FRANCE.	POPES.
992 Christianity established in Denmark. 991 Christianity established in Norway. The Scandinavian pirates formidable to Southern and Western Europe. Iceland and Greenland discovered and colonized	975 Wladimir the Great extends the Russian monarchy, and 988 Establishes Christianity. 942 Poland becomes a kingdom.	994 Christianity introduced into Hungary. 997 Stephen I. establishes the Hungarian monarchy. 990 Bodeslaus III. independent in Bohemia. The Letti, &c., established in Lithuania and Prussia.	912 Conrad I. of Franconia. 919 Henry the Fowler. 936 Otho the Great. 962 Empire of the West restored and given to Otho. 973 Otho II. 983 Otho III. Jealousies begin to arise between the emperors and the popes.	922 Robert. 923 Rodolph. 933 Louis Outremer. 954 Lothaire. 986 Louis V. the Idle. 987 Hugh Capet, founder of a new dynasty. 996 Robert the Wise. The province of Neustria assigned to the Normans, and thence called Normandy.	904 Leo V. — Christopher. 905 Sergius III. 913 Anastasius [III. 914 Lando 915 John X. 928 Leo VI. 929 Stephen VIII 931 John XI. 936 Leo VII. 939 Stephen IX. 943 Martin III. 946 Agapetus II. 956 John XII. 963 Leo VIII. 964 Benedict V. 965 John XIII. 972 Benedict VI. 974 Donus II. 975 Benedict VII 982 John XIV. 985 John XV. — John XVI. [illegible] V 999 Sylvester II.

CENTURY.

ENGLAND.	SCOTLAND.	EASTERN EMPIRE.	SARACENS.	Progress of Civilization
The Heptarchy still continues, but the states frequently vary both in number and extent 717 Ethelbald in Mercia. 707 Offa unites East Anglia to Mercia; but toward the close of the century Wessex becomes the predominant state.	702 Ambes Keleth. 704 Eugene VII. 721 Mordach. 730 Elfinius. 761 Eugene VIII. 764 Fergus III. 767 Salvathus. 787 Achaius.	705 Justinian II. restored. 711 Philippicus Bardanes. 713 Anastasius II. 716 Theodosius III. 718 Leo III. Isauricus. 741 Constantine V. Copronymus. 775 Leo IV. 780 Constantine VI. Porphyrogennetus. (Irene. Nicephorusi). During the greater part of this century the empire is distracted by the Iconoclast controversy.	705 Walid I. 714 Suleiman. 717 Omar II. 719 Yezid II. 723 Hashem. 742 Walid II. 743 Merwan; Yezid III. 750 Abu l'Abbas, founder of the Abasside dynasty. 753 Almanzor. 775 Mohadi. 785 Al Hadi. 786 Harun-al-Rashid. The seat of the Khaliphate fixed at Bagdad, A. D. 762.	Paper made from cotton. Carpets introduced. Schools of learning founded by the Saracens. Greek works of science translated into Arabic.

CENTURY.

SOUTHERN ITALY.	SPAIN.	ENGLAND.	SCOTLAND.	EASTERN EMPIRE.	SARACENS.	Progress of Civilization.
The islands of Sicily, Corsica and Sardinia, and a considerable part of the kingdom of Naples, occupied by the Saracens.	Gradual decay of the Saracenic power. Foundation of the Christian kingdoms of Navarre and Leon.	828 End of the Heptarchy. Egbert the Great, king of England. 838 Ethelwolf. 857 Ethelbald. 866 Ethelred 872 Alfred the Great. England frequently ravaged by Danish and Norwegian pirates.	819 Congal III. 824 Dongal. 831 Alpin. 833 Kenneth II. 831 Alpin. 854 Donald V. 858 Constantine II. 874 Ethus. 875 Gregory the Great. 892 Donald VI. The Picts subdued and expelled by Kenneth II.	811 Michael I. 813 Leo V. 820 Michael II. 829 Theophilus. 841 Harun. 842 Michael III 867 Basilius I. 886 Leo VI.	809 Al Amin. 814 Al Mamun. 833 Motassem. 846 Motawakkel 861 Montaser. 862 Mostain. Fall and division of the Khaliphate. Fatimate dynasty founded 768, by Motaz. The seat of the Fatimites transferred in the next century to Egypt.	Streets of Cordova paved. Saxon code of laws formed. Clocks brought to Western Europe. Oxford university founded. Agriculture and horticulture encouraged in Germany.

CENTURY.

ENGLAND.	SCOTLAND.	EASTERN EMPIRE.	SARACENS.	Progress of Civilization.
901 Edward I. the Elder. 925 Athelstan. 941 Edmund I. 946 Edred. 955 Edwy. 959 Edgar. 975 Edward II. the Martyr. 978 Ethelred II. The Danes acquire possession of a great portion of England.	903 Constantine III. 943 Malcolm I. 958 Indulph. 968 Duffus. 972 Cullen. 977 Kenneth III. 994 Constantine IV. 995 Grimus.	900 Alexander. 911 Constantine VII. Porphyrogennetus. 919 Romanus I. — Constantine VIII. 959 Romanus II. 963 Nicephorus II. 969 John Zimisces 976 Basilius II. and Constantine IX. The prosperity of the empire partially restored in consequence of the decline of the Saracenic power.	The Khaliphs in subjection to their Turkish mercenaries, whose chief 935 Takes the title of Emir al Omrah 997 The Ghaznevid dynasty founded. The Fatimite Khaliphs possess a powerful empire in Egypt.	University of Cambridge founded. Figures of arithmetic introduced from the Arabs. Mining in the Hartz mountains. Wine presses first introduced into Italy.

ELEVENTH

NORWAY.	DENMARK.	SWEDEN.	RUSSIA.	POLAND.	HUNGARY	GERMANY.	FRANCE
Sweyn, king of both countries. 14 Canute the Great, king of England.		1 Olaus. 19 Amund I. 35 Edmund II. 40 Hacquin III. 61 Sturkill. 75 Ingo the Good.	15 Svatopole I. 16 Jarolaus. 54 Isilaus I. 78 Vsevolod I. 93 Svatopole II Russia scarcely yet emerged from barbaism.	25 Miesko II. 37 Casimir I. Anarchy. 41 Casimir recalled. 58 Boleslaus II. the Bold. 77 Boleslaus takes the title of king. 81 Wladislaus I.	38 Peter. 41 Expelled, and succeeded by Otto. 44 Peter restored 47 Anchar I. 61 Bela I. 63 Solomon. 74 Gieza I. 77 Ladislaus I. 95 Coloman.	2 Henry II. 24 Conrad II. of Franconia, who 32 Inherits Burgundy. 39 Henry III 56 Henry IV Wars with the Saxons: and with the Popes on the question of ecclesiastical investitures.	31 Henry I. 60 Philip I. the Amorous.
11 Olavus II. 32 Sueno. 36 Magnus Oleron. 47 Harold III Haardrade. 66 Olavus II. 70 Magnus I. 87 Hacon. 89 Magnus II.	36 Hardicanute. 42 Magnus. 47 Sweyn Elpisden. 74 Harold VII. 76 Canute the Saint. 85 Olaus II. 95 Eric III.						
The nations of the North abandon their piratical habits, and make great advances in civilization.						95 Commencement of the Crusades, first preached by Peter the Hermit, and then sanctioned by the Popes.	

TWELFTH

NORTHERN NATIONS.	RUSSIA.	POLAND	HUNGARY & BOHEMIA.	GERMANY	FRANCE	POPES.
Norway. 3 Sigurd. 62 Magnus III. *Denmark.* 7 Nicholas. 35 Eric IV. 39 Eric V. 47 Canute V. 55 Sueno IV. 57 Waldemar I. 82 Canute VI. *Sweden.* 10 Ingo IV. 29 Ragwald. 40 Suercher II. 60 Eric X. the Holy. 61 Charles VII. 68 Canute. 92 Suercher III.	14 Wlademir II. 25 Motislaus 32 Jaropolik. 38 Vzevolod II. 46 Isialaus II 56 Jourje or George I. the founder of Moscow. 57 Andrew I. reigning at Wladimir. 75 Michael I.	2 Boleslaus III. Civil dissensions and constant wars with the Letti in Lithuania and Prussia. 38 Wladislaus II. 46 Boleslaus IV. 73 Miesko III. 77 Expelled by Casimir II., the Just 95 Lescho V.	*Hungary.* 14 Stephen II. 31 Bela II. 41 Gieza II. 61 Stephen III. 74 Bela III. 96 Emeric. *Bohemia.* 40 Wladislaus III duke. 75 Frederick, duke. 90 Conrad II. duke. 97 Premislaus Ottoacre I. king.	6 Henry V. 25 Lothaire II. the Saxon. 37 Conrad III. 52 Frederic I. Barbarossa 90 Henry VI. Asper. 98 Philip (Otho).	6 Louis VI. the Fat. 37 Louis VII. the Young. 80 Philip II. Augustus. The great feudatories of the crown gradually reduced to obedience, and the royal authority established.	18 Gelasius II. 19 Calixtus II. 24 Honorius II. 30 Innocent II. 43 Celestine II. 44 Lucius II 45 Eugenius III. 53 Anastasius IV. 54 Adrian IV. 59 Alexander II. 81 Lucius III. 85 Urban III. 87 Gregory VIII. — Clement III. 91 Celestine III. 98 Innocent III.

CENTURY.

POPES.	Southern ITALY.	SPAIN.	ENGLAND.	SCOTLAND	EASTERN EMPIRE.	TURKS.	Progress of Civilization.
3 John XVII. — John XVIII. 9 Sergius IV. 12 Benedict VIII. 24 John XIX. 33 Benedict IX 45 Gregory VI. 46 Clement II. — Benedict X. 48 Damasus II — Leo IX. 55 Victor II. 57 Stephen X. 58 Nicholas II 61 Alexander II 73 Gregory VII 86 Victor III. 88 Urban II. 99 Pascal II.	*Norman dukes of Naples.* 43 William 59 Robert. 85 Roger. ——— 90 Roger, *Count of Sicily.* ——— 22 Sardinia and Corsica recovered from the Saracens by the citizens of Pisa.	10 Sancho the Great *Aragon.* 34 Ramirez. 67 Sancho I. 94 Peter I. *Castile.* 35 Ferdinand I. 65 Sancho II. 72 Alphonso VI. 85 The kingdom of Castile greatly enlarged. *Portugal.* 88 Henry, count of Portugal.	2 Massacre of the Danes. 14 Sweyn of Denmark. 17 Canute. 35 Harold Harefoot. 39 Hardicanute. 41 Edward the Confessor. 66 Harold II. — William the Conqueror. 87 William II. Rufus. 66 The Norman dynasty established by William the Conqueror.	4 Malcolm II. 34 Duncan 40 Macbeth. 57 Malcolm III. 93 Donald VII. 94 Duncan II. — Donald restored. 97 Edgar.	25 Constantine IX. alone. 20 Romanus III. 34 Michael IV. V. 41 Michael 54 Theodora. — Constantine X 56 Michael VI. 57 Isaac I. 59 Constantine XI 67 Romanus III. Diogenes. 71 Michael VII. — Constantine XII. 78 Nicephorus III. 81 Alexius I Comnenus	The power of the Seljukian Turks established by Togrul Beg, Alp Arslan, and Malek Shah, but subsequently weakened by internal divisions. The Khorasmians become formidable.	Musical notes invented. Tournaments legally constituted. Windmills first used. Danegelt remitted in England. Doomsday book finished. Chivalrous spirit fostered by the Crusades. Clocks with wheels introduced.

CENTURY.

SOUTHERN ITALY	SPAIN.	ENGLAND AND SCOTLAND.	EASTERN EMPIRE.	TURKS AND TARTARS.	Progress of Civilization.
2 Roger II. of Naples. 30 Roger III., king of Naples and Sicily. 54 William I. the Good. 66 William II. the Bad. 89 Tancred. 94 William III. The Two Sicilies united to the Empire.	*Aragon.* 4 Alphonso I. 34 Ramirez II. 37 Petronillo and Raymond. 62 Alphonso II. 95 Peter II. *Castile.* 9 Alphonso VII. 22 Alphonso VIII 57 Ferdinand II. 58 Alphonso IX. the Noble. *Portugal.* 29 Alphonso I. Henriques king. 85 Sancho I. Continued wars with the Moors.	0 Henry I. Beauclerk. 35 Stephen of Blois, Usurper. 54 Henry II. first of the Plantagenets 89 Richard I. Cœur-de-Lion 99 John Lackland. Ireland conquered by Henry II. *Scotland.* 7 Alexander I 24 David I. 53 Malcolm IV 65 William the Lion.	18 John Comnenus. 43 Manuel Comnenus. 80 Alexius II. 83 Andronicus. 85 Isaac II. Angelus. *Kingdom of Jerusalem.* 1099 Godfrey of Bouillon. 1 Baldwin I. 18 Baldwin II. 31 Foulke. 44 Baldwin III. 62 Almeric. 73 Baldwin IV. 85 Baldwin V. 86 Guy. 92 Conrad. — Henry of Champagne. 87 The kingdom overthrown by Saladin.	The monarchy of the Seljukian Turks gradually destroyed by internal divisions. Rise of the Moguls under Temujin, afterward Jenghiz Khan.	The cultivation of the sugar-cane introduced into Sicily. Glass windows used in England.

THIRTEENTH

NORTHERN NATIONS.	RUSSIA.	POLAND.	HUNGARY AND BOHEMIA.	GERMANY.	FRANCE.
Norway. 7 Hacon II. 63 Magnus IV. 80 Eric II. 99 Hacon III. *Denmark* 2 Waldemar II. 42 Eric VI. 51 Abel. 52 Christopher. 59 Eric VII. 86 Eric VIII. *Sweden.* 10 Eric XI. 20 John. 23 Eric XI. 50 Waldemar I. 76 Magnus II. 81 Birger II.	13 Jourje II Constantine 38 Jarolaus II. 50 Alexander I. 63 Jarolaus III 71 Vasili I. 75 Demetrius I 94 Andrew at Moscow. 38 Conquered by the Mongolian horde.	2 Wladislaus II. 6 Lesko V. restored. 27 Boleslaus V 79 Lesko VI. 89 Anarchy. 95 Przemislaus. 96 Wladislaus IV. The conquest of Prussia by the Teutonic knights begun 1230, completed 1823.	4 Ladislaus II — Andrew II. 35 Bela IV. 40 Mogul invasion. 70 Stephen IV. 72 Ladislaus III 90 Andrew III. *Bohemia.* 30 Wenceslaus III. 53 Premislaus Ottoacar II. 78 Anarchy. 84 Wenceslaus IV.	8 Otho IV. 12 Frederic II. 52 Conrad IV. 54 William, count of Holland 56 Richard, earl of Cornwall. —Alphonso of Spain. 73 Rodolph of Hapsburg. 91 Adolphus of Nassau. 98 Albert I. of Austria.	23 Louis VIII., the Lion. 26 Louis IX. the Saint. 70 Philip III. the Hardy. 85 Philip IV. the Fair.
				The Crusades. 68 Capture of Antioch. 91 and of Acre, by the Egyptian sultan. End of the Crusades.	

FOURTEENTH

NORTHERN NATIONS.	RUSSIA.	POLAND.	HUNGARY AND BOHEMIA.	GERMANY.	FRANCE.	POPES.
Norway. 15 Magnus V. 26 Hacon III. 28 Magnus VI. 58 Hacon IV. 75 Olaus IV. *Denmark.* 21 Christopher II 32 Waldemar III 75 Margaret. *Sweden.* 26 Magnus III. 63 Albert of Mecklenburg. 97 Norway, Denmark, and Sweden, joined by the Union of Calmar.	The country subject to the Mongolian horde.	0 Wenceslaus. 35 Casimir the Great. 70 Louis, king of Hungary. 85 Hedwige and Uladislaus Jagellon. *Prussia.* Subject to the grand master of the Teutonic knights.	1 Wenceslaus. 5 Otho of Bavaria. 13 Charles, Robert. 42 Louis I. 82 Mary and 86 Sigismund. *Bohemia.* 5 Wenceslaus V. 6 Henry. 10 John of Luxemburg. 46 Charles IV. — Joined to the empire.	8 Henry VII. of Luxemburg. 13 Louis of Bavaria, & — Frederic III., of Austria. [IV. 47 Charles 78 Wenceslaus. 15 The independence of Switzerland proclaimed, & 86 established by the battle of Sempach.	14 Louis X 15 John I. 16 Philip V 23 Charles the Fair. 28 Philip VI. 50 John II. 56 He is taken by the English. 64 Charles V. the Wise. 80 Charles VI.	3 Benedict XI 5 Clement V. 16 John XXII. 34 Benedict XII. 42 Clement VI. 52 Innocent VI 62 Urban V. 71 Gregory XI SCHISM OF THE WEST. *Popes at Rome.* 78 Urban VI. 89 Boniface IX *Popes at Avignon.* 78 Clement VII. [XIII. 94 Benedict

FIFTEENTH

DENMARK.	RUSSIA AND POLAND.	GERMANY.	FRANCE.	POPES.	SOUTHERN ITALY.
12 Eric IX. 41 Christopher III. 48 Christian I 81 John II. The Swedes engaged in almost incessant wars to recover their independence from **the Danes.**	*Russia.* 25 Vasali the Blind. 62 Ivan Vasilievitch I. 74 Tartar Yoke broken. *Poland.* 34 Wladislaus V. 47 Casimir IV. 92 John I.	0 Rupert. 10 Jodochus. 11 Sigismond, king also of Hungary and Bohemia. 37 Albert II. 39 Frederic III. 93 Maximilian I. During the greater part of this century, the dukes of Burgundy acquire great political influence. At the close, their possessions pass by marriage into the royal family of Austria.	22 Henry VI., of England. — Charles VII of Valois. 61 Louis XI. 83 Charles VIII 98 Louis XII. Rapid increase of the royal power in France during this century. Wars in Italy at the close.	4 Innocent VII. 6 Gregory XII. 9 Alexander V. 10 John XXIII. 17 Martin V. 31 Eugenius IV. 39 Felix V. 47 Nicholas V. 55 Calixtus III. 58 Pius II. 64 Paul II. 72 Sixtus IV. 84 Innocent VIII 92 Alexander VI.	Sicily and Naples lose their political importance. Both merge in the kingdom of Spain: the former at the beginning, the latter at the close of the century.

CENTURY.

Popes.	Southern Italy.	Spain.	England & Scotland.	Eastern Empire.	Turks and Tartars.	Progress of Civilization
16 Honorius III. [IX. 27 Gregory 41 Celestine IV. [IV. 43 Innocent 54 Alexander IV. 61 Urban IV. 65 Clement IV. [X. 71 Gregory 76 Innocent V — Adrian V. — John XXI. 77 Nichol. III 81 Martin IV. 85 Honorius IV. 88 Nicho. IV. 94 Celestine V. [VIII. — Boniface	52 Conrad IV (Emperor.) 54 Manfred. 66 Conradin. —Charles of Anjou. 82 Sicily conquered by the king of Aragon. 85 Charles II in Naples. 85 James of Aragon in Sicily. 96 Frederic II. in Sicily.	*Aragon.* 13 James I. 76 Peter III. 85 Alphonso III. 91 James II. *Castile.* 14 Henry I. 17 Alphonso X. 26 Ferdinand III. 52 Alphonso XI., the Wise. 84 Sancho IV. 95 Ferdinand IV. *Portugal.* 12 Alphonso II., the Fat. 33 Sancho II. 46 Alphonso III. 79 Dionysius, the father of his country.	*England.* 16 Henry III 65 House of Commons formed. 72 Edward I. Wales subdued. *Scotland.* 14 Alexander II. 49 Alexander III. 85 Anarchy. 92 John Baliol. 94 Anarchy (Sir Wm. Wallace.)	1203 Constan inople taken by the Latin Crusaders, and the empire broken into fragments. It was partially restored in the middle of the century by Michael Paleologus.	1298 The dynasty of the Ottoman Turks is founded in Bithynia by Othman I. The Moguls subdue the greater part of Asia and North-eastern Europe, but in the middle of the century their empire is broken up.	Establishment of the Inquisition Magna Charta. Representatives of the Commons in parliament Spectacles invented. Glass mirrors used. Clocks to strike made in Europe.

CENTURY.

Southern Italy.	Spain.	England and Scotland.	Eastern Empire.	Ottoman Empire.	Progress of Civilization.
Naples. 9 Robert I. 43 Joan I. 82 Charles III., of Durazzo. *Sicily.* 28 Frederic I. 37 Peter II. 42 Louis. 55 Frederic II 67 Mary.	*Aragon.* 27 Alphonso IV. 36 Peter IV. 87 John I. 95 Martin. *Castile.* 12 Alphonso XII. 50 Peter the Cruel. 69 Henry II. 79 John I. 90 Henry III. *Portugal.* 25 Alphonso IV. 57 Peter the Cruel. 67 Ferdinand. 85 John I., the Great.	*England.* 7 Edward II. 27 Edward III. Edward claims the crown of France. 75 Death of the Black Prince. 77 Richard II. 99 Henry IV. of Lancaster. *Scotland.* 6 Robert Bruce. 29 David II. 70 Robert II., the first of the Stuarts. 90 Robert III.	Throughout this century the Eastern empire gradually declines, and at the close becomes tributary to the Turks.	26 The empire of the Turks. established by Othman at Prusa. 25 Orkhan. 58 Amurath I. 89 Bayezid I. Timur Lenk subdues Western and Central Asia, and establishes a mighty empire.	Mariner's compass introduced into Europe. Paper made from linen rags. Gunpowder and cannon used in war. New Testament translated by Wickliffe. Pins and playing cards invented.

CENTURY.

Spain.	England & Scotland.	Eastern & Ottoman Empires.	Progress of Civilization
Aragon. 10 Ferdinand. 16 Alphonso V. 58 John II. 74 Ferdinand the Catholic. *Castile.* 6 John II. 54 Henry IV. 74 Isabella, who marries Ferdinand of Aragon, and thus unites the two crowns. *Portugal.* 33 Edward. [African. 38 Alphonso V., the 81 John II. [tunate. 95 Emmanuel the For-	*England.* 13 Henry V. 22 Henry VI. *Wars of the Roses.* 61 Edward IV. (York.) 83 Edward V. — Richard III. 85 Henry VII., the first of the Tudors. *Scotland.* 6 James I. 37 James II. 60 James III. 88 James IV. Great civil commotions in Scotland.	The Greek empire gradually sinks into ruin, being assailed by the Turkish sultans; 3 Soleiman. 10 Moussa. 13 Mohammed I. 21 Amurath II. 51 Mohammed II., who 53 takes Constantino- 81 Bayezid II. [ple. The empire of Timûr destroyed by the civil wars of his descendants, one of whom, Baber, founds the empire of Delhi, or of the Great Mogul, in India	Maritime enterprises encouraged. Air-gun and musket invented. The art of printing. Vatican library founded. Greek philosophers seek refuge in Italy. Algebra borrowed from the Arabs. Discovery of America. Passage round the the Cape of Good Hope discovered.

SIXTEENTH

DENMARK AND SWEDEN.	RUSSIA AND POLAND.	GERMANY, &c.	FRANCE.	POPES.
Denmark. 13 Christian II. 23 Frederic I 34 Christian III. 59 Frederic II. 88 Christian IV.	*Russia.* 5 Vasili Ivanovitch. 33 IvanVasiliovitchII 84 Feodor. 98 Buris Gudonof.	*Empire.* 19 Charles V. king of Spain, &c. 58 Ferdinand I. 64 Maximilian II. 76 Rodolph II. Prussia rises gradually into importance. Holland rejects the yoke of Spain, and 84 Maurice, prince of Orange, is chosen Stadtholder of the United Provinces.	15 Francis I. 47 Henry II. 59 Francis II. 60 Charles IX. 74 Henry III. *Wars of the League.* 89 Henry IV. of Bourbon.	3 Pius III. — Julius II. 13 Leo X. 22 Adrian VI. 23 Clement VII. 34 Paul III. 50 Julius III. 55 Marcellus III. — Paul IV. 59 Pius IV. 66 Pius V. 72 Gregory XIII. 85 Sixtus V. 90 Urban VII. — Gregory XIV. 91 Innocent IX. 92 Clement VIII. 40 Order of Jesuits established.
Sweden. 23 Gustavus Vasa establishes the independence of Sweden. 60 Eric XVI. 68 John III. 92 Sigismund, king of Poland. 99 Charles IX.	*Poland.* 1 Alexander. 6 Sigismund I. 48 Sigismund II. Augustus. 73 Henry of Valois. 75 Stephen. 87 Sigismund III. who also became king of Sweden.			

SEVENTEENTH

DENMARK AND SWEDEN.	RUSSIA AND POLAND.	GERMANY, &c.	FRANCE.
Denmark. 48 Frederic III. 70 Christian V. 99 Frederic IV.	*Russia.* 5 Demetrius. 6 Vassili Shuiski. 13 Michael Romanof. 45 Alexis. 76 Feodor. 82 Ivan and Peter. 96 Peter alone.	*Empire.* 12 Matthias. 19 Ferdinand II. 37 Ferdinand III. 58 Leopold I. The Thirty Years'War. The dutchy of Prussia increases in power. Holland takes a prominent place among the European States.	10 Louis XIII. 43 Louis XIV. The monarchy of France attains the summit of its greatness, and the ambition of the king excites the jealousy of the principal European states.
Sweden. 11 Gustavus Adolphus the Great. 32 Christina. 54 Charles X. 60 Charles XI. 97 Charles XII. Great Northern War.	*Poland.* 32 Wladislaus VI. 48 John Casimir. 69 Michael Coryleat. 74 John Sobieski. 97 Frederic Augustus I. of Saxony.		

EIGHTEENTH AND

DENMARK.	SWEDEN.	RUSSIA AND POLAND.	GERMANY, &c.	FRANCE.	POPES.
30 Christian VI. 46 Frederic V. 66 Christian VII. 84 Regency.	18 Ulrica Leonora. 20 Frederic I. of Hesse Cassel. 51 Adolphus Frederic of Holstein. 71 Gustavus III. 92 Gustavus Adolphus II.	*Russia.* 21 Peter the Great takes the title of Emperor. 25 Catherine I. 27 Peter II. 30 AnneIvanofna — Ivan, a minor. 41 Elizabeth. 61 Peter II. 62 Catherine II. 96 Paul I.	*Empire.* 5 Joseph I. 11. Charles VI. 42 Charles VII. of Bavaria. 45 Francis I. of Lorraine and Maria Theresa. 65 Joseph II. 90 Leopold II. 92 Francis II.	14 LouisXV. 74 Louis XVI. 92 Republic Sanguinary tumults and civil wars. 99Napoleon, First Consul.	0 Clement XI. 21 Innocent XIII 24 Benedict XIII 30 Clement XII. 40 Benedict XIV 58 Clement XIII 69 Clement XIV 75 Pius VI. 98 Roman republic.
		Poland. Having been long distracted by civil commotions, is in 1772 dismembered by Russia, Prussia, and Austria.	*Prussia.* 1 Becomes a kingdom. 40 Frederick II. the Great. 86 Fred. Wm. II. 97 Fred. Wm. III.		
8 Frederic VI. 14 Norway united to Sweden. 39 Christian VIII.	9 Charles XIII. 10 Bernadotte chosen Crown prince 19 Becomes king, as Charles John.	*Russia.* 1 Alexander. 25 Nicholas. 31 Attempted Polish revolution.	*Austria.* 4 Francis 35 Ferdinand I. Emperor of Austria.	4 Napoleon Emperor. 14 Louis XVIII. 15 Napoleon restored. — Louis XVIII. restored. 25 CharlesX 30 L. Philip.	0 Pius VII. 8 Pope deposed 14 —— restored. 23 Leo XII. 31 Gregory XVI.
			Prussia. 40 Fred. Wm.IV		*Holland.* 1814 William I. 1840 William II. on the abdication of his father.

CENTURY.

SPAIN.	ENGLAND AND SCOTLAND.	TURKS AND PERSIANS.	Progress of Civilization.
4 Ferdinand the Catholic, alone. — Philip I. of Austria. 16 Charles I., or V., as emperor of Germany. 56 Philip II. 98 Philip III.	*England.* 9 Henry VIII. 47 Edward VI. 53 Jane Grey. — Mary. 58 Elizabeth.	*Turkey.* 12 Selim I. 20 Soleiman II. 66 Selim II. 74 Amurath III. 95 Mohammed III.	The Reformation. The Copernican system. Reformation of the calendar. Stocking-frame. Newspapers. Telescopes. Toleration legally established in France by the Edict of Nantes.
Portugal. 21 John III. 57 Sebastian. 78 Henry the Cardinal. 80 Portugal is united to Spain.	*Scotland.* 13 James V. 42 Mary. 67 James VI. who, at the beginning of the next century, unites the kingdoms of England and Scotland, which are henceforth called Great Britain.	*Persia.* 1 The Suffavean dynasty founded by Ismael. 25 Shah Taurasp. 77 Mohammed. 84 Abbas the Great.	

CENTURY.

POPES.	SPAIN, &c.	GREAT BRITAIN.	TURKS AND PERSIANS.	Progress of Civilization.
5 Leo XI. — Paul V. 21 Gregory XV. 23 Urban VIII. 44 Innocent X. 55 Alexander VII. 67 Clement IX. 70 Clement X. 76 Innocent XI. 89 Alexander VIII. 91 Innocent XII.	*Spain.* 21 Philip IV. 65 Charles II. *Portugal.* Separates from Spain under 40 John IV. of Braganza. 56 Alphonso IV. 68 Peter II.	3 James VI., of Scotland, and I. of England. 25 Charles I. 42 Civil war. 49 Commonwealth 53 Cromwell, Lord Protector. 58 Richard, ditto. 60 Charles II. 85 James II. 88 Revolution. 89 William III. and Mary.	*Turkey.* 4 Ahmed I. 17 Mustapha I. 23 Amurath IV. 40 Ibrahim. 55 Mohammed IV. 87 Soleiman III. 90 Ahmed II. 98 Mustapha II. *Persia.* Declines rapidly under the later Suffavean princes.	Logarithms. Steam-engines. Circulation of the blood. Regular posts. Thermometer and barometer. Air-pump. Jesuits' bark. Bayonets. Plate glass. Bank of England projected. National Debt begun.

NINETEENTH CENTURIES.

SPAIN.	PORTUGAL.	GREAT BRITAIN.	TURKS AND PERSIANS.	INDIA, &c.	Progress of Civilization.
0 Philip V. of Anjou. 24 Louis. 25 Philip V. restored. 46 Ferdinand VI. 59 Charles III 88 Charles IV The Spanish monarchy gradually declines, the court imbecile and profligate.	6 John V. 50 Joseph Emmanuel. 77 Mary. 96 John, Regent. The Portuguese monarchy declines like the Spanish.	2 Anne (Stuart). 14 George I. of Hanover. 27 George II. 60 George III. 83 The American colonies become independent states, and about the same time the foundation is laid of the British empire in Hindustan. England during the close of the century establishes its naval supremacy.	*Turkey.* 3 Ahmed III. 30 Mohammed V. 54 Ottoman III 57 Mustapha III. 74 Ahmed IV. 89 Selim III. The power of Turkey gradually declines. *Persia.* For a while becomes powerful under Nadir Shah, but after his death it is again distracted by civil wars, & the sovereignty is seized by the Turkish tribe of the Kajars.	After the death of Aurungzebe (1707), the power of the empire of Delhi is destroyed, and the provinces form independent states; most of which have been successively rendered subject to the British East India Company.	Porcelain manufactured in Europe. Inoculation introduced. Chronometers. Cook's voyages. Colonization of Australia. Spinning jennies Galvanism. Planet Herschel discovered. Air balloons. Telegraphs. Steam-boats discovered, but not used until the next century.
8 Ferdinand VII. — Joseph. Napoleon. 14 Ferdinand VII. restored. **33 Isabella II**	9 Royal family emigrate. 14 French expelled. 21 John VI. 28 Miguel. **31 Maria da Gloria.**	11 George, Prince Regent. 20 George IV. 30 William IV. 37 Victoria. *Belgium.* **1831 Leopold elected king.**	*Turkey.* 7 Mustapha IV. 8 Mohammed VI. 19 Abdul Medjid. *Greece.* **31 Otho of Bavaria.**	0 Runjit Sing, ruler of Punjâb. 39 Shah Sujah, restored to the throne of Cabul. 40 English murdered in Cabul. Shah Sujah slain.	Steam-vessels. Gas-lights. Lithography. New processes of engraving. Arctic voyages. Railroads. **Locomotive Engines.**

GENEALOGICAL TABLE OF THE BOURBONS.

The names printed in capital letters, in these Tables, denote the sovereigns: the mark, †, is prefixed to the date of a death.

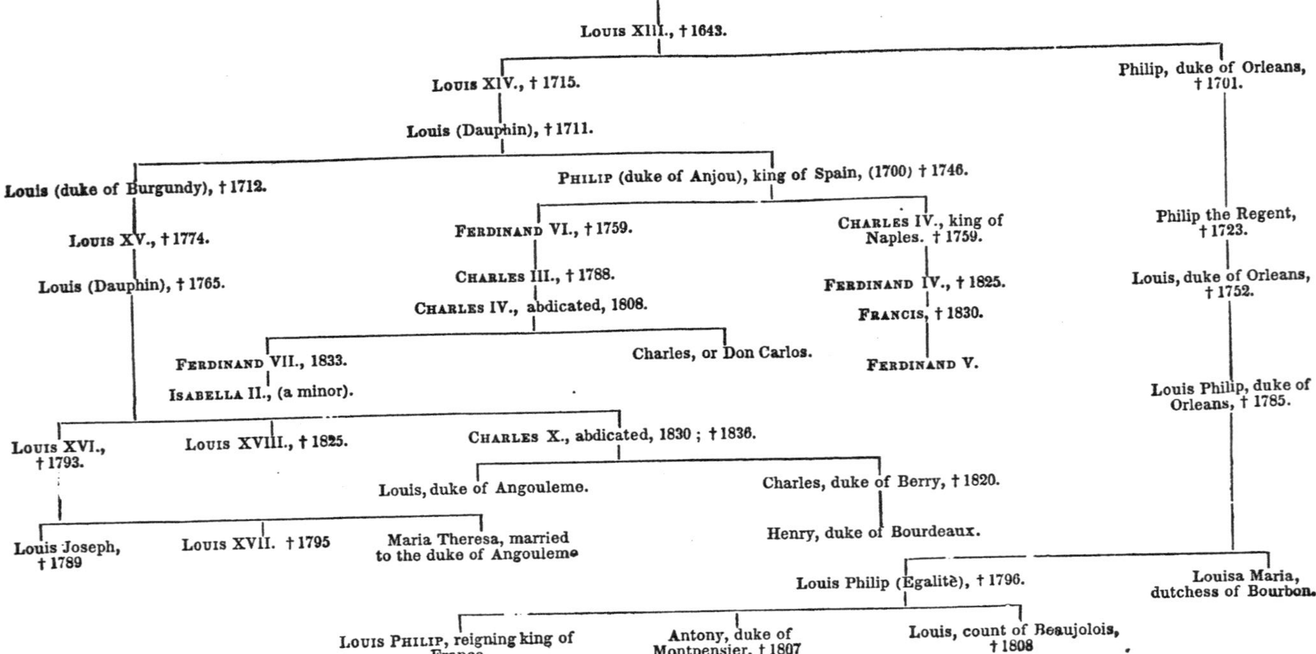

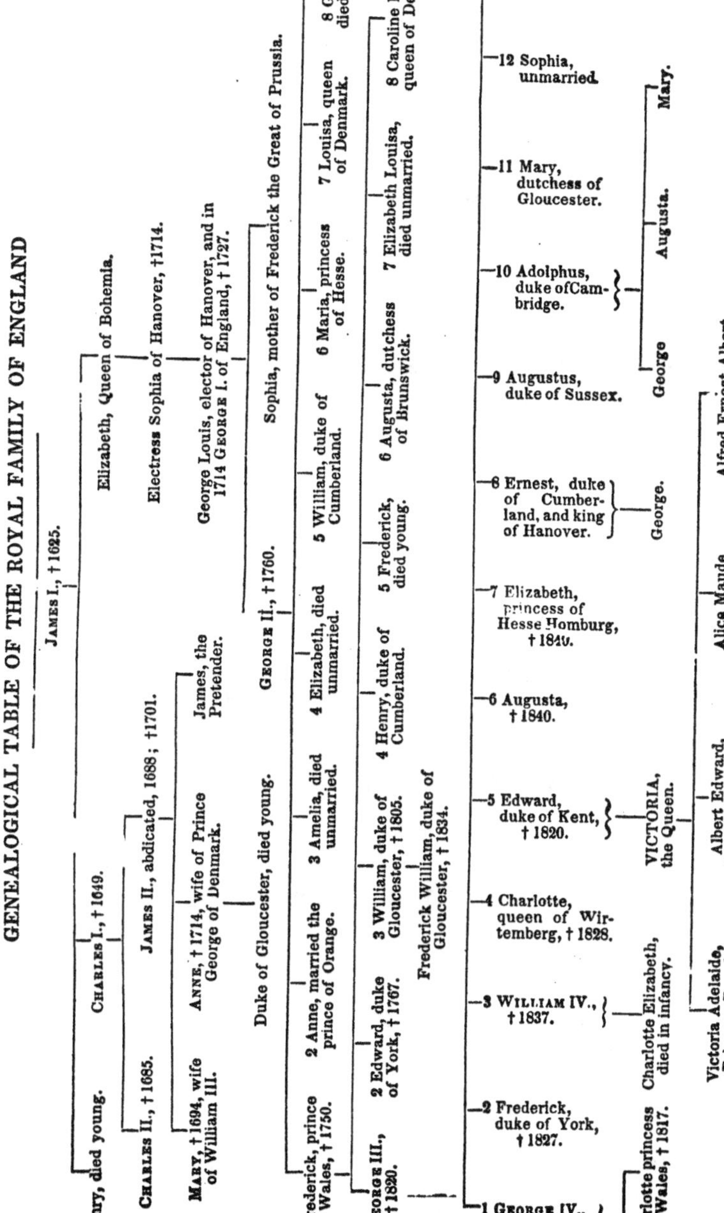
GENEALOGICAL TABLE OF THE ROYAL FAMILY OF ENGLAND
JAMES I., † 1625.
Henry, died young.
CHARLES I., † 1649.
Elizabeth, Queen of Bohemia.
CHARLES II., † 1685.
JAMES II., abdicated, 1688; † 1701.
Electress Sophia of Hanover, † 1714.
MARY, † 1694, wife of William III.
ANNE, † 1714, wife of Prince George of Denmark.
James, the Pretender.
George Louis, elector of Hanover, and in 1714 GEORGE I. of England, † 1727.
Duke of Gloucester, died young.
GEORGE II., † 1760.
Sophia, mother of Frederick the Great of Prussia.
1 Frederick, prince of Wales, † 1750.
2 Anne, married the prince of Orange.
3 Amelia, died unmarried.
4 Elizabeth, died unmarried.
5 William, duke of Cumberland.
6 Maria, princess of Hesse.
7 Louisa, queen of Denmark.
8 George, died young.
1 GEORGE III., † 1820.
2 Edward, duke of York, † 1767.
3 William, duke of Gloucester, † 1805.
Frederick William, duke of Gloucester, † 1834.
4 Henry, duke of Cumberland.
5 Frederick, died young.
6 Augusta, dutchess of Brunswick.
7 Elizabeth Louisa, died unmarried.
8 Caroline Matilda, queen of Denmark.
1 GEORGE IV., † 1830.
2 Frederick, duke of York, † 1827.
3 WILLIAM IV., † 1837.
4 Charlotte, queen of Wirtemberg, † 1828.
5 Edward, duke of Kent, † 1820.
6 Augusta, † 1840.
7 Elizabeth, princess of Hesse Homburg, † 1840.
8 Ernest, duke of Cumberland, and king of Hanover.
9 Augustus, duke of Sussex.
10 Adolphus, duke of Cambridge.
11 Mary, dutchess of Gloucester.
12 Sophia, unmarried.
13 Amelia, † 1809
Charlotte princess of Wales, † 1817.
Charlotte Elizabeth, died in infancy.
VICTORIA, the Queen.
George.
George
Augusta.
Mary.
Victoria Adelaide, Princess Royal
Albert Edward, Prince of Wales
Alice Maude
Alfred Ernest Albert.

QUESTIONS

ON

MODERN HISTORY.

TO ACCOMPANY

A MANUAL OF MODERN HISTORY,

BY W. C. TAYLOR.

COMPILED BY REV. L. L. SMITH.

NEW YORK:
D. APPLETON & CO., 200 BROADWAY.
PHILADELPHIA:
GEORGE S. APPLETON, 164 CHESNUT-STREET.
MDCCCLI.

QUESTIONS

ON

MODERN HISTORY.

CHAPTER I.

CONSEQUENCES OF THE FALL OF THE WESTERN EMPIRE.

Sec. 1.—*The Gothic Kingdom of Italy.*

1. What is said of the Visigoths in Spain?
2. What, of the Ostrogoths?
3. What tribes came from the German Forests?
4. What is said of them?
5. What tribes were still more barbarous?
6. For what were the Germanic tribes remarkable?
7. From what part of Europe did the Sclavonic tribes come?
8. How did they resemble the Tartars?
9. Their form of government?
10. How long did the court of Constantinople remain in obscurity?
11. Who restored its supremacy?
12. How was Zeno made emperor?
13. Who excited a revolt against him?
14. Who restored him to the throne?
15. What excited hostilities between him and Theodoric?
16. How was peace obtained by Zeno?
17. What is said of the march of Theodoric?
18. Who opposed him?
19. What city sustained a long siege?
20. What became of Odoacer?
21. How did Theodoric secure his conquest?
22. What were the limits of his empire?
23. What heresy did he embrace?
24. The consequence of this?
25. What crimes did he commit?
26. How did he die? and at what age?

Sec. 2.—*Reign of Justinian.*

1. Who was Justin?
2. What office did he hold?
3. How did he secure the throne?
4. Whom did he make his associate?
5. Whom did Justinian marry?
6. Her character?
7. Mention a singular folly of the Eastern Empire.
8. What result followed Justinian's partiality to one of the factions?
9. How did this happen?
10. How did Justinian restore order?
11. How many of the rioters were killed?
12. What war did Justinian now engage in?
13. His commander?
14. What was done before the armament set sail?
15. What happened to Gelimer?
16. How did he console himself?
17. What afforded Belisarius a pretext for attacking Italy?
18. How did Theodotus act?
19. How did his subjects treat him?
20. How did Vitiges commence his reign?
21. His course afterwards?
22. How did the bishop of Rome act?
23. How was he punished?
24. Who succeeded him, and by what means?
25. The success of Belisarius?
26. What prevented him from taking Ravenna?
27. Who was Theodobert? and his exploits?
28. The fate of Belisarius?
29. The Lombards, why so called?
30. What protected the empire for forty years?
31. Who were the Avars?
32. Their actions, &c.?
33. By whom conquered?
34. Their origin and original condition?
35. For what celebrated?
36. The rival of Justinian, who?
37. How did he secure the tranquillity of Persia?
38. His favourite project?
39. Who first checked his career?
40. What happened to the provinces of Italy and Africa?
41. Why was Belisarius less successful than formerly?
42. How did he disgrace himself?
43. Who succeeded him in the command?
44. His success?
45. How was Italy governed after this?

46. How long did Narses govern it?
47. How was Belisarius employed in the mean time?
48. How was he treated by Justinian?
49. What hastened his death?
50. The character of Justinian?

SEC. 3.—*The Establishment of the Civil Law.*

1. What project did Justinian form?
2. What led him to do this?
3. What lawyer was appointed to prepare the code?
4. His qualifications for this duty?
5. The instructions given to the commission?
6. How long were they employed in this Herculean undertaking?
7. What more difficult work yet remained to be performed?
8. To whom was it entrusted, and what powers were given him?
9. The recommendation of the emperor?
10. How many books did the code contain?
11. How many, the Digest, or Pandects?
12. Why so called?
13. How many years did it occupy?
14. How many laws did it contain?
15. How many volumes was it necessary to examine, in order to prepare it?
16. State the substance of the emperor's decree.
17. With what other works was Tribonian charged?
18. What is said of it?
19. Were these works perfect?
20. What were the Novels?
21. How many of them were there?
22. How long were these law volumes lost?
23. When, how, and by whom, discovered?
24. The use that has been made of them?

SEC. 4.—*History of the Silk Trade.*

1. How was silk first obtained in Europe?
2. What nations had the first monopoly of it?
3. What were silk robes first called?
4. Whence did the silk first come?
5. How is this known?
6. Show the difficulties of its importation from China?
7. What is mentioned as a proof of Julius Cæsar's magnificent spectacles?
8. The price of silk at Rome?
9. What law was made in the reign of Tiberius?
10. What curious circumstance is mentioned, in the history of silk?
11. The decision of the Sonnite Doctors?
12. Who was the first Roman emperor, that wore a silk garment?
13. What had diminished the price of silk by this time?
14. Whose successors did the Persian sovereigns consider themselves?
15. And whose, did the Byzantine emperors consider themselves?
16. What is said of the Red Sea?
17. Of the straits of Bab-el-Mandeb?
18. The common proverb with Eastern sailors, respecting the Yam Suph?
19. What advantage did the Persians take of their local position, with respect to the silk trade?
20. How did Justinian attempt to obviate this inconvenience?
21. What unforeseen event secured to him his great object?
22. What unnoticed fact in natural theology is mentioned?
23. How did these monks carry the silkworms' eggs to Constantinople?
24. What singular circumstance shows the success of the Greeks in the manufacture of silk?
25. How was the Sogdian trade annihilated?
26. How long did the Greeks monopolize the silk trade?
27. How was the manufacture of it extended in Europe?
28. To whom is France indebted for her present superiority in this trade?
29. Who endeavoured to introduce it into England?

SEC. 5.—*The Monarchy of the Franks under the Merovingian Dynasty.*

1 Who was the first king of the Franks?
2. What were his descendants called?
3. Who was his successor?
4. What cost him his throne?
5. Who succeeded Hilderik?
6. The modern name of Clovis?
7. Whom did he marry?
8. What benefit did she confer on him?
9. What fee did he give the bishop that baptized him?
10. What anecdote is related, illustrative of the little real authority enjoyed by the Frank kings?
11. The extent of the kingdom of Clovis?
12. By whom was he succeeded?
13. Relate the story of the death of Chlodomer's infant children?
14. Who succeeded Theodoric?
15. His character and exploits?
16. Under whom was all France again united?
17. Who succeeded him?
18. The state of the kingdom, during their reign?
19. Under whom was France once more united?
20. How did he punish Brunilda?
21. Who succeeded him?
22. His character, &c., and why canonized?

23. Who were the real sovereigns of France, during the reign of his successors?
24. Who was the greatest of these nominal ministers?
25. Who was Charles Martel?
26. What rendered his name illustrious?
27. For what victory is he still more justly celebrated?
28. His successor?
29. The name of the dynasty, that succeeded the Merovingian?

SEC. 6.—*The Lombard Monarchy.*

1. By whom, and why, were the Lombards encouraged to settle on the frontiers of the empire?
2. Who became head of the Lombards?
3. In what war did he engage?
4. How did he treat Cunimund?
5. The real object of Alboin's ambition?
6. What led to this enterprise?
7. On what condition did the Lombards resign their lands to the Avars?
8. What imprudent act did the Empress Sophia commit?
9. The consequence of it?
10. What city alone resisted Alboin?
11. Why was it spared?
12. The end of Alboin?
13. Who succeeded him?
14. His character and end?
15. The nature of the government established by his successor?
16. What tended to reconcile the Italians to the supremacy of the Lombards?
17. What ambitious design did Luitprand conceive?
18. Of what did he take advantage?
19. Who instigated the Venetians against him?
20. How was the pope treated by the Emperor Leo?
21. Who saved him from this fate?
22. Why did the Italians revolt against Leo?
23. To whom did the pope have recourse in his extremities?
24. Under what king did the Lombards reach the summit of their greatness?
25. By whom was Astulphus subdued?
26. Who finally destroyed the power of the Lombards?
27. How was their king treated?
28. Who received the iron crown of Lombardy?

SEC. 7.—*The Anglo-Saxons.*

1. What befell the Britons when they were finally deserted by the Romans?
2. What imprudent advice did they adopt?
3. Whom did they invite over?
4. Who were the Saxons and Angles?
5 Their two chiefs?
6. Where did they land?
7. How many followers did they bring with them?
8. What induced them to send for more?
9. How did they treat the Britons?
10. Where are their descendants now?
11. How long did the struggle last?
12. What was the Saxon heptarchy?
13. In which of these kingdoms was the Christian religion first established?
14. Mention the circumstance that induced Gregory to send missionaries into England.
15. Who was the head of the mission?
16. Who founded the monastery of St. Alban's?
17. Whom did he send to instruct Charlemagne?
18. For what is France indebted to Alcuin?
19. What universities did he found?
20. Who was the first king of all England?
21. In what year did this great event occur?
22. How long after the first arrival of the Anglo-Saxons in Britain?

CHAPTER II.

THE RISE AND ESTABLISHMENT OF THE SARACENIC POWER.

SEC. 1.—*Political and Social Condition of the East at the coming of Mohammed.*

1. Who succeeded Justinian?
2. For what was his reign remarkable?
3. Who succeeded Justin II.?
4. His character?
5. Tiberius' successor?
6. His character?
7. The condition of Persia at this time?
8. How did the Emperor Maurice act toward the royal fugitive?
9. How did Khosrú evince his gratitude?
10. Against whom did the emperor then turn his arms?
11. What led to a mutiny of his soldiers?
12. Who was Phocas?
13. How did he commence his reign?
14. What noble act did Maurice perform?
15. Who sanctioned the usurpation of Phocas?
16. What title did he receive from him in consequence?
17. What was the end of Phocas?
18. Who succeeded him?
19. How did Khosrú, king of Persia, act when he heard of the death of Maurice, his benefactor?
20. What supplied him with allies in every province?
21. What enterprise did his successes now encourage him to undertake?
22. How did the Jews act in Jerusalem?
23. The fate of Egypt?
24. How long was Khosrú's camp in sight of Constantinople?

25. What letter did he now receive?
26. Who was the writer?
27. How was the letter treated?
28. Mohammed's remark when he heard of this treatment?
29 How were the Avars employed at this time?
30. What purpose did the emperor form?
31. Who dissuaded him from executing it?
32. On what condition did Khosrú promise peace to the empire?
33. How was the emperor affected by this insult?
34. His first step?
35. What bold enterprise did he form?
36. Show what was his success.
37. How did Khosrú act during this desolation of his kingdom?
38. The consequences to himself of such conduct?
39. What excuse did his son offer for his unnatural conduct?
40. What trophy did Heraclius bring with him from Jerusalem?
41. The fate of Persia?
42. What flame was now beginning to spread?
43. How was victory fatal to Heraclius?
44. His conduct?
45. What new enemies appeared on the confines of Persia?
46. The fate of the empire during the last eight years of the reign of Heraclius?

Sec. 2.—*State of Arabia at the coming of Mohammed.*

1. The geographical position of Arabia?
2. Its dimensions?
3. The soil and climate, &c.?
4. Character and position of Arabia Felix?
5. Character and position of Arabia Petræa?
6. What once gave it importance and wealth?
7. From whom are the Arabs descended?
8. What is their boast?
9. Why has their country never been conquered?
10. What parts have been conquered?
11. The physical and intellectual constitution of the Arab?
12. What is said of the camel?
13. Of the Arab horse?
14. The ancient religion of the Arabs?
15. Their religious condition before the coming of Mohammed?
16. What did an ancient father say of Arabia?
17. In what province were the principal cities, in remote ages?
18. The chief cities now?
19. What has always given Mecca importance?
20. How has their temple of Mecca been always regarded?
21. What tribe had the custody of it?
22. What consequence did this give them?
23. What gave a check to Christianity in Arabia?
24. In what year did this happen?
25. How is Mecca situated?
26. Its soil and water, &c.?
27. How far have its inhabitants to send for good fruit?
28. By whom was Mecca founded?
29. By whom was its temple erected?
30. To whom is its early prosperity ascribed?
31. Why did Ishmael make it his residence?
32. What proves it to be an ancient city?
33. The ancient name of Medina?
34. How does it compare with Mecca?
35. Why did its citizens espouse the cause of Mohammed?
36. The literature of the Arabs?
37. How was a literary spirit kept up?
38. What was done with their best poems?
39. The title of their seven best poems?
40. How were they written?
41. Where kept?
42. Their history, what?
43. Their astronomy?
44. Their mechanical arts?
45. What four peculiarities has God given them?

Sec. 3.—*The Preaching of Mohammed.*

1. Where was Mohammed born?
2. Who was his father?
3. His mother?
4. The religion of both?
5. His uncles, who?
6. Where did he become an orphan?
7. Whither did he go at the age of thirteen?
8. His course from this time?
9. The consequence of his mercantile talent?
10. Whom did he marry?
11. What consideration did this give him?
12. What use did he immediately make of his good fortune?
13. What did he do for his family?
14. What was he doing for the next fifteen years?
15. His yearly practice?
16. What made him acquainted with the principal forms of religion then prevailing?
17. The names of some of these sects?
18. What led him to think himself a prophet?
19. To whom did he first announce his mission?
20. Did she recognize his claims?
21. Who followed her example?
22. What led them to believe in him so readily?

23 What were these converts called?
24. The meaning of the word?
25. What confirmed their faith?
26. Why did he communicate them orally?
27. Is it probable so eminent a merchant did not know how to read and write?
28. Why did he then pretend ignorance?
29. In what book were these revelations preserved?
30. The meaning of the term?
31. How soon did he publicly proclaim himself a prophet?
32. How was he received?
33. Under what circumstances did he make the avowal?
34. How did Ali act?
35. Where did Mohammed begin to preach?
36. Why did the guardians of the city oppose him?
37. How were some of his most zealous followers treated?
38. Was he alarmed by these demonstrations?
39. What did he say, when requested to suspend his preaching?
40. On what great occasion did he preach?
41. What rendered the inhabitants of Medina that were present peculiarly attentive?
42. What was Mahommed's first step in imposture?
43. What was he all along an impostor or an enthusiast?
44. What doctrine did he now preach in opposition to his former doctrines?
45. What personal interview did the angel Gabriel afford him?
46. How did the Meccan chiefs act after this?
47. Whither did he flee?
48. What is his flight called?
49. How old was he at this time?
50. How was he received in Medina?
51. The meaning of the term "Medina"?
52. How did his converts act?
53. What attracted warriors to his standard?
54. What occurred near the well Bedr?
55. How did he now extend his religion?
56. What sublime orientalism was long the war cry of his followers?
57. Who were the special objects of his hatred?
58. Why were they so?
59. What effect did a defeat at Ohod have on him?
60 To what did he ascribe it?
61. What character did the war now assume?
62. How did the Meccans suffer?
63. What did they do?
64. What did Mohammed say?
65. What did Mohammed become?
66. His character?
67. Did he take Mecca?
68. To whom did he send ambassadors?
69. The king of Persia's treatment of the letter sent him?
70. How did Heraclius treat it?
71. What sowed the seeds of disease in his constitution?
72. How did he enter Mecca?
73. How did he show homage to the national faith?
74. The effect produced by his presence?
75. In what war did he now engage?
76. The consequence of his success?
77. How did he treat the Kaaba?
78. What emblem was permitted to remain?
79. What was the black stone?
80. The consequence of the capture of Mecca?
81. What two great objects did he thus effect?
82. How many warriors did he now have?
83. What led to his death?
84. At what age and in what year?
85. His dying words?
86. His favourite wife?
87. Why did he make no will?
88. Who was Fatima?

Sec. 4.—*Early Progress of the Saracens.*

1. What shook the fabric of Islamism to its foundation?
2. Who had the best hereditary claims?
3. What rendered him unpopular?
4. How was the controversy decided?
5. What surname did he assume?
6. The meaning of it?
7. His first exploit?
8. What purpose did he then form?
9. The success of his army?
10. Its general, who?
11. Why did he wish to take Jerusalem?
12. His instructions to his army?
13. What renders them so remarkable?
14. Quote Rev. 9. 4.
15. What other city did he wish to take
16. Did Heraclius succour it?
17. How often was his army routed?
18. What dispute arose between the Saracen generals?
19. Why was the memory of the Khaliph Abú Bekr venerated?
20. His character?
21. His successor?
22. How did he evince his jealousy of Khaled?
23. What empire fell next?
24. The result of the battle of Kadesia?
25. Describe the standard of Persia?
26. What was done with it?
27. What foolish act did an Arabian soldier perform?
28. Where was the final battle fought, which decided the fate of Persia?

29 The fate of the Persian king?
30. What dynasty ended with him?
31. What country fell next?
32. The equipage of the khaliph as he came to the surrender of Jerusalem?
33. What did he do when he reached his camp?
34. What proofs of his moderation are given?
35. Where did he build his mosque?
36. What cities were next taken?
37. How many years did the conquest of Syria occupy?
38. What country fell next?
39. The fate of the famous library at Alexandria?
40. The fate of Omar?
41. The results of his reign of ten years?
42. By whom is his memory venerated?
43. By whom execrated?
44. His habits?
45. For what are the Arabs indebted to him?
46. What customs, &c., did he introduce?
47. His successor?
48. What exploits were performed in his reign?
49. The fate of the Colossus of Rhodes?
50. How many camel-loads did it contain?
51. The fate of Othman?
52. His successor?
53. Who revolted, and her fate?
54. How was the difficulty with Moawiyáh settled? Relate the circumstances.
55. Who thus became khaliph?
56. Ali's character?
57. What tradition is mentioned?
58. The fate of his posterity?
59. Whose martyrdom is yearly celebrated in Persia?
60. The conquests of the Saracens?
61. What country in Europe did they subdue?
62. How long did they hold it?
63. What plans did they design to accomplish?
64. Who rescued Europe from their yoke?
65. In what battle?
66. How long did it last?
67. What led to the dismemberment of their empire?
68. The three standards?
69. What did Abûl Abbas do?
70. Relate the circumstances of the assassination of the Ommiade family.
71. Who escaped, and his subsequent fortune?
72. The capital of the Abbasside dynasty?
73. The hero of the Arabian Nights' Entertainment?
74. The literary character of the Saracens?
75. The end of the matter?

CHAPTER III.

RESTORATION OF THE WESTERN EMPIRE.

Sec. 1.—*The Life of Charlemagne.*

1. What circumstances conspired to give power and authority to the pope?
2. Why did the Italians desire to have the pope recognised as the head of the Christian church?
3 What favour did the pope show Pepin?
4. How was it returned?
5. Who commanded the French armies in Italy?
6. To whom did Pepin leave his kingdom?
7. What circumstance made Charlemagne sole monarch?
8. What were the grounds of hostility, between Charlemagne and the king of the Lombards?
9. What induced Charlemagne to declare war against the Saxons?
10. What lead him into Italy?
11. What exploits did he perform there?
12. What led him into Spain?
13. What recalled him home, before he had conquered the Saracens?
14. Describe the battle of Roncesvalles.
15. What is said of the song of Roland?
16. Relate the legend of Roncesvalles.
17. The anecdote of John, king of France.
18. What is said of the devastation of the Saxons, at this time?
19. Who was their leader?
20. His fate?
21. How did Charlemagne employ the intervals of tranquillity?
22. By whom was he assisted?
23. What circumstance proves the renown of Charlemagne?
24. What presents were sent him?
25. What new enemy now appeared?
26. How was Charlemagne affected by their appearance?
27. How did these Normans act in England?
28. What led Charlemagne again into Italy?
29. What title did the pope confer on him?
30. What project was now formed?
31. How was it defeated?
32. Who succeeded Charlemagne?
33. How long did Charlemagne live?
34. The character of Louis?

Sec. 2.—*Decline and Fall of the Carlovingian Dynasty.*

1. The boundaries of the Western empire?
2. What crimes did Louis commit, at the instigation of his wife?
3. The consequences of them?
4. How did he show his remorse?
5. What led to a civil war?
6. What civil war ensued after his death?
7. Who may be considered the founder of the French monarchy?

8. What kingdoms and states were formed out of the fragments of the Western empire?
9. To what did they owe their origin?
10. How did Charlemagne endeavour to remedy this evil?
11. What nullified his wise policy?
12. What principle was the foundation of the feudal system?
13. Of what great race were the Normans a branch?
14. What exasperated them against the Franks?
15. What was their character as sailors?
16. How did they find the land when they were far out at sea?
17. What title did their leaders assume?
18. How did these sea-kings get followers?
19. Their usual conduct, &c.?
20. Why were they specially hostile to the clergy, &c.?
21. Thierry's description of a sea-king?
22. From what ballads do we obtain all our information of these sea-kings?
23. Recite the enactments of an ancient law among them.
24. Who were the Kempe?
25. How did Hiorolf act?
26. His success?
27. How did Half act?
28. What was necessary in order to obtain admission into this number?
29. What were they forbidden to do?
30. What circumstance proved the devotion of his crew to Half?
31 Who were the *berseker?*
32. How did Sivald's sons act, when they were in this state?
33. Their fate?
34. What other exploits did Halfdan perform?
35. How did the sons of Arngrim act, during their *berserk* madness?
36. How did the sea-kings procure wives for themselves?
37. Show how Moalda was treated.
38. What sufferings did these pirates inflict on France?
39. How did tne Franks defend themselves?
40. The consequences of such folly?
41. By whom was the Russian monarchy founded?
42. What foothold did they obtain in other countries?
43. The story of Charles and Rollo?
44. How did Rollo afterwards act?
45. What incident is mentioned, as showing the security of property?
46 What new enemy appeared at this time?
47 Who saved England for a time?
48 The last of the Carlovingian dynasty?
49 The founder of the present race of French kings?
50. The state of France at this period?

Sec. 3.—*The Foundation of the Germanic Empire.*

1. What oath were the German emperors obliged to take?
2. Where did the custom of electing emperors commence?
3. How long did it continue?
4. What emperor raised Germany to the highest rank among European states?
5. From what disgraceful tribute did he free his kingdom?
6. How did the Germans show their sense of the importance of this victory?
7 What incident shows the character of this age?
8 How did Otho become king of Italy?
9. Why did the pope acknowledge him as Roman emperor and supreme head of the church?
10 Why did he afterwards oppose him?
11 How did Otho resent this conduct?
12 What hastened the death of Otho II.
13 How was Otho III. killed?
14. What anecdote is related of Conrad's generosity?
15. What proofs of energy did Henry III. give?
16 In whose reign did the great struggle between the papal and imperial power begin?
17 The condition of affairs in England favourable to the pope?
18. The condition of affairs in Spain?
19. The condition of affairs in Northern Europe?
20. Whom did Edward the Confessor nominate as his successor?
21. Whom did the English prefer?
22. What oath did Harold take?
23. Under what circumstances?
24. What artifice was employed to give sanctity to it?
25. Did he adhere to it?
26. What induced William to invade England?
27. What battle decided the contest?
28. How did William treat the English?
29. How did some Normans lay the foundation of the kingdom of the two Sicilies?
30. How did all these events strengthen the pope?

Sec. 4.—*State of the East from the Establishment to the Overthrow of the Khaliphate.*

1. What is said of the history of the Byzantine empire during the middle ages?
2. Its condition, &c.?
3 Whence did the Turks and Tartars come?
4. When was their country invaded and by whom?

5. What dangerous practice did the Khaliph Al Moutassem introduce?
6. The consequence of it?
7. How was the revolution completed?
8. What new horde now appeared?
9. Their victories?
10. The extent of the dominions of Malek Shah?
11. What little circumstance now occurred, which led to mighty consequences?
12. The conduct of the assassins?
13. What shows the extent of the evil?
14. How was the kingdom of Malek Shah divided?
15. Of what benefit to the Christians was this division?

CHAPTER IV.

GROWTH OF THE PAPAL POWER.

Sec. 1.—*The Origin of the Papacy.*

1. What is remarkable in the clerical organization of Christianity?
2. What statement is made on this subject?
3. What two great principles were fully recognized at a very early period?
4. The opinion of infidels on this point?
5. The general outline of the apostolic model.
6. To what two different lines of temptation were the clergy exposed?
7. Show how they tended to the same result?
8. The only bond that held nations together?
9. What led to the persecution of the pagans?
10. How did this tend to increase the power of the clergy?
11. How was the discipline of the church injured?
12. How were the doctrines of Christianity corrupted?
13. What miserable practices were thus introduced?
14. What bodies have always been prominent in introducing and supporting superstitions, &c.?
15. Was the charge of idolatry urged against the Christians true?
16. What proves it to be so?
17. Who were the Iconoclasts?
18. The decrees of the synod of Constantinople?
19. How did the pope act?
20. Who made the pope a temporal prince?
21. When does the proper history of the papacy begin?
22. What three transactions combined to give it form?
23. What naturally led to the temporal sovereignity of the pope?
24. What is said of the pope's confirmation of Pepin as king of France?
25. On what is popery founded?
26. Separate the two parts?
27. What happened ere one generation had passed away?

Sec. 2.—*The early Development of the Political System of the Papacy.*

1. The important links between ancient and modern history?
2. Was the French monarchy originally elective or hereditary?
3. Why did Pepin then wish to be recognized by the pope?
4. What is said of the measures of the pope?
5. What ceremony did they revive?
6. How did Pepin regard it?
7. How did the pope regard it?
8. Its effect?
9. How did the Frank nobles regard it?
10. What new act did pope Stephen perform?
11. Its effect?
12. What return did the Carlovingians make to Stephen?
13. What fraud did the holy father commit in order to secure these acquisitions?
14. Its effect?
15. Is it now acknowledged to have been a fraud?
16. What pontiff first combined the elements of the papacy into a system?
17. What difficulty met him at the outset?
18. How did the pope attempt to ward off the danger?
19. How did Leo III. act?
20. How has his act been interpreted?
21. What is said of it?
22. What benefits did Leo experience from this moderation?
23. How did he show his gratitude?
24. The dangers and benefits to the papal see, of the re-establishment of the empire?
25. What is said of the struggles between the bishops of Rome and of Constantinople?
26. The effect on the papacy of the death of Charlemagne?
27. What is said of the usurpations of the church during the wars between the successors of Charlemagne?
28. What shameful acknowledgment did Charles the Bald make?
29. What canon did the bishops make?
30. How did king and people regard it?
31. What right did the pope assume?
32. Why did he depose the archbishop of Ravenna?
33. How did he treat King Lothaire?
34. What acknowledgment did the pope exact of the king of France?

35. How was he recognized as emperor?
36. What letter did the pope write to the king?
37. How did the feudal lords treat the pontiffs?
38. To what are the vices of this period attributable?
39. The great error of the pontiffs?
40. What rendered popery, as a system, inoperative?

Sec. 3.—*The Struggle for Supremacy between the Popes and Emperors.*

1. For what services was Otho rewarded with the iron crown of Lombardy and the title of emperor of the West?
2. How did Otho show his jealousy of the designs of the pope against him, even in his coronation?
3. How did the pope treat Otho?
4. Otho's conduct in return?
5. The character of Pope John?
6. Who was elected in his room?
7. What bull did he issue?
8. What did the bishops think and say of it?
9. What led to John's restoration?
10. His subsequent conduct?
11. His end?
12. What did the people think of his death?
13. Who succeeded him?
14. The condition of the papacy at this time?
15. To what did the papacy owe its first success?
16. What now gave it strength for a new struggle?
17. How was Pope John treated?
18. His successors, and who prevailed?
19. What traitorous act did Boniface VII. commit?
20. The death of Boniface?
21. The death of his rival?
22. What shows how low the papacy had now sunk?
23. How did Sylvester act?
24. How did Benedict VIII. treat the Emperor Henry?
25. The state of the popedom soon after this?
26. How old was Benedict IX. when raised to the popedom?
27. Who induced him to resign, and by what means?
28. Who was Hildebrand?
29. What became of him?
30. His character?

Sec. 4.—*Revival of the Papal Power.*

1. What led to the success of the papal usurpation?
2. How did it endeavour to secure its acquisitions?
3. What is said of the nobles of Italy?
4. What opinion was the papacy during this time generating?
5. Under what pressure was its organization completed?
6. How did it link itself with every class of the community?
7. How was the clerical identified with the popular cause?
8. Who was the first that clearly perceived the tendency and strength of this current?
9. What is said of his personal character?
10. Of his measures?
11. His design?
12. What is said of Leo IX.?
13. Hildebrand's first interview with him?
14. What had the pontiff dreaded?
15. What service did Hildebrand render him?
16. How was he rewarded?
17. Why were the clergy and people of Rome pleased at these things?
18. Leo's conduct?
19. His fate?
20. What led to his death?
21. Who succeeded him?
22. Hildebrand's views and conduct?
23. How did the new pope treat him?
24. How did he conduct himself in France?
25. How did the people act on the death of Pope Stephen?
26. How did Hildebrand?
27. Why did the emperor aid Nicholas?
28. How did Nicholas act?
29. How did he act towards the Normans in the south of Italy?
30. How did they serve him in turn?
31. The effect of this?
32. What is said of the church of Milan?
33. Peter Damian's boldness?
34. The result of it?
35. How was Nicholas' successor chosen?
36. Who was the real governor of the church?
37. How did he treat the Milanese?
38. How did it happen that two archbishops of Milan were chosen?
39. The contest that ensued?
40. How had Hildebrand been preparing for the contest?
41. How did he contribute to the Norman conquest of England?
42. How did he act towards William?
43. What did he send him?
44. How did he act towards Matilda?
45. What daring act threw all these political struggles into the shade?
46. The real author of all these acts?

Sec. 5.—*Pontificate of Gregory VII.*

1. What is said of the accession of Hildebrand to the papacy?
2. How did he obtain the emperor's ratification of his irregular election?
3. What favourite plan of his did he begin at once to put in execution?

4 For what purposes did he send a legate to Spain?
5. What effect did his energy produce on the emperor?
6. What were the two great objects of the pope?
7. What were the arguments for the celibacy of the clergy?
8. What against it?
9. What were lay-investitures?
10. The objections to them?
11. What seemed to make it necessary that these appointments in the church should be independent of the state?
12. What blasphemous claim did the pope put forth?
13. What canon was passed on this subject in a general council held at Rome?
14. What is said of the letters of the pope in which he communicated these decrees to the European sovereigns?
15. Mention some of his actions corresponding to his words.
16. How did the emperor relish these things?
17. What conspiracy was formed in Rome against the pope?
18. What daring act was perpetrated by the prefect of the city?
19. The consequences of it?
20. How did the pope treat the emperor?
21. How did the emperor act in return?
22. What did the pope then do?
23. Mention the most important of the resolutions that he passed.
24. What reply did he make when advised not to excommunicate the emperor?
25. What did both parties now prepare to do?
26. What circumstance happened, at this time, very opportunely for the pope?
27. How was Henry situated?
28 What hardships did he endure in crossing the Alps?
29. How did he act when he reached Lombardy?
30. To what indignities was he subjected by the pope?
31. Their effect on his mind?
32. What led him to repent of his degradation?
33. How did he renew the war?
34. How was he treated at home?
35. Why did this disconcert the pope?
36. How did he act, &c.?
37. What is the doctrine of transubstantiation?
38. Why were the clergy zealous in the support of it?
39. What remark was made to a discontented nobleman of the queen of Spain by her confessor?
40. Who assailed the doctrine vigorously in the eleventh century?
41. What induced the pope to depart from his neutrality between Henry and Rodolph?
42 How did Henry act thereupon?
43. How did he act after Rodolph was defeated and slain?
44. What did Gregory do after his departure from Rome?
45. How did he view his conduct on his death-bed?
46. His frequent remark?
47. Of what may he be regarded as the founder?
48. How has he been spoken of by historians?
49. Of what may he be called the representative?
50. How was he regarded by the soldiers, the people, and the clergy?
51. What is said of his faults?
52. How did he act with reference to criminals whom he sentenced to death?
53. Give a summary of his history and character.

SEC. 6.—*The War of Investitures.*

1. How did Urban II. commence his pontificate?
2. Whom did Matilda now marry?
3. Of what illustrious family are they the ancestors?
4. What domestic trouble now afflicted the Emperor Henry?
5. To what threatening danger was the attention of the Christian world now directed?
6. Whose eloquence led to the first crusade?
7. What new oath did the clergy take in A.D. 1104?
8. What grievous misfortune now befel Henry?
9. How did the bishop of Liege act, and how was he treated in consequence?
10. Did Henry V. yield to the pope, in the matter of investitures?
11. How did he treat Pope Paschal?
12. How was the matter finally compromised?
13. What schism now took place in the church?
14. Owing to whose exertions was Pope Anacletus stigmatized as an antipope?
15. How many bishops assembled at the general council in Rome A.D. 1139?
16. Who was Abelard, and by whom opposed?
17. Of what was this controversy the first symptom?
18. The doctrines of Arnold?
19. What struggle now commenced in Italy?
20. Why did it so speedily cease?

SEC. 7.—*The Crusades.*

1. When did pilgrimages to Jerusalem begin.

2. When did they begin to multiply and why?
3. How did the Saracens treat the pilgrims, whilst they possessed Jerusalem?
4. How did the Turks treat them?
5. Who first proposed a general crusade against the Turks?
6. Who actually excited the first crusade?
7. How did he do it?
8. Who were the first crusaders?
9. Why were they so called?
10. How did they act on their march?
11. The consequences to themselves?
12. Their treatment of the Jews?
13. Who commanded the first regular army against the Turks?
14. What noblemen joined his standard?
15. How were they received and treated by the Greek emperor?
16. Their career in Asia?
17. When was Jerusalem taken?
18. How was it defended by the Mohammemedans?
19. By what stratagem did Godfrey excite his troops to deeds of valour?
20. How was their triumph sullied?
21. What boast did the knights make?
22. How long did the massacre last?
23. What suddenly put a stop to it?
24. Their conduct thereupon?
25. Who was chosen king of Jerusalem?
26. What noble declaration did he make?
27. How long did this new kingdom last?
28. How many crusades were there?
29. How long did they last?
30. Give the history of the second crusade.
31. Through whose influence had it been undertaken?
32. His conduct under the storm of public indignation that burst upon him?
33. What kings joined in a new crusade on the news of the capture of Jerusalem by Saladin?
34. What prevented their success?
35. What led king Philip to return home?
36. What, king Richard?
37. What befel Richard on his return?
38. At whose instigation was the fourth crusade undertaken?
39. Their first departure from their original design?
40. Their second?
41. How did they act toward Constantinople?
42. By whom was the fifth crusade undertaken?
43. The history of it?
44. How did Frederick II. of Germany act?
45. Why was he twice excommunicated by the pope?
46. His success?
47. What caused him to return home?
48. Why was he a third time excommunicated?
49. How did he act on his return?
50. Who led the ninth crusade?
51. What led to the ruin of this crusade?
52. The pope's address to the clergy of Sicily, on hearing of the death of the emperor?
53. The fate of Louis?
54. When was Acre, the last stronghold of the Christians in Palestine, taken?

SEC. 8.—*The Crusade against the Albigenses.*

1. What is a general council?
2. Who were the Albigenses?
3. What decree had been pronounced against them?
4. Why were the feudal lords unwilling to execute it?
5. Why did some persons maintain that the Old Testament was written by the Spirit of Evil?
6. Against what Romish doctrines did the Albigenses protest?
7. The moral character of the Albigenses?
8. What relation did they wish to hold to the Romish church?
9. Explain this.
10. Innocent III.'s first step in his endeavours to crush them?
11. What is said of his emissaries?
12. How did Castelnau, the papal legate, act?
13. His conduct to Raymond, on his refusal to treat with him?
14. What inflamed the Pope against Raymond?
15. How was he treated?
16. How did Philip Augustus, the king of France, act?
17. What promises did the monks make to the crusaders?
18. What new monastic order was instituted by the Pope, Innocent III?
19. Their special object?
20. By what dreaded name is this institution best known?
21. How did Raymond act at the approach of danger?
22. How did his nephew act?
23. Raymond's conduct at the approach of the hostile army of the crusaders?
24. The conduct of the crusaders towards their prisoners?
25. The barbarous answer of the abbot of Citeaux, when asked by the army, how they should distinguish catholics from heretics?
26. How did the army act?
27. Who interfered in behalf of young Raymond?
28. His advice to him?
29. His fate, and that of the townsmen?
30. What had the country been made by these crusaders?

31 How were the Albigenses still treated?
32. How much better were the monks of Citeaux than robbers?
33 Simon de Montfort's conduct?
34. What did Raymond do?
35. How was he treated in Rome?
36. What was Montfort doing in the meantime?
37. How did the king of Aragon attempt to secure his friendship?
38. Why was not peace made?
39. The fate of the defenders of the stronghold of Raymond—the castle of Lavaur?
40. What now interrupted the friendship between the monks of Citeaux and the crusaders?
41. How did Arnold, the papal legate, act?
42. How was the pope set at defiance by his creatures?
43. The fate of the king of Aragon and the citizens of Toulouse?
44. The cause of the quarrel between the legate and Montfort?
45. What more formidable enemy now appeared?
46. How did Montfort lose Toulouse?
47. His fate?
48. The subsequent fate of Toulouse?
49. What institution was now established in this country?
50. The effects of these wars?

Sec. 9.—*Consequences of the Crusades.*

1. What advantages did the popes derive from the crusades?
2. What effect had the increase of the papal power on that of the kings of Europe?
3 What peculiar circumstances led to a contrary result in France?
4. How did the kings of Spain profit by the fanaticism of the age?
5. The effects of the crusades on chivalry?
6. Describe the Hospitallers, or knights of St. John, or knights of Malta.
7. The knights Templars.
8. The Teutonic Order.
9. The Order of St. Lazarus.
10. The effects of the crusade on the Italian cities?
11. What laid the foundation of the present Hanseatic league?
12. What led to the establishment of municipal institutions?
13. How did the royal authority gain by the extension of municipal freedom?
14. What followed as a necessary consequence of this freedom?
15 The state of Germany at this period?
16. What brave emperor restored tranquillity?
17. To whom did the pope give the kingdom of Naples?
18 The effect of his cruelties?
19 The fate of Conradin?
20. The effect of the severance of Italy from the German empire?
21. What proved a more formidable foe to the Romish church than the sovereigns of Germany?

Sec. 10.—*Formation and Constitutional History of the Spanish Monarchy.*

1. The condition of Spain for several hundred years after the invasion of the Saracens?
2. In what four states were they comprised after the fourteenth century?
3. What is said of the kingdom of Granada?
4. What is said of Navarre?
5. What is said of Aragon?
6. What is said of Castile?
7. How did they begin to secure their conquests?
8. What is said of their dissensions?
9. The complaint of the soldiers of Fernan Gonçales?
10. How long did it take the Spaniards to reach the Douro?
11. How long to reach the Tagus?
12. To what circumstances should be imputed the liberal charters of communities in Castile and Leon?
13. Some of their enactments?
14. The date of popular representation in Castile?
15. How much sooner than the first convocation of the English house of commons?
16. What powerful check on the operations of the crown did they fail to avail themselves of?
17. What important principle of the constitution was recognised?
18. What prerogative long survived the wreck of their liberties?
19. What anomalous institution was peculiar to Castile?
20. Describe it.
21. What were these associations called?
22. The state of the cities of Castile?
23. The state of the nobles, &c.?
24. How did the over-weening confidence of the nobles prove their ruin?
25. The effects of the long minorities in Castile?

Sec. 11.—*Survey of the Constitution of Aragon.*

1. What first raised Aragon to political importance?
2. Where were the seeds of liberty planted and brought to maturity?
3. Which of the maritime republics was eminently conspicuous?
4. What is said of its navy?

5. What countries did it conquer?
6. What city did it conquer?
7. What is said of the authority of their monarchs?
8. How were they chosen?
9. What did they swear to do before assuming the sceptre?
10. Some of the privileges of the nobles?
11. What is said of the commons of Aragon?
12. What of the triennial Cortes?
13. What of the committee of interim?
14. The privileges and functions of the cortes?
15. What is said of Barcelona?
16. How was its wealth exhibited?
17. Its *peculiar* glory?
18. Its government and privileges?
19. The influence of these democratic institutions on the character of the Catalonians?
20. What did the Venetian ambassador say of them in the sixteenth century?
21. The policy of the kings of Spain when Castile and Aragon were united?
22. What did Ferdinand say of the nobles of Aragon?
23. How did they lose their privileges?
24. What is said of the connexion between freedom of trade and freedom of institutions?
25. Of what great truth is Spain a memorable and sad example?
26. With whom did the Austrian line of Spanish monarchs begin?

SEC. 12.—*State of Western Europe at the commencement of the Fourteenth Century.*

1. Rodolph of Hapsburg's first step after becoming emperor of Germany?
2. Who founded the imperial house of Austria?
3. How and when was Venice founded?
4. When did it first rise into importance?
5. Who conferred on them the sovereignty of the Adriatic?
6. What ceremony thence arose?
7. How did the crusades extend their power?
8. What change of government did the increasing wealth of Venice occasion?
9. What led to the terrible council of ten?
10. To what did Genoa owe its prosperity?
11. How were they rewarded by the Greek emperors for the help afforded by them?
12. What led to the war between them and the Pisans, and its result?
13. Why was Charles of Anjou, king of Naples, hated?
14. What led to the Sicilian vespers?
15. Who were massacred, and who spared?
16. Who protected the islanders?
17. The pope's doings in consequence?
18. How did Peter, king of Aragon, outwit Charles?
19. Did the Catalonians regard the pope's fulminations?
20. What naval victory did Peter's admiral gain?
21. The end of Charles?
22. What saved the Mohammedans at this time from Alphonzo, king of Castile?
23. To what new kingdom in Europe did the crusade in Spain lead?
24. How was this result produced?
25. The policy of the French kings after Hugh Capet's usurpation?
26. What error did Philip I. commit?
27. How was this danger increased?
28. Who was the founder of the greatness of the French monarchy?
29. What is said of the Plantagenets?
30. Of Richard I.?
31. Of John?
32. The battle of Bouvines?
33. Of the papacy after the death of Nicholas?
34. How did the doctrine of infallibility injure it?
35. How long was the holy see vacant?
36. Whom did the cardinals elect?
37. What is said of him?
38. How did he show his pride?
39. Who forced him to resign, and how?
40. His successor?
41. How did he act?

SEC. 13.—*Pontificate of Boniface.*

1. What is said of the manner in which Boniface obtained the resignation of Celestine?
2. What declaration did Celestine make of him? See p. 446.
3. How did he treat Celestine?
4. His character and designs?
5. His letters to Philip, Edward, and Adolphus?
6. The conduct of James of Aragon?
7. How did the Sicilians view this conduct in their sovereign?
8. How was Philip of France acting at this time?
9. The pope's command to him?
10. What did the pope do, when Philip refused to obey him?
11. How was this bull received in Europe?
12. How did Edward of England act?
13. How did Philip?
14. The effect of their conduct?
15. Arbitration of Boniface, and how was his decision treated?
16. His treatment of the Colonnas?
17. How did he endeavour to lull the king's vigilance?
18. How did Philip treat his proposal?
19. How did Boniface induce persons to come to Rome to attend the celebration of the jubilee?

20. The secret object of the jubilee?
21. Who was the pope's messenger to Philip, after the jubilee was over?
22. How did the king treat him?
23. Boniface's subsequent proceedings?
24. Peter Flotte's summary of the bull, *Ausculta fili?*
25. Philip's treatment of it?
26. His letter? Repeat it.
27. The substance of the manifestoes of the three orders?
28. Boniface's command to Edward of England?
29. Edward's reply?
30. Conduct of some of the French clergy, and Philip's proceedings thereupon?
31. Demands of Boniface on Philip?
32. Philip's retaliation?
33. Boniface's violent proceeding?
34. Philip's retaliation?
35. What did Boniface then proceed to do?
36. How was his purpose of vengeance thwarted?
37. What alone saved him from being carried a prisoner to France?
38. His end?
39. The effect of his reign on the papal power?
40. Show how this was produced?
41. What change was occasioned, &c., by the death of Boniface?
42. How did Benedict XI. act?

SEC. 14.—*State of England and the Northern Kingdoms at the Commencement of the Fourteenth Century.*

1. How did William the Conqueror treat the Saxon population of England?
2. Who was the first of the Plantagenet dynasty?
3. The situation of Ireland at this time?
4. What suggested to William the idea of conquering Ireland?
5. Who was the only English pope?
6. On what condition did he permit Henry to invade Ireland?
7. What right had he over Ireland or the Irish church?
8. What led Henry to invade Ireland?
9. What is said of the great charter?
10. How did the pope treat John?
11. What saved England from becoming a French province?
12. Character of Henry III.?
13. What laid the basis of the house of commons?
14. The chief object of Edward's ambition?
15. Why is the eldest son of the king of England called prince of Wales?
16. What gave Edward a pretence to invade Scotland?
17. The three competitors?
18. Who was chosen, and on what condition?
19. His end?
20. What Scottish hero arose to sustain his country?
21. Who finally secured the crown?
22. What produced innumerable civil wars in the north of Europe?
23. Who subdued Prussia and Livonia?

SEC. 15.—*Revolutions in the East in consequence of the Mongolian Invasion.*

1. What is said of the Mongolian empire?
2. Of Jenghiz Khan?
3. His early history?
4. His first expedition?
5. His conquests?
6. His maxim?
7. The conquests of his successors?
8. Who were the Mamelukes?
9. Their career?
10. How long did their dominion over Egypt last?
11. When did they finally expel the Christians from Syria and Palestine?

CHAPTER V.

THE REVIVAL OF LITERATURE; THE PROGRESS OF CIVILIZATION AND INVENTION.

SEC. 1.—*Decline of the Papal Power.—The great Schism of the West.*

1. Where did Clement V fix his residence, and why, &c.?
2. What further did Philip require of him?
3. How did he act on the occasion?
4. What sacrifice was he forced to make to gratify Philip?
5. How were these knights treated?
6. What was their only crime?
7. What inspired Philip with the hope of obtaining the empire for his brother?
8. Did the pope aid him?
9. How did he act, and why?
10. How did the new emperor begin his reign?
11. For what purpose had the council of Vienne been summoned?
12. What was proved?
13. Why was Clement unwilling that Boniface should be condemned?
14. The sentence of the council?
15. The decrees of the council?
16. What had nearly brought on a war between the emperor and the king of France?
17. Henry's death, how occasioned?
18. What important personages died about this time?
19. The consequences, &c.?
20. How long were the cardinals in electing a pope?
21. What happened at their first meeting?

22. How were they forced to come to a decision?
23. Who was elected, and by what means?
24. The state of Europe at this time?
25. How did the pope act?
26. What did the emperor Louis do?
27. What excited the indignation of the Germans against the pope?
28. How did Louis treat him?
29. What prevented the destruction of the pope?
30. The fate of the antipope?
31. By what religious dispute was the church now disturbed?
32. Who compelled the pope to retract his doctrines?
33. (Could the pope then be infallible?)
34 What is said of the pope's wealth?
35. What was the pope's sojourn at Avignon called, and why?
36. To what did the successor of John owe his election?
37. How was he regarded by the kings of Europe?
38. How did Philip, king of France, treat him?
39. Who was chosen his successor?
40. What deputation was sent him?
41. How did he treat Naples?
42. How the emperor Louis V.?
43. How the church of England?
44. How did Louis V. act?
45. The effect of his humiliations?
46. What events now took place in Italy?
47. How did Jane conciliate the pontiff?
48. What did the king of Hungary do?
49. What did the pope do to avert the danger?
50. The history of Rienzi?
51. The doings of the king of Hungary?
52. How did Clement avail himself of the opportunity?
53. How did he act towards the archbishop of Milan?
54. His decision with regard to the dispute between the king of Hungary and the queen of Naples?
55. Why is the eldest son of the king of France called the dauphin?
56. What is said of the power of the papacy at this time?
57. How did the pope endeavour to recover the ancient patrimony of St. Peter?
58. The end of Rienzi?
59. Actions of Charles IV.?
60. What events were now taking place in France?
61. How did John, the king of France, replenish his coffers?
62. Give some account of the origin and doings of the Free Companies?
63. How did the pope keep them from plundering Avignon?
64. How did his successor Urban V. keep them away?
65. How did the emperor Charles demean himself toward the pope?
66. What was thought of his conduct?
67. Why was the pope unwilling to live in Rome?
68. What had he gained by going thither?
69. Gregory's great object?
70. By what infamous means did he endeavour to gain over the Florentines?
71. The consequence of this conduct?
72. How did Gregory retaliate?
73. The reply of the papal legate to the Bolognese when they sued for pardon?
74. What reformer now arose in England?
75. How did Gregory order him to be treated?
76. Who protected him?
77. His doctrines?
78. Why was Gregory so enraged with him?
79. Why did he think of returning to Avignon?
80. What prevented him?
81. Of what was the death of Gregory XI. a new era?
82. What attached the Romans to the papacy?
83 Who succeeded Gregory?
84. By what means was he elected?
85. What expectations had been formed of Urban's conduct?
86. Were they realized?
87. How did he act?
88. How did the cardinals act?
89. How was the fate of the church now to be determined?
90. How did Urban treat the count of Fondi?
91. The consequence?
92. Whom did the cardinals think of choosing as antipope?
93. Whom did they choose?
94. Why was he hated by the Italians?
85. For whom did the emperor declare?
96. For whom the queen of Naples?
97. What became of Clement?
98. Whom did the king of France favour and why?
99. How did Urban treat the queen of Naples?
100. How did the two popes treat one another?
101. What states favoured each?
102. How did France suffer in the contest?
103. How did Jane, queen of Naples, suffer for the part she took in the contest?
104. Who undertook to avenge her?
105. His fate, and that of his barons?
106. How did Urban treat the king of Naples?
107. How did the king act thereupon?
108. What conspiracy was now detected?
109. How were the cardinals treated?
110. How did he treat Durazzo?

111. How did Durazzo retort?
112. Whither did he escape?
113. His conduct during his flight?
114. How was Clement VII., the antipope, acting all this while?
115. What kingdom suffered most from the schism?
116. How was it treated?
117. What doctrinal dispute was now added to the schism?
118. What became of Monçon?
119. How did the pope resolve the question?
120. Who undertook to decide it?
121. Bull of Clement VII. on the subject?
122. How was Urban VI. now acting?
123. His end?
124. The conduct of his successor?
125. How did Clement propose to strengthen himself?
126. How did the doctors of the Sorbonne propose to terminate the schism?
127. The effect on Clement?
128. Letter of the French ministers to the cardinals?
129. How did they act?
130. The decision of the French court thereupon?
131. Benedict's obstinacy?
132. The state of the Western governments?
133. What advantage did Boniface take of these circumstances?
134. How did the cardinals attempt to put an end to the schism?
135. Who recognised the several popes?
136. The effect of these disputes?
137. Who, in Germany, advocated Wickliffe's doctrine?
138. Alexander's successor?
139. His qualifications?
140. How was the schism now to be terminated?
141. John's remark on Constance?
142. Sigismond's infamous treatment of John Huss?
143. How was Pope John treated?
144. How were Huss and Jerome treated?
145. What hero sustained the cause of the Hussites, in Germany?
146. The result of the deliberations of the council?
147. What council succeeded that of Constance?
148. The result of it?
149. The good effects of these councils?
150. What enemy, still more formidable than councils, was now arising?

SEC. 2.—*First Revival of Literature, and Inventions in Science.*

1. Who first employed literary talent against the church?
2. The founder of Italian literature?
3. The first reviver of experimental science?
4. His great merit, what?
5. What was thought of his discoveries?
6. Who followed Dante in reviving literature?
7. What new inventions were now made?
8. What was used before paper?
9. What did the Arabs find in Bokhara?
10 What answered instead of cotton for paper?
11. The first manufactory of linen paper, when and where?
12. What is said of the invention of oil painting?
13. What of the invention of printing?
14. The first printing-press, where?
15. How did Faustus treat Gutenberg?
16. What is said of the invention of gunpowder?
17. The first account of it, in what year?
18. Who first used powder in mines, &c.?
19. Cannon, how first made?
20. The discoverer of the polarity of the needle?
21. Of the compass?
22. How did the old Danish sailors direct their course?
23. To whom are we indebted for the improvement of the compass?

SEC. 3.—*Progress of Commerce.*

1. Who engrossed the commerce of Europe from A.D. 1300 to 1450?
2. Who the trade of the Levant?
3. What led to the wars between the Italian cities?
4. Who finally became supreme?
5. Where was the largest silk manufactory?
6. With what did Venice supply Europe?
7. What made them the chief bankers and money-lenders every where?
8. The origin of the three balls, exhibited over pawnbrokers' shops?
9. What led to dissensions, &c., among the Italian republics?
10. What houses became chief in the several cities?
11. The last war between Venice and Genoa, called what; and its effects?
12. What else contributed to the decline of Genoa?
13. How long did it remain a dependency of the dutchy of Milan?
14. What saved Venice from internal convulsions?
15. What secured and fostered its trade?
16. The greatest advantage gained by Venice over its commercial rivals arose from what?
17. Of what advantage was this treaty to them?

18. What is said of the territorial acquisitions of Venice?
19. What is said of its power and conduct?
20. What is said of the Hanseatic confederation?
21. What cities joined the confederacy?
22. At what city did the representatives regularly meet, and how often?
23. How many cities sent delegates in the fifteenth century?
24. Were these all that belonged to the confederacy?
25. What rights did they exercise?
26. The principal marts?
27. What misfortune befel Novogorod? and when?
28. What became of its merchants?
29. What took place annually at Bruges?
30. To what did this intercourse, &c., naturally lead?
31. What gave commerce a new direction?
32. What else injured the confederation?
33. What led the northern sovereigns to assail the confederation?
34. The result of this?
35. What cities finally remained united?
36. On what was commercial prosperity based in Flanders?
37. In what did they trade?
38. What is said of the earls of Flanders?
39. With whom did Edward I. of England seek an alliance?
40. What is said of Philippa?
41. How did Philip, the Fair, treat her and her father?
42. How did Guy, the earl, act after his escape?
43. Of what was this the commencement?
44. What is said of the burgesses of Flanders?
45. How did the nobles view their progress?
46. At what were they grieved?
47. What brought on war?
48. Who directed the mercantile Flemings?
49. The results of the war?
50. What powerful rival appeared?
51. What manufacture flourished there?
52. What proportion of the exports of the kingdom did it constitute?
53. How did Edward I. obtain workmen from Flanders?
54. How were they regarded?
55. Of what did the petitions complain?
56. What was the conduct of the landowners?
57. The law passed on the subject?
58. The effect of it?
59. What is said of the woolen manufactures in the reign of Henry VI.?
60. The reciprocity law?
61. What foolish attempt was made to limit the supply of labour?
62. The besetting error of legislators at this period?
63. The real use of money?
64. The essence of all commerce?
65. What laws did the ignorance of the legislators lead them to pass?
66. What check to industry did Henry VII. remove?
67. What proved the necessity of legislative interference?
68. What other law did he make?
69. What was thought of it at the time?
70. What kept the parliaments from troubling commerce, &c., in Henry VIII.'s time?
71. What circumstance deserves to be mentioned in connection with the woolen trade?
72. The effect of hostilities between England and Flanders in 1528?
73. How did Wolsey act?
74. The true remedy?
75. What act was passed under Edward VI.?
76. The effect of it?
77 The effect of the persecutions in France and Flanders?
78. What is said in the remonstrance of the Hanse towns concerning the exports of England?
79. What did the English begin to do in this reign?
80. What is said of their success?
81. What is said of Elizabeth's monopolies?
82. What right did the company of merchant adventurers possess?
83. How did they secure their patent?
84. The trade in woolen goods in the reign of James I?
85. In what state was the cloth exported?
86. How much did the Dutch gain by dressing it?
87. How did James endeavour to prevent this?
88. How did the Germans and Dutch meet this piece of legislation?
89. The consequence?
90. The recommendation to the commissioners?
91. Why did English commerce increase under the commonwealth?
92. The effect of the restoration?
93. Report of the merchant adventurers?
94. What is said of the Walloons?
95. What evils are illustrated in the history of manufactures so far?
96. Was this folly peculiar to England?
97. When did the system of protection begin?
98. From what did it derive its support?
99. When did England enter into the spirit of maritime discovery?
100. Why was the progress of commerce so slow?

SEC 4.—*Revolutions of Germany, France, and Spain.*

1. From what period did the German empire begin to be consolidated?
2. Under whose government did an important change take place in Switzerland?
3. How was the revolution effected?
4. Where did the Austrians suffer a ruinous defeat?
5. The results of it?
6. The successor of Albert and his character?
7. What led the German princes to form written constitutions?
8. What led to the Golden Bull?
9. What did it fix?
10. How was the crown given?
11. To whom was the right of voting restricted?
12. Who administered the empire during an interregnum?
13. How did the electors show their authority in the next reign?
14. Who succeeded Sigismond?
15. (What breach of faith did Sigismond once commit?)
16. Who succeeded Albert?
17. What is said of Frederic's posterity?
18. The policy of Philip Augustus of France?
19. Who pursued it with the most vigour?
20. On what did Edward found his claims to the crown of France?
21. The success of Edward's invasion?
22. What terrible calamities visited France at this period? Mention *seven.*
23. Conduct of Edward, the Black Prince, in his French dominions?
24. The result of his wars?
25. What saved the English from being expelled from all their continental possessions?
26. Between whom was the battle of Agincourt fought?
27. The terms of the treaty?
28. Who overthrew the power of England?
29. How did she manage it?
30. What alone remained of England's possessions?
31. The consequences of the destruction of the French nobility?
32. What change was made in ecclesiastical affairs?
33. What was the Pragmatic Sanction?
34. The state of Spain at this period?
35. What Castilian monarch defeated the Moors?
36. How was the power of Castile weakened?
37. What made Aragon almost equally important with Castile?
38. What kingdom did the Aragonese monarchs acquire?
39. What fortunate event united the two crowns of Aragon and Castile?

SEC. 5.—*The State of England and the Northern Kingdoms in the Fourteenth and Fifteenth Centuries.*

1. One benefit of the inglorious reign of Edward II.
2. To what was he forced by his barons?
3. What clause was added to the great charter?
4. Who succeeded?
5. What made his name illustrious?
6. What three fundamental principles of government were established in this reign?
7. How did his parliament treat him when in the midst of victory?
8. How when the tide was turned?
9. What great poet flourished in England in this reign?
10. In what language were the laws now written?
11. In what language had they been written up to this time?
12. Edward's successor?
13. By what was the early part of his reign troubled?
14. What dangerous insurrection occurred?
15. What reformer in the church now appeared?
16. The success of his doctrines?
17. What misfortune now befell Richard?
18. Who succeeded him?
19. Who was the rightful heir?
20. Why then was Henry chosen?
21. What discovery did Henry IV. make?
22. Why did the Percies take up arms?
23. Who maintained a stout resistance for several years?
24. Who succeeded Henry IV.?
25. His character both before and after his accession?
26. What alienated the nation from the house of Lancaster?
27. What led Richard, duke of York, to take up arms against Henry VI.?
28. The cognizance of the Yorkites?
29. Of the Lancastrians?
30. The successor of Henry VI.?
31. His character?
32. Who usurped the crown after his death?
33. How did he endeavour to secure it?
34. Who now revived the claims of the Lancastrian family?
35. What extinguished the hostility between the two families?
36. How were the wars excited by disputed succession terminated in Scotland?
37. (Who was the first of the Stuart family that sat on the throne of England?)
38. What was Queen Margaret of Denmark called?

39. What kingdoms did she unite under one government?
40. Why did the Swedes separate from it?
41. In what family has the Danish crown continued?
42. The state of Russia in the fourteenth and fifteenth centuries?
43. How did the Teutonic knights add to their dominions at this time?
44. Could they retain these provinces?
45. What revolution proved fatal to Poland?
46. How was it occasioned?
47. From what family were the Polish kings chosen?
48. When did this family become extinct?

SEC. 6.—*Rise and Progress of the Ottoman Empire.*

1. What is said of the Byzantine empire under the administration of the Palæologi?
2. What would have ruined the state, even had the Mohammedans left it to itself?
3. What delayed the triumph of the Mohammedans?
4. Where did the power of the Ottoman Turks commence?
5. What caused a small wandering tribe of the Turks to settle in Armenia?
6. How long did they stay there?
7. What occurred on their return to their own country?
8. Who returned back into Asia Minor?
9. What motive induced him to do so?
10. What occurred on his return?
11. The reward of his services?
12. The founder of the Turkish empire?
13. When born?
14. Who instructed him how to govern?
15. What family descended from this renegade?
16. His exploits?
17. What military force did Othman's son establish?
18. Exploits of Soliman?
19. Who captured Adrianople?
20. Where did he fall?
21. Exploits of Bayezíd?
22. The limits of the empire of Constantinople?
23. How long besieged?
24. What saved it?
25. Who was Tamerlane?
26 What is said of him?
27. Why was he called Timúr the Tartar?
28. His descendants, called what?
29. Extent of his empire?
30. How did he treat Sebaste?
31 How, Damascus?
32. Fate of Bayezíd?
33. End of Timúr?
34. Fate of his empire after his death?
35. Baber's empire, where established, and its name and duration?
36. Bayezíd's successor?
37. The greater part of his reign, how spent?
38. Exploits of Amurath II.?
39. What two Christian heroes arrested his progress?
40. Who was Hunniades?
41. Who was Scanderbeg?
42. Mohammed II.'s great aim?
43. Army and navy, how large?
44. The last of the Greek emperors?
45. Who assisted him?
46. Duration of the siege of Constantinople?
47. When was it taken?
48. Fate of its inhabitants?
49. How was Europe affected, &c.?
50. Mohammed's treatment of his Christian subjects?

CHAPTER VI.

THE REFORMATION, AND COMMENCEMENT OF THE STATES-SYSTEM IN EUROPE.

SEC. 1.—*Progress of Maritime Discovery.*

1. The scene of the earliest navigation?
2. Its location in the opinion of the ancients?
3. How long did it take the ancients to explore this sea?
4. What discovery was made by them, which assisted their navigation?
5. Who first availed himself of these winds?
6. How much did they shorten voyages?
7. The fruit of this discovery?
8. How was the navigation to the Indies changed under the emperor Claudius?
9. What advantages did the Arabians see could be derived from a port on the Euphrates?
10. What city did they build?
11. In what year?
12. The enterprise of the Arabian merchants?
13. The author of the Christian Topography?
14. The design of the work?
15. Its doctrines?
16. Who discovered the Feroe Islands?
17. Who, Iceland?
18. What proved that Iceland had been known before?
19. The first discoverers of it?
20. What do the Icelandic chronicles relate?
21. When was Greenland discovered?
22. The income of the pope from Greenland?
23. How many years were occupied in a voyage from Greenland to Iceland and Norway, and back again?
24. How long was news sometimes on its way from Greenland to Norway?
25. (How long would it take us now to carry news between the two countries?)

26. Early name of Greenland ?
27. Why so called ?
28. The opinion of some on this point ?
29. What is said of this, &c. ?
30. The effect of the fall of Constantinople on the learning of Europe ?
31. How was this effect produced ?
32. What old belief existed with respect to the globe ?
33. What have Augustine and Lactantius written on the subject, and why ?
34. The first discovery that followed the introduction of the mariner's compass ?
35. Character of Prince Henry, of Portugal ?
36. What seaport town did he found ?
37. What did he do there ?
38. To what point did he direct his chief attention ?
39. How much did he accomplish ?
40. The southernmost cape of Africa known in those days ?
41. Why so named ?
42. What cape was found beyond it ?
43. What is said of it ?
44. What did the sailors say of it ?
45. What river was next discovered ?
46. What islands ?
47. When did Prince Henry die ?
48. What grant did the pope make him ?
49. Who revived the passion for discovery after his death ?
50. What error of the ancients was now discovered ?
51. What common belief did the Portuguese practically refute ?
52. What ambassadors did the king send out ?
53. What is said of the rituals and ceremonies of Buddhism ?
54. What reports were prevalent in the thirteenth century ?
55. The supposed name of this king ?
56. (Of what was "Prester" a contraction ?)
57. What Venetian visited Pekin ?
58. What Englishman followed ?
59. What discovery did Bartholomew Diaz make in 1483 ?
60. What did he name the cape ?
61. What did King John name it ?
62. What letters were received from the monks ?
63. What diverted men's minds at this time from the voyage around Africa ?
64. Who first rounded the Cape of Good Hope ?
65. How many years after its discovery did he do this ?
66. In what harbour did he anchor ?
67. What distinguished Genoese joined the Portuguese ?
68. What led him to think he might reach India by going west ?
69. From whom did he obtain his armament ?
70. When did he set sail ?
71. From what port, and with how many ships ?
72. Why were the West India Islands so named ?
73. How was Columbus received on his return ?
74. How was the world divided by the pope ?
75. What has always been a characteristic of the Spaniards ?
76. To what did they devote themselves in America ?
77. When did they begin to pay some attention to agriculture ?
78. What is said of the commercial and colonial policy of the Spaniards ?
79. The cause of the low state of civilization in Spain and her colonies ?
80. What Englishman made new discoveries in America ?
81. Who first attempted to circumnavigate the world ?
82. What followed this exploit ?

Sec. 2.—*Origin of the Reformation.*

1. What first excited a repugnance to ecclesiastical supremacy ?
2. What increased it ?
3. What compelled men to exercise the right of private opinion ?
4. What spread the disrespect for the Roman See still further ?
5. What convinced the people that there was a power superior to that of the pope's ?
6. The effect of their feeble efforts to correct abuses ?
7. Character of Alexander VI. ?
8. (Story of his death ? Cæsar Borgia, his son's ring ?) See Ranké's history.
9. His successor ? His character ?
10. What was thought of papal pretensions at this time ?
11. Character of Romish ecclesiastics ?
12. Who had exhausted the treasury of the church ?
13. How did Leo X. propose to replenish it ?
14. The origin of indulgences ?
15. Doctrine of indulgences ?
16. When first issued, and to whom ?
17. Subsequently to whom ?
18. Finally to whom ?
19. To whom was the monopoly of indulgences granted ?
20. The chief agent in retailing them ?
21. How did he execute his commission ?
22. How was his conduct viewed ?
23. The author of the reformation ?
24. To what order of monks did he belong ?
25. How had he prepared his mind for the noble career on which he entered ?
26. (How did he get a Bible ?)
27. His first move ?
28. What is said of Luther ?

29. What excuse is made for his violence?
30. His character?
31. Who commenced the reformation *before* Luther?
32. Who prepared the way for both?
33. Leo's bull?
34. How did Luther treat it?
35. How did he treat the volumes of the canon law?
36. How did he engage the princes on his side?
37. The first among his *great* converts?
38. For what purpose were corruptions in doctrine introduced into the Roman church?
39. Illustrate.
40. What French reformer appeared, a follower of Zuinglius?
41. His native place?
42. The year in which he commenced publishing?
43. Title of his followers?
44. In what Swiss city did he establish himself?
45. Of what system was he the author?
46. What is said of the conduct of the ecclesiastical courts?
47. Who was burned for his opinions?
48. What is said of the differences between the Calvinists and Lutherans?
49. Decree of the diet of Spires?
50. What is said of the confession of Augsburgh?
51. What countries adopted the reformed doctrines?
52. What the Romish?
53. What council was assembled to decide differences?
54. How many years did it sit?
55. What Roman Catholic country rejected its decrees?

Sec. 3.—*History of the Negotiations and Wars Respecting Italy.*

1. What is meant by the balance of power?
2. Where did the theory have its origin?
3. Its chief members in Italy?
4 How did Renè, the last monarch of the house of Anjou, act?
5. To whom did Provence revert on the death of Renè?
6. Prudent conduct of Louis XI.?
7. Folly of his son Charles VIII.?
8. What induced him to act thus?
9. His success at first?
10. What caused his hasty retreat?
11 The parties to the league?
12. The fate of his men left behind in Italy?
13. How did Louis XII. prepare for a subsequent invasion of Italy?
14. His success?
15. Ferdinand's intention?
16 The name of the great captain?
17. Who now formed a design against Venice?
18. Who aided him?
19. What averted the danger?
20. What left it defenceless?
21. How did Julius treat the Venetians?
22. How did Ferdinand?
23. What saved them?
24. How did the Venetians appease the pope and Ferdinand?
25. What design had the pope formed?
26. What confederacy was formed against France out of the fragments of the league of Cambray?
27. What part was assigned to Henry VIII.?
28. One master-stroke of the pope's policy.
29. What is said of their infantry?
30. Louis' conduct?
31. What relieved Louis?
32. How did the war terminate?

Sec. 4.—*The History of Burgundy under the Princes of the House of Valois.*

1. What is said of Burgundy?
2. Why is its history an episode?
3. To whom did King John give it?
4. Whom did he marry?
5. How did he bring about a peace between the nobles and merchants of Flanders?
6. Message of the ambassadors of Hungary?
7. Sultan Bayezíd's boast?
8. What crusade was proclaimed?
9. Its commander?
10. How did Sigismund relish his allies?
11. The count of Nevers' imprudence?
12. Proof of his carelessness?
13. How did the knights act in the first alarm?
14. Advice of the Hungarians?
15. Why was it not taken?
16. How had Bayezíd arranged his army?
17. With what object?
18. The success of his plan?
19. How did Sigismund act?
20. What is said of the valour of the French knights on the day of the battle?
21. The object of Bayezíd in taking prisoners?
22. Who was set at liberty, and why?
23. The duty assigned him?
24. Fate of the rest?
25. How was the money raised to pay the ransom?
26. What increased the difficulty?
27. How was it obviated?
28. Who were the Frisons?
29. Who now attacked them?
30. The success of the enterprise?
31. What is said of Philip's administration of the government of France?
32. His great fault?
33. Why was his death regretted?

SEC. 5.—*The History of Burgundy (continued).*

1. Who succeeded Philip?
2. His first step?
3. By whom opposed?
4. John's treachery?
5. How was a party arrayed against him?
6. His fate?
7. Why regretted by his Flemish subjects?
8. His successor?
9. His first step?
10. What changed the aspect of affairs?
11. Who delivered France?
12. What order of knighthood did Philip the Good institute?
13. What is said of the brilliancy of his court?
14. Why did Philip encourage this taste for display among his subjects?
15. How were the Swiss now engaged?
16. What league was now formed against them?
17. Why?
18. How was an army raised?
19. Result of the first battle?
20. How was the war terminated?
21. How was the duke of Burgundy engaged at this time?
22. The result?
23. Why did the dauphin flee from his father's court?
24. With whom did he take refuge?
25. His gratitude?
26. How did Charolais endeavour to avenge himself?
27. What is said of Philip the Good's reign?
28. Why was he the more lamented?

SEC. 6.—*The History of Burgundy (concluded).*

1. What disturbance took place immediately on the installation of Charles the Bold?
2. What secret vow did he make?
3. What increased his indignation?
4. How did the citizens of Liege act?
5. How did Charles avenge himself on the king of France?
6. What did Louis XI. do thereupon?
7. What advantage did Louis have over Charles in this kind of warfare?
8. What memorable piece of folly did Louis commit?
9. How did Charles profit by it?
10. The most mortifying condition of his liberation?
11. How was the city of Liege treated?
12. What saved it from utter ruin?
13. How did Louis avenge the indignities put on him?
14. How did Charles alienate from him the chivalry of Burgundy?
15. How did he change the Swiss from being his friends into foes?
16. Charles' design against them?
17. Size and condition of his army?
18. His baseness to the governor, &c. of Granson?
19. The vengeance of the Swiss?
20. Their war-cry and the meaning of it?
21. What was now heard in the distance?
22. What were they?
23. Fate of Charles and his army?
24. The booty taken?
25. Distribution of the three diamonds?
26. Effect of the defeat on Charles?
27. His measures for renewing the war?
28. How were the Swiss employed?
29. Account of the siege of Morat?
30. Folly of Charles?
31. Fate of his army?
32. Describe the battle?
33. What proverb took its origin in this battle?
34. What further disasters befel Charles?
35. Who had sold him to his enemies?
36. How did he treat him in time of battle?
37. The end of Charles?
38. His successor?
39. The designs of Louis XI.
40. Conduct of the Flemings?
41. Whom did Mary marry?
42. Who conquered Burgundy?
43. To what hostilities did this lead?

SEC. 7.—*The Age of Charles V.*

1. What caused the political idea of the balance of power to spread in Europe?
2. What had Maximilian added to his dominions by marriage?
3. Whom did his son marry?
4. Their sons?
5. Inheritance of Charles?
6. What other good fortune befell him?
7. His power?
8. To whom did he resign his German dominions?
9. When did Ferdinand's dynasty end?
10. When that of Charles V.?
11. Whom did Ferdinand marry?
12. Whom Charles V.?
13. What two monarchs determined to resist the house of Austria?
14. What is said of Henry VIII.?
15. His prime minister?
16. Character of Francis I.?
17. His conduct soon after his accession to the throne?
18. What aggravated the mutual jealousies of Charles and Francis?
19. Their power, how balanced?
20. Their allies?
21. Where did the war begin?
22. What led to the loss of Milan?
23. What other calamities befel Francis?
24. What other evil did the queen-mother do him?

25. Plan of Charles to invade France?
26. How and by whom defeated?
27. Francis' plan and its success?
28. What misfortune befell him?
29. What led to his capture?
30. The battle of Pavia—describe.
31. What led to the defeat of Francis?
32. Describe his capture.
33. Describe his surrender of his sword.
34. How was he treated?
35. Francis' expectations?
36. How did Charles receive the news?
37. His first demand?
38. How did Francis receive these proposals?
39. What step did he then take?
40. How was he treated in Spain?
41. The effect of this triumph?
42. Conduct of Henry VIII.?
43. Effect of imprisonment on Francis?
44. The chief obstacle to a treaty between him and Charles?
45 What resolution did he take?
46. Its effect on Charles?
47. Francis' insincerity?
48. How did Charles manifest his suspicion of Francis' insincerity?
49. Describe his departure.
50. How was the river crossed?
51. Francis' actions on reaching France?
52. How long had he been a prisoner?
53. First violation of the treaty?
54. How did Francis excuse himself?
55. Who absolved him of his oath?
56. What dreadful insurrection afflicted Germany at this time?
57. The leader of it?
58. Had the reformation any thing to do with it?
59. How had Luther diminished his influence?
60. What league did Francis organize against Charles?
61. Why called "Holy?"
62. Who joined it?
63. How was Rome treated by Charles?
64. How did Charles receive the news?
65. What prayers were offered in all the Spanish churches?
66. Francis' success?
67. His reverses, and the cause of them?
68 Who was Andrew Doria?
69. The treaty of Cambray, by whom negotiated?
70. League of Smalkald, by whom made?
71. Cause of Charles' concessions?
72. How had Francis secured the friendship of the pope?
73. What led Henry VIII. to break off from the league?
74. What acts were passed in England?
75. What now employed men's minds for a season?
76. What crowned the emperor with glory?
77. Challenge of Charles?
78. What other folly was committed?
79. What brought about a truce?
80. What now filled Charles with anxiety?
81. What added to it?
82. What foolish expedition did he now undertake?
83. The consequence of his failure?
84. Francis' designs?
85. What gave him a pretext to take up arms?
86. Francis' plan of operations?
87. What opened the way for an alliance between Charles and Henry?
88. What marriage excited jealousy and alarm in England?
89. The fruit of this marriage?
90. How were Henry's plans changed by the birth of Mary?
91. What alliances were now formed?
92. What aid did the sultan afford Francis?
93. Who now invaded France?
94. Charles' projects?
95. What favoured them?
96. Who first seized on church property?
97. What compelled the Protestants to renew the league of Smalkald?
98. Who deserted the league?
99. Why did he act so basely?
100. Conduct of the pope?
101. What was the "Interim," and why so called?
102. What city refused it?
103. Maurice's designs?
104. His actions?
105. The result of them?
106. What offended the pope?
107. His conduct?
108. What surprising event astonished Europe?
109. What is said of him and his career?
110. What was calculated to make him regretted?
111. In whose reign was the protestant religion established in England?
112. Who succeeded Edward VI.?
113. Whom did she marry?
114. (Their relationship?)
115. Her successor?
116. Of what folly were the Lutherans guilty?
117. To whom did Charles give his several dominions?
118. Whither did he retire?
119. How long afterwards did he die?
120. What society was now established for the purpose of sustaining the cause of popery?
121 What made it formidable?
122. When suppressed, and why?
123. (When re-established?)
124. The condition of Venice at this time?
125. What had exhausted their resources?

126. How were they injured by the discovery of the new route to India?
127. What endeavours did they make to avert the danger?
128. Success of the Portuguese?
129. What city became the staple for the commodities of the East?
130. What befell the Venetians?
131. What proved no less fatal to the inferior branches of their commerce?
132. When did Venice cease to be one of the principal powers of Europe?
133. What still caused it to be considered and respected?
134. Who became the head of Florence?
135. Who established his supreme authority over it, and under what title?
136. The extent of his dominions?

SEC. 8.—*The Age of Elizabeth.*

1. The crisis of the reformation in England?
2. How did Elizabeth strengthen herself?
3. Who assumed the arms and title of England?
4. What prevented any hostile attempt against England?
5. The champion of the Protestants in Europe?
6. The champion of the Roman Catholics?
7. Of what importance to England was the ancient rivalry between France and Spain?
8 Relationship of Mary, queen of Scots to Elizabeth?
9 Mary's husband who?
10 What reasons had she to hope for success in establishing herself on the throne of England?
11 What induced Philip of Spain to acknowledge Elizabeth's title?
12 The great object of the alliance between Spain and France?
13. To what did it lead, and how did it end?
14. What compelled Mary to return to Scotland?
15. Was she willing to go?
16. What had she to endure at home?
17. What prevented an immediate outbreak?
18. What led to the first open breach between her and her subjects?
19. What aroused her husband's jealousy?
20. His conduct towards her?
21. What reconciled them?
22 How was the hollowness of this reconciliation proved?
23 How was Darnley murdered?
24 What confirmed the suspicions that his wife was the author of the deed?
25. The result?
26. What constraint was put on Mary?
27. Whither did she escape?
28. What befell her there?
29. What made it necessary for Elizabeth to keep her in close confinement?
30. What is said of Francis II. of France?
31. The leading object of the Guises?
32. Who was trying to do the same thing in the Netherlands?
33. The object of Philip's ambition?
34. How did he aim to attain it?
35. His fatal error?
36. What proud title did it give the reformed?
37. What precipitated the civil war in France?
38. What conspiracy was formed?
39. What confirmed opposition to the Guises?
40. What showed the power of the Huguenots?
41. What synod was talked of?
42. How was it prevented?
43. What sentence was passed on the prince of Condé?
44. What saved him?
45. Of what insincerity was she guilty?
46. Her fatal error, and its effect?
47. Policy of the duke of Guise?
48. His aims and plans?
49. What were the bishops doing at Trent?
50. Whom alone did it terrify?
51. How did Maximilian act toward the pope?
52. What plans were concocting at the council of Trent?
53. What letter was read from Mary?
54. What did the cardinal declare of her intentions?
55. How were the Italians engaged?
56. Philip's opinion of Protestants?
57. How long had this council sat?
58. Its results?
59. The last acts of the council?
60. What great change in the papacy did this council produce?
61. What remark is made of European sovereigns favourable to despotism?
62. What law was established in relation to priests?
63. The effect of this law on the papacy?
64. What were made articles of faith?
65. How did the pope excite disturbances in Europe?
66. On what points was the pope inflexible, and why?
67. What general suspicion was diffused through Europe soon after the rising of the council?
68. Was it groundless?
69. Design of Pius IV.?
70. What interview did he urge?
71. The designs contemplated?
72. How were the days and nights spent?
73. In what did they agree, and in what did they differ?
74. Alva's plans?
75. Why did the queen oppose them?

76 On what did she rely to retain her power?
77 Why did she hate the Huguenots?
78. Of what was she more afraid than of the progress of heretical opinions?
79. What interfered with the spread of protestantism in France?
80. How did Philip begin to execute his part of the plan?
81. His lord lieutenant, who?
82. The consequence?
83. Effects of this on England?
84. Alva's conduct?
85. Was it liked at Rome?
86. Who undertook to protect the Flemings?
87. Where, and by whom, were they defeated?
88. Design of Pius V. against the Turks?
89. Why did Philip refuse to come into the scheme?
90. Conduct of this pontiff?
91. His successor?
92. What conspiracy was detected in France in A. D. 1560?
93. What ensued?
94. When was it terminated?
95. What marriage was proposed?
96. How was the proposal received?
97. Who were among the invited guests?
98. What is said of the populace of Paris at this period?
99. What feelings did the presence of Coligni inspire in them?
100. Who fostered it?
101. What alone restrained them?
102. Who was the nominal king of France?
103. Who possessed the authority?
104. What led to Coligni's assassination?
105. How was the author discovered?
106. Of what imprudence were the protestants guilty?
107. Catherine's scheme to defeat their vengeance?
108. How numerous were the conspirators?
109. From whom was the secret kept?
110 Catherine's story to the king?
111. Its effect on him?
112. His conduct?
113. When did the work begin?
114. How were most of the Huguenots killed?
115. Charles' conduct?
116. How long did the massacre last?
117. On whom was it attempted to throw the blame?
118. How many Huguenots survived?
119. The effect of it?
120. How was the news received at Rome and at Madrid?
121. What was thought of the deed in the north of Europe?
122. The head of the revolters in the Netherlands?
123. What were they styled?
124. What city captured gave them a naval station?
125. The effect of the massacre of St. Bartholomew on them?
126. Who succeeded Alva?
127. What decisive battle did he gain?
128. What distinguished persons fell in this battle?
129. What prevented its proving fatal to the Netherlanders?
130. What excited the indignation of both Catholics and Protestants?
131. What confederacy was formed?
132. What caused it to fall through?
133. How only could freedom be secured?
134. Who organized the confederacy of Utrecht?
135. Of what commonwealth was it the basis?
136. What had well nigh ruined the projects of the prince of Orange?
137. What defection from the confederacy took place, and why?
138. How did the Hollanders act?
139. Whom did they choose as their sovereign?
140. Why did they not elect the prince of Orange?
141. Who was elected after the duke of Anjou deserted them?
142. What important city did they lose?
143. Did they despair?
144. To whom did they offer the sovereignty?
145. How did she assist them?
146. What gave them a decided advantage by sea and land?
147. When was their independence secured and recognised?
148. Who succeeded Charles IX.?
149. His course?
150. His conduct?
151. The head of the Catholic party?
152. Advantages of the duke of Guise?
153. What encouraged him to raise the cry of religion?
154. Object of the Holy league?
155. By whom drawn up?
156. By whom signed?
157. Its head?
158. Its protectors?
159. The consequence of it?
160. Whose fate did it precipitate?
161. What led to her death?
162. Relate the circumstances?
163. What assassinations took place in France?
164. The consequence of this crime?
165. Philip's great undertaking?
166. Size of his army, and its general?
167. Name of the armament?
168. How did Elizabeth prepare to meet it?
169. Her only ally?
170. When did the armada sail?

171 When did it reach the English channel?
172 What disappointment awaited the admiral there?
173. How was his fleet assailed?
174. The result?
175. How assailed in the harbour?
176. How did he attempt to return home?
177. What befell him?
178. How many ships reach home in safety?
179. How was this glorious success regarded?
180. Its effect?
181. Its effect on the Spanish state and people?
182. End of Henry III. of France?
183. What house became extinct by his death?
184. What house succeeded?
185. From whom descended?
186. Its representative?
187. His character?
188. What did he find it necessary to do in order to secure his crown?
189. How did he atone to the Huguenots for this desertion?
190. Who aided him?
191. What clouded the close of Elizabeth's reign?
192. What war did she still maintain?
193. What gave Philip command of the India trade?
194. What ruined his commerce?
195. When did the English first reach India?
196. When was the East India Company founded?
197. Of what did the Hanseatic league complain?
198. By what measures did they destroy their own power?
199. The state of England during Elizabeth's reign?
200. What proves that this was owing to her energy and wisdom?

Sec. 9.—*The Age of Gustavus Adolphus.*

1. The object of Rudolph's anxiety?
2. What prevented?
3. What new league was formed, and why?
4. What to oppose it?
5. What came near involving Europe in a general war?
6. The prime minister of Henry IV.?
7. His administration?
8. Henry's grand scheme?
9. His more immediate object?
10. What gave him a pretext for interfering in the affairs of Germany?
11. What alliances did he form?
12. What put an end to all his schemes?
13. What contributed to avert a general war?
14. Fate of Rudolph?
15. His end?
16. Matthias' conduct towards the Protestants?
17. Ferdinand's treatment of his protestant subjects?
18. Matthias' successor?
19. The effect of the union of Spain and Portugal?
20. Its popularity in Portugal?
21. The influence of Philip's reign on the peninsula?
22. Fatal error of Philip III.?
23. Power of Spain at his death?
24. Who completed its ruin?
25. What revolutions took place?
26. The ruling house of Portugal?
27. Frederick the elector-palatine's misfortune?
28. Conduct of James I., his father-in-law?
29. What led to it?
30. His reputation in Europe?
31. What had occurred to change his neutral policy?
32. What inflamed the nation against the papists?
33. The object of this plot?
34. (How was it discovered?)
35. Of what was James now convinced?
36. The head of the new protestant union?
37. The imperial generals and their success?
38. On what terms did the king of Denmark purchase peace?
39. Wallenstein elevation?
40. What kept England aloof from this contest?
41. The principal causes of this?
42. The head of the French administration?
43. The effect of his administration?
44. His first operations?
45. What strong city of the Huguenots did he capture?
46. What war ensued?
47. Effect of the treaty of Chierasio?
48. What war was renewed in Germany?
49. Edict of the Emperor Ferdinand?
50. To whom was the execution of the decree committed?
51. His conduct?
52. The effect of the clamour against him?
53. Who declared war against the emperor?
54. When did he land in Germany?
55. What alliances did he form?
56. Who afterwards joined them?
57. What prevented Gustavus' decisive success?
58. Fate of Magdeburg?
59. What remained of it?
60. The effect of this cruelty?
61. Conduct of the elector of Saxony?
62. Battle of Leipsic?
63. Where was Count Tilly killed?
64. To whom did the emperor again have recourse?
65. Battle of Nuremburg?
66. Battle of Lutzen and its results?
67. Who succeeded Gustavus?

68. To whom was the management of the German war entrusted?
69. His character?
70. His success?
71. What added to the confidence of the evangelical union?
72. How was Wallenstein treated?
73. Who succeeded him?
74. Battle of Nordlingen?
75. How did the emperor improve it?
76. On whom now was the whole weight of the war thrown?

SEC. 10.—*Administration of the Cardinals Richelieu and Mazarine.*

1. Richelieu's popularity?
2. What prevented him from cordially co-operating with Gustavus?
3 How was he induced to take an active part in the war?
4. His energy?
5. Success of the confederates?
6. Death of Saxe Weimar?
7. Battle of Leipsic, between whom?
8. What, for a time, inclined the Swedes to peace?
9. What gave them new courage?
10. The result of the war?
11. Peace of Westphalia, what of it?
12. What was now going on in England?
13. What had caused discontent there?
14. What of the petition of right?
15. Charles I.'s folly?
16. What aggravated political animosities?
17. The head of the church in England?
18. Object of the high commission court?
19. Opinions of many in England concerning the reformation there?
20. Their wishes?
21. What were these reformers called?
22. What more serious cause of complaint did they have?
23. What new sect now started up?
24. What gave them power and influence?
25. What return did they make for Charles' favours to them?
26. How did parliament regard these doctrines, and why?
27. Charles' two ministers?
28. Their character?
29. Their measures?
30. What produced an outbreak in Scotland?
31. The design of the solemn league and covenant?
32. Richelieu's measures in Scotland?
33. Effect of the treaty at Berwick?
34. What did Charles do in order to obtain a grant to carry on the war against Scotland?
35. The doings of Parliament?
36. Charles' conduct thereupon?
37. Measures of the Scots?
38. What did Charles then do?
39. How did Parliament manifest its disposition?
40. Their first step?
41. How were the Scots described?
42. Fate of Strafford?
43. The next bill passed by the commons?
44. Conduct of the bishops?
45. The consequence of this step?
46. Charles' next step?
47. What change, fatal to his interests, was now produced, and how?
48. The Norman settlers in Ireland, their conduct?
49. What prevented the Tudor monarchs from breaking the power of the aristocracy?
50. How did Elizabeth treat the nobles?
51. How did James I. treat the province of Ulster?
52. What rendered property insecure?
53. Strafford's conduct?
54. What means did he use to expel the Irish from their property?
55. Why did the English nation countenance this injustice?
56. Who were the new settlers?
57. How were the papists treated?
58. How did Charles treat them?
59. Strafford's plan in Ireland?
60. What induced the Irish to rebel?
61. What hastened the rebellion?
62. How were the Irish regarded in England?
63. How their efforts to right themselves?
64. What report was studiously circulated?
65. How did he refute this suspicion?
66. What resolution did parliament pass?
67. The history of the civil war?
68. What foolish attempt did Charles now make?
69. The result?
70. Why was not a treaty formed between Charles and his parliament?
71. When did the civil war commence?
72. What alliance did parliament make?
73. The parliamentary leader?
74. What city did he besiege?
75. The royalist leader?
76. (His relationship to Charles?)
77. Where was the great battle fought?
78. Whose skill secured the victory?
79. What prevented the immediate submission of Charles?
80. What caused dissensions in the ranks of his adversaries?
81. How did the Presbyterians act?
82. Where did they have the majority?
83. Where the Independents?
84. The Self-denying ordinance?
85. Who gained the battle of Naseby?
86. Its results?
87. Charles' next step?
88. How was he treated by them?

89. Object of the anxiety of the Presbyterians and Independents?
90. Who succeeded?
91. What alarmed them?
92. Who stimulated the soldiers to disobey the parliament?
93 What bold measure did he take?
94 Cromwell's measures and the result?
95. Charles' injudicious course?
96. How did Cromwell become master of his fate?
97. Who then took up arms in his favour, and with what success?
98. How did the parliament act, and why?
99. Charles' folly?
100. How was the parliament treated?
101. What proposals were then made?
102. What resolution was adopted?
103. Charles' spirit?
104. His sentence?
105. When and where executed?
106. What followed his death?
107. His government?

SEC. 11.—*Formation of the States-System in the Northern Kingdoms of Europe.*

1. Who kept Sweden in continual agitation?
2. Whom did they choose as administrators of the kingdom?
3. Who undertook to destroy Swedish independence?
4. His base and treacherous conduct?
5. Of what was this massacre the signal?
6. Who headed it?
7. The reward of his heroism?
8. The fate of Christian II.?
9. For how long a time did the Danish kings attempt to recover Sweden?
10. The state of Denmark at this time?
11. In whose reign was the Reformation established in Denmark?
12. Who completed it?
13. What became of the domains of the bishops?
14. Fate of Norway about this time?
15. By what was Christian IV. distinguished among the sovereigns of northern Europe?
16. What commercial establishment was founded in his reign?
17. What caused the failure of his wars against Austria and Sweden?
18. Prosperity of Sweden?
19. To whom was it owing?
20. What did Vasa substitute in the place of the aristocratic senate?
21. What religion did he introduce?
22. What did he establish?
23. Who raised Sweden to the summit of greatness?
24. To what distinction was he raised?
25. In what battle did he fall?
26. What advantages did Sweden gain by the peace of Bromsebro?
27 What elector of Brandenburg was the true founder of the greatness of his house?
28. The first king of Prussia?
29. Who achieved the independence of Russia?
30. To whom was it in subjection?
31. By what khan was Iwan III. attacked?
32. His conduct?
33. His success?
34. Attempts of Iwan IV.?
35. What country did he discover and annex to his dominions?
36. Who founded the city of Tobolsk?
37. Who succeeded Fédor?
38. How did he obtain peace from Sweden and Poland?
39. During whose reigns was Poland a flourishing country?
40. What prevented the Reformation from taking deep root in Poland?
41. How was the sovereign chosen in Poland?
42. By what were these elections marked?
43. The condition of Poland under its constitution?
44. Which of its monarchs distinguished himself by foreign conquests?

SEC. 12.—*Progress of the Turkish Power in Europe.*

1. The policy of the successors of Mohammed II.?
2. Fate of Bayezíd II.?
3. How was Selim obliged to maintain his throne?
4. What country did he conquer?
5. What people did he next subdue?
6. What country did he then invade and conquer?
7. Give an account of the invasion.
8. The fate of Túmán, the sultan?
9. The object of Soleyman's ambition?
10. What kingdom did he invade?
11. What signal victory did he gain?
12. How did he treat the country?
13. What still greater triumph did he gain during this war?
14. What is said of the siege?
15. When was it taken?
16. What country did Soleyman then invade, and with what success?
17. Who attempted to form a confederation against the Turks?
18. What prevented?
19. What opportunity did Charles V. avail himself of to take Tunis?
20. How did Soleyman determine to avenge himself?
21. What turned his wrath on Venice?
22. What conquests did he make in the East in the meantime?

23 Who commanded the allied navies against him?
24. What became of the knights of St. John after their expulsion from Rhodes?
25. Soleyman's attempt against them?
26. His success?
27. What revenge did he try to take?
28. When and where did he die?
29. What island did his successor take from the Venetians?
30. The fate of the Turkish fleet?
31. The results of the diet of Presburg?

CHAPTER VII.

THE AUGUSTAN AGES OF ENGLAND AND FRANCE.

SEC. 1.—*State of the Continental Kingdoms after the peace of Westphalia.*

1. The prime mover in the civil broils of France at this time?
2. His object?
3. What were the parliaments of France?
4. Its conduct on this occasion?
5. The conduct of the queen-regent?
6. The result of it?
7. To what condition was the queen soon reduced?
8. To what did such intrigues lead?
9. Mazarine's movements?
10. His success?
11. Movements of Condé?
12. Proclamation of the parliament of Paris?
13. How was the danger, with which the monarchy was now threatened, averted?
14. Louis' conduct?
15. What were the Spaniards doing at this time?
16. What French general excelled Condé in military skill?
17. How did Mazarine engage England to take a share in the contest?
18. Their movements?
19. To whom was Dunkirk given?
20. Mazarine's favourite policy?
21. Who was chosen Emperor of Germany, and why?
22. His first measure?
23. Character of Christina?
24. Whom did her senate wish her to marry?
25. Why did she refuse?
26. How did she act?
27. Her conduct during the remainder of her life?
28. Against whom did Charles X. declare war?
29. His success?
30. What excited indignation against the Swedes?
31. What powers united against them?
32. What city did he besiege?
33. What disposed him to peace?
34. What made the Swedes desirous of peace?

SEC. 2.—*History of England under the Commonwealth.*

1. The consequence of the execution of Charles I.?
2. The feelings of the nation thereupon?
3. What restrained them from evincing their dissatisfaction?
4. In whom was vested the supreme authority?
5. What soon claimed the attention of the new government?
6. How was Ireland regarded in England?
7. Who was appointed lord-lieutenant of Ireland?
8. Why did he covet the appointment?
9. What circumstances rendered the conquest of Ireland easy?
10. Whom had Charles I. appointed lord-lieutenant?
11. His doings?
12. The grounds of the dissatisfaction of the different parties with the treaty he concluded?
13. Who induced them to reject it?
14. What step, fatal to the royal authority, did he take?
15. How was the nuncio treated, and why?
16. Who then resumed the authority?
17. His first step?
18. Cromwell's first success?
19. His cruelty?
20. Its effect?
21. What soon distressed him?
22. How was he relieved?
23. By what means did he conquer the country?
24. How many catholics went into voluntary exile?
25. Movements of Charles II.?
26. To what terms did he submit?
27. The fate of Montrose, and who was he?
28. Who was sent for to oppose him?
29. What general headed his troops?
30. What saved Cromwell?
31. The results of the battle?
32. Why was not this defeat disagreeable to Charles?
33. His resolute conduct?
34. Its success?
35. Where defeated?
36. What became of the prisoners?
37. Charles' movements?
38. Fate of the presbyterian clergy?
39. In what foreign war was England now engaged?
40. How had their ambassador been treated at the Hague?
41. The terms of the celebrated navigation act?
42. How did it affect the Dutch?
43. How did the war commence?
44. The number on each side?

45. The result of the battle, and of the war?
46. Who was now the ruler of England?
47. What had brought the long parliament into disrepute?
48. How did Cromwell treat it?
49. How was his conduct viewed by the people?
50. His next step, and the reason of it?
51. The title of this parliament?
52. Cromwell's treatment of it?
53. The nature of the new constitution?
54. Spirit of the new parliament?
55. Cromwell's treatment of it?
56. How did he at length secure a pliant parliament?
57. How did they gratify Cromwell's ambition?
58. What restrained him from assuming the title?
59. How did he endeavour to divert the attention of the nation from domestic affairs?
60. What decided him to attack Spain instead of France?
61. His demands of the Spanish ambassador, and why made?
62. The ambassador's reply?
63. The effect of the demand on the English nation?
64. Admiral Blake's first step?
65. His next step?
66. His treatment of Tunis?
67. Success of Penn and Venables?
68. Their treatment on their return?
69. Blake's further success?
70. Blake's political principles?
71. Feelings of the nation respecting Cromwell's usurpation?
72. Cromwell's treatment of parliament?
73. What experiment did he determine to hazard?
74. By whom was he opposed?
75. What sobered him for life?
76. His fears, how manifested?
77. When did he die?
78. How did the populace evince their feelings?
79. Evelyn's report of the funeral?
80. His successor?
81. His difficulties?
82. What parliament was now re-assembled?
83. How was it fettered?
84. Richard's conduct?
85. The state of the nation at this time?
86. Who resolved to act a decided part?
87. What letter did Cromwell once write to him?
88. What declaration did he make that caused the re-assembling of the long parliament?
89. What was it called?
90. Its doings?
91. When did Monk commence his march to London, and with what force?
92. How was he received?
93. How did he first show his intentions?
94. His subsequent conduct?
95. When did the long parliament conclude its sittings?
96. When did a new house of commons meet?
97. Who attempted to raise an army against it?
98. What became of him?
99. The question to be decided, and how was it decided?
100. When did Charles II. enter London?
101. How was he received?
102. His age?

SEC. 3.—*History of England, from the Restoration to the Revolution; and Rise of the Power of Louis XIV.*

1. What is said of Charles?
2. His first measures?
3. By what was the harmony of the nation disturbed?
4. What act was passed?
5. How many of the clergy rejected these conditions?
6. How were they treated?
7. By what three measures did Charles render himself very unpopular?
8. What province did Charles take from the Dutch in America?
9. The head of the Dutch at that time?
10. Why did he seek the alliance of France?
11. What naval victory was gained by the English?
12. What dreadful calamity now afflicted London?
13. How many died in one year?
14. De Witt's efforts?
15. What second calamity afflicted London?
16. Describe it.
17. The effect of the treatment of the nonconformists?
18. The state of Ireland at this time?
19. What unwise act was passed relating to it?
20. De Witt's movements?
21. Why did the treaty of peace increase the discontent of the people?
22. What is said of Louis XIV.?
23. What country did he claim, and on what ground?
24. His success?
25. Why were the Dutch alarmed?
26. From what unexpected quarter did they receive assistance?
27. The effect of this alliance?
28. What other mortification did he have to endure?
29. How did Louis win over Charles?
30. The terms of the agreement?

31. By what atrocious acts was the war commenced?
32. Louis' career?
33. On whom did the Dutch vent their rage, and how?
34. Who was chosen stadtholder?
35. Noble resolution of the Dutch?
36. Noble reply of the stadtholder to those that tried to corrupt him?
37. The effects of this stubborn spirit?
38. How did Charles now act, and why?
39. Effect of Turenne's cruelty in the Palatinate?
40 Why did Louis bribe Charles?
41. The efforts of parliament, and the cause of their failure?
42. Louis' success?
43 How did Charles attempt to conciliate the nation?
44. What spread a gloom over England?
45. Tale of Titus Oates?
46. Was there really a plot formed to restore the Romish religion?
47. What completed the delusion?
48. What law was passed by the parliament?
49. How did the Covenanters act?
50. How were they punished?
51. State of Ireland at this time?
52. What was the title of the supporters of the court?
53. What was the title of the leaders of the opposition?
54. What bill passed the house of commons?
55. How did Charles treat the parliament?
56. And the new one also?
57. How did he obtain the support of the clergy?
58. How did he treat London?
59. Who were executed?
60. The death of Charles?
61. How was Louis XIV. acting at this time?
62. Conduct of the Emperor Leopold?
63. The head of the insurgents?
64. Who aided Leopold against the Turks?
65. The progress of the Turks?
66. How was Vienna saved?
67. Leopold's conduct to his deliverers?
68. Why did Louis raise the siege of Luxemburg at this time?
69. His successes?
70. How did he weaken his kingdom
71. What edict did he first issue?
72. The effect of this?
73. The next step?
74 The crowning act of cruelty?
75. How many abandoned their country?
76. The consequences of this treatment of them?
77. What countries united against France?
78. Who conspired against James II.?
79. The fate of Argyle?
80. The fate of Monmouth?
81. Manner of his death?
82. The effect of Judge Jeffries' cruelty?
83. James' conduct with respect to the Catholics?
84. His folly?
85. His first step?
86. What kept the nation quiet?
87. His daughters, and to whom married?
88. What edict did James now issue?
89. His design in so doing?
90. How was it received by the dissenters themselves?
91. Its folly?
92. Conduct of the bishops?
93. Their treatment?
94. What event now took place?
95. What report was circulated?
96. How was he treated by his daughter?
97. What trial now took place?
98. The question at issue?
99. The verdict?
100. How received?
101. James' remark?
102. State of things throughout England on the receipt of the news?
103. What project was now formed?
104. The object of the whig party?
105. How had the lower orders been alienated from the Presbyterians?
106. Another reason for this?
107. How did they excuse themselves for so doing?
108. How were matters in Scotland?
109. How did James view Scotland?
110. What far more powerful party existed?
111. Their rallying cry?
112. In what awkward position did the tories find themselves on James' accession?
113. The crisis of their loyalty?
114. How was it regarded?
115. Why were the first movements of the tories slow and unsteady?
116. The most they looked for?
117. The state of Europe at this time?
118. Why was the reign of James odious to the princes of Germany?
119. Why to the pope, also?
120. Why, particularly so, to the Dutch?
121. Why did William make so vigorous efforts to take advantage of the crisis in England?
122. What now excited universal alarm and indignation in Europe?
123. The consequence?
124. What is said of William's landing?
125. James' conduct?
126. The conduct of William?
127. The motive that led James to leave his kingdom?
128. The cause of his ruin?
129. What three proposals were made to the convention?

130. To whom was the first proposal most agreeable?
131 Why was it not adopted?
132. What proverb was current?
133. The difficulties of the second proposal?
134. Were William and Mary heartily elected?
135. What completed the ruin of James' cause?
136. The effect of Louis' efforts in his behalf?
137. Who, in after times, committed the same folly?

Sec. 4.—*General History of Europe, from the League of Augsburg to the Formation of the Grand Alliance.*

1. Demand of the Scottish convention?
2. Hopes of the dissenters?
3. State of Ireland?
4. Conduct of the Irish Protestants?
5. Movements and acts of James?
6. His party in Scotland?
7. Siege of Londonderry?
8. Battle of Boyne, describe.
9. Conduct of the Irish after the desertion of their monarch?
10. Final success of William?
11. Terms of the treaty?
12. How many Irish joined James?
13. What act brought great odium on William's government?
14. Relate the circumstances.
15. What hopes did Louis found on it?
16. His attempt, and its fate?
17. James' remark on witnessing the burning of the French ships?
18. What was the title of the partizans of the Stuarts?
19. Their plan?
20. The effect of the attempt?
21. How was the act of succession changed?
22. Who was Sophia?
23. Character of the Emperor Leopold?
24. His conduct to the Hungarians?
25. Horrible conduct of Louis XIV.?
26. Did it benefit his cause?
27. His subsequent success?
28. What kept the emperor quiet?
29. The probable consequence, had he long remained so?
30. The success of Louis in Flanders?
31. His success at sea?
32 The state of things in France?
33. What effect did a knowledge of these things have on the allies?
34. With what success?
35 What led to a peace?
36. What is said of it?
37. Conduct of the emperor?
38. The name of his distinguished general?
39. Describe the great battle of Zenta.
40 The terms of the peace of Carlowitz.
41. The three candidates for the throne of Spain?
42. Conduct of William and Louis, kings of England and France?
43. Conduct of the king of Spain in consequence?
44. How were the affections of the Scotch alienated from William?
45. Who was proclaimed king of Spain?
46. Conduct of Louis?
47. How was it received?
48. Conduct of the emperor?
49. What alliance was formed?
50. Its avowed objects?
51. Great imprudence of Louis?
52. Death of William, how occasioned?
53. Effect of it on the allies?
54. How were their fears quieted?

Sec. 5.—*The War of the Spanish Succession.*

1. How was Anne's accession received?
2. Why was William disliked?
3. Why did both whigs and tories dislike him?
4. What suspicion was circulated of him?
5. What interest had England in the war against Louis?
6. Why did she engage in it?
7. What discovery did they subsequently make?
8. The commander-in-chief of the English army?
9. Where and when was war declared against France?
10. Which of the generals of the allied armies obtained success?
11. Who hampered his movements?
12. Splendid action of Rooke and Ormond?
13. Their trophies?
14. The battle of Hochstet, between whom fought, and the result?
15. Doings of the emperor?
16. Movements of the allies in the next campaign?
17. Battle of Blenheim, describe.
18. The consequences of this victory?
19. What signal conquest did Rooke make?
20. What victory did he gain?
21. What prevented the ruin of Louis?
22. Louis' success in Italy?
23. Success of the allies in Spain?
24. The effect of these variations of success?
25. Describe the battle of Ramillies?
26. The results of this victory?
27. How were its effects felt in Italy?
28. The deliberations of the French marshals?
29. The consequences?
30. The results of the battle?
31. To what was the ill success of the allies in Spain attributable?
32. The movements of the different armies

33. What losses were sustained by Louis in the Mediterranean Sea?
34. What prevented peace?
35. What important treaty was made in England?
36. What advantage did Louis derive from his recent misfortunes?
37. What victory did the duke of Berwick gain?
38. What success did the French obtain in Germany?
39. What naval enterprise did the allies undertake?
40. What evils did the French suffer from the invasion?
41. Feelings of the nation toward Godolphin and Marlborough?
42. What did he do in order to regain his popularity?
43. What city did he take?
44. What island did the English take?
45. The effect of these victories on the allied powers?
46. The effect on Louis?
47. Why was peace not obtained?
48. What victory was obtained?
49. The effect of the capture of Mons?
50. Conduct of the Archduke Charles?
51. The success of Louis in Spain?
52. What revolution in the English cabinet was of great service to Louis?
53. Give an account of the manner in which it was brought about.
54. What cry did the tories raise?
55. Conduct of the whigs?
56. Give an account of Dr. Sacheverell's sermon and the proceedings thereupon.
57. The consequence of his persecution?
58. Doings of the new parliament?
59. What unexpected event changed entirely the aspect of affairs?
60. The result of it?
61. What was Philip forced to do, and why?
62. Who continued the war?
63. When and where was the final treaty made?
64. How was it relished in England?
65. Why?
66. By what means did the whigs regain much of their lost popularity?
67. What disappointed the hopes of the Pretender?
68. Who succeeded Anne?

Sec. 6.—*Peter the Great of Russia.—Charles XII. of Sweden.*

1. Doings of Alexis, czar of Russia?
2. Doings of his son Theodore?
3. His character and popularity?
4. His successor?
5. How was she treated by Peter?
6. What extraordinary revolution took place in Denmark?
7. Conduct of Christian V.?
8. What title has been given to Charles XII.?
9. How did Peter the Great commence his reign?
10. Magnificent plans of Peter?
11. His wisdom, how displayed?
12. The first place he visited?
13. His conduct there?
14. Whither then did he go?
15. What present was made him?
16. How long had he been absent from home?
17. What alliance did he form, and with what object?
18. Who commenced the war, and how?
19. What arrested their progress?
20. Charles' measures?
21. Their success?
22. The battle of Narva, describe?
23. Peter's remark?
24. Charles' next movements?
25. What project did he form?
26. What victory did he gain?
27. The result of the battle of Pultusk to Augustus?
28. Who was elected king of Poland?
29. What was Peter doing in the meantime?
30. Under what circumstances was St. Petersburgh founded?
31. What new scheme was formed between Augustus and Peter?
32. Their success?
33. His boldness to the emperor?
34. Joseph's facetious remark when informed of the pope's displeasure?
35. How did the allies feel at the departure of Charles?
36. The duke of Marlborough's politic course toward Charles?
37. The haughty reply of Charles to Peter's ambassador?
38. The answer of Peter?
39. How did Peter prevent his advance?
40. Charles' folly?
41. His disappointment?
42. What still greater misfortune befell him?
43. The severity of the winter?
44. What city did Charles besiege?
45. What news reached him there?
46. What terrible misfortune overtook him?
47. The spoils that Peter took?
48. Whither did Charles escape?
49. Repeat Campbell's description of this catastrophe?
50. The results of this victory?
51. What became of the prisoners?
52. What saved Sweden?
53. What new plan did Charles form in Turkey?
54. What frustrated it for a time?
55. How did Charles thereupon act?
56. What new war now broke out?
57. Into what danger was Peter now placed?

58. Who saved him, and how ?
59. Disappointment of Charles?
60. His foolhardiness ?
61. His folly ?
62. Victory of Steenbock ?
63. How sullied ?
64. His disaster ?
65. What great victory did Peter gain?
66. How did he celebrate it ?
67. What carried Charles home?
68. How did he travel ?
69. His enemies ?
70. His misfortune ?
71. His next step ?
72. Plan of his minister ?
73. Charles' death, how and where?
74. How regarded by the Swedish senate ?
75. Fate of his minister ?
76. His successor ?
77. What oath was exacted of the sovereigns?
78. When was peace made, and on what conditions ?

CHAPTER VIII.

GROWTH OF THE MERCANTILE AND COLONIAL SYSTEM.

Sec. 1.—*Establishment of the Hanoverian Succession in England.*

1. What system had been established in England during the wars with Louis XIV. ?
2. When was the bank of England founded?
3. The effect of it ?
4. Its internal effect ?
5. When did the mercantile system begin to manifest its strength ?
6. In what manner ?
7. What is said of the effects of the treaty of Utrecht ?
8. Of what did it contain the germs ?
9. What was the first commercial state in Europe at the commencement of the eighteenth century ?
10. What change was made in the English administration at the accession of George I. ?
11. How did the whigs use their power ?
12. What favourable opportunity was thus afforded ?
13. Why did not Louis XIV. avail himself of it ?
14. Course of the regent of France ?
15. Imprudence of the Pretender ?
16. What were his supporters called ?
17. What took place in the north of England ?
18. The treatment of the leaders ?
19. Course of the Pretender ?
20. What title did Peter assume after his peace with Sweden ?
21. How did he extend his dominions ?
22. How did he treat his eldest son, and why ?
23. Peter's successor ?
24. Doings of the Turks ?
25. By whom opposed, and with what result ?
26. The results of the next campaign ?
27. The fruits of the peace of Passarowitz ?
28. What interests depended on the preservation of the terms of the treaty of Utrecht ?
29. Who was opposed to them, and why ?
30. The grand scheme of Alberoni ?
31. How frustrated ?
32. How was the pope mortified ?
33. What society began now to be suspected ?
34. What is said of the doctrines of the other secret societies ?
35. What new war now arose ?
36. The result of it ?
37. Law's scheme ?
38. His success ?
39. Its result ?
40. The object of the South Sea scheme ?
41. Its progress and the results ?
42. What new effort was made, and its results ?
43. What now preserved the peace of Europe, and for how long a time ?
44. Why did Walpole lose his popularity ?
45. How did he contend against the opposition ?
46. Course of the Emperor Charles, in order to secure the throne to his daughter, Maria Theresa ?
47. What was this law called ?
48. How was the guarantee of France obtained ?
49. What brought on the war ?
50. What led to a second war ?
51. What involved Europe in new contentions ?
52. What forced Walpole to commence hostilities against Spain ?
53. The consequence of Vernon's success ?
54. The results, and their causes ?
55. Anson's success ?
56. Enemies of Maria Theresa ?
57. Who commenced the war ?
58. What offer did he make the queen, and how was it received ?
59. Her conduct, and its results ?
60. What kingdom aided her ?
61. Conduct of the new ministers of England ?
62. Revolution in Russia ?
63. Conduct of Elizabeth ?
64. Course of affairs in Germany ?
65. Repeat Dr. Johnson's description of the fate of the Bavarian prince ?
66. Exploit of the count of Bellisle ?
67. Why did Maria Theresa refuse to make peace with France ?

68. Fate of the elector of Bavaria?
69. Battle of Dettingen, and the results?
70. Effect of the haughtiness and ambition of Maria Theresa?
71. Object of the family compact?
72. Plan of the monarchs of Spain and France?
73. His success?
74. Naval fight, and the cause of the defeat of the English?
75. Consequences to the admirals?
76. What should have put an end to the war?
77. What parties continued to fight?
78. What battle was fought, and with what results?
79. What now terminated the war?
80. Give an account of the young Pretender?
81. What victory did he gain?
82. His misconduct?
83. His subsequent movements?
84. What mistake did he commit?
85. His movements in Scotland?
86. What victory did he gain?
87. A second mistake?
88. Where was his cause ruined?
89. What saved his life?
90. The conduct of the royalists after the the battle?
91. Fate of the young Pretender?
92. Success of Marshal Saxe?
93. Movements in Italy?
94. Results of the animosity between the French and English?
95. What paralyzed the exertions of the allies?
96. Fruit of the popular revolt in Holland?
97. Describe the battle of Val.
98. What strong fortress did the French take?
99. The advantage it gave them?
100. What naval engagement took place, and the fruits of it?
101. What second loss at sea did the French sustain?
102. A third loss?
103. The result?
104. Where was the treaty signed?
105. The basis of the treaty?
106. What did it leave unsettled?
107. The only advantage of the war to England?
108. What folly had England committed?
109. Whose policy had led to it?
110. The fruits of the folly?

Sec. 2.—*The Colonial Struggle between France and Great Britain.*

1. What is said of the peace of Aix-la-Chapelle?
2. What two causes tended to produce a new and fiercer struggle?
3. What injury had the court of Austria to complain of?
4. What prevented Frederick from gaining any permanent friend?
5. Of what two powerful personages was he the personal enemy?
6. What prevented Austria from declaring war against Prussia?
7. Who was the real guide of the court of Vienna at this time?
8. What grand project did he form?
9. What is said of Louis XV.?
10. Why was England jealous of France?
11. What were the chief subjects contested between them?
12. How did the partiality of George II. for Hanover affect his policy?
13. What state of things in India led both the French and English to enlarge their territories in that country?
14. Who was the French governor in India?
15. What afforded him an opportunity of interfering in the politics of India?
16. What effect did his doings have on the English?
17. Who was the English leader in India?
18. How was Dupleix treated by the French?
19. What treaty did his successor make with the English authorities?
20. By what means, and for what purpose, did the British ministry endeavour to secure Nova Scotia?
21. How did the French view these measures?
22. What object did the French have in view in the interior of N. America?
23. By what means was it necessary to effect this object?
24. Who commenced hostilities?
25. What caused the defeat of the expedition against the French forts on the Ohio?
26. What remark is made of the Virginia troops under Washington?
27. What other expeditions were undertaken, and their success?
28. What successes did the English obtain at sea?
29. What excited the jealousy of the provincial governors of India against the English?
30. What enraged Suraja Dowla against them?
31. The conduct of the English?
32. How were the captives among them treated?
33. Who recovered Calcutta?
34. Describe the battle of Plassy.
35. The fate of Suraja Dowla?
36. The consequences of this victory of the English?

Sec. 3.—*The Seven Years' War.*

1. The actions of the French government when intelligence was received of the

events that had taken place in India and America?
2. How did the British view these preparations?
3. What honourable act did the British government perform at this time?
4. Object of the French in menacing an invasion of England?
5. Conduct of Admiral Byng?
6. What aggravated the popular discontent?
7. Movements of the king of Prussia?
8. His treatment of King Augustus and Saxony?
9. The fate of Admiral Byng?
10. What attempt was made against the life of Louis?
11. The treatment of the assassin?
12. Conduct of George II.?
13. The condition of Prussia at the commencement of the campaign?
14. Skilful movements of Frederic?
15. Describe the battle of Prague.
16. The consequence of his delay before the walls of the city?
17. How was he now situated?
18. How was Berlin treated?
19. What plans of Pitt were defeated, and the cause?
20. Why did this fail to destroy the ministry?
21. The good effect of the failure?
22. What brilliant exploit did Frederic perform?
23. What other exploit did he perform?
24. What third one, a week afterwards?
25. Frederic's subsequent movements?
26. The successes of the British?
27. Their effect on the nation?
28. What three expeditions did General Abercrombie plan in America?
29. Describe the battle of Minden?
30. What fault was committed in this battle, and by whom?
31. By what defeat was this victory counterbalanced?
32. What rendered even the Austrian victories useless?
33. The effect of this indecisive campaign?
34. What place was justly considered the key of Canada?
35. What had prepared the colonists in Canada to submit to a change of masters?
36. What places were captured by General Amherst and Sir William Johnson?
37. The object of Wolfe's expedition?
38. What daring plan did he adopt?
39. Describe the battle.
40. Describe Wolfe's death.
41. Montcalm's, the French general
42. The fruit of this battle?
43. What is said of the success of the English in the East Indies?
44. Who were the generals on each side? and compare them.
45. What defeats did the French sustain?
46. What is said of the Dutch armaments and of Clive's promptness?
47. Threat of the French court?
48. Exploit of Admiral Boscawen?
49. Of Sir Edward Hawke?
50. Doings of Commodore Thurot?
51. What beautiful incident occurred during the attack on Carrickfergus?
52. The fate of himself and his fleet?
53. The conduct of the people of France to their sovereign?
54. What untoward event caused the failure of the campaign?
55. The movements of Frederic?
56. What deranged his plans?
57. How did he out-manœuvre Count Daun?
58. The disaster of Berlin?
59. Describe the battle of Torgau and its results.
60. What efforts were made by the French to recover Canada?
61. By whom baffled?
62. The successes of the English in India?
63. The complaints of the English?
64. The age of George III. at his accession to the throne?
65. To what results did the death of the king of Spain lead?
66. What contributed to the hostility of Spain to England?
67. The doings of the combatants on the continent?
68. How did Pitt propose to anticipate the hostile designs of Spain?
69. What led to his resignation?
70. The consequences?
71. How did the allies propose to attack Britain?
72. What was the state of Portugal at this period?
73. How had the king offended the Jesuits?
74. Their attempt against him, and its consequences?
75. What demand was made of him, and under what circumstances?
76. The consequence of his refusal?
77. What unexpected event delivered the king of Prussia from ruin?
78. Conduct of the emperor of Russia?
79. His subsequent fate?
80. Conduct of his successor?
81. Movements of Frederic?
82. Movements of the English in the West Indies?
83. In the East Indies?
84. What did they gain by the war?
85. On what basis was peace made between Prussia and Austria?
86. The result of the continental war?
87. What had Britain gained by the colonial war?
88. What question arose during the sever

years' war that led to important discussions?
89. By what system was the internal condition of England greatly improved?
90. The effect of the increase of the national debt?

CHAPTER IX.

THE AGE OF REVOLUTIONS.

SEC. 1.—*Change in the Relations of the Catholic Powers to the Holy See.—Dismemberment of Poland.*

1. What is said of the sufferings of France during the late war?
2. Character and conduct of Louis XV.?
3. Conduct of the parliaments?
4. What ecclesiastical order was suppressed in France, A.D. 1762?
5. What occasioned popular discontent in Spain?
6. Conduct of Charles III.?
7. Of the marquis of Pombal in Portugal?
8. What is said of his reforms?
9. How were the Jesuits treated in Spain?
10. In Mexico, Peru, and Paraguay?
11. Where else were they treated in the same way?
12. Who tried to protect them?
13. What island did the French get possession of in the Mediterranean?
14. Who endeavoured to maintain its independence?
15. How did the French minister attempt to strengthen his influence with Louis XV.?
16. What accident interrupted the festivities of the occasion?
17. To what did Choiseul owe his disgrace?
18. What empire was now rapidly rising in Europe?
19. How did Catherine treat Poland?
20. The king of Prussia's conduct?
21. Between whom did a war now break out?
22. Frederic's remark on it?
23. Catherine's plans?
24. Her treatment of the Greeks?
25. What great naval defeat did the Turks sustain?
26. Who was forced to join in the war against them?
27. Who now became jealous of the Russians?
28. Whom did the king of Denmark marry?
29. Her subsequent fate?
30. Who usurped the royal authority?
31. For what did the Danish court become remarkable?
32. What bloodless revolution was now effected in Sweden?
33. How was it effected?
34. How were the efforts of the king of Poland thwarted?
35. What gave Catherine a right to interfere?
36. What base act was now perpetrated on Poland, and by what powers?
37. What did Russia gain by the war with Turkey?
38. The exclamation of Louis XV. when he heard of the partition of Poland?
39. How did D'Aquillon endeavour to atone for his negligence?
40. When was the order of Jesuits finally suppressed?
41. What crimes were subsequently charged on them?

SEC. 2.—*History of England from the Peace of Paris to the Commencement of the American War.*

1. Why did the Brunswick dynasty at first rely on the whigs for support?
2. Why were the tories afterwards more favoured?
3. What led to the resignation of the prime minister?
4. Who assailed the English ministry with bitterness in a periodical?
5. Their conduct thereupon?
6. What became of Wilkes?
7. Conduct of the East India Company at this time?
8. Why was it now proposed to tax America?
9. On what ground was the tax resisted?
10. Whose appointment aggravated party animosities?
11. Conduct of Wilkes?
12. Conduct of the house of commons?
13. What gave importance to this contest?
14. What circumstances added to the exasperation of parties?
15. What kept alive the dispute with America?
16. The only beneficial results of these disputes?
17. Conduct of the Bostonians?
18. Retaliation of the English government?
19. Acts of the colonists?
20. What defeated all hopes of an accommodation?
21. Feelings of the continental powers with reference to this contest?
22. Who prevented France from interfering?
23. What kept Spain quiet?
24. Why was Frederic of Prussia rejoiced at the contest?
25. Why, Catherine of Russia?
26. How was the colonial revolt regarded in England?

SEC. 3.—*The American War.*

1. What completed the alienation of the colonies?
2. When did they declare their independence?

3. How did the first campaign terminate?
4. What nation first recognized the independence of the United States?
5. What, for a time, menaced the peace of the continent?
6. What compelled Joseph to relinquish his prey?
7. The policy of Washington?
8. What lowered the character of the English among foreign nations?
9. The effect of them?
10. What formidable enemy now appeared in Hindostan?
11. His successes?
12. Exploits of Sir Charles Rodney?
13. What dispute now arose between England and all the European maritime powers?
14. What nations united against England?
15. Against whom, and why, did England declare war?
16. Disasters of the Dutch?
17. What led the English ministry to despair of conquering America?
18. What two signal triumphs shed lustre on the British arms?
19. What successes attended them in the East Indies?
20. When was the independence of America recognized?

Sec. 4.—*The British Empire in India.*

1. On what was the British empire in India founded?
2. Who were the first to interfere in the East?
3. Under whose government did the English obtain a preponderating influence in the East?
4. What disputes arose between the directors at home and the officers in India?
5. What roused Hyder Ali against the English?
6. Conduct of Warren Hastings?
7. Condition of affairs in Ireland?
8 What averted a civil war?
9. Mr. Fox's plan for the government of India?
10. His design in this plan?
11. What defeated it?
12. Under whose auspices was a new ministry formed?
13. The new bill for the government of India?
14. What branch of commerce did the East India company monopolize?
15. What governor-general of India was now impeached?
16. The result of the trial?
17. What is said of Capt. Cook's three voyages?
18 What suggestion of Cook was acted upon?
19. What dangers did the illness of the king disclose?
20. What did Mr. Pitt determine upon in consequence?

Sec. 5.—*History of Europe, from the end of the American War to the commencement of the French Revolution.*

1. What took place in Europe during the progress of the American war?
2. Who was the most enterprising of the royal reformers?
3. With whom did his measures involve him in a contest?
4. How did the pope act?
5. What now prevented the dismemberment of Turkey?
6. The measures of Frederic?
7. The effect of the success of the Americans on the Dutch?
8. Who encouraged them, and why?
9. What brought matters to a crisis?
10. The consequence of Frederic William's interference?
11. The condition of France?
12. Who aggravated the disorder, and how?
13. What measures did he recommend?
14. Who demonstrated their inadequacy?
15. Conduct of Louis?
16. Feelings of the French soldiers that had fought for American independence?
17. How did the connexion of the court of France with Austria cause discontent?
18. Who, in consequence, became unpopular?
19. What mortified the French?
20. The progress of reform in other states?
21. How did the French minister of finance offend the parliaments?
22. Their great object?
23. Their demand?
24. Who took up the matter in earnest?
25. Who superseded the archbishop as minister?
26. How many years had elapsed since the last assembly of the states-general?
27. When and where did they now meet?
28. What demand did the democratic party make?
29. What excited a spirit of insubordination in Paris?
30. Against whom was the popular indignation directed?
31. What act of violence was now committed?
32. How did Louis endeavour to conciliate his subjects?
33. The commander of the National Guards?
34. The treatment of Louis?
35. Of what was this outrage the commencement?

Sec. 6.—*The French Revolution.*

1. What measures established popular sovereignty?
2. What club was formed?
3. Conduct of the nobility?
4. What conference took place at Pilnitz?
5. What attempt did Louis now make?
6. What, for a time, restored his popularity?
7. Conduct of the Emperor Leopold?
8. The great object of the revolutionary party?
9. What proceedings furnished them a plausible pretext for hostilities?
10. What forced Louis to declare war?
11. Effect of the defeat of his armies in Paris?
12. What new incident gave fresh strength to the Jacobin party?
13. What declaration proved still more injurious to Louis?
14 Its effect in Paris?
15. Conduct of La Fayette?
16. His successor?
17. What diabolical plot was executed in Paris, and by whom?
18. Success of the allies?
19. Success of Dumouriez?
20. What decree of the convention was a virtual declaration of war against all the kings of Europe?
21. The fate of Louis?
22. The date of his execution?
23. The effect of this act on the other powers?
24. Who united against France?
25. Catherine's policy?
26. Conduct of Dumouriez?
27. The fate of his successor?
28. Movements of the allies?
29. The effect of this revolutionary excitement in St. Domingo?
30. What was Catherine doing at this time?
31. Who joined in the iniquitous scheme?
32. What Polish patriot attempted to avert the fate of his country?
33. In what year was Poland blotted from the list of nations?
34. The fate of Marie Antoinette?
35. What civil war broke out in France?
36. The fate of the Lyonese revolters?
37. What were *assignats?*
38. What city in southern France revolted?
39. Who directed the artillery of the besiegers?
40. How were the inhabitants of Toulon punished?
41. Whose enormities in Paris became now insupportable?
42. His fate?
43. What revived the spirits of the English?
44. The fate of the Dutch?
45. What is said of Burke?
46. How had the king of Prussia treated the English?
47. The condition of France?
48. What colonies did the Dutch lose?
49. Who subdued a formidable insurrection in Paris?
50. Who was now entrusted with the executive functions of government?
51. What French general made a celebrated retreat in Germany?
52. Where was Bonaparte commanding?
53. On what terms did he force the king of Sardinia to purchase peace?
54. How was the pope treated?
55. Conduct of the Corsicans?
56. Condition of Ireland?
57. What new enemy now appeared against England?
58. What formidable mutiny broke out in the fleet?
59. The end of it?
60. Napoleon's progress in Italy?
61. His treatment of Genoa and Venice?
62. What naval victory did the English gain over the Spaniards?
63. What Spanish island did they take?
64. What loss did the Dutch sustain?
65. What new revolution broke out in France?
66. With whom was peace made?
67. What threat alarmed Great Britain?
68. What expedition did Napoleon plan?
69. His success there?
70. What brilliant naval victory did Lord Nelson achieve?
71. Condition of Ireland?
72. Who was now lord-lieutenant of Ireland?
73. The results of the victory of Lord Nelson?
74. The movements of the allies in Italy?
75. What was Napoleon doing?
76. Under what circumstance did he arrive in Paris?
77. How had the duke of York been compelled to purchase a safe retreat from Holland?
78. Bonaparte's conduct in Paris?
79. His exaltation?
80. What important change was made in the constitution of the British empire?
81. In what year?
82. What daring plan did Napoleon form?
83. What two great victories did he gain?
84. What induced the emperor to continue the war?
85. What defeat dashed his hopes?
86. With what new enemy was Great Britain threatened?
87. Conduct of the Russian emperor?
88. What induced Mr. Pitt to retire from the cabinet?
89. Naval victory of the British in the Baltic?
90. Fate of the Russian emperor.
91. Expedition of Abercrombie?

92. Terms of the treaty of Amiens?
93. Doings of the English in India?
94. Condition of France?

CHAPTER X.

THE FRENCH EMPIRE.

Sec. 1.—*Renewal of the War between England and France.*

1. To what did Napoleon now direct his attention?
2. What power was conferred on him?
3. Why did not Great Britain interfere to protect St. Domingo?
4. What gave rise to angry discussions?
5. Who renewed the war, and how?
6. How did Napoleon retaliate?
7. The leaders of the insurrection in Ireland?
8. The first movements of the hostile powers?
9. Doings of the English in India?
10. Condition of St. Domingo?
11. Who was made prime minister of England?
12. Of what base attempt were the English ministers guilty?
13. What crime did Napoleon commit in retaliation?
14. What new dignity was conferred on Bonaparte?
15. What power refused to recognise him?
16. Who was anxious to avenge the death of the Duke D'Enghien?
17. How was war commenced against Spain?
18. How did Pitt attempt to justify his conduct?
19. What powers united against Napoleon?
20. What new title did Napoleon assume?
21. How did Austria commence the war?
22. What signal victory was gained by Lord Nelson?
23. What success did Napoleon meet with in Austria?
24. What revived the courage of France?
25. What capital did Napoleon capture?
26. Where did he gain a brilliant victory?
27. How were a large body of Russians destroyed?
28. How did Napoleon keep the king of Prussia quiet?
29. What hastened the death of Pitt?
30. What honours were paid him?

Sec. 2.—*Progress of Napoleon's Power.*

1. What British general was distinguishing himself in India?
2. Who succeeded him?
3. What great measure did Mr. Fox carry?
4. Movements of the British in South America?
5. What king did Napoleon dethrone?
6. On whom did he confer the vacant throne?
7. Whom did he make king of Holland?
8. His character?
9. Why was peace refused by the English?
10. What circumstances exasperated the king of Prussia against Napoleon?
11. What enraged the Germans?
12. Folly of Frederic, and its fruits?
13. What fatal defeat did he sustain?
14. What was worse than this defeat?
15. Fate of Berlin?
16. The Berlin decrees?
17. What three successive defeats did the British sustain?
18. How did the ministers displease the king?
19. How did the Turks treat their sultan?
20. What sanguinary battle was fought between the French and Russians?
21. What important city was taken by Napoleon?
22. How did the two emperors meet?
23. What treaty was made, and at whose expense?
24. What reply was made to the remonstrances of Frederic?
25. How was he treated?

Sec. 3.—*The French Invasion of Spain.*

1. How were the Danes treated by the English?
2. The effect of this base conduct on the maritime powers?
3. What imperious edict did Napoleon issue respecting the reigning family of Portugal?
4. How did the British government retaliate on France for the Berlin decrees?
5. How did it embroil itself with America?
6. What proclamation did the American government issue?
7. The condition of Spain?
8. How did Godoy treat Ferdinand?
9. How did Napoleon win Godoy's support?
10. How did he treat Ferdinand?
11. How did Murat act in Madrid?
12. What new kings did Napoleon make?
13. How did the Spanish people relish these measures?
14. How did England avail herself of this altered state of things?
15. The fate of Marshal Dupont?
16. How did Joseph Bonaparte act when he heard of it?
17. Noble conduct of the citizens of Saragossa?
18. Sir Arthur Wellesley's success in Portugal?
19. The conduct of King Gustavus?
20. How was he treated by his subjects?
21. What three defeats did the Spaniards sustain?

22. With what forces did Napoleon invade Spain ?
23. Conduct of the English under Sir John Moore ?
24. Of what misconduct was the duke of York accused ?
25. Who succeeded him as commander-in-chief?
26. What new enemy now appeared against France ?
27. What led Francis to take this step.
28. What baffled his calculations ?
29. Success of Napoleon against him ?
30. The result of the campaign ?
31. Fate of the Tyrolese ?
32. Sentence of their chieftains ?
33. What efforts were made to shake off the French yoke in Germany?
34 What expedition was planned by the British ministry?
35. The result of it?
36. How did England offend the sultan of Turkey ?
37. What, notwithstanding, induced him to court an alliance with England ?
38. On what other power did the same motive operate ?
39. How was Austria treated by Napoleon ?
40. Why was he so moderate ?
41. Who was now the English commander in Spain ?
42. What great battle did he fight ?
43. The offence of Sir Francis Burdett ?
44. How was it punished ?
45. The effect of Napoleon's marriage ?
46. Who was his wife ?
47. Movements of the hostile powers in Portugal ?
48. What prevented the French from taking Cadiz ?
49. What extraordinary revolution now took place in Sweden ?
50. Calamity of George III. ?
51. Massena's conduct in Portugal ?
52. Movements of Wellington and Soult in Spain ?
53 How did Spain offend her South American colonies ?
54. What important island was wrested from the Dutch ?
55. Policy of Bernadotte ?
56. What was Alexander of Russia engaged in doing ?
57 Condition of Turkey ?
58. Treachery of Mohammed Ali, pacha of Egypt ?
59. Condition of Sicily ?
60. What victories did Wellington gain in Spain ?
61. The results of the battle of Salamanca ?
62. What led the South American colonies to return to their allegiance ?
63. What formidable enemy was now arming against Napoleon ?

Sec. 4.—*The Russian War.*

1. What act of Napoleon alarmed Alexander?
2. What alarmed the Austrian emperor ?
3. What system did Alexander wish relaxed ?
4. Why was not peace made ?
5. What mistake did Napoleon commit with reference to Poland ?
6. Why did he refuse the independence of Poland ?
7. To what capital did he first advance ?
8. How did the Russians act ?
9. To what capital did he then direct his march ?
10. What dreadful battle did he gain ?
11. Near what village was a still more dreadful battle fought ?
12. How many of the combatants were killed ?
13. How did the Russians regard Moscow ?
14. How did they destroy the hopes of Napoleon ?
15. What was he now compelled to do ?
16. What sufferings did his army experience in their retreat ?
17. Describe the passage of the Borodino.
18. Napoleon's course.
19. In what war was Great Britain engaged ?
20. What country did the Americans invade ?
21. What victories did they gain ?
22. What domestic transactions took place in England ?
23. What new enemy did Napoleon have to encounter ?
24. Who abandoned his cause ?
25. What great battle liberated Germany ?
26. Describe it.
27. Conduct of Bernadotte.
28. Of the Hanoverians.
29. Of the Dutch.
30. Where was Wellington, and what was he doing ?
31. Who exercised the real authority in Spain ?
32. What is said of Joseph Bonaparte ?
33. What marshal was sent to Spain to aid the French ?
34. What country was now about to be invaded ?
35. Conduct of Soult ?
36. What prevented Spain from reaping the benefits of her freedom ?
37. Progress of the war in America ?
38. What powers invaded France ?
39. Conduct of Napoleon ?
40. Progress of Bernadotte ?
41. What general alarmed Bonaparte most ?
42. What friend forsook him ?
43. When was Paris taken ?
44. When was Bonaparte deposed ?

45. Who was made king?
46. When did he reach France?
47. What provision was made for Bonaparte?

Sec. 5.—*History of Europe from the Dethronement of Napoleon to the Conclusion of the Treaty of Vienna.*

1. First proceedings of Ferdinand in Spain?
2. Mistakes of the allies?
3. What battles were fought in America?
4. What distinguished personages visited England?
5. What threw a shade of gloom over the general joy?
6. How did Louis XVIII. give offence?
7. Resolution of Bonaparte?
8. When did he land in France?
9. With how many men?
10. His progress?
11. Course of Louis?
12. Proclamation of the congress of Vienna?
13. Terms of the treaty between the four allied powers?
14. Conduct of Napoleon?
15. The first battle?
16. Describe the battle of Waterloo.
17. Whither did Napoleon flee?
18. His fate?
19. Conduct and end of Murat?
20. Fate of Ney and Labedoyère?
21. Terms of the treaty of Vienna?
22. Avowed object of the holy alliance?
23. Its real object?

CHAPTER XI.

HISTORY OF THE PEACE.

Sec. 1.—*State of Europe at the Close of the War.*

1. Immediate results of peace?
2. What country felt them most sensibly?
3. Why so?
4. What states were humbled?
5. Whose marriage diffused joy in England?
6. How was the nation affected at her death?
7. What other deaths occurred?
8. Condition of France?
9. Of the Netherlands?
10. Of Germany?
11. Of Spain?
12. Who revolted from the Spanish dominion?
13. What change took place in the Spanish Constitution?
14. In what other places did similar revolutions take place?
15. Effect of these changes on the monarchs of Europe?
16. Conduct of Louis XVIII.?
17. Of the Austrian emperor?
18. Condition of Sweden?
19. Between what principles was a struggle going on in the civilized world?

Sec. 2.—*History of Europe during the Reign of George IV.*

1. What conspiracy was detected in England?
2. Character of the conspirators?
3. How were they treated?
4. What suspended the preparations for the king's coronation?
5. Where had she been?
6. Why did she return to England?
7. What inducement was offered her to stay away?
8. Describe her trial.
9. Her melancholy end?
10. Condition of Ireland?
11. When and where did Bonaparte die?
12. Distracted condition of Spain?
13. Who composed the insurgents?
14. Resolution of the congress of Verona?
15. Who opposed it?
16. Who undertook to carry it into execution, and why?
17. Conduct of Ferdinand?
18. Course of the English ministers?
19. What struggle was going on in the south-east of Europe?
20. How was it viewed by the Holy Alliance?
21. What celebrated poet went to their aid?
22. Commercial embarrassments in England?
23. What association was formed in Ireland?
24. What event now excited attention in Europe?
25. The conduct of the British government?
26. Through whose influence was Donna Maria established on her throne?
27. What British nobleman died in A. D 1827?
28. Conduct of the cabinet on Canning's appointment as premier?
29. Why did they resign?
30. Why did the European powers interfere in the struggle of the Greeks for freedom?
31. Why did Austria keep aloof?
32. How did the emperor act on the occasion?
33. Movements of the combined fleet.
34. When, and where, and why was the Turkish navy annihilated?
35. The effect of this victory?
36. How was it regarded in France and Russia?
37. How in England?
38. Conduct of the sultan?
39. Doings of the allies?
40. Movements of Russia?
41. Describe their second campaign.
42. Terms of the treaty?

43. To whom was the crown of Greece offered?
44. Who finally accepted it?
45. What revolution now took place in Portugal?
46. Treachery of Don Miguel?
47. Conduct of Charles X. of France?
48. Conduct of his ministry?
49. What made them unpopular?
50. How was the appointment of Prince Polignac to office regarded?
51. What contest was going on in England?
52. Who resisted all change?
53. Object of the emancipation bill?
54. What brought matters to a crisis?
55. When did the bill receive the royal assent?
56. When did George IV. die?

SEC. 3.—*History of Europe during the Reign of William IV.*

1. Who succeeded George IV.?
2. Causes of his popularity?
3. Which of the two great parties, whig or tory, did he favour?
4. Condition of France?
5. What rendered Charles X. exceedingly unpopular?
6. Conduct of Polignac?
7. What threat did the royal speech contain?
8. Character of the reply?
9. Conduct of Charles thereupon?
10. How did he hope to overcome his unpopularity?
11. Success of the expedition?
12. Conduct of Polignac thereupon?
13. Consequences of it?
14. Why did the commercial classes dread the renewal of civil commotion?
15. How might Charles have averted the storm?
16. His course?
17. The three ordinances of July?
18. How was the intelligence received in Paris?
19. Doings of the opponents of the ministry?
20. Of the principal journalists?
21. By what act was the first disturbance occasioned?
22. What proved that no insurrection was anticipated?
23. Events of the 27th of July?
24. Conduct of the citizens at night?
25. Appearance of things on the morning of the 28th?
26. Conduct of the marshal?
27. Events of the day?
28. Situation of the troops in the evening?
29. Orders of the king?
30. What defection took place on the 29th?
31. The effect of it?
32. Fate of Charles?
33. Who was chosen lieutenant-general of the kingdom?
34. To what dignity was he elected by the chambers?
35. The effect of this revolution in Europe?
36. Declaration of the duke of Wellington?
37. Its effect?
38. What event proved still more injurious to the Wellington administration?
39. Its results?
40. How did the people excuse their vain terrors?
41. Principles of the new administration?
42. Views of the European sovereigns?
43. Conduct of the emperor of Russia?
44. In what country did this revolutionary spirit produce the more decisive effects?
45. When and why did the revolution break out there?
46 Policy of the king of Holland?
47. Course of Prince Frederick?
48. The result of the revolution?
49. Who was elected king?
50. Whom did he marry?
51. What changes took place in Germany?
52. Condition of Spain?
53. Of Portugal?
54. Of Italy and Switzerland?
55. Where did the flame of insurrection rage most furiously?
56. Whose cruelties had provoked them?
57. The continuance and result of the struggle?
58. Explain the state of parties in France.
59. What body sustained the king?
60. What severely tested the stability of the government?
61. The sentence of the late ministers?
62. State of things in England?
63. How long did the debate on the first reading of the bill last?
64. Character of the members of the new parliament?
65. Fate of the reform bill in the house of lords?
66. What calmed the excitement in London?
67. What dreadful scourge now made its appearance?
68. Fate of the new reform bill in the house of lords?
69. How did the premier propose to carry it?
70. Consequence of his refusal?
71. The new premier?
72. State of the country?
73. Conduct of Wellington?
74. What secret compact was made?
75. When was the bill carried?
76. To what dangers was the new French monarchy exposed?
77. Conduct of the republican party?
78. What insurrection took place in the south of France?
79. Who was taken captive?

80. What revolt took place in Paris?
81. Its effect?
82. What transactions now took place in Belgium?
83. What exposed Turkey to great danger?
84. Proceedings of the pacha of Egypt?
85. What saved Constantinople?
86. What events were taking place in Spain?
87. Conduct of Ferdinand on discovering how he had been treated?
88. Fate of Don Carlos?
89. What revolution broke out in Brazil?
90. Pedro's measures thereupon?
91. His success?
92. Whom did his daughter marry?
93. What disturbances took place in the papal states?
94. State of the papal power?
95. What measures occupied the attention of the British parliament?
96. What rendered the second session of this body memorable?
97. What changes took place in the cabinet?
98. Why was Peel soon forced to resign?
99. Who was left out of the Melbourne cabinet?
100. Course of Don Carlos?
101. Who organized a revolt in his favour?
102. What were the terms of the treaty between the four powers?
103. What was the court of Madrid forced to do?
104. What aid was granted?
105. What alienated the king of the French from the cause of the Spanish queen?
106. Course of the Carlists?
107. Of Don Carlos?
108. Of the queen-regent?
109. Course of events in Canada?
110. What produced embarrassment in the commercial world?
111. When did William IV. die?
112. What is said of his reign?
113. Who succeeded him?

CHAPTER XII.

HISTORY OF COLONIZATION.

SEC. 1.—*The Establishment of the Spaniards in Mexico.*

1. Where was the first Spanish colony established?
2. The orders of Isabella?
3. The consequence of them?
4. The effects of slavery on the Indians?
5. The second island occupied?
6. The third one?
7. Its extent and populousness?
8. How many Spaniards were sufficient to conquer it?
9. By whose intrepidity were more important conquests made?
10. Under whose command was an expedition fitted out against the continent?
11. When and where did he land?
12. How was he received?
13. To what degree of civilization had the Mexicans attained?
14. Cortez' first step?
15. How was his demand received?
16. The effect of these gifts?
17. His next step?
18. What city grew up from his encampment?
19. What did he do in order to inspire his men with courage?
20. His forces?
21 With whom was his first encounter?
22. [illegible] what cruelty was he guilty?
23. The effect of [illegible]?
24. His description of the ancient city of Tlascala?
25. How did Montezuma receive him?
26. The perils of his situation?
27. What bold resolution did he adopt?
28. What did he do to secure his retreat if necessary?
29. His ostensible pretext for seizing Montezuma?
30. The treatment of Qualpopoca?
31. His letter to the emperor?
32. His description of the city of Mexico?
33. What danger impended over him?
34. His prudent measures?
35. What dangers surrounded him on his return to Mexico?
36. Fate of the emperor?
37. Losses of the Spaniards during their retreat?
38. What victory restored their confidence?
39. Conduct of Guatimozin?
40. His cruel fate?
41. Result of his capture?
42. How was Cortez treated by his sovereign?
43. The first thought of the conquerors?
44. Conduct of Sahagun and Las Casas?
45. The results of their protection of the Mexicans?
46. Who were the *conquistadores?*
47. What were *haciendas?*
48. What fortunate circumstance contributed to the preservation of the Indians?
49. Why did not the *conquistadores* enter into mining speculations?
50. What were *audiencias?*
51. What abuses grew up?
52. How long did they continue?
53. What first led to the assertion of Mexican independence?
54. Conduct of the viceroy?
55. The cause of the enthusiasm with which his proclamation was received?
56. What proposition was made?
57. Why rejected?

58 Conduct of the *audiencia* ?
59. Feelings of the Creoles and Indians at this usurpation ?
60 Common remark of Bataller, one of the members of the council ?
61. Decrees of the juntas of Spain ?
62. Who raised the standard of revolt ?
63. What declaration did he make to his congregation ?
64. His progress and conduct ?
65. Acts of the Viceroy Venegas?
66. What stopped the career of Hidalgo ?
67. His further career and end ?
68. Conduct of his dispersed army ?
69. Manifesto of Rayon ?
70. The treatment it received ?
71. Who succeeded to the influence of Hidalgo ?
72. His prudent course ?
73. What rendered the royalist cause odious ?
74. By whom was Morelos finally defeated ?
75. His end ?
76. Exploits of Mina and his end ?
77. Conduct of the Viceroy Apodaca ?
78. Whom did he employ to draw up his plan ?
79. Substance of his draft of a constitution ?
80. How was it received by the old Spaniards ?
81. Their conduct thereupon ?
82. Effects of this false step ?
83. Success of Iturbide ?
84. Conduct of the cortes of Madrid ?
85. Effects of it ?
86. Elevation of Iturbide ?
87. How long did he reign ?
88. His end ?
89. When did Mexico become independent ?
90. Its progress since ?

SEC. 2.—*The Establishment of the Spaniards in Peru.*

1. Who discovered the passage around South America ?
2. Who conquered Peru ?
3. When did he land there ?
4. The civil condition of the country when the Spaniards first appeared in it ?
5. Who was the reigning inca ?
6. How was he treated by Pizarro ?
7. How did he receive the Spaniards ?
8. Subject of the priest's discourse to him at their first interview ?
9. Relate the circumstances of the interview.
10. Cruel and treacherous conduct of the Spaniards.
11 Fate of the inca.
12. Fate of Pizarro.
13 How long after the first conquest was it before the royal authority was established ?
14. Treatment of the Peruvians ?
15. What proportion of the labourers perished annually ?
16. How else were they oppressed ?
17. What is said of the insurrections at the close of the last century ?
18. How did Chili become annexed to the Spanish dominions ?
19. Loyalty of the Spanish colonies when Joseph Bonaparte was proclaimed king of Spain ?
20. Describe the struggle for independence in Chili and Peru.
21. When did the last Spanish garrison surrender ?
22. To what province was Upper Peru attached previous to the revolution ?
23. What name did it then assume ?
24. What tribute of national gratitude was paid to Bolivar ?
25. His noble conduct ?
26. Condition of Bolivia ?
27. By whom was Florida discovered ?
28. Who discovered the Mississippi ?
29. Plan of the French Huguenots ?
30. When and why was Florida annexed to the United States ?
31. The date of its cession ?

SEC. 3.—*Portuguese Colonies in South America.*

1. How was Brazil discovered ?
2. How long was it neglected ?
3. Condition and character of the natives ?
4. Why were the Portuguese in Brazil attacked, and by whom ?
5. The policy of the Portuguese ?
6. How long did this policy continue ?
7. How was Brazil governed ?
8. Restriction on the chief officers ?
9. Judicial power of the captains-general ?
10. How were the regular troops recruited ?
11. How officered ?
12. Who were the ordenanças ?
13. Their duty ?
14. Who were the fidalgos ?
15. The orders of knighthood ?
16. The privileges of the grand master of the order of Christ ?
17. Salaries of the clergy ?
18. Why so small ?
19. How did this jealousy of the Portuguese government show itself ?
20. Describe the conspiracy of 1769.
21. The fate of Tiradentas.
22. What conspiracy was organized in A.D. 1801 ?
23. What created a new era in the history of Brazil ?
24. How did Don John govern the country ?
25. The progress under his government ?
26. The first cause of discontent ?
27. What formal proposition was made by a Portuguese general ?

28. When was the constitution proclaimed in Rio Janeiro?
29. What projects were the Portuguese forming with reference to Brazil?
30. How were they received?
31. What led to Brazilian independence?
32. What is said of Paraguay?
33. How did the Jesuits rule it?
34. Who headed the revolution in it?
35. His policy?

SEC. 4.—*The English in America.*

1 The great object of the English adventurers?
2. How did they seek to accomplish it?
3. What port in Russia did Chancellor discover?
4. What was accomplished by the company of merchant adventurers?
5 With what Asiatic power did Queen Elizabeth conclude a commercial treaty?
6. How were the English navigators disappointed?
7. What successful enterprise encouraged them?
8. What gave importance to the information obtained by Sir Francis Drake?
9. How did the English avail themselves of it?
10. By whom was Canada first settled?
11. What is said of the early progress of the colony?
12. What of the contests of the French with the Indians?
13. When was Louisiana settled, and by whom?
14. Why was it more valued than Canada?
15. How did the French propose to connect Canada and Louisiana?
16. The consequence of the attempt?
17. The subsequent fate of the two colonies?
18. What do the British colonies in America now form?

SEC. 5.—*Colonization of the West Indies.*

1. What is said of Barbadoes when the English first took possession of it?
2. When were negroes first imported as slaves?
3. What is said of their increase?
4. What is said of the settlement of St. Lucia?
5. Of Martinico and Guadaloupe?
6. Of Tobago?
7. Of Trinidad?
8. Of the Bahama islands?
9. Of the Bermuda islands?
10. What little animal came near destroying the colony?
11. What use do the English make of these islands?
12. What is said of Jamaica?
13. Why was it made the great rendezvous of the bucaniers?
14. The conduct of these men?
15. What is said of Morgan, their most noted leader?
16. From what has Jamaica suffered?
17. What is said of Guiana?
18. What of Hispaniola?

SEC. 6.—*The Portuguese in India.*

1. Who discovered the passage around the Cape of Good Hope?
2 Policy of the Portuguese under Albuquerque?
3. Conduct of the Mohammedans?
4. By whom were they assisted?
5. What city became the seat of the Portuguese government?
6. What system was strongly deprecated by Vasco de Gama?
7. How did Albuquerque defend himself?
8. What other places did he subdue?
9. What people attempted to establish themselves on the coasts of Malabar?
10. What would have been the consequence of their success?
11. What progress did the Portuguese make in sixty years?
12. What occasioned the ruin of this mighty empire?
13. Explain the cause?
14. The most remarkable of their possessions?
15. Describe it?
16. What gave it importance?
17. Of what did it give the world a memorable example?
18. Describe it, as it was during the busy seasons?
19. What led to its destruction?
20. What is it now?

SEC. 7.—*The Spaniards in the East Indies.*

1. The object of the first voyage of Columbus?
2. What prevented the Spaniards from occupying the Moluccas?
3. Who settled the Philippine islands?
4. Why so named?
5. What city did he build?
6. By whom was it attacked?
7. What rivals soon appeared?
8. Who now owns these islands?

SEC. 8.—*The Dutch in the East Indies.*

1. What drove the Dutch to revolt from Spain?
2. What laid the foundation of their commercial prosperity?
3. How did the Spaniards seek to check the growing spirit of freedom in the Netherlands?
4. The consequence?

5. How did they seek to humble the Portuguese?
6. The consequence?
7. What fruitless expeditions were made?
8. The story of Cornelius Houtman?
9. How did the Spaniards first attempt to defeat the enterprise he started?
10. Their next attempt?
11. How was their calumny refuted?
12. The first islands occupied by the Dutch?
13. For what island did they and the English contend?
14. Which succeeded?
15. What city did they build?
16. What trade did they wrest from the Portuguese?
17. The next island they obtained possession of?
18. Of what trade did this give them the monopoly?
19. To whom does Ceylon now belong?
20. What baffled their efforts to open a trade with the Chinese?
21. On what island did they establish a flourishing settlement?
22. How did they lose this island?
23. To whom does it now belong?
24. What caused the ruin of the Dutch empire in the East?
25. How was their dominion maintained in Java?
26. What trade do they still monopolize?

Sec. 9.—*The Danes in the East Indies.*

1. What led to the Danish association for trade in the East Indies?
2. Where was an establishment made?
3. What checked the prosperity of the company?
4. For what did the Danes distinguish themselves?

Sec. 10.—*The French in the East Indies.*

1 When was the French East India company formed?
2. Why was the India trade abandoned?
3. In what island did the French attempt a settlement?
4. What town did they purchase?
5. What islands did they subsequently acquire?
6. What opened to them a new career of ambition?
7 The designs of M. Dupleix?
8. By whom were they completely baffled?
9. Their subsequent attempts?

Sec. 11.—*The English in India.*

1. The settlements of the English in India a hundred years ago?
2. The number of British subjects there now?
3. The annual revenue obtained from them?
4. The army maintained by the English company?
5. What is said of Calcutta, Bombay, Madras?
6. When was the London company incorporated?
7. When was the English company incorporated?
8. Why, and when, and under what name were the two companies united?
9. The first settlement of any importance?
10. What grant of land did they obtain in A.D. 1658?
11. How did they secure it?
12. What island did they obtain in 1668?
13. When was a settlement made at Calcutta?
14. What fortunate circumstance secured them valuable privileges over other Europeans?
15. Conduct of the viceroy of Bengal?
16. By whom was Calcutta retaken?
17. Bold resolution of Clive?
18. To whom did he give the viceroy's post?
19. To whom was the government of Calcutta afterwards entrusted?
20. To what was the council bribed?
21. What claim did the servants of the East India company make?
22. The effect of granting it?
23. How did Cossim act?
24. What rash act did he commit?
25. Its consequences?
26. Who was his successor?
27. Who was now made governor-general?
28. The condition of the affairs of the presidency?
29. The consequence of his zeal in reforming abuses?
30. Who first rose against him?
31. By whom was the plot instigated?
32. How was he treated?
33. How was another of the mutineers rewarded by the council?
34. Effect of Clive's firmness?
35. What removed the chief source of intrigue?
36. Who nearly ruined the presidency of Madras?
37. Who retrieved the losses of the English?
38. What serious constitutional question arose?
39. How was the right of the British Parliament virtually asserted?
40. Whose administration greatly extended the territories of the company?
41. What is said of the means he employed for this purpose?
42. Proposition of Mr. Fox, and how defeated?
43 What important change was made in the government of India by Mr. Pitt?
44. The object of the new measure?

45. The first governor-general under the new system?
46. Whose ambitious projects excited his suspicions?
47. By whom instigated?
48. What led to their interference?
49. What dispute arose between Mr. Pitt and the court of directors?
50. The result of the war with Tippoo Saib?
51. The most remarkable events of Sir John Shore's administration?
52. The third governor-general?
53. The object of his first efforts?
54. Against whom did he declare war, and with what result?
55. In what points of policy was he thwarted by the home government?
56. Conduct of Lord Clive?
57. Of Lord Wellesley?
58. What gave rise to serious embarrassments?
59. What led to an angry controversy with the English ministry?
60. What compromise was effected?
61. The cause of the mutiny of the native Indian army?
62. Who aggravated their feelings of natural discontent?
63. The pretext for revolt?
64. Lord Bentinck's conduct towards the mutineers?
65. What system of policy did Lord Minto propose to introduce?
66. Why was his success impossible?
67. What is said of his administration?
68. What war broke out under his successor?
69. Condition of central India?
70. What important settlement was made in A.D. 1819?
71. Who succeeded the marquis of Hastings?
72. In what war did he engage?
73. What strong fortress did he take?
74. Earl Amherst's successor?
75. For what was his administration remarkable?
76. What important change was made in the government of India, A.D. 1833?
77. What two new kingdoms were founded on the ruins of the Mogul empire?
78. What is said of the Afghans?
79. Who restored the Persian supremacy?
80. How long did the Afghan monarchy continue?
81. By what was it then distracted?
82. Its condition under the Baurikzye brothers?
83. For what purpose was an embassy sent to Cabul?
84 Why was it changed to a political legation?
85 Demand of the ruler of Cabul?
86 What resolution did the British Indian government then adopt?
87. What is said of Shah Sujáh's government?
88. Result of the insurrection in Cabul in 1841?
89. The result of the war that ensued?
90. What is said of the importance of this annexation?

CHAPTER XIII.

HISTORY OF CHINA.

1. When does the authentic history of the Chinese commence?
2. When did Confucius flourish?
3. Condition of China in his time?
4. What use did he make of the old traditions of the country?
5. His main principle?
6. What is said of his ritual?
7. Who first united all the Chinese under one sovereign?
8. What great work did he perform?
9. Its object?
10. How was this service overbalanced?
11. Who invaded China under the Han dynasty?
12. Why is the memory of the Hans still cherished in China?
13. When did the Mongols invade China?
14. When was the conquest completed?
15. Describe the naval fight between the Mongols and the Chinese.
16. Conduct of the Chinese admiral?
17. Government of the Mongols?
18. When were they driven from the country?
19. Who was the conqueror of the Mongols?
20. Describe his rise from rank to rank.
21 Character of his government.
22. The last of his dynasty?
23. Who invaded the empire in his reign?
24. His end and dying request?
25. Who avenged his death, and by whose assistance?
26. Conduct of the Tartars?
27. How did they treat the country?
28. Who was Coxinga, and his actions?
29. Character and acts of Kang-he, the second of the Tartar emperors?
30. Conduct of his successor?
31. Conduct of Keën-lung his successor?
32. What inscription did he engrave on the stone tablet of Ele?
33. What is said of his fame?
34. How long did he reign?
35. Character of his successor?
36. Conduct of the British squadron!
37. Object of the British embassy?
38. Who is the reigning emperor?
39. The cause of the late war between China and England?
40. What is said of Chinese military prowess?
41. Terms of the treaty?

42. Opinions of the Chinese respecting themselves?
43. How are the Tartar conquerors regarded by the natives?
44. What secret societies now exist throughout China?

CHAPTER XIV

HISTORY OF THE JEWS.

1. What is said of Jewish colonies?
2. Of Jewish philosophers at Alexandria?
3. What was Gnosticism?
4. In what distant countries did the Jews settle themselves?
5. What is said of the Jews of Arabia, in the time of Mohammed?
6. Why did they ever act in concert with Mohammedans?
7. How were they treated by the Abbaside khaliphs?
8. By Almanzor, and Mamun?
9. For what were they noted?
10. How were they treated under the Mongols?
11. Condition of Persia at the accession of Shah Abbas?
12. What led the Jews to his country?
13. How did he treat them?
14. What saved them from ruin?
15. How were they treated in Spain?
16. How by the Spanish Moslems?
17. What distinguished Jews belong to this era?
18. How were they treated in the more northern countries?
19. How by Charlemagne and his immediate successors?
20. Decree of the council of Meaux?
21. Conduct toward them of Philip Augustus, in A.D. 1180?
22. Of St. Louis IX.?
23. Of the parliament of Paris in 1288?
24. Of Philip the Long?
25. Of King John in 1350?
26. Of Pope Honorius III.?
27. Of Pope Gregory IX.?
28. The condition of the Jews at Avignon?
29. Conduct towards them of Gregory XIII.?
30. Of Sixtus V.?
31. Their sufferings during the crusades?
32 Their condition in England?
33. What circumstances confirm this?
34. When were they expelled from Spain?
35. How many left the country?
36. What took place at the era of the Reformation?
37. Their condition in England at the present time?
38 Conduct towards them of Maria Theresa of Austria?
39 Their condition in France?
40. In Russia?
41. In Mohammedan countries?
42 Their number?
43 How many in Europe?
44 In Asia?
45. In Africa?
46. In America?

CHAPTER XV.

HISTORY OF THE UNITED STATES OF AMERICA

Sec. 1.—*Colonial History.*

1. When was the first permanent attempt made to plant a colony within the limits of the United States?
2. The last colony planted?
3. The dimensions of Virginia, in the reign of Elizabeth?
4. Why so named?
5. How was it afterwards divided?
6. In what year was Jamestown settled?
7. When and where, and by whom was the settlement of New-York begun?
8. When was it occupied by the English?
9. When, and by whom was the colony of Plymouth planted?
10. What attempts had been previously made to form settlements in New England?
11. When was the Massachusetts colony established?
12. The first settlement
13. When was the Plymouth colony incorporated with that of Massachusetts?
14. When, and where was the settlement of New Hampshire begun?
15. What three other settlements were made?
16. Under the government of what colony were they at first?
17. When was New Hampshire formed into a separate province?
18. When, and by whom was New Jersey settled?
19. By whom was it first conquered?
20. When did the English occupy it?
21. When, and by whom was Delaware first occupied?
22. Who afterwards seized it?
23. When was Maine settled?
24. The first town built in it?
25. How long did it remain a part of Massachusetts?
26. When, and by whom was Maryland settled?
27. Where did Lord Baltimore first plant his colony?
28. When, and by whom was Connecticut settled?
29. When New Haven?
30 When was it united to the colony of Connecticut?
31 When, and by whom was Rhode Island settled?

32. Under what circumstances?
33. What credit is due to him?
34. When, and by whom was North Carolina settled?
35 When did it become a distinct colony?
36 When was South Carolina settled?
37 When was the city of Charleston commenced?
38. When, and by whom was Pennsylvania settled?
39. Why was its growth more rapid than that of the other colonies?
40. When was Georgia colonized?
41. The first place founded?
42. What union was formed in 1643?
43. The motives of this confederation?
44. Why was Rhode Island excluded?
45. What war broke out in 1675?
46. The loss sustained by New England in it?
47. The causes of Bacon's rebellion?
48. The condition of the New England colonies during the reign of James II.?
49. Their governor?
50. What finally became of him?
51. What three kinds of government prevailed in the colonies?
52. Where did the charter governments prevail?
53. Describe them?
54. The royal governments?
55. The sources of grievance in these colonies?
56. The proprietary governments?
57. The causes of the quarrels in them?
58. The population of the colonies in 1689?
59. Their trade with whom?
60. Their chief employment?
61. For what is the year 1692 signalized?
62. How many were the sufferers?
63. The principal theatre of the delusion?
64. The effect on the colonies of the revolution of 1688?
65. What is said of *King William's war?*
66. Of *Queen Anne's war?*
67. The result of the peace of Utrecht in 1713?
68. The principal event of the war commenced 1744?
69. The effect of this war on the colonies?
70. The cause of the war that followed soon after?
71. The fate of the first expedition against the French?
72. Its commander?
73. The singular fate of the "Plan of Union," adopted in 1754?
74. What is said of Braddock's expedition?
75. What victory made amends for this defeat?
76. The parties in the *seven years' war*?
77. The campaign of 1756 in America?
78 Of 1757?
79 Of 1758?
80. Of 1759?
81. Of 1760?
82. The terms of the treaty of 1763?
83. How many wars, occupying how many years, were the colonies engaged in, during the seventy years terminating A.D. 1760?
84. The increase in population during this time?
85. In trade and commerce?
86. How had a *national* spirit been created?

SEC. 2.—*Revolutionary History.*

1. In what year did the revolutionary war commence?
2. What doctrine was established among the colonists so early as the middle of the seventeenth century?
3. What restrictions had been imposed upon them?
4. When was America first taxed by Great Britain for the purpose of raising a revenue?
5. The object of the *stamp act?*
6. How was it received in the colonies?
7. The proceedings of the colonists?
8. By what declaration was the repeal of the act accompanied?
9. What new act was passed?
10. How were the cargoes of *tea* treated in the different ports to which they were sent?
11. The *Boston port bill?*
12. Its effect?
13. The first proceedings of the colonies?
14. What did they next do?
15. The proceedings of the government of Great Britain thereupon?
16. The first hostile proceedings, when, where, and how occasioned?
17. What fortresses were taken, and what memorable battle was fought?
18. Who was now appointed the American commander-in-chief?
19 Size of the American army?
20 What expedition was next planned, and its success?
21. How were the British driven from Boston?
22. When was American independence declared?
23. Washington's head-quarters, and size of his army?
24. British army, how large?
25. What victory did Lord Howe gain?
26. Policy of Washington?
27. What fort was taken by the enemy?
28. What is said of Washington's retreat?
29. How was his army diminished?
30. Number of his troops?
31. What succession of victories did he gain?
32. The effect of them?
33. Conduct of the American congress dur-

ing the darkest period of the revolutionary struggle?
34. What French nobleman embarked in the struggle?
35 What battle was fought for the purpose of protecting Philadelphia, and the result?
36. What other battle was fought nearly a month later, and the result?
37 Objects of Burgoyne's invasion?
38. Fate of his army?
39. Consequences of the surrender?
40. Describe the battle of Monmouth?
41. What was doing in the South?
42. Describe the campaign of 1779.
43. Object of the enemy?
44. What were the causes of the inactivity of the Americans?
45. What is said of the depreciation of the currency?
46. What American general capitulated in 1780?
47. What defeat did the Americans sustain?
48. What foreign help arrived this year?
49. For what was this year memorable?
50. Fate of Arnold and of Andre?
51. By what inauspicious event was the campaign of 1781 opened?
52. From what was Virginia suffering?
53. What signal victory was achieved by the Americans in South Carolina?
54. What two battles were subsequently fought by General Greene?
55. What on the September following?
56. Whither did Cornwallis retire, and with what forces?
57. What was Washington's original plan of the campaign?
58. How and why did he change it?
59. When did the siege commence, and when and how did it terminate?
60. Clinton's movements?
61. Action of congress?
62. Subsequent resolution of the British house of commons?
63. What commissioners were appointed to negotiate a peace?
64. When was the treaty signed?
65. The conclusion of Washington's farewell address?
66. Effect of the war on the trade, commerce, agriculture, and manufactures of the country?

SEC 3.—*Constitutional History.*

1. Debt of the country at the return of peace?
2. Powers of the confederation?
3. What plan to redeem the credit of the country was defeated, and by what states?
4. Conduct of Massachusetts?
5. When was the constitution ratified and adopted?
6. Our first President?
7. Where did the first congress assemble?
8. What measures occupied its attention?
9. What measure did Hamilton propose in order to restore public credit?
10. What tax was imposed at the second session of congress?
11. What institution was established?
12. The two parties in the country?
13. Where did Indian hostilities break out?
14. What generals were defeated by the Indians?
15. On what ground was the bill for adding to the army resisted?
16. By what difficulties was Washington's second term embarrassed?
17. Proclamation of Washington?
18. How was it received by the anti-federalists?
19. Conduct of Genet?
20. Of the democratic party?
21. What bill passed in 1794?
22. Conduct of Great Britain?
23. Who subdued the Indians?
24. Cause of the "Whiskey insurrection?"
25. How was it put down?
26. Objections to Jay's treaty?
27. What treaty was made with Spain?
28. What is said of Jay's treaty?
29. Concluding remarks of Washington's farewell address?
30. Results of Washington's administration?
31. Conduct of the French government?
32. Our second president?
33. Opposition to France, how manifested?
34. Its effect?
35. Date of Washington's death?
36. His character?
37. What laws killed the federalist party?
38. Our third president?
39. The most important event of this period?
40. Object of Burr's conspiracy?
41. His subsequent history?
42. How were the interests of the United States becoming complicated with the policy of the belligerent powers of Europe?
43. What right had Great Britain always claimed and exercised?
44. What special outrage was committed?
45. Action of the American government thereupon?
46. Of the British government?
47. The *Milan decree?*
48. Our fourth president?
49. The state of the country?
50. Object of the non-intercourse act?
51. Napoleon's *Rambouillet decree?*
52. Act of May 1st of the American congress?
53. Conduct of the British government?
54. How many American vessels had been thus captured?

55. When was war declared against Great Britain?
56. The grounds of the war?
57. Was it popular with all parties?
58. How long did it last?
59. The campaign of 1812?
60. What brilliant naval victories were gained?
61. Military and naval operations of 1813?
62. What victory put an end to the Indian war in the northwest?
63. Jackson's victory over the Indians, in the south?
64. Naval operations in 1814?
65. What forces did the British send over in 1814?
66. What battles were fought in the north?
67. Actions of the British fleet in the Chesapeake?
68. Attempt on Baltimore?
69. Engagement on Lake Champlain?
70. Battle of Plattsburgh?
71. Object of the Hartford convention?
72. Its statement of grievances?
73. Describe the battle of New Orleans?
74. When was the United States bank incorporated?
75. Our fifth president?
76. Condition of the country?
77. What Indian war broke out in 1818?
78. Terms of the convention made with Great Britain in 1819?
79. Treaty with Spain?
80. What distinguished foreigner visited the United States in 1824?
81. How was he sent home?
82. Our sixth president?
83. Relate the affair of the Indians and the state of Georgia.
84. What ex-presidents died July 4, 1826?
85. What important bill was passed by the twentieth congress?
86. Mr. Adams' administration?
87. What is said of party spirit during the election?
88. Our seventh president?
89. How did he signalize his accession to office?
90. What important measures engaged the attention of the twenty-first congress?
91. What bills did Jackson veto?
92. When and where did nullification commence?
93. Jackson's proclamation?
94. Conduct of South Carolina?
95. What led to a repeal of the nullifying ordinances?
96. How were the "deposites" removed from the United States bank?
97. With what country was a war threatened?
98. How was it prevented?
99. How was the city of New-York afflicted in the winter of 1835?
100. Value of the property destroyed?
101. What Indian war now broke out?
102. Benton's "expunging resolution?"
103. Our eighth president?
104. State of the country?
105. What occasioned it?
106. Amount of failures in New-York?
107. Conduct of the banks?
108. How did congress endeavour to remedy the difficulty?
109. Our ninth president?
110. How long did he survive his inauguration?
111. His successor?
112. *The treaty of Washington?*
113. The difficulties in Rhode Island?
114. How were they settled?
115. The fate of Dorr?
116. The present president?

English.

A MANUAL

OF

GRECIAN AND ROMAN ANTIQUITIES.

BY DR. E. F. BOJESEN,

Professor of the Greek Language and Literature in the University of **Soro.**

Translated from the German.

EDITED, WITH NOTES AND A COMPLETE SERIES OF QUESTIONS, BY THE

REV. THOMAS K. ARNOLD, M. A.

REVISED WITH ADDITIONS AND CORRECTIONS.

One neat volume, 12mo. Price $1.

The present Manual of Greek and Roman Antiquities is far superior to any thing on the same topics as yet offered to the American public. A principal Review of Germany says:—Small as the compass of it is, we may confidently affirm that it is a great improvement on all preceding works of the kind. We no longer meet with the wretched old method, in which subjects essentially distinct are herded together, and connected subjects disconnected, but have a simple, systematic arrangement, by which the reader easily receives a clear representation of Roman life. We no longer stumble against countless errors in detail, which though long ago assailed and extirpated by Niebuhr and others, have found their last place of refuge in our Manuals. The recent investigations of philologists and jurists have been extensively, but carefully and circumspectly used. The conciseness and precision which the author has every where prescribed to himself, prevents the superficial observer from perceiving the essential superiority of the book to its predecessors, but whoever subjects it to a careful examination will discover this on every page."

The Editor says:—"I fully believe that the pupil will receive from these little works a correct and tolerably complete picture of Grecian and Roman life; what I may call the POLITICAL portions—the account of the national constitutions and their effects—appear to me to be of great value; and the very moderate extent of each volume admits of its being thoroughly mastered—of its being GOT UP and RETAINED."

"A work long needed in our schools and colleges. The manuals of Rennet, Adam, Potter, and Robinson, with the more recent and valuable translation of Eschenburg, were entirely too voluminous. Here is neither too much, nor too little. The arrangement is admirable—every subject is treated of in its proper place. We have the general Geography, a succinct historical view of the general subject; the chirography, history, laws, manners, customs, and religion of *each* State, as well as the points of union for all, beautifully arranged. We regard the work as the very best adjunct to classical study for youth that we have seen, and sincerely hope that teachers may be brought to regard it in the same light. The whole is copiously digested into appropriate questions."—*S. Lit. Gazette.*

From Professor Lincoln, of Brown University.

"I found on my table after a short absence from home, your edition of Bojesen's Greek and Roman Antiquities. Pray accept my acknowledgments for it. I am agreeably surprised to find on examining it, that within so very narrow a compass for so comprehensive a subject, the book contains so much valuable matter; and, indeed, so far as I see, omits noticing no topics essential. It will be a very useful book in Schools and Colleges, and it is far superior to any thing that I know of the same kind. Besides being cheap and accessible to all students, it has the great merit of discussing its topics in a consecutive and connected manner."

Extract of a letter from Professor Tyler, of Amherst College.

"I have never found time till lately to look over Bojesen's Antiquities, of which you were kind enough to send me a copy. I think it an excellent book; learned, accurate, concise, and perspicuous; well adapted for use in the Academy or the College, and comprehending in a small compass, more that is valuable on the subject than many extended treatises"

HAND BOOK

OF

MEDIÆVAL GEOGRAPHY AND HISTORY.

BY

WILHELM PUTZ,

PRINCIPAL TUTOR IN THE GYMNASIUM OF DUREN.

Translated from the German by

REV. R. B. PAUL, M. A.,

Vicar of St. Augustine's, Bristol, and late Fellow of Exeter College, Oxford.

1 volume, 12mo. 75 cts.

HEADS OF CONTENTS.

I. Germany before the Migrations.
II. The Migrations.

THE MIDDLE AGES.

FIRST PERIOD.—From the Dissolution of the Western Empire to the Accession of the Carlovingians and Abbasides.

SECOND PERIOD.—From the Accession of the Carlovingians and Abbasides to the first Crusade.

THIRD PERIOD.—Age of the Crusades.

FOURTH PERIOD.—From the Termination of the Crusades to the Discovery of America.

"The characteristics of this volume are: precision, condensation, and luminous arrangement It is precisely what it pretends to be—a manual, a sure and conscientious guide for the student through the crooks and tangles of Mediæval history. * * * * All the great principles of this extensive Period are carefully laid down, and the most important facts skilfully grouped around them. There is no period of History for which it is more difficult to prepare a work like this. and none for which it is so much needed. The leading facts are well established, but they are scattered over an immense space; the principles are ascertained, but their development was slow, unequal, and interrupted. There is a general breaking up of a great body, and a parcelling of it out among small tribes, concerning whom we have only a few general data, and are left to analogy and conjecture for the details. Then come successive attempts at organization, each more or less independent, and all very imperfect. At last, modern Europe begins slowly to emerge from the chaos, but still under forms which the most diligent historian cannot always comprehend. To reduce such materials to a clear and definite form is a task of no small difficulty, and in which partial success deserves great praise. It is not too much to say that it has never been so well done within a compass so easily mastered, as in the little volume which is now offered to the public."—*Extract from American Preface.*

"This translation of a foreign school-book embraces a succinct and well arranged body of facts concerning European and Asiatic history and geography during the middle ages. It is furnished with printed questions, and it seems to be well adapted to its purpose, in all respects. The mediæval period is one of the most interesting in the annals of the world, and a knowledge of its great men, and of its progress in arts, arms, government and religion, is particularly important, since this period is the basis of our own social polity."—*Commercial Advertiser.*

"This is an immense amount of research condensed into a moderately sized volume, in a way which no one has patience to do but a German scholar. The beauty of the work is its luminous arrangement. It is a guide to the student amidst the intricacy of Mediæval History, the most difficult period of the world to understand, when the Roman Empire was breaking up and parcelling out into smaller kingdoms, and every thing was in a transition state. It was a period of chaos from which modern Europe was at length to arise.

The author has briefly taken up the principal political and social influences which were acting on society, and shown their bearing from the time previous to the migrations of the Northern nations, down through the middle ages to the sixteenth century. The notes on the crusades are particularly valuable, and the range of observation embraces not only Europe but the East. To the student it will be a most valuable Hand-book, saving him a world of trouble in hunting up authorities and facts."—*Rev. Dr. Kip, in Albany State Register.*

English.

MANUAL

OF

ANCIENT GEOGRAPHY AND HISTORY.

BY WILHELM PÜTZ,

PRINCIPAL TUTOR IN THE GYMNASIUM OF DUREN

Translated from the German.

EDITED BY THE REV. THOMAS K. ARNOLD, M. A.,

AUTHOR OF A SERIES OF "GREEK AND LATIN TEXT-BOOKS."

One volume, 12mo. $1.

"At no period has History presented such strong claims upon the attention of the learned, as at the present day; and to no people were its lessons of such value as to those of the United States. With no past of our own to revert to, the great masses of our better educated are tempted to overlook a science, which comprehends all others in its grasp. To prepare a text-book, which shall present a full, clear, and accurate view of the ancient world, its geography, its political, civil, social, religious state, must be the result only of vast industry and learning. Our examination of the present volume leads us to believe, that as a text-book on Ancient History, for Colleges and Academies, it is the best compend yet published. It bears marks in its methodical arrangement, and condensation of materials, of the untiring patience of German scholarship; and in its progress through the English and American press, has been adapted for acceptable use in our best institutions. A noticeable feature of the book, is its pretty complete list of 'sources of information' upon the nations which it describes. This will be an invaluable aid to the student in his future course of reading."

"Wilhelm Pütz, the author of this 'Manual of Ancient Geography and History,' is Principal Tutor (*Oberleher*) in the Gymnasium of Duren, Germany. His book exhibits the advantages of the German method of treating History, in its arrangement, its classification, and its rigid analysis. The Manual is what it purports to be, 'a clear and definite outline of the history of the principal nations of antiquity,' into which is incorporated a concise geography of each country. The work is a text-book; to be *studied*, and not merely *read* It is to form the groundwork of subsequent historical investigation,—the materials of which are pointed out, at the proper places, in the Manual, in careful references to the works which treat of the subject directly under consideration. The list of references (especially as regards earlier works) is quite complete,—thus supplying that desideratum in Ancient History and Geography, which has been supplied so fully by Dr. J. C. I. Gieseler in Ecclesiastical History.

"The nations whose history is considered in the Manual, are: in *Asia*, the Israelites, the Indians, the Babylonians, the Assyrians, the Medes, the Persians, the Phœnicians, the States of Asia Minor; in *Africa*, the Ethiopians, the Egyptians, the Carthaginians; in *Europe*, the Greeks, the Macedonians, the Kingdoms which arose out of the Macedonian Monarchy, the Romans. The order in which the history of each is treated, is admirable. To the whole are appended a 'Chronological Table,' and a well-prepared series of 'Questions.' The pronunciation of proper names is indicated,—an excellent feature. The accents are given with remarkable correctness. The typographical execution of the American edition is most excellent."—*S. W. Baptist Chronicle.*

"Like every thing which proceeds from the editorship of that eminent Instructor, T. K. Arnold, this Manual appears to be well suited to the design with which it was prepared, and will, undoubtedly, secure for itself a place among the text-books of schools and academies thoughout the country. It presents an outline of the history of the ancient nations, from the earliest ages to the fall of the Western Empire in the sixth century, the events being arranged in the order of an accurate chronology, and explained by accompanying treatises on the geography of the several countries in which they transpired. The chief feature of this work, and this is a very important one, is, that it sets forth ancient history and ancient geography in their connection with each other.

"It was originally prepared by Wilhelm Pütz, an eminent German scholar, and translated and edited in England by Rev. T. K. Arnold, and is now revised and introduced to the American public in a well written preface, by Mr George W. Greene, Teacher of Modern Languages in Brown University."—*Prov. Journal.*

MANUAL
OF
MODERN GEOGRAPHY AND HISTORY.

BY WILHELM PÜTZ,

Author of Manuals of "Ancient Geography and History," "Mediæval Geography and History," &c.

TRANSLATED FROM THE GERMAN. REVISED AND CORRECTED.

One volume, 12mo. $1.

"*Preface.*—The present volume completes the series of Professor Pütz's Handbooks of Ancient, Mediæval, and Modern Geography and History. Its adaptation to the wants of the student will be found to be no less complete than was to be expected from the former Parts, which have been highly approved by the public, and have been translated into several languages besides the English. The difficulty of compressing within the limits of a single volume the vast amount of historical material furnished by the progress of modern states and nations in power, wealth, science, and literature, will be evident to all on reflection; and they will find occasion to admire the skill and perspicacity of the Author of this Handbook, not only in the arrangement, but also in the facts and statements which he has adopted.

"In the American edition several improvements have been made; the sections relating to America and the United States have been almost entirely re-written, and materially enlarged and improved, as seemed on every account necessary and proper in a work intended for general use in this country; on several occasions it has been thought advisable to make certain verbal corrections and emendations; the facts and dates have been verified, and a number of explanatory notes have been introduced. It is hoped that the improvements alluded to will be found to add to the value of the present Manual."

FIRST LESSONS IN COMPOSITION,

IN WHICH THE PRINCIPLES OF THE ART ARE DEVELOPED IN CONNECTION WITH THE PRINCIPLES OF GRAMMAR;

Embracing full Directions on the subject of Punctuation: with copious Exercises.

BY. G. P. QUACKENBOS, A.M.

Rector of the Henry Street Grammar School, N. Y.

One volume, 12mo. 45 cts.

EXTRACT FROM PREFACE.

"A county superintendent of common schools, speaking of the important branch of composition, uses the following language: 'For a long time I have noticed with regret the almost entire neglect of the art of original composition in our common schools, and the want of a proper text book upon this essential branch of education. Hundreds graduate from our common schools with no well-defined ideas of the construction of our language.' The writer might have gone further, and said that multitudes graduate, not only from common schools, but from some of our best private institutions, utterly destitute of all practical acquaintance with the subject; that to many such the composition of a single letter is an irksome, to some an almost impossible task. Yet the reflecting mind must admit that it is only this practical application of grammar that renders that art useful—that parsing is secondary to composing, and the analysis of our language almost unimportant when compared with its synthesis.

"One great reason of the neglect noticed above, has, no doubt, been the want of a suitable text-book on the subject. During the years of the Author's experience as a teacher, he has examined, and practically tested the various works on composition with which he has met: the result has been a conviction that, while there are several publications well calculated to advance pupils at the age of fifteen or sixteen, there is not one suited to the comprehension of those between nine and twelve; at which time it is his decided opinion that this branch should be taken up. Heretofore, the teacher has been obliged either to make the scholar labor through a work entirely too difficult for him, to give him exercises not founded on any regular system, or to abandon the branch altogether—and the disadvantages of either of these courses are at once apparent.

"It is this conviction, founded on the experienee not only of the Author, but of many other teachers with whom he has consulted, that has led to the production of the work now offered to the public. It claims to be a first-book in composition, and is intended to initiate the beginner, by easy and pleasant steps, into that all important, but hitherto generally neglected, art."

COURSE OF MATHEMATICAL WORKS,

BY GEORGE R. PERKINS, A. M.,

Professor of Mathematics and Principal of the State Normal School

I. PRIMARY ARITHMETIC. Price 21 cts.

A want, with young pupils, of rapidity and accuracy in performing operations upon written numbers; an imperfect knowledge of Numeration; inadequate conceptions of the nature and relations of Fractions, and a lack of familiarity with the principles of Decimals, have induced the author to prepare the PRIMARY ARITHMETIC.

The first part is devoted to MENTAL EXERCISES and the second to *Exercises on the Slate and Blackboard.*

While the minds of young pupils are disciplined by mental exercises (if not wearisomely prolonged), they fail, in general, in trusting to "head-work" for their calculations; and in resorting to written operations to solve their difficulties, are often slow and inaccurate from a want of early familiarity with such processes: these considerations have induced the Author to devote part of his book to *primary written exercises.*

It has been received with more popularity than any Arithmetic heretofore issued.

II. ELEMENTARY ARITHMETIC. Price 42 cts.

Has recently been carefully revised and enlarged. It will be found concise, yet lucid. It teaches the radical relations of numbers, and presents fundamental principles in analysis and examples. It leaves nothing obscure, yet it does not embarrass by multiplied processes, nor enfeeble by minute details.

In this work *all of the examples or problems are strictly practical,* made up as they are in a great measure of important statistics and valuable facts in history and philosophy, which are thus unconsciously learned in acquiring a knowledge of the Arithmetic.

Fractions are placed immediately after Division; Federal Money is treated as and with Decimal Fractions; Proportion is placed before Fellowship, Alligation, and such rules as require its application in their solution. Every rule is marked with verity and simplicity. The answers to all of the examples are given.

The work will be found to be an improvement on most, if not all, previous elementary Arithmetics in the treatment of Fractions, Denominate Numbers, Rule of Three, Interest, Equation of Payments, Extraction of Roots, and many other subjects.

Wherever this work is presented, the publishers have heard but one opinion in regard to its merits, and that most favorable.

III. HIGHER ARITHMETIC. Price 84 cts.

The present edition has been revised, many subjects rewritten, and much new matter added; and contains an APPENDIX of about 60 pages, in which the philosophy of the more difficult operations and interesting properties of numbers are fully discussed. The work is what its name purports, a *Higher* Arithmetic, and will be found to contain many entirely new principles which have never before appeared in any Arithmetic. It has received the strongest recommendations from hundreds of the best teachers the country affords.

IV. ELEMENTS OF ALGEBRA. Price 84 cts.

This work is an introduction to the Author's "Treatise on Algebra," and is designed especially for the use of Common Schools, and universally pronounced "admirably adapted to the purpose."

V. TREATISE ON ALGEBRA. Price $1 50.

This work contains the higher parts of Algebra usually taught in Colleges; a new method of cubic and higher equations as well as the THEOREM OF STURM, by which we may at once determine the number of real roots of any Algebraic Equation, with much more ease than by previously discovered method.

In the present *revised edition,* one entire chapter on the subject of CONTINUED FRACTIONS has been added.

VI. ELEMENTS OF GEOMETRY, WITH PRACTICAL APPLICATIONS. $1.

The author has added throughout the entire Work, PRACTICAL APPLICATIONS, which, in the estimation of Teachers, is an important consideration.

An eminent Professor of Mathematics, in speaking of this work, says: "We have adopted it, because it follows more closely the best model of pure geometrical reasoning, which ever has been, and perhaps ever will be exhibited; and because the Author has *condensed* some of the important principles of the great master of Geometricians, and more especially has shown that his *theorems* are not mere *theory,* by many *practical applications:* a quality in a text-book of this science no less uncommon than it is important."

PERKINS' COURSE OF MATHEMATICS.

TESTIMONIALS.

From the numerous recommendations of these works, received from the highest sources, the following selections are deemed sufficient to call the attention of Teachers, and those connected with Education, to a thorough trial of their merits.

From PROF. COOK *and* DR. CAMPBELL, *of Albany Academy.*

"From all who have used the ELEMENTARY ARITHMETIC here, both teachers and scholars, we hear but one opinion, and that is most favorable. It is an excellent text-book, and we have no hesitation in recommending it to parents and pupils."

Extract from the Minutes of the Board of School Commissioners of the City of Albany, April 11th, 1850.

"The Committee on text-books made a report, recommending Perkins' SERIES OF ARITHMETICS as superior text-books for the use of schools; whereupon it was unanimously resolved, that Perkins' Primary and Elementary Arithmetics be adopted as the Arithmetical text-books of the Albany District Schools."

From I. W. JACKSON, A. M., *Professor of Mathematics, Union College.*

'The Higher Arithmetic is a work of an order superior to any that has been issued from the American press. Indeed, I am acquainted with no work on Arithmetic in the English language equal to it. I am confident that its general adoption as a text-book, by our seminaries, would be considered by all who feel an interest in the promotion of the exact sciences, as an omen of good."

The following was unanimously adopted by the Chenango County Teachers' Institute, in October, 1849.

"That we consider Perkins' Elementary Arithmetic, Higher Arithmetic and Elements of Algebra, better adapted to the use of schools than any other works on these subjects; that we highly recommend their use throughout the country, and that we will each use our endeavors to secure their adoption in our several schools."

From SAMUEL CROSS, *Principal of Classical Institute, Warren, R. I.*

"After a thorough examination, I *must* say, in all candor, that I am much pleased with the Elementary Arithmetic."

From GEORGE W. MEEKER, ESQ., *Secretary of the Board of School Inspectors, Chicago.*

"I consider them better adapted to the wants of our Schools and Seminaries than any other series extant. I am happy to add, that the Arithmetics have recently been unanimously adopted as the text-books of the Public Schools of this City.

From each of the Principals of the Public Schools of Chicago.

"We have examined Perkins' Arithmetics, and consider them the best before the public."

Extract from a Letter from GEO. P. WILLIAMS, *Professor of Mathematics and Natural Philosophy, University of Michigan.*

"After an examination of the last editions of these works, I am prepared to repeat the opinion formerly expressed, that they are the best arithmetics in use."

From C. M. WRIGHT, *Principal of South Bend (Ind.) Academy.*

"I have adopted Perkins' Mathematical Series, and say unhesitatingly that they need only be examined to be liked."

From JOHN F. NICHOLS, *Principal of the High School, Detroit.*

"I have examined, with great care, the revised edition of Perkins' Elementary Arithmetic; and I hesitate not in saying, that in my opinion, it is much superior to any other work on the subject, with which I am acquainted."

From O. S. TAYLOR, *Principal of Branch University, Michigan.*

"The Elementary Arithmetic is the most practical work in the English language."

From N. BRITTAIN, *Principal of Rochester Collegiate Institute.*

I have examined with considerable care "Perkins' Elementary Arithmetic," and regard it a work of great merit. In several important points, I consider it preferable to any work of the kind now in use.

From I. F. MACK, ESQ., *late Sup. P. Schools of Rochester.*

I concur in the sentiment above expressed in reference to "Perkins' Elementary Arithmetic." The "Higher Arithmetic," and Algebra, by the same Author, have been adopted by the Board of Education of this city, and introduced into the public schools with entire satisfaction.

From CHARLES AVERY, A. M., A. A. S., *Prof. of Chemistry and Nat. Phil., Hamilton College*

I have examined Perkins' Algebra, and am pleased with it. I esteem it a valuable work of the kind; and do, therefore, cheerfully recommend it to the confidence and patronage of the public.

PROF. MANDEVILLE'S READING BOOKS.

I. PRIMARY, OR FIRST READER. Price 10 cents.

II. SECOND READER. Price 16 cents.

These two Readers are formed substantially on the same plan; and the second is a continuation of the first. The design of both is, to combine a knowledge of the meaning and pronunciation of words, with a knowledge of their grammatical functions. The parts of speech are introduced successively, beginning with the articles, these are followed by the demonstrative pronouns; and these again by others, class after class, until all that are requisite to form a sentence have been separately considered; when the common reading lessons begin.

The Second Reader reviews the ground passed over in the Primary, but adds largely to the amount of information. The child is here also taught to read writing as well as printed matter; and in the reading lessons, attention is constantly directed to the different ways in which sentences are formed and connected, and of the peculiar manner in which each of them is delivered. All who have examined these books, have pronounced them a decided and important advance on every other of the same class in use.

III. THIRD READER. Price 25 cents.

IV. FOURTH READER. Price 38 cents.

In the first two Readers, the main object is to make the pupil acquainted with the meaning and functions of words, and to impart facility in pronouncing them in sentential connection: the leading design of these, is to form a natural, flexible, and varied delivery. Accordingly, the Third Reader opens with a series of exercises on articulation and modulation, containing numerous examples for practice on the elementary sounds (including errors to be corrected) and on the different movements of the voice, produced by sentential structure, by emphasis, and by the passions. The habits formed by these exercises, which should be thoroughly, as they can be easily mastered, under intelligent instruction, find scope for improvement and confirmation in the reading lessons which follow, in the same book and that which succeeds.

These lessons have been selected with special reference to the following peculiarities: 1st, Colloquial character; 2d, Variety of sentential structure; 3d, Variety of subject matter; 4th Adaptation to the progressive development of the pupil's mind; and, as far as possible, 5th, Tendency to excite moral and religious emotions. Great pains have been taken to make the books in these respects, which are, in fact, characteristic of the whole series, superior to any others in use; with what success, a brief comparison will readily show.

V THE FIFTH READER; OR, COURSE OF READING. Price 75 cents.

VI. THE ELEMENTS OF READING AND ORATORY. Price $1.

These books are designed to cultivate the literary taste, as well as the understanding and vocal powers of the pupil.

THE COURSE OF READING comprises three parts; the *first part* containing a more elaborate description of elementary sounds and the parts of speech grammatically considered than was deemed necessary in the preceding works; here indispensable: *part second*, a complete classification and description of every sentence to be found in the English, or any other language; examples of which in every degree of expansion, from a few words to the half of an octavo page in length, are adduced, and arranged to be read; and as each species has its peculiar delivery as well as structure, both are learned at the same time; *part third*, paragraphs; or sentences in their connection unfolding general thoughts, as in the common reading books. It may be observed that the selections of sentences in part second, and of paragraphs in part third, comprise some of the finest gems in the language: distinguished alike for beauty of thought and facility of diction. If not found in a school book, they might be appropriately called "elegant extracts."

The ELEMENTS OF READING AND ORATORY closes the series with an exhibition of the whole theory and art of Elocution exclusive of gesture. It contains, besides the classification of sentences already referred to, but here presented with fuller statement and illustration, the laws of punctuation and delivery deduced from it: the whole followed by carefully selected pieces for sentential analysis and vocal practice.

THE RESULT.—The student who acquaints himself thoroughly with the contents of this book, will, as numerous experiments have proved; 1st, Acquire complete knowledge of the structure of the language; 2d, Be able to designate any sentence of any book by name at a glance; 3d, Be able to declare with equal rapidity its proper punctuation; 4th, Be able to declare, and with sufficient practice to give its proper delivery. Such are a few of the general characteristics of the series of school books which the publishers now offer to the friends and patrons of a sound common school and academic education. For more particular information, reference is respectfully made to the "Hints," which may be found at the beginning of each volume.

N. B. The punctuation in all these books conforms, in the main, to the sense and proper delivery of every sentence, and is a guide to both. When a departure from the proper punctuation occurs, the proper delivery is indicated. As reading books are usually punctuated, it is a matter of surprise that children should learn to read at all.

⁎ The above series of Reading Books are already very extensively introduced and commended by the most experienced Teachers in the country. "Prof. Mandeville's system is eminently original, scientific and practical, and destined wherever it is introduced to supersede at once all others."

MANDEVILLE'S READING BOOKS.

A FEW OPINIONS OF THEIR MERITS.

At the Quarterly Meeting of the Committee on Text-Books of the Common School Association of Ashtabula County, Ohio, it was unanimously resolved:

"We recommend Professor Mandeville's series of Reading Books, comprising 'Primary Reader,' 'Second Reader,' 'Third Reader,' 'Fourth Reader,' 'Course of Reading,' and Elements of Reading and Oratory,' for the following among other reasons:—

"1. They contain a greater variety of matter and style than any other series with which we are acquainted; and the selections are peculiarly well adapted to interest the young, and to form the habit of reading in an easy, natural manner, instead of the stiff, mechanical mode prevalent in our schools.

"2. The punctuation throughout the series is in accordance with sentential structure; and coinciding with the delivery, a guide to it. This admirable system of punctuation is fully developed in the sixth book of the series.

"3. The fifth and sixth books contain a complete classification and description of all the sentences of the English language, with numerous examples; in the sixth are definite rules, derived from the structure of sentences, for their proper delivery; and throughout the series signs are introduced, so far as necessary, to guide the pupil in giving the proper inflections, and the various evolutions or movements of the voice.

"4. The nature of Emphasis is fully and philosophically explained; and its vocal effects are so clearly pointed out, that learners, with ordinary instructions, will be in little danger of forming the habit of reading in a monotonous manner.

"5. In short, these works, being eminently scientific and practical, are well calculated to make intelligent and accomplished readers; to lead pupils to think, and to give to thought its appropriate rhetorical and vocal expression; and we are fully of the opinion, that with the use of these books in the hands of teachers acquainted with the system, the labor of learning to read will be very much abridged: and consequently their introduction will prove a great saving to the community in a pecuniary point of view."

At a meeting of the BOARD OF EDUCATION of the City of BROOKLYN, it was unanimously resolved, that Professor MANDEVILLE'S SERIES OF READING BOOKS be exclusively adopted as text-books in the Common Schools of the city.

From the Teachers of the Public School Society of New-York.

"NEW-YORK, July 9th, 1849.

"The Teachers of the New-York Public School Society have listened with much pleasure to Prof. Mandeville's Course of Lectures on Reading, and it appears to them that his system, as explained in the 'Elements of Reading and Oratory,' presents the following advantages:

"1st. A series of Rules for punctuation easily learned and readily applied.

"2d. This punctuation is so applied as to prove in most cases a guide to the delivery of the sentence.

"3d. The system introduces the student to a thorough analysis of the grammatical structure of sentences.

"4th. It is equally valuable as a Rhetorical exercise, since it places the subject of '*Style*' in a clearer light than any elementary work with which the Teachers are acquainted.

"5th. A classification of the different sentences in the language, with a description of their distinctive peculiarities of structure, and this classification successfully illustrated by examples drawn from a great number of the best English writers.

"6th. While other systems are content with laying down some general principles, and leave so much to caprice or momentary impulse on the part of the reader, this system, on the other hand, considers minute details of the utmost importance to general effect; and by giving reasons for the particular delivery of every form of sentence, recommends itself by its clearness, precision, and unity.

"7th. These views apply to the 'Elements of Reading and Oratory,' the only work of Prof. Mandeville's that has come under the notice of the Teachers as a body.

"It is therefore,

"*Resolved*, That the Teachers of the P. S. Society recommend the system of Prof. Mandeville, contained in his 'Elements of Reading and Oratory,' as worthy of the very highest attention of their fellow-teachers every where.

"*Resolved*, That the excellent illustrations of his principles given by the Professor, have conveyed to us a correct and clear idea of the practical benefits of his very excellent system."

www.ingramcontent.com/pod-product-compliance
Lightning Source LLC
LaVergne TN
LVHW021301110826
845150LV00003B/450